MOTIVATIONAL
SCIENCE

Key Readings in Social Psychology

General Editor: ARIE W. KRUGLANSKI, University of Maryland at College Park

The aim of this series is to make available to senior undergraduate and graduate students key articles in each area of social psychology in an attractive, user-friendly format. Many professors want to encourage their students to engage directly in research in their fields, yet this can often be daunting for students coming to detailed study of a topic for the first time. Moreover, declining library budgets mean that articles are not always readily available, and course packs can be expensive and time-consuming to produce. **Key Readings in Social Psychology** aims to address this need by providing comprehensive volumes, each one of which will be edited by a senior and active researcher in the field. Articles will be carefully chosen to illustrate the way the field has developed historically as well as current issues and research directions. Each volume will have a similar structure, which will include:

- An overview chapter, as well as introductions to sections and articles,
- Questions for class discussion,
- Annotated bibliographies,
- Full author and subject indexes.

Published Titles

The Self in Social Psychology	Roy F. Baumeister
Stereotypes and Prejudice	Charles Stangor
Motivational Science	E. Tory Higgins and Arie W. Kruglanski

Titles in Preparation

Social Psychology	Arie W. Kruglanski and E. Tory Higgins
Social Cognition	David Hamilton
Close Relationships	Harry Reis and Caryl Rusbult
Group Processes	John Levine and Richard Moreland
Intergroup Relations	Michael Hogg and Dominic Abrams
Language and Communication	Gün R. Semin
Attitudes and Persuasion	Richard E. Petty, Shelly Chaiken, and Russell Fazio
Social Psychology of Emotions	W. Gerrod Parrott
Social Psychology of Culture	Hazel Markus and Shinobu Kitayama
Social Psychology of Health	Peter Salovey and Alexander J. Rothman

MOTIVATIONAL SCIENCE
Social and Personality Perspectives

Edited by

E. Tory Higgins
Columbia University
New York, NY

Arie W. Kruglanski
University of Maryland
at College Park, MD

USA	Publishing Office:	PSYCHOLOGY PRESS
		A member of the Taylor & Francis Group
		325 Chestnut Street
		Philadelphia, PA 19106
		Tel: (215) 625-8900
		Fax: (215) 625-2940
	Distribution Center:	PSYCHOLOGY PRESS
		A member of the Taylor & Francis Group
		7625 Empire Drive
		Florence, KY 41042
		Tel: 1-800-634-7064
		Fax: 1-800-248-4724
UK		PSYCHOLOGY PRESS
		A member of the Taylor & Francis Group
		27 Church Road
		Hove
		E, Sussex, BN3 2FA
		Tel: +44 (0)1273 207411
		Fax: +44 (0)1273 205612

MOTIVATIONAL SCIENCE: Social and Personality Perspectives

1 2 3 4 5 6 7 8 9 0

Printed by Sheridan Books–Braun-Brumfield, Ann Arbor, MI, 2000.
Flin-Flon XIII, 1970. Acrylic on canvas.   Frank Stella
  © Courtesy The Kreeger Museum, Washington, D.C. All rights reserved.

A CIP catalog record for this book is available from the British Library.
∞ The paper in this publication meets the requirements of the ANSI Standard Z39.48-1984 (Permanence of Paper).

Library of Congress Cataloging-in-Publication Data

Motivational science : social and personality perspectives / edited by E. Tory Higgins

Arie Kruglanski.
        p. cm.— (Key readings in social psychology)
     Includes bibliographical references and index.
        ISBN 0-86377-696-5 (alk. paper) — ISBN 0-86377-697-3 (pbk. : alk. paper)
     1. Motivation (Psychology) 2. Motivation (Psychology)—Social aspects. 3. Personality and motivation. I. Higgins, E. Tory (Edward Tory), 1946– II. Kruglanski, Arie W.
III. Series

     BR503.M69 2000
     153.8—dc21   CIP
                                                         00-025430

ISBN: 0-86377-696-5 (case)
ISBN: 0-86377-697-3 (paper)

Contents

About the Editors

E. Tory Higgins is Professor and Chair of Psychology at Columbia University where he received his Ph.D. in 1973. He has taught at Princeton University, University of Western Ontario and New York University. He was a co-founder of the Ontario Symposium on Personality and Social Psychology (with M. P. Zanna & C. P. Herman) and co-editor of the *Handbook of Motivation and Cognition* (with R. M. Sorrentino). He has been a Fellow at the Center for Advanced Studies in the Behavioral Sciences and received a National Institute of Mental Health MERIT Award (1989). He is also the recipient of the Donald T. Campbell Award For Outstanding Contributions to Social Psychology (1996), the Thomas M. Ostrom Award For Outstanding Contributions to Social Cognition (1999), the American Psychological Society's William James Fellow Award For Distinguished Contributions to Psychology (2000), and the American Psychological Association's Distinguished Scientific Contribution Award (2000).

Arie W. Kruglanski is Professor of Psychology at the University of Maryland. He received his Ph.D in Psychology at UCLA in 1968, and taught at Tel Aviv University, Israel, where he founded the social psychology program. He is the recipient of the National Institute of Mental Health Research Scientist Award, and the Donald Campbell Award (2000) for Outstanding Contributions to Social Psychology. He has been a Fellow at the Center for Advanced Studies in the Behavioral Sciences, as well as Fellow of the American Psychological Association and the American Psychological Society. He has served as editor of the *Personality and Social Psychology Bulletin*, and of the *Journal of Personality and Social Psychology: Attitudes and Social Cognition* section. His work has been disseminated in over 150 articles, chapters and books, and has been supported by grants from the National Science Foundation, the National Institute of Mental Health, Deutsche Forschungs Gemeineschaft, the Ford Foundation and the Israeli Academy of Sciences.

Acknowledgements

The Authors and Publishers are grateful to the following for permission to reproduce the articles in this book:

Reading 1: T. Pyszczynski, J. Greenberg, & S. Solomon, Why do we need what we need?: A terror management perspective on the roots of human social motivation. Psychological Inquiry, 8, 1–20. Copyright © 1997 by Lawrence Erlbaum Associates. Reprinted with permission.

Reading 2: R. F. Baumeister and M. R. Leary, The Need to Belong: Desire for interpersonal attachments as a fundamental human motivation. Psychological Bulletin, 117, 497–529. Copyright © 1995 by the American Psychological Association. Reprinted with permission.

Reading 3: M. B. Brewer, The social self: On being the same and different at the same time. Personality and Social Psychology Bulletin, 17, 475–482. Copyright © 1991 by Sage Publications. Reprinted with permission.

Reading 4: A. Tesser, M. Millar, & J. Moore, Some affective consequences of social comparison and reflection processes: The pain and pleasure of being close. Journal of Personality and Social Psychology, 54, 49–61. Copyright © 1988 by the American Psychological Association. Reprinted with permission.

Reading 5: N. Cantor, Life task problem-solving: Situational affordances and personal needs. Personality and Social Psychology Bulletin, 20, 235–243. Copyright © 1994 by Sage Publications. Reprinted with permission.

Reading 6: S. Folkman, R. S. Lazarus, C. Dunkel-Schetter, A. DeLongis, & R. Gruen, The dynamics of a stressful encounter. Journal of Personality and Social Psychology, 50, 992–1003. Copyright © 1986 by the American Psychological Association. Reprinted with permission.

Reading 7: E. L. Deci and R. M. Ryan, The support of autonomy and the control of behavior. Journal of Personality and Social Psychology, 55, 1024–1037. Copyright © 1987 by the American Psychological Association. Reprinted with permission.

Reading 8: J. W. Atkinson, Motivational determinants of risk-taking behavior. Psychological Review, 64, 359–372. Copyright © 1957 by the American Psychological Association. Reprinted with permission.

Reading 9: I. Ajzen and M. Fishbein, The prediction of behavior from attitudinal and normative variables. Journal of Experimental Social Psychology, 6, 466–487, copyright © 1970 by Academic Press, reprinted by permission of the publisher.

Reading 10: A. Bandura and D. Cervone, Self-evaluative and self-efficacy mechanisms governing the motivational effects of goal systems. Journal of Personality and Social Psychology, 45, 1017–1028. Copyright © 1983 by the American Psychological Association. Reprinted with permission.

Reading 11: R. R. Vallacher and D. M. Wegner, What do people think they are doing?: Action identification and human behavior. Psychological Review, 94, 3–15. Copyright © 1987 by the American Psychological Association. Reprinted with permission.

Reading 12: W. Mischel and Y. Shoda, A cognitive-affective system theory of personality: Reconceptualizing situations, dispositions, dynamics, and invariance in personality structure. Psychological Review, 102, 246–268. Copyright © 1995 by the American Psychological Association. Reprinted with permission.

Motivational Science: The Nature and Functions of Wanting

E. Tory Higgins and Arie W. Kruglanski

I t is rare for a textbook in social psychology to have even one chapter with motivation in its title. Even definitions of the field of social psychology rarely mention motivation. Instead, social psychologists historically have taken a cognitive approach to understanding social behavior (see Zajonc, 1980a). For example, early on Krech and Crutchfield (1948) stated that "if we are to understand social behavior, we must know how all perceptions, memories, fantasies are combined or integrated or organized into present **cognitive structures**" (p. 77), and later Ostrom (1984) pointed out that the "cognitive approach to understanding social behavior has always ruled over social psychology" (p. 29). Although the cognitive variables changed from Gestalt principles (e.g., Krech & Crutchfield, 1948) to information processing principles (e.g., Ostrom, 1984), the dominant approach remained cognitive. Yet motivational variables were typically included in basic social psychological theories. For example, the cognitive consistency theories of the 1950s and 1960s (for a source-book see Abelson, Aronson, McGuire, Newcomb, Rosenberg, & Tannenbaum, 1968) postulate a motive to have psychologically coherent relations among one's cognitions. Social comparison theory (Festinger, 1954) posits the drive to evaluate one's opinions, abilities, and emotions (cf. Schachter & Singer, 1962). Attribution theory posits the need to apprehend the causal structure of one's environment (Kelley, 1967). Social cognition models posit various information processing goals (e.g., impression formation, or memory goals) on the part of the cognizing individual (cf. Wyer & Srull, 1989). Mostly, however, the motivational variables in social psychological theories were left relatively unarticulated, and remained at the background of the theoretical treatments whose focus was predominantly cognitive.

Yet without a thorough understanding of motivation, the cognitive approach cannot explain the intricacies of human psychology. Investigators have recognized this for a long time, as in Guthrie's (1935) famous criticism of Tolman's (1932) original expectancy theory that seemed to leave actors lost in thought and unable to act. In criticizing the concept of habit as a determinant of behavior, Lewin (1951) argued that it was necessary to distinguish the motivational aspect of habit from the cognitive aspect and then examine the special role of each in behavior. Bandura (1965) distinguished between the cognitive learning of how to behave in certain ways (acquisition) and the motivation to enact the behaviors (performance). Nisbett and Ross (1980), in their highly influential book on social cognition, acknowledged that "we share our field's inability to bridge the gap between cognition and behavior, a gap that in our opinion is the most serious failing of modern cognitive psychology" (p. 11). There are good reasons to believe that such a gap may only be bridged by the consideration of motivation.

To say that cognitive analyses need to take full account of motivational factors does not mean that motivation functions independently of cognition. It is equally misleading to treat motivation and cognition as completely separable. Motivational variables like goals have cognitive properties like accessibility, and cognitive variables like beliefs have motivational properties like importance (for a discussion, see Kruglanski, 1996). By operating together to produce combined effects, motivation and cognition are synergistic (Sorrentino & Higgins, 1986). It is critical, therefore, to recognize the commonalities of motivation and cognition as well as their differences, and to examine how they interact to produce joint effects.

What is it about motivation, then, that is different than but works together with cognition? There is a long history of different ways of thinking about motivation. Given that the root of the term "motivation" is "to move" the first notion that comes to mind concerns the movement's destination; it is not surprising then that one classic way of thinking about motivation has been in terms of approach or avoidance of desired and undesired states, respectively. Motivation as approach and avoidance is found in theories of regulatory anticipation that concern expectancies of pleasant versus painful outcomes (e.g., Atkinson, 1964; Freud, 1920/1950; Mowrer, 1960), theories of regulatory reference that concern desired end-states versus undesired end-states as the reference point for self-regulation (e.g., Carver and Scheier, 1981; Powers, 1973), and, more recently, in regulatory focus theory that concerns approach and avoidance as strategic means for goal attainment (see Higgins, 1997).

Although approach and avoidance has been a major way to think about motivation, there have been other ways as well (for reviews, see Pittman, 1998; Weiner, 1972). Inspired by Darwin's ideas (e.g., 1871), Freud (1915/1957), McDougall (1923) and others proposed that people are propelled to action by basic biological instincts. The notion of drives was a homeostatic concept in which disruptions or disequilibria in basic needs induce driving forces that instigate action to reestablish equilibrium (see Woodworth, 1918). From this perspective, behavior is motivated by drive reduction or discharge of tension in relation to physiological needs or quasi-needs that include goals (e.g., Hull, 1943; Lewin, 1935; Spence, 1956).

If one were to choose a single term for what most people mean by motivation, however, it would probably be the verb "to want." This one term captures in everyday language a wide variety of relevant meanings: to have or feel a need of, to be necessary (require); to wish or demand the presence of; to desire to come, go, or be; to have a strong desire for or inclination toward (like); to fail to possess (lack); to hunt or seek in order to seize (see, for example, Webster's Dictionary, 1989). Motivational science is concerned with the nature and functions of wanting and their relation to knowing, feeling, and doing. As such, it naturally raises such questions as: What are the basic wants of people? What is the interplay between biological and socialization factors in determining what people want? When do people change what they want? How do different wants facilitate or interfere with one another, and what are the consequences? How does wanting function with knowing to bridge the gap to behavior? Do people know what they want, and does knowing influence what they want and getting what they want? How does knowing the likelihood of getting what one wants influence how much one tries to get it? Do people not want to know about some wants, and what are the consequences of trying not to know? Do different kinds of wants influence what one wants to know? Does getting what one wants proceed in a stage-like sequence, and are there ways of proceeding at each stage that make getting what one wants more likely? Does getting or not getting what one wants influence how one feels about it, and does the nature of the feelings depend on what it is that one wants? Are there different strategies for getting what one wants, and are some strategies better than others for fulfilling different kinds of wants? Does one's past history and future expectations of getting what one wants influence what one wants now?

Wanting is not only a process but also a structure within which a vast gamut of experiences unfolds that itself merits investigation. Different kinds of wants involve different kinds of experience (e.g., hunger versus thirst versus belonging). Different experiences accompany trying to get what one wants (e.g., experiences of ease versus difficulty; eagerness versus vigilance). Getting or not getting what one wants produces different emotions (e.g., happiness versus sadness; a sense of relaxation versus that of tension). Motivational science needs to be concerned with personal experiences and not just behaviors (see, for example, Weiner, 1986). After all, quality of life has a lot to do with people's motivational experiences of pleasure and pain (see Kahneman, Diener, & Schwarz, 1999). Motivational science must examine the pleasures and pains of wanting that form the texture of our experience, determine the extent of our life satisfaction, and constitute a fundamental part and parcel of the human predicament.

Motivational science extends not only across the various areas of psychology, including social/personality, abnormal, developmental, organizational, community, animal learning, and physiological, but also beyond psychology to other disciplines encompassing law, business, education, and health. It is not possible in one volume to represent the full range of motivational science. Indeed, it is difficult to represent even the contributions of only social/personality psychology to motivational science in a single volume. To provide some boundary conditions, we have identified the following six major themes found in the research and theories of social/personality motivational scientists over the past half century. These are represented in the various sections of the present volume respectively labeled as: 1) basic wants; 2) when wants change; 3) bridging the gap between knowing and doing; 4) getting what one wants; 5) knowing from wanting; and 6) wanting from knowing. To provide some general background for the articles included in this volume, we will briefly review each of these themes, as illustrated by the included articles as well as related papers.

Basic Wants

A science of wanting must consider whether there are basic wants and, if so, what might they be. This can be a daunting task. When wants were conceptualized as instincts, some theorists described a small number of basic wants, such as Freud's (1915/1957) life and death instincts while other theorists like McDougall (1923) proposed a very large number of instincts. Because instincts could be postulated as propelling each specific end-state, there were only weak constraints on how many could be postulated.

The original concept of drive (Woodworth, 1918) provided greater constraints by relating basic wants to basic physiological deficits. However, this physiological equilibrium notion of drive might be too constraining. Although all basic wants must have some biological underpinnings, these underpinnings need not be directly related to physiological disequilibriums. It is not clear, for example, what the relation is between a basic need to belong with other people as part of a group and some physiological disequilibrium. Moreover, it is possible to consider basic wants in relation to general survival without postulating specific physiological substrates.

Relating basic needs to general survival has been the most common approach in the social/personality literature. Not surprisingly, basic survival wants that relate to getting along in the social world have received special attention (see Stevens & Fiske, 1995). Different basic wants related to getting along with others have been also proposed. It has been postulated that there is a basic human need to form and maintain strong and stable interpersonal relationships (see Baumeister & Leary, 1995). It has been proposed that in an undifferentiated social environment that provides no guidelines for action, there is a motivation for intergroup categorization that can provide order and coherence to the social situation (see Tajfel, Flament, Billig, & Bundy, 1971). Also relevant to the issue of in-group and out-group relations, it has been suggested that social identity and group loyalty are strongest for those self-categorizations that fulfill simultaneously the basic needs for individuals to belong and to be distinctive (see Brewer, 1991). The basic desire to maintain self-esteem, in combination with closeness to others, is said to jointly influence strategic use of reflection and social comparison processes (see Tesser, Millar, & Moore, 1988).

There are other basic human wants that have been described in the social/personality literature. Perhaps the one that has received the most attention is the need for consistency as postulated in Festinger's (1957) theory of cognitive dissonance, Heider's (1958) balance model, Osgood and Tannenbaum's (1955) congruity principle, Abelson and Rosenberg's (1958) symbolic psycho-logic model, and other theories. Generally inspired by Gestalt notions of good form or good fit, these theories in different ways postulate a basic human need for coherence among beliefs, feelings, and actions—in other words, a social world that makes sense.

A notion related to the need for consistency is that people have a basic need for a social world that is predictable and controllable, a social world in which one believes one can effectively interact with others. This basic set of wants has been postulated in social-psychological attribution theories (e.g., Heider, 1958; Jones & Davis, 1965; Kelley, 1967), personality theories of the self (e.g., Kelly, 1955; Lecky, 1961), and in theories of effectance or control motivation (e.g., Brehm, 1966; Deci & Ryan, 1987; Lerner, 1970; Pittman & Pittman, 1980; Seligman, 1975; White, 1959; Woodworth, 1958). Indeed, consistency models themselves have been reinterpreted in terms of an underlying need for effective interpersonal relationships (Abelson, 1983), as well as in terms of the basic need for a valued self-image (see Aronson, 1969; Cooper & Fazio, 1984; Steele & Lui, 1981; Tesser & Cornell, 1991). Moreover, in order to achieve coherence and a sense of objective reality, as well as to maintain strong and effective relationships, a basic need for shared reality has been posited (see Hardin & Higgins, 1996). Finally, to the extent that consistency, coherence, and predictability relate to closure and certainty, there are theories proposing that needs for closure and certainty vary across individuals and across situations (see Kruglanski, 1989; Sorrentino & Short, 1986).

Some wants are postulated to be basic in the sense that they are heritable, such as Tesser's (1993) heritability of attitudes. Other wants are postulated to be basic because they are relevant to all people even if the specific optimal level of the want that is preferred varies across people. These basic wants represent motivational parameters that all persons possess albeit at different degrees; one example of such a general want may be Zuckerman's (1984) sensation-seeking dimension (cf. Berlyne, 1960; Hunt, 1965) on which persons might vary. Still other wants are postulated to be basic because they concern nothing less than life and death, such as Freud's corresponding instincts mentioned earlier and Pyszczynski, Greenberg, and Solomon's (1997) mortality anxiety, which, according to the terror management theory, is rooted in the relation between the fundamental instinct for self-preservation and humans' unique awareness of their inevitable demise, and gives rise to numerous human motivations. Before determining what might be the basic human wants, motivational scientists will need to decide what criteria are most appropriate to use in order to proclaim a given want as basic.

When Wants Change

The notion that there are basic wants does not imply that people's motivations are fixed. If one were to postulate a relatively small set of basic drives, for example, one would still posit that people's motivations would vary depending on the level of disequilibrium of each of the physiological needs. Wants would change as a function of need fulfillment. In control theories as well (e.g., Carver and Scheier, 1981; Powers, 1973), wants change as the magnitude of discrepancy between one's current state and one's desired end-state changes, and this is true whether the desired end-states constitute basic wants or not (see also Atkinson, 1964; Bandura & Cervone, 1983; Klinger, 1975; Locke, 1968).

In addition to the changes within wants that are inherent in need fulfillment, the literature describes conditions when wants change because of the influence of other wants upon them. Developmental shifts provide classic examples of such conditions. Psychodynamic models, for instance, propose that there are biologically-linked developmental shifts in the basic preoccupations or problems to which people attend, and these changes influence which wants are emphasized at each stage (e.g., Erickson, 1963; Freud, 1905/1953). The developmental shifts that have received the most attention in the social/personality literature are those related to life transitions or social life phases (e.g., Higgins & Eccles-Parsons, 1983; Ruble, 1994). Each life phase has basic tasks that need to be fulfilled, and changes in life tasks change the nature of individuals' goals or current concerns and the relative emphasis they receive (see Cantor, 1994; Frey & Ruble, 1985; Klinger, 1975).

Life transitions involve long-term changes in relatively chronic wants of people. New situations can also produce temporary changes in the momentary wants of people. For example, one major area of interest in the social/personality literature has been in how situations increase people's need for accuracy, which in turn alters the kind of information they want. Studies have found, for example, that people are more likely to form impressions of others using specific individuating attributes rather than general stereotypes when their need for accuracy is increased by entering a situation in which they are dependent on their interaction partner for important outcomes (see Fiske & Neuberg, 1990). Need for accuracy can also increase when people are in a situation in which they believe other people will evaluate them or hold them accountable for their judgments, which has been shown to change not only what type of information is wanted but also how much information is wanted (see Kruglanski & Webster, 1996; Tetlock, 1992).

Another major area of interest in the social/personality literature has been on how situations induce self-evaluative or self-appraisal needs that in turn have motivational consequences. Particular situations, for example, can increase individuals' awareness of themselves as objects in the world, such as knowing that one is being observed by others or seeing oneself in a mirror. Objective self-awareness increases self-evaluation in relation to standards salient or accessible in the immediate situation, that in turn increases the motivation to meet the standard (see Carver & Scheier, 1981; Wicklund & Duval, 1971). Stressful encounters represent another situation that increases self-evaluative or self-appraisal needs. A primary appraisal concerned with basic needs such as one's own self-esteem or protecting a loved one induces secondary appraisals of different coping options, and specific combinations of primary and secondary appraisals relate to specific ways of coping, such as planful problem-solving, that produce more or less satisfactory outcomes (e.g., Folkman, Lazurus, Dunkel-Schetter, DeLongis, & Gruen, 1986).

Thus far, we have seen that current concerns or motivational states can change when there are changes in basic wants. There can also be more than one current concern in a situation and these alternative concerns can influence one another. The notion of instincts had the decided advantage of relating current clusters of feelings, thoughts, and actions backwards to specific motivational entities directed toward particular end-states. The contemporary story of motivation, however, is considerably more complicated because current motivational states are often the product of the interrelations among different wants in the immediate situation. The classic example of this is the state of conflict as a motivational variable.

The self-regulatory notion of conflict subsumes different types of incompatibility between approaching pleasure and avoiding pain. There is the general psychodynamic conflict (see Freud, 1923/1961) between individual instinctual wishes (Id) and societal pressures (Superego), and more specific conflict among a person's own desires and the desires held for that person by his or her significant others (Horney, 1946). There are also immediate situational conflicts between approaching pleasure and avoiding pain (see Berlyne, 1960; Lewin, 1935; Miller, 1944), including approach/approach conflict, avoidance/avoidance conflicts, approach/avoidance conflicts, and even double approach/avoidance conflicts in which moving toward one of two alternative desired goals (a pleasure to be approached) means moving away from the other goal (a pain to be avoided). The product of conflict between different wants is itself a motivational state—the state of confusion. There is evidence, for example, that independent of the extent to which people are attaining their goals, conflict between goals produces a confusion-related motivational syndrome of vacillation, distractibility, and feeling unsure of oneself (see Van Hook & Higgins, 1988). Such confusion can be an aversive motivational state that one strives to avoid in order to reach epistemic closure (Kruglanski & Webster, 1996).

There is another case of wants changing wants that has received particular attention in the social/personality literature. The traditional viewpoint in psychology was that the fulfillment of wants via rewards for engaging in an activity increases subsequent motivation to engage in that particular activity (e.g., Hull, 1943; Skinner, 1938; Thorndike, 1911). But in the early 1970s a series of papers in the social/personality literature proposed that introducing rewards as one type of want for activity engagement can reduce another type of want for activity engagement, thereby undermining subsequent motivation to engage in the rewarded activity (e.g., Deci, 1971; Kruglanski, Friedman, & Zeevi, 1971; Lepper, Greene, & Nisbett, 1973; Ross, 1975).

Most generally, such undermining can be understood in terms of the extrinsic motivation of reward interfering with intrinsic motivation to engage in the activity (for a review, see Pittman & Heller, 1987), although the distinction between intrinsic and extrinsic motivation has been conceptualized in different ways. For example, these two wants can be related to different kinds of basic needs or incentives, such as distinguishing between (intrinsic) wants related to autonomy or self-determination and (extrinsic) wants related to control or pressure from others (e.g., Deci & Ryan, 1987), or these two wants can be related to different kinds of inferences about the nature of the activity engagement (e.g., deCharms, 1968; Kruglanski, 1975; Lepper et al., 1973), such as whether the engagement was an end in itself (intrinsic) or a means to an end (extrinsic). Subsequent research has shown that how extrinsic wants influence intrinsic wants also varies as a function of different kinds of expectancies and feedback (e.g., Harackiewicz, Sansone, & Manderlink, 1985).

Wants that are undermined by events can also produce reactions that change the level of other wants. For example, when needs for consistency are undermined, as when imbalance or dissonance occurs (see Festinger, 1957; Heider, 1958; Wicklund & Brehm, 1976), people's motivation to approach or avoid certain objects or activities will change in a direction that reduces the inconsistency. Events that are experienced as threatening people's need for freedom or control can also increase approach or avoidance motivations so as to restore the threatened freedom, such as an increased attraction to an object that was taken away as a choice alternative (see Brehm, 1966). Such reactance can also decrease people's motivation to cooperate with others or even produce a motivation to go against others' desires (Brehm & Mann, 1975).

This last example involves a change in the effectiveness of social influence as a function of a change in another motivation (i.e., a threat to perceived freedom or control). There is a vast literature on social influence that is clearly relevant to this section on when wants change. Because attitudes concern objects and activities to be approached or avoided, for example, the literature on processes underlying attitude change is directly relevant to when wants change (e.g., Chaiken, 1980; Kelman, 1958; McGuire, 1964; Petty & Cacioppo,

1986; for a review, see Eagly & Chaiken, 1993). Also relevant is the literature on how dyadic and group contact influences people's motivations, including the mere presence of other people (e.g., Zajonc, 1966) and majority or minority direct influence attempts (for a review, see Levine & Moreland, 1998). Because this volume is concerned mainly with self-regulation of individual wants (rather than what someone else desires the individual to want), this social influence literature will not be reviewed here. The reader can learn about these areas by reading other volumes in this series.

Bridging the Gap Between Knowing and Doing

Cognitive variables are not enough to understand social behavior. The challenge for motivational science is to bridge the gap between knowing and doing. People take action because they want something. When their wants change, their actions change correspondingly. Because people have wants to be fulfilled that require action, they rarely remain lost in thought. But what is the nature of the bridge that wants provide between knowing and doing? What is the nature of the motivation-cognition interface that underlies action?

One approach to bridging the gap between knowing and doing is to reconsider the nature of knowing itself. Do people engage in cognitive activity simply for its own sake, as an end in itself, or do they engage in it as a means to an end? James (1890/1948) stated: "Primarily then, and fundamentally, the mental life is for the sake of action of a preservative sort" (p. 4). The first step, then, in bridging the gap between knowing and doing is to recognize that individuals' mental life has fundamental survival value through its contribution to adaptive action. This relation to adaptive action has been emphasized in the social/personality literature as well (see Fiske, 1992; Higgins, 2000; Ostrom, 1984). Ostrom (1984) argued that action is the root of social knowledge: "American social psychologists shared the view that human action was the basis of social knowledge. . . . It was obvious to these social psychologists that humans were 'doers' rather than 'watchers'" (p. 17).

The motivated nature of cognition is intertwined with its social functions. When people enter into association with others their mental life is transformed, which in turn transforms their associations with others (see Allport, 1968; Higgins, 2000; Levine, Resnick, & Higgins, 1993). People do not learn how the world works all on their own. They learn it in association with others. Such learning is socially shared and the shared reality aspect of the knowledge is one of its most critical properties (see Hardin & Higgins, 1996; Levine, Resnick, & Higgins, 1993). It is critical that people learn what matters to others about objects, such as what it is about the furniture in a home that parents care about. It is particularly important to learn what it is about oneself as an object that other people care about. Children are motivated to learn how their appearance and behaviors influence caretakers' responses to them in order to increase the likelihood that the caretakers will provide them the nurturance and security they need in order to survive (see Bowlby, 1969, 1973; Cooley, 1902/1964; Mead, 1934; Sullivan, 1953).

Other people continue to be vital for individuals striving to meet their goals and satisfy their needs, and thus individuals need to learn how their social world works and impacts on them. In other words, social cognition is in the service of social interaction. Social cognition depends on individuals' goals, and these goals are influenced by their social roles and positions in the larger culture (see Higgins, 2000). Evidence for the functional nature of social cognition includes the fact that people are less interested in maximizing accuracy as such than being accurate enough to get along and find consensus with others in order to facilitate social interaction. Even stereotypes as representations of social categories can be understood as serving social interaction goals, such as allowing for rapid responses in situations where such responses are required (see Fiske, 1992).

From this functional perspective, people learn what they need to know to make the world work for them. The gap between knowing and doing is bridged by connecting knowing to wanting. There are various ways of doing so. A classic approach is to identify the kinds of knowing that people need to regulate their actions. Perhaps the major form of such knowing is anticipating the future or developing expectancies. Freud (1920/1950), Tolman (1932), Lewin (1935), Mowrer (1960), Atkinson (1957, 1964), and other psychologists proposed that anticipated pleasure and anticipated pain are fundamental determinants of action.

Regulatory anticipation is a specific case of expectancy functioning, and expectancy is used in a variety of ways as a motivational variable (see Higgins, 1997; Olson, Roese, & Zannd, 1996). It has been used in relation to events or outcomes that vary in their likelihood of occurrence or attainability. This includes expectancies concerning the likelihood of effective performance from self-percepts of efficacy (e.g., Bandura & Cervone, 1983), achievement motives (e.g., Atkinson, 1957, 1964; Feather, 1961), or perceptions of task difficulty or luck (e.g., Weiner et al., 1971). It also includes expectancies concerning the outcomes or consequences of performing some action (e.g., Rotter, 1954) or engaging in some activity (e.g., Ajzen & Fishbein, 1970). Expectancies about others' characteristics and behaviors has also been used when considering interpersonal motivations (e.g., Downey, Freitas, Michaelis, & Khouri, 1998; Zanna & Pack, 1975). Another cognitive process related to expectancy is simulation of possible events, including not only what might happen but what *might have* happened (see Kahneman & Miller, 1986; Kahneman & Tversky, 1982). Such simulations not only influence predictions about the likelihood of specific events or outcomes, but they also motivate actions such as coping responses (e.g., Taylor & Schneider, 1989).

Expectancy has also been used in relation to value. It has been postulated that as expectancy decreases, value increases (e.g., Atkinson, 1957, 1964), because the difficult to attain task or hard to get goals are often valued more than easier accomplishments or attainments. It has also been proposed that what is normally expected establishes a neutral value (e.g., Kahneman & Miller, 1986), and that small discrepancies from the norm are pleasant whereas larger ones are painful (e.g., McClelland, Atkinson, Clark, & Lowell, 1953). Another kind of value-laden expectancy is knowing what actions others expect of you. These normative or prescriptive expectancies establish goals to be fulfilled or standards to be met and have been postulated as a distinct motivational force on behavior (e.g., Ajzen & Fishbein, 1970; for a review, see Stryker & Statham, 1985).

People not only have knowledge about the likelihood of certain events or outcomes, they also have knowledge about how pleasant or painful those events or outcomes will be. This knowledge constitutes the value component of expectancy-value models (see Edwards, 1955; Festinger, 1942; for a review, see Ajzen, 1996). In Ajzen and Fishbein's (1970) attitude-behavior model, for example, an individual's attitude toward performing the act is predicted by the product of the individual's beliefs about the consequences of the act and the individual's evaluation of each such consequence (i.e., its subjective desirability).

A different way to bridge the gap between knowing and doing is to link knowing what you are doing to the means and ends of goal attainment. Roger Brown (1958), for example, proposed that people name objects and events, such as calling a dime "money," a "coin," or a "dime," at whatever level of categorization is most useful for a current objective. Vallacher and Wegner (1987) distinguished between higher levels of action identification that were ends in themselves and lower levels that were just means to an end. Low levels of action identification specify *how* an action can be performed, whereas high levels signify the *purpose* of the action. Lower level identities support effective action procedures, whereas higher level identities increase understanding of the action.

The bridges between knowing and doing discussed thus far involve people knowing what to expect, knowing what they want, and knowing what one is doing (and why one is doing it). The relation between knowing and doing need not involve such controlled, effortful processing, however. Knowing can translate into action in more automatic ways as well.

Beliefs and encodings can be affectively laden so that they are themselves "hot" cognitions (see Mischel & Shoda, 1995). These hot cognitions can be activated preconsciously and effortlessly (see Zajonc, 1980b). They provide a bridge between knowing and action because the knowing assigns meaning to an activity which creates a psychological situation that itself constitutes a motivational state (see Mead, 1934; Weber, 1967).

Attitudes as stored knowledge structures connecting objects or activities with personal evaluations of them also function as a bridge between knowing and action. By knowing that one likes or dislikes some object, one is motivated to approach or avoid it (Fazio, 1990; for a review, see Eagly & Chaiken, 1993). Stored attitudes can be used to make action decisions with less effort than a detailed expectancy-value analysis (see Fazio, 1990; Sanbonmatsu & Fazio, 1990). Stored knowledge structures can even more directly bridge knowing and action by containing information about how to act in a particular type of situation. Responding repeatedly in the same manner to the same stimulus event can create a stored association between the event and the response, similar to Hull's (1943) notion of habit. Because of such procedural learning (see Smith, 1993), exposure to the event can automatically produce action. Indeed, even activating the stored association by priming the event can produce the associated response without mediation by attitudes or evaluative judgments of the event (see Bargh, Chen, & Burrows, 1996).

Getting What One Wants

Habits or situation-response associations of the kind studied by Bargh et al. (1996) are unusual in bridging the gap from cognition to a specific designated action. Usually the bridge from cognition to action involves activating specific wants whose fulfillment requires action, but the action to be taken is not specified. The bridge says what is wanted but not how specifically to get it. This "How" question is another critical part of motivational science (for reviews, see Cantor & Khilstrom, 1987; Gollwitzer & Moscowitz, 1996; Mischel, Cantor, & Feldman, 1996; for a review of how people fail to get what they want, see Baumeister & Heatherton, 1996).

The most general answer to the how question is that people *approach* pleasant end-states and *avoid* painful end-states. As mentioned earlier, this classic hedonic principle provides the underpinning of a broad range of motivational theories from the ancient Greeks, through 17th and 18th century British philosophers, to 20th century psychologists (for a review, see Higgins, 1997). It is not enough, however, to want to approach or avoid something. It is also necessary to monitor or evaluate where one is in relation to where one wants to be. Cybernetic and control process models postulate a monitoring system that compares current states to reference point end-states. For desired end-states, the monitoring system provides feedback about whether there is a need to reduce any perceived discrepancy. For undesired end-states, the monitoring system provides feedback about whether there is a need to amplify any perceived discrepancy (see Carver & Scheier, 1990; Miller, Galanter, & Pribram, 1960; Powers, 1973; Wiener, 1948). The process of self-evaluation provides this important monitoring and feedback function ("How am I doing?"), and thus is essential to effective self-regulation as well as being a major determinant of people's emotional experiences (see Bandura, 1986; Carver & Scheier, 1990; Higgins, 1987)

Another important perspective on the how question derives from German "Will Psychology" (see Gollwitzer & Moscowitz, 1996; Mischel, Cantor, & Feldman, 1996). How are intentions to do something effective in producing the intended action? One solution is to treat intentions, such as the intention to mail a letter, as if they were a kind of need that assigns valence to objects and events that then become end-states to be approached or avoided (see Lewin, 1951). This solution helps to explain responses to task interruption and the substitute value of alternative actions. It is silent, however, with respect to issues of how people become committed to specific actions and what strategies are effective or ineffective at maintaining commitment (or changing commitment when appropriate; see Klinger, 1975). These issues have been addressed in terms of willpower and mind-sets.

People can intend to do something, like prepare a delicious dinner, and then get distracted by their children or a phone call so that the meal is overcooked. They can intend to lose weight by eating only healthy food and then nibble candy bars all day. How do people maintain concentration on their task despite distractions, barriers, and temptations? What processes or strategies underlie effective self-control or willpower? Some early research into these basic questions observed how children respond to a basic test of self-control—the ability to resist the temptation of a goodie available now in order to get a better goodie later (e.g., Mischel & Patterson, 1978). This strategic ability to effectively delay gratification increases developmentally, and individual differences found early on among children predict self-control later in life (see Mischel, Shoda, & Rodriguez, 1989). One general strategy for delaying gratification is to try not to think about the tempting properties of the alternative that is available now. Effective tactics include distracting oneself by thinking about other things, or symbolically transforming the alternative in ways that make it less tempting (e.g., Mischel & Moore, 1980; Mischel & Patterson, 1978).

Attempting to delay gratification is not the only mental control problem in which people use such tactics. Indeed, the classic mental control problem in psychology is people trying to control unwanted thoughts from entering consciousness. This problem was a central concern in the early psychodynamic literature, but it has recently received renewed attention in the social/personality literature as well (for a review, see Wegner & Wenzlaff, 1996). One especially interesting phenomenon is that in attempting to suppress unwanted thoughts, people can make the thoughts more accessible so that they later rebound to dominate their conscious awareness more than ever (e.g., Wegner, Schneider, Carter, & White, 1987; for a review, see Wegner, 1994).

People need strategies not only for self-control, but also to assign sufficient resources to a task and to proceed smoothly with its execution. There are several phases in an action sequence and effective action requires appropriate mind-sets at the different phases (see Heckhausen & Gollwitzer, 1987; Kuhl, 1984; Lewin, Dembo, Festinger, & Sears, 1944). For example, a deliberative mind-set is most appropriate in the predecisional phase in which potential goals are considered and a decision to pursue one of them is made; an implemental mind-set is most appropriate for the postdecisional-preactional phase in which the execution of goal-directed actions is planned and strategic alternatives for goal attainment are selected (see Gollwitzer, Heckhausen, & Stellar, 1990). Moreover, implementation intentions not only facilitate planning and getting started but they also mobilize effort, ward off distractions, and improve resumption of disrupted tasks (see Gollwitzer, 1996). The process of mobilizing effort itself involves strategic decisions. For example, it is important to mobilize no more and no less effort (or motivational energy) than is required by the difficulty of the task (e.g., Brehm & Self, 1989). Positive illusions about the kind of person one is and how much control one has in life can serve the function of mobilizing effort and are especially adaptive for maintaining effort in the face of setbacks (see Taylor & Brown, 1988).

An important aspect of task execution is information seeking. Information seeking is also a fundamental component of problem-solving and hypothesis-testing. The social/personality literature has paid special attention to alternative information-processing strategies used in hypothesis testing (see Kruglanski, 1989; Sedikides, 1993; Swann, 1984; Trope & Liberman, 1996). The different strategies relate to different motives. In testing hypotheses about oneself or another person, for example, a diagnostic strategy might be used when the motive is simply accuracy, a confirming (or hypothesis-matching) strategy might be used when the motive is verification, and a valence-sensitive strategy might be used when the motive is enhancement (e.g., see Sedikides, 1993; Swann, 1987; Trope & Bassok,

1983). Motives also influence strategic concerns with the exhaustiveness of the information-seeking process, such as fear of invalidity increasing and time pressure decreasing the number of alternative hypotheses considered (see Kruglanski, 1989).

In addition to specific strategic actions used in self-control—task execution and information seeking—there are general strategic inclinations for attaining desired end-states. Regulatory focus theory (Higgins, 1997) distinguishes between two general strategic inclinations that depend on an individual's regulatory focus during goal attainment. When individuals have a promotion focus on accomplishment or advancement, they are eager to act in ways that facilitate goal attainment. When they have a prevention focus on safety or responsibility, they are vigilant to act in ways that avoid goal impairment. When people succeed in attaining their goals, they feel joyful in a promotion focus and feel relaxed in a prevention focus. When people fail to attain their goals, they feel disappointed in a promotion focus and feel nervous in a prevention focus.

Different strategic inclinations influence decision-making and problem-solving. When making decisions, for example, people in a promotion focus differ from those in a prevention focus in how they combine expectancy and value information (see Shah & Higgins, 1997) and the extent to which they have a risky versus a conservative bias (see Crowe & Higgins, 1997). Different strategic inclinations can also be related to different styles of solving life tasks. One important life task of students, for example, is to maintain high motivation to achieve good grades. One important source of motivational support is friends. Individuals differ in whether they seek out or avoid friends telling them that they are likely to succeed on an upcoming test (Cantor, 1994). Prevention focus individuals, for example, might avoid reassurance because it could make them too relaxed in anticipating success, thereby causing them to study less than they believe is necessary to succeed on the test.

Social/personality psychologists have been especially interested in the tactics that people use to impress other people or to fulfill personal needs in their relationships with others. There are a wide variety of ingratiation and impression management techniques whose effectiveness depends on the qualities of the interaction partner and the context of interaction (see Baumeister, 1982; Goffman, 1959; Jones, 1964; Leary & Kowalski, 1990; Schlenker, 1980). Some of the techniques are quite sophisticated. For example, sometimes individuals who believe they have little control over whether they will succeed use self-handicapping strategies, such as drinking or staying up late before an exam, whose purpose is to get others to attribute any failure on their part to situational causes rather than to a lack of ability (e.g., Jones & Berglas, 1978; see also Adler, 1954).

There are also individual differences in the extent to which people use self-presentational strategies in their social interactions. For example, high self-monitors are more likely than low self-monitors to use the standards associated with their current social interaction to regulate their actions, whereas low self-monitors are more likely than high self-monitors to use their personal standards to regulate their actions (e.g., Snyder, 1974, 1979). People also differ in the strategies they use for selecting partners and maintaining relationships. It has been suggested, for example, that evolutionary processes created a difference in the social strategies used by males and females to fulfill the basic social relationship needs of mating successfully and having surviving offspring, such as men devoting a greater proportion of their mating effort to short-term relationships (see Buss & Schmitt, 1993).

Knowing From Wanting

With exceptions such as evolutionary predispositions, usually individuals' strategic and tactical decisions are strongly influenced by what they know. As discussed earlier, the automatic and controlled use of stored knowledge and input information is a fundamental part of self-regulation. In a later section, we review additional ways that knowing influences wanting. It is important to recognize, however, that the relation between knowing and wanting is reciprocal. Not only does knowing influence wanting, but wanting also influences knowing. This reciprocal relation has fascinated psychologists since unconscious motives were discovered. It means that people can do exactly what they want to do and still believe that it is simply the rational thing to do because their wants unconsciously bias the knowledge they use to instigate (and later justify) the action.

There are several ways to conceptualize how wants influence knowing. The psychodynamic perspective emphasizes how unconscious needs, drives, and defense mechanisms determine which thoughts, and in which form, enter conscious awareness (see, for example, Erdelyi, 1974; Freud, 1937; Freud, 1923/1961; Klein, 1970). Gestalt-inspired consistency theories emphasize how needs for mental coherence transform beliefs and opinions (e.g., Festinger, 1957; Heider, 1958). These viewpoints on how wants influence knowing have not gone unchallenged in the social/personality literature, however (for reviews, see Kruglanski, 1996; Kunda, 1990).

Self-perception theory (Bem, 1967) challenged dissonance theory's (Festinger, 1957) motivational account for why people subsequently express an attitude congruent with a position they agreed to advocate in a message despite the fact that the advocated position contradicts the attitude they had expressed prior to their message. According to self-perception theory, there is no need to postulate an unpleasant state of dissonance that motivates attitude change to reduce the dissonance. Instead, the theory postulates that people use inferential processes to determine the attitudinal significance of their action. They infer that their action (i.e., advocating a particular position), given that it was unconstrained by external factors (i.e., freely chosen), must reflect an internal intention that agrees with their action (i.e., an attitude corresponding to the advocated position).

There are conditions in which the inferential processes postulated by self-perception theory are especially likely to influence attitudes (e.g., Fazio, Zanna, & Cooper, 1977; Salancik & Conway, 1975). Nonetheless, there is substantial evidence to support the conclusion that attitude-discrepant actions do produce an unpleasant state that motivates attitude change or some other action to reduce it (e.g., Cooper & Fazio, 1984; Steele & Liu, 1981; Zanna & Cooper, 1974; for reviews, see Kruglanski, 1996; Kunda, 1990).

The notion that people are motivated to have positive rather than negative thoughts enter consciousness has received most attention in the social/personality literature in its application to self-knowledge. Classic phenomena include people being more willing to take credit when they succeed than to take blame when they fail, and people being more likely to attribute success to high ability, and less likely to attribute failure to low ability, when it comes to explaining their own performance rather than another person's performance (for a review, see Snyder, Stephan, & Rosenfield, 1978). Once again, some questions were raised about whether motivational biases underlie such phenomenon or whether they can be accounted for in terms of information processing variables (see Miller & Ross, 1975; Tetlock & Levi, 1982).

There are a variety of cognitive alternative explanations for such apparently motivated asymmetries. For example, it can be argued that most individuals are likely to have a history of succeeding more often than failing, which would produce a stronger expectation of success than failure. For each individual, this expectation could produce selective attention to positive versus negative acts during performance and better retrieval of positive versus negative acts after performance. Partly inspired by such critiques, studies were subsequently designed that did provide convincing evidence that motives could, indeed, bias self-knowledge. For example, evidence of self-serving self-judgments was found in studies that controlled for past history and experimentally manipulated personal involvement in a performance or the personal relevance of a self-attribute (for reviews, see Kruglanski, 1996; Kunda, 1990). There is evidence, then, of wanting influencing knowing that is consistent with both the Gestalt and psychodynamic viewpoints on motivation. Evidence of wanting influencing knowing, however, is not restricted to these motives. Indeed, the findings viewed as supporting the Gestalt and psychodynamic viewpoints could be due, at least in part, to other motives.

Several other motives were discussed earlier. For example, it has been postulated that people have a basic need for effectance or perceived control. When people are deprived of control, they are strongly motivated to reinstate it. Studies have found that control deprivation changes people's attributional processes (e.g., Pittman & Pittman, 1980) and their judgments (e.g., Brehm & Brehm, 1981). A valued self-image is a desired end-state. Thus, from the perspective of control theory, people should be motivated to reduce any discrepancy from a valued self-image that their behavior has produced, such as reaffirming a valued self-attribute threatened by counterattitudinal advocacy (e.g., Steele & Lui, 1981). People also have a need for accuracy. There is evidence that when people's need for accuracy changes, their impression formation and attributional processes change (e.g., Fiske & Neuberg, 1990; Kruglanski & Ajzen, 1983; Tetlock, 1992).

The social roles that people enact also establish motives for their actions that can influence information processing and subsequent knowledge. An early study by Jones and deCharms (1958), for example, found that individuals assigned different (imaginary) roles before observing the same behaviors of an ex-prisoner of war attributed different personality characteristics to him. Even preparation for role enactment can influence how information is processed. In another early study, for example, Zajonc (1960) showed that even prior to communication, individuals assigned the role of "transmitter" of information represented the information in a more unified and organized way than individuals assigned the role of "recipient." In the transmitter role, people are also motivated to tailor their message to suit the characteristics of their audience, at least in part because such convergence creates a shared reality with their audience. When communicators tune their messages in this way, their own subsequent memory and judgments are influenced—the "saying is believing" effect (Higgins & Rholes, 1978; for a review, see Hardin & Higgins, 1996).

There are also individual differences in people's motives that influence what they know. People vary, for example, in their motivation to engage in situations in which uncertainty about the self or the world can be resolved through exploration (uncertainty-oriented persons) versus situations that provide certainty about the self or the world (certainty-oriented persons). This individual difference has been found to influence how information is processed and used, such as the extent to which the quality of the arguments in a persuasive message is given more weight than the characteristics of the message source (e.g., Sorrentino, Bobocel, Gitta, Olson, & Hewitt, 1988). People also vary in wanting to find closure on some topic (high need for closure) versus wanting to avoid closure and keep an open mind (low need for closure). Compared to low need for closure individuals, high need for closure individuals are more likely to use information that is highly available or accessible ("seize") and to ignore new or contradictory information once closure has been attained ("freeze"; e.g., Kruglanski & Webster, 1996).

Wanting From Knowing

We have described in previous sections how people learn about what matters in the world and use their stored knowledge of how the world works to make strategic and tactical decisions. People learn about how the world works in order to survive in it. People have knowledge of future events, outcome contingencies, and how they feel about things that are fundamental components of motivation. In all these respects, then, we have already described several ways in which wanting is influenced by knowing. In this section, we briefly review some other, more specific ways in which what one wants is influenced by the type of knowledge one possesses.

Since Heider's (1958) discussion of how people's lay theories about the social world influence their perceptions of and attributions for social actions, social/personality psychologists have recognized that people's mental models of the world are an important determinant of their responses to themselves and others. The attributions that people make for social actions are themselves motivationally significant. For example, people's motivation to punish (blame) or reward (credit) others for their actions depends on the type of person or situation attribution they make, such as whether they believe an action by another person that harmed them or someone else was due to the person's low ability, low effort, or bad intentions or was accidental, unforeseeable, or unlucky (e.g., Hamilton, Blumenfeld, & Kushler, 1988; Seligman, Finegan, Hazlewood, & Wilkinson, 1985).

People's own subsequent motivation to engage in an activity or the effort they put into performing a task also depends on how they explained their initial engagement or performance. Children, for example, are less interested in doing an activity again if they attributed their initial engagement to seeking an award for doing it than if they attributed it to their liking of the activity (e.g., Lepper, Greene, & Nisbett, 1973; Ross, 1975; see also Kruglanski, 1975). This phenomenon of rewards for engaging in an activity undermining later interest in the activity was discussed earlier as an example of wants changing wants. According to attributional accounts of this phenomenon, the undermining is mediated by the actors' explanations for their activity engagement.

People also can engage in more than one activity at a time. Even a single object, such as a coloring storybook or computer learning game, can incorporate more than one activity so that the actor switches back and forth between them. The inferences that people make from their switching back and forth can influence their subsequent interest in the alternative activities. It has been found that switching back and forth between two initially liked activities decreases subsequent interest in them, whereas switching back and forth between two initially disliked activities increases subsequent interest in them (Higgins, Trope, & Kwon, 1999).

Attributions for performance on a task can also undermine or enhance subsequent effort on the task. Subsequent effort and performance increases, for example, if actors attribute an earlier failure to their lack of effort than if they attribute it to their low ability on the task (Dweck, 1975). Indeed, this might account for the superior performance of individuals high in achievement motivation because they are more likely than individuals low in achievement motivation to attribute failure to a lack of effort (Weiner & Kukla, 1970; for a review relating attributions to depressives' lack of motivation, see Weary, Elbin, & Hill, 1987).

Reasons for one's actions are not restricted to explanations for activity engagement or performance outcomes. People also have reasons for their attitudes and opinions. We have discussed earlier how reasons in the form of likelihood and outcome expectancies can influence attitudes. There is also evidence that simply thinking of reasons for one's opinion on some topic or why one would prefer a particular object over an alternative can change one's attitudes and preferences. Moreover, this influence of knowing on wanting has been shown to polarize attitudes and produce poorer choices (e.g., Tesser, 1978; Wilson & Schooler, 1991).

Mental models of why people engage in activities or why they perform well or poorly are not the only mental models they have about the social world (see, for example, Wegener & Petty, 1998). These other mental models can also have motivational consequences. For example, people can have different theories about the nature of intelligence. They can believe that intelligence is a controllable and increasable quality (an incremental theory), or they can believe that intelligence is a fixed and uncontrollable trait (an entity theory). When individuals have an incremental theory they are more likely to want to increase their competence (a learning goal). In contrast, when individuals have an entity theory they are more likely to want positive evaluations of their competence (a performance goal). The former relation between knowing and wanting has been found to produce a more adaptive pattern of achievement behavior than the latter pattern of knowing and wanting (e.g., Dweck & Leggett, 1988).

People can also have faulty explanations for their actions or states that nonetheless influence their motivation and actions. Individuals, for example, can experience a high state of arousal or excitation that has a specific cause, such as some drug they ingested or some exercise they performed, but mistakenly believe that its cause is something else, such as some feeling they have. This misattribution, in turn, can make them want to behave in ways that fit their misattribution, such as behaving aggressively because of a misattribution to anger (e.g., Schachter & Singer, 1962; Zillman, Johnson, & Day, 1974).

Not only can wanting be influenced by knowing that is faulty, it can be influenced by knowing that does not recognize what is known. There are different ways of knowing something that relate to different kinds of knowledge. Episodic knowledge (e.g., autobiographical knowledge) is different from declarative knowledge (e.g., encyclopedic knowledge), which in turn is different from procedural knowledge (e.g., intuitive or tacit knowledge). Thus, life experiences can produce a kind of knowing that cannot be easily explained, justified, or evidentially supported but nevertheless influences motivation. For example, repeated exposure to an object can produce a feeling of familiarity when it is presented again later without any conscious recollection of having seen it before. Nonetheless, this feeling of familiarity increases people's liking for the object—a very different kind of wanting from knowing (see Zajonc, 1980b). As another example, people's knowledge of a significant other, such as their mother, can be unconsciously transferred to a newly encountered person, along with the positive or negative feelings associated with the significant other, thus influencing motivations to approach or avoid the new person (see Andersen, Reznik, & Manzella, 1996; Chen & Andersen, 1999).

Concluding Remarks

Motivational science is concerned with the nature and functions of wanting and their relation to knowing, feeling, and doing. The domain of motivational science extends across psychological areas and beyond to other disciplines. This chapter and volume concentrate on those issues that have been most central in the social/personality literature: basic wants, when wants change, bridging the gap between knowing and doing, getting what one wants, knowing from wanting, and wanting from knowing. Compared to other scientific domains that interface with psychology, like neuroscience and cognitive science, the domain of motivational science has not been well articulated or made accessible to scientists or the public. This is both surprising and unfortunate given that a major goal of families, businesses, and schools is to motivate others, and behavioral problems with motivational roots are consistently included among the public's major societal concerns. The present volume of social/personality articles is intended to provide access to some basic ideas and research findings in motivational science that are relevant to these goals and concerns.

REFERENCES

Abelson, R. P. (1983). Whatever became of consistency theory? *Personality and Social Psychology Bulletin, 9*, 37–54.

Abelson, R. P., Aronson, E., McGuire, W. J., Newcomb, T. M., Rosenberg, M. J., & Tannenbaum, P. H. (Eds.). (1968). *Theories of cognitive consistency: A sourcebook*. Chicago: Rand McNally.

Abelson, R. P., & Rosenberg, M. J. (1958). Symbolic psychologic: A model of attitudinal cognition. *Behavioral Science, 3*, 1–13.

Adler, A. (1954). *Understanding human nature*. New York: Fawcett.

Ajzen, I. (1996). The social psychology of decision making. In E. T. Higgins & A. W. Kruglanski (Eds.), *Social psychology: Handbook of basic principles* (pp. 297–325). New York: Guilford.

Ajzen, I., & Fishbein, M. (1970). The prediction of behavior from attitudinal and normative variables. *Journal of Experimental Social Psychology, 6*, 466–487.

Allport, G. W. (1968). The historical background of modern social psychology. In G. Lindzey & E. Aronson (Eds.), *The handbook of social psychology* (Vol. 1, pp. 1–80). Reading, MA: Addison-Wesley.

Andersen, S. M., Reznik, I., & Manzella, L. M. (1996). Eliciting facial affect, motivation, and expectancies in transference: Significant-other representations in social relations. *Journal of Personality and Social Psychology, 71,* 1108–1129.

Aronson, E. (1969). The theory of cognitive dissonance: A current perspective. In L. Berkowitz (Ed.), *Advances in experimental social psychology,* (Vol. 4, pp. 1–34). New York: Academic Press.

Atkinson, J. W. (1957). Motivational determinants of risk-taking behavior. *Psychological Review, 64,* 359–372.

Atkinson, J. W. (1964). *An introduction to motivation.* Princeton, NJ: D. Van Nostrand.

Bandura, A. (1965). Vicarious processes: A case of no-trial learning. In L. Berkowitz (Ed.), *Advances in experimental social psychology* (pp. 1–55). New York: Academic Press.

Bandura, A. (1986). *Social foundations of thought and action: A social cognitive theory.* Englewood Cliffs, NJ: Prentice-Hall.

Bandura, A., & Cervone, D. (1983). Self-evaluative and self-efficacy mechanisms governing the motivational effects of goal systems. *Journal of Personality and Social Psychology, 45,* 1017–1028.

Bargh, J. A., Chen, M., & Burrows, L. (1996). Automaticity of social behavior: Direct effects of trait construct and stereotype activation on action. *Journal of Personality and Social Psychology, 71,* 230–244.

Baumeister, R. F. (1982). A self-presentational view of social phenomenon. *Psychological Bulletin, 91,* 3–26.

Baumeister, R. F., & Heatherton, T. F. (1996). Self-regulation failure: An overview. *Psychological Inquiry, 7,* 1–15.

Baumeister, R. F., & Leary, M. R. (1995). The need to belong: Desire for interpersonal attachments as a fundamental human motivation. *Psychological Bulletin, 117,* 497–529.

Bem, D. J. (1967). Self-perception: An alternative interpretation of cognitive dissonance phenomena. *Psychological Review, 74,* 183–200.

Berlyne, D. E. (1960). *Conflict, arousal and curiosity.* New York: McGraw-Hill.

Bowlby, J. (1969). *Attachment* (Attachment and loss, Vol. 1). New York: Basic Books.

Bowlby, J. (1973). *Separation: Anxiety and anger* (Attachment and loss, Vol. 2). New York: Basic Books.

Brehm, J. W. (1966). *A theory of psychological reactance.* New York: Academic Press.

Brehm, J. W., & Mann, M. (1975). The effect of importance of freedom and attraction to group members on influence produced by group pressure. *Journal of Personality and Social Psychology, 31,* 816–824.

Brehm, J. W., & Self, E. A. (1989). The intensity of motivation. *Annual Review of Psychology, 40,* 109–131.

Brehm, S. S., & Brehm, J. W. (1981). *Psychological reactance: A theory of freedom and control.* New York: Academic Press.

Brewer, M. B. (1991). The social self: On being the same and different at the same time. *Personality and Social Psychology Bulletin, 17,* 475–482.

Brown, R. W. (1958). *Words and things.* New York: Free Press.

Buss, D. M., & Schmitt, D. P. (1993). Sexual strategies theory: A contextual evolutionary analysis of human mating. *Psychological Review, 100,* 204–232.

Cantor, N. (1994). Life task problem-solving: Situational affordances and personal needs. *Personality and Social Psychology Bulletin, 20,* 235–243.

Cantor, N., & Kihlstrom, J. F. (1987). *Personality and social intelligence.* Englewood Cliffs, NJ : Prentice-Hall.

Carver, C. S., & Scheier, M. F. (1981). *Attention and self-regulation: A control-theory approach to human behavior.* New York: Springer-Verlag.

Carver, C. S., & Scheier, M. F. (1990). Origins and functions of positive and negative affect: A control-process view. *Psychological Review, 97,* 19–35.

Chaiken, S. (1980). Heuristic versus systematic information processing and the use of source versus message cues in persuasion. *Journal of Personality and Social Psychology, 39,* 752–766.

Chen, S., & Andersen, S. M. (1999). Relationships from the past in the present: Significant-other representations and transference in interpersonal life. In M. P. Zanna (Ed.), *Advances in experimental social psychology* (Vol. 31, pp. 123–190). New York: Academic Press.

Cooley, C. H. (1964). *Human nature and the social order.* New York: Schocken Books. (Original work published 1902)

Cooper, J., & Fazio, R. H. (1984). A new look at dissonance theory. In L. Berkowitz (Ed.), *Advances in Experimental Social Psychology* (Vol. 17, pp. 229-265). New York: Academic Press.

Crowe, E., & Higgins, E. T. (1997). Regulatory focus and strategic inclinations: Promotion and prevention in decision-making. *Organizational Behavior and Human Decision Processes, 69,* 117–132.

Darwin, C. (1871). *The descent of man and selection in relation to sex.* London: Murray.

deCharms, R. (1968). *Personal causation.* New York: Academic Press.

Deci, E. L. (1971). Effects of externally mediated rewards on intrinsic motivation. *Journal of Personality and Social Psychology, 18,* 105–115.

Deci, E. L., & Ryan, R. M. (1987). The support of autonomy and the control of behavior. *Journal of Personality and Social Psychology, 55,* 1024–1037.

Downey, G., Freitas, A. L., Michaelis, B., & Khouri, H. (1998). The self-fulfilling prophecy in close relationships: Rejection sensitivity and rejection by romantic partners. *Journal of Personality and Social Psychology, 75,* 545–560.

Dweck, C. S. (1975). The role of expectations and attributions in the alleviation of learned helplessness. *Journal of Personality and Social Psychology, 31,* 674–685.

Dweck, C. S., & Leggett, E. L. (1988). A social-cognitive approach to motivation and personality. *Psychological Review, 95,* 256–273.

Eagly, A. H., & Chaiken, S. (1993). *The psychology of attitudes.* New York: Harcourt Brace Jovanovich.

Edwards, W. (1955). The prediction of decisions among bets. *Journal of Experimental Psychology, 51,* 201–214.

Erdelyi, M. H. (1974). A new look at the new look: Perceptual defense and vigilance. *Psychological Review, 81,* 1–25.

Erikson, E. H. (1963). *Childhood and society* (Revised edition. Original edition, 1950). New York: W. W. Norton & Co.

Fazio, R. H. (1990). Multiple processes by which attitudes guide behavior: The mode model as an integrative framework. In M. P. Zanna (Ed.), *Advances in Experimental Social Psychology* (Vol. 23, pp. 75–109). New York: Academic Press.

Fazio, R. H., Zanna, M. P., & Cooper, J. (1977). Dissonance and self-perception: An integrative view of each theory's proper domain of application. *Journal of Experimental Social Psychology, 13,* 464–479.

Feather, N. T. (1961). The relationship of persistence at a task to expectation of success and achievement-related motives. *Journal of Abnormal and Social Psychology, 63,* 552–561.

Festinger, L. (1942). A theoretical interpretation of shifts in level of aspiration. *Psychological Review, 49,* 235–250.

Festinger, L. (1954). A theory of social comparison processes. *Human Relations, 1,* 117–140.

Festinger, L. (1957). *A theory of cognitive dissonance.* Evanston, IL: Row, Peterson.

Fiske, S. T. (1992). Thinking is for doing: Portraits of social cognition from daguerreotype to laser photo. *Journal of Personality and Social Psychology, 63,* 877–889.

Fiske, S. T., & Neuberg, S. L. (1990). A continuum of impression formation, from category-based to individuating processes: Influences of information and motivation on attention and interpretation. In M. P. Zanna (Ed.), *Advances in experimental social psychology* (Vol. 23. pp. 1–74). New York: Academic Press.

Folkman, S., Lazarus, R. S., Dunkel-Schetter, C., DeLongis, A., & Gruen, R. (1986). The dynamics of a stressful encounter. *Journal of Personality and Social Psychology, 50,* 992–1003.

Freud, A. (1937). *The ego and the mechanisms of defense.* New York: International Universities.

Freud, S. (1950). *Beyond the pleasure principle.* New York: Liveright. (Original work published 1920)

Freud, S. (1953). Three essays on the theory of sexuality. *Standard Edition,* Volume 7. London: Hogarth Press. (Original work published 1905)

Freud, S. (1957). Instincts and their vicissitudes. *Standard Edition,* Volume 14. London: Hogarth Press. (Original work published 1915)

Freud, S. (1961). The ego and the id. In J. Strachey (Ed. and Trans.), *Standard edition of the complete psychological works of Sigmund Freud* (Vol. 19, pp. 3–66). London: Hogarth Press. (Original work published 1923)

Frey, K. S., & Ruble, D. N. (1985). What children say when the teacher is not around: Conflicting goals in social comparison and performance assessment in the classroom. *Journal of Personality and Social Psychology, 48,* 550–562.

Goffman, E. (1959). *The presentation of self in everyday life.* Garden City, NY: Doubleday.

Gollwitzer, P. M. (1996). The volitional benefits of planning. In P. M. Gollwitzer & J. A. Bargh (Eds.), *The psychology of action: Linking cognition and motivation to behavior* (pp. 287–312). New York: Guilford.

Gollwitzer, P. M., Heckhausen, H., & Stellar, B. (1990). Deliberative vs. implemental mind-sets: Cognitive tuning toward congruous thoughts and information. *Journal of Personality and Social Psychology, 59,* 1119–1127.

Gollwitzer, P. M., & Moskowitz, G. B. (1996). Goal effects on action and cognition. In E. T. Higgins & A. W. Kruglanski (Eds.), *Social psychology: Handbook of basic principles* (pp. 361–399). New York: Guilford.

Guthrie, E. R. (1935). *The psychology of learning.* New York: Harper.

Hamilton, V. L., Blumenfeld, P. C., & Kushler, R. H. (1988). A question of standards: Attributions of blame and credit for classroom acts. *Journal of Personality and Social Psychology, 54,* 34–38.

Harackiewicz, J. M., Sansone, C. , & Manderlink, G. (1985). Competence, achievement orientation, and intrinsic motivation: A process analysis. *Journal of Personality and Social Psychology, 48,* 493–508.

Hardin, C., & Higgins, E. T. (1996). Shared reality: How social verification makes the subjective objective. In R. M. Sorrentino & E. T. Higgins (Eds.), *Handbook of motivation and cognition: The interpersonal context* (Vol. 3, pp. 28–84). New York: Guilford Press.

Heckhausen, H., & Gollwitzer, P. M. (1987). Thought contents and cognitive functioning in motivational versus volitional states of mind. *Motivation and Emotion, 11,* 101–120.

Heider, F. (1958). *The psychology of interpersonal relations.* New York: Wiley.

Higgins, E. T. (1987). Self-discrepancy: A theory relating self and affect. *Psychological Review, 94,* 319–340.

Higgins, E. T. (1997). Beyond pleasure and pain. *American Psychologist, 52,* 1280–1300.

Higgins, E. T. (2000). Social cognition: Learning about what matters in the social world. *European Journal of Social Psychology, 30,* 3–39.

Higgins, E. T., & Eccles-Parsons, J. (1983). Social cognition and the social life of the child: Stages as subcultures. In E. T. Higgins, D. N. Ruble, & W. W. Hartup (Eds.), *Social cognition and social development: A socio-cultural perspective* (pp. 15–62). New York: Cambridge University Press.

Higgins, E. T., & Rholes, W. S. (1978). "Saying is believing": Effects of message modification on memory and liking for the person described. *Journal of Experimental Social Psychology, 14,* 363–378.

Higgins, E. T., Trope, Y., & Kwon, J. (1999). Augmentation and undermining from combining activities: The role of choice in activity engagement theory. *Journal of Experimental Social Psychology, 35,* 285–307.

Horney, K. (1946). *Our inner conflicts: A constructive theory of neurosis.* London: Routledge & Kegan Paul.

Hull, C. L. (1943). *Principles of behavior.* New York: Appleton-Century-Crofts.

Hunt, J. M. (1965). Intrinsic motivation and its role in psychological development. *Nebraska Symposium on Motivation, 13,* 189–282.

James, W. (1948). *Psychology.* New York: The World Publishing Company. (Original publication, 1890)

Jones, E. E. (1964). *Ingratiation: A social psychological analysis.* New York: Appelton-Century-Crofts.

Jones, E. E., & Berglas, S. (1978). Control of attributions about the self through self-handicapping strategies: The appeal of alcohol and the role of under-achievement. *Personality and Social Psychology Bulletin, 4,* 200–206.

Jones, E. E., & Davis, K. E. (1965). From acts to dispositions: The attribution process in person perception. In L. Berkowitz (Ed.), *Advances in experimental social psychology* (Vol. 2, pp. 219–266). New York: Academic Press.

Jones, E. E., & deCharms, R. (1958). The organizing function of interaction roles in person perception. *Journal of Abnormal and Social Psychology, 57,* 155–164.

Kahneman, D., Diener, E., & Schwarz, N. (1999). *Well-being:*

The foundations of hedonic psychology. New York: Russell Sage.

Kahneman, D., & Miller, D. T. (1986). Norm theory: Comparing reality to its alternatives. *Psychological Review, 93,* 136–153.

Kahneman, D., & Tversky, A. (1982). The simulation heuristic. In D. Kahneman, P. Slovic, & A. Tversky (Eds.), *Judgment under uncertainty: Heuristics and biases* (pp. 201–208). New York: Cambridge University Press.

Kelley, H. H. (1967). Attribution theory in social psychology. In D. Levine (Ed.), *Nebraska Symposium of Motivation, 15,* 192–238.

Kelly, G. A. (1955). *The psychology of personal constructs.* New York: W. W. Norton.

Kelman, H. C. (1958). Compliance, identification, and internalization: Three processes of attitude change. *Journal of Conflict Resolution, 2,* 51–60.

Klein, G. S. (1970). *Perception, motives and personality.* New York: Knopf.

Klinger, E. (1975). Consequences of commitment to and disengagement from incentives. *Psychological Review, 82,* 1–25.

Krech, D., & Crutchfield, R. S. (1948). *Theory and problems of social psychology.* New York: McGraw-Hill.

Kruglanski, A. W. (1975). The endogenous-exogenous partition in attribution theory. *Psychological Review, 82,* 387–406.

Kruglanski, A. W. (1989). *Lay epistemics and human knowledge: Cognitive and motivational bases.* New York: Plenum.

Kruglanski, A. W. (1996). Motivated social cognition: Principles of the interface. In E. T. Higgins & A. W. Kruglanski (Eds.), *Social psychology: Handbook of basic principles* (pp. 493–520). New York: Guilford.

Kruglanski, A. W, & Ajzen, I. (1983). Bias and error in human judgment. *European Journal of Social Psychology, 13,* 1–44.

Kruglanski, A. W., & Webster, D. M. (1996). Motivated closing of the mind: "Seizing" and "freezing." *Psychological Review, 103,* 263–283.

Kruglanski, A. W., Friedman, I., & Zeevi, G. (1971). The effects of extrinsic incentive on some qualitative aspects of task performance. *Journal of Personality, 39,* 606–617.

Kuhl, J. (1984). Volitional aspects of achievement motivation and learned helplessness: Toward a comprehensive theory of action control. In B. A. Maher (Ed.), *Progress in experimental personality research* (Vol. 12, pp. 99–170). New York: Academic Press.

Kunda, Z. (1990). The case for motivated reasoning. *Psychological Bulletin, 108,* 480–498.

Leary, M. R., & Kowalski, R. M. (1990). Impression management: A literature review and two-component model. *Psychological Bulletin, 107,* 34–47.

Lecky, P. (1961). *Self-consistency: A theory of personality.* New York: The Shoe String Press.

Lepper, M. R., Greene, D., & Nisbett, R. E. (1973). Undermining children's intrinsic interest with extrinsic reward: A test of the overjustification hypothesis. *Journal of Personality and Social Psychology, 28,* 129–137.

Lerner, M. J. (1970). The desire for justice and reaction to victims. In J. R. Macaulay & L. Berkowitz (Eds.), *Altruism and helping behavior* (pp. 205–229). New York: Academic Press.

Levine, J. M., & Moreland, R. L. (1998). Small groups. In D.

T. Gilbert, S. T. Fiske, & G. Lindzey (Eds.), *The handbook of social psychology,* (Vol. 2, pp. 415–469). New York: McGraw-Hill.

Levine, J. M., Resnick, L. B., & Higgins, E. T. (1993). Social foundations of cognition. *Annual Review of Psychology, 44,* 585–612.

Lewin, K. (1935). *A dynamic theory of personality.* New York: McGraw-Hill.

Lewin, K. (1951). *Field theory in social science.* New York: Harper.

Lewin, K., Dembo, T., Festinger, L., & Sears, P. S. (1944). Level of aspiration. In J. McHunt (Ed.), *Personality and the behavior disorders* (Vol. 1, pp. 333–378). New York: Ronald Press.

Locke, E. A. (1968). Toward a theory of task motivation and incentives. *Organizational Behavior and Human Performance, 3,* 157–189.

McClelland, D. C., Atkinson, J. W., Clark, R. A., & Lowell, E. L. (1953). *The achievement motive.* New York: Appleton-Century-Crofts.

McDougall, W. (1923). *Outline of psychology.* New York: Scribner.

McGuire, W. J. (1964). Inducing resistance to persuasion: Some contemporary approaches. In L. Berkowitz (Ed.), *Advances in experimental social psychology* (Vol. 1, pp. 191–229). New York: Academic Press.

Mead, G. H. (1934). *Mind, self, and society.* Chicago: University of Chicago Press.

Miller, D. T., & Ross, M. (1975). Self-serving biases in the attribution of causality: Fact or fiction? *Psychological Bulletin, 82,* 213–225.

Miller, N. E. (1944). Experimental studies of conflict. In J. McV. Hunt (Ed.), *Personality and the behavior disorders* (Vol. 1, pp. 431–465). New York: Ronald Press.

Miller, G. A., Galanter, E., & Pribram, K. H. (1960). *Plans and the structure of behavior.* New York: Holt, Rinehart, & Winston.

Mischel, W., Cantor, N., & Feldman, S. (1996). Principles of self-regulation: The nature of willpower and self-control. In E. T. Higgins & A. W. Kruglanski (Eds.), *Social psychology: Handbook of basic principles* (pp. 329–360). New York: Guilford.

Mischel, W., & Moore, B. (1980). The role of ideation in voluntary delay for symbolically presented rewards. *Cognitive Therapy and Research, 4,* 211–221.

Mischel, W., & Patterson, C. J. (1978). Effective plans for self-control in children. In W. A. Collins (Ed.), *Minnesota symposia on child psychology* (Vol. 11, pp. 199–230). Hillsdale, NJ: Erlbaum.

Mischel, W., & Shoda, Y. (1995). A cognitive-affective system theory of personality: Reconceptualizing situations, dispositions, dynamics, and invariance in personality structure. *Psychological Review, 102,* 246–268.

Mischel, W., Shoda, Y., & Rodriguez, M. L. (1989). Delay of gratification in children. *Science, 244,* 933–938.

Mowrer, O. H. (1960). *Learning theory and behavior.* New York: John Wiley.

Nisbett, R. E., & Ross, L. D. (1980). *Human inference: Strategies and shortcomings of informal judgment* (Century Series in Psychology). Englewood Cliffs, NJ: Prentice-Hall.

Olson, J. M., Roese, N. J., & Zanna, M. P. (1996). Expectancies. In E. T. Higgins & A. W. Kruglanski (Eds.), *Social psychology: Handbook of basic principles* (pp. 211–238). New York: Guilford.

Osgood, C. E., & Tannenbaum, P. H. (1955). The principle of congruity in the prediction of attitude change. *Psychological Review, 62*, 42–55.

Ostrom, T. M. (1984). The sovereignty of social cognition. In R. S. Wyer, Jr. & T. K. Srull (Eds.), *Handbook of social cognition* (Vol. 1, pp. 1–38). Hillsdale, NJ: Erlbaum.

Petty, R. E., & Cacioppo, J. T. (1986). *Communication and persuasion: Central and peripheral routes to attitude change*. New York: Springer-Verlag.

Pittman, T. S. (1998). Motivation. In D. T. Gilbert, S. T. Fiske, & G. Lindzey (Eds.), *The handbook of social psychology* (Vol. 1, pp. 549–590). New York: McGraw-Hill.

Pittman, T. S., & Heller, J. F. (1987). Social motivation. *Annual Review of Psychology, 38*, 461–489.

Pittman, T. S., & Pittman, N. L. (1980). Deprivation of control and the attribution process. *Journal of Personality and Social Psychology, 39*, 377–389.

Powers, W. T. (1973) *Behavior: The control of perception*. Chicago: Aldine.

Pyszczynski, T. A., Greenberg, J., & Solomon, S. (1997). Why do we need what we need?: A terror management perspective on the roots of human social motivation. *Psychological Inquiry, 8*, 1–20.

Ross, M. (1975). Salience of reward and intrinsic motivation. *Journal of Personality and Social Psychology, 32*, 245–254.

Rotter, J. B. (1954). *Social learning and clinical psychology*. Englewood Cliffs, NJ: Prentice-Hall.

Ruble, D. N. (1994). A phase model of transitions: Cognitive and motivational consequences. In M. P. Zanna (Ed.), *Advances in experimental social psychology* (Vol. 26, pp. 163–214). New York: Academic Press.

Salancik, G. R., & Conway, M. (1975). Attitude inferences from salient and relevant cognitive content about behavior. *Journal of Personality and Social Psychology, 32*, 829–840.

Sanbonmatsu, D. M., & Fazio, R. H. (1990). The role of attitudes in memory-based decision making. *Journal of Personality and Social Psychology, 59*, 614–622.

Schachter, S., & Singer, J. E. (1962). Cognitive, social and physiological determinants of emotional state. *Psychological Review, 69*, 379–399.

Schlenker, B. R. (1980). *Impression management: The self-concept, social identity, and interpersonal relations*. Monterey, CA: Brooks/Cole.

Sedikides, C. (1993). Assessment, enhancement, and verification determinants of the self-evaluation process. *Journal of Personality and Social Psychology, 65*, 317–338.

Seligman, C., Finegan, J. E., Hazlewood, J. D., & Wilkinson, M. (1985). Manipulating attributions for profit: A field test of the effects of attributions on behavior. *Social Cognition, 3*, 313–321.

Seligman, M. E. P. (1975). *Helplessness: On depression, development, and death*. San Francisco: Freeman.

Shah, J., & Higgins, E. T. (1997). Expectancy × value effects: Regulatory focus as a determinant of magnitude *and* direction. *Journal of Personality and Social Psychology, 73*, 447–458.

Skinner, B. F. (1938). *The behavior of organisms: An experimental analysis*. New York: Appleton-Century-Crofts.

Smith, E. R. (1993). Procedural knowledge and processing strategies in social cognition. In R. S. Wyer & T. K. Srull (Eds.), *Handbook of social cognition* (Second Ed., Vol. 1, pp. 99–151). Hillsdale, NJ: Erlbaum.

Snyder, M. (1974). The self-monitoring of expressive behavior. *Journal of Personality and Social Psychology, 30*, 526–537.

Snyder, M. (1979). Self-monitoring processes. In L. Berkowitz (Ed.), *Advances in experimental social psychology* (Vol. 12, pp. 85–128). New York: Academic Press.

Snyder, M. L., Stephan, W. G., & Rosenfeld, D. (1978). Attributional egotism. In J. H. Harvey, W. Ickes, & R. F. Kidd (Eds.), *New directions in attribution research* (Vol. 2, pp. 91–117). Hillsdale, NJ: Erlbaum.

Sorrentino, R. M., Bobocel, D. R., Gitta, M. Z., Olson, J. M., & Hewitt, E. L. (1988). Uncertainty orientation and persuasion: Individual differences in the effects of personal relevance on social judgments. *Journal of Personality and Social Psychology, 55*, 357–371.

Sorrentino, R. M., & Higgins, E. T. (1986). Motivation and cognition: Warming up to synergism. In R. M. Sorrentino & E. T. Higgins (Eds.), *Handbook of motivation and cognition: Foundations of social behavior* (pp. 3–19). New York: Guilford.

Sorrentino, R. M., & Short, J. C. (1986). Uncertainty orientation, motivation, and cognition. In R. M. Sorrentino & E. T. Higgins (Eds.), *Handbook of motivation and cognition: Foundations of social behavior* (Vol. 1, pp. 379–403). New York: Guilford Press.

Spence, K. W. (1956). *Behavior theory and conditioning*. New Haven, CT: Yale University Press.

Steele, C. M., & Liu, T. J. (1981). Making the dissonance act unreflective of the self: Dissonance avoidance and the expectancy of a value affirming response. *Personality and Social Psychology Bulletin, 45*, 5–19.

Stevens, L. E., & Fiske, S. T. (1995). Motivation and cognition in social life: A social survival perspective. *Social Cognition, 13*, 189–214.

Stryker, S., & Statham, A. (1985). Symbolic interaction and role theory. In G. Lindzey & E. Aronson (Eds.), *Handbook of social psychology* (Vol. I, pp. 311–378). New York: Random House.

Sullivan, H. S. (1953). *The collected works of Harry Stack Sullivan: The interpersonal theory of psychiatry* (Vol. 1). Edited by H. S. Perry & M. L. Gawel. New York: W. W. Norton.

Swann, W. B., Jr. (1984). Quest for accuracy in person perception: A matter of pragmatics. *Psychological Review, 91*, 457–477.

Swann, W. B., Jr. (1987). Identity negotiation: Where two roads meet. *Journal of Personality and Social Psychology, 53*, 1038–1051.

Tajfel, H., Flament, C., Billig, M., & Bundy, R. P. (1971). Social categorization and intergroup behavior. *European Journal of Social Psychology, 1*, 149–178.

Taylor, S. E., & Brown, J. D. (1988). Illusion and well-being: A social psychological perspective on mental health. *Psychological Bulletin, 103*, 193–210.

Taylor, S. E., & Schneider, S. K. (1989). Coping and the simulation of events. *Social Cognition, 7*, 174–194.

Tesser, A. (1978). Self-generated attitude change. In L. Berkowitz (Ed.), *Advances in experimental social psychology* (Vol. 11, pp. 289–338). New York: Academic Press.

Tesser, A. (1993). The importance of heritability in psychological research: The case of attitudes. *Psychological Review, 100*, 129–142.

Tesser, A., & Cornell, D. P. (1991). On the confluence of self-processes. *Journal of Experimental Social Psychology*, 27, 501–526.

Tesser, A., Millar, M., & Moore, J. (1988). Some affective consequences of social comparison and reflection processes: The pain and pleasure of being close. *Journal of Personality and Social Psychology*, 54, 49–61.

Tetlock, P. E. (1992). The impact of accountability on judgment and choice: Toward a social contingency model. In M. P. Zanna (Ed.), *Advances in Experimental Social Psychology* (Vol. 25, pp. 331–376). New York: Academic Press.

Tetlock, P. E., & Levi, A. (1982). Attribution bias: On the inconclusiveness of the cognition-motivation debate. *Journal of Experimental Social Psychology*, 18, 68–88.

Thorndike, E. L. (1911). *Animal intelligence.* New York: Macmillan.

Tolman, E. C. (1932). *Purposive behavior in animals and men.* New York: Appleton-Century-Crofts.

Trope, Y., & Bassok, M. (1983). Information gathering strategies in hypothesis testing. *Journal of Experimental Social Psychology*, 19, 560–576.

Trope, Y., & Liberman, A. (1996). Social hypothesis testing: Cognitive and motivational mechanisms. In E. T. Higgins & A. W. Kruglanski (Eds.), *Social psychology: Handbook of basic principles* (pp. 239–270). New York: Guilford.

Vallacher, R. R., & Wegner, D. M. (1987). What do people think they are doing?: Action identification and human behavior. *Psychological Review*, 94, 3–15.

Van Hook, E., & Higgins, E. T. (1988). Self-related problems beyond the self-concept: The motivational consequences of discrepant self-guides. *Journal of Personality and Social Psychology*, 55, 625–633.

Weary, G., Elbin, S. D., & Hill, M. G. (1987). Attribution and social comparison processes in depression. *Journal of Personality and Social Psychology*, 52, 605–610.

Weber, M. (1967). Subjective meaning in the social situation. In G. B. Levitas (Ed.), *Culture and consciousness: Perspectives in the social sciences* (pp. 156–169). New York: Braziller.

Webster's Ninth New Collegiate Dictionary. (1989). Springfield, MA: Merriam-Webster.

Wegener, D. T., & Petty, R. E. (Eds.). (1998). Mental models. *Social Cognition* (Special Issue), 8(3). New York: Guilford Press.

Wegner, D. M. (1994). Ironic processes of mental control. *Psychological Review*, 101, 34–52.

Wegner, D. M., Schneider, D. J., Carter, S., & White, T. (1987). Paradoxical effects of thought suppression. *Journal of Personality and Social Psychology*, 53, 5–13.

Wegner, D. M., & Wenzlaff, R. M. (1996). Mental control. In E. T. Higgins & A. W. Kruglanski (Eds.), *Social psychology: Handbook of basic principles* (pp. 466–492). New York: Guilford.

Weiner, B. (1972). *Theories of motivation: From mechanism to cognition.* Chicago: Rand McNally.

Weiner, B. (1986). Attribution, emotion, and action. In R. M. Sorrentino & E. T. Higgins (Eds.), *Handbook of motiva-*

tion and cognition: Foundations of social behavior (Vol. 1, pp. 281–312). New York: Guilford Press.

Weiner, B., Frieze, I., Kukla, A., Reed, L., Rest, S., & Rosenbaum, R. M. (1971). Perceiving the causes of success and failure. In E. E. Jones, D. E. Kanouse, H. H. Kelley, R. E. Nisbett, S. Valins, & B. Weiner (Eds.), *Attribution: Perceiving the causes of behavior* (pp. 95–120). Morristown, NJ: General Learning Press.

Weiner, B., & Kukla, A. (1970). An attributional analysis of achievement motivation. *Journal of Personality and Social Psychology*, 15, 1–20.

White, R. W. (1959). Motivation reconsidered: The concept of competence. *Psychological Review, 66,* 297–333.

Wicklund, R. A., & Brehm, J. W. (1976). *Perspectives on cognitive dissonance.* Hillsdale, NJ: Erlbaum.

Wicklund, R. A., & Duval, S. (1971). Opinion change and performance facilitation as a result of objective self awareness. *Journal of Experimental Social Psychology*, 7, 319–342.

Wiener, N. (1948). *Cybernetics: Control and communication in the animal and the machine.* Cambridge, MA: M.I.T. Press.

Wilson, T. D., & Schooler, J. W. (1991). Thinking too much: Introspection can reduce the quality of preferences and decisions. *Journal of Personality and Social Psychology*, 60, 181–192.

Woodworth, R. S. (1918). *Dynamic psychology.* New York: Columbia University Press.

Woodworth, R. S. (1958). *Dynamics of behavior.* New York: Holt, 1958.

Wyer, R. S., & Srull, T. K. (1989). *Memory and cognition in its social context.* Hillsdale, NJ: Erlbaum.

Zajonic, R. B. (1960). The process of cognitive tuning and communication. *Journal of Abnormal and Social Psychology, 61,* 159–167.

Zajonc, R. B. (1966). *Social psychology: An experimental approach.* Belmont, CA: Brooks/Cole.

Zajonc, R. B. (1980a). Cognition and social cognition: A historical perspective. In L. Festinger (Ed.), *Retrospections on social psychology* (pp. 180–204). New York: Oxford University Press.

Zajonc, R. B. (1980b). Feeling and thinking: Preferences need no inferences. *American Psychologist*, 35, 151–175.

Zanna, M. P., & Cooper, J. (1974). Dissonance and the pill: An attribution approach to studying the arousal properties of dissonance. *Journal of Personality and Social Psychology*, 29, 703–709.

Zanna, M. P., & Pack, S. J. (1975). On the self-fulfilling nature of apparent sex differences in behavior. *Journal of Experimental Social Psychology*, 11, 583–591.

Zillmann, D., Johnson, R. C., & Day, K. D. (1974). Attribution of apparent arousal and proficiency of recovery from sympathetic activation affecting excitation transfer to aggressive behavior. *Journal of Experimental Social Psychology*, 10, 503–515.

Zuckerman, M. (1984). Sensation seeking: A comparative approach to a human trait. *The Behavioral and Brain Sciences*, 7, 413–471.

Basic Wants

A common idea in the field of motivation is that some of our wants are more basic than others. Presumably, these basic wants provide the foundation on which subsequent motives, desires and wishes may be constructed. But a major problem has been to decide which particular wants are the basic ones, what exactly makes them basic, and how many such basic wants there are. Different theorists provided different answers to these questions. Conceptualizing wants as instincts Freud (1915/1957) distinguished two that seemed particularly basic, namely the life and the death instincts. McDougall (1923), however, proposed a very large number of instincts which cast some doubt on whether they all could be very basic.

In partial response to the criticisms brought against the instinct concept, Woodworth (1918) proposed the notion of a drive state assumed to be engendered by basic physiological deficits. But other theorists have felt that a direct relation to physiological deficits is too narrow a requirement to define a motivation as basic, and that some wants may be truly basic, not necessarily because they stem from tissue deficits but because they fulfill a fundamental function without which survival would be in jeopardy. One such want may be the desire to belong with other people and be a member of a group. The desire to belong with others is basic because the tendency of humans to coalesce in groups may have been a major factor that contributed to our survival and dominance within the animal kingdom (Caporael & Brewer, 1991). A related basic want is the need to get along with others (see Stevens & Fiske, 1995), without which effective group functioning is unlikely. In the present section, Baumeister and Leary (1995) examine the social psychological implications of the need to belong and its intriguing consequences for the degree to which stable interpersonal relationships are more gratifying overall than transient or discontinuous relations.

However, the need to belong and form part of a group may be in tension with another basic want, the desire to distinguish oneself and be different from others. This latter want is also fundamental from the evolutionary perspective because personal distinctiveness may be important for attracting the attention of potential mating partners, hence increasing the likelihood of propagating one's genes. The tension between the want to belong and that to be distinctive are discussed in the paper by Brewer (1991). She proposes that a strong social identity, whereby one's uniqueness derives from the special character of the group to which one belongs, provides a solution to this conflict that has far-reaching conse-quences for human social behavior.

A closely related theme is addressed in the paper by Tesser, Millar, and Moore (1988); namely, the tension between the joy of belonging with successful others and the dread that their success will outshine one's own successes and detract from one's distinctiveness and attention-drawing potential. The authors theorize that we

may want to shine on some dimensions only (those in regard to which we feel competent or endowed) and not on all dimensions. It is in regard to the former, self-relevant, dimensions only that one feels competitive with one's friends and close relations, whereas with respect to other dimensions one is pleased to bask in their reflected glory.

But there are other basic wants besides the desire to belong and to be distinctive. Some such wants relate to the highly cognitive nature of humans as a species and the great evolutionary advantages that our highly developed brains have bestowed upon us. A particularly interesting want relates to the fact that among the many species, the human species is probably the only one whose members are consciously aware of their own mortality. Such awareness runs the risk of engendering abject terror that needs to be managed or else it could totally dominate the human experience and paralyze our ability to act. The article by Pyszczynski, Greenberg, and Solomon (1997) featured in this section explores the notion of terror management and its implications for a broad variety of social psychological phenomena.

REFERENCES

Baumeister, R. F., & Leary, M. R. (1995). The need to belong: Desire for interpersonal attachments as a fundamental human motivation. *Psychological Bulletin, 117,* 497–529.

Brewer, M. B. (1991). The social self: On being the same and different at the same time. *Personality and Social Psychology Bulletin, 17,* 475–482.

Caporael, L. R., & Brewer, M. B. (1991). Reviving evolutionary psychology: Biology meets society. *Journal of Social Issues, 47,* 187–195.

Freud, S. (1957). Instincts and their vicissitudes. *Standard Edition,* Volume 14. London: Hogarth Press. (Original work published 1915)

McDougall, W. (1923). *Outline of psychology.* New York: Scribner.

Pyszczynski, T. A., Greenberg, J., & Solomon, S. (1997). Why do we need what we need?: A terror management perspective on the roots of human social motivation. *Psychological Inquiry, 8,* 1–20.

Stevens, L. E., & Fiske, S. T. (1995). Motivation and cognition in social life: A social survival perspective. *Social Cognition, 13,* 189–214.

Tesser, A., Millar, M., & Moore, J. (1988). Some affective consequences of social comparison and reflection processes: The pain and pleasure of being close. *Journal of Personality and Social Psychology, 54,* 49–61.

Woodworth, R. S. (1918). *Dynamic psychology.* New York: Columbia University Press.

Suggested Readings

Pittman, T. S., & Pittman, N. L. (1980). Deprivation of control and the attribution process. *Journal of Personality and Social Psychology, 39*, 377–389.

Stevens, L. E., & Fiske, S. T. (1995). Motivation and cognition in social life: A social survival perspective. *Social Cognition, 13*, 189–214.

Tajfel, H., Flament, C., Billig, M., & Bundy, R. P. (1971). Social categorization and intergroup behavior. *European Journal of Social Psychology, 1*, 149–178.

Tesser, A. (1993). The importance of heritability in psychological research: The case of attitudes. *Psychological Review, 100*, 129–142.

Wicklund, R. A., & Brehm, J. W. (1976). *Perspectives on cognitive dissonance*. Hillsdale, NJ: Erlbaum.

Zuckerman, M. (1984). Sensation seeking: A comparative approach to a human trait. *The Behavioral and Brain Sciences, 7*, 413–471.

The Need to Belong: Desire for Interpersonal Attachments as a Fundamental Human Motivation

Roy F. Baumeister • Department of Psychology, Case Western Reserve University

Mark R. Leary • Department of Psychology, Wake Forest University

Editors' Notes

Is there a basic human need to form and maintain strong, stable, interpersonal relationships? If there is a need to belong, then (nonaversive) repeated interactions with the same partner should be more satisfying than (nonaversive) discontinuous interactions with many changing partners; satisfaction of the belonging need in one set of relationships should reduce the motivation to satisfy it in other relationships; failures to satisfy it should cause distress; interpersonal relationships should influence cognition and emotion, and should operate across a wide variety of situations and cultures. Evidence is reviewed that supports each of these predictions.

Discussion Questions

1. Describe the need to belong.
2. What kind of evidence supports the conclusion that there is a basic need to belong?

Authors' Abstract

A hypothesized need to form and maintain strong, stable interpersonal relationships is evaluated in light of the empirical literature. The need is for frequent, nonaversive interactions within an ongoing relational bond. Consistent with the belongingness hypothesis, people form social attachments readily under most conditions and resist the dissolution of existing bonds. Belongingness appears to have multiple and strong effects on emotional patterns and on cognitive processes. Lack of attachments is linked to a variety of ill effects on health, adjustment, and well-being. Other evidence, such as that concerning satiation, substitution, and behavioral consequences, is likewise consistent with the hypothesized motivation. Several seeming counterexamples turned out not to disconfirm the hypothesis. Existing evidence supports the hypothesis that the need to belong is a powerful, fundamental, and extremely pervasive motivation.

The purpose of this review is to develop and evaluate the hypothesis that a need to belong is a fundamental human motivation and to propose that the need to belong can provide a point of departure for understanding and integrating a great deal of the existing literature regarding human interpersonal behavior. More precisely, the belongingness hypothesis is that human beings have a pervasive drive to form and maintain at least a minimum quantity of lasting, positive, and significant interpersonal relationships. Satisfying this drive involves two criteria: First, there is a need for frequent, affectively pleasant interactions with a few other people, and, second, the interactions must take place in the context of a temporally stable and enduring framework of affective concern for each other's welfare. Interactions with a constantly changing sequence of partners will be less satisfactory than repeated interactions with the same person(s), and relatedness without frequent contact will also be unsatisfactory. A lack of belongingness should constitute severe deprivation and cause a variety of ill effects. Furthermore, a great deal of human behavior, emotion, and thought is caused by this fundamental interpersonal motive.

The hypothesis that people are motivated to form and maintain interpersonal bonds is not new, of course. John Donne (1975) has been widely quoted for the line "No [person] is an island." In psychology, the need for interpersonal contact was asserted in several ways by Freud (e.g., 1930), although he tended to see the motive as derived from the sex drive and from the filial bond. Maslow (1968) ranked "love and belongingness needs" in the middle of his motivational hierarchy; that is, belongingness needs do not emerge until food, hunger, safety, and other basic needs are satisfied, but they take precedence over esteem and self-actualization. Bowlby's (e.g, 1969, 1973) attachment theory also posited the need to form and maintain relationships. His early thinking followed the Freudian pattern of deriving attachment needs from the relationship to one's mother; he regarded the adult's need for attachment as an effort to recapture the intimate contact that the individual had, as an infant, with his or her mother.[1] Horney (1945), Sullivan (1953), Fromm (1955, 1956), de Rivera (1984), Hogan (1983), Epstein (1992), Ryan (1991), Guisinger and Blatt (1994), and others have made similar suggestions. The existence of a need to belong is thus a familiar point of theory and speculation, although not all theorists have anticipated our particular formulation of this need as the combination of frequent interaction plus persistent caring. Moreover, most theorists have neglected to provide systematic empirical evaluation of this hypothesis. For example, Maslow's (1968) influential assertion of a belongingness need was accompanied by neither original data nor review of previous findings. Thus, despite frequent, speculative assertions that people need to belong the belongingness hypothesis needs to be critically evaluated in light of empirical evidence. A main

---

[1] His later thinking may, however, have moved beyond this view to regard attachment needs as having a separate, even innate basis rather than being derived from the contact with one's mother; in this later view, he created the relationship to one's mother as simply an influential prototype of attachment.

goal of the present article is to assemble a large body of empirical findings pertinent to the belongingness hypothesis to evaluate how well the hypothesis fits the data.

Another goal of this article is to demonstrate the broad applicability of the need to belong for understanding human motivation and behavior. Even though many psychological theorists have noted human affiliative tendencies in one form or another, the field as a whole has neglected the broad applicability of this need to a wide range of behaviors. Thus, for example, the motive literature has been dominated by research on the respective needs for power, achievement, intimacy, approval, and, to a lesser extent, affiliation. But the need for power may be driven by the need to belong, as we suggest later. Likewise, people prefer achievements that are validated, recognized, and valued by other people over solitary achievements, so there may be a substantial interpersonal component behind the need for achievement. And the needs for approval and intimacy are undoubtedly linked to the fact that approval is a prerequisite for forming and maintaining social bonds, and intimacy is a defining characteristic of close relationships. The need to belong could thus be linked to all of them.

Furthermore, even a quick glance at research on social behavior from the perspective of the belongingness hypothesis raises the possibility that much of what human beings do is done in the service of belongingness. Thus, the belongingness hypothesis might have considerable value for personality and social psychology and even for psychology as a whole. As a broad integrative hypothesis, it might help rectify what some observers have criticized as fragmentation and atomization in the conceptual underpinnings of the field (see Vallacher & Nowak, 1994; West, Newsom, & Fenaughty, 1992). [. . .]

Conceptual Background

Fundamental Motivations: Metatheory

Before proceeding with our examination of the need to belong, we must consider briefly the metatheoretical requirements of our hypothesis. That is, what criteria must be satisfied to conclude that the need to belong, or any other drive, is a fundamental human motivation? We suggest the following. A fundamental motivation should (a) produce effects readily under all but adverse conditions, (b) have affective consequences, (c) direct cognitive processing, (d) lead to ill effects (such as on health or adjustment) when thwarted, (e) elicit goal-oriented behavior designed to satisfy it (subject to motivational patterns such as object substitutability and satiation), (f) be universal in the sense of applying to all people, (g) not be derivative of other motives, (h) affect a broad variety of behaviors, and (i) have implications that go beyond immediate psychological functioning. We consider each of these criteria in turn.

The first criterion is that a fundamental motivation should operate in a wide variety of settings: any motive that requires highly specific or supportive circumstances to produce effects cannot properly be called fundamental. Certain circumstances may retard or prevent its operation, but in general the more widely it can produce effects, the stronger its claim to being a fundamental motivation.

The second and third criteria refer to emotional and cognitive patterns. Cognitive and emotional responses reflect subjective importance and concern, and a motivation that fails to guide emotion and cognition (at least sometimes) can hardly be considered an important one. In addition, most motivational and drive systems involve hedonic consequences that alert the individual to undesired state changes that motivate behavior to restore the desired state and whose removal serves as negative reinforcement for goal attainment.

The fourth criterion is that failure to satisfy a fundamental motivation should produce ill effects that go beyond temporary affective distress. A motivation can be considered to be fundamental only if health, adjustment, or well-being requires that it be satisfied. Also, motivations can be sorted into wants and needs, the difference being in the scope of ill effects that follow from nonsatisfaction: Unsatisfied needs should lead to pathology (medical, psychological, or behavioral), unlike unsatisfied wants. Thus, if belongingness is a need rather than simply a want, then people who lack belongingness should exhibit pathological consequences beyond mere temporary distress.

Substitution and satiation are two familiar hallmarks of motivation. If the need to belong is a fundamental need, then belonging to one group should satisfy it and hence obviate or reduce the need to belong to another group. People may be driven to form social bonds until they have a certain number, whereafter the drive to form attachments would presumably subside. Furthermore, attachment partners should be to some degree interchangeable. Of course, this does not mean that a 20-year spouse or friend can be simply replaced with a new acquaintance. In the long run, however, a new spouse or friend should do as well as the previous one.

The sixth and seventh criteria involve universality and nonderivativeness. Any motivation that is limited to certain human beings or certain circumstances, or any motivation that is derived from another motive, cannot be regarded as fundamental. Universality can be indicated by transcending cultural boundaries. Establishing that a motive is not derivative is not easy, although path-analytic models can suggest derivative patterns. Satisfying the first criterion may also help satisfy the seventh, because if the motivation operates in a broad variety of situations without requiring particular, favorable circumstances, then it may be presumed to be fundamental. Meanwhile, if the evidence contradicts evolutionary patterns or fails to indicate physiological mechanisms, then the hypothesis of universality or innateness would lose credibility.

The eighth criterion is the ability to affect a wide and diverse assortment of behaviors. The more behaviors that appear to be influenced by a particular motive, the stronger its case for being one of the fundamental motives. Lastly, we suggest that a fundamental motive should have implications that go beyond psychological functioning. If a motivation is truly fundamental, it should influence a broad range of human activity, and hence it should be capable of offering viable and consistent interpretations of patterns observed in historical, economic, or sociological studies.

Falsification is only one relevant approach to evaluating a broad hypothesis about belongingness being a fundamental motivation. The belongingness hypothesis could indeed be falsified if it were shown, for example, that many people can live happy, healthy lives in social isolation or that many people show no cognitive or emotional responses to looming significant changes in their belongingness status. In addition to such criteria, however, hypotheses about fundamental motivations must be evaluated in terms of their capacity to interpret and explain a wide range of phenomena. Part of the value of such a theory is its capac-

ity to provide an integrative framework, and this value is a direct function of the quantity and importance of the behavior patterns that it can explain in a consistent, intelligible fashion. We therefore pay close attention to the potential range of implications of the belongingness hypothesis, in addition to examining how many falsification tests the hypothesis has managed to survive.

The Need to Belong: Theory

In view of the metatheoretical requirements listed in the previous section, we propose that a need to belong, that is, a need to form and maintain at least a minimum quantity of interpersonal relationships, is innately prepared (and hence nearly universal) among human beings. Thus, unlike the Freudian (1930) view that regarded sexuality and aggression as the major driving psychological forces, and unlike the most ambitious behaviorist views that considered each newborn a tabula rasa, our view depicts the human being as naturally driven toward establishing and sustaining belongingness. The need to belong should therefore be found to some degree in all humans in all cultures, although naturally one would expect there to be individual differences in strength and intensity, as well as cultural and individual variations in how people express and satisfy the need. But it should prove difficult or impossible for culture to eradicate the need to belong (except perhaps for an occasional, seriously warped individual).

The innate quality presumably has an evolutionary basis. It seems clear that a desire to form and maintain social bonds would have both survival and reproductive benefits (see Ainsworth, 1989; Axelrod & Hamilton, 1981; Barash, 1977; Bowlby, 1969; D. M. Buss, 1990, 1991; Hogan, Jones, & Cheek, 1985; Moreland, 1987). Groups can share food, provide mates, and help care for offspring (including orphans). Some survival tasks, such as hunting large animals or maintaining defensive vigilance against predatory enemies, are best accomplished by group cooperation. Children who desired to stay together with adults (and who would resist being left alone) would be more likely to survive until their reproductive years than other children because they would be more likely to receive care and food as well as protection. Cues that connote possible harm, such as illness, danger, nightfall, and disaster, seem to increase the need to be with others (see also Rofe, 1984), which again underscores the protective value of group membership. Adults who formed attachments would be more likely to reproduce than those who failed to form them, and long-term relationships would increase the chances that the offspring would reach maturity and reproduce in turn (see also Shaver, Hazan, & Bradshaw, 1988).[2]

Competition for limited resources could also provide a powerful stimulus to forming interpersonal connections. There are several potential, although debatable, advantages to forming a group under conditions of scarcity. For example, groups may share resources and thus prevent any individual from starving (although sharing deprives other group members of some of their resources), and groups may appropriate resources from nonmembers (although there is the problem of how to distribute them in the group). What appears less debatable is the severe competitive disadvantage of the lone individual confronting a group when both want the same resource. When other people are in groups, it is vital to belong to a group oneself, particularly a group of familiar, cooperative people who care about one's welfare. Thus, an inclination to form and sustain social bonds would have important benefits of defending oneself and protecting one's resources against external threats.

The likely result of this evolutionary selection would be a set of internal mechanisms that guide individual human beings into social groups and lasting relationships. These mechanisms would presumably include a tendency to orient toward other members of the species, a tendency to experience affective distress when deprived of social contact or relationships, and a tendency to feel pleasure or positive affect from social contact and relatedness. These affective mechanisms would stimulate learning by making positive social contact reinforcing and social deprivation punishing.

Our version of the belongingness hypothesis does not regard the need as derived from a particular relationship or focused on a particular individual. In this, it differs from the early, Freudian version of Bowlby's work, in which the relationship to the mother was regarded as the cause of the desire for attachment. Thus, Bowlby suggested that adult attachments to work organizations, religious groups, or others are derived from the child's tie to mother and revolve around personal attachment to the group leader or supervisor (Bowlby, 1969, p. 207). In contrast, we propose that the need to belong can, in principle, be directed toward any other human being, and the loss of relationship with one person can to some extent be replaced by any other. The main obstacle to such substitution is that formation of new relationships takes time, such as in the gradual accumulation of intimacy and shared experience (see Sternberg, 1986, on the time course of intimacy). Social contact with a long-term intimate would therefore provide some satisfactions, including a sense of belonging, that would not be available in interactions with strangers or new acquaintances.

The belongingness hypothesis can be distinguished from a hypothesized need for mere social contact in terms of whether interactions with strangers or with people one dislikes or hates would satisfy the need. It can be distinguished from a hypothesized need for positive, pleasant social contact in terms of whether nonhostile interactions with strangers would satisfy it. The need to belong entails that relationships are desired, so interactions with strangers would mainly be appealing as possible first steps toward long-term contacts (including practicing social skills or learning about one's capacity to attract partners), and interactions with disliked people would not satisfy it.

Additional differences between the belongingness hypothesis and attachment theory could be suggested, although it may be a matter of interpretation whether these are merely differences of emphasis or fundamental theoretical differences. In our understanding, the (very real) strengths of attachment theory are two fold. First, attachment theory has emphasized the task of elaborating individual differences in attachment style (e.g., Hazan & Shaver, 1994a, 1994b; Shaver et al., 1988), whereas we focus on the commonality of the overarching need to belong. Second, attachment theory has emphasized certain emotional needs and satisfactions implicit in certain kinds of relationships, whereas we regard it as at least plausible that the need to belong could be satisfied in other ways. For example, one might imagine a

---

[2]A possible sex difference could be suggested in the mode of experiencing this need, however, in that men may be more oriented toward forming relationships, whereas women may be more oriented toward maintaining them. Men can reproduce many times by forming many brief relationships, whereas women can reproduce only about once per year, and so their most effective reproductive strategy would be to enable each child to receive maximal care and protection (D. M. Buss, 1991).

young fellow without any family or intimate relationships who is nonetheless satisfied by being heavily involved in an ideologically radical political movement. There are undoubtedly strong emotional mechanisms associated with belongingness, as we show later, but these could be understood as mediating mechanisms rather than as essential properties.

As a fundamental motivation, the need to belong should stimulate goal-directed activity designed to satisfy it. People should show tendencies to seek out interpersonal contacts and cultivate possible relationships, at least until they have reached a minimum level of social contact and relatedness. Meanwhile, social bonds should form easily, readily, and without requiring highly particular or conducive settings. (Indeed, if social attachments form through shared unpleasant experiences, contrary to what simple association models might predict, this would be especially compelling support for the belongingness hypothesis.) Cognitive activity should reflect a pervasive concern with forming and maintaining relationships. Emotional reactions should follow directly from outcomes that pertain to the need to belong. More precisely, positive affect should follow from forming and solidifying social bonds, and negative affect should ensue when relationships are broken, threatened, or refused.

If belongingness is indeed a fundamental need, then aversive reactions to a loss of belongingness should go beyond negative affect to include some types of pathology. People who are socially deprived should exhibit a variety of ill effects, such as signs of maladjustment or stress, behavioral or psychological pathology, and possibly health problems. They should also show an increase in goal-directed activity aimed at forming relationships.

In addition, the belongingness hypothesis entails that people should strive to achieve a certain minimum quantity and quality of social contacts but that once this level is surpassed, the motivation should diminish. The need is presumably for a certain minimum number of bonds and quantity of interaction. The formation of further social attachments beyond that minimal level should be subject to diminishing returns: that is, people should experience less satisfaction on formation of such extra relationships, as well as less distress on terminating them. Satiation patterns should be evident, such that people who are well enmeshed in social relationships would be less inclined to

seek and form additional bonds than would people who are socially deprived. Relationships should substitute for each other, to some extent, as would be indicated by effective replacement of lost relationship partners and by a capacity for social relatedness in one sphere to overcome potential ill effects of social deprivation in another sphere (e.g., if strong family ties compensate for aloneness at work).

We propose that the need to belong has two main features. First, people need frequent personal contacts or interactions with the other person. Ideally these interactions would be affectively positive or pleasant, but it is mainly important that the majority be free from conflict and negative affect.

Second, people need to perceive that there is an interpersonal bond or relationship marked by stability, affective concern, and continuation into the foreseeable future. This aspect provides a relational context to one's interactions with the other person, and so the perception of the bond is essential for satisfying the need to belong. When compared with essentially identical interactions with other people with whom one is not connected, a strictly behavioral record might reveal nothing special or rewarding about these interactions. Yet an interaction with a person in the context of an ongoing relationship is subjectively different from and often more rewarding than an interaction with a stranger or casual acquaintance. To satisfy the need to belong, the person must believe that the other cares about his or her welfare and likes (or loves) him or her.

Ideally this concern would he mutual, so that the person has reciprocal feelings about the other. M. S. Clark and her colleagues (e.g., Clark, 1984; Clark & Mills, 1979; Clark, Mills, & Corcoran, 1989; Clark, Mills, & Powell, 1986) have shown that a framework of mutual concern produces a relationship qualitatively different from one based on self-interested social exchange. Still, it is plausible that mutuality is merely desirable rather than essential. The decisive aspect may be the perception that one is the recipient of the other's lasting concern.

Viewed in this way, the need to belong is something other than a need for mere affiliation. Frequent contacts with nonsupportive, indifferent others can go only so far in promoting one's general well-being and would do little to satisfy the need to belong. Conversely, relationships characterized by strong feelings of attachment, intimacy, or commitment but lacking regular contact will also fail to satisfy the need. Simply knowing that a bond exists may be emotionally reassuring, yet it would not provide full belongingness if one does not interact with the other person. Thus, we view the need to belong as something more than either a need for affiliation or a need for intimate attachment.

The notion that people need relationships characterized by both regular contact and an ongoing bond has been anticipated to some degree by Weiss (1973; see also Shaver & Buhrmester, 1983), who suggested that feelings of loneliness can be precipitated either by an insufficient amount of social contact (social loneliness) or by a lack of meaningful, intimate relatedness (emotional loneliness). Weiss's distinction has been criticized on conceptual and empirical grounds (e.g., Paloutzian & Janigian, 1987; Perlman, 1987), and efforts to operationalize and test the distinction have met with mixed results (DiTommaso & Spinner, 1993; Saklofske & Yackulic, 1989; Vaux, 1988). In our view, the difficulty with this distinction arises from the assumption that people have a need for mere social contact and a separate need for intimate relationship. Rather, the need is for regular social contact with those to whom one feels connected. From an evolutionary perspective, relationships characterized by both of these features would have greater survival and reproductive value than would relationships characterized by only one. Accordingly, the need to belong should be marked by both aspects.

Review of Empirical Findings

We searched the empirical literature of social and personality psychology for findings relevant to the belongingness hypothesis. The following sections summarize the evidence we found pertaining to the series of predictions about belongingness.

Forming Social Bonds

A first prediction of the belongingness hypothesis is that social bonds should form relatively easily, without requiring specially conducive circumstances. Such evidence not only would attest to the presence and power of the need to belong but would suggest that the need is not a derivative of other needs (insofar as it is not limited to circum-

stances that meet other requirements or follow from other events).

There is abundant evidence that social bonds form easily. Indeed, people in every society on earth belong to small primary groups that involve face-to-face, personal interactions (Mann, 1980). The anthropologist Coon (1946) asserted that natural groups are characteristic of all human beings. Societies differ in the type, number, and permanence of the groups that people join, but people of all cultures quite naturally form groups.

The classic Robbers Cave study conducted by Sherif, Harvey, White, Hood, and Sherif (1961/1988) showed that when previously unacquainted boys were randomly assigned to newly created groups, strong loyalty and group identification ties ensued rapidly. In fact, later in that study, the two strongly opposed groups were recombined into a single group with cooperative goals, and emotional and behavioral patterns quickly accommodated to the new group (although the prior antagonistic identifications did hamper the process).

The tendency for laboratory or experimentally created groups to quickly become cohesive has also been noted in the *minimal intergroup* situation (Brewer, 1979). Tajfel and his colleagues (Billig & Tajfel, 1973: Tajfel, 1970; Tajfel & Billig, 1974; Tajfel, Flament, Billig, & Bundy, 1971) showed that assigning participants to categories on a seemingly arbitrary basis was sufficient to cause them to allocate greater rewards to in-group members than to out-group members. Indeed, the original goal of Tajfel et al. (1971) was not to study group formation but to understand the causes of in-group favoritism. To do this, they sought to set up an experimental group that would be so trivial that no favoritism would be found, intending then to add other variables progressively so as to determine at what point favoritism would start. To their surprise, however, in-group favoritism appeared at once, even in the minimal and supposedly trivial situation (see also Turner, 1985).

This preferential treatment of in-group members does not appear to be due to inferred self-interest or to issues of novelty and uncertainty about the task (Brewer & Silver, 1978; Tajfel, 1970; Tajfel & Billig, 1974). Inferred similarity of self to in-group members was a viable explanation for many of the early findings, but Locksley, Ortiz, and Hepburn (1980) ruled this out by showing that people show in-group favoritism even when they have been assigned to groups by a random lottery. Thus, patterns of in-group favoritism, such as sharing rewards and categorizing others relative to the group, appeared quite readily, even in the absence of experiences designed to bond people to the group emotionally or materially.

Several other studies suggest how little it takes (other than frequent contact) to create social attachments. Bowlby (1969) noted that infants form attachments to caregivers very early in life, long before babies are able to calculate benefits or even speak. Festinger, Schachter, and Back (1950) found that mere proximity was a potent factor in relationship formation; people seemed to develop social bonds with each other simply because they lived near each other. Nahemow and Lawton (1975) replicated those findings and also showed that pain of best friends who differed by age or race were particularly likely to have lived very close together, suggesting that extreme proximity may overcome tendencies to bond with similar others. Wilder and Thompson (1980) showed that people seem to form favorable views toward whomever they spend time with, even if these others are members of a previously disliked or stereotyped outgroup. In their study, intergroup biases decreased as contact with members of the out-groups increased (and as in-group contact decreased).

We noted that the formation of social attachments under adverse circumstances would be especially compelling evidence because it avoids the alternative explanations based on classical conditioning (i.e., that positive associations breed attraction). Latane, Eckman, and Joy (1966) found that participants who experienced electric shock together tended to like each other more than control participants who did not experience shock, although the effect was significant only among firstborns. Kenrick and Johnson (1979) found that participants rated each other more positively in the presence of aversive than nonaversive noise. Elder and Clipp (1988) compared the persistence of attachments among military veterans and found that the greatest persistence occurred among groups that had undergone heavy combat resulting in the deaths of some friends and comrades. Although it would be rash to suggest that all shared negative experiences increase attraction, it does appear that positive bonding will occur even under adverse circumstances.

The development of interpersonal attraction under fearful circumstances has been explained in terms of both misattribution (i.e., people may misinterpret their anxious arousal as attraction to another person) and reinforcement theory (i.e., when the presence of some other person reduces one's distress, a positive emotional response becomes associated with that person; Kenrick & Cialdini, 1977). The misattribution explanation is largely irrelevant to the belongingness hypothesis, but the reinforcement explanation is germane. Specifically, although others may reduce one's distress through various routes (such as distraction, humor, or reassurance), evidence suggests strongly that the mere presence of other people can be comforting (Schachter, 1959). Such effects may well be conditioned through years of experience with supportive others, but they also may indicate that threatening events stimulate the need to belong.

The fact that people sometimes form attachments with former rivals or opponents is itself a meaningful indicator of a general inclination to form bonds. Cognitive consistency pressures and affective memories would militate against forming positive social bonds with people who have been rivals or opponents. Yet, as we have already noted, the Robbers Cave study (Sherif et al., 1961/ 1988) showed that people could join and work together with others who had been bitterly opposed very recently, and Wilder and Thompson (1980) showed that social contact could overcome established intergroup prejudices and stereotypes. Orbell, van de Kragt, and Dawes (1988) likewise showed that impulses toward forming positive attachments could overcome oppositional patterns. In their study using the prisoner's dilemma game, having a discussion period led to decreased competition and increased cooperation, as a result of either the formation of a group identity that joined the potential rivals together or explicit agreements to cooperate. Thus, belongingness motivations appear to be able to overcome some antagonistic, competitive, or divisive tendencies.

Similar shifts have been suggested by M. S. Clark (1984, 1986; Clark, Mills, & Powell, 1986; Clark, Ouellette, Powell, & Milberg, 1987), who showed that people move toward a communal orientation when there is a chance to form a relationship. When participants were confronted with a person who seemingly would not be amenable to relationship formation (i.e., because she was already married), they interacted with her on the basis of norms of equitable exchange and individuality; when they believed she would be a possible relationship partner, however, they interacted with her on a communal basis (i.e., mutuality and sharing, without respect to individual equity concerns).

The remarkable ease with which social bonds form has been shown with experimental methods and confirmed by other methods. The main limitation would be that people do not always form relationships with all available or proximal others, which could mean that satiation processes limit the number of relationships people seek and which also indicates that other factors and processes affect the formation of relationships. Some patterns (e.g., ingroup favoritism in minimal groups) have been well replicated with careful efforts to rule out alternative explanations.

CONCLUSION

In brief, people seem widely and strongly inclined to form social relationships quite easily in the absence of any special set of eliciting circumstances or ulterior motives. Friendships and group allegiance seem to arise spontaneously and readily, without needing evidence of material advantage or inferred similarity. Not only do relationships emerge quite naturally, but people invest a great deal of time and effort in fostering supportive relationships with others. External threat seems to increase the tendency to form strong bonds.

Not Breaking Bonds

The belongingness hypothesis predicts that people should generally be at least as reluctant to break social bonds as they are eager to form them in the first place. A variety of patterns supports the view that people try to preserve relationships and avoid ending them. In fact, Hazan and Shaver (1994a, p. 14) recently concluded that the tendency for human beings to respond with distress and protest to the end of a relationship is nearly universal, even across different cultures and across the age span.

Some relationships are limited in time by external factors, and so these are logically the first place to look for evidence that people show distress and resistance to breaking bonds. Encounter groups and training groups, for example, are often convened with the explicit understanding that the meetings will stop at a certain point in the future. Even so, it is a familiar observation in the empirical literature (e.g., Egan, 1970; Lacoursiere, 1980; Lieberman, Yalom, & Miles, 1973) that the members of such groups resist the notion that the group will dissolve. Even though the group's purpose may have been fulfilled, the participants want to hold on to the social bonds and relationships they have formed with each other. They promise individually and sometimes collectively to stay in touch with each other, they plan for reunions, and they take other steps to ensure a continuity of future contacts. In actuality, only a small minority of these envisioned reunions or contacts take place, and so the widespread exercise of making them can be regarded as a symptom of resistance to the threatened dissolution (Lacoursiere, 1980, p. 216).

Other relationships are limited in time by external transitions such as graduating from college, moving to a different city, or getting a new job. As such transitions approach, people commonly get together formally and informally and promise to remain in contact, to share meals or other social occasions together, to write and call each other, and to continue the relationship in other ways. They also cry or show other signs of distress over the impending separation (Bridges, 1980). These patterns seem to occur even if the dissolving relationship (e.g., with neighbors) had no important practical or instrumental function and there is no realistic likelihood of further contact.

More generally, many social institutions and behavior patterns seem to serve a need to preserve at least the appearance of social attachment in the absence of actual, continued interaction. Reunions constitute an occasion for people to see former acquaintances. The massive exchange of greeting cards during the Christmas holiday season includes many cases in which the card is the sole contact that two people have had during the entire year, but people still resist dropping each other's name from the mailing list because to do so signifies a final dissolution of the social bond. In fact, most people will send Christmas cards to perfect strangers from whom they receive cards (Kunz & Woolcott, 1976). People seem not to want to risk damaging a relationship even if they do not know the identity of the other person!

Likewise, social rituals involving greetings and farewells serve to assure others of the continuation of one's relationships with them. Many greetings, particularly those directed at family members and close friends, seem designed to indicate that one's relationship has remained intact since the last contact, and farewells often include some hint that the relationship will be maintained until the people see one another again (Goffman, 1971). The importance of such rituals in the maintenance of belongingness is reflected in the distress people sometimes experience when they feel that another's greeting is inadequately warm or that the other's farewell expresses insufficient concern about the impending separation.

In many cases, people seem reluctant to dissolve even bad or destructive relationships. The apparent unwillingness of many women to leave abusive, battering spouses or boyfriends (Roy 1977; Strube, 1988) has prompted several generations of speculative explanations, ranging from masochistic or self-destructive liking for abuse to calculations of economic self-interest that supposedly override considerations of physical harm. The belongingness hypothesis offers yet one more potential perspective: The unwillingness to leave an abusive intimate partner is another manifestation of the strength of the need to belong and of the resulting reluctance to break social bonds. The fact that people resist breaking off an attachment that causes pain attests to how deeply rooted and powerful the need to belong is.

Moreover, when people do decide to break off an intimate relationship, they typically experience considerable distress over the dissolution (which we cover in more detail in the later section on emotion). This is ironic: Although goal attainment is usually marked by positive affect such as satisfaction and joy, attaining the goal of getting a divorce is generally accompanied by negative affect. To be sure, in some cases the distress over divorce is accompanied by an admixture of positive affect, but the negative affect nonetheless indicates the resistance to breaking the bond.

It is also relevant and noteworthy that the social bond often continues despite the divorce. In her study on divorce, Vaughan (1986) concluded that "in most cases [marital] relationships don't end. They change, but they don't end" (p. 282). Weiss (1979) also found that some form of (often ambivalent) attachment persists after divorce. The persistence of intimate relationships past the occasion or mutually agreed and formally institutionalized dissolution may be yet another indication of people's reluctance to break social bonds.

CRITICAL ASSESSMENT

Because ethical and practical constraints prevent laboratory experimentation on the ending of significant relationships, the evidence in this section was drawn from observational studies and other methods, and so the hypothesis of resistance to relationship dissolution is not as conclusively supported as might be desired. Alternative explanations exist for some of the findings. For example, the persistence of relatedness after divorce is partly due to ongoing practical concerns, such as joint responsibility for child care; although Vaughan (1986) was emphatic in asserting that such pragmatic concerns fall far short of explaining the extent of continuing attachments, she was vague about the evidence to back up her assertion. Also, as we noted, the tendency for battered women to return to their abusive partners has been explained in many ways, and the hypothesized reluctance to break off a relationship is only one of them.

On the positive side, however, the persistence of such bonds has been observed by a variety of researchers. The fact that these researchers are from different disciplines suggests that these conclusions do not stem from a single methodological or theoretical bias. More systematic research on possible boundary and limiting conditions of the resistance to dissolve bonds would be desirable.

CONCLUSION

Despite some methodological weaknesses and ambiguities, the weight of the evidence does favor the conclusion that people strongly and generally resist the dissolution of relationships and social bonds. Moreover, this resistance appears to go well beyond rational considerations of practical or material advantage.

Cognition

Intelligent thought is generally recognized as the most important adaptive trait among human beings, and so it seems reasonable to assume that issues of fundamental concern and importance are likely to be the focus of cognitive activity. The belongingness hypothesis therefore would predict that people will devote considerable cognitive processing to interpersonal interactions and relationships.

Basic patterns of thought appear to reflect a fundamental concern with social relationships. Sedikides, Olsen, and Reis (1993) showed that relationships are natural categories; that is, people spontaneously classify incoming information in terms of social relationships. Participants stored information about relationship partners together, and they did this more for strong, close relationships (marriage) than for weak or distant ones (e.g., acquaintanceship). Pryer and Ostrom (1981) showed that people use the individual person as a cognitive unit of analysis for familiar people more than for unfamiliar people. These researchers began by questioning the basic assumption that the person is the fundamental unit of social perception. That is, information is not necessarily or inherently processed and stored in memory on a person-by-person basis, but it is, in fact, processed and stored on such a basis when it pertains to significant others. Ostrom, Carpenter, Sedikides, and Li (1993) provided evidence that information about out-group members tends to be stored and organized on the basis of attribute categories (such as traits, preferences, and duties), whereas in-group information is processed on the basis of person categories. Thus, social bonds create a pattern in cognitive processing that gives priority to organizing information on the basis of the person with whom one has some sort of connection.

Several studies have pursued the notion that people process information about close relationship partners differently from the way they process information about strangers or distant acquaintances. For example, research has shown that, when a group of people take turns reading words aloud, they each have high recall for the words they personally speak but have poor recall for the words preceding and following their performance. Brenner (1976) found that this next-in-line effect occurs not only for one's own performance but also for words spoken by one's dating partner (and the words immediately preceding and following).

In a series of studies, Aron, Aron, Tudor, and Nelson (1991) showed that close relationship partners, unlike strangers, have cognitive effects similar to those of the self. Thus, when people form an image of themselves or their mothers interacting with some object, they have more difficulty recalling that object than if they imagined a famous but personally unacquainted person interacting with that same object. In another study, participants had more difficulty in making me–not me

judgments about traits on which they differed from their spouse than in making judgments about traits on which they resembled the spouse. These results suggest that cognitive processes tend to blur the boundaries between relationship partners and the self, in the form of "including [the] other in the self" (p. 241). In short, these studies confirm that information about relationship partners is singled out for special processing, and they raise the possibility that the need to belong leads to a cognitive merging of self with particular other people. Such patterns of subsuming the individual in the interpersonal unit indicate the importance of these relationships.

Many of the special biases that people exhibit for processing information in ways that favor and flatter themselves are extended to partners in close relationships. Fincham, Beach, and Baucom (1987) showed that self-serving biases that take credit for success and refuse blame for failure operate just as strongly—or even more strongly—when people interpret their spouses' outcomes as when they interpret their own outcomes. That is, events are interpreted in a way that is maximally flattering to the spouse, just as they are interpreted in ways that enhance and protect the self. (These patterns are extended only to partners in good, strong, happy relationships, however; high marital distress is correlated with a breakdown in these partner-serving attributions.)

Likewise, the "illusion or unique invulnerability" (Perloff & Fetter, 1986) turns out not to be as unique as first thought. Although people are more extremely and unrealistically optimistic about themselves than about some vague target such as the average person, they are equally optimistic about their closest friends and family members. That is, they think that bad things are not as likely to happen either to themselves or to their close friends as to strangers or to a hypothetical average person.[3] Along the same lines, Brown (1986) showed that people (particularly those with high

---

[3]Perloff and Fetzer (1986) favored an interpretation for their results in terms of the vagueness of the comparison target over the motivational explanation that people want to regard their closest relationship partners as equally invulnerable (equal to themselves). Their discrimination between the two hypotheses rested on the "one of your friends" condition in their second study: They found that the "closest friend" was seen as being highly invulnerable, whereas when participants chose one of their other friends, this person was seen as more vulnerable.

self-esteem) tend to extend self-serving biases to their friends. Specifically, people rate both self and a same-sex friend more favorably than they rate people in general.

Group memberships also appear to exert important influences on cognitive patterns. People expect more favorable and fewer objectionable actions by their in-group than by out-group members, and these expectations bias information processing and memory, leading people to forget the bad things (relative to good things) that their fellow in-group members do (Howard & Rothbart, 1980). People also make group-serving or "sociocentric" attributions for the performance of the groups to which they belong. Members of a successful group may make group-serving attributions that put the entire group in a good light, whereas, after failure, group members may join together in absolving one another of responsibility (Forsyth & Schlenker, 1977; Leary & Forsyth, 1987; Zander, 1971).

Linville and Jones (1980) showed that people tend to process information about out-group members in extreme, black-and-white, simplistic, polarized ways, whereas similar information about members of their own group is processed in a more complex fashion. Thus, the mere existence of a social bond leads to more complex (and sometimes more biased) information processing. [. . .]

CONCLUSION

Concern with belongingness appears to be a powerful factor shaping human thought. People interpret situations and events with regard to their implications for relationships, and they think more thoroughly about relationship (and interaction) partners than about other people. Moreover, the special patterns of processing information about the self are sometimes used for information about relationship partners as well. Thus, both actual and potential bonds exert substantial effects on how people think.

Their findings suggested that participants in that condition selected a friend who seemed most likely to have the problem asked about, so it is difficult to evaluate the motivational hypothesis. Thus, the interpretation emphasized here is consistent with all of Perloff and Fetzer's findings, as they acknowledged, even though their own interpretations tended to favor explanation in terms of vague versus specific targets.

Emotion

The main emotional implication of the belongingness hypothesis is that real, potential, or imagined changes in one's belongingness status will produce emotional responses, with positive affect linked to increases in belongingness and negative affect linked to decreases in it. Also, stable or chronic conditions of high belongingness should produce a general abundance of positive affect, whereas chronic deprivation should produce a tendency toward abundant negative affect.

POSITIVE AFFECT

In general, the formation of social bonds is associated with positive emotions. Perhaps the prototype of relationship formation is the experience of falling in love, which is typically marked by periods of intense bliss and joy, at least if the love is mutual (e.g., Sternberg, 1986). When love arises without belongingness, as in unrequited love, the result is typically distress and disappointment (Baumeister & Wotman, 1992). Belongingness is thus crucial if love is to produce bliss.

Likewise, occasions such as new employment, childbirth, fraternity or sorority pledging, and religious conversion, all of which are based on the entry into new relationships and the formation of new social bonds, are typically marked by positive emotions and celebrated as joyous. Childbirth is especially significant in this regard because the data show that parenthood reduces happiness and increases stress, strain, and marital dissatisfaction (e.g., S. A. Anderson, Russell, & Schumm, 1983; Campbell, Converse, & Rodgers, 1976; Glenn & McLanahan, 1982; for reviews, see Baumeister, 1991; Bernard, 1982; Campbell, 1981; Spanier & Lewis, 1980), yet people nonetheless retain a positive image of it, celebrate it, and feel positive about it, both in advance and in retrospect. It is plausible that the formation of the new social bond is directly responsible for the joy and positive feelings, whereas the negative aspects and feelings associated with parenthood arise indirectly from the hassles, conflicts, and stresses that accompany the social bond.

If the formation of bonds is one occasion for joy, a second occasion comes when the bond is formalized into a more recognizably permanent status. A wedding for example, does not create a new relationship, at least in modern Western cultures, because the bride and groom typically have known each other intimately for some time. The wedding does, however, signify an increase in commitment to maintaining the relationship permanently, and the joyful celebration of the wedding can be regarded as an affective consequence of solidifying the social bond. It is noteworthy that many traditional wedding vows include an actuarially implausible pledge that the marriage will never end ("till death do us part"). In essence, such vows are an institutionalized mechanism for committing people to meet their spouse's belongingness needs.

Although we have emphasized the view of affect as a result of attachment, positive affect may in turn help solidify social attachment. Probably the most influential view of this sort was developed by Shaver et al. (1988), who portrayed romantic love as a kind of glue designed by nature to solidify the attachment between two adults whose interaction is likely to lead to parenting. In their view, love elaborates on sexual attraction in a way that will hold the couple together when their sexual intercourse leads to reproduction. Along the same lines, various studies have found that positive affective experiences increase attraction and solidify social bonds (L. A. Clark & Watson, 1988; Gouaux, 1971; May & Hamilton, 1980; Veitch & Griffitt, 1976). Moreland (1987) concluded that the development of shared emotions is one of the principal causes of the formation of small groups.

More generally, happiness in life is strongly correlated with having some close personal relationships. Research suggests that it does not seem to make a great deal of difference what sort of relationship one has, but the absence of close social bonds is strongly linked to unhappiness, depression, and other woes (e.g., Argyle, 1987; Freedman, 1978; Myers, 1992). People with high levels of intimacy motivation tend to enjoy higher levels of happiness and subjective well-being (McAdams & Bryant, 1987), which is likely a result of their tendency to form and maintain a rich network of friendships and other social bonds (McAdams, 1985). Having some intimate bond appears to be important and perhaps even necessary for happiness. Social isolation is practically incompatible with high levels of happiness.

NEGATIVE AFFECT

Threats to social attachments, especially the dissolution of social bonds, are a primary source of negative affect. People feel anxious at the prospect of losing important relationships, feel depressed or grief stricken when their connections with certain other people are severed, and feel lonely when they lack important relationships (Leary, 1990; Leary & Downs, in press; Tambor & Leary, 1993).

Anxiety is often regarded as the extreme or prototype of negative affect, and it is clearly linked to damaged, lost, or threatened social bonds. In fact, social exclusion may well be the most common and important cause of anxiety (Baumeister & Tice, 1990). Horney (1945) identified the source of "basic anxiety" as the feeling of "being isolated and helpless in a potentially hostile world" (p. 41); of course, that formula mixes two different sources, insofar as isolation is a function of the belongingness need, whereas helplessness is a frustration of control (which is probably another fundamental motivation). Anxiety and general distress seem to be a natural consequence of being separated from important others. Children as young as 1 year old show extreme distress—separation anxiety—on being separated from their mothers (Bowlby, 1973), and adults show similar reactions when they must leave loved ones for an extended period of time. Furthermore, people's memories of past rejections are tainted with anxiety (Tambor & Leary, 1993), and even just imagining social rejection increases physiological arousal (Craighead, Kimball, & Rehak, 1979).

Consistent with the social exclusion theory of anxiety, Barden, Garber, Leiman, Ford, and Masters (1985) found that anxiety ensues if people are excluded from social groups, but experiences of social inclusion appear to counteract the effects of exclusion and remove the anxiety. Mathes, Adams, and Davies (1985) predicted that a threat to self-esteem would mediate the link between jealousy and anxiety, but their results did not support their hypothesis. Instead, they found that the loss of relationship led directly to anxiety.

Like anxiety, depression may be precipitated by a variety of events, but failing to feel accepted or included is certainly one of them. Both general depression and social depression (i.e., dysphoria about the nature or one's social relationships) are inversely related to the degree to which one feels included and accepted by others (Tambor & Leary, 1993). Hoyle and Crawford (in press) found that both depression and anxiety were significantly correlated (negatively) with students' sense of belonging to their university.

Jealousy is another negative affective state that is a common response to threats to one's relationships. Pines and Aronson (1983) reported that, in a series of surveys, some experience of jealousy was essentially universal, in the sense that everyone experiences it sooner or later. Moreover, more than half of their respondents described themselves as being "a jealous person" and correctly estimated that slightly more than half of the other participants would respond in that same way; however, they also said that the true incidence of jealous people was even higher, because some jealous people deny their jealousy. Pines and Aronson emphasized that "feeling excluded" is a major cause of jealousy.

Regarding jealousy, perhaps the most relevant finding for our purposes was that of Reiss (1986), who concluded that jealousy is cross-culturally universal. Reiss carefully investigated the extravagant claims made by some observers and anthropologists that, in certain cultures, people are able to exchange sexual partners and intimate partners without any possessiveness or jealousy, and in every case the claim turned out to be unwarranted. Cultures may indeed vary as to which particular actions or signs of affection are regarded as justifying jealous reactions, and they may differ in how people express their jealousy, but sexual jealousy is found in all cultures.

Loneliness reflects "an individual's subjective perception of deficiencies in his or her social relationships"(Russell, Cutrona, Rose, & Yurko, 1984, p. 1313). In other words, people feel lonely when their belongingness needs are being insufficiently met. Moreover, it appears that belongingness, rather than mere social contact, is the crucial factor. Mere social contact does not, by itself, buffer people against loneliness. Lonely and nonlonely people do not differ markedly in the amount of time they spend with other people. However, lonely people spend less time with friends and family—those who are most likely to fulfill their needs to belong—than nonlonely people (Jones, 1981). Furthermore, loneliness is much more strongly related to one's sense of social isolation than to objective indexes of one's social network, such as one's sheer number of friends (Williams & Solano, 1983). In one study, the correlation between self-reported loneliness and the degree to which people felt included and accepted by others was found to be –.71 (Spivey, 1990). Generally, loneliness seems to be a matter more of a lack of intimate connec-

tions than of a lack of social contact (Reis, 1990: Wheeler, Reis, & Nezlek, 1983).

Yet another highly aversive emotional state is guilt. Despite a long tradition of analyzing guilt in terms of self-evaluation according to abstract moral standards, recent work has increasingly emphasized the interpersonal structure of guilt (Baumeister, Stillwell, & Heatherton, 1994; Cunningham, Steinberg, & Grev, 1980; Jones & Kugler, in press: Jones, Kugler, & Adams, 1995; Miceli, 1992: Tangney, 1992). Empirical studies of how people induce guilt in others have found that such inductions are almost entirely confined to close interpersonal relationships and that a major reason for inducing guilt is to cause one's partner to exert himself or herself more to maintain the interpersonal relationship (e.g., by spending more time with or paying more attention to oneself; Baumeister, Stillwell, & Heatherton, in press; Vangelisti, Daly, & Rudnick, 1991). Many episodes of guilt can thus be understood as responses to disturbances or threats to interpersonal attachments. [. . .]

CONCLUSION

Many of the strongest emotions people experience, both positive and negative, are linked to belongingness. Evidence suggests a general conclusion that being accepted, included, or welcomed leads to a variety of positive emotions (e.g., happiness, elation, contentment, and calm), whereas being rejected, excluded, or ignored leads to potent negative feelings (e.g., anxiety, depression, grief, jealousy, and loneliness). The near universality of distress associated with divorce and bereavement is consistent with the belongingness hypothesis; indeed, there is no firm evidence in those literatures that significant social bonds can ever be broken without suffering or distress, even though (as noted) not every recently divorced or bereaved person will necessarily be suffering acutely when the interviewer happens to call.

Although the evidence was not equally abundant or equally strong for all emotions, the consistency across multiple emotions was impressive. It seems quite safe to conclude that both positive and negative emotional reactions are pervasively linked to relationship status. The existence of an interpersonal bond changes the way one responds emotionally to the performances and actions of a relationship partner and indeed intensifies many emotional reactions. Moreover, actual or possible changes in belongingness status constitute an important cause of emotions. The evidence is sufficiently broad and consistent to suggest that one of the basic functions of emotion is to regulate behavior so as to form and maintain social bonds.

Consequences of Deprivation

The general argument is that deprivation of belongingness should lead to a variety or affiliative behaviors and cause various undesirable effects, including decrements in health, happiness, and adjustment. We have already documented (in the preceding section) that loss of social bonds causes emotional distress, which is sufficient to show that belongingness is something people want. To regard it as a need, however, it is necessary to show effects that go beyond mere frustration and emotional distress.

Considerable research shows that people who do not have adequate supportive relationships experience greater stress than those who do. In part, this is because having other people available for support and assistance can enhance coping and provide a buffer against stress. However, evidence suggests that simply being part of a supportive social network reduces stress, even if other people do not provide explicit emotional or practical assistance (Cohen & Wills, 1985). Although this finding has been interpreted in terms of the stress-reducing effects of social support, an equally plausible explanation is that the deprivation of the need to belong is inherently stressful.

Direct evidence that deprivation of belongingness is maladaptive was provided by DeLongis, Folkman, and Lazarus (1988). They found that happily married couples were less likely to experience psychological and somatic health problems, both on and after stressful days, than other participants. Medical research has suggested that these beneficial effects extend beyond mere health complaints. Lynch (1979) summarized the evidence from many studies by stating that "U.S. mortality rates for all causes of death . . . are consistently higher for divorced, single, and widowed individuals" than for married individuals (p. 38). Lynch's own data showed the greater incidence of fatal heart attacks among unattached individuals than among married people, but he noted that similar effects can be found for tuberculosis, cancer, and many other illnesses, as well as overall patterns.

Of course, there are multiple possible explanations for such an effect that might have nothing to do with belongingness, but efforts to control for these variables have often found a persistent, independent, robust effect of social relations. Goodwin, Hunt, Key, and Samet (1987) found that married participants survived cancer better than single ones even after the timing of diagnosis, likelihood of receiving treatment, and cigarette smoking had been controlled, and they cited other evidence that the effect remains after family income has been controlled.

Indeed, being deprived of belongingness may have direct effects on the immune system. Kiecolt-Glaser, Garner, et al. (1984) found that loneliness was associated with a decrease in immunocompetence, specifically in natural killer cell activity, and this effect was independent of changes in perceived distress. Kiecolt-Glaser, Ricker, et al. (1984) replicated this effect and also round elevated urinary cortisol levels among lonely participants. Kiecolt-Glaser et al. (1987) found poorer immune function on several measures among women suffering from marital disruption, including divorce, separation, and unhappy marriage.

The effects of belongingness on mental illness parallel those on physical illness. Rejected children have a higher incidence of psychopathology than other children (Bhatti, Derezotes, Kim, & Specht, 1989; Hamachek, 1992). Children who grow up without receiving adequate attention from caregivers show emotional and behavioral pathologies, as demonstrated experimentally by Harlow, Harlow, and Suomi (1971) with animals and as corroborated by observations of human children by Bowlby (1969, 1973; we also Rutter, 1979).[4]

Marital status also has strong correlations with mental illness. Bloom, White, and Asher (1979) reviewed the literature and concluded that, in all studies, mental hospital admission rates are highest among divorced and separated people, intermediate among never-married people, and lowest among married people. In fact, as measured by admissions to mental hospitals,[5] mental illness is

---

[4] Semal studies have shown that physically unattractive people have a higher incidence of psychopathology than attractive people (e.g., Barocas & Vance, 1974: Cash, 1985; Farina, Burns, Austad, Bugglin, & Fischer, 1986; O'Grady, 1989). One reason may be that they lack belongingness, because society tends to reject unattractive individuals (Berscheid & Walster, 1974).

[5] Admittedly, hospital admissions is an imprecise measure.

at least 3 and possibly up to 22 times higher among divorced people than among married people.

Even problems that might at first seem unrelated to social interaction and relationships are sometimes found to have social deprivation or failed belongingness as an underlying cause. Problems with attachment have been identified as a major factor in eating disorders. Sours (1974), for example, noted that patients with eating disorders tended to have been (as children) overly sensitive to separation from their mothers. Armstrong and Roth (1989) found that women with eating disorders had significantly more intense and severe separation and attachment difficulties than a normal comparison group.

Combat-related stress is also moderated by belongingness. Veterans who perceive that they have a high degree of social support are significantly less likely to experience post-traumatic stress disorder than those who have lower perceived support (Hobfall & London, 1986; Solomon, Waysman, & Mikulincer, 1990). In fact, the authors of one study concluded that loneliness "is the most direct antecedent of psychopathology and social dysfunction" in combat stress reactions (Solomon et al., 1990, p. 468).

Crime may also be affected by belongingness. Sampson and Laub (1993) showed that having a good marriage and a stable job each had a strong negative effect on adult crime, consistent with other evidence. Other evidence suggests that social bonds to other criminals or to criminal groups may foster crime. Recent news coverage of gangs has repeatedly suggested that a need to belong attracts unattached young people to join violent gangs, which tend to serve as a surrogate "family" (Olmos, 1994; cf. Jankowski, 1991). Sampson and Laub likewise found that having social relationships with delinquent peers was one of the strongest independent predictors of juvenile delinquency, consistent with plenty of previous evidence. They did, however caution that this well-established link is based on largely correlational data and that ambiguities about the direction of

One might object that married people can stay out of institutions because they have someone at home to take care of them. On the other hand, many people are admitted to such institutions at the behest of family members, and so one could argue that the true difference is even larger. Given the size and consistency of the effect, it seems reasonable to conclude that marital status is related to mental illness, although further and methodologically better evidence is needed.

causality remain to be addressed. Still, for present purposes, the link is important evidence that belongingness needs are important among deviants, regardless of whether the link arises because having delinquent peers causes delinquent activity or because delinquent activity leads to bonding with delinquent peers.

Meanwhile, in laboratory experimentation, Geis and Moon (1981) sought to involve participants in lying, cheating, and stealing at the behest of an assigned group partner (a confederate). They found that 67% of a sample of college students acquiesced in an act of cheating and in a monetary theft by their partner and that they actively lied to conceal the theft. Thus, it appears that even recently formed group bonds may be strong enough to overcome some salient prohibitions of traditional morality. (It is noteworthy that the group loyalty in that study may have been intensified by the presence of a hostile rival group.) More extreme versions of the phenomenon of going along with objectionable actions by fellow group members because of loyalty have been commonly observed as central factors in group violence, such as spontaneous atrocities committed by the Ku Klux Klan (Wade, 1987), Nazi police guards (Browning, 1992), and others (Staub, 1989; see also Groth, 1979, on gang rape).

The relevance of belongingness to suicide was suggested nearly a century ago by Durkheim (1897/1963). His seminal work proposed that suicide could be explained as a result of a failure of social integration. People who are well integrated into society by multiple and strong relationships are unlikely to commit suicide, whereas unintegrated people are much more likely to kill themselves. Durkheim's hypothesis has held up far better than most social science hypotheses over the decades, and the evidence continues to show that a lack of social integration increases the likelihood of suicide (Trout, 1980). For example, single, divorced, and widowed people are more likely to commit suicide than married people (e.g., Rothberg & Jones, 1987). Those who are unemployed have a higher suicide rate than those who are employed. People who belong to subcultural groups that are shrinking have increased suicide rates. People who work in occupations that are shrinking are also more likely than others to commit suicide. Indeed, the main criticism that can be leveled against Durkheim's hypothesis is that it is incomplete in the sense that it does not explain everything about suicide (e.g., Baumeister, 1990; Douglas, 1967), but it is correct as far as it goes. For present purposes, the important point is that strong social ties are associated with a lower risk of suicide, probably because such ties help restrain people from killing themselves.

Social support research is relevant to the belongingness hypothesis because social support is based on relationships and positive interactions with others, and so any benefits of such support would constitute further confirmation of the belongingness hypothesis. The benefits of social support appear to be well established. Thus, for example, Cohen, Sherrod, and Clark (1986) showed that the availability of social support—which can be restated as the existence of social bonds—buffers people against the ill effects of stress. Cutrona (1989) showed that social support reduced depression during pregnancy and postpartum depression among adolescent girls. Responding to methodological criticisms that had attacked social support research as merely self-report bias, Cutrona's study included ratings of each girl's support network by an adult informant who knew the girls well, and these external informants' ratings predicted health outcomes (in some cases, even better than the girls' own ratings of their support). Thus, the benefits of belongingness in coping with major life stress appear to go beyond mere self-report bias.

Older adults who have a close, intimate friend (i.e., a "confidant") maintain higher morale in the face of life stresses such as retirement and spousal death than individuals who lack such a relationship. For example, Lowenthal and Haven (1968) found that widows who have a confidant have been found to be only slightly more depressed than married women, whereas those without a confidant have been found to be much more dysphoric. These researchers also found that the majority of older adults who recently lost a confidant were depressed, but the majority who currently had a confidant were satisfied.

Rook (1987) distinguished between social support and companionship. Social support was in this case rather narrowly interpreted in terms of direct help, whereas companionship meant the expressive aspects of social interaction. Both were found to be important and beneficial, but companionship may be the more important of the two, especially for psychological well-being, social satisfaction, and coping with minor stress. These data are par-

ticularly important for the relevance of social support research to the belongingness hypothesis because one could conceivably argue that belongingness per se is irrelevant and that the practical, material help that people derive from their social networks is solely responsible for the benefits of social support. Rook's data suggested, on the contrary, that the practical help is secondary (except in extreme circumstances in which major assistance is needed), whereas belongingness is highly beneficial by itself.

Perhaps most generally, general well-being and happiness in life depend on having some close social ties. Social isolation is strongly related to various patterns of unhappiness (for reviews, see Argyle, 1987; Baumeister, 1991; Freedman, 1978; Myers, 1992). Indeed, Baumeister (1991) noted that it is about the only objective factor that shows a substantial correlation with subjective well-being. Happiness also appears to be fairly stable across time and circumstance (e.g., Costa, McCrae, & Zonderman, 1987), leading many to conclude that it is linked to personality factors. The broad trait of extraversion appears to be strongly related to happiness and positive affectivity (see Costa & McCrae, 1980, 1984), and extraversion encompasses several factors, such as sociability, gregariousness, warmth, and social involvement, that seem likely to enhance the tendency to form and maintain social ties. Moreover, belongingness appears to be sufficient to overcome the relative deficit in happiness that introverts suffer. Hotard, McFatter, McWhirter, and Stegall (1989) found that introverts who have a good network of social relationships are just as happy as extraverts. Thus, introverts' deficit in happiness may be a result of their experiencing less belongingness.

Further support for the importance of belongingness to psychological well-being is provided by the fact that the pychotherapeutic process is facilitated by close personal bonds. Numerous therapeutic orientations stress the importance of the relationship between the therapist and the client. Rogers (1959), for example, urged psychotherapists to display a willingness to accept and support the client regardless of his or her behavior or contribution to the relationship. Such "unconditional positive regard" is perhaps the ultimate way to fulfill another person's belongingness needs. From the standpoint of the belongingness hypothesis, however, the essential ingredient in client-centered therapy is not unconditional positive regard (i.e., appraisal) but unconditional social acceptance (i.e., belongingness).[6]

Furthermore, some have suggested that one goal of psychotherapy should be to enhance clients' ability to elicit social support in their everyday lives (Brehm, 1987). To the extent that people who have strong connections with others are happier, healthier, and better able to cope with the stresses of everyday life, most clients would presumably benefit from enhancing their belongingness.

The psychotherapeutic usefulness of belonging can also be seen in the effectiveness of group therapy. As Lewin (1951) flatly stated, "It is easier to change individuals formed into a group than to change them separately" (p. 228). In part, the effectiveness of group therapy seems to depend on engendering a sense of belongingness, as some authors have asserted (Larkin, 1972; Yalom, 1985). Forsyth (1991), in his review of research on group therapy, observed that therapeutic groups provide the member "with a sense of belonging, protection from harm, and acceptance" (p. 675).

People differ, of course, in the degree to which they believe that their belongingness needs are being met irrespective of the extensiveness of their social networks or the strength of social support they receive. Lakey and Cassady (1990) provided data suggesting that perceived social support operates much like a cognitive schema. People have relatively stable, organized beliefs about the extent and quality of their interpersonal relationships. These belief systems lead to biased interpretation of social interactions, as well as to a biased recall of past interpersonal events. As a result, some people have a predisposition to perceive others as unsupportive, leading them to experience belongingness deprivation even when others are in fact being supportive.

CRITICAL ASSESSMENT

The diversity of methodologies and the multiplicity of disciplines that have furnished the evidence reviewed in this section make it highly implausible to suggest that all such evidence can be explained away as the result of confounds or artifacts. At worst, some of the findings have alternate explanations. Not all studies have maintained careful distinction between the pragmatic benefits of certain relationships and the direct benefits of belongingness. The fact that happily married people commit fewer crimes than other adults, for example, might be partly (or even wholly) due to the material benefits of being married. Even so, researchers who have maintained such distinctions (such as several of the social support researchers) have found pragmatic benefits to be a secondary factor. Belongingness thus has important and direct benefits.

A more serious limitation is that several of the findings are correlational. The higher rates of mental and physical illness among loners could reflect a tendency for people to reject deviants as potential relationship partners. By the same token, the higher levels of life satisfaction found among happily married people could be partly due to a tendency for chronically unhappy people to be rejected as marriage partners. Still, those studies that have provided evidence about the direction of causality have consistently identified belongingness as the causal factor.

CONCLUSION

Deprivation of stable, good relationships has been linked to a large array of aversive and pathological consequences. People who lack belongingness suffer higher levels of mental and physical illness and are relatively highly prone to a broad range of behavioral problems, ranging from traffic accidents to criminality to suicide. Some of these findings may be subject to alternative explanations, and for some the direction of causality has not been established; however, the weight of evidence suggests that lack of belongingness is a primary cause of multiple and diverse problems. It therefore seems appropriate to regard belongingness as a need rather than simply a want. [. . .]

Innateness, Universality, and Evolutionary Perspectives

We proposed that a fundamental need would presumably be innate, which would entail that it is found in all human beings and is not derivative of other motives. This will, of course, be quite difficult to verify, because empirical criteria for testing such a hypothesis are not widely recognized. One approach, however, would be to examine how

---

[6] The two overlap in many ways, of course. Cutrona (1986) has noted that esteem support is an important element of social support, particularly for helping people avoid depressive reactions to stressful events.

well the empirical evidence conforms to evolutionary arguments. If evolution has instilled the motivation, then it is presumably universal among human beings and will be present in each person without needing to be derived from other motives.

Barchas (1986) has asserted that "over the course of evolution, the small group became the basic survival strategy developed by the human species" (p. 212). He went on to suggest that the brain and small groups evolved and adapted together, with multiple interrelationships. The evidence reviewed by Barchas remains preliminary, but it does seem that any link between brain structures and small-group formation would strengthen the case for an innate motivation.

Although the psychobiological systems involved in social attachment are not yet well understood, early evidence implicates the brain opioid system. According to Panksepp, Siviy, and Normansell (1985), both the tendency to form social bonds and the emotional effects of social loss (e.g., sadness or grief) are mediated by opioids. The formation and validation of relationships apparently stimulate opioid production, whereas the dissolution of relationships impedes it. As Panksepp et al. put it, "social affect and social bonding are in some fundamental neurochemical sense opioid addictions" (p. 25). Thus, in their view, the tendency to seek social connections with others is based not only on the secondary reinforcements that other people provide but on psychophysiological mechanisms as well.

Multiple evolutionary reasons could be suggested for the readiness to form groups easily. Groups can share labor, resources, and information; diffuse risk; and cooperate to overcome stress or threat (Hogan et al., 1985). Defense against rival groups would also be a significant factor: If other people form into groups, lone individuals would be at a competitive disadvantage in many situations, and so evolution may have selected for people who would form groups defensively. Hence, the evolutionary argument would fit any evidence that group formation or cohesion patterns are increased by external threat.

It has long been noted that external threats increase group cohesion, and some writers have treated this as axiomatic. Stein (1976) reviewed these views in light of the evidence and found that a broad variety of methods have yielded generally consistent findings; that is, external threats do in-

crease cohesion most of the time. There are some circumstances in which groups disintegrate under threat, especially if the threat pertains only to some members of the group or if group members must compete against each other to survive the threat (e.g., if there are too few lifeboats). Staw, Sandelands, and Dutton (1981) also found evidence that group cohesion is sometimes weakened in the aftermath of a threat, especially if the group has failed to defeat the threat and the group members blame each other. Apart from these circumscribed exceptions, however, it is safe to conclude that external threats do generally increase group cohesion.

A remarkable demonstration of the power or external threat to forge lasting bonds was provided by Elder and Clipp's (1988) study of World War II veterans' groups. In Elder and Clipp's results, the effects of maximum threat were discernible 40 years later. That is, four decades after the war, the most enduring and strongest ties were found among veterans who had experienced heavy combat together and had suffered the deaths of some close comrades. Units that had experienced combat without fatalities were less close 40 years later, but they retained stronger ties than the units that had not been in combat together. In other words, the sharing of military experience provided some lasting bonds, these bonds were intensified by shared experience of combat, and they were especially strong if it had been heavy combat that had killed some members of the group. It seems clear that there would be survival benefits to a pattern in which the death of a group member strengthened the ties among the survivors, especially in the face of external danger.

The group formation effects in the Robbers Cave study (described earlier; Sherif et al., 1961/1988) accelerated rapidly after the mutual discovery of the existence of the two rival groups; that is, the implicit threat posed by the opposing group seemed to motivate each boy to cling to his own group more strongly. Similar processes have been observed in terrorist groups, which mainly become cohesive in the face of external threat and danger. During periods when the conflict with outsiders lapses, terrorist groups experience internal dissent and conflict and may fall apart (see McCauley & Segal, 1987).

Compelling evidence in favor of emphasizing the competitive disadvantage motive for affiliating was provided by Hoyle, Pinkley, and Insko

(1989). These researchers noted the irony that encounters between individuals are generally pleasant and supportive, whereas encounters between groups are frequently unpleasant and confrontational, and their first study confirmed these general expectations and stereotypes empirically. In their second study, they sought to determine the decisive factor by comparing interactions between persons, between groups, and between one person and one group. To their surprise, they found that participants' expectations about the interaction were determined mainly by the other party rather than by participants' own belongingness status. When participants expected to interact with a group, they expected an abrasive interaction; when they expected to interact with an individual, they anticipated a pleasant, agreeable interaction. Identical effects were found regardless of whether the participant expected to be alone or to be part of a group. Thus, apparently, the presence of an outgroup causes people to anticipate conflict and problematic interactions. Such an expectation could well elicit a motivation to form a group to protect oneself.

A similar conclusion was suggested by Lauderdale, Smith-Cunnien, Parker, and Inverarity (1984). Following Schachter's (1951) studies on group rejection of deviants, they found that increasing an external threat led to increased rejection. The implication was that groups become increasingly oriented toward solidarity when confronted with an external threat.

Apart from threat, the possibility of gaining resources also seems to trigger group cohesion, even when it is functionally irrelevant. Rabbie and Horwitz (1969) assigned participants randomly to two groups. The random assignment alone yielded no effects of group cohesion on their measures of in-group preference, but they did find significant effects after a manipulation in which one group was given a prize (transistor radio) based on a coin flip. The rewarded group and the deprived group both showed increased in-group preference. The prize was logically irrelevant to subsequent group activities and preferences. The implication is apparently that the combination of limited resources and multiple groups triggers an in-group preference response that has no apparent practical or rational basis, which is consistent with the view that it is a deeply rooted and possibly innate tendency rather than a strategic or rational choice.

CRITICAL ASSESSMENT

The evidence linking external threat to increased group cohesion is convincing but does not prove an evolutionary hypothesis of innateness or universality. The evidence for brain mechanisms is likewise supportive but inadequate to prove innateness. The evidence in this section is perhaps best described by stating that the evolutionary hypothesis nicely survived several tests that could have contradicted it.

CONCLUSION

Several patterns seem consistent with evolutionary reasoning. It remains plausible (but unproven) that the need to belong is part of the human biological inheritance. If so, the case for universality and nonderivativeness would be strong. At present, it seems fair to accept these hypotheses as tentative working assumptions while waiting for further evidence. [. . .]

General Discussion

We have considered a broad assortment of evidence pertaining to the hypothesis that the desire for interpersonal attachments—the need to belong—is a fundamental human motivation. Most of the metatheoretical requirements we outlined for evaluating such a hypothesis appear to be satisfied, although some issues remain. We begin by reviewing the major conclusions.

Again and again, we found evidence of a basic desire to form social attachments. People form social bonds readily, even under seemingly adverse conditions. People who have anything in common, who share common (even unpleasant) experiences, or who simply are exposed to each other frequently tend to form friendships or other attachments. Moreover, people resist losing attachments and breaking social bonds, even if there is no material or pragmatic reason to maintain the bond and even if maintaining it would be difficult.

Abundant evidence also attests that the need to belong shapes emotion and cognition. Forming or solidifying social attachments generally produces positive emotion, whereas real, imagined, or even potential threats to social bonds generate a variety of unpleasant emotional states. In short, change in belongingness is a strong and pervasive cause of emotion in ways that support the hypothesis of a need to belong. It is also evident that people think a great deal about belongingness. They devote a disproportionate amount of cognitive processing to actual or possible relationship partners and interaction partners, and they reserve particular, more extensive, and more favorable patterns of information processing for people with whom they share social bonds.

Deficits in belongingness apparently lead to a variety of ill effects, consistent with the view that belongingness is a need (as opposed to merely a want). Both psychological and physical health problems are more common among people who lack social attachments. Behavioral pathologies, ranging from eating disorders to suicide, are more common among people who are unattached. Although most of these findings are correlational and many alternative explanations can be suggested, recent efforts have begun controlling for these other factors, and the pure, primary effects of belongingness appear to remain strong. It appears, then, that belongingness is not only pleasant but also apparently very beneficial to the individual in multiple ways.

We proposed two aspects of the need to belong, and both appear to be important. That is, people seem to need frequent, affectively pleasant or positive interactions with the same individuals, and they need these interactions to occur in a framework of long-term, stable caring and concern. People who can satisfy one component but not the other tend to be less satisfied and less well off then people who can satisfy both, but they do seem to derive some benefits from satisfying the one component (as opposed to satisfying neither). More and better evidence is needed on this point, however; most evidence pertains to people who have the bond and lack interactions, rather than the reverse. Also, it is unclear whether the interactions must be pleasant or can be satisfactory if they are merely neutral. The evidence suggests merely that aversive or conflictual interactions fail to satisfy the need. Some evidence suggests that a framework of mutual, reciprocal concern is best, but the effects and importance of mutuality need further investigation.

The need to belong also appears to conform to motivational patterns of satiation and substitution. People need a few close relationships, and forming additional bonds beyond those few has less and less impact. Having two as opposed to no close relationships may make a world of difference to the person's health and happiness; having eight as opposed to six may have very little consequence. When a social bond is broken, people appear to recover best if they form a new one, although each individual life tends to involve some particularly special relationships (such as filial or marital bonds) that are not easily replaced. People without intimate partners engage in a variety of activities to find partners, but people who have partners already are much less active at seeking additional relationships, consistent with the satiation hypothesis.

We reviewed evidence that the need to belong affects a broad variety of behaviors; indeed, the range is sufficiently broad as to render less plausible any notion that the need to belong is a product of certain other factors or motives. We also noted that evidence about belongingness seems to implicate some brain mechanisms and to conform to patterns that evolutionary theory would suggest, both of which seem consistent with the argument that the need is innate in humans. Still, the nonderivative hypothesis is probably the least well supported aspect of our theory, not because of any clear evidence deriving the need to belong from other motives but simply perhaps because it is relatively difficult to collect compelling data to show that a motive is not derivative. The issue of which motives derive from which others appears to be an important challenge for future motivation research.

We also considered several counterexamples that at least superficially suggested tendencies to reject social attachment. On close inspection, these patterns did not stand up as counterexamples, and indeed there was generally strong evidence of a positive need to belong that increased the subjective difficulty of rejecting or avoiding attachment.

We conclude, then, that the present state of the empirical evidence is sufficient to confirm the belongingness hypothesis. The need to belong can be considered a fundamental human motivation. [. . .]

Concluding Remarks

At present, it seems fair to conclude that human beings are fundamentally and pervasively motivated by a need to belong, that is, by a strong desire to form and maintain enduring interpersonal attachments. People seek frequent, affectively positive interactions within the context of long-term, caring relationships. As a speculative point of theory or impressionistic observation, the need to belong is not a new idea; indeed, we noted a variety of previous psychological theorists who have proposed it in one form or another. What is new, however, is the existence of a large body of empirical evidence with which to evaluate that hypothesis.

If psychology has erred with regard to the need to belong, in our view, the error has not been to deny the existence of such a motive so much as to underappreciate it. This review has shown multiple links between the need to belong and cognitive processes, emotional patterns, behavioral responses, and health and well-being. The desire for interpersonal attachment may well be one of the most far-reaching and integrative constructs currently available to understand human nature.

REFERENCES

Ainsworth, M. D. (1989). Attachments beyond infancy. *American Psychologist, 44,* 709–716.

Anderson, S. A., Russell, C. S., & Schumm, W. R. (1983). Peceived marital quality and family lifecycle categories: A further analysis. *Journal of Marriage and the Family, 45,* 127–139.

Argyle, M. (1987). *The psychology of happiness.* London: Methuen.

Armstrong, J. G., & Roth, D. M. (1989). Attachment and separation in eating disorders: A preliminary investigation. *International Journal of Eating Disorders, 8,* 141–155.

Aron, A., Aron, E. N., Tudor M., & Nelson, G. (1991). Close relationships as including other in the self. *Journal of Personality and Social Psychology, 60,* 241–253.

Axelrod, R., & Hamilton, W. D. (1981). The evolution of cooperation. *Science, 11,* 1390–1396.

Barash, D. P. (1977). *Sociobiology and behavior.* New York: Elsevier.

Barchas, P. (1986). A sociophysiological orientation to small groups. In E. Lawler (Ed.), *Advances in group processes* (Vol. 3, pp. 209–246). Greenwich, CT: JAI Press.

Barden, R. C., Garber, J., Leiman, B., Ford, M. E., & Masters, J. C. (1985). Factors governing the effective remediation of negative affect and its cognitive and behavioral consequences. *Journal of Personality and Social Psychology, 49,* 1040–1053.

Barocas, R., & Vance, F. L. (1974). Physical appearance and personal adjustment counseling. *Journal of Counseling Psychology, 21,* 96–100.

Baumeister, R. F. (1990). Suicide as escape from self. *Psychological Review, 97,* 90–113.

Baumeister, R. F. (1991). *Meanings of life.* New York: Guilford Press.

Baumeister, R. F., Stillwell, A. M., & Heatherton, T. F. (1994). Guilt: An interpersonal approach. *Psychological Bulletin, 115,* 243–267.

Baumeister, R. F., Stillwell, A. M., & Heatherton, T. F. (in press). Personal narratives about guilt: Role in action control and interpersonal relationships. *Basic and Applied Social Psychology.*

Baumeister, R. F., & Tice, D. M. (1990). Anxiety and social delusion. *Journal of Clinical Psychology, 9,* 165–195.

Baumeister, R. F., & Wotman, S. R. (1992). *Breaking hearts: The two sides of unrequited love.* New York: Guilford Press.

Bernard, J. (1982). *The future of marriage.* New Haven, CT: Yale University Press.

Berscheid, E., & Walster, E. (1974). Physical attractiveness. In L. Berkowitz (Ed.), *Advances in experimental social psychology* (Vol. 7, pp. 158–215). New York: Academic Press.

Bhatti, B., Derezotes, D., Kim, S., & Specht, H. (1989). The association between child maltreatment and self-esteem. In A. M. Mecca, N. J. Smelser, & J. Vasconcellos (Eds.), *The social importance of self-esteem* (pp. 24–71). Berkeley: University of California Press.

Billig, M., & Tajfel, H. (1973). Social categorization and similarity in intergroup behavior. *European Journal of Social Psychology, 3,* 27–51.

Bloom, B. L., White, S. W., & Asher, S. J. (1979). Marital disruption as a stressful life event. In G. Levinger & O. C. Moles (Eds.), *Divorce and separation: Context, causes and consequences* (pp. 184–200). New York: Basic Books.

Bowlby, J. (1969). *Attachment and loss: Vol. 1. Attachment.* New York: Basic Books.

Bowlby, J. (1973). *Attachment and loss: Vol. 2. Separation anxiety and anger.* New York: Basic Books.

Brehm, S. S. (1987). Social support and clinical practice. In J. E. Maddux, C. D. Stoltenberg, & R. Rosenwein (Eds.), *Social processes in clinical and counseling psychology* (pp. 26–38). New York: Springer-Verlag.

Brenner, M. W. (1976). *Memory and interpersonal relations.* Unpublished doctoral dissertation. University of Michigan, Ann Arbor.

Brewer, M. B. (1979). Ingroup bias in the minimal intergroup situation. A cognitive–motivational analysis. *Psychological Bulletin, 86,* 307–324.

Brewer M. B., & Silver, M. (1978). Ingroup bias as a function of task characteristics. *European Journal of Social Psychology, 8,* 393–400.

Bridges, W. (1980). *Transitions: Making sense of life's changes.* Reading, MA: Addison-Wesley.

Brown, J. D. (1986). Evaluations of self and others: Self-enhancement biases in social judgments. *Social Cognition, 4,* 353–376.

Browning, C. R. (1992). *Ordinary men: Reserve Police Battalion 101 and the final solution in Poland.* New York: Harper Collins.

Buss, D. M. (1990). The evolution of anxiety and social exclusion. *Journal of Social and Clinical Psychology, 9,* 196–210.

Buss, D. M. (1991). Evolutionary personality psychology. *Annual Review of Psychology, 42,* 459–491.

Campbell, A. (1981). *The sense of well-being in America.* New York: McGraw-Hill.

Campbell, A., Converse, P .E., & Rodgers, W. L. (1976). *The quality of American life: Perceptions, evaluations, and satisfactions.* New York: Russell Sage Foundation.

Cash, T. F. (1985). Physical appearance and mental health. In J. A. Graham & A. Kligman (Eds.), *The psychology of cosmetic treatments* (pp. 196–216). New York: Praeger.

Clark, L. A., & Watson, D. (1988). Mood and the mundane: Relations between daily life events and self-reported mood. *Journal of Personality and Social Psychology, 54,* 296–308.

Clark, M. S. (1984). Record keeping in two types of relationships. *Journal of Personality and Social Psychology, 47,* 549–557.

Clark, M. S. (1986). Evidence for the effectiveness of manipulations of communal and exchange relationships. *Personality and Social Psychology Bulletin, 12,* 414–425.

Clark, M. S., & Mills, J. (1979). Interpersonal attraction in exchange and communal relationships. *Journal of Personality and Social Psychology, 37,* 12–24.

Clark, M. S., Mills, J., & Corcoran, D. M. (1989). Keeping track of needs and inputs of friends and strangers. *Personality and Social Psychology Bulletin, 15,* 533–542.

Clark, M. S., Mills J., & Powell, M. C. (1986). Keeping track of needs in communal and exchange relationships. *Journal of Personality and Social Psychology, 51,* 333–338.

Clark, M. S., Ouellette, R., Powell, M. C., & Milberg, S. (1987). Recipient's mood, relationship type, and helping. *Journal of Personality and Social Psychology, 53,* 94–103.

Cohen, S., Sherrod, D. R., & Clark, M. S. (1986). Social skills and the stress-protective role of social support. *Journal of Personality and Social Psychology, 50,* 963–973.

Cohen, S., & Wills, T. A. (1985). Stress, social support, and the buffering hypothesis. *Psychological Bulletin, 98,* 310–357.

Coon, C. S. (1946). The universality of natural grouping in human societies. *Journal of Educational Sociology, 20,* 163–168.

Costa, P. T., & McCrae, R. R. (1980). Influence of extraversion and neuroticism on subjective well-being: Happy and unhappy people. *Journal of Personality and Social Psychology, 38,* 668–678.

Costa, P. T., & McCrae, R. R. (1984). Personality as a lifelong determinant of wellbeing. In C. Z. Malatesta & C. E. Izard (Eds.), *Emotion in adult development* (pp. 141–157). Beverly Hills. CA: Sage.

Costa, P. T., McCrae, R. R., & Zonderman, A. B. (1987). Environmental and dispositional influences on well-being: Longitudinal follow-up of an American national sample. *British Journal of Psychology, 78,* 299–306.

Craighead, W. E., Kimball, W. H., & Rehak, R. S. (1979). Mood changes, physiological responses, and self-statements during social rejection imagery. *Journal of Consulting and Clinical Psychology, 47,* 385–396.

Cunningham, M. R., Steinberg, J., & Grev, R. (1980). Wanting to and having to help: Separate motivations for positive mood and guilt-induced helping. *Journal of Personality and Social Psychology, 38,* 181–192.

Cutrona, C. E. (1986). Behavioral manifestations of social support: A microanalytic investigation. *Journal of Personality and Social Psychology, 51,* 201–208.

Cutrona, C. E. (1989). Ratings of social support by adolescents and adult informants: Degree of correspondence and prediction of depressive symptoms. *Journal of Personality and Social Psychology, 57,* 723–730.

DeLongis, A., Folkman, S., & Lazarus, R. S. (1988). The impact of daily stress on health and mood: Psychological and social resources as mediators. *Journal of Personality and Social Psychology, 54,* 486–495.

de Rivera, J. (1984). The structure of emotional relationships. In P. Shaver (Ed.), *Review of personality and social psy-* *chology, Vol. 5: Emotions, relationships, and health* (pp. 116–145). Beverly Hills, CA: Sage.

DiTommaso, E., & Spinner, B. (1993). The development and initial validation of the social and emotional loneliness scale for adults. *Personality and Individual Differences, 11,* 127–134.

Donne, J. (1975). *Devotions on emergent occasions.* Montreal, Canada: McGill Queens University Press.

Douglas, J. D. (1967). *The social meanings of suicide.* Princeton, NJ: Princeton University Press.

Durkheim, E. (1963). *Suicide.* New York: Free Press. (Original work published 1897)

Egan, G. (1970). *Encounter: Group processes for interpersonal growth.* Monterey, CA: Brooks/Cole.

Elder, G. H., & Clipp, E. C. (1988). Wartime losses and social bonding: Influence across 40 years in men's lives. *Psychiatry, 51,* 177–198.

Epstein, S. (1992). The cognitive self, the psychoanalytic self, and the forgotten selves. *Psychological Inquiry, 3,* 34–37.

Farina, A., Burns, G. L., Austad, C., Bugglin, C. S., & Fischer, E. H. (1986). The role of physical attractiveness in the readjustment of discharged psychiatric patients. *Journal of Abnormal Psychology, 86,* 510–517.

Festinger, L., Schachter, S., & Back, K. (1950). *Social pressures in informal groups: A study of a housing community.* Palo Alto, CA: Stanford University Press.

Fincham, F. D., Beach, S. R., & Baucom, D. H. (1987). Attribution processes in distressed and nondistressed couples: 4. Self-partner attribution differences. *Journal of Personality and Social Psychology, 52,* 739–748.

Forsyth, D. R. (1991). Change in therapeutic groups. In C. R. Snyder & D. R. Forsyth (Eds.), *Handbook of social and clinical psychology* (pp. 664–680). New York: Pergamon Press.

Forsyth, D. R., & Schlenker, B. R. (1977). Attributing the causes of group performance: Effects of performance quality, task importance, and future testing. *Journal of Personality, 45,* 220–236.

Freedman, J. (1978). *Happy people: What happiness is, who has it, and why.* New York: Harcourt Brace Jovanovich.

Freud, S. (1930). *Civilization and its discontents* (J. Riviere, Trans.). London: Hogarth Press.

Fromm, E. (1955). *The sane society.* New York: Holt, Rinehart & Winston.

Fromm, E. (1956). *The art of loving.* New York: Harper & Brothers.

Geis, F. L., & Moon, T. H. (1981). Machiavellianism and deception. *Journal of Personality and Social Psychology, 41,* 766–775.

Glenn, N. D., & McLanahan, S. (1982). Children and marital happiness: A further specification of the relationship. *Journal of Marriage and the Family, 44,* 63–72.

Goffman, E. (1971). *Relations in public.* New York: Harper Colophon.

Goodwin, J. S., Hunt, W. C., Key, C. R., & Samet, J. M. (1987). The effect of marital status on stage, treatment, and survival of cancer patients. *Journal of the American Medical Association, 258,* 3125–3130.

Gouaux, C. (1971). Induced affective states and interpersonal attraction. *Journal of Personality and Social Psychology, 16,* 253–260.

Groth, A. N. (1979). *Men who rape.* New York: Plenum Press.

Guisinger, S., & Blatt, S. J. (1994). Individuality and relatedness: Evolution of a fundamental dialectic. *American Psychologist, 49,* 104–111.

Hamachek, D. (1992). *Encounters with the self* (4th ed.). San Diego, CA: Harcourt Brace Jovanovich.

Harlow, H. F., Harlow, M. K., & Suomi, S. J. (1971). From thought to therapy: Lessons from a primate laboratory. *American Scientist, 59,* 538–549.

Hazan, C., & Shaver, P. R. (1994a). Attachment as an organizational framework for research on close relationships. *Psychological Inquiry, 5,* 1–22.

Hazan, C., & Shaver, P. R. (1994b). Deeper into attachment theory. *Psychological Inquiry, 5,* 68–79.

Hobfall, S. E., & London, P. (1986). The relationship of self-concept and social support to emotional distress among women during the war. *Journal of Social and Clinical Psychology, 4,* 189–203.

Hogan, R. (1983). A socioanalytic theory of personality. In M. Page & R. Dienstbier (Eds.), *Nebraska Symposium on Motivation, 1982* (pp. 55–89). Lincoln: University of Nebraska Press.

Hogan, R., Jones, W. H., & Cheek, J. M. (1985). Socioanalytic theory: An alternative to armadillo psychology. In B. R. Schlenker (Ed), *The self and social life* (pp. 175–198). New York: McGraw-Hill.

Horney, K. (1945). *Our inner conflicts: A constructive theory of neurosis.* New York: Norton.

Hotard, S. R., McFatter, R. M., & McWhirter, R. M, & Stegall, M. E. (1989). Interactive effects of extraversion, neuroticism, and social relationships on subjective well-being. *Journal of Personality and Social Psychology, 57,* 321–331.

Howard, J. W., & Rothbart, M. (1980). Social categorization and memory for in-group and out-group behavior. *Journal of Personality and Social Psychology, 38,* 301–310.

Hoyle, R. H., & Crawford, A. M. (in press). Use individual-level data to investigate group phenomena: Issues and strategies. *Small Group Research.*

Hoyle, R. H., Pinkley, R. L., & Insko, C. A. (1989). Perceptions of social behavior: Evidence of differing expectations for interpersonal and intergroup interaction. *Personality and Social Psychology Bulletin, 15,* 365–376.

Jankowski, M. S. (1991). *Islands in the street: Gangs and American urban society.* Berkeley: University of California Press.

Jones, W. H. (1981). Loneliness and social contact. *Journal of Social Psychology, 113,* 295–296.

Jones, W. H., & Kugler, K. (in press). Interpersonal correlates of the guilt inventory. *Journal of Personality Assessment.*

Jones, W. H., Kugler, K., & Adams, P. (1995). You always hurt the one you love: Guilt and transgressions against relationship partners. In K. Fischer & J. Tangner (Eds.), *Self-conscious emotion* (pp. 301–321). New York: Guilford Press.

Kenrick, D. T., & Cialdini, R. B. (1977). Romantic attraction: Misattribution versus reinforcement explanations. *Journal of Personality and Social Psychology, 35,* 381–391.

Kenrick, D. T., & Johnson. G. A. (1979). Interpersonal attraction in aversive environments: A problem for the classical conditioning paradigm? *Journal of Personality and Social Psychology, 37,* 572–579.

Kiecolt-Glaser, J. K., Fisher, L. D., Ogrocki, P., Stout, J. C., Speicher, C. E., & Glaser, R. (1987). Marital quality, marital disruption, and immune function. *Psychosomatic Medicine, 49,* 13–34.

Kiecolt-Glaser, J. K., Garner, W., Speicher, C., Penn, G. M., Holliday, J., & Glaser, R. (1984). Psychosocial modifiers of immunocompetence in medical students. *Psychosomatic Medicine, 46,* 7–14.

Kiecolt-Glaser, J. K., Ricker, D., George, J., Messeck, G., Speicher, C. E., Garner, W., & Glaser, R. (1984). Urinary cortisol levels, cellular immunocompetency, and loneliness in psychiatric inpatients. *Psychosomatic Medicine, 46,* 15–23.

Kunz, P. R., & Woolcott, M. (1976). Season's greetings: From my status to yours. *Social Science Research, 5,* 269–278.

Lacoursiere, R. B. (1980). *The life cycles of groups: Group developmental stage theory.* New York: Human Sciences Press.

Lakey, B., & Cassady, P. B. (1990). Cognitive processes in perceived social support. *Journal of Personality and Social Psychology, 59,* 337–343.

Larkin, M. (1972). *Experimental groups: The uses of interpersonal encounter, psychotherapy groups, and sensitivity training.* Morristown, NJ: General Learning Press.

Latane, B., Eckman, J., & Joy, V. (1966). Shared stress and interpersonal attraction. *Journal of Experimental Social Psychology, 1*(Suppl.), 80–94.

Lauderdale, P., Smith-Cunnien, P., Parker, J., & Inverarity, J. (1984). External threat and the definition of deviance. *Journal of Personality and Social Psychology, 46,* 1058–1068.

Leary, M. R. (1990). Responses to social exclusion: Social anxiety, jealousy, loneliness, depression, and low self-esteem. *Journal of Social and Clinical Psychology, 9,* 221–229.

Leary M. R., & Downs, D. L. (in press). Interpersonal functions of the self-esteem motive: The self-esteem system as a sociometer. In M. Kernis (Ed.), *Efficacy, agency, and self-esteem.* New York: Plenum Press.

Leary, M. R., & Forsyth, D. R. (1987). Attributions of responsibility for collective endeavors. In C. Hendrick (Ed.), *Review of personality and social psychology, Vol. 8: Group processes* (pp. 167–188). Newbury Park. CA: Sage.

Lewin, K. (1951). *Field theory in social sciences.* New York: Harper & Row.

Lieberman, M. A., Yalom, I. D., & Miles, M. B. (1973). *Encounter groups: First facts.* New York: Basic Books.

Linville, P. W., & Jones, E. E. (1980). Polarized appraisals of out-group members. *Journal of Personality and Social Psychology, 38,* 689–703.

Locksley, A., Ortiz, V., & Hepburn, C. (1980). Social categorization and discriminatory behavior: Extinguishing the minimal intergroup discrimination effect. *Journal of Personality and Social Psychology, 39,* 773–783.

Lowenthal, M. F., & Haven, C. (1968), Interaction and adaptation: Intimacy as a critical variable. *American Sociological Review, 33,* 20–30.

Lynch, J. J. (1979). *The broken heart: The medical consequences of loneliness.* New York: Basic Books.

Mann, L. (1980). Cross-cultural studies of small groups. In H. Triandis & R. Brislin (Eds.), *Handbook of cross-cultural psychology: Social psychology* (Vol. 5, pp. 155–209). Boston: Allyn & Bacon.

Maslow, A. H. (1968). *Toward a psychology of being.* New York: Van Nostrand.

Mathes, E. W., Adams, H. E., & Davies, R. M. (1985). Jealousy: Loss of relationship rewards, loss of self-esteem, depression, anxiety, and anger. *Journal of Personality and Social Psychology, 48,* 1552–1561.

May, J. L., & Hamilton, P. A. (1980). Effects of musically evoked affect on women's interpersonal attraction and perceptual judgments of physical attractiveness of men. *Motivation and Emotion, 4,* 217–228.

McAdams, D. P. (1985). Motivation and friendship. In S. Duck & D. Perlman (Eds.), *Understanding personal relationships: An interdisciplinary approach* (pp. 85–105). Beverly Hills, CA: Sage.

McAdams, D. P., & Bryant, F. B. (1987). Intimacy motivation and subjective mental health in a nationwide sample. *Journal of Personality, 55,* 395–413.

McCauley, C. R., & Segal, M. E. (1987). Social psychology of terrorist groups. In C. Hendrick (Ed.), *Group processes and intergroup relations: Review of personality and social psychology* (Vol. 9, pp. 231–256). Newbury Park, CA: Sage.

Miceli, M. (1992). How to make someone feel guilty: Strategies of guilt inducement and their goals. *Journal for the Theory of Social Behavior, 22,* 81–104.

Moreland, R. L. (1987). The formation of small groups. In C. Hendrick (Ed.), *Group processes: Review of personality and social psychology* (Vol. 8, pp. 80–110). Newbury Park, CA: Sage.

Myers, D. (1992). *The pursuit of happiness.* New York: Morrow.

Nahemow, L., & Lawton, M. P. (1975). Similarity and propinquity in friendship formation. *Journal of Personality and Social Psychology, 32,* 205–213,

O'Grady, K. E. (1989). Physical attractiveness, need for approval, social self-esteem, and maladjustment. *Journal of Social and Clinical Psychology, 8,* 62–69.

Olmos, E. (Producer). (1994, April 8). *Lives in hazard.* New York: National Broadcasting Company.

Orbell, J. M., van de Kragt, A., & Dawes, R. M. (1988). Explaining discussion-induced cooperation. *Journal of Personality and Social Psychology, 54,* 811–819.

Ostrom, T. M., Carpenter, S. L., Sedikides, C., & Li, F. (1993). Differential processing of in-group and out-group information. *Journal of Personality and Social Psychology, 64,* 21–34.

Paloutzian, R. F., & Janigian, A. S. (1987). Models and methods in loneliness research: Their status and direction. In M. Hoja & R. Crandall (Eds.), *Loneliness: Theory, research, and applications* (pp. 31–36). San Rafael, CA: Select Press.

Panksepp, J., Siviy, S. M., & Normansell, L. A. (1985). Brain opioids and social emotions. In M. Reite & T. Field (Eds.), *The psychobiology of attachment and separation* (pp. 3–49). New York: Academic Press.

Perlman, D. (1987). Further reflections on the present state of loneliness research. In M. Hoja & R. Crandall (Eds.), *Loneliness: Theory, research, and applications* (pp. 17–26). San Rafael, CA: Select Press.

Perloff, L. S., & Fetzer, B. K. (1986). Self–other judgments and perceived vulnerability to victimization. *Journal of Personality and Social Psychology, 50,* 502–510.

Pines, M., & Aronson, E. (1983). Antecedents, correlates, and consequences of sexual jealousy. *Journal of Personality, 51,* 108–135.

Pryor, J. M., & Ostrom, T. M. (1981). The cognitive organization of social life: A converging-operations approach. *Journal of Personality and Social Psychology, 41,* 628–641.

Rabbie, J. M., & Horwitz, M. (1969). Arousal of ingroup-outgroup bias by a chance win or loss. *Journal of Personality and Social Psychology, 13,* 269–277.

Reis, H. T. (1990). The role of intimacy in interpersonal relations. *Journal of Social and Clinical Psychology, 9,* 15–30.

Reiss, I. L. (1986). A sociological journey into sexuality. *Journal of Marriage and the Family, 48,* 233–242.

Rofe, Y. (1984). Stress and affiliation: A utility theory. *Psychological Review, 91,* 235–250.

Rogers, C. R. (1959). A theory of therapy personality and interpersonal relationships as developed in the client-centered framework. In S. Koch (Ed.), *Psychology: A study of a science* (Vol. 3, pp. 184–256). New York: McGraw-Hill.

Rook, K. S. (1987). Social support versus companionship: Effects on life stress, loneliness, and evaluations by others. *Journal of Personality and Social Psychology, 52,* 1132–1147.

Rothenberg, J. M., & Jones, F. D. (1987). Suicide in the U.S. Army: Epidemiological and political aspects. *Suicide and Life-Threatening Behavior, 17,* 119–132.

Roy, M. (Ed.). (1977). *Battered women.* New York: Van Nostrand.

Russell, D., Cutrona, C., Rose, J., & Yurko, K. (1984). Social and emotional loneliness: An examination of Weiss's typology of loneliness. *Journal of Personality and Social Psychology, 46,* 1313–1321.

Rutter, M. (1979). Maternal deprivation, 1972–1978: New findings, new concepts, new approaches. *Child Development, 50,* 283–305.

Ryan, R. M. (1991). The nature of the self in autonomy and relatedness. In J. Strauss & G. R. Goethals (Eds.), *The self: Interdisciplinary approaches* (pp. 208–238). New York: Springer-Verlag.

Saklofske, D. H., & Yackulic, R. A. (1989). Personality predictors of loneliness. *Personality and Individual Differences, 10,* 467–472.

Sampson, R. J., & Laub, J. H. (1993). *Crime in the making. Pathways and turning points through life.* Cambridge, MA: Harvard University Press.

Schachter, S. (1951). Deviance, rejection, and communication. *Journal of Abnormal Social Psychology, 16,* 190–207.

Schachter, S. (1959). *The psychology of affiliation.* Stanford, CA: Stanford University Press.

Sedikides, C., Olsen, N., & Reis, H. T. (1993). Relationships as natural categories. *Journal of Personality and Social Psychology, 64,* 71–82.

Shaver, P., & Buhrmester, D. (1983). Loneliness, sex-role orientation, and group life: A social needs perspective. In P. Paulus (Ed.), *Basic group processes* (pp. 259–288). New York: Springer-Verlag.

Shaver, P., Hazan, C., & Bradshaw, D. (1988). Love as attachment. The integration of three behavioral systems. In R. J. Sternberg & M. L. Barnes (Eds.), *The psychology of love* (pp. 68–99). New Haven, CT: Yale University Press.

Sherif, M., Harvey, O. H., White, B. J., Hood, W. R., & Sherif, C. W. (1988). *The Robbers Cave experiment: Intergroup conflict and cooperation.* Middletown, CT: Wesleyan University Press. (Original work published 1961)

Solomon. Z., Waysman, M., & Mikulincer, M. (1990). Family functioning, perceived social support, and combat-related psychopathology: The moderating role of loneliness. *Journal of Social and Clinical Psychology, 9,* 456–472.

Sours, J. A. (1974). The anorexia nervosa syndrome. *International Journal of Psychoanalysis, 55,* 567–576.

Spanier, G. B., & Lewis, R. A. (1980). Marital quality: A review of the seventies. *Journal of Marriage and the Family, 42,* 825–839.

Spivey, E. (1990). *Social exclusion as a common factor in social anxiety, loneliness, jealousy, and social depression.* Unpublished master's thesis. Wake Forest University, Winston-Salem, NC.

Staub, E. (1989). *The roots of evil: The origins of genocide and other group violence.* Cambridge, England: Cambridge University Press.

Staw, B. M., Sandelands, D. E., & Dutton, J. E. (1981). Threat-rigidity effects in organizational behavior: A multi-level analysis. *Administrative Science Quarterly, 26,* 501–524.

Stein, A. A. (1976). Conflict and cohesion: A review of the literature. *Journal of Conflict Resolution, 20,* 143–172.

Sternberg, R. J. (1986). A triangular theory of love. *Psychological Review, 93,* 119–135.

Strube, M. J. (1988). The decision to leave an abusive relationship: Empirical evidence and theoretical issues. *Psychological Bulletin, 104,* 236–250.

Sullivan, H. S. (1953). *The interpersonal theory of psychiatry.* New York: Norton.

Tajfel, H. (1970). Experiments in intergroup discrimination. *Scientific American, 223,* 96–102.

Tajfel, H., & Billig, M. (1974). Familiarity and categorization in intergroup behavior. *Journal of Experimental Social Psychology, 10,* 159–170.

Tajfel, H., Flament, C., Billig, M. G., & Bundy, R. F. (1971). Social categorization and intergroup behaviour. *European Journal of Social Psychology, 1,* 149–177.

Tambor, E. S., & Leary, M. R. (1993). *Perceived exclusion as a common factor in social anxiety: Loneliness, jealousy, depression, and low self-esteem.* Manuscript submitted for publication.

Tangney, J. P. (1992). Situational determinants of shame and guilt in young adulthood. *Personality and Social Psychology Bulletin, 18,* 199–206.

Trout, D. L. (1980). The role of social isolation in suicide. *Suicide and Life-Threatening Behavior, 10,* 10–23.

Turner, J. C. (1985). Social categorization and the self-concept: A social cognitive theory of group behavior. In F. J. Lawler (Ed.), *Advances in group processes: Theory and research* (Vol. 2, pp. 77–121). Greenwich, CT: JAI Press.

Vallacher, R. R., & Nowak, A. (1994). The chaos in social psychology. In R. Vallacher & A. Nowak (Eds.), *Dynamical systems in social psychology* (pp. 1–16). San Diego, CA: Academic Press.

Vangelisti, A. L., Daly, J. A., & Rudnick, J. R. (1991). Making people feel guilty in conversations: Techniques and correlates. *Human Communication Research, 18,* 3–39.

Vaughan, D. (1986). *Uncoupling.* New York: Oxford University Press.

Vaux, A. (1988). Social and emotional loneliness: The role of social and personal characteristics. *Personality and Social Psychology Bulletin, 14,* 722–734.

Veitch, R., & Griffitt, W. (1976). Good news, bad news. Affective and interpersonal effects. *Journal of Applied Social Psychology, 6,* 69–75.

Wade, W. C. (1987). *The fiery cross: The Klu Klux Klan in America.* New York: Touchstone/Simon & Schuster.

Weiss, R. S. (1973). *Loneliness: The experience of emotional and social isolation.* Cambridge, MA: MIT Press.

Weiss, R. S. (1979). The emotional impact of marital separation. In G.. Levinger & O. C. Moles (Eds.), *Divorce and separation: Context, causes, and consequences* (pp. 201–210). New York: Basic Books.

West, S., Newsom, J. T., & Fenaughty, A. M. (1992). Publication trends in *Journal of Personality and Social Psychology:* Stability and change in topics. methods, and theories across two decades. *Personality and Social Psychology Bulletin, 18,* 473–484.

Wheeler, L., Reis, H. T., & Nezlek, J. (1983). Loneliness, social interaction, and sex roles. *Journal of Personality and Social Psychology, 45,* 943–953.

Wilder, D. A., & Thompson, J. E. (1980). Intergroup contact with independent manipulations of in-group and out-group interaction. *Journal of Personality and Social Psychology, 8,* 589–603.

Williams, J. G., & Solano, C. H. (1983). The social reality of feeling lonely: Friendship and reciprocation. *Personality and Social Psychology Bulletin, 9,* 237–242.

Yalom, I. (1985). *The theory and practice of group psychotherapy.* New York: Basic Books.

Zander, A. (1971). *Motives and goals in groups.* New York: Academic Press.

The Social Self: On Being the Same and Different at the Same Time

Marilynn B. Brewer • Department of Psychology, University of California at Los Angeles

Editors' Notes

The author proposes that social identity and group loyalty are strongest for those self-categorizations that simultaneously fulfill the need for individuals to belong and the need for individuals to be distinctive. Strong social identities are social selves that reconcile these opposing needs for assimilation and differentiation from others. The need for belongingness is fulfilled by assimilation to an in-group, whereas the need for distinctiveness is fulfilled by differentiating the in-group from out-groups through intergroup comparisons. Two determinants of the strength of social identification are examined—depersonalization and group size. As predicted, there was an interaction between these variables, with strength of social identification (operationalized as in-group bias) being stronger for a larger than a smaller group only when the individual group members were depersonalized. This model of optimal distinctiveness demonstrates how motivational strength can derive from resolving conflicting needs. Moreover, because the self can be defined at different levels of social identification, this model accounts for how self-interest and self-serving motivations can produce actions that seem irrational at the individual level.

Discussion Questions

1. What determines strength of social identification?
2. How can one account for self-sacrifice by individuals for the sake of groups to which they belong if people are simply motivated by self-interest?

Authors' Abstract

Most of social psychology's theories of the self fail to take into account the significance of social identification in the definition of self. Social identities are self-definitions that are more inclusive than the individuated self-concept of most American psychology. A model of *optimal distinctiveness* is proposed in which social identity is viewed as a reconciliation of opposing needs for assimilation and differentiation from others. According to this model, individuals avoid self-construals that are either too personalized or too inclusive and instead define themselves in terms of distinctive category memberships. Social identity and group loyalty are hypothesized to be strongest for those self-categorizations that simultaneously provide for a sense of belonging and a sense of distinctiveness. Results from an initial laboratory experiment support the prediction that depersonalization and group size interact as determinants of the strength of social identification.

In recent years, social psychologists have become increasingly "self"-centered. The subject index of a typical introductory social psychology text contains a lengthy list of terms such as *self-schema, self-complexity, self-verification, self-focusing, self-referencing, self-monitoring*, and *self-affirmation,* all suggesting something of a preoccupation with theories of the structure and function of self. The concept of self provides an important point of contact between theories of personality and theories of social behavior. Yet there is something peculiarly *un*social about the construal of self in American social psychology.[1]

The *self* terms listed above are representative of a highly *individuated* conceptualization of the self. For the most part, our theories focus on internal structure and differentiation of the self-concept rather than connections to the external world. Particularly lacking is attention to the critical importance of group membership to individual functioning, both cognitive and emotional. The human species is highly adapted to group living and not well equipped to survive outside a group context. Yet our theories of self show little regard for this aspect of our evolutionary history. As a consequence, most of our theories are inadequate to account for much human action in the form of collective behavior. The self-interested, egocentric view of human nature does not explain why individuals risk or sacrifice personal comfort, safety, or social position to promote group benefit (Caporael, Dawes, Orbell, & van de Kragt, 1989).

Even a casual awareness of world events reveals the power of group identity in human behavior. Names such as *Azerbaijan, Serbia, Lithuania,* *Latvia, Estonia, Tamil, Eritrea, Basques, Kurds, Welsh,* and *Quebec* are currently familiar because they represent ethnic and national identities capable of arousing intense emotional commitment and self-sacrifice on the part of individuals. Furthermore, they all involve some form of separatist action—attempts to establish or preserve distinctive group identities against unwanted political or cultural merger within a larger collective entity. People die for the sake of group distinctions, and social psychologists have little to say by way of explanation for such "irrationality" at the individual level.

Social Identity and Personal Identity

It is in this context that I have been interested in the concept of social identity as developed by European social psychologists, particularly Henri Tajfel and John Turner and their colleagues from the University of Bristol (e.g., Tajfel & Turner, 1986; Turner, Hogg, Oakes, Reicher, & Wetherell, 1987). Although social identity theory has been introduced to U.S. social psychology, as a theory of self it is often misinterpreted. Americans tend to think of social identities as *aspects* of individual self-concept—part of internal differentiation. But the European conceptualization is one involving

---

[1]Here I join many other critics who have pointed to the highly individuated conceptualization of self as an ethnocentric product of the Western worldview (e.g., Caporael, Dawes, Orbell, & van de Kragt 1989; Sampson, 1988, 1989). My point is that such a conceptualization is not adequate to an understanding of American selves either.

extension of the self beyond the level of the individual.

A schematic representation of social identity theory is presented in Figure 1. The concentric circles represent definitions of the self at different levels of inclusiveness within some particular domain. *Personal identity* is the individuated self—those characteristics that differentiate one individual from others within a given social context. *Social identities* are categorizations of the self into more inclusive social units that *depersonalize* the self-concept, where *I* becomes *we*. Social identity entails "a shift towards the perception of self as an interchangeable exemplar of some social category and away from the perception of self as a unique person" (Turner et al., 1987, p. 50).

The concentric circles in Figure 1 also illustrate the contextual nature of social identity. At each point in the figure, the next circle outward provides the frame of reference for differentiation and social comparison. To take a concrete example, consider my own identity within the occupation domain. At the level of personal identity is me as an individual researcher and teacher of social psychology. For this conceptualization of myself, the most immediate frame of reference for social comparison is my social psychology colleagues at UCLA. The most salient features of my self-concept in this context are those research interests, ideas, and accomplishments that distinguish me from the other social psychologists on my faculty.

My social identities, by contrast, *include* the interests and accomplishments of my colleagues. The first level of social identity is me as member of the social area within the department of psychology at UCLA.[2] Here, the department provides the relevant frame of reference, and social comparison is with other areas of psychology. At this level the most salient features of my self-concept are those which I have in common with other members of the social area and which distinguish *us* from cognitive, clinical, and developmental psychology. At this level of self-definition my social colleague and I are interchangeable parts of a common group identity—my self-worth is tied to the reputation and outcomes of the group as a whole.

A yet higher level of social identity is the De-

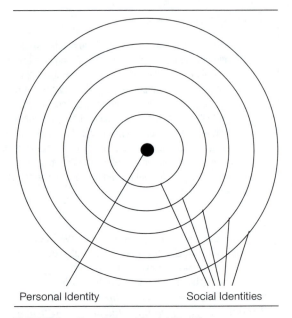

Personal Identity   Social Identities

FIGURE 1 ■ Personal and Social Identities.

partment of Psychology within UCLA. At this level, the campus becomes the frame of reference and other departments the basis of comparison. The next level of identification is represented by UCLA as institution, with other universities providing the relevant comparison points. And, finally, there is my identification with academia as a whole, as compared with nonacademic institutions in the United States or the world.

The point to be made with this illustration is that the self-concept is *expandable and contractable* across different levels of social identity with associated transformations in the definition of self and the basis for self-evaluation. When the definition of self changes, the meaning of self-interest and self-serving motivation also changes accordingly.

Social Identity and Self-Esteem

In American psychology, social identity theory is associated with self-esteem. Most of the experimental research derived from the theory has focused on the consequences of being assigned to membership in a particular social group or category. Within this research tradition, category identity is imposed either by experimental instructions or by manipulation of the salience of natural group

---

[2]The use of this particular illustration should not imply that social identity requires spatial contiguity. I also have a strong sense of identification with social psychologists all over the world who share my research specialty.

distinctions, and the emphasis is on the effect of such categorization on in-group favoritism in the service of positive self-esteem (e.g., Lemyre & Smith, 1985; Oakes & Turner, 1980). In general, social identity research has concentrated on the evaluative implications of in-group identification to the exclusion of research on why and how social identities are established in the first place (Abrams & Hogg, 1988; Doise, 1988).

Social identity should not be equated with membership in a group or social category. Membership may be voluntary or imposed, but social identities are chosen. Individuals may recognize that they belong to any number of social groups without adopting those classifications as social identities. Social identities are selected from the various bases for self-categorization available to an individual at a particular time. And specific social identities may be activated at some times and not at others.

Available research leaves unanswered the question of the direction of causal relationship between identification and positive in-group evaluation. Do individuals select a particular social identity because it has positive value or status, or does identification produce a bias toward positive in-group evaluation? In-group bias may not be a method of *achieving* self-esteem so much as an *extension* of self-esteem at the group level (Brown, Collins, & Schmidt, 1988; Crocker & Luhtanen, 1990).

Particularly problematic to self-esteem explanations of social identity are those situations in which individuals choose to identify with groups that are of low status or negatively valued by the population at large. In the real world, individuals who belong to disadvantaged minorities do not consistently reject their group identity despite its possible negative implications, nor do they suffer from excessively low self-esteem (Crocker & Major, 1989). Even though evaluative bias in favor of own-group identities may be an inevitable *consequence* of social identification, it does not fully account for the *selection* of social identities.

Optimal Distinctiveness Theory

My position is that social identity derives from a fundamental tension between human needs for validation and similarity to others (on the one hand) and a countervailing need for uniqueness and individuation (on the other). The idea that individuals need a certain level of both similarity to

and differentiation from others is not novel. It is the basis of uniqueness theory, proposed by Snyder and Fromkin (1980), as well as a number of other models of individuation (e.g., Codol, 1984; Lemaine, 1974; Maslach, 1974; Ziller, 1964). In general, these models assume that individuals meet these needs by maintaining some intermediate degree of similarity between the self and relevant others.

The theory of social identity provides another perspective on how these conflicting drives are reconciled. Social identity can be viewed as a compromise between assimilation and differentiation from others, where the need for deindividuation is satisfied within in-groups, while the need for distinctiveness is met through *inter*-group comparisons. Adolescent peer groups provide a prototypical case. Each cohort develops styles of appearance and behavior that allow individual teenagers to blend in with their age mates while "sticking out like a sore thumb" to their parents. Group identities allow us to be the same and different at the same time.

The model underlying this view of the function of social identity is a variant of *opposing process* models, which have proved useful in theories of emotion and acquired motivation (Solomon, 1980). Instead of a bipolar continuum of similarity-dissimilarity, needs for assimilation and differentiation are represented as opposing forces, as depicted in Figure 2.

As represented along the abscissa of the figure, it is assumed that within a given social context, or

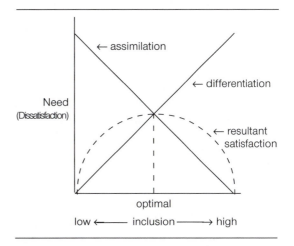

FIGURE 2 ■ The Optimal Distinctiveness Model.

frame of reference, an individual can be categorized (by self or others) along a dimension of social distinctiveness-inclusiveness that ranges from uniqueness at one extreme (i.e., features that distinguish the individual from any other persons in the social context) to total submersion in the social context (deindividuation) at the other. The higher the level of inclusiveness at which self-categorization is made, the more depersonalized the self-concept becomes.[3]

Each point along the inclusiveness dimension is associated with a particular level of activation of the competing needs for assimilation and individuation. Arousal of the drive toward social assimilation is inversely related to level of inclusiveness. As self-categorization becomes more individuated or personalized, the need for collective identity becomes more intense. By contrast, arousal of self-differentiation needs is directly related to level of inclusiveness. As self-categorization becomes more depersonalized, the need for individual identity is intensified.

At either extreme along the inclusiveness dimension, the person's sense of security and self-worth is threatened. Being highly individuated leaves one vulnerable to isolation and stigmatization (even excelling on positively valued dimensions creates social distance and potential rejection). However, total deindividuation provides no basis for comparative appraisal or self-definition. As a consequence, we are uncomfortable in social contexts in which we are either too distinctive (Frable, Blackstone, & Scherbaum, 1990; Lord & Saenz, 1985) or too undistinctive (Fromkin, 1970, 1972).

In this model, equilibrium, or *optimal distinctiveness*, is achieved through identification with categories at that level of inclusiveness where the degrees of activation of the need for differentiation and of the need for assimilation are exactly equal. Association with groups that are too large or inclusive should leave residual motivation for greater differentiation of the self from that group identity, whereas too much personal distinctiveness should leave the individual seeking inclusion in a larger collective. Deviations from optimal distinctiveness in either direction—too much or too little personalization—should drive the individual

to the same equilibrium, at which social identification is strongest and group loyalties most intense.

The basic tenets of the optimal distinctiveness model are represented in the following assumptions:

1. Social identification will be strongest for social groups or categories at that level of inclusiveness which resolves the conflict between needs for differentiation of the self and assimilation with others.
2. Optimal distinctiveness is independent of the evaluative implications of group membership, although, other things being equal, individuals will prefer positive group identities to negative identities.
3. Distinctiveness of a given social identity is context specific. It depends on the frame of reference within which possible social identities are defined at a particular time, which can range from participants in a specific social gathering to the entire human race.
4. The optimal level of category distinctiveness or inclusiveness is a function of the relative strength (steepness) of the opposing drives for assimilation and differentiation. For any individual, the relative strength of the two needs is determined by cultural norms, individual socialization, and recent experience.

This last assumption makes the model consistent with theories that emphasize cultural differences in definition of the self (Markus & Kitayama, in press; Triandis, McCusker, & Hui, 1990). However, it is unlikely that any societies exist in which either the extreme of individuation or that of assimilation is optimal, except as a cultural ideal. There is a limit to the cultural shaping of fundamental human needs.

Distinctiveness and Level of Identification

The primary implication of this model of social identity is that distinctiveness per se is an extremely important characteristic of groups, independent of the status or evaluation attached to group memberships. To secure loyalty, groups must not only satisfy members' needs for affiliation and belonging *within* the group, they must also maintain clear boundaries that differentiate them from other groups. In other words, groups must maintain distinctiveness in order to survive—effective

---

[3]In this article, the terms *deindividuation* and *depersonalization* are used more or less interchangeably, although the former refers to the identifiability of the individual to others whereas the latter refers to self-perception.

groups can not be too large or too heterogeneous. Groups that become overly inclusive or ill-defined lose the loyalty of their membership or break up into factions or splinter groups.

To return to the concentric circle schematic of Figure 1, the optimal distinctiveness model implies that there is one level of social identity that is dominant, as the primary self-concept within a domain. In contrast to theories that emphasize the prepotency of the individuated self, this model holds that in most circumstances personal identity will *not* provide the optimal level of self-definition. Instead, the prepotent self will be a collective identity at some intermediate level of inclusiveness, one that provides both shared identity with an in-group and differentiation from distinct out-groups.

Evidence for the relative potency of group identity over personal identity is available from a number of research arenas. Studies of the growth of social movements, for instance, reveal that activism is better predicted by feelings of *fraternal deprivation* (i.e., the perception that one's group is disadvantaged relative to other groups) than by feelings of personal deprivation (Dubé & Guimond, 1986; Vanneman & Pettigrew, 1972). Individual members of disadvantaged groups frequently perceive higher levels of discrimination directed against their group than they report against themselves personally (Taylor, Wright, Moghaddam, & Lalonde, 1990), but it is the former that motivates participation in collective action (Taylor, Moghaddam, Gamble, & Zellerer, 1987; Wright, Taylor, & Moghaddam, 1990).

Individuals also respond in terms of group identity when they are placed in social dilemma situations and faced with a conflict between making profit for themselves and helping to preserve a collective resource (Caporael et al., 1989). My own research in this area demonstrates that the choice subjects make is affected by the group identities available to them. If there is no collective identity *or* if the collective is too large and amorphous, then most individuals behave selfishly, pocketing as much money as they can for themselves before the public good runs out. However, when an intermediate group identity is available, individuals are much more likely to sacrifice self-interest in behalf of collective welfare (Brewer & Schneider, 1990). When a distinctive social identity is activated, the collective self dominates the individuated self.

Recognizing the motivational properties of group distinctiveness makes sense of a number of research findings from the intergroup literature, including the seemingly paradoxical self-esteem of members of some disadvantaged minorities or deviant groups and the accentuation of small differences in intergroup stereotypes.

In a particularly relevant study, Markus and Kunda (1986) found that subjects who had been made to feel uncomfortably unique increased their self-ratings of similarity to referent in-groups but also increased their ratings of *dis*similarity to out-groups. This is exactly what would be predicted from the optimal distinctiveness model. Overindividuation should not lead to an indiscriminate preference for similarity to all other people but to a selective need for assimilation to a distinct in-group.

Effects of Group Size Versus Status

The distinctiveness of a particular social category depends in part on the clarity of the boundary that distinguishes category membership from nonmembership and in part on the number of people who qualify for inclusion. Although group size and distinctiveness are not perfectly negatively correlated, categories that include a vast majority of the people in a given social context are not sufficiently differentiated to constitute meaningful social groups.[4] In general, then, optimal distinctiveness theory predicts that mobilization of in-group identity and loyalty will be achieved more easily for minority groups than for groups that are in the numerical majority. This prediction fits well with results of research on in-group bias and group size. In both real and laboratory groups, evaluative biases in favor of the in-group tend to increase as the proportionate size of the in-group relative to the out-group decreases (Mullen, Brown, & Smith, 1990). Further, strength of identification and importance attached to membership in experimentally created groups are greater for minority than for majority categories (Simon & Brown, 1987; Simon & Pettigrew, 1990).

The effects of relative group size are more com-

---

[4]Take as an illustration the idea of classifying persons by the number of arms they have. It is easy to imagine one-armed individuals as a meaningful social category. Having two arms, however, is not sufficiently distinctive to provide a basis for social identity, even though it is a well-defined classification.

plicated, however, when intergroup differences in status are taken into consideration (Ng & Cram, 1988). Because minority size is often associated with disadvantages in status or power, in many contexts group distinctiveness and positive evaluation may be in conflict. Although membership in a high-status majority may satisfy needs for positive social identity, it does not optimize distinctiveness. Accordingly, members of large high-status groups should seek further differentiation into subgroups, which permits greater distinctiveness without sacrificing the positive evaluation associated with membership in the superordinate category.

Members of low-status minority groups are also faced with a conflict between positive social identity and distinctiveness, but in a way that is less easily resolved than in the case for high-status majorities. On the other hand, minority individuals can dissociate themselves from their group membership and seek positive identity elsewhere. This strategy, however, often violates optimal distinctiveness. Dissociation may be achieved either at the cost of loss of distinctiveness (e.g., "passing") or at the cost of too much individual distinctiveness (e.g., as a "solo" representative of a deviant group). On the other hand, minority group members can embrace their distinctive group identity, but at the cost of rejecting or defying majority criteria for positive evaluation (Steele, 1990). This latter strategy has particularly interesting implications because once group identity has been established, disadvantage may actually enhance group loyalties rather than undermine them.

Deindividuation and Social Identity: Initial Evidence

Data collection is just beginning on a series of research projects designed to test general hypotheses regarding the interrelationship between social category distinctiveness and strength of group identification. We have already completed one laboratory experiment on the interactive effects of deindividuation and group distinctiveness as joint determinants of strength of identification with a social group or category. In this initial experiment, distinctiveness was operationalized as relative group size so that distinctive and nondistinctive groups could be studied in the same experimental context.

As in our previous research on intergroup rela-

tions, we created artificial category identities in the laboratory by giving subjects a dot estimation task and then informing each of them that he or she was an "underestimator" or an "overestimator." To vary inclusiveness of the two social categories, we informed all subjects that more than and only 20% as overestimators. Thus, assignment to one of the categories meant assignment to either a majority or a minority group.

Our primary purpose in this first experiment was to determine how the preference for minority category membership is affected by loss of distinctiveness in the experimental context. At the outset of the experiment, we created conditions designed to alter subjects' placement on the continuum from individuated to inclusive social identity. To manipulate this variable, we made use of confidentiality instructions that precede data collection in our experimental paradigm.

In the control condition, subjects received standard assurances of confidentiality and generated an ID number that served to protect their personal identity. In the *depersonalization* condition, the subject was assigned an arbitrary ID number in the context of written instructions that emphasized membership in a large, impersonal category. The wording of the depersonalized instructions was as follows:

> Since in this study we are not interested in you as an individual but as a member of the college student population, we do not ask for any personal information. However, for statistical purposes we need to match up different questionnaires completed by the same person. In order to do this, we have assigned you an arbitrary code number that is to be used throughout this session. . . . We are running this study in order to assess the attitudes and perceptions of students in general. For the purposes of this study you represent an example of the average student no matter what your major is. We are only interested in the general category and not in individual differences.

By immersing the subject in the broadly inclusive category of college student, we hoped to overindulge the need for assimilation relative to the need for differentiation for most of our subjects. In accord with an opposing-process model, such overindulgence should inhibit further activation of the assimilation drive and disinhibit or excite the opposing drive, resulting in devaluation of inclusive group memberships and enhanced preference for smaller, more distinctive social identities.[5]

After assignment to the overestimator and underestimator categories, subjects made a series of ratings designed to assess favoritism in their perceptions of the two social groups. In-group bias is the mean rating of the subject's own category (overestimator or underestimator) on a series of evaluative rating scales minus the rating of the out-group category on the same scales. A difference score in the positive direction constitutes one measure of strength of identification with the in-group. Figure 3 depicts the results for the in-group bias measure obtained from the four experimental conditions generated by the factorial combination of minority-majority in-group size and initial depersonalization.

Analysis of the in-group bias measure revealed a significant interaction between the effects of depersonalization and in-group size, $F(1,91) = 4.62$, $p < .05$. Under control conditions, subjects expressed significant in-group bias in favor of their own group in both minority and majority conditions, but more so when the in-group was in the majority. This latter effect was somewhat surprising in light of previous research on the relationship between group size and in-group bias. Apparently, in our laboratory setting, assignment to either of two mutually exclusive and distinct categories activates social identity regardless of relative group size. And in the absence of explicit information about group status, subjects may assume that majority categories are superior to minority groups.

The direction of effect of in-group size was clearly reversed, however, under conditions of deindividuation. When subjects had been exposed to depersonalizing instructions at the outset of the experiment, in-group bias was enhanced for those assigned to the minority category but virtually eliminated in the majority condition. As predicted by an opposing-process model, making subjects feel excessively depersonalized reduced valuation of identity with large social categories compared with more distinctive groups.

We are currently undertaking a series of field studies designed to parallel the laboratory experiment in a natural setting. For this purpose, we are studying student organizations at UCLA under the assumption that a large, urban university campus

[5]A complete description of the full design and results of this experiment is currently in preparation (Brewer & Manzi, 1990).

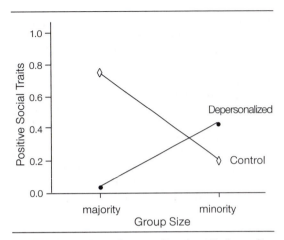

FIGURE 3 ■ In-Group Bias as a Function of In-Group Size and Depersonalization.

provides a natural deindividuated context for assessing formation of differentiated social identities. As a first step in this research, we have compiled an inventory of campus groups based on listings of student organizations registered with the UCLA Associated Students, which has proved to be an interesting data set in its own right. More than 425 organizations are registered, which range from social clubs (including sororities and fraternities) to interest groups based on ethnicity, religion, political positions, and sexual orientation. Both the number and the differentiation of these organizations tell an interesting story about needs for social group identification on a campus where the student body numbers more than 30,000.

The initial lab and field experiments are designed to test one side of the opposing-process model—the effects of excessive deindividuation on sensitivity to in-group size and preference for distinctive social identities. Further experiments will address the other side of the equation—the effects of too high a degree of individuation on preference for assimilation to a distinctive social category. This aspect of optimal distinctiveness theory has potential implications for the way in which people cope with being deviant or stigmatized.

The basic tenet is that excessive individuation is undesirable—having any salient feature that distinguishes oneself from everyone else in a social context (even if otherwise evaluatively neutral or positive) is at least uncomfortable and at worst devastating to self-esteem. One way to combat the nonoptimality of stigmatization is to convert the stigma from a feature of *personal identity* to a basis of *social identity*. Witness the current popularity of support groups for individuals with almost any kind of deviant characteristic or experience. Among other functions such groups serve is that of creating a categorical identity out of the shared feature. What is painful at the individual level becomes a source of pride at the group level—a badge of distinction rather than a mark of shame. Collective identities buffer the individual from many threats to self-worth, and it is time that their motivational significance is clearly recognized in social psychology's understanding of the self.

REFERENCES

Abrams, D., & Hogg, M. A. (1988). Comments on the motivational status of self-esteem in social identity and intergroup discrimination. *European Journal of Social Psychology, 18,* 317–334.

Brewer, M. B., & Manti, J. (1990). *Ingroup identification as a function of depersonalization, distinctiveness, and status.* Unpublished manuscript, University of California, Los Angeles.

Brewer, M. B., & Schneider, S. (1990). Social identity and social dilemmas: A double-edged sword. In D. Abrams & M. Hogg (Eds.), *Social identity theory: Constructive and critical advances.* London: Harvester-Wheatsheaf.

Brown, J. D., Collins, R. L., & Schmidt, G. W. (1988). Self-esteem and direct versus indirect forms of self-enhancement. *Journal of Personality and Social Psychology, 55,* 445–455.

Caporael, L., Dawes, R., Orbell, J., & van de Kragt, A. (1989). Selfishness examined: Cooperation in the absence of egoistic incentives. *Behavioral and Brain Sciences, 12,* 683–699.

Codol, J-P. (1984). Social differentiation and nondifferentiation. In H. Tajfel (Ed.), *The social dimension.* Cambridge: Cambridge University Press.

Crocker, J., & Luhtanen, R. (1990). Collective self-esteem and ingroup bias. *Journal of Personality and Social Psychology, 58,* 60–67.

Crocker, J., & Major, B. (1989). Social stigma and self-esteem: The self-protective properties of stigma. *Psychological Review, 96,* 609–630.

Doise, W. (1988). Individual and social identities in intergroup relations. *European Journal of Social Psychology, 18,* 99–111.

Dubé, L., & Guimond, S. (1986). Relative deprivation and social protest: The person-group issue. In J. Olson, C. P. Herman, & M. Zanna (Eds.), *Relative deprivation and social comparison: The Ontario Symposium* (Vol. 4, pp. 201–216). Hillsdale, NJ: Lawrence Erlbaum.

Frable, D., Blackstone, T., & Scherbaum, C. (1990). Marginal and mindful: Deviants in social interaction. *Journal of Personality and Social Psychology, 59,* 140–149.

Fromkin, H. L. (1970). Effects of experimentally aroused feelings of undistinctiveness upon valuation of scarce and novel experiences. *Journal of Personality and Social Psychology, 16,* 521–529.

Fromkin, H. L. (1972). Feelings of interpersonal undistinctiveness: An unpleasant affective state. *Journal of Experimental Research in Personality, 6,* 178–182.

Lemaine, G., (1974). Social differentiation and social originality. *European Journal of Social Psychology, 4,* 17–52.

Lemyre, L., & Smith, P. M. (1985). Intergroup discrimination and self-esteem in the minimal group paradigm. *Journal of Personality and Social Psychology, 49,* 660–670.

Lord, C., & Saenz, D. (1985). Memory deficits and memory surfeits: Differential cognitive consequences of tokenism for tokens and observers. *Journal of Personality and Social Psychology, 49,* 918–926.

Markus, H., & Kitayama, S. (in press). Culture and the self: Implications for cognition, emotion, and motivation. *Psychological Review.*

Markus, H., & Kunda, Z. (1986). Stability and malleability of the self-concept. *Journal of Personality and Social Psychology, 51,* 858–866.

Maslach, C. (1974). Social and personal bases of individuation. *Journal of Personality and Social Psychology, 29,* 411–425.

Mullen, B., Brown, R., & Smith, C. (1990, August). *Ingroup bias as a function of salience: The effects of proportionate ingroup size and the reality of the group.* Paper presented at the annual meeting of the American Psychological Association, Boston.

Ng, S. H., & Cram, F. (1988). Intergroup bias by defensive and offensive groups in majority and minority conditions. *Journal of Personality and Social Psychology, 55,* 744–757.

Oakes, P. J., & Turner, J. C. (1980). Social categorization and intergroup behaviour: Does minimal intergroup discrimination make social identity more positive? *European Journal of Social Psychology, 10,* 295–301.

Sampson, E. E. (1988). The debate on individualism: Indigenous psychologies of the individual and their role in personal and societal functioning. *American Psychologist, 43,* 15–22.

Sampson, E. E. (1989). The challenge of social change for psychology: Globalization and psychology's theory of the person. *American Psychologist, 44,* 914–921.

Simon, B., & Brown, R. (1987). Perceived intragroup homogeneity in minority-majority contexts. *Journal of Personality and Social Psychology, 53,* 703–711.

Simon, B., & Pettigrew, T. F. (1990). Social identity and perceived group homogeneity: Evidence for the ingroup homogeneity effect. *European Journal of Social Psychology, 20,* 269–286.

Snyder, C. R., & Fromkin, H. L. (1980). *Uniqueness: The human pursuit of difference.* New York: Plenum.

Solomon, R. (1980). The opponent process theory of acquired motivation. *American Psychologist, 35,* 691–712.

Steele, C. M. (1990, August). *Protecting the self: Its role in decisions and minority involvement.* Paper presented at the annual meeting of the American Psychological Association, Boston.

Tajfel, H., & Turner, J. C. (1986). The social identity theory of intergroup behavior. In S. Worchel & W. Austin (Eds.), *Psychology of intergroup relations.* Chicago: Nelson-Hall.

Taylor D. M., Moghaddam, F. M., Gamble, I., & Zellerer E. (1987). Disadvantaged group responses to perceived inequality: From passive acceptance to collective action. *Journal of Social Psychology, 127,* 254–272.

Taylor, D. M., Wright, S. C., Moghaddam, F. M., & Lalonde, R. N. (1990). The personal/group discrimination discrepancy: Perceiving my group, but not myself, to be a target for discrimination. *Personality and Social Psychology Bulletin, 16,* 254–262.

Triandis, H. C., McCusker, C., & Hui, C. H. (1990). Multimethod probes of individualism and collectivism. *Journal of Personality and Social Psychology, 59,* 1006–1020.

Turner, J. C., Hogg, M., Oakes, P., Reicher, S., & Wetherell, M. (1987). *Rediscovering the social group: A self-categorization theory.* Oxford: Basil Blackwell.

Vanneman, S., & Pettigrew, T. F. (1972). Race and relative deprivation in urban United States. *Race, 13,* 461–486.

Wright, S. C., Taylor, D. M., & Moghaddam, F. M. (1990). Responding to membership in a disadvantaged group: From acceptance to collective protest. *Journal of Personality and Social Psychology, 58,* 994–1003.

Ziller, R. C. (1964). Individuation and socialization. *Human Relations, 17,* 341–360.

Some Affective Consequences of Social Comparison and Reflection Processes: The Pain and Pleasure of Being Close

Abraham Tesser, Murray Millar and Janet Moore
• Institute for Behavioral Research, University of Georgia

Editors' Notes

What are some costs and benefits of close relationships? The authors propose a self-evaluation mainte-nance (SEM) model to address this question. The model predicts that the pain from social comparison with another who outperforms oneself on a task that is high in self-relevance will be greater when one has a close relationship with the other (because the self-evaluative threat is greater). The model also predicts that the pleasure from basking in the reflected glory of another who outperforms oneself on a task that is low in self-relevance will be greater when one has a close relationship with the other (because the promise of self-augmentation is greater). The results of the studies generally supported both of these predictions. Thus, a close relationship with another person who outperforms one on a task can either increase the pain of social comparison or the pleasure of basking in reflected glory depending on whether the task is high or low in self-relevance, respectively.

Discussion Questions

1. What are two interpersonal processes of self-evaluation that can produce pleasure or pain?
2. How does the closeness of one's relationship with another person and the self-relevance of a task influence one's response to being outperformed by that person on the task?

Authors' Abstract

A self-evaluation maintenance (SEM) model of social behavior was described. According to the comparison process, when another outperforms the self on a task high in relevance to the self, the closer the other the greater the threat to self-evaluation. According to the reflection process, when another outperforms the self on a task low in relevance to the self, the closer the other the greater the promise of augmentation to self-evaluation. Affect was assumed to reflect threats and promises to self-evaluation. In three studies, subjects were given feedback about own performance and the performance of a close (friend) and distant (stranger) other on tasks that were either low in self-relevance (Study 2) or that varied in self-relevance (Studies 1 and 3). In Study 1 (N = 31), subjects' performance on simple and complex tasks after each feedback trial served as a measure of arousal. Being outperformed by a close other resulted in greater arousal than being outperformed by a distant other. In Study 2 (N = 30), evaluative ratings of words unrelated to task performance served as an indirect measure of affect. Results indicated that when relevance is low, more positive affect is associated with a friend's outperforming the self than either a friend's performing at a level equal to the self or being outperformed by a stranger. In Study 3 (N = 31), subjects received feedback while their facial expressions were monitored. Pleasantness of expression was an interactive function of relevance of task, relative performance, and closeness of comparison other. The results of all three studies were interpreted as being generally consistent with the SEM model.

After a decade of research on cold cognition, social psychology is beginning to enjoy the warm embrace of affect and emotion (Abelson, 1983; Clark, Milberg, & Ross, 1983; Fiske, 1982; Roseman, 1984; Zajonc, 1980). The research described here also deals with emotion. It emphasizes the role of social circumstances in producing affect.

Affect and emotion have played an important mediating role in several theories of social phenomena, such as aggression (e.g., Geen & Quanty, 1977; Zillman, 1978), helping behavior (e.g., Batson, Duncan, Ackerman, Buckley, & Birch, 1981; Cialdini & Kenrick, 1976; Isen & Levin, 1972; Piliavin, Dovidio, Gaertner, & Clark, 1982), and close relationships (Berscheid, 1983; Gottman & Levenson, 1984). Our studies examine the role of affect in social comparison and reflection processes.

The notion of social comparison (Festinger, 1954; Goethals, 1984; Suls & Miller, 1977), an important perspective in social psychology, has been with us for a long time. The concept of basking in reflected glory, although less influential, was introduced some 10 years ago (Cialdini et al., 1976). Our studies are based on a self-evaluation maintenance (SEM) model that integrates these two ideas into a system in which affect may play a crucial role.

Self-Evaluation Maintenance (SEM) Model

The SEM model assumes that persons behave in a manner that will maintain or increase self-evaluation and that one's relationships with others have a substantial impact on self-evaluation. The SEM model is composed of two dynamic processes. Both the *reflection process* and the *comparison process* have as component variables the closeness of another and the quality of that other's performance. These two variables interact in affecting self-evaluation but do so in opposite ways in each of the processes.

Self-evaluation may be raised to the extent that a close (in a unit-relation sense; Heider, 1958) other performs very well on some activity; that is, one can bask in the reflected glory of the close other's good performance. For example, one can point out (to oneself and others) one's close relationship with one's friend the rock star and thereby increase one's own self-evaluation. The better the other's performance and the closer the psychological relationship, the more one can gain in self-evaluation through the reflection process.

The outstanding performance of a close other can, however, cause one's own performance to pale by comparison and decrease self-evaluation. Being close to another invites comparison, and the other's good performance could result in one's own performance looking bad, thereby adversely affecting self-evaluation. Again, the better the other's performance and the closer the psychological relationship, the greater the loss in self-evaluation through the comparison process.

It should be apparent from the description that the reflection and comparison processes depend on the same two variables but have opposite effects on self-evaluation: When closeness and performance are high, there is a potential gain in self-evaluation through the reflection process but there is a potential loss through the comparison process. According to the SEM model, the relevance of another's performance to one's self-definition determines the relative importance of the reflection and comparison processes. Following social comparison theory, another's performance is relevant to an individual's self-definition to the extent that the performance is on a dimension that is important to the individual's self-definition and to the extent that the other's performance is not so much better or worse than the individual's own performance that comparisons are rendered difficult. If the other's performance is highly relevant, the comparison process will be relatively important and one will suffer by comparison with a close other's better performance. If the other's performance is minimally relevant, the reflection process will be relatively important and one can enhance self-evaluation by basking in the reflected glory of a close other's better performance. (A more elaborated treatment of the model's constructs and dynamics can be found in Tesser, 1986, and Tesser & Campbell, 1983.)

On the Mediating Process

Direct empirical tests of the model have focused only on behavior: changes in closeness (e.g., Pleban & Tesser, 1981), attempts to change another's performance (e.g., Tesser & Smith, 1980), and changes in relevance (e.g., Tesser & Campbell, 1980). There has been no attempt to measure self-evaluation. We viewed self-evaluation as

a hypothetical construct, a theoretical fiction which is used to organize and make comprehensible the relationships among the variables that have empirical indicants, i.e., relevance, performance, closeness. Similarly, self-evaluation maintenance is viewed as a hypothetical process much

like "dissonance reduction" is viewed as a hypothetical process in dissonance theory. Neither dissonance reduction nor self-evaluation maintenance is directly measured or observed, but both models are testable because they make specific predictions concerning the observable antecedents and observable consequences of the hypothesized process. (Tesser & Campbell, 1983, pp. 8–9)

Although the SEM model has been useful in accounting for the relevant behaviors (see Tesser, 1986, for a review), there have been no tests directed at its mediating processes. If self-evaluation processes are real, how might they be detected? We believe that the operation of these processes is often relatively fast and, even more important, outside of conscious awareness (see Tesser's, 1986, section on awareness). Therefore, self-reports may have limited utility. However, if these processes are real, they should also manifest themselves in more unobtrusive measures of change in affect and arousal. Threats to self-evaluation should result in negative affect, whereas enhancements to self-evaluation should lead to positive affect.

The SEM Model and Affect

There is some previous research using self-reported affect that is consistent with the SEM assumption. In studying social-comparison jealousy, Salovey and Rodin (1984) gave participants feedback that they performed well or poorly on a dimension that was relevant or irrelevant to their self-definition. They also provided information that another participant had performed well on either the relevant or irrelevant dimension. From the perspective of the SEM model, the condition that poses the greatest threat to self-evaluation is the one in which the participant performs poorly on a relevant dimension and the other performs well on this dimension. Salovey and Rodin found that participants in this condition reported more anxiety, more depression, and less positivity of mood than did participants in any of the seven other conditions.

When one person helps another, the person receiving help is implicitly demonstrating inferior performance. When the help takes place on a dimension relevant to the recipient's self-definition, comparison processes should come into play, and the closer the relationship of the helper, the greater the threat to self-evaluation. Nadler, Fisher, and Ben-Itzhak (1983) had participants try to solve a mystery. The task was described as tapping important skills (high relevance) or luck (low relevance). The participant's solution was wrong and he was given a clue from either a friend (close other) or a stranger (distant other). Some participants went through this experience once and some went through it twice. Participants then rated their affect on a series of scales. From the perspective of the model, the most threatening condition is the one in which help was received twice from a friend on the relevant task. This condition was indeed associated with the most negative affect, and none of the other conditions appeared to differ from one another.

Although these two studies suggest that conditions presumed to result in threat to self-evaluation are associated with negative affect, more research is needed. For example, do conditions presumed to maximize self-evaluation (i.e., the outstanding performance of a close other on a low-relevance dimension) produce positive affect? Furthermore, the studies depended on self-reports of affect. The studies to be described examine both threatening and enhancing conditions and unobtrusive behavioral outcroppings of arousal and facial expressions to index affect.

Study I: SEM and Arousal

The SEM model is a motivational model. Theoretically, persons strive to maintain a positive self-evaluation. Therefore, threats to self-evaluation or promises of gain in self-evaluation ought to be arousing. A number of models of emotion suggest that both positive and negative emotion are arousing (e.g., Clark et al., 1983; Russell's, 1980, circumplex model; the jukebox models of Mandler, 1975, and Schacter, 1964). The SEM model is quite specific about the conditions that threaten a loss and those that promise a gain in self-evaluation. High-relevance activities activate the comparison process and create the potential for threat (by the better performance of a close other). Low-relevance activities activate the reflection process and create the promise of a gain (also by the better performance of a close other).

Arousal has known effects on task performance. It tends to facilitate or speed up the performance of simple (low response competition) tasks and to interfere with or slow down the performance of complex (high response competition) tasks (e.g.,

Spence, 1956; Zajonc, 1965). We consider here two tasks. The *primary task* is either high or low in personal relevance and is the task with which the individual is concerned. The *secondary task* is incidental to the primary task but varies in complexity. It is included in order to detect changes in arousal.

According to the SEM model, when a primary performance dimension is high in relevance, the comparison process is activated and threat increases with the relative performance of another, particularly a close other. If arousal results from this threat, performance on a simple secondary task should be facilitated, and performance on a complex secondary task should be degraded with the other's, particularly a close other's better performance. When a primary performance dimension is low in relevance, the promise of gain to self-evaluation should increase with the other's relative performance, particularly a close other. If arousal is associated with the promise of gain in self-evaluation, we should expect to find that simple secondary tasks are facilitated and complex secondary tasks are degraded with the other's, particularly a close other's, better performance.

In statistical terms, these predictions lead to the expectation of a three-factor interaction on performance: Closeness × Other's Performance × Task Complexity. If the comparison process or the reflection process are differentially effective in producing arousal, the relevance variable should also enter into the interaction, that is, Relevance × Closeness × Performance × Complexity. However, we have no specific hypotheses about the relative strengths of the comparison and reflection processes.

Research (e.g., Spence, Farber, & McFann, 1956) concerning arousal and task performance has benefited from the inclusion of the Taylor (1953) Manifest Anxiety Scale, a scale that has been construed as a measure of general drive (arousal). It is included because it is expected to facilitate performance on the simple task and interfere with performance on the complex task. Research on sociopathy has shown that persons who score low on the Socialization scale of the California Psychological Inventory (Gough, 1964) show less arousal (electrodermal response) to noxious stimuli (e.g., Hare, 1978). Furthermore, Waid and Orne (1982) have shown that these subjects also perform less well on a nonstressful, high-response-conflict task. Because persons who score low on the Socialization scale show fewer arousal effects, this scale was included with the expectation that the predictions from the model would be better supported among more socialized individuals. Finally, we also included a measure of self-esteem (Rosenberg, 1965), although we had no directional predictions concerning this measure. (See Tesser & Campbell, 1982a and 1983, for a discussion of individual differences in self-esteem and self-evaluation maintenance processes.)

Method

OVERVIEW

Subjects reported to the experiment location with a friend. After measuring the relevance of social sensitivity and creativity to their self-definition, we separated the two and seated each before a microcomputer. The computer administered a series of items purporting to measure creativity and social sensitivity. After the subject responded to each item, she was given feedback that she had done either better or worse than either her friend or a stranger. Following the feedback, subjects completed a simple or complex motor task (typing a single digit five times or five different digits as fast as they could). Item type (social sensitivity vs. creativity), relative performance, comparison other (friend vs. stranger), and complexity of task were systematically manipulated such that each subject was exposed once to all 16 possible combinations.

SUBJECTS

Seventeen pairs of female friends ($N = 34$) were recruited from an introductory psychology pool. They signed up for a study on "social sensitivity, creativity, and social judgment" and received course credit for their participation.

PROCEDURE

Subjects participated in one friendship pair at a time. When they arrived for their session, they were told that the study concerned the relationships among social sensitivity, creativity, and social judgment. They were also given an overview of the tasks that they would be asked to complete. Each subject then filled out a questionnaire intended to measure the relevance of creativity and

social sensitivity to their self-definition. There were two 7-point items to measure each: To what extent do you consider yourself a creative (socially sensitive) person? How important is it for you to be a creative (socially sensitive) person?

Subjects were then taken to separate rooms and seated before a microcomputer. They were told that they would be given a series of items that accurately measured social sensitivity and creativity. They were also told that they would be receiving feedback following their response to each item concerning their performance and the performance of their friend or a stranger (someone who had previously participated in the study). They were told to pay attention to the feedback. After the item feedback, subjects were told they would have to type a number into the computer as quickly as they could in order to "keep participants [i.e., themselves] alert during the feedback period." Subjects were then given examples to familiarize them with this aspect of the procedure.

Design. Each subject was confronted with 16 trials conforming to a completely balanced 2 (item type: creativity vs. social sensitivity) × 2 (performance feedback: self better than other vs. other better than self) × 2 (closeness: friend vs. stranger) × 2 (task complexity: simple vs. complex). The order of trials was randomized for each subject. The social sensitivity items provided subjects with an interpersonal problem and a solution to which they could respond yes or no. For example, "An older brother dominates his younger sister. Whenever the sister tries to show her independence, the older brother becomes aggressive. Should the younger sister be encouraged to limit her contacts with her older brother?" The creativity items asked subjects to indicate whether one word had something to do with three other words. For example, subjects were asked to indicate whether the word red was related to the three words *happy, selfish,* and *heart.* Following the subjects' response to each item, they learned that their answer was either better or worse than that of the other (friend or stranger), that is, self was correct and other incorrect or vice versa.

Measuring arousal. After the feedback had been visible for 10 s, it disappeared from the screen and the subject was prompted to type in five numerical digits as quickly as possible. The simple task (low response competition) consisted of a single, randomly selected digit repeated 5 times. The complex task (high response competition) consisted of five randomly selected (with replacement) digits. The dependent variable, recorded by the computer, was the speed with which these numbers were entered.

Postexperimental questionnaires. On completion of the computer task, subjects returned to the first room and completed several additional questionnaires. One asked them to indicate how well they, their friend, and the stranger did on the social sensitivity and creativity items. These items were framed in terms of percentage correct (free response) and "compared to the average subject" (7-point scale anchored with *bad/good*). Subjects also filled out Rosenberg's (1965) Self-Esteem Scale, the Socialization scale of the California Personality Inventory (Gough, 1964), and Taylor's (1953) Manifest Anxiety Scale. Finally, subjects were completely debriefed and all their questions answered.

Results

Recall our expectations. The threat of comparison results from the better performance of another, particularly a close other, on a relevant dimension. The promise of reflection also results from the good performance of another, particularly a close other, but on an irrelevant dimension. Both the threat of comparison and the promise of reflection should result in arousal. Because closeness and performance interact to produce comparison (when relevance is high) and reflection (when relevance is low), closeness and performance should interact in producing arousal. Arousal, in turn, should facilitate performance on the simple task and interfere with performance on the complex task. Because these effects go in opposite directions, the overall prediction is for a three-factor interaction: Performance × Closeness × Complexity.

Our index of secondary task performance was the amount of time taken to complete the task. The analysis of variance (ANOVA) of this index included four within-subjects factors: 2 (relevance) × 2 (performance) × 2 (closeness) × 2 (complexity). Relevance was defined as a within-subjects factor (i.e., idiographically) by separately summing the responses to the two items included to measure the relevance of social sensitivity and the two items included to measure the relevance of creativity. For each subject, the topic that had the larger sum was classified as high in relevance and the one with the smaller sum was classified as low

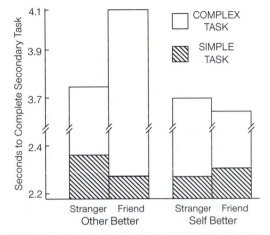

FIGURE 1 ■ Study 1: Time taken (in seconds) to complete simple and complex secondary tasks as a combined function of performance feedback (self better vs. other better) and closeness of other (friend vs. stranger). (This figure originally appeared in Tesser, in press, and is reproduced here by permission.)

in relevance. (Three subjects were dropped because there was no difference in the relevance of the two areas.)

Several effects emerged. First, there was a huge task-complexity effect, $F(1, 30) = 378.78, p < .001$. Although this effect is not surprising, it serves to validate the complexity manipulation: The simple task ($M = 2.3$ s) took substantially less time than the complex task ($M = 3.8$ s). The next two effects, a performance main effect, $F(1, 30) = 6.44$, $p < .02$, and a Complexity × Performance interaction, $F(1, 30) = 4.65, p < .05$, should be interpreted in terms of the final, more interesting effect. As predicted, the Performance × Closeness × Complexity interaction was also significant, $F(1, 30) = 4.52, p < .05$. As seen in Figure 1, the interaction is of the appropriate form.

Because arousal is inferred from the differential effects on simple and complex tasks, the three-factor interaction is decomposed in terms of the simple interactions with task complexity, that is, the Closeness × Complexity interactions and the Performance × Complexity interactions.[1] Where other outperforms self, as closeness increases

---

[1] It is worth noting that although both simple and complex tasks show the expected pattern of means, as seen in Figure 1, most of the variance in differences between tasks comes from the complex task. Indeed, a separate analysis of the simple task yields no significant effects. Perhaps there is a floor effect at work with this task.

(from stranger to friend), there is a slowing down on the complex task and a speeding up on the simple task, $t(60) = 2.60$, $p < .01$.[2] This effect is slightly reversed ($t < 1$) when the self outperforms the other. Similarly, if we look only at the close other, the friend, as performance increases (from self better to other better), there is a viewing down on the complex task and a speeding up on the simple task, $t(60) = 3.02$, $p < .01$. This effect is slightly reversed ($t < 1$) when the other is distant, the stranger.

The relevance of a topic to one's self-definition determines the relative importance of the comparison and reflection processes. Because we assumed that comparison and reflection processes would have similar effects on arousal, we did not expect relevance necessarily to moderate the predicted interaction. In fact, it did not ($F < 1$). To make this lack of effect meaningful, however, it is important to show that relevance was adequately varied.

First, as noted, each of the subjects included in the analysis rated one of the topics as more relevant than the other: On a scale varying from 2 to 14 with 8 as the midpoint, the mean rating of the low-relevance activity was 8.87 and the mean rating of the high-relevance activity was 11.52.[3] Second and more important, relevance must have been adequately varied because it had a significant impact on other variables. Subjects were asked on the postexperimental questionnaire to rate performance and indicate the percentage correct for themselves, their friend, and the stranger on the computer tasks. Recall that subjects received feedback that they and the others did better than one another an equal number of times, and that was

true for both the high and low-relevance topics. These responses were analyzed in a 2 (relevance) × 3 (person: self vs. friend vs. stranger) within-subjects ANOVA. Focusing on the rating of performance, there was an effect of person, $F(2, 54) = 8.27$, $p < .001$: Friends ($M = 2.95$) were rated as performing better than self ($M = 3.52$) or stranger ($M = 3.54$). Furthermore, there was a significant main effect of relevance, $F(1, 27) = 10.93$, $p < .01$. Because the interaction approached significance, $F(2, 27) = 3.65$, $p = .08$, and is meaningful, we probed the simple effects. It was only for self that high-relevance performance ($M = 3.18$) was significantly better than low-relevance performance ($M = 3.86$), $F(1, 81) = 5.29$, $p < .05$. The corresponding comparisons for friend ($Ms = 2.93$ vs. 2.96) and stranger ($Ms = 3.50$ vs. 3.57) did not approach significance. The outcomes for the percentage-correct measure were similar. The person effect was only marginally significant, $F(2, 54) = 2.56$, $p < .10$, but there was a significant overall relevance effect, $F(1, 27) = 6.73$, $p < .02$. Because the interaction did not approach significance, we did not follow up with formal statistical tests. However, it is worth noting that the effect of relevance for self ($Ms = 63\%$ vs. 57%) was larger than that for friend ($Ms = 66\%$ vs. 63%) or stranger ($Ms = 61\%$ vs. 50%). In sum, the relevance variable had effects on perceptions of performance, and these effects were most pronounced for the self, as might be expected.

Subjects responded to a number of personality measures including self-esteem, the Socialization scale of the California Psychological Inventory, and the Taylor Manifest Anxiety Scale. Each was split at the median and, in turn, added as a between-subjects factor to the basic ANOVA of the response times. The predicted interaction (Performance × Closeness × Complexity) was not moderated by any of these variables. For some subjects, social sensitivity was more relevant than creativity ($n = 24$), whereas the reverse was true for the remaining subjects ($n = 7$). This classification was also added as a between-subjects factor to the basic ANOVA. Again, there was no moderating effect.

---

[2]Because the direction of these simple interaction effects was predicted, one-tailed t tests were used for assessing their significance. These t tests are simply the square root of the F test for the appropriate simple effect. (The relation between t and F with 1 degree of freedom is $F = t^2$.) There are 60 degrees of freedom because the appropriate error term in this repeated-measures analysis is the pooled error terms from the three-factor interaction (with 30 df) and the relevant two-factor interaction (with 30 df) in this case, Closeness × Complexity (Winer, 1962).

[3]Both means are on the high side of the scale midpoint, yet we are arguing that one is high and the other low in relevance. Perhaps our argument is wrong. On the other hand, it seems very difficult to interpret these scale values in absolute terms. Clearly, it is socially desirable to say that these dimensions are important. The scales have no fixed origin. Also, there are no norms on a representative set of dimensions for comparison. Perhaps, then, the numbers should be interpreted in relative terms.

Discussion

When a close other does better than the self, performance on a complex task worsens but performance on a simple task is facilitated. From these data we conclude that arousal results when a close other performs better than the self. Furthermore, the relevance of the performance domain does not appear to moderate this effect. In short, the superior performance of close others affects our emotion more than does the superior performance of distant others. Indeed, there is some evidence that the mere anticipation of a close other's performance can be arousing. For example, Brenner (1973) found that when individuals in a group take turns reading words, they have a difficult time remembering the words read just before their own turn. More interesting from our perspective, they also have a difficult time remembering the words read just before a friend's turn.

We interpret the arousal results to indicate that both the loss in self-evaluation associated with the social comparison process and the gain in self-evaluation associated with the social reflection process manifest themselves in arousal. Although we have some evidence that the relevance manipulation was successful, we have no directional evidence of the operation of these two processes. That is, arousal can index both positive and negative effect, and we argue that it is doing that in this study. Another interpretation, one that could be derived from a social comparison perspective,[4] is simply that being outperformed by another, particularly a close other, produces negative affect (and arousal) regardless of the level of relevance. What seems to be needed now to make the case for the reflection process is a demonstration that being outperformed by another can sometimes reduce negativity. Specifically, according to the SEM model, reduced negativity (or increased positivity) should be associated with being outperformed by a close other on a low-relevance dimension. Study 2 was run in an attempt to provide such evidence. Before turning to that study, however, we address briefly the question of self-reports.

Subjects' self-reports, in addition to providing evidence concerning the validity of the relevance variable, showed an interesting pattern of distortion. Although they received feedback that each of the actors (self, friend, stranger) had performed equally well, subjects indicated that their friend had performed better than self or stranger. Such charitable but distorted self-reports have also been observed by Tesser and Campbell (1982b). We take these reports to mean that persons often like to say nice things about those who are close to them. Perhaps this is simply a generalization from the kind of interaction that may go on inside a close relationship in attempts to maintain that relationship (see Brickman & Bulman, 1977).

Study 2: Positive Affect and the Reflection Process

The results of Study 1 are quite consistent with the SEM model, but they are consistent with other theoretical positions as well, most notably a social comparison perspective. When relevance is high, the predictions of the social comparison perspective and the SEM model are the same: Being outperformed by another, particularly a close other, will produce negative affect (and arousal). The predictions diverge for affect (but not necessarily arousal) in the low-relevance case. The social comparison perspective continues to predict negative affect (and arousal) with the better performance of a close other. The SEM model, on the other hand, posits a reflection process. A close other's better performance when relevance is low provides the opportunity for basking in the reflection of the other's good performance and hence should be associated with relatively more positive affect (and arousal).

What is needed, then, for interpretive clarity is a set of low-relevance conditions that vary with respect to relative performance and closeness and a directional measure of affect, that is, one that is sensitive to differences in positivity and negativity. Under such low-relevance conditions both the social comparison perspective and the SEM model predict a Performance × Closeness interaction, but the form of those interactions differ: Stating it in terms of positivity of affect, the social comparison perspective predicts the least positivity when the close other outperforms the self; the SEM model predicts the most positivity when the close other outperforms the self.

This study provides a site for examining the relative merit of these opposing predictions. Subjects received feedback that a close (friend) or distant (stranger) other performed about the same or bet-

---

[4]The label *social comparison perspective* is used to refer to a broad view on social behavior rather than any single statement of social comparison theory (e.g.. Festinger, 1954). Although this alternative explanation has the flavor of social comparison theory, we know of no particular version that makes this specific prediction, nor are we aware of any studies of arousal per se conducted in the social comparison tradition.

ter than the self on a low-relevance test. After receiving feedback, subjects made evaluative ratings of unfamiliar words. Because we believe that affective changes are often fast and not subject to conscious awareness, we wanted a non-self-report measure of affect. Positivity and negativity of the ratings of words unrelated to the performance dimension, an indirect index of affect (e.g., Clark & Isen, 1982; Isen & Shalker, 1977), was therefore used as our primary measure. Subjects also responded to a self-report measure of affect on the postexperimental questionnaire.

The only individual difference measure used in the study was a measure of self-esteem (Rosenberg, 1965). No specific predictions were made about the influence of this variable.

Method

SUBJECTS

Thirty-four female undergraduates comprising 17 friendship pairs were recruited for a study ostensibly on the relation between personality and the perception of others. Four subjects were dropped because of experimenter errors in procedure, leaving a total of 30 participants in the study.

PROCEDURE

Subjects were scheduled in groups of 4 (two friendship pairs).[5] When they arrived, they were asked to fill out the self-esteem scale and a questionnaire designed to measure their interests. The interest measure actually measured the relevance of a number of dimensions (e.g., movies, science, television, health and fitness, photography) to the subject's self-definition. For each dimension, subjects were asked on a 7-point scale anchored with *strongly agree* and *strongly disagree* how interested they were (e.g., "I enjoy movies a great deal and go to the movies whenever I can") and how knowledgeable they were (e.g., "I know more about movies than most people").

After completing these measures, each subject was given an opportunity to say a little about herself so that the others might form a first impression. While the subjects were engaged in this activity, the experimenter determined each subject's least relevant dimension from the interest inventory. Subjects' ratings on the question concerning their contact with the particular topic

and the question concerning their knowledge about the topic were summed to form one score. Subjects also were asked to rank order the six interest areas according to knowledge about the topic. This rank ordering was used to determine the subjects' least relevant dimension when there was a tie between summed scores. The mean rating of the selected dimension was 12.78 on a scale that varied from 2 (high relevance) to 14 (low relevance). The topic that subjects rated lowest in terms of interest and knowledge was the topic about which they were subsequently quizzed.

Subjects then were given the following cover story:

> In the next phase of the study you will be interacting with a computer that will produce questions about an area to be randomly selected from among those on the interest inventory. The computers are interconnected so that some of you will be getting feedback about how another is responding to the same questions. Although you will know who the feedback concerns, you will not know who, if anyone, is getting feedback on your performance. Finally, some of you may not get feedback on anyone.

In order to forestall questions, subjects were told that after the computer phase they would be given another exercise in which they would learn a little more about one another before giving their final impressions of each other. Subjects then were taken to separate booths and seated before a microcomputer.

MANIPULATING THE INDEPENDENT VARIABLES

Each subject was confronted with 30 questions from an area that she had marked as least relevant to her self-definition. After each block of five items, subjects were told how many of the preceding items they had answered correctly and how many of these same items their friend (close condition) or one of the new acquaintances (distant condition) had answered correctly. In the *equal* performance condition, subjects learned, with some variability over trials to bolster credibility,

---

[5]If only one friendship pair arrived for the study, those subjects assigned to feedback about a distant other were told that they were receiving feedback on the performance of the last participant who had answered questions on that particular topic.

that they had correctly answered approximately the same number of items (15) that the other had answered correctly (16). In the *other-better* condition, the subject learned that the other (23 correct) had outperformed her (7 correct).

MEASURING AFFECT

While subjects remained in the booths, the experimenter returned and told each subject that it would take a few more minutes to get the materials ready for the next phase of the study. Furthermore, each subject was told that while she was waiting she might wish to help out a graduate student by doing some ratings. Subjects were shown a stack of cards with an unfamiliar word printed on each card (e.g., *Catarhh, Obol, Perdol*) and paper containing places to write and rate each word on a 7-point semantic differential scale (*pleasant–unpleasant*). They were shown how to use the scale to rate the pleasantness of the words.[6] The experimenter then left. The average rating given on the pleasantness scale served as an indirect measure of subjects' affect (Clark & Isen, 1982; Isen & Shalker, 1977).

When the experimenter returned, approximately 7 min later, a final questionnaire designed to check on the performance manipulation and to assess self-reported affect was administered. Finally, all 4 subjects were brought back together, probed for suspicion regarding the hypotheses, and thoroughly debriefed.

Results

PERFORMANCE MANIPULATION

When subjects had been outperformed by the other, they rated their performance as significantly poorer ($M = 6.01$) than when they performed equal to the other ($M = 4.00$), $F(1, 25) = 13.05, p < .001$. When subjects were outperformed by the other, they rated the other's performance as significantly better ($M = 2.73$) than when they had performed equally ($M = 4.00$), $F(1, 25) = 6.55, p < .02$. When asked to

rate who had done better on a scale with endpoints *I did much better* and *She did much better*, subjects who had been outperformed were more inclined to rate toward the other-did-better end of the scale ($M = 6.31$) than when they performed equally ($M = 3.94$), $F(1, 25) = 51.43, p < .0001$. Neither the closeness nor the Closeness × Performance effects were significant in any of these analyses. Performance appears to have been successfully manipulated.

AFFECT

Our major measure of affect was the mean evaluative rating of the first five words subsequent to the feedback. (Two subjects used in this analysis rated fewer than five words.) These data were analyzed in terms of a 2 (performance) × 2 (closeness) ANOVA. The means associated with these conditions are illustrated in Figure 2.

Both the social comparison perspective and the SEM model predict a Closeness × Performance interaction. This component is significant, $F(1, 21) = 6.44, p < .02$. The theoretical perspectives differ, however, with respect to the expected pattern of the interaction: The SEM model anticipates the most positivity and the social comparison perspective the least positivity in the close-other-better cell. As seen in Figure 2, the pattern of means is consistent with the SEM prediction. Analyses of simple effects revealed that the close-other-better cell ($M = 3.57$) was more positive than the close-other-equal cell ($M = 4.29$), $F(1, 21) = 5.06, p <$

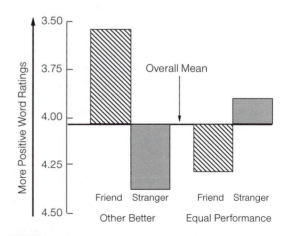

FIGURE 2 ■ Study 2: Effects of closeness (friend vs. stranger) and relative performance (other vs. equal) on pleasantness ratings of words unrelated to task performance.

---

[6]Subjects were told that the number they completed, or even whether they worked at all, was completely up to them. Originally we had hoped to use helping as an indirect index of positive affect/mood (e.g., Isen & Levin, 1972). Because almost all subjects rated some of the words, this was not possible. The 5 (of 20) subjects who rated no words came from each of the four conditions, so differential selection does not seem to be an important problem.

.05, and more positive than the distant-other-better cell ($M = 4.38$), $F(1, 21) = 5.94$, $p < .05$. Neither of the remaining simple effects was significant ($F < 1$).

A self-report affect measure was taken on the postexperimental questionnaire. Subjects responded to four 7-point semantic differential scales (*pleasant–unpleasant, proud–not proud, dissatisfied–satisfied,* and *angry–not angry*) to indicate their feelings while working on the interest test. These ratings were summed and subjected to an ANOVA similar to the one just reported. None of the effects were significant.

Both of the analyses reported here were also run with a median split on the self-esteem scale as an additional factor. In no case did self-esteem significantly affect the outcomes.

Discussion

This study dealt with the effects of closeness and performance on affect when a performance dimension is low in personal relevance. Different theoretical viewpoints can be seen as making differing predictions concerning these effects. A simple social comparison perspective might predict that being outperformed by another, particularly a close other, should result in negative affect (even when relevance is low), whereas the SEM model assumes that the reflection process becomes important when relevance is low and the better performance of a close other has the potential for joy. The pattern of results was consistent with the latter expectation. A close other's better performance was associated with the most positive affect, even though that performance was associated with the self's poorer performance in both relative and absolute terms (see Tesser & Campbell, 1980).

The measure of affect that showed the predicted effects was indirect and immediate. A more direct, self-report measure given approximately 7 min after the feedback revealed no systematic effects. Obviously, there are a number of potential explanations for this discrepancy. Perhaps the effects are rather short-lived and would have shown themselves on an immediate self-report, or perhaps the effect is so subtle that it doesn't register in conscious awareness.

Study 2 was undertaken to help clarify the results of Study 1. In Study 1 closeness and performance interacted to produce arousal, and relevance had no impact. We argued, however, that the arousal was indexing negative affect in the case of high relevance and positive affect in the case of low relevance. Study 2 showed the pattern of affect predicted to be associated with low relevance. However, Study 2 focused only on low-relevance conditions, and the operations used in Studies 1 and 2 differed somewhat, making comparisons difficult. What is needed now is a study in which both high and low relevance conditions are present and in which it is possible to track differences in positivity and negativity in affect.

Study 3: SEM and Facial Expression

Study 3 was designed to provide more evidence for the comparison and reflection processes by examining the positivity and negativity of affect in all the conditions relevant to the SEM model. The primary measure of affect used in this study was the pleasantness of facial expressions. Facial indexes of affect have been found useful in a variety of contexts (e.g., Barden, Garber, Duncan, & Masters, 1981; Ekman & Oster, 1979; Zuckerman, Klorman, Larrance, & Spiegel, 1981).

The SEM model assumes that threats to self-evaluation are unpleasant and increases in self-evaluation are pleasant. Furthermore, the theory is explicit in specifying the conditions that promise to reduce or augment self-evaluation. When the task is high in relevance, the comparison process is important and a close other's better performance should lead to more negative affect than should a distant other's better performance. On the other hand, when relevance is low, the reflection process is important, and a close other's better performance should lead to more positive affect than should a distant other's better performance. In sum, all three factors (relative performance, relevance, and closeness) should interact in producing affective responses.

Study 3 uses a paradigm similar to that used in Study 1: Subjects take a test high in relevance to their self-definition and a test low in relevance. A friend (close other) and a stranger (distant other) are purported to respond to the same test items. For each item, subjects are given feedback containing three elements of information: type of item (high or low relevance), relative performance (self better vs. other better), and the closeness of the comparison other (friend vs. stranger). These variables define eight trials that represent a complete replication of a factorial design composed of the complete crossing of the three elements. Subjects' affective response, as registered in their facial expression, was monitored continuously during each trial.

As in Study 1, the Taylor Manifest Anxiety scale, the Rosenberg Self-Esteem Scale, and the Socialization scale of the California Psychological Inventory were administered.

Method

SUBJECTS

Forty-six undergraduate women (23 pairs of friends) taking introductory psychology classes received extra course credit for participation. One participant was dropped from further consideration because of failure to follow experimental instructions.

PROCEDURE

Each friendship pair was informed by a male experimenter that the purpose of the study was to measure esthetic judgment and logical thinking ability. The experimenter gave a short definition of each ability and explained that participants would be required to complete two computer tasks designed to measure these abilities. Before completing the tasks, the participants were asked to fill out a four-item questionnaire. The questionnaire was designed to assess the relevance of each domain to the participant's self-definition. They rated on 7-point scales the extent to which they thought of themselves as having good esthetic judgment (logical thinking ability) and how important it was for them to have good esthetic judgment (logical thinking ability).

Each friend was then escorted to a separate room and seated at a microcomputer. The experimenter explained that the microcomputer would require them to perform eight games: four logical thinking games and four esthetic judgment games. After they finished playing each game, the computer would automatically score their performance and provide feedback. In addition, the computer would tell them how well their friend, who was working on the terminal in the next room, performed on the same game. However, if their friend had not completed or was not assigned a similar game, they would receive information on the performance of

a subject who had participated earlier in the study. The experimenter then left the room and the microcomputer gave participants directions on how to play the games as well as an opportunity to practice both the logical thinking and esthetic judgment games. After the practice games, four logical thinking and four esthetic judgment trials were presented with preassigned feedback randomly ordered.

Participants were given a questionnaire designed to assess their perceptions of their performance, their friend's performance, and the stranger's performance on the esthetic judgment and logical thinking games. A further questionnaire asked participants to report how they felt in each of the eight feedback conditions; they rated on 7-point scales the extent to which they felt good or bad when they received the eight types of feedback. Participants then completed the Rosenberg Self-esteem Scale (Rosenberg, 1965), the Socialization scale of the California Psychological Inventory, and the Taylor Manifest Anxiety Scale. Finally, participants were questioned concerning the experimental hypotheses, debriefed, and released.

COMPUTER TASKS

An interception task that ostensibly measured logical thinking and a pattern creation task that ostensibly measured esthetic judgment were used. The logical thinking task required participants to intercept a target airplane in a 12×11 matrix. Each time participants moved one unit, the target airplane moved one unit. The target airplane's movements were random except when participants were to receive poor performance feedback. On these trials the computer moved the target so that it was impossible to hit. Participants were informed that the computer evaluated their logical ability not only by whether they intercepted the target but also by examining the pattern or strategy they used to intercept the target.

The esthetic judgment game required participants to take an existing pattern and make it more esthetically pleasing by changing the symbols used to make the pattern and the amount of space between symbols. With each pattern, participants were given four chances to make it look pleasing. After each attempt, the modified pattern was presented to the participant. Participants were informed that the computer would evaluate their esthetic judgment not only on the basis of the final pattern they created but on the basis of the means in which they attempted to make the pattern esthetically pleasing.

FEEDBACK

At the end of each trial, the computer presented information ostensibly reporting on the participants' performance and the performance of either their friend or an earlier participant. Each participant received feedback representing each level of the three variables (friend vs. stranger, logical thinking vs. esthetic judgment; self better vs. other better), creating eight feedback conditions. Self-better feedback was created by giving the participant a score between 70th and 90th percentile and the comparison person a score between 20th and 50th percentile; other-better feedback was created by reversing these scores. The order in which the feedback conditions were presented was counterbalanced across subjects. After the feedback had been presented, subjects could terminate the feedback and initiate the next trial by pressing a designated key on the computer. The time spent examining the feedback was recorded by the computer.

DEPENDENT MEASURE

Cameras behind a one-way mirror in the experimental rooms recorded the participants' facial responses during the game-playing behavior and feedback. The computer illuminated a light recorded on the videotape to signal when the participant was receiving feedback. Two raters later viewed the tapes and, when the light signal was on, rated the pleasantness of participants' facial responses to the feedback by using a 7-point scale anchored by *unpleasant* (7) and *pleasant* (1). Raters were blind to feedback conditions.

Results

RELIABILITY OF FACIAL RATINGS

Two persons independently rated the pleasantness of each subject's face in each condition; these ratings were summed to yield a pleasantness score. (Because of difficulty with the video equipment, data for 2 subjects were deleted, leaving 43 subjects.) Reliability of ratings was assessed for each subject by computing a coefficient alpha over the eight conditions in which each subject was ob-

served. Reliability was satisfactory. Only 5 subjects had alphas under .60; the mean alpha was .81 and the median alpha .93.

Analysis of Facial Ratings

Relevance was defined as in Study 1: The two relevance items for each topic were summed (2 = maximal relevance; 14 = minimal relevance), and the topic that had the larger sum was classified as high relevance ($M = 4.48$) and the topic that had the smaller sum was classified as low relevance ($M = 6.45$; see Footnote 3). For 17 subjects logical ability was more relevant; for 14 subjects esthetic judgment was more relevant. Twelve subjects were dropped because there was no difference in the relevance of the two areas.

Pleasantness ratings were analyzed in a 2 (relevance) × 2 (closeness) × 2 (performance) repeated-measures ANOVA. The means associated with this analysis are presented in Table 1. The SEM model predicts both a two-way interaction (Relevance × Performance) and a three-way interaction (Relevance × Closeness × Performance). The two-factor interaction was not significant ($F < 1$), but the three-factor interaction was significant, $F(1, 30) = 4.72$, $p < .04$. The only other effect even to approach significance was that due to closeness, $F(1, 30) = 3.18$, $p = .08$. Facial expressions were more pleasant in connection with feedback to a friend than a stranger.

As one might guess, knowing that the predicted Relevance × Performance interaction did not emerge, the pattern of means producing the three-factor interaction does not, in absolute terms, completely conform to predictions. On the other hand, the pattern does conform to theoretical expectations in relative terms (see Tesser, in press, for a

TABLE 1. Pleasantness of Facial Expressions as a Function of Relative Performance, Personal Relevance, and Closeness of Other

| Other (closeness) | Self-better performance | | Other-better performance | | |
	High relevance	Low relevance	High relevance	Low relevance	M
Friend	7.10	7.77	7.97	7.39	7.56
Stranger	8.71	7.74	8.03	8.55	8.26
M	7.90	7.76	8.00	7.97	7.91

Note. Numbers have a potential range of 2 (most pleasant) to 14 (most unpleasant).

discussion of the importance of relative prediction or interactions in testing SEM predictions).

We assume that SEM functioning is not the only thing that determines behavior in general or pleasantness of facial expression in this particular instance. For example, the SEM model makes some absolute predictions about the difference in pleasantness between friend and stranger. It predicts that being outperformed by a friend should be more threatening (more unpleasant) than being outperformed by a stranger on a relevant task. As seen in Table 1, this was not the case. However, independent of SEM functioning, as noted, more pleasant expressions tend to be associated with feedback about a friend than with feedback about a stranger. This effect is not anticipated by the SEM model but it is not particularly surprising. Because it is present, we must look at this closeness effect relative to the closeness effect in other conditions. (The closeness effect is defined as the difference in pleasantness to friend vs. stranger, with positive numbers meaning more pleasantness to friend.)

Fortunately, the SEM model is unambiguous in telling us where to look for relative differences. When the self outperforms the other, there should be no threat due to comparison even if the performance dimension is self-relevant. Thus, the closeness effect under other-better, high-relevance conditions should be less positive than under self-better, high-relevance conditions. Figure 3 illustrates these closeness effects as deviations from the overall difference in pleasantness to the friend and stranger. As can be seen, the difference in these effects is in the predicted direction and is significant, $t(60) = 1.74$, $p < .04$ (see Footnote 2).

When relevance is low the reflection process is important. So, in absolute terms, there should be more pleasantness associated with a friend than with a stranger when the other performs better. Although this absolute difference is in the appropriate direction, it could be due to the general difference in facial pleasantness alluded to earlier. So, again, we pursue our strategy of relative comparisons. On a low-relevance dimension, if the self outperforms the other then one cannot bask in the other's good performance. Thus, the closeness effect under other-better, low-relevance conditions should be more positive than the closeness effect under self-better, low-relevance conditions. As shown in Figure 3, this difference is in the predicted direction although not significant, $t(60) = 1.30$, $p < .10$.

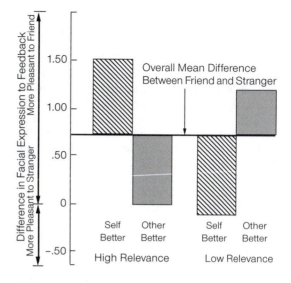

FIGURE 3 ▪ Study 3: Differences in pleasantness of facial expression to close (friend) and distant (stranger) other as a combined function of performance feedback (self better vs. other better) and relevance of task to subjects' self-definition.

The comparison of closeness effects between other-better, high-relevance conditions and self-better, high-relevance conditions is actually the simple Closeness × Performance interaction at high relevance. The comparison of closeness effects between other better, low relevance and self better, low relevance is actually the simple Closeness × Performance interaction at low relevance. These simple interactions go in opposite directions as predicted. Thus, an overall test of the entire set of relative predictions is the Closeness × Performance × Relevance interaction. As reported earlier, this source of variation was clearly significant.

Still focusing on Figure 3, another set of comparisons is possible. Earlier we compared closeness effects as a function of performance while holding relevance constant. The model also has something to say about the effects of relevance while holding performance constant. It suggests that the other-better, high-relevance condition should be associated with a smaller closeness effect than should the other-better, low-relevance condition. That is, in the former condition closeness should increase the loss due to comparison, and in the latter it should increase the gain due to reflection. The relative sizes of the effect are in the expected direction but do not approach significance, $t(60) = 1.14$. When the dimension is high in relevance, there is a potential threat of comparison. If self outperforms other, then threat is avoided. When the dimension is low in relevance, there is a potential gain due to reflection. When self outperforms other, that promise is unfulfilled. Thus, the closeness effect associated with the former condition (threat avoidance) should be more positive than that associated with the latter condition (loss of potential gain). It is, $t(60) = 1.71$, $p < .05$. These predictions, like those made earlier, are also confirmed as a set by the presence of the significant Closeness × Performance × Relevance interaction. [. . .]

General Discussion

We have suggested that much social behavior can be understood as the result of two antagonistic processes: A comparison process and a reflection process. We have also suggested that the motive underlying these processes is the maintenance of a positive self-evaluation. Finally, we argued that threats and promises to self-evaluation should result in changes of affect. Thus, tracking affect could help evaluate the tenability of the model. This was the goal of our research.

The results of the three studies are encouraging. When another outperforms the self compared with when the self outperforms the other, the closer the other, the greater the threat if the task is high in relevance (comparison process) and the greater the promise if the task is low in relevance (reflection process). Study 1 showed that conditions presumed to lead to increased threat or increased promise seemed to be associated with greater arousal (speeded-up performance of simple tasks and slowed-down performance of complex tasks). Interpreting the low-relevance results of Study 1 was difficult. The SEM model suggests that the better performance of a close other produces arousal because of the positivity of reflection. A social comparison perspective suggests that the better performance of a close other generates threat (negative affect and arousal) even on low-relevance tasks. In Study 2, closeness and relative performance on a low-relevance task were manipulated. Results favored the SEM model. An indirect measure of affect revealed the most positivity and least negativity when the self was outperformed by a close other on a low-relevance task.

In Study 3 we used a different measure of directional changes in affect and pleasantness of facial expression, and we explored these changes in both high- and low-relevance circumstances. When the task was high in relevance, pleasantness of affect associated with the close other (relative to the distant other) decreased as performance changed from self better to other better. On the other hand, when the task was low in relevance, pleasantness of affect associated with the close other (relative to the distant other) increased as performance changed from self better to other better. These results offer partial support for the SEM model and suggest that the closeness of others increases the pain of comparison and the pleasure of reflection.

REFERENCES

Abelson, R. P. (1983). Whatever became of consistency theory? *Personality and Social Psychology Bulletin, 9,* 37–54.

Barden, R. C., Garber, J., Duncan, S. W. & Masters, J. C. (1981). Cumulative effects of induced affective states in children: Accentuation, inoculation, and remediation. *Journal of Personality and Social Psychology, 40,* 750–760.

Batson. C. D., Duncan, B. D., Ackerman, P., Buckley, T., & Birch, K. (1981). Is empathic emotion a source of altruistic motivation? *Journal of Personality and Social Psychology, 40,* 290–302.

Berscheid, E. (1983). Emotion. In H. H. Kelley, E. Berscheid, A. Christensen, J. H. Harvey, T. L. Huston, G. Levinger, E. McClintock, L. A. Peplau, & D. R. Peterson (Eds.), *Close relationships* (pp. 110–168). New York: Freeman.

Brenner, M. (1973). The next-in-line effect. *Journal of Verbal Learning and Verbal Behavior, 12,* 320–323.

Brickman, P., & Bulman, R. J. (1977). Pleasure and pain in social comparison. In J. Suls & R. L. Miller (Eds.), *Social comparison processes: Theoretical and empirical perceptions* (pp. 149–186). Washington, DC: Hemisphere.

Cialdini, R. B., Borden, R. J., Thorne, A., Walker, M. R., Freeman, S., & Slaon, L. R. (1976). Basking in reflected glory: Three (football) field studies. *Journal of Personality and Social Psychology, 34,* 366–375.

Cialdini, E., & Kenrick, D. T. (1976). Altruism as hedonism: A social development perspective on the relationship of negative mood state and helping. *Journal of Personality and Social Psychology, 34,* 907–914.

Clark, M. S., & Isen, A. M. (1982). Toward understanding the relationship between feeling states and social behavior. In A. Hastorf & A. M. Isen (Eds.), *Cognitive social psychology* (pp. 73–108). New York: Elsevier North-Holland.

Clark, M. S., Milberg, S., & Ross, J. (1983). Arousal cues arousal-related material in memory: Implications for understanding effects of mood on memory. *Journal of Verbal Learning and Verbal Behavior, 22,* 633–649.

Ekman, P., & Oster, H. (1979). Facial expressions of emotions. *Annual Review of Psychology, 30,* 527–554.

Festinger, L. (1954). A theory of social comparison processes. *Human Relations, 7,* 117–140.

Fiske, S. T. (1982). Schema triggered affect: Applications to social perception. In M. S. Clark & S. T. Fiske (Eds.), *Affect and cognition: The 17th Annual Carnegie Symposium on Cognition* (pp. 55–78). Hillsdale, NJ: Erlbaum.

Geen, R. G., & Quanty, M. B. (1977). The catharsis of aggression: An evaluation of a hypothesis. In L. Berkowitz (Eds.), *Advances in experimental social psychology* (Vol. 10, pp. 2–23). New York: Academic Press.

Goethals, G. R. (1984, August). *Social comparison theory: Psychology from the lost and found*. Paper presented at the annual convention of the American Psychological Association, Toronto.

Gottman, J. M., & Levenson, R. W. (1984). Why marriages fail: Affective and physiological patterns in marital interaction. In J. C. Masters & K. Yarkin-Levin (Eds.), *Boundary areas in social and developmental psychology* (pp. 67–106). New York: Academic Press.

Gough, H. G. (1964). *Manual of the California Psychological Inventory*. Palo Alto, CA: Consulting Psychologists Press.

Hare, R. D. (1978). Electrodermal and cardiovascular correlates of psychopathy. In R. E. Hare & D. Schalling (Eds.), *Psychopathic behavior: Approaches to research* (pp. 126–139). London: Wiley.

Heider, F. (1958). *The psychology of interpersonal relations*. New York: Wiley.

Isen, A. M., & Levin, P. F. (1972). The effect of feeling good on helping: Cookies and kindness. *Journal of Personality and Social Psychology, 21,* 384–388.

Isen, A. M., & Shalker, T. E. (1977). *Do you "accentuate the positive, eliminate the negative" when you are in a good mood?* Unpublished manuscript. University of Maryland, Baltimore County, Catonsville.

Mandler, G. (1975). *Mind and emotion*. New York: Wiley.

Nadler, A., Fisher, J. D., & Ben-Itzhak, S. (1983). With a little help from a friend: Effect of single or multiple act aid as a function of domain and task characteristic. *Journal of Personality and Social Psychology, 44,* 310–321.

Piliavin, J. A., Dovidio, J. F., Gaertner, S. L., & Clark, R. D. (1982). Responsive bystanders: The process of intervention. In V. J. Derlega & J. Grzelak (Eds.), *Cooperation and helping behavior* (pp. 281–304). New York: Academic Press.

Pleban, R., & Tesser, A. (1981). The effects of relevance and quality of another's performance on interpersonal closeness. *Social Psychology Quarterly, 44,* 278–285.

Rosenberg, M. (1965). *Society and the adolescent self-image*. Princeton, NJ: Princeton University Press.

Roseman, I. (1984). Cognitive determinants of emotion: A structural theory. In P. Shaver (Ed.), *Review of Personality and Social Psychology* (Vol. 5, pp. 11–36). Beverly Hills, CA: Sage.

Russell, J. A. (1980). A circumplex model of affect. *Journal of Personality and Social Psychology, 39,* 1161–1178.

Salovey, P., & Rodin, J. (1984). Some antecedents and consequences of social-comparison jealousy. *Journal of Personality and Social Psychology, 17,* 780–792.

Schacter, S. (1964). The interaction of cognitive and physiological determinants of emotional state. In L. Berkowitz (Ed.), *Advances in experimental social psychology* (Vol. 1, pp. 49–79). New York: Academic Press.

Spence, K. W. (1956). *Behavior theory and conditioning*. New Haven, CT: Yale University Press.

Spence, K. W., Farber, I. E., & McFann, H. H. (1956). The relation of anxiety (drive) level to performance in competitional and noncompetitional paired-associates learning. *Journal of Experimental Psychology, 52,* 296–305.

Suls, J. M., & Miller, R. L. (Eds.). (1977). *Social comparison processes: Theoretical and empirical perspectives*. Washington, DC: Hemisphere.

Taylor, J. A. (1953). A personality scale of manifest anxiety. *Journal of Abnormal and Social Psychology, 48,* 285–290.

Tesser, A. (1986). Some effects of self-evaluation maintenance on cognition and action. In R. M. Sorrentino & E. T. Higgins (Eds.), *The handbook of motivation and cognition: Foundations of social behavior* (pp. 435–464). New York: Guilford Press.

Tesser, A. (in press). Toward a self-evaluation maintenance model of social behavior. In L. Berkowitz (Ed.), *Advances in experimental social psychology* (Vol. 20). New York: Academic Press.

Tesser, A., & Campbell, J. (1980). Self-definition: The impact of the relative performance and similarity of others. *Social Psychology Quarterly, 43,* 341–347.

Tesser, A., & Campbell, J. (1982a, August). Self-evaluation maintenance processes and individual differences in self-esteem. Paper presented at the annual convention of the American Psychological Association, Washington, DC.

Tesser, A., & Campbell, J. (1982b). Self-evaluation maintenance and the perception of friends and strangers. *Journal of Personality, 50,* 261–279.

Tesser, A., & Campbell, J. (1983). Self-definition and self-evaluation maintenance. In J. Suls & A. Greenwald (Eds.), Social psychological perspectives on the self (Vol. 2, pp. 1–31).

Tesser, A., & Smith, J. (1980). Some effects of friendship and task relevance on helping: You don't always help the one you like. *Journal of Experimental Social Psychology, 16,* 583–590.

Waid, W. W., & Orne, M. T. (1982). Reduced electrodermal response to conflict, failure to inhibit dominant behaviors, and delinquency proneness. *Journal of Personality and Social Psychology, 13,* 769–774.

Winer, B. J. (1962). *Statistical principles in experimental design*. New York: McGraw-Hill.

Zajonc, R. B. (1965). Social facilitation. *Science, 149,* 269–274.

Zajonc, R. B. (1980). Feeling and thinking: Preferences need no inferences. *American Psychologist, 35,* 151–176.

Zillman, D. (1978). Attribution and misattribution of excitatory reactions. In J. H. Harvey, W. Ickes, & R. E. Kidd (Eds.), *New directions in attribution research* (Vol. 2, pp. 335–368). New York: Wiley.

Zuckerman, M., Klorman, R., Larrance, D. T., & Spiegel, N. H. (1981). Facial, autonomic, and subjective components of emotion: The facial feedback hypothesis vs. the externalizer-internalizer distinction. *Journal of Personality and Social Psychology, 41,* 929–944.

READING 4

Why Do We Need What We Need?
A Terror Management Perspective on the Roots
of Human Social Motivation

Tom Pyszczynski • Department of Psychology, University of Colorado at Colorado Springs
Jeff Greenberg • Department of Psychology, University of Arizona
Sheldon Solomon • Department of Psychology, Skidmore College

Editors' Notes

People are motivated to have positive beliefs about themselves, their in-group members, and the world in which they live. What is the origin and relation among these and other motivations? In their terror management theory, the authors propose that many human motivations are rooted in the relation between the fundamental instinct for self-preservation and humans' unique awareness of their inevitable mortality. The basic nature of human motivation concerns dealing with the potentially paralyzing knowledge of one's inevitable death while fulfilling the prime directive for continued goal-directed behavior. Positive beliefs serve the function of controlling the basic anxiety, and thus these beliefs are energetically maintained and defended. The authors point out that such maintenance and defense, like the worldview defense of responding more favorably to those upholding than those violating cultural values, does not require that reminders of mortality induce emotional upheavals or that one be conscious of the problem of death. The authors discuss three main motivational systems for self-preservation and terror management: 1) direct homeostatic motives to keep the biological systems of the body functioning properly; 2) defensive motives to cope with the terror of knowing about the inevitability of death; and 3) self-expansive motives to adapt to a complex and changing environment. The authors postulate that various social-psychological phenomena, including self-enhancement, impression management, consensus building, and cognitive consistency, can be understood as symbolic means of terror management.

Discussion Questions

1. Describe three motivational systems for self-preservation and terror management.
2. From the perspective of terror management theory, what functions are served by impression management, belief in a just world, and cognitive consistency?

Authors' Abstract

In this article, we use terror management theory to address the question of why people are motivated to achieve a variety of specific psychological endstates. We argue that the most basic of all human motives is an instinctive desire for continued life, and that all more specific motives are ultimately rooted in this basic evolutionary adaptation. We propose a tripartite motive system through which this prime directive for continued life is achieved, along with a hierarchical model of the relation between motives at different levels of abstraction. This analysis specifies the relation between the self-presentation instinct and various more specific and concrete psychological motives. The three major branches of this motivational hierarchy consist of (a) direct biological motives, which are oriented toward attaining the biological necessities of life (e.g., food, air, water); (b) symbolic-defensive motives, which are oriented toward controlling the potential for existential terror brought on by awareness of the ultimate impossibility of continued satisfaction of the self-preservation instinct; and (c) self-expansive motives, which are oriented toward the growth and expansion of the individual's competencies and internal representations of reality. To illustrate the integrative utility of this analysis, we discuss the role of superordinate symbolic terror management needs in the pursuit of cognitive consistency, belief in a just world, self-awareness related behavior, self-esteem, social identity, impression management, and the control of others' worldviews.

Why do people do what they do when they do it? To answer this question, it is often assumed that, in addition to the satisfaction of biological needs, people are motivated to attain a variety of distinctly psychological endstates, and that these motives mediate a broad range of human behaviors. Convincing evidence now exists that people are motivated to obtain (among other things) positive evaluations of themselves and the groups to which they belong, favorable public images, consistency among their cognitions, and benign beliefs about the world in which they live (e.g., that the world is just). Much literature exists that documents the many ways in which these needs influence social cognition and interpersonal behavior.

The primary appeal of motivational theorizing is the hope of explaining the causal relations among large sets of variables with a few relatively simple constructs. Thus, a single motivational state can be invoked to account for a wide range of behaviors. For example, hunger can be posited to account for such diverse behaviors as driving to Jack-in-the Box at 3:00 a.m., shoplifting a candy bar, and barbecuing a burger. Similarly, the need for self-esteem has been proposed as a driving force behind such seemingly disparate forms of behavior as altruism and aggression, accuracy and bias in inferences, and conformity and deviance in response to others.

Motivational states can also help account for how a diverse set of stimulus conditions can lead to the same behavior. For example, a motive state of thirst can help explain massive consumption of liquids in response to such diverse conditions as being stranded in the Sonoran Desert, consuming a bag of salty potato chips, or running a marathon. Similarly, the self-esteem motive construct can account for an overly positive global evaluation of oneself after having a paper rejected from the *Journal of Personality and Social Psychology*, performing poorly on the squash court, or spilling one's drink at a party.

Because motivational constructs can be such powerful explanatory tools, theorists have invoked a variety of psychological needs to explain and guide the investigation of specific forms of behavior. However, inquiry concerning these needs has evolved historically out of separate and distinct theoretical perspectives into independent and isolated research programs, with little attention directed toward understanding the origins of and relations among these needs. This state of conceptual isolationism may impede progress toward understanding the basic nature of human motivation by leading to a Tower of Babel–like assortment of overlapping need states that are ultimately explained tautologically—not unlike the problem that developed with the proliferation of instinct labels early in the 20th century. The purpose of this article is to propose a hierarchical analysis of human motivation, derived from terror management theory (TMT; Greenberg, Pyszczynski, & Solomon, 1986; Solomon, Greenberg, & Pyszczynski, 1991a), that addresses the question of why a variety of distinct psychological motives exist and how these various motives are related to each other.

TMT

From the perspective of TMT (for a more complete exposition, see Solomon et al., 1991a), many psychological needs are ultimately rooted in the existential dilemma into which our species was born. Although humans share with other forms of life a basic instinct for self-preservation, they are unique in their possession of intellectual capacities that make them explicitly and painfully aware of the inevitability of their mortality. Because of this juxtaposition of animal instinct with sophisticated intellect, humans must live with the knowledge that the most basic of their needs and desires ultimately will be thwarted. Knowledge of the inevitability of death gives rise to the potential for paralyzing terror, which would make continued goal-directed behavior impossible.

The theory posits that this terror is managed by a dual-component cultural anxiety buffer, consisting of (a) an individual's personalized version of the cultural worldview, which consists of a set of benign concepts for understanding the world and one's place in it, a set of standards through which one can attain a sense of personal value, and the promise of literal and/or symbolic immortality to those who live up to these standards; and (b) self-esteem, or a sense of personal value, which is attained by believing that one is living up to the standards of value that are part of the cultural worldview. Because of the role these structures play in controlling anxiety, a great deal of energy is devoted to their maintenance and defense.

We believe that TMT is useful because:

1. It is parsimonious and requires only one commonly accepted and rather noncontroversial a priori assumption: specifically, that living organisms are oriented toward self-preservation,
2. It provides a conceptual account of the nature and function of culture and self-esteem, and thus explains what other social psychological theories presume as the starting point for their analyses.

3. It can account for a great deal of existing empirical evidence on social psychological phenomena such as self-esteem maintenance, prejudice, attraction, interpersonal relationships, conformity, obedience, aggression, and altruism.
4. It can be used to derive a wide range of novel hypotheses, many of which have been supported by empirical findings that cannot be readily explained by existing alternative theoretical perspectives.

Empirical Evidence

Initial empirical tests of TMT were based on two basic hypotheses derived from the theory. *The anxiety-buffer hypothesis* states that if a psychological structure functions to provide protection against anxiety, then strengthening that structure should make one less prone to exhibit anxiety and anxiety-related behavior in response to threats, and weakening that structure should make one more prone to do so. In support of this hypothesis, research has shown that increasing self-esteem reduces self-reports of anxiety in response to graphic death-related stimuli, physiological arousal in response to the threat of painful electric shock, and defensive distortions to deny vulnerability to an early death (Greenberg et al., 1992; Greenberg, Pyszczynski, et al., 1993). In addition, both chronically high and experimentally enhanced self-esteem have been shown to reduce the extent of defensive responses engendered by reminders of one's mortality (Harmon-Jones, Simon, Greenberg, Pyszczynski, Solomon, & McGregor, in press); consistent with these findings, depressed individuals, who tend to be especially low in self-esteem, have been shown to engage in especially strong worldveiw defense in response to mortality salience (Simon, Harmon-Jones, Solomon, & Pyszczynski, 1996). It has also been shown that threats to one's worldview make one more prone to exhibit both physiological and self-report indicators of anxiety in response to subtle death-related questions (Pyszczynski, Becker, et al., 1994).

The *morality salience hypothesis* states that if a psychological structure provides protection against anxiety, then reminding people of the source of this anxiety should increase the need for that structure. This will in turn lead to especially positive reactions to anyone or anything that supports it, and especially negative reactions to anyone or anything that threatens it. In support of this hypothesis, reminders of death have been shown to lead to more favorable evaluations of those who exemplify cultural values or praise the culture and of members of the ingroup; and to especially negative evaluations of those who violate cultural values or criticize the culture and of members of the outgroup (e.g., Florian & Mikulincer, 1994; Greenberg et al., 1990; Ochsmann & Reichelt, 1993; Rosenblatt, Greenberg, Solomon, Pyszczynski, & Lyon, 1989). Mortality salience has also been shown to lead to behavioral avoidance of outgroup members (Ochsmann & Mathay, 1994), overestimation of consensus for one's attitudes on culturally relevant issues (Pyszczynski, Wicklund, et al., in press), increased conformity to cultural standards (Greenberg, Simon, et al., 1992), and increased difficulties and emotional distress when behaving counter to cultural norms (Greenberg, Porteus, Simon, Pyszczynski, & Solomon, 1995). These effects have been demonstrated in the United States, Canada, Germany, and Israel; thus there is at least some evidence of cross-cultural generalizability.

The effects of mortality salience appear to be specific to the problem of death. Comparison conditions in which participants are induced to think about anxiety-provoking events other than death (e.g., giving a speech in front of a large audience, intense physical pain, general worries about life after college, taking a test in an important class, or failing such a test, or to actually experience failure on a supposed intelligence test) do not produce effects parallel to that of thinking about one's own mortality (Greenberg, Pyszczynski, Solomon, Simon, & Breus, 1994; Greenberg, Simon, et al., 1995; Harmon-Jones, Simon, et al., in press). These findings are important because they remove the morality salience results from the domain of theories that might be able to explain increased cultural affiliation in response to general threats to self.

Taken together, these studies suggest that the problem of death plays a significant role in many distinct domains of human social behavior, and that self-esteem and cultural worldviews play a role in controlling the anxiety that results from awareness of one's mortality. Of course, TMT is a relatively recent development, and there are many questions within the domain of the theory yet to be subjected to empirical test. Although additional research on these issues is sorely needed, the evidence available to date is highly encouraging for the theory.

Role of Consciousness in Terror Management Processes

One of the most common reactions to TMT is that it couldn't possibly be correct because people just don't think about death all that often. Although we suspect that death-related concerns enter consciousness more often than most people realize, we agree that such thoughts occupy relatively little of our conscious attention. Nonetheless, we maintain that the problem of death exerts an ongoing influence on a broad range of socially important behavior. Recently we have begun conducting research that might help explain how that could be true.

Interestingly, although the reminders of mortality used in our mortality salience studies have consistently been shown to affect responses to people and ideas that impinge on the cultural worldview, these reminders have just as consistently been shown not to produce anxiety or negative affect. Furthermore, regression analyses have shown repeatedly that the effect of mortality salience on responses to those who impinge on the cultural worldview are not mediated by participants' current emotional state. Indeed, studies that have compared mortality salience with the salience of other aversive events have shown that although mortality salience does not produce negative affect and does produce increased worldview defense (i.e., more favorable reactions to those who uphold cultural values and less favorable reactions to those who violate cultural values), the salience of other aversive events often does produce negative affect but consistently does not produce increased worldview defense. This is not to suggest that the problem of death is not emotionally upsetting to people. Many studies, conducted in our laboratories and elsewhere, have shown that confrontation with mortality often produces both physiological and subjective indicators of anxiety (Alexander, Colley, & Adlerstein, 1957; Greenberg, Solomon, et al., 1992). Rather, the finding of increased worldview defense in the absence of signs of emotional upheaval suggest that subjectively experienced emotion is not necessary for these effects to occur and that even relatively subtle reminders of mortality seem to engage the terror management system.

Recently we have compared the relatively subtle mortality salience induction used in most of our studies with a more blatant and powerful induction, and found that the subtle induction produces stronger effects (Greenberg, Pyszczynski, et al., 1994, Study 1). This led us to hypothesize that the problem of death may exert its effect primarily when it is on the fringes of consciousness: that is, when it is highly accessible but outside of current focal attention or working memory. Consistent with this possibility, we found that although strong mortality salience effects were found when participants were distracted from the problem of death after a mortality salience induction, no such effects were found when they were forced to keep death-related concepts in working memory (Greenberg, Pyszczynski, et al., 1994, Studies 2 & 3). Moreover, we found that the accessibility of death-related themes is higher after a delay and distraction than it is immediately after the mortality salience induction (Greenberg, Pyszczynski, et al., 1994, Study 4). These studies suggest that the problem of death must be activated and then removed from consciousness to affect interpersonal judgments and behavior.

From the perspective of TMT, the problem of death is an ongoing source of concern, regardless of whether one is currently consciously focused on it or not. The cultural anxiety buffer (cultural worldview and self-esteem) functions to control the potential for anxiety that arises as a result of the implicit knowledge of our ultimate mortality. Encounters with death-related stimuli lead to increased pursuit of self-esteem and faith in the cultural worldview because they signal a need for increased protection from this most basic of all fears. The findings that mortality salience exerts its effects most clearly after participants have been distracted from the problem of death, and that the problem of death is most accessible after such a distraction, suggest that the terror management system functions to control death-related fear primarily when the problem of death is highly accessible but not in current focal consciousness, in what Freud referred to as the *preconscious*.

This, of course, is consistent with the psychoanalytic roots of TMT. Rank (1936/1976), Becker (1973), and Freud (1933), whose thinking provided the primary inspiration for the theory, all posited that basic biological needs exert a strong influence on behavior and that these influences occur primarily when these needs are outside of consciousness. In our view, the findings that mortality salience leads to increased worldview defense only after participants have been distracted from the issue of death provide some of the strongest evidence available to date for the operation of such unconscious forces. Studies showing that subliminally presented stimuli can produce both physiological and subjective signs of anxiety (e.g., Robles, Smith, Carver, & Wellens, 1987) and influence behavior and judgment (e.g., Baldwin, Carrell, & Lopez, 1990; Silverman & Weinberger, 1985) also suggest that threatening material outside of consciousness can exert a motivating influence on people.

Although the notion of unconscious sources of motivation has been a highly controversial and hotly debated issue since Freud's original propositions along these lines, it remains an essential but often unacknowledged assumption that is the cornerstone of most contemporary motivational psychology, including our own. It is hard to imagine a compelling argument that people always know why they are doing what they are doing. A student who fails an important test and responds by derogating that test or making other excuses is hardly likely to be aware that his excuse making is driven by a need for self-esteem. A woman who buys an expensive new car and later finds herself praising her purchase to friends and derogating the almost-chosen alternative is similarly unlikely to realize that her behavior is driven by a need to reduce cognitive dissonance. A man who assumes a rape victim to be seductive and responsible for her plight is certainly not likely to think of his judgment as rooted in a desire to see the world as just. Indeed, the available evidence suggests that people are rarely, if ever, aware of the psychological forces underlying such motivated behavior (cf. Nisbett & Wilson, 1977).

Indeed, we have argued that for defensive motives to be effective in serving their functions, it is essential that people not be aware of their operation—people must maintain "an illusion of objectivity" and view their thoughts and actions as following rationally from the situation they are in (Pyszczynski & Greenberg, 1987). Kunda (1990) recently reviewed a broad range of evidence consistent with this basic notion. More recently, we have shown that encouraging participants to express the threatening emotion from which a defensive behavior presumably provides protection can eliminate the defensive response (Pyszczynski, Greenberg, Solomon, Sideris, & Stubing, 1993). The underlying point here is that if people knew why they do what they do, much of their behavior no longer would be able to fulfill the function that it is oriented toward serving. Clearly, then, the notion of unconscious motivation is critical to most, if not all, well-supported existing motivational theories; it also paves the way for the hierarchical analysis of human motivation to be presented next.

A Tripartite Model of Basic Human Motive Systems

From the perspective of TMT, a wide variety of psychological needs ultimately are rooted in the pursuit of self-esteem and faith in the cultural worldview, which in turn function to provide protection from the fear of death. The fear of death itself ultimately serves the instinct for self-preservation, which we view as a very basic and primitive psychological adaptation that functions to perpetuate the organism's genes. The self-preservation instinct can be viewed as the "master motive" that is the desired end state for virtually all systems within the organism. Although modern evolutionary theorists generally agree that natural selection occurs on the level of the gene rather than the individual, instinctive programming for the continued existence of the individual is one highly adaptive way of facilitating survival of one's genes. Individuals with behavioral tendencies oriented toward self-preservation are likely to live longer than those without such propensities, making it more likely that they will reproduce and protect their offspring, and thereby pass their genes on to future generations. The assumption of a self-preservation instinct follows directly from evolutionary and sociobiological theory and is shared with a broad range of previous theorists (e.g., Darwin, Dawkins, Freud, Rank, Wilson, Zilboorg).

According to TMT, the self-preservation instinct—the goal of staying alive—is the superordinate goal toward which all behavior is oriented. All other motives are, in one way or another, derived from and subservient to this "prime directive." We posit three main motivational systems that serve to facilitate survival: direct, symbolic, and self-expansive.[1]

Direct Motives

The most basic branch of the motivational system encompasses the biological processes and innate behavioral proclivities that keep us alive. For example, the maintenance of appropriate temperature, oxygen, and blood sugar levels ultimately all work toward sustaining life for the individual, as do instinctive tendencies to recoil from a loud noise, move away from the source of physical pain, and seek social attachments. These and other innate domain specific mechanisms (cf. Buss, 1994) function to keep the organism alive and enhance the likelihood of gene perpetuation. In some cases, these homeostatic biological mechanisms and innate response patterns give rise to subjective need states, in which people feel desire for food, water, relief from pain, or social contact, and these subjective desires instigate overt behavior oriented toward acquiring these entities. In other cases, these systems instigate adjustments in internal state or behavior without any mediation of consciously experienced needs or desires. We refer to these biological self-regulatory systems as the *direct means of self-preservation,* because they facilitate the organism's continued existence in a direct and straightforward manner. In the absence of abundant natural resources or modern technology, most of the daily activities of the typical human would

---

[1]It is important to acknowledge two general influences on our hierarchical thinking about motivation. First, Abraham Maslow's compelling and influential need hierarchy introduced to psychology the very concept of a hierarchy of psychological needs. Certainly his characterization of biological deficit motives as the most basic, followed by psychological deficit motives such as for self-esteem, followed by growth motives to actualize the self, has influenced virtually all subsequent thinking about the relations among human motives. However, our hierarchical conception differs from Maslow's in one fundamental way. Although Maslow ordered motives in terms of priority or prepotency for the organism such that lower order needs had to be relatively satisfied before higher order needs become active, he did not propose that the higher order motives were actually derived from and serving the more basic motives. In contrast, we argue that most psychological motives ultimately serve and are derived from three basic motive systems, which brings us to the second general influence. Although the history of psychology is replete with theorists who have focused on either defensive motives or growth motives, Otto Rank was the first to consider the integration of these two distinct types of motives. Although TMT is clearly focused on defensive motivation, following Rank we have recently proposed an integrative framework that considers the relation between defensive and growth motives (Greenberg, Pyszczynski, & Solomon, 1995).

be directed toward biological self-preservation. Although less time and energy is devoted to these needs in societies rich in such resources, the procurement of food, water, comfort, and shelter remain major ongoing goals even among the privileged elite in technologically advanced societies.

Defensive Motives

Although the pursuit of the biological necessities of life is clearly important in all societies, much of what people spend their time on (in small tribal cultures as well as large, technologically advanced ones) seems to be focused on the pursuit of meaning and value rather than self-preservation. It is our position, however, that the pursuit of meaning and value is just as surely linked to self-preservation as are hunting and food gathering. From the perspective of TMT, the pursuit of meaning and value, or faith in the cultural worldview and self-esteem, is the primary means of coping with the potential for terror that results when an animal instinctively programmed for self-preservation becomes aware that inevitably it will die. We refer to such pursuits as *symbolic means of self-preservation* because, although they do not keep the individual alive in any direct biological sense, they function to control the terror that results from knowledge of the inevitability of death. As we argue later in this article, most (but not all) of the motives studied by social psychologists are symbolic means of managing existential terror.

Although the symbolic defensive needs for meaning and value are distinct from the direct biological needs discussed in the previous section, they often impinge on the way our more basic biological proclivities are expressed. Whereas biological needs may drive us to seek food, sex, and social contact, terror-driven cultural proscriptions play an important role in determining what we eat, how we have sex, and with whom we affiliate. Thus, although internal homeostatic processes and innate behavioral proclivities play an important role in much socially significant behavior, the symbolic terror management needs for meaning and value often determine the specific ways in which our biological proclivities are expressed.

Self-Expansive Motives

A human being with a capacity to do nothing other than maintain an interior homeostasis and defend against physical and psychological threats would have little chance of long-term survival in a complex and changing environment. Such an animal must also be inclined to explore, assimilate new information, and integrate that information with its existing conception of the world, because survival depends on the development of an adequate understanding of the environment and a complex set of skills for interacting with that environment. Thus it seems clear that a motive for growth and expansion of one's capacities (e.g., Deci & Ryan, 1991; Maslow, 1943: Rank, 1932/1989; White, 1959) would make good evolutionary sense in that it would greatly increase the animal's chances of surviving long enough to reproduce.

Self-expansive motives are different from biological-homeostatic and symbolic-defensive motives in that there is less of a sense of urgency about them. Unlike these other motives, they do not stem from a sense of discomfort, distress, or deficit that the individual desires to minimize (cf. Maslow, 1943). Rather than operating in a drivelike manner, expansive motives entail a potential to derive pleasure from the maximal engagement of one's cognitive and behavioral capacities with the environment. The integrative activity that occurs when our capacities are maximally engaged produces change or growth within the individual—a simultaneous improvement in organization that entails increases in both complexity and simplicity. Complexity increases in the sense that the internal representation becomes differentiated and comes to encompass more and finer distinctions. Simplicity increases in the sense that the internal representation becomes more orderly and elegant; individual elements are organized into more coherent structures that increase the efficiency of the representation. Expansive activities are motivating because of the pleasure that such engagement produces. For a more thorough presentation of our perspective on self-expansive motivation, see Greenberg, Pyszczynski, and Solomon (1995) and Pyszczynski, Solomon, Greenberg, and Stewart-Fouts (1995).

Hierarchical Organization of Social Motives

The relation between the self-preservation instinct and various other psychological needs can be illuminated by thinking in terms of a hierarchical organization of goals and standards for self-regulation, similar to that proposed by Carver and Scheier

(1981), Powers (1978), and Vallacher and Wegner (1987). From this perspective, goals and behavior are seen as organized in a hierarchical manner, with abstract goals at the top of the hierarchy and concrete behavior at the bottom. As one moves up the hierarchy, the goal underlying a given behavior becomes the behavioral means through which the next more abstract goal is met. For example, as one moves up the hierarchy, the behavior of going to the library can be thought of as motivated by the goal of getting a book, preparing for an examination, working toward the successful completion of a class, pursuing a college degree, pursuing a career, demonstrating one's intelligence, acquiring self-esteem, or ameliorating the anxiety associated with the awareness of death. Similarly, one moves down the hierarchy toward the increasingly concrete behavioral means through which one's goals are met. Thus the behavior of going to the library can also be seen as the goal that motivates a variety of increasingly concrete behaviors, such as taking the bus, going to the bus stop, walking down Third Avenue, moving one's body, and changing the level of tension in the muscles of one's legs. Any behavior can be seen as simultaneously motivated by a variety of motives that operate at different levels of abstraction. Similarly, any behavior can be seen as the desired end state that motivates a variety of more concrete actions that also vary in their level of abstraction. From this perspective, the question of why we need what we need can be addressed by examining the superordinate goals that a particular desired state ultimately serves. Vallacher and Wegner's (1985) action identification theory and research explicitly address the antecedents and consequences of the level of abstraction at which people consciously think of their own behavior.

All of this implies that, at any given time, the individual is aware of only a small subset of the multitude of goals that he or she is currently pursuing and a similarly small subset of the more concrete behavioral means through which this pursuit takes place. Although most observers probably would agree that the behavior of a student studying for an exam is probably rooted in a desire to demonstrate his or her competence, which is in turn probably rooted (at least in part) in a need for self-esteem, the student actively involved in studying is unlikely to be aware of anything more abstract than a desire to get a good grade on the test or the class, or perhaps to maintain a high enough grade point average to get into graduate school. Concerns about self-esteem are, in most instances, probably outside of the student's conscious awareness.

We argue that all psychological motives facilitate the survival of the human organism. Direct homeostatic motives instigate adjustments that keep the biological systems of the body functioning at their proper levels. Defensive motives ameliorate the emotional distress produced by human awareness of the inevitability of death. Self-expansive motives facilitate survival by improving the human organism's capacity to adapt and prosper in a complex and changing environment. Viewing human motivation from this perspective reveals the basic functions served by the many motives that influence human behavior and highlights their interrelatedness. In the following section, we explore the implications of the defensive terror management system for understanding various specific social motives in the context of the hierarchical model of motivation presented previously (because of space limitations, we leave consideration of the implications of the self-expansive system for specific motives to another endeavor).

Theories of Social Motivation

Many important and influential theories that explore the influence of specific motives on social cognition and behavior have been proposed. In the following sections, we argue that a wide variety of social motives can be viewed as serving a terror management function. We begin with theories concerning cognitive consistency and justice, because these are two essential characteristics of any cultural worldview that are likely to be effective in controlling anxiety. It would be hard to imagine how one could derive security from any system of meaning lacking either of these two qualities. Although a variety of theories have claimed that people are motivated to seek cognitive consistency (e.g., Heider, 1944; Newcomb, 1953), our primary focus will be on what is undoubtedly the most influential and well-researched of the consistency theories: Festinger's (1957) theory of cognitive dissonance. In the justice domain—although there are a number of influential theories concerning the desire for fairness, justice, or equity (e.g., Homans, 1961; Lerner, 1980; Walster, Walster, & Berscheid, 1978)—our central focus will be on what we view as the most general and psychological of these: Lerner's just-world hypothesis (Lerner, 1980).

We then consider theoretical perspectives concerned with the functioning and protection of the self; the self-esteem or value component of terror management. We begin with theories of self-awareness and self-regulation that focus on how the individual is directed toward achieving that component's goals and meeting its self-referent standards (e.g., Carver & Scheier, 1981; Duval & Wicklund, 1972). We then discuss a number of prominent theories that assume that the need for self-esteem or a positive self-image is a dominant force that drives a diverse range of behaviors (e.g., Horney, 1950; James, 1890/1950; Steele, 1988; Tesser, 1988). We also consider social identity theory, which posits that because self-esteem is partly determined by evaluations of the social groups to which one does and does not belong, people also need positive conceptions of the groups to which they belong (Tajfel & Turner, 1979). Many theorists have argued that because people are highly dependent on the behavior of others, they are strongly motivated to control the impressions that others form of them. Thus, we then turn our attention to impression management and self-presentational theories, which argue that a great deal of human behavior is oriented toward controlling the impressions that others form of us (e.g., Baumeister, 1982; Goffman, 1959; Schlenker, 1980; Tedeschi, Schlenker, & Bonoma, 1971). Finally, we consider theories concerned with reactions to, and social influence attempts to control, the way others perceive the external world (Allport, 1954).

We agree that people work hard to maintain consistency among their cognitions, a belief that the world is just, minimal discrepancies between self and standards, positive evaluations of themselves and their groups, and positive impressions from others. Large bodies of evidence exist to support each of these basic motivational propositions. However, from the perspective of TMT, all of these motives ultimately are derived from the more basic goal of maintaining the integrity of the cultural anxiety buffer, which in turn functions to control the potential for abject terror that results from our awareness of our vulnerability and mortality. All of the social motives just noted can be considered symbolic means of self-preservation.

Of course there have been a number of scientific turf wars among the proponents of these different motive systems. For example, it has been argued that the pursuit of cognitive consistency is really just a matter of self-esteem maintenance (e.g., Greenwald & Ronis, 1978; Steele, 1988); or, vice versa, that the pursuit of self-esteem is really just a matter of people with preexisting positive self-images seeking information to confirm or verify those conceptions (e.g., Swann, 1983). Similarly, it has been argued that both consistency-seeking and esteem-enhancing behavior ultimately boil down to a matter of controlling the impressions that others form of oneself (e.g., Tedeschi et al., 1971; Weary, 1979). Conversely, it has been argued that self-presentational behavior is ultimately just one more attempt to convince oneself of one's value (Greenberg et al., 1986). It seems that every time these controversies arise, convincing evidence is marshaled in favor of a specific position, only to be subsequently contradicted by additional evidence in favor of the alternative. Although temporary states of near-consensus on these issues do occasionally emerge, they are generally rather short lived.

We suggest that the solution to this quandary is not likely to be found in a clear victory of one theory over the other (see also Tetlock & Levi, 1982). Under certain conditions, people are indeed motivated to seek all of these frequently cited end states. Rather than attempting to determine which is the most basic of these various motives, it might be better to look for what they have in common—that is, the common needs they are all directed toward meeting. From the perspective of a hierarchical analysis of motivation, all of the motives just cited are important and none can be reduced to a special case of another. Each motive serves its intended purpose at the hierarchical level specified by the respective theorist. Our goal here is to consider the superordinate needs that all of these widely recognized psychological motives are oriented toward satisfying. We suggest that, although manifested in different ways, all of these social motives entail attempts on the part of the individual to maintain the integrity of the cultural anxiety buffer. All ultimately entail the pursuit of faith in a particular conception of the world and/or the belief that one is a person of primary value in that world. Thus, they all function to reduce the individual's proneness to anxiety concerning his or her vulnerability and ultimate mortality.

We are not claiming that TMT says all there is to say about these motives, nor are we proposing

TMT as a replacement for the extant theories that address them. For the most part, we believe that the existing theories do a good job of explaining the dynamics of behavior driven by the specific motive in question. More important, these theories operate at a different level of analysis and thus address important questions not addressed by TMT. We are suggesting, however, that it is important to ask the question, "Why do we need what we need?"; and that attempting to answer this question will reveal the root relatedness of many distinct social motives.

Cognitive Consistency

According to Festinger's (1957) original theory of cognitive dissonance, holding two mutually exclusive cognitions produces an aversive tension state that people are motivated to reduce. Although Festinger was never particularly clear about why people seek to reduce inconsistency, he seemed to imply that motivation to reduce inconsistencies may be an inherent, "hardwired" aspect of cognitive systems. A similar assumption was made in the balance theories proposed by Heider (1944) and Newcomb (1953), which view the pursuit of consistency as a basic property of perceptual systems. People prefer consistency because it forms a pleasing gestalt and because inconsistency or imbalance is psychologically discombobulating. In this sense, the need for consistency is a psychological outgrowth of biological homeostasis. Just as certain physiological parameters must be sustained within circumscribed limits to promote physical stability in the service of continued existence, so too must cognitive consistency be maintained to promote psychological stability (also in the service of continued existence).

The alternative to viewing consistency as an innate need is to argue that people attempt to minimize inconsistencies because doing so serves a more basic psychological function. Over the years theorists have argued that inconsistencies may be minimized to sustain a positive self-image, deny responsibility for aversive consequences, or sustain a favorable public image (Cooper & Fazio, 1984; Steele, 1988; Tedeschi et al., 1971), and we have previously argued (Greenberg et al., 1986; Solomon et al., 1991b) that these interpretations of dissonance phenomena bring them within the domain of TMT. If dissonance results from a threat to the individual's sense of value and motivates

defense to restore that sense of value, it is an important mechanism by which the self-esteem component of the cultural anxiety buffer is sustained.

However, on empirical and conceptual grounds, we have recently come to believe that inconsistency may be disturbing to people, irrespective of its implications for public or private self-image. Empirically, recent evidence has shown that dissonance reduction can occur even when the counterattitudinal behavior has no aversive consequences (Aronson, Fried, & Stone, 1991; Harmon-Jones, Brehm, Greenberg, & Simon, 1994). In addition, whereas Steele's (1988) self-affirmation findings have provided the clearest support for the self-esteem view of dissonance phenomena, Simon, Greenberg, and Brehm (in press) have recently presented empirical support for an interpretation of these findings based on Festinger's original version of dissonance theory. Finally, the strongest existing evidence for the consistency version of dissonance theory may be Swann's self-verification findings (for a review, see Swann, 1987), which show that people sometimes prefer information consistent with self-beliefs over information supporting an inconsistent but more positive view of the self.

From a TMT perspective, consistency among cognitions is a necessary prerequisite for faith in an orderly and stable conception of reality that imbues life with meaning. If cognitions do not seem to follow from one another, then one is living an absurd Alice-in-Wonderland type existence in which nothing is sensible or explicable. In such a meaningless universe, there would be no basis for valuing oneself and feeling safe and secure. In addition, once the individual has become committed to a particular worldview as a basis for security, he or she becomes motivated to maintain faith in it. Thus, information consistent with that worldview is sought and information inconsistent with it is avoided or explained away because of the effect such information would have on faith in, and thus the effective functioning of, that conception. Inconsistency undermines the very foundation of the individual's potentially fragile psychological equanimity. [. . .]

Belief in a Just World

Although consistency is necessary for a worldview to be psychologically useful, it is not sufficient. Knowing that there is order and stability in life in no way guarantees that one will not be annihilated soon and possibly forever by events beyond one's personal control. To effectively serve its terror management function, one's worldview must provide a sense that behavior and outcomes are related in a just way, that if one lives up to cultural values, one will experience positive outcomes and ultimately qualify for death transcendence. This contingency between goodness and security is a key component of any worldview capable of assuaging existential terror.

According to Lerner's just-world hypothesis, people are motivated to believe that the world is a fair and just place where people deserve what they get and get what they deserve. Viewing the world in this way makes it seem safer, more manageable, and less frightening. Encounters with injustice, in which good people suffer or bad people reap rewards, threatens this conception and thus set off defensive reactions to restore our sense of justice. If justice cannot be restored behaviorally, then to reduce the threat, victims are blamed or derogated and the well off are elevated or seen as superior to those who are less fortunate. A large body of research has supported this view by showing that people become emotionally upset when they encounter injustice and that such encounters motivate them to do something to restore justice (for a review, see Lerner, Miller, & Holmes, 1976).

From the perspective of TMT, people need to believe that the world is just because such a conception makes emotional equanimity possible. Conceiving of the world as a just place, where the good are rewarded and the evil are punished, makes it possible for self-esteem to provide its anxiety-buffering function, because in a just world, the good do not suffer. Neither self-esteem nor a belief in justice alone is capable of providing this protection from anxiety. Being a valuable person in an absurd and chaotic universe is not particularly comforting, and a just world is not likely to be much of a source of comfort for a person who conceives of himself as evil and unlovable. From the perspective of TMT, just world beliefs are seen as part of the cultural worldview that provides protection from existential terror.

Consistent with this analysis are studies showing that mortality salience increases allocations of reward for persons who exemplify cultural standards and punishment for persons who violate such standards (e.g., Florian & Mikulciner, 1994; Ochsmann & Reichelt, 1993; Rosenblatt et al.,

1989). For example, it has been shown that thoughts of one's mortality lead participants to recommend harsher bond for a prostitute and more severe punishment for a man who abandons his wife and children. Likewise, it has been shown that mortality salience leads participants to recommend larger rewards for a person who provides police with information useful in apprehending a violent criminal or for a person who finds a wallet on the street and returns it to its owner. In general, mortality salience encourages people to favor larger rewards for the good and harsher punishment for the wicked.

Like Lerner (1980), we conceive of the just-world belief as more of an implicit, preconscious operating assumption than an explicit, consciously held attitude. Lerner has argued that the psychologically active aspect of just-world beliefs are largely unconscious, and that people's conscious beliefs about justice are probably mere cognitive overlays of relatively minor importance in providing psychological security. We have similarly argued that terror management operates outside of consciousness to serve unconscious needs (Solomon et al., 1991a). Consistent with this idea are recent studies showing that the effects of mortality salience are strongest when death thoughts are outside of current focal attention (Greenberg et al., 1994) and when participants are responding experientially rather than rationally. [. . .]

Objective Self-Awareness and Self-Regulation

Beliefs in consistency and justice are essential for sustaining faith in a terror-assuaging cultural worldview, but for most people, the social milieu in which they live provides an effective validating shield against threats to these fundamental beliefs. What is probably more often at issue in day-to-day life is sustaining the other component of the cultural anxiety-buffer: the valued self. A number of highly influential social psychological theories are focused on behavior that serves this function. Theories of self-awareness posit that when attention is focused on the self, people become motivated to reduce discrepancies between current state and salient standards (Carver & Scheier, 1981; Duval & Wicklund, 1972; Wicklund, 1975). From the perspective of TMT, this attempt to meet either one's own or one's audience's standards is viewed as an attempt to attain self-esteem by meeting cultural standards of value (either by living up to one's own standards or by enhancing the esteem with which one is held by the audience).

Although both Duval and Wicklund's (1972) and Carver and Scheier's (1981) formulations assume that self-focused attention leads to comparison of current state with standards—and indeed, there is evidence supporting this assumption (Scheier & Carver, 1983)—neither theory provides an explanation for why this is the case. TMT provides what we believe is a simple and straightforward explanation for this tendency (Pyszczynski & Greenberg, 1992; Pyszczynski, Greenberg, Solomon, & Hamilton, 1990). We have argued that the capacity for self-reflective thought is one of the cognitive building blocks that gives rise to the potential for existential terror. It is because we are capable of perceiving ourselves as separate and distinct objects, and because through imagination we can project these perceptions in time and space, that we are forced to realize that we will someday die. The theory posits that the potential for terror that arises out of our capacity for self-awareness is minimized by accepting and living up to cultural standards of value. Thus from our perspective, it is the potential for terror to which self-awareness gives rise that instigates the comparison with standards. Only by such comparisons and evaluations can we be sure that we actually are living up to the standards of our worldviews. Self-awareness leads to comparisons with standards because such comparisons short-circuit the potential for terror that would otherwise result. By comparing ourselves with cultural standards and working to make sure that our behavior conforms to them, we safely embed ourselves in the cultural drama and ensure that we are protected from our deep existential fears. [. . .]

Self-Esteem and Positive Social Identity

Whereas self-awareness and self-regulation theories focus on how people adjust their behavior to match their standards of value and the affective consequences of discrepancies, other theories focus on how people cope with existing self–standard discrepancies to protect self-esteem. The initial impetus for the development of TMT was to address the heretofore unasked question (in empirically oriented psychology) of why people need self-esteem. We posited that self-esteem, which is achieved by accepting a cultural conception of re-

ality and believing that one is living up to the standards of value that are part of that conception, functions to provide protection from deeply rooted fears concerning our vulnerability and mortality. Thus, from the perspective of TMT, people seek self-esteem because of the protection from anxiety that self-esteem provides. Similarly, to the extent that pride in the social groups to which one belongs ultimately functions to preserve one's self-esteem (Tajfel & Turner, 1979), the pursuit of a positive group identity is also ultimately rooted in the fear of death.

This terror management analysis is consistent with a broad range of findings concerning the pursuit and defense of self-esteem:

1. Self-esteem is negatively correlated with anxiety, anxiety-related behavior, and a wide range of physical and psychological disorders widely thought to be related to or caused by anxiety or stress (for a review, see Solomon et al., 1991b).
2. Situationally imposed threats to self-esteem engender anxiety (e.g., Leary, Barnes, & Griebel, 1986) and defensive responses, such as self-serving attributions and self-handicapping (for a review, see Greenberg et al., 1986).
3. Defense of self-esteem is mediated by negatively labeled arousal—in our terms, anxiety (e.g., Gollwitzer, Earle, & Stephan, 1982).
4. Successful defense of self-esteem minimizes the affective impact of failure and other threats to self-esteem (e.g., McFarland & Ross, 1982; Mehlman & Snyder, 1985). [. . .]

It could certainly be argued that people fear death because death implies the dissolution of self, that fear of biological death is rooted in a fear of the loss of one's identity. This is an interesting possibility, worthy of serious consideration, that essentially reverses the logic of our theory. Perhaps not surprisingly, we find this alternative view less compelling for several reasons. First, if one accepts the assumption that human psychological processes evolved out of simpler processes that existed in our prehuman ancestors (cf. Erchak, 1992), the precedence of the loss of self over loss of life seems difficult to conceive of. To the extent that the self is a linguistically based structure that depends on a variety of sophisticated cognitive capacities for its operation (cf. Pyszczynski et al., 1995), it is highly unlikely that even our closest primate cousins possess a true sense of self. Instinctive pursuit of continued life and avoidance of that which threatens one's continued existence, on the other hand, seems common to even the most primitive species. Thus motivation for life and the complementary avoidance of death seems to predate the existence of self ontogenetically. It seems unlikely that a relatively recent adaptation, such as the emergence of the self as the control center for goal-directed behavior, would be responsible for something likely to have existed long before the emergence of that particular adaptation.

The available empirical evidence also seems to favor the notion that the fear of death is a primary concern that cannot be reduced to a concern with self-esteem or self-integrity. Consistent with this view, research has shown that although thoughts about one's mortality consistently lead to increased worldview defense, thoughts of self-esteem threatening events (e.g., giving a speech or failing a test) or the actual experience of failure on a supposed test of intelligence—although capable of creating negative affect—do not produce parallel effects (Greenberg, Pyszczynski, et al., 1994; Greenberg, Simon, et al., 1995). Although the case is far from closed on this issue, we feel that the weight of both empirical evidence and conceptual argument favors the view that the need to manage existential terror is superordinate to and provides a compelling explanation for the need for self-esteem.

Self-Verification Theory

Although there is a great deal of conceptual and empirical convergence on the idea that people desire a positive self-image, there is one prominent line of theory and research that stands in stark contrast to this consensus—the work on self-verification tendencies. We address this work in some detail because it seems to challenge any theory that posits a need for self-esteem. Swann (1983, 1987) has argued that, because people need a consistent understanding of themselves for effective functioning, they employ a variety of self-verification strategies to confirm their existing self-images. Initially, proponents of self-verification theory argued that self-esteem-enhancing behavior is actually a special case of the pursuit of self-verification. If the majority of participants in experiments that purport to demonstrate the operation of a self-esteem motive initially had positive opinions of themselves, self-enhancing behavior might in fact be driven by a self-verification motive. That is,

participants in these studies behaved in a manner likely to prove their value only because they initially believed in their value; in fact, they were motivated to provide evidence consistent with their initially held self-conceptions. [. . .]

From the perspective of TMT, self-esteem is a means to an end rather than an end in and of itself. People—at least most people—pursue validation of their positive self-images because of the role that such self-conceptions play in controlling anxiety. Swann and colleagues' demonstrations of the pursuit of negative information about the self among low-self-esteem individuals usually entails selecting participants with low self-esteem from among the lowest 10 or 20% of the distribution of college students. Thus even this research suggests that the vast majority of people strive to maintain a positive self-image. However, the fact that most people control their anxiety through the maintenance of a positive self-image in no way implies that this is the only way that anxiety can be controlled, or that the pursuit of self-esteem is even the most adaptive way of accomplishing this.

We have posited that self-esteem acquires its anxiety-buffering properties by virtue of early experiences interacting with one's parents or primary caregivers (for a more complete account of this process, see Solomon et al., 1991a). Primitive associations formed early in life between the child's behavior, which meets or violates the parents' (and culture's) standards of goodness, and the parents' display of affection or displeasure, lead to the preconscious assumption of a contingency between valued behavior and warmth, protection, and safety. Later, more explicit teachings from the culture, in the form of fairy tales, stories, and religious teachings, reinforce the notion that the world is a just place where good behavior is rewarded and bad behavior is punished (cf. Lerner et al., 1976). As a consequence, the child learns to feel safe and secure when his or her behavior meets cultural standards and to experience a general sense of fear and anxiety when his or her behavior falls short of such standards.

This developmental analysis is intended to be a very general depiction of the typical way in which the socialization process unfolds. Unfortunately, there are some cases that do not fit this pattern. Some children get very little in the way of love, approval, or attention from their parents; some get exactly the opposite. Others receive random doses of rewards and punishments unconnected to their behavior or based on inconsistently applied standards. The child must nonetheless develop some means of controlling his or her fears and budding anxieties. It may be that in the absence of sufficient affection or consistently applied standards, these children develop negative self-conceptions and begin to use these conceptions as a means of controlling anxiety. It may be that from relatively early on, these children learn that by viewing themselves as worthless and behaving and speaking in a manner consistent with this view, they can minimize the abusive responses of their parents, and perhaps even elicit small displays of affection and sympathy from them (cf. Becker, 1964). In addition, these children may learn to derogate themselves as a way of making sense of their negative outcomes and sustaining a belief that the world is just (cf. Becker, 1973; Lerner & Simmons, 1966). [. . .]

We suggest, then, that there are indeed instances in which people are not motivated to maintain a positive self-image and also some in which they are motivated to maintain a negative self-image. In this sense, they can be said to be motivated to maintain consistency in their self-conceptions. However, it is not consistency per se that is the superordinate goal that they are pursuing, but rather, the protection from anxiety that is provided by whatever conception of themselves they have become invested in.

Our discussion thus far has focused on concerns about one's private self-image; however, if the self is ultimately a cultural construction, then much social behavior is also motivated by concerns about the way one is viewed by others. This, of course, is the domain of theories of self-presentation or impression management.

Theories of Self-Presentation and Impression Management

People live in a social world in which they are heavily dependent on others for a wide range of outcomes. Everything we need and want in life, from tangible commodities such as money and sex, to more abstract entities like respect, admiration, and social power, depends on the way others view us. Impression management or self-presentation theories argue that, because of this dependence on others, people are strongly motivated to control the impressions that others form of them (e.g., Baumeister, 1982; Goffman, 1959; Jones, 1964;

Schlenker, 1980). A great deal of evidence has accumulated to support this general contention. There is good evidence that people do indeed alter their behavior in ways likely to create a desired impression on others. It is also clear that this impression management process can be a very subtle and complex one, involving the use of intricate strategies that can vary widely from setting to setting (cf. Goffman, 1959; for a recent review of impression management research, see Leary & Kowalski, 1990). [. . .]

What is it that people are seeking when they attempt to control the way that other's view them? We suggest that, in most cases, their penultimate goal is that of maintaining either a positive self-image or faith in their cultural worldview. We care about what others think because we are heavily dependent on them for the maintenance of our own conceptions of self and world. We need them to validate us, to tell us that we really are as bright, attractive, and wonderful as we would like to believe we are, and that the world is really as we perceive it. If no one but ourselves could see these qualities, it would be very difficult indeed to maintain faith that they are as we perceive them. Thus, as a variety of other theorists have suggested (cf. Baumeister, 1982; Goffman, 1955; Mead, 1934), people use others as a means of creating and validating their identities and worldviews. Our sense of meaning, personal value, and identity all arise out of, and are sustained through, our interactions with others.

Research has provided evidence consistent with this view of the pursuit of public image being rooted in a more basic quest for self-esteem. For example, Greenberg and Pyszczynski (1985) showed that the presence of an audience observing a person's failure increased the extent of that person's later defensive reactions in a completely anonymous and private setting. Others have also found increased private defense following a threat to public self-image (e.g., Apsler, 1975; Tesser & Paulhus, 1983). This evidence suggests that what is at stake in public is often not so much one's image in the eyes of the specific present audience, but the underlying private self-esteem that is affected by the public impressions one makes. From a terror management perspective, this is a crucial concern because others who share one's basic worldview are the ultimate validators of the fragile social fiction that is our private sense of meaning and value.

Note we said that the pursuit of identity and value is the *penultimate* goal underlying *a great deal* of self-presentational behavior. As should be clear by this point, we view the pursuit of self-esteem and faith in one's worldview as a means to an end rather than an end in and of itself. Self-esteem is needed because of its central role in controlling anxiety concerning our vulnerability and mortality. Thus we seek others' approval and confirmation of our beliefs in order to maximize our self-esteem and faith in our worldviews; we seek these psychological entities because of the role they play in protecting us from deeply rooted fears about life, death, and existence. Recent findings that subtle death-related stimuli lead to an overestimation of consensual support for one's attitudes is consistent with this view (Pyszczynski, Wicklund, et al., in press). [. . .]

In sum, we suggest that people care about what others think, and alter their behavior to create favorable impressions in others, because they are heavily dependent on others for the maintenance of their symbolic fictions. Impression management theory is concerned with our motivation to influence the way that others perceive and evaluate us. From the perspective of TMT, impression management behavior is seen as helping us validate or verify one aspect of the cultural anxiety buffer, self-esteem. As much as we might like to, we can't simply believe whatever we want (cf. Festinger, 1957). To be confident that our perceptions and evaluations reflect the world "as it really is," we need other people to perceive and evaluate things as we do. As Carlos Casteneda's fictional Don Juan observed, "The average person seeks approval in the eyes of others and calls it self-confidence."

Reacting to and Managing Others' Impressions of External Reality: Social Influence

Closely related to the desire to control the impressions that others form of ourselves is the desire to control the way that others view external reality. Because of our dependence on others for validation, it is important that others' perceptions of the world line up nicely with our own, thus "proving" the correctness and validity of our own perceptions and enhancing their effectiveness for the management of existential terror. Just as faith in our personal value depends on others sharing our positive self-evaluations, so too does faith in our conception of external reality depend on others sharing these conceptions.

We have derived two basic implications from this analysis, one well supported and the other yet to be studied. The first implication is that thoughts of death should lead to positive reactions to those who support one's worldview and negative reactions to those who challenge one's worldview. In support of this notion, a substantial body of research has shown that mortality salience increases the favorability of reactions to fellow ingroupers and decreases the favorability of reactions to outgroupers, whether the group distinctions are based on long-standing religious, national, or political distinctions (Greenberg, et al., 1990, 1992; Ochsmann & Mathay, 1994), or are based on minimal categorization criteria such as aesthetic preferences (Harmon-Jones, Simon, et al., in press). These findings suggest that prejudice is motivated at least in part by the desire to sustain faith in one's worldview.

Although TMT is consistent with the core tenets of social identity theory, we believe it provides a more complete explanation of prejudice.[2] The theories concur that intergroup bias is often rooted in the need for self-esteem; from a terror management perspective, intergroup bias can help sustain the self-esteem component of the cultural anxiety buffer. However, TMT also specifies a second motivation for intergroup bias that may play an even larger role in prejudice—the motivation to maintain the other component of the cultural anxiety buffer, faith in one's cultural worldview.

The available research is highly consistent with the terror management view of intergroup bias in showing that mortality salience increases ingroup favoritism and prejudice (e.g., Greenberg et al., 1990; Ochsman & Mathay, 1994). In contrast, the evidence for the role of self-esteem concerns, the only determinant of intergroup bias proposed by social identity theory, suggests that these effects are much more limited and circumscribed than originally proposed (e.g., Crocker, Thompson, McGraw, & Ingerman, 1987; Meindl & Lerner, 1984). The existing evidence suggests that threats

---

[2]Social identity theorists and researchers should be lauded for their study of specific aspects of intergroup relations as they relate to social identity concerns. This work is on a level of analysis different from that of TMT; in fact, TMT is largely silent on many of these aspects of intergroup relations

to self-esteem increase intergroup bias only if the individual's identity as a member of the relevant group is highly salient when the threat is experienced. Thus social identity concerns can lead to an increase in intergroup bias, but only when the implications of such bias for self-evaluation are especially clear.

In contrast, the implications of others for faith in one's worldview are very often likely to be clear. When others are members of our group or share our beliefs, they help validate our worldview; when others are members of groups with different beliefs, when they express different views, they challenge our worldviews. This can account not only for the many demonstrations of mortality-salience effects on reactions to similar and dissimilar others, but also brings us to the second implication of TMT for intergroup relations: that people should be strongly motivated to control the way others perceive aspects of external reality that are central to their worldviews. Because of our need for consensual validation of our worldviews, we are often strongly motivated to manage the perceptions of external reality held by others. Thus a great deal of energy is devoted to persuading others to join us in sharing our beliefs, attitudes, and values— that our worldview is ultimately the best and most correct of all possible worldviews.

Evangelical activity is probably the clearest and most direct example of this desire to control the worldviews of others. Throughout history, many cultures have sent out messengers to proselytize and convert those from other cultures who see the world differently. By converting others to the correctness of one's faith, one increases one's own confidence in it. Less dramatic but equally relevant are the endless arguments that people engage in over politics, social issues, religion, art, music— almost anything that people care about can be a source of contention and lead to fervent attempts at influence. We suggest that the desire to persuade is usually rooted in a more basic desire to convince oneself of the correctness of one's own position. Whereas the existence of others who see things differently threatens this faith, the active conversion of such people to one's own view both eliminates the threat imposed by their deviance and demonstrates the superiority and correctness of one's own perspective—if my view wasn't right, why did the other guy come around to it when I explained it in terms he could understand?

Unfortunately, there has been little in the way of systematic research on the antecedents of the social influence process. Although hundreds of studies have been conducted to investigate the effects of social-influence attempts and the processes through which such influence occurs, relatively little attention has been focused on the roots of the desire to influence. Perhaps this emphasis on understanding how social influence occurs over the reasons why people are so motivated to engage in social influence reflects the importance society places on learning how to better influence others to perceive the world and behave in "appropriate" ways.

What Do We Need the Most?

If all of the social motives previously discussed are ultimately oriented toward controlling deeply rooted fears concerning human vulnerability and mortality, one might ask which of these more circumscribed social motives is most basic—what do we need the most? This question has cropped up in many different forms over the years: Is consistency more important than self-enhancement? Is public image more important than private self-concept? Is individual self-concept more important than social identity? In contrast to Maslow's (1943) hierarchy of motives, the current hierarchical model offers no clear ranking of the prepotency of motives.

From our perspective, questions of whether consistency, self-esteem, justice, or public image are more important to the individual's psychological well-being are analogous to questions of whether food, water, or shelter are more important to the individual's physical well-being. They are all basic needs that ultimately serve the same superordinate psychological (or biological) function. Just as food, water, and shelter are different but essential ways of keeping one's body alive and functioning, consistency, justice, esteem, and approval are different but essential ways of controlling the fear associated with the ultimate impossibility of staying alive and functioning.

Which motive is strongest in any individual at any point in time depends on a host of historical and situational factors that ultimately boil down to a matter of how this particular individual learned to control basic fears early in life, and what this particular individual is most deprived of at this particular point in time. Although, because of their early interactions with their primary caregivers, most people learn to use a positive self-image as a central component of their armor against existential fear, others learn to rely more heavily on other psychological entities. Early difficulties in attaining or sustaining particular psychological states may also channel certain individuals to be particularly sensitive to their current maintenance. For example, as Bowlby (1969) has suggested, the formation of insecure attachments with one's primary caregivers may make one especially dependent on the approval of others in one's adult life. Recent priming of particular needs and current situational pressures may also help tip the balance toward one or another particular desired psychological end state. For example, a recent failure in the pursuit of an ego-relevant goal may make one especially needy of self-esteem-enhancing feedback for days or weeks. Likewise, a current threat to any aspect of the anxiety-buffering system is likely to make that particular need come immediately to the forefront of one's psychological functioning. Thus from our perspective, the answer to questions concerning the dominance among motives is to be found in understanding the genesis and functioning of these motives in concert with an understanding of the dispositions, socialization, and unique psychological situation of the individual rather than in the motives themselves.

Conclusion

The purpose of this article has been to address the question of why people are motivated to obtain and sustain a variety of specific and distinct psychological entities. To this end, we discussed the role of terror management concerns in a variety of important symbolic social motives and attempted to place these symbolic motives in a broader evolutionary and self-regulatory context. We argue that all motivational processes are ultimately oriented toward the survival of the individual, and that many symbolic social motives are ultimately oriented toward controlling existential terror by sustaining faith in a culturally derived worldview and one's sense of value based on the standards of that worldview. TMT provides an integrative framework that can be used to explain the function and relatedness of many specific social motives. Although many hypotheses remain to be tested concerning the relation between terror management needs and other more specific motives, we have

accumulated a substantial body of evidence to support the role of terror management concerns in various specific domains that cannot be readily accounted for in other ways. Although generally complementary with other theories of social motivation, we believe that TMT makes a unique contribution to the study of each of the social motives we have discussed.

We believe that the question of why people need what they need is a very important one. Any complete account of a particular social motive ought to explain why that need exists, what more basic psychological function it serves. Although many extant motivational theories do address this question, others take the focal need as an unexplained postulate. By tying many social motives to the basic existential concerns of the human species, which in turn are tied to an even more basic animal instinct for survival, the terror management framework provides a linkage between the psychological and biological sides of the human organism. In addition, the hierarchical terror-management framework provides conceptual links between what have been considered quite different forms of social behavior. Given that the same organism is involved in the pursuit of consistency, justice, self-esteem, and favorable public images, it should be advantageous to be able to explain much of what we know about these diverse phenomena with a few motivational constructs rather than with topic specific mini-theories that do not examine the more basic motivational programming underlying the individual's needs.

This is not to imply that more concrete theories of the dynamics of specific motives are unnecessary. Although TMT may provide a unifying framework that explains the functions of many psychological motives, there are many questions about the dynamics of specific motivational processes that the theory does not address. For example, TMT provides little in the way of insight into the conditions under which inconsistent cognitions will be motivating, the specific cognitive distortions that will be engaged to defuse threats to self-esteem, or the particular self-presentational tactics that will be used to impress a given audience. For these and many other questions, domain-specific theories are needed that explicate the precise workings of specific motivational systems.

Nonetheless, we feel that a terror management analysis provides useful insights into all of the specific motives to which it can be applied. Our hope is that this article will provoke lively discussion that will help move us toward a fuller understanding of the nature and functioning of human social motivation. Beyond the theoretical utility of moving toward such a goal, understanding the superordinate functions of particular motives should enable us to help individuals who are having difficulties with any specific motive. Understanding what people are really seeking when they pursue self-esteem, pride in the groups to which they belong, a consistent and just conception of the world, or favorable regard from others ultimately may have the liberating effect of providing alternative means of achieving the basic functions that these more specific psychological motives are designed to serve.

REFERENCES

Alexander, I. E., Colley, R. W., & Adlerstein, A. M. (1957). Is death really a matter of indifference? *Journal of Psychology, 43,* 277–283.

Allport, G. W. (1954). *The nature of prejudice.* Garden City, NY: Addison-Wesley.

Apsler, R. (1975). Effects of embarrassment on behavior toward others. *Journal of Personality and Social Psychology, 32,* 145–153.

Aronson, E., Fried, C., & Stone, J. (1991). AIDS prevention and dissonance: A new twist on an old theory. *American Journal of Public Health, 81,* 1636–1638.

Baldwin, M. W., Carrell, S. E., & Lopez, D. F. (1990). Priming relationship schemas: My advisor and the Pope are watching me from the back of my mind. *Journal of Experimental Social Psychology, 26,* 435–460.

Baumeister, R. F. (1982). A self-presentational view of social phenomena. *Psychological Bulletin, 91,* 3–26.

Becker, E. (1964). *The revolution in psychiatry: The new understanding of man.* New York: Free Press.

Becker, E. (1973). *The denial of death.* New York: Free Press.

Bowlby, J. (1969). *Attachment and loss: Vol. 1.* New York: Basic Books.

Buss, D. (1994). *The evolution of desire.* New York: Basic Books.

Carver, C. S., & Scheier, M. F. (1981). *Attention and self-regulation: A control theory approach to human behavior.* New York: Springer-Verlag.

Cooper, J., & Fazio, R. H. (1984). A new look at dissonance theory. In L. Berkowitz (Ed.), *Advances in experimental social psychology,* (Vol. 10. pp 229–267). New York: Academic.

Crocker, J., Thompson, L. L., McGraw, K. M., & Ingerman, C. (1987). Downward comparison, prejudice, and evaluation of others. Effects of self-esteem and threat. *Journal of Personality and Social Psychology, 52,* 907–916.

Deci, E. L., & Ryan, R. M. (1991). A motivational approach to self: Integration in personality. In R. A. Dienstbier (Ed.), *Nebraska symposium on motivation: Perspectives in motivation* (Vol. 38, pp. 237–288). Lincoln: University of Nebraska Press.

Duval, S., & Wicklund, R. A. (1972). *A theory of objective self-awareness.* New York: Academic.

Erchak, G. M. (1992). *The anthropology of self and behavior.* New Brunswick, NJ: Rutgers University Press.

Festinger, L. (1957). *A theory of cognitive dissonance.* Evanston, IL: Row, Peterson.

Florian, V., & Mikulciner, M. (1994). *Fear of personal death and the judgment of social transgressions: An expansion of terror management theory.* Unpublished manuscript. Bar-Ilan University, Ramat Gan, Israel.

Freud, S. (1933). *New introductory lectures on psycho-analysis.* New York: Norton.

Goffman, E. (1955). On face-work: An analysis of ritual elements in social interaction. *Journal of the Study of Interpersonal Processes, 18,* 211–231.

Goffman, E. (1959). *The presentation of self in everyday life.* New York: Anchor.

Gollwitzer, P. B., Earle, W. B., & Stephan, W. G. (1982). Affect as a determinant of egotism: Residual excitation and performance attributions. *Journal of Personality and Social Psychology, 43,* 702–709.

Greenberg, J., & Pyszczynski, T. (1985). Compensatory self-inflation: A response to the threat to self-regard of public failure. *Journal of Personality and Social Psychology, 49,* 273–280.

Greenberg, J., Pyszczynski, T., & Solomon, S. (1986). The causes and consequences of the need for self-esteem: A terror management theory. In R. F. Baumeister (Ed.), *Public self and private self* (pp. 189–212). New York: Springer-Verlag.

Greenberg, J., Pyszczynski, T., & Solomon, S. (1995). Towards a dual motive depth psychology of self and social behavior. In M. Kernis (Ed.), *Self-efficacy and self-regulation.* New York: Plenum.

Greenberg, J., Pyszczynski, T., Solomon, S., Pinel, E., Simon, L., & Jordan, K. (1993). Effects of self-esteem on vulnerability-denying defensive distortions: Further evidence of an anxiety-buffering function of self-esteem. *Journal of Experimental Social Psychology, 29,* 229–251.

Greenberg, J., Pyszczynski, T., Solomon, S., Rosenblatt, A., Veeder, M., Kirkland S., & Lyon, D. (1990). Evidence for terror management theory II: The effects of mortality salience reactions to those who threaten or bolster the cultural worldview. *Journal of Personality and Social Psychology, 58,* 308–318.

Greenberg, J., Pyszczynski, T., Solomon, S., Simon, L., & Breus, M. (1994). The role of consciousness and the specificity to death of mortality salience effects. *Journal of Personality and Social Psychology, 67,* 627–637.

Greenberg, J., Porteus, J., Simon, L., Psyzczynski, T., & Solomon, S. (1995). Evidence of a terror management function of cultural icons: The effects of mortality salience on the inappropriate use of cherished cultural symbols. *Personality and Social Psychology Bulletin, 21,* 1221–1228.

Greenberg, J., Simon, L., Harmon-Jones, E., Solomon, S., Pyszczynski, T., & Lyon, D. (1995). Testing alternative explanations for mortality salience effects: Terror management, value accessibility, or worrisome thoughts. *European Journal of Social Psychology, 25,* 417–433.

Greenberg, J., Simon, L., Pyszczynski, T., Solomon, S., & Chatel, D. (1992). Terror management and tolerance: Does mortality salience always intensify negative reactions to others who threaten one's worldview? *Journal of Personality and Social Psychology, 63,* 212–220.

Greenberg, J., Solomon, S., Pyszczynski, T., Rosenblatt, A., Burling, J., Lyon, D., Simon, L., & Pinel, E. (1992). Why do people need self-esteem? Converging evidence that self-esteem serves an anxiety-buffering function. *Journal of Personality and Social Psychology, 63*, 913–922.

Greenwald, A. G., & Ronis, D. L. (1978). Twenty years of cognitive dissonance: Case study of the evolution of a theory. *Psychological Review, 85*, 53–57.

Harmon-Jones, E., Brehm, J., Greenberg, J., & Simon, L. (1994). *Evidence of dissonance reduction in the absence of aversive consequences.* Unpublished manuscript. University of Arizona, Tucson.

Harmon-Jones, E., Greenberg, J., Solomon, S., & Simon, L. (1994). *The effects of mortality salience on intergroup discrimination in the minimal group paradigm.* Unpublished manuscript. University of Arizona. Tucson.

Harmon-Jones, E., Simon, L., Greenberg, J., Pyszczynski, T., & Solomon, S., & McGregor, H. (in press). Assessing the terror management analysis of self-esteem. Evidence that self-esteem undermines mortality salience effects. *Journal of Personality and Social Psychology.*

Heider, F. (1944). Social perception and phenomenal causality. *Psychological Review, 51*, 358–374.

Homans, G. C. (1961). *Social behavior: Its elementary forms.* New York: Harcourt Brace.

Horney, K. (1970). *Neurosis and human growth: The struggle toward self-realization.* New York: Norton. (Original work published 1950)

Jones, E. E. (1964). *Ingratiation.* New York: Appleton-Century-Crofts.

Kunda, Z. (1990). The case for motivated reasoning. *Psychological Bulletin, 108*, 480–498.

Leary, M. R., Barnes, B. D., & Griebel, C. (1986). Cognitive, affective, and attributional effects of potential threats to self-esteem. *Journal of Social and Clinical Psychology, 4*, 461–474.

Leary, M. R., & Kowalski, R. M. (1990). Impression management: A literature review and two-component model. *Psychological Bulletin, 107*, 34–47.

Lerner, M. J. (1980). *The belief in a just world: A fundamental delusion.* New York: Plenum.

Lerner, M. J., Miller, D. T., & Holmes, J. G. (1976). Deserving and the emergence of forms of justice. In L. Berkowitz (Ed.), *Advances in experimental social psychology* (Vol. 9, pp. 134–160). New York: Academic.

Lerner, M. J., & Simmons, C. H. (1966). Observers' reactions to the "innocent victim": Compassion or rejection? *Journal of Personality and Social Psychology, 4*, 203–210.

Maslow, A. H. (1943). A theory of human motivation. *Psychological Review, 50*, 370–396.

McFarland, C., & Ross, M. (1982). Impact of causal attributions on affective reactions to success and failure. *Journal of Personality and Social Psychology, 43*, 937–946.

Mead, G. H. (1934). *Mind, self and society.* Chicago: University of Chicago Press.

Mehlman, R. C., & Snyder, C. R. (1985). Excuse theory: A test of the self-protective role of attributions. *Journal of Personality and Social Psychology, 4*, 994–1001.

Meindl, J. R., & Lerner, M. J. (1984). Exacerbation of extreme responses to an outgroup. *Journal of Personality and Social Psychology, 47*, 71–84.

Newcomb, T. M. (1953). An approach to the study of communicative acts. *Psychological Review, 60*, 393–404.

Nisbett, R. E., & Wilson, T. D. (1977). Telling more than we can know: Verbal reports on mental processes. *Psychological Review, 84*, 231–259.

Ochsmann, R., & Mathay, M. (1994). *Depreciating and distancing from foreigners: Effects of mortality salience.* Unpublished manuscript. University of Mainz, Germany.

Ochsmann, R., & Reichelt, K. (1994). *Evaluation of moral and immoral behavior: Evidence for terror management theory.* Unpublished manuscript. University of Mainz, Germany.

Powers, W. T. (1978). Quantitative analysis of purposive systems—Some spadework at foundations of scientific psychology. *Psychological Review, 85*, 417–435.

Pyszczynski, T., Becker, L. A., Greenberg, J., Solomon, S., Vandeputte, D., & Stewart-Fouts, M. (1994). *Evidence that the cultural worldview provides a buffer against death-related anxiety.* Unpublished manuscript. University of Colorado, Colorado Springs.

Pyszczynski, T., & Greenberg, J. (1987). Self-regulatory perseveration and the depressive self-focusing style: A self-awareness theory of reactive depression. *Psychological Bulletin, 102*, 1–17.

Pyszczynski, T., & Greenberg, J. (1992). *Hanging on and letting go: Understanding the onset, progression and remission of depression.* New York: Springer-Verlag.

Pyszczynski, T., Greenberg, J., Solomon, S., & Hamilton, J. (1990). A terror management analysis of self-awareness and anxiety: The hierarchy of terror. *Anxiety Research, 2*, 177–195.

Pyszczynski, T., Greenberg, J., Solomon, S., Sideris, J., & Stubing, M. J. (1993). Emotional expression and the reduction of motivated cognitive bias: Evidence from cognitive dissonance and distancing from victim paradigms. *Journal of Personality and Social Psychology, 64*, 177–186.

Pyszczynski, T., Solomon, S., & Greenberg, J., Stewart-fouts, M. (1995). The liberating and constraining aspects of self: Why the freed bird finds a new cage. In A. Oosterwegel & R. A. Wicklund (Eds.), *The self in European and North American culture: Development and processes.* Amsterdam: Kluwer.

Pyszczynski, T., Wicklund, R. A., Floresku, S., Koch, S., Gauch, G., Solomon. S., & Greenberg, J. (in press). Whistling in the dark: Exaggerated consensus estimates in response to incidental reminders of mortality. *Psychological Science.*

Rank, O. (1976). *Will therapy and truth and reality.* New York: Knopf. (Original work published 1936)

Rank, O. (1989). *Art and artist: Creative urge and the personality development.* New York: Norton. (Original work published 1936)

Robles, R., Smith, R., Carver, C. S., & Wellens, A. R. (1987). Influence of subliminal visual images on the experience of anxiety. *Personality and Social Psychology Bulletin, 13*, 399–410.

Rosenblatt, A., Greenberg, J., Solomon, S., Pyszczynski, T., & Lyon, D. (1989). Evidence for terror management theory I: The effects of mortality salience on reactions to those who violate or uphold cultural values. *Journal of Personality and Social Psychology, 57*, 681–690.

Scheier, M. F., & Carver, C. S. (1983). Self-directed attention and the comparison of self with standards. *Journal of Experimental Social Psychology, 19*, 205–222.

Schlenker, B. R. (1980). *Impression management.* Belmont, CA: Wadsworth.

Silverman, L. H., & Weinberger, J. (1985). Mommy and I are one: Implications for psychotherapy. *American Psychologist, 40,* 1296–1308.

Simon, L., Greenberg, J., & Brehm, J. (in press). Trivialization: The forgotten mode of dissonance reduction. *Journal of Personality and Social Psychology.*

Simon, L., Harmon-Jones, E., Solomon, S., & Pyszczynski, T. (1996). Mild depression, mortality salience, and defense of the cultural worldview: Evidence of intensified terror management in the mildly depressed. *Personality and Social Psychology Bulletin, 22,* 81–90.

Solomon, S., Greenberg, J., & Pyszczynski, T. (1991a). A terror management theory of social behavior: The psychological functions of self-esteem and cultural worldviews. In M. Zanna (Ed.), *Advances in experimental social psychology* (Vol. 24, pp. 93–159). San Diego: Academic.

Solomon, S., Greenberg, G., & Pyszczynski, T. (1991b). Terror management theory of self esteem. In C. R. Snyder & D. Forsyth (Eds.), *Handbook of social and clinical psychology: The health perspective* (pp. 21–40). New York: Pergamon.

Steele, C. M. (1988). The psychology of self-affirmation: Sustaining the integrity of the self. In L. Berkowitz (Ed.), *Advances in experimental social psychology* (Vol. 21, pp. 261–302). San Diego, CA: Academic.

Swann, W. B., Jr. (1983). Self-verification: Bringing social reality into harmony with the self. In J. Suls & A. G. Greenwald (Eds.), *Social psychological perspectives on the self* (Vol. 2, pp. 33–66). Hillsdale, NJ: Lawrence Erlbaum Associates, Inc.

Swann, W. B., Jr. (1987). Identity negotiation: Where two roads meet. *Journal of Personality and Social Psychology, 53,* 1038–1051.

Tajfel, H., & Turner, J. (1979). An integrative theory of intergroup conflict. In W. G. Austin & S. Worchel (Eds.), *The social psychology of intergroup relations.* Pacific Grove, CA: Brooks/Cole.

Tedeschi, J. T., Schlenker, B. R., & Bonoma, T. V. (1971). Cognitive dissonance: Private ratiocination or public spectacle? *American Psychologist, 26,* 685–695.

Tesser, A. (1988). Toward a self-evaluation maintenance model of social behavior. In L. Berkowitz (Ed.), *Advances in experimental social psychology* (Vol. 21, pp. 181–227). San Diego, CA: Academic.

Tesser, A., & Paulhus, D. (1983). The definition of self: Private and public self-evaluation maintenance strategies. *Journal of Personality and Social Psychology, 44,* 672–682.

Tetlock, P. E., & Levi, A. (1982). Attribution bias: On the inconclusiveness of the cognition–motivation debate. *Journal of Experimental Social Psychology, 18,* 68–88.

Vallacher, R. R., & Wegner, D. M. (1985). *Action identification theory.* Hillsdale, NJ: Lawrence Erlbaum Associates, Inc.

Walster, E., Walster, G. W., & Bencheid, E. (1978). *Equity: Theory and research.* Boston: Allyn & Bacon.

Weary, G. (1979). Self-serving attributional biases: Perceptual or response distortions. *Journal of Personality and Social Psychology, 37,* 1418–1420.

White, R. W. (1959). Motivation reconsidered: The concept of competence. *Psychological Review, 66,* 297–333.

Wicklund, R. A. (1975). Objective self-awareness. In L. Berkowitz (Ed.), *Advances in experimental social psychology* (Vol. 8, pp. 233–275). New York: Academic.

INTRODUCTION TO PART 2

When Wants Change

A particularly interesting feature of human motivation is its malleability. We may have strong wants at a given moment that decline or entirely disappear the next moment or are replaced by other wants that then move our behavior in a different direction. It is common knowledge that wants can be fulfilled. For example, physiological deficits can be eliminated through appropriate activities (such as eating or drinking in the cases of hunger or thirst), and discrepancies from desired states of affairs can be removed once those particular states are attained (e.g., one is accepted to a firm one aspired to join, one is offered the job of which one had dreamt, or one finally completes the requirements for a coveted academic degree).

But there are other, perhaps more interesting, ways in which our wants may change. Developmental shifts are one factor that determines the changes in our wants at the different points in our lives. Psychodynamic models, for instance, discuss biologically-linked developmental shifts in the basic preoccupations or problems to which people attend, and these influence which wants are emphasized at any given stage (e.g., Erikson, 1963; Freud, 1905/1953). Beyond physiological and psychological maturation, there exist transitions and life phases dictated by culture and society (e.g., the phases of education, work, establishing a family, retirement), which are the changes that have received the most attention in the social and personality literature. Each life phase includes basic tasks that need to be fulfilled, and changes in life-tasks alter the nature of individuals' goals or current concerns and the relative emphasis they receive.

97

It is of interest, moreover, that such life tasks may be approached very differently by different people depending on their other goals and their relative importance, and depending on the strategic means they have learned to apply toward goal attainment. Cantor's (1994) paper in the present section demonstrates how different individuals approach the same life-tasks through vastly different strategies. Cantor's paper also demonstrates that we often seek out social situations in which particular affordances match our personal wants. In that sense the profile of our wants may account in part for the great variety of behavioral styles (i.e., what we do, where we go, with whom we associate) that people may exhibit.

Social and personality psychologists have strongly emphasized that motivated behavior, that is, activities we pursue en route to our goals, is typically accompanied by a considerable amount of appraisal. Even though our basic needs may be relatively fixed and universal, the subordinate objectives that derive from these activities are selected carefully on the basis of extensive appraisal. The article by Folkman et al. (1986) featured in the present section illustrates this with respect to a negative goal, the desire to extricate oneself from stressful circumstances. These authors distinguish between a primary appraisal related to the determination of whether the situation involves potential harm, and hence is stressful, whereas secondary appraisal involves the evaluation of various coping options such as ways of altering the situation, or leaving it altogether. The option ultimately chosen would depend on the individual's perceived resources, for example her or his skills in a particular domain, the necessary effort, and the likelihood and degree of the harm involved.

The final article in this section by Deci and Ryan (1987), discusses another way in which situations may interact with the individual's characteristics to determine her or his wants and actions. These authors discuss the basic human need for autonomy and the way persons react to controlling situations that put autonomy in jeopardy. External threats, rewards, surveillance, or critical commentary can be controlling and may put the individual under pressure. Personal states may also undermine autonomy such as public self-consciousness, competitive orientation, and external locus of control. The authors demonstrate that autonomously motivated activities have several important psychological advantages over activities where the individual feels externally controlled. Autonomously performed activities are enjoyed more, performed more creatively and flexibly, as well as in a more relaxed manner than are controlled activities.

REFERENCES

Cantor, N. (1994). Life task problem-solving: Situational affordances and personal needs. *Personality and Social Psychology Bulletin, 20,* 235–243.

Deci, E. L., & Ryan, R. M. (1987). The support of autonomy and the control of behavior. *Journal of Personality and Social Psychology, 55,* 1024–1037.

Erikson, E. H. (1963). *Childhood and society* (Revised edition. Original edition, 1950). New York: W. W. Norton.

Folkman, S., Lazarus, R. S., Dunkel-Schetter, C., DeLongis, A., & Gruen, R. (1986). The dynamics of a stressful encounter. *Journal of Personality and Social Psychology, 50,* 992–1003.

Freud, S. (1953). Three essays on the theory of sexuality. *Standard Edition*, Volume 7. London: Hogarth Press. (Original work published 1905)

Suggested Readings

Brehm, J. W., & Mann, M. (1975). The effect of importance of freedom and attraction to group members on influence produced by group pressure. *Journal of Personality and Social Psychology, 31,* 816–824.

Frey, K. S., & Ruble, D. N. (1985). What children say when the teacher is not around: Conflicting goals in social comparison and performance assessment in the classroom. *Journal of Personality and Social Psychology, 48,* 550–562.

Harackiewicz, J. M., Sansone, C., & Manderlink, G. (1985). Competence, achievement orientation, and intrinsic motivation: A process analysis. *Journal of Personality and Social Psychology, 48,* 493–508.

Kruglanski, A. W. (1975). The endogenous-exogenous partition in attribution theory. *Psychological Review, 82,* 387–406.

Wicklund, R. A., & Duval, S. (1971). Opinion change and performance facilitation as a result of objective self awareness. *Journal of Experimental Social Psychology, 7,* 319–342.

Life Task Problem-Solving: Situational Affordances and Personal Needs

Nancy Cantor • Princeton University

Editors' Notes

Can personality be reconceptualized from a situation-centered perspective? The author proposes that the same general activity, such as receiving support from others, can take different situational forms that afford different needs to be fulfilled, and individuals strategically select whichever situation affords their personal needs to be fulfilled. Evidence is presented of how late adolescents are strategic in selecting social support situations that afford fulfilling their particular achievement needs. For example, defensive pessimists seek social support situations with friends who will listen to their pessimistic anticipations of failure without reassuring them by reminding them of their past success, whereas individuals with a discrepancy between their past performance and their aspirations seek situations with successful friends who serve as models of what they desire to be like. This paper demonstrates how people are strategically motivated to engage in situations where their personal needs match the situational affordances.

Discussion Questions

1. How can situations be conceptualized as being a part of personality?
2. Provide examples of the strategic selection of situations to fulfill personal needs.

Authors' Abstract

An analysis of life task problem solving provides an illustration of a common language for personality and social psychologies. The personal needs of individuals and the situational affordances of social life interactively define strategic solutions to life task problems. Research on situations that encourage agentic or communal goals in late adolescents' pursuit of the intimacy life task and on three achievement strategies in which social support takes different forms to serve different individuals' needs exemplifies the coordination of what people need to do and what situations afford to be done in daily-life problem solving.

Personality and social psychologists seem increasingly to be working from what Higgins (1990) called a "common language." There is much common cause in our interests, there is much common fate in our outcomes, and as scientists of social behavior, we often ask (surprisingly) similar questions. In other words, it seems clearer than ever that the caricatures of personality psychology, on the one hand, as concerned with "the person" and of social psychology, on the other hand, as concerned with "the situation" are descriptively inaccurate now (as they probably have been for quite some time), as well as being roadblocks to this emerging common language.

From the perspective of personality psychology, a situation-centered strategy for understanding personality is flourishing (e.g., see Snyder & Ickes's, 1985, situationist strategy). In this view, individuals' personalities are defined by the situations they choose and influence in their daily lives (e.g., Buss, 1987; Emmons, Diener, & Larsen, 1986). This is illustrated in Fleeson's (1992) experience-sampling study of individual differences in implicit motive dispositions and self-regulation in daily life. Individuals high in need for power, for example, can be characterized as those for whom the opportunity in a situation to strongly influence others is critical to their enjoyment of and involvement in the situation, whether it is a classroom discussion or an intimate talk with a friend. Some situations readily provide that specific opportunity to be influential, and individuals high in need for power will seize it. That is, individuals' personalities are distinguished by their selective responsiveness to the opportunities in particular kinds of situations (Mischel, 1990).

From the perspective of social psychology, the complementary person-centered strategy for understanding situational effects is also flourishing. Following the Lewinian tradition, situations are understood as exerting an impact through their psychological significance for the individuals in them (see Higgins, 1990). For example, Niedenthal and her colleagues (e.g., Setterlund & Niedenthal, 1993) find that individuals' decisions in daily life, ranging from which restaurant to eat in to which kind of therapist to see, are often based on the degree of fit between their self-concepts and an image of the prototypic person for that situation. These situation prototypes signal for people the kinds of opportunities for self represented by a choice to be in that situation. For example, a prototype for a particular fancy restaurant may suggest the opportunity to be a gourmet. However, only individuals who have a clear concept of what they are like (or would like to be like) in relevant domains pay attention to these situational opportunities in their choices. For others, these situational opportunities for self are not important, because they make these choices on the basis of non-self-relevant criteria (e.g., "I choose restaurants by convenience"). That is, the psychological significance of situational opportunities strongly depends on the needs and goals of individual participants (Dweck, 1986).

Thus, as personality psychology increasingly embraces a situation-centered approach and social psychology takes a person-centered perspective, the traditional boundaries become ever more ill-defined. That is, the presence and influence of a common language are, more than ever, apparent in a variety of literatures. Baron and Boudreau (1987), for example, use the Gibsonian language of affordances to provide a compelling unifying description of persons and their matching situations. This commonality in approach emerges quite clearly as we consider the situations that define personality and the personalities that define situations.

Before trying to illustrate this commonality, I

should point out that I will be using the terms *situation* and *personality* in an inclusive, rather than a restrictive, way. Situations can be defined at the macro level of culture and social organizations or at the day-to-day micro level as the temporal, spatial, and interpersonal situations in which individuals take part (Cantor & Fleeson, 1991). Accordingly, I will take a situation-centered look at personality at both the macro and the micro levels. Similarly, personality can be alternatively defined by the macrolevel goals and dispositions of an individual or by his or her micro-level problems and behavioral strategies in specific situations (Cantor, 1990). Again, I will be drawing on both levels of analysis in considering the personalities that define situations.

Personality and Social Life as Problem Solving

In 1987, John Kihlstrom and I wrote a book, *Personality and Social Intelligence* (Cantor & Kihlstrom, 1987), in which we outlined a problem-solving approach to personality and social behavior. Our basic argument was that regularities in social behavior are connected to people's problem-solving efforts in daily life. To understand those regularities, we must understand the problems on which people work in their daily lives—which we called *life tasks*—and the *strategies* that characterize their attempted solutions. More to my point here, we argued that these life tasks and strategies represent the coming together of the individual and his or her current life situation. That is, the "situation" (both as macro-level culture and as micro-level situations) affords and encourages certain life tasks to be the problems for a person in each life period. Yet the "person," with his or her self-concept and autobiographical knowledge, finds a personal "problem" within that broader task and shapes those situations to help provide a strategic "solution." In other words, both the tasks and the strategies, the problems and the solutions, are jointly constructed by person and situation.

Although several traditions serve as a background for this interactionist, problem-solving perspective (Cantor & Zirkel, 1990), the framework for human development proposed by Erik Erikson seems especially valuable. Erikson (1950) argued that *both* individuals and their sociocultural environments work jointly on a successive set of life tasks—tasks that foster individual and group life (see also Havighurst, 1953). Life tasks take form largely in the micro-level rituals of home and schools and social organizations (Higgins & Parsons, 1983; Veroff, 1983). Individuals' tasks are defined in large part by the social rituals of a given life stage. Thus Erikson's is a situation-centered theory of personality development. For example, through rules and norms of social dating, families not only signal the task of intimacy to their older adolescents but also make it a particular kind of problem (e.g., group vs. couple dating). Conversely, those rituals also take different concrete forms according to the personal needs and developmental readiness of the individual participants, so that Erikson offers a person-centered theory of socialization. For example, an adolescent with a crisis over separating from family may enter the rituals of dating as a way of declaring independence. Individuals' particular problems will have an impact on the ways in which they work on the task in those age-graded rituals, changing the very nature of the situational affordances.

Erikson did not entirely follow his mentor's view of "civilization and its discontents" (cf. Freud, 1930/1961). He did not endorse the portrayal of an intractable discord between the interests, desires, and needs of organized society and of individuals. Although he too portrayed the process of personality development as an arduous one, he carefully emphasized the mutuality of purpose between individuals and society. He portrayed the normative journey as full of crises, incomplete solutions to normative tasks, and even perversions of rituals. Nonetheless, in his portrait, individuals and society muddle through this process together, as many recent self theorists have also emphasized (see, e.g., Markus & Cross, 1990).

This Eriksonian perspective informs much of the work that my students and I have done over the past several years. For example, for some years now, we have studied the transition into and through college in a variety of student subcultures, including a 5-year project with an Honors College sample and a semester-long project with women in a college sorority (Cantor et al., 1991; Cantor, Norem, Niedenthal, Langston, & Brower, 1987). Not surprisingly, the life tasks that our culture proclaims as age typical for college students, those of independence-identity and of intimacy, do indeed emerge as personally relevant to many in our samples (e.g., Cantor, Acker, & Cook-

Flannagan, 1992; Zirkel & Cantor, 1990). These age-typical life tasks, however, represent fairly broad problem-solving agendas within which particular life task problems get shaped by individuals in line with different situational opportunities and personal needs. Zirkel (1992) has documented this constructive alternativism for the independence life task, and Sanderson and I (e.g., Sanderson & Cantor, 1993) are currently doing the same for the intimacy life task.

In reviewing some of the work from these studies, I will start with our work on the intimacy life task in order to illustrate a situation-centered view of personality. I will consider how older adolescents pursue the intimacy life task as either a communal or an agentic problem in different age-typical situations. Thus the signature of the person can be seen in his or her selective responsiveness to different situational opportunities for intimacy. Conversely, taking a person-centered view of situations, I will also consider how individuals create situational opportunities in their strategic solutions to their particular task problems. In that case, I will focus on the clever ways in which the college students in these studies create different versions of social support to address their particular academic "problems"—thus making the people in their lives work for them, day to day.

A Situation-Centered Look at Personality

I begin, then, with a situation-centered look at how *the* intimacy life task becomes different "problems" in line with alternative opportunities in an age-typical context.

For older adolescents, in high school and college, the macro-level cultural context presents intimacy largely as a communal problem to be tackled. For example, Erikson (1950) framed the intimacy task as a communal pursuit to follow the more agentic strivings for identity and independence of earlier adolescence. In most descriptions of the pursuit of intimacy, the objective even in casual dating is to find, eventually, a close, serious relationship in which intimacy can be obtained (e.g., Hazan & Shaver, 1987). The serious relationship is, thus, the normative social ritual or situation within which to work on intimacy. In recent years, our cultural concerns with the ever-decreasing modal age for involvement in sexual relationships reflect in part this belief that intimacy should

be conditional on a serious commitment (although they also reflect public health concerns). As a result of making the serious relationship the microlevel situation for the pursuit of intimacy, the particular goals of communion (interdependence, trust, mutuality) are emphasized (McAdams, 1984).

Therefore, one situation-centered framing of the intimacy task is as a problem about communion in serious relationships. There is, however, another problem in the intimacy task that also makes some sense even for older adolescents. This is still, after all, a life period largely focused on self-development and independence, and the new-found freedoms of life away from home may encourage the pursuit of intimacy as an agentic problem with more agentic goals. Casual dating may provide a situation, for example, in which to try out different selves, to test a newly developed sense of independence from family, and to experiment with sexuality. In this situation, sexual activity, for example, can reinforce a personal sense of maturity and independence, even including the rewards of feeling skilled at protecting the self by engaging in safer sex. In other words, casual dating situations, rather than simply being steppingstones to the "real" pursuit of intimacy in serious relationships, may afford a different, more agentic meaning to the intimacy life task.

The social rituals of late adolescence, including casual as well as steady dating, afford the pursuit of agentic or communal goals in the intimacy life task. For the more agentic goals, the casual dating situation with many partners should provide the best opportunities for goal pursuit. In contrast, for the more communal goals, a serious relationship should provide a better situation for sharing, trust, and close communication. Moreover, because this is a life period full of expanding interest in both independence and interdependence, individual adolescents' personalities may well be marked by a stronger interest in one or the other goal and its associated dating situation. We may, therefore, see the signature of personality in the situations late adolescents pursue.

Sanderson and I have recently observed just such a situational marking of communal and agentic orientations to the intimacy life task. That is, we have been investigating the situations for pursuing intimacy and regulating sexual behavior that are more typically associated with a more communal orientation in this task ("In my dating relationships, I try to share my most intimate thoughts and feelings") or a more agentic one ("In my dating relationships, I try to maintain a strong sense of independence"). In a variety of college and high school student samples, we find that individuals' intimacy orientations (as measured on a brief, 14-item self-report scale) can be characterized by their responsiveness in different dating situations.

We find, for example, that different dating situations are more likely to be associated with participants who see the intimacy task as a problem of agency and with those who see it as one of communion. Longer-duration serious relationships are associated with a more communal orientation, whereas greater numbers of casual partners and lifetime sexual partners are associated with the more agentic orientation. Moreover, opportunities for engaging in safer sex within these different dating situations are differentially seized on by individuals with different intimacy orientations. Individuals with stronger agentic orientations report engaging in safer sexual activity in casual relationships—where they are more likely to feel comfortable being self-assertive and self-protective—than in more serious dating relationships. In contrast, individuals with stronger communal orientations report engaging in safer sexual activity in serious dating relationships—where they are more likely to feel comfortable negotiating and communicating about sex with their partner—than in casual dating situations (Sanderson & Cantor, 1993).

These situational patterns make sense if one thinks of the "problems" being pursued by individuals who report more communal or more agentic intimacy goals. In the serious relationship, the situation encourages interdependence and communication, and the regulation of sexual intimacy would best follow through that communication. In casual dating, the situation encourages self-assertion, and accordingly, safer sexual activity would be more likely to occur through that route than through interpersonal negotiation. In this way, these situations define alternative routes to safer sexual activity that are more or less congruent with communal or agentic goals for the intimacy task. Therefore, if you are a person who defines the intimacy task as mostly about interpersonal communion, then you will do better at regulating your sexual activity in a dating situation that encourages discussion and closeness (i.e., a serious relationship). However, if you are a person for whom

intimacy is more about personal agency than interpersonal communication, then you will be better able to regulate sexual activity in a casual dating situation that encourages you to focus on self-assertion.

We tested this differential responsiveness more directly with data from an HIV/AIDS intervention program that Catherine Sanderson designed with John Jemmott at Princeton (Sanderson & Cantor, 1993). In this program, she designed two intervention conditions: one to fit communally oriented goals (e.g., focusing on skills of negotiation and communication with partner about condom use) and another to fit agentically oriented goals (e.g., teaching technical skills to make a person feel efficacious in condom use). In a 3-month follow-up testing, participants were significantly more responsive on attitudinal measures of vulnerability to HIV/AIDS, and on measures of intentions to use condoms in the future, when the intervention was structured around their preferred goal orientation (i.e., technical skills for agentic and communication for communal).

All the participants in this program were highly motivated to learn about HIV/AIDS and to develop intentions to engage in safer sexual activity. Nonetheless, we believe that when they were exposed to an intervention that afforded them a better opportunity to pursue their typical intimacy goal, they were then also better able to actively take part in the program—that is, to engage the material, to turn the situation to their optimal advantage.

In other words, by examining differential responsiveness, we also see how individuals make optimal use of particular kinds of situations—namely, those that afford and encourage their particular purposes (cf. Baron & Boudreau, 1987). This brings us to individuals' strategies and to the person-centered analysis of situational affordances, to which I now turn.

A Person-Centered Look at Situations

As this analysis of intimacy task pursuit suggests, the problems on which individuals work are defined in the context of their typical daily life situations. Different situations afford, encourage, demand, and discourage particular problems to be pursued, and individuals' personalities are marked by their responsiveness to those particular affordances. In fact, just such an association of personality with situation prompted Snyder and Ickes (1985) to refer to this situation-centered approach as a social psychological analysis of personality.

Of course, there is also another perspective to take on this same interweaving of person and situation. To fill out the picture, we need to consider a person-centered analysis of situations. This alternative perspective, rather than emphasizing the meaning that is given to personality through the situations of daily life, highlights the structuring of situations around the problems of individuals. This person-centered approach emphasizes what people need to do in situations and the influences of their particular problems on those situations.

In a problem-solving analysis, we focus on *strategies* to see how individuals' problems in the task define the situation. Strategies are individuals' characteristic ways of handling problems in a task. One way to think of strategies is that they represent what a particular person needs out of a situation in order to keep working on the task. For example, consider the strategy of defensive pessimism, which both Norem (e.g., Norem & Illingworth, 1993) and Showers (1992) have elegantly analyzed. Defensive pessimists need to harness their anxiety before a task so that they can actually face the task (Norem, 1989). Simultaneously, they need to protect the self in the event of a poor performance (Showers, 1992). To do this, they set low expectations and do worst-case analyses before a task; these strategic maneuvers seem to free them to be quite task-focused during the task and not to ruminate after the task.

Strategies, such as defensive pessimism, enlist the help of situations; they require specific temporal, spatial, and interpersonal situations as props. For example, before a task, the defensive pessimist has to be able to anticipate possible worst-case outcomes without being reassured by others, whereas after the task, the same pessimist will not want to labor over what went wrong (Norem & Cantor, 1986). Situations, often defined by the people in them, have to cooperate with individuals' strategic efforts if they are to serve their "functions."

In the case of defensive pessimism, for example, a supportive situation for task pursuit clearly has to involve some fairly patient people—those who are willing both to put up with anticipatory pessimism and then not to be surprised by post hoc repression. In this case, a supportive situation is one

in which others listen but do not encourage, as attempts at encouragement interrupt defensive pessimists' strategic efforts. Notice, of course, that, from the outside, the presence of a nonreassuring other in the face of a highly successful defensive pessimist engaged in anticipatory gloom would look like anything but a scenario for functional social support. However, from a person-centered or "inside," perspective, the success of the strategy for overcoming the pessimist's particular problem depends crucially on just that sort of benign neglect as social support (e.g., as Norem & Cantor, 1986, demonstrated).

Understanding the pessimist's problem and his or her strategic solution tells us much about the form that functional social support can sometimes take. Of course, social support takes different forms for different individuals, depending on their particular problems (e.g., House & Kahn, 1985). Therefore, one way of understanding this support process is to investigate how different problems define different strategies that rely on varying forms of social support.

In studying such strategies, we have engaged in what might be called an ecological analysis of the daily-life pursuits of our college student samples. We use a variety of methods to try to piece together the individual's particular problem, his or her particular strategic response, and the situational conditions that support that response. For example, participants in our studies fill out a social network measure in which they tell us about the specific people in their current support network and the different roles they play (e.g., people who encourage me; people who discourage me; people whom I'd like to be more like; people who make me feel happy). By cross-referencing these social support reports with experience-sampling event reports, in which participants report on daily-life events as they occur, we can see how particular problems define the supportive situation. To expand on this point, I turn now to different strategic uses to which participants in our studies have put their social networks.

"Time with Friends": Turning a Communal Situation Toward Agentic Purposes

Some of the dearest examples in our research of how situations can be defined by the problems of individuals are in the domain of achievement strategies. In these strategies, the help of others is enlisted in very particular ways at very specific times in the face of particular problems. Consider the common situation in daily life of spending time with friends, defined in our studies through subjects' diary and event reports of what they were doing and/or who was with them. We have observed three quite different ways that this "situation" can serve a supportive function in the achievement pursuits of our college student subjects. These three strategies are of interest in part because they clearly illustrate the different ways that individuals utilize situational affordances in line with personal needs. Additionally, they are of unique interest as strategies because they implicate a set of commonly available social supports (e.g., Butler, 1992; Hill, 1987) that are used here quite discriminatively to meet a set of acute personal needs that are commonly observed to bring problem solving to a standstill without such strategic intervention (Cantor & Blanton, 1993).

Strategic Reassurance Seeking

Harlow (Harlow & Cantor, 1994), for example, has analyzed a strategy of reassurance seeking in the face of academic setbacks. In this strategy, individuals seek the company of friends in social situations like parties and relaxing in the dorm when things are not going well academically. Unlike defensive pessimists, these individuals seek specific reassurances from their friends in the face of academic obstacles. They were especially likely at these critical times to be with people from their network whom they view as "encouragers." Their diary and experience-sampling reports suggest that they did not engage in a variety of other possible responses to such setbacks. They did not study with friends when they were unhappy in academic pursuits; they did not ruminate alone in the face of these academic setbacks. Instead, they specifically reacted to academic setbacks by turning ostensibly *social* events into avenues for academic reassurance.

Why do they stretch these social events into forums for academic reassurance rather than engaging help more instrumentally? Harlow labeled these subjects *outcome focused* because of their particular problem in academics. Analysis of their life task appraisals (and other self-concept measures) suggested that they are excessively concerned with academic outcomes and quite uncertain about maintaining progress in this task. For them, therefore, academic setbacks triggered this problem by shaking up their confidence. To get back on track, they required reassurance from friends, which they obtained in social situations. When things were going well in their classroom pursuits, they did not seek this reassurance in social situations; instead, they studied with others. In the face of an obstacle, though, they turned their social life into a forum for strategic reassurance seeking.

Ironically, the outcome-focused subjects' strategy serves their academic pursuits reasonably well but takes a toll on their social-life satisfaction. By turning otherwise relaxing social events into arenas for academic reassurance, the outcome-focused subjects diluted their experience of social life and even lost relatively many friends over the course of a college semester (Harlow & Cantor, 1994). Reassurance seeking is not necessarily the situation that one wants ideally to create on a regular basis with one's friends—at least if they are to remain as friends in addition to being encouragers (see Coyne, 1976, on the social costs of depression). For example, Langston (1990) has shown that people profit from regularly telling their friends about positive task performances, as compared with engaging in the kind of "negative marking" that must precede strategic reassurance seeking. Whereas strategic reassurance seeking may solve one problem—that of reestablishing confidence in the face of academic setbacks—it may also make the problem of maintaining friendships all the more difficult.

Studying with "Idols"

There is another, perhaps less costly, way that one could use the help of friends when academic pursuits are not going particularly well. Instead of turning to others for reassurance during social events, one could face challenges in academics by increasing the time spent studying with others, a more instrumental form of social support (Thoits, 1986). Who could afford to create this form of social support? Harlow's outcome-focused subjects were too shaken by setbacks to react in such an instrumental way. However, this more instrumental strategy is used in this same sample by those who have a different problem. These individuals perceive a relatively large gap between their current academic self-characteristics and what they would ideally like to be (self-concept discrepancy; Higgins, 1987). Their problem is a more positive one of self-improvement, not the more negative one of repairing a shaky self-image (Higgins, 1993). They do not require reassurances (e.g., they did not increase time with encouragers after setbacks). In this case, the strategic response to unhappiness in classroom pursuits was to gather with others and study. Moreover, particular others played this role—namely, those in the subjects' networks who served as "idols" (i.e., "people I would like to be more like"). In other words, once again, the situation of social support takes a form that fits the individual's problem. Fortunately, in this case, these students' instrumental needs to better match their ideal standards could be met by studying with others, without alienating those others in the process.

Friends for Friends' Sake Helps Academics

Finally, perhaps the least intrusive way in which we have seen people use "time with friends" as part of an achievement strategy is in mood enhancement. Blanton (Blanton & Cantor, 1993), for example, studied a group of summer school students at Virginia Tech University who significantly increased their participation in (enjoyable) social events during times of particular academic challenge. In this diary study, spending time socializing was systematically associated, for everyone, with a positive mood in academic events during the same period. However, some students systematically increased these social activities during times of academic challenge. Why? We think the reason is again related to the function served by these social events for their particular academic problem. For these students, "simply" spending time socializing serves a strategic function because the problem for them is being excessively debilitated in their academic work when they are in a bad mood. Because socializing is associated with positive mood in academic events, this purely social strategy serves a good academic purpose. (For those inclined to concrete analogies, it is a bit like having ice cream before one's vegetables to avoid fleeing from the table; or, at least, thinking about the rewards of ice cream as one eats those vegetables.) Moreover, this social support strategy serves its academic purpose while also increasing the experience of enjoyable social pursuits.

In a general sense, these comparisons point to the obvious but, I think, not trivial point that different people need different things from ostensibly similar situations. The functional significance of "time with friends" was different in each of these strategies because the individuals' problems differed. Many researchers have noted these different functions of social support, including opportunities for disclosure, for reassurance seeking, for instrumental gains, and for fun and relaxation (e.g., Butler, 1992; Cohen & Wills, 1985). Others, most notably Craig Hill (1987), have begun to specify the different needs for specific forms of affiliation that individuals have in their social life. However, the literature is generally less clear in putting these two parts of strategic support seeking together, by specifying why certain forms of support are effective in certain situations and which people will benefit in those situations. For this purpose, it really helps to take the person-centered perspective of the individual's particular problem and the strategy used to address that problem in particular situations. Sometimes, as in the case of defensive pessimism, it is difficult (if not impossible) to predict what would constitute support without an understanding of the problem at issue. Therefore, one contribution of a person-centered perspective on situations is to provide a systematic guide to how ostensibly similar situations are enlisted differently in social support precisely because they are addressing different problems.

Building a Common Language: Joining Personality and Social Psychologies

In conclusion, I want to return to the similarity in objectives between personality psychology and social psychology as they are commonly practiced these days. At the least, these enterprises seem to share a strong family resemblance, and so it seems worthwhile to break down the boundaries as much as possible. It is often difficult these days to tell who is taking the situation-centered and who is taking the person-centered perspective in the analysis of social behavior (perhaps because these may be artificial distinctions).

I have emphasized a problem-solving analysis because I think it makes a special contribution to the overlapping of these traditions. The language of problems, tasks, and strategies provides a way of specifying the needs and affordances that unite persons and situations in daily life (cf. Baron &

Boudreau, 1987). As I illustrated in the case of the intimacy task of older adolescents, it is virtually impossible to define life tasks independent of the age-typical opportunities. Particular adolescents, for example, will think about intimacy in different life situations—in families that stress agency or communion; in school settings with social norms that emphasize casual or steady dating. These life situations will help to shape their intimacy orientations. People's problems are partly defined by *what they can do* in their life situations—by the pragmatics of their lives. As Fiske (1992) has argued, people think and feel in order to do things.

Nevertheless, there is an equally pressing need to work from the other direction—to take what Snyder (1993) labeled the functionalist perspective in his work on volunteerism. Clearly, something about the personal needs of an adolescent (the self-concept, the autobiographical memories, the motives or dispositions) contributes to making him or her more or less responsive to the different opportunities for different types of intimacy in those age-typical situations. Therefore, it is critical to show that the needs of particular people also define the problems that they have in particular situations—define *what they need to do* in those situations.

These two directions of influence, as schematized in Figure 1, can also be seen in the analysis of problem-solving strategies. For example, on one hand, I have emphasized the different ways that individuals use others as support to solve the particular achievement problems that

follow from their personal needs (a functionalist analysis). Accordingly, what is reassuring social support for an outcome-focused individual is debilitating interference for a defensive pessimist. On the other hand, these same analyses reveal how dependent strategic problem solving is on the opportunities in the social situation (a pragmatic analysis). For example, the strategy of the outcome-focused subjects would not be so risky if it did not depend so strongly on the availability and willingness of others to provide the necessary reassurance. Similarly, Blanton's mood-dependent subjects would presumably suffer in their academic pursuits without readily available fun social opportunities. In this way, strategies are defined in line with what a person *needs to do* and what he or she *can do* in the situation.

Moreover, what makes problem solving so complex is that people's strategic behavior—*what they do*—comes to influence both their future personal needs and the opportunities in their daily-life situations. (These reverberations from problem-solving efforts are illustrated in Figure 1 as influences *from* strategies *to* personal needs and situational affordances.) For example, the strategic reassurance seeking of the outcome-focused students created, over time, both new personal needs (such as social problems) and new situational affordances (parties now served academic functions). Strategies come to influence what individuals now *need to do* as well as what they actually *can do*.

The problem-solving analysis inevitably goes in both directions, from situation to person and from person to situation. As such, it provides a common language in which strategic solutions cut across both persons and situations. That is why, in writing in 1990 about personality and problem solving, I borrowed from Gordon Allport's characterization of the "having" and the "doing" in personality. Yes, people may "have" dispositions and self-concepts and strivings, but those personalities are marked most by what they do in situations. The same can be said about situations—they have affordances, but those affordances are often difficult to see because they are defined by what people need to do, and people often need to do surprising things. It should not always be the job of personality psychologists to carve personality from its situational joints (cf. Caspi & Bem, 1990), nor should social psychologists necessarily try to find those "pure" strong situational effects that capture all people (Ickes, 1982). Instead, as

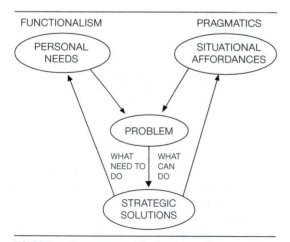

FIGURE 1 ■ Personality and Social Perspectives.

Higgins (1990), Snyder and Ickes (1985), and others have suggested, we may want to continue to work on and embrace one or many common languages for our joint enterprise. I am confident that the language of problem solving speaks to one such common ground.

REFERENCES

Baron, R. M., & Boudreau, L. A. (1987). An ecological perspective on integrating personality and social psychology. *Journal of Personality and Social Psychology, 53,* 1222–1228.

Blanton, H., & Cantor, N. (1993). *Regulating mood in daily life: The case for social instrumentality.* Manuscript submitted for publication.

Buss, D. M. (1987). Selection, evocation, and manipulation. *Journal of Personality and Social Psychology, 53,* 1214–1221.

Butler, R. (1992). What young people want to know when: Effects of mastery and ability goals on interest in different social comparisons. *Journal of Personality and Social Psychology, 62,* 934–943.

Cantor, N. (1990). From thought to behavior: "Having" and "doing" in the study of personality and cognition. *American Psychologist, 45,* 735–350.

Cantor, N., Acker, M., & Cook-Flannagan, C. (1992). Conflict and preoccupation in the intimacy life task. *Journal of Personality and Social Psychology, 6,* 644–655.

Cantor, N., & Blanton, H. (1993). Effortful goal pursuit in daily life. In J. A. Bargh & P. M. Gollwitzer (Eds.), *Thought, motivation, and action.* New York: Guilford.

Cantor, N., & Fleeson, W. (1991). Life tasks and self-regulatory processes. In M. Maehr & P. Pintrich (Eds.), *Advances in motivation and achievement* (Vol. 7, pp. 327–369). Greenwich, CT: JAI Press.

Cantor, N., & Kihlstrom, J. F. (1987). *Personality and social intelligence.* Englewood Cliffs, NJ: Prentice-Hall.

Cantor, N., Norem, J. K., Langston, C., Zirkel, S. Fleeson, W., & Cook-Flannagan, C. (1991). Life tasks and daily life experience. *Journal of Personality, 59,* 435–451.

Cantor, N., Norem, J. K., Niedenthal, P. M., Langston, C. A., & Brower, A. M. (1987). Life tasks, self-concept ideals, and cognitive strategies in a life transition. *Journal of Personality and Social Psychology, 53,* 1178–1191.

Cantor, N., & Zirkel, S. (1990). Personality, cognition, and purposive behavior. In L. A. Pervin (Ed.), *Handbook of personality* (pp. 135–159). New York: Guilford.

Caspi, A., & Bem, D. J. (1990). Personality continuity and change across the life course. In L. A Pervin (Ed.), *Handbook of personality* (pp. 549–569). New York: Guilford.

Cohen, S., & Wills, T. A. (1985). Stress, social support, and the buffering hypothesis. *Psychological Bulletin, 8,* 310–357.

Coyne, J. C. (1976). Depression and the response of others. *Journal of Abnormal Psychology, 85,* 186–193.

Dweck, C. S. (1986). Motivational processes affecting learning. *American Psychologist, 41,* 1040–1048.

Emmons, R. A., Diener, E., & Larsen, R. J. (1986). Choice and avoidance of everyday situations and affect congruence: Two models of reciprocal interactionism. *Journal of Personality and Social Psychology, 51,* 815–826.

Erikson, E. H. (1950). *Childhood and society.* New York: Norton.

Fiske, S. T. (1992). Thinking is for doing: Portraits of social cognition from daguerreotype to laserphoto. *Journal of Personality and Social Psychology, 63,* 877–889.

Fleeson, W. (1992). *Life tasks, implicit motives, and self-regulation in daily life.* Unpublished doctoral dissertation, University of Michigan, Ann Arbor.

Freud, S. (1961). Civilization and its discontents. In J. Strachey (Ed. and Trans.), *The standard edition of the complete psychological works of Sigmund Freud* (Vol. 21). London: Hogarth Press. (Original work published 1930)

Harlow, R., & Cantor, N. (1994). The social pursuit of academics: Side-effects and "spillover" of strategic reassurance seeking. *Journal of Personality and Social Psychology, 66,* 388–397.

Havighurst, R. J. (1953). *Human development and education.* New York: Longmans, Green.

Hazan, C., & Shaver, P. (1987). Romantic love conceptualized as an attachment process. *Journal of Personality and Social Psychology, 52,* 511–524.

Higgins, E. T. (1987). Self-discrepancy: A theory relating self and affect. *Psychological Review, 94,* 319–340.

Higgins, E. T. (1990). Personality, social psychology, and person-situation relations: Standards and knowledge activation as a common language. In L. A. Pervin (Ed.), *Handbook of personality* (pp. 301–332). New York: Guilford.

Higgins, E. T. (1993, July). *Self-discrepancies: Beyond valence in motivation and cognition.* Paper presented at the Ringberg Conference on Motivation and Action, Munich, Germany.

Higgins, E. T., & Parsons, J. E. (1983). Social cognition and the social life of the child: Stages as subcultures. In E. T. Higgins, D. N. Ruble, & W. W. Hartup (Eds.), *Social cognition and social developments: A sociocultural perspective* (pp. 15–62). New York: Cambridge University Press.

Hill, C. A. (1987). Affiliation motivation: People who need people . . . but in different ways. *Journal of Personality and Social Psychology, 52,* 1008–1018.

House, J. S., & Kahn, R. L. (1985). Measures and concepts of social support. In S. Cohen & L. Syme (Eds.), *Social support and health* (pp. 83–108). Orlando, FL: Academic Press.

Ickes, W. (1982). A basic paradigm for the study of personality roles and social behavior. In W. Ickes & E. S. Knowles (Eds.), *Personality, roles and social behavior.* New York: Springer-Verlag.

Langston, C. A. (1990). *The dynamics of daily life: Responses to positive and negative events, life-task activity, mood and well-being.* Unpublished doctoral dissertation. University of Michigan.

Markus, H., & Cross, S. (1990). The interpersonal self. In L. A. Pervin (Ed.), *Handbook of personality* (pp. 576–602). New York: Guilford,

McAdams, D. P. (1984). Human motives and personal relationships. In V. J. Derlega (Ed.), *Communication, intimacy and close relationships* (pp. 41–70). Orlando, FL: Academic Press.

Mischel, W. (1990). Personality dispositions revisited and revised: A view after three decades. In L. A. Pervin (Ed.), *Handbook of personality* (pp. 111–152). New York: Guilford.

Norem, J. K. (1989). Cognitive strategies as personality: Effectiveness specificity, flexibility and change. In D. M. Buss

& N. Cantor (Eds.), *Personality psychology: Recent trends and emerging directions* (pp. 45–60). New York: Springer-Verlag.

Norem, J. K., & Cantor, N. (1986). Defensive pessimism: "Harnessing" anxiety as motivation. *Journal of Personality and Social Psychology, 51,* 1208–1217.

Norem, J. K., & Illingworth, K. S. S. (1993). Strategy-dependent effects of reflecting on self and tasks: Some implications of optimism and defensive pessimism. *Journal of Personality and Social Psychology, 65,* 822–835.

Sanderson, C., & Cantor, N. (1993). *Intimacy orientation and sexual behavior: How late adolescents take on the intimacy life task.* Manuscript submitted for publication.

Setterlund, M. B., & Niedenthal, P. M. (1993). "Who am I? Why am I here?": Self-esteem, self-clarity and prototype matching. *Journal of Personality and Social Psychology, 61,* 764–780.

Showers, C. (1992). The motivational and emotional consequences of considering positive and negative possibilities for an upcoming event. *Journal of Personality and Social Psychology, 63,* 471–484.

Snyder, M. (1993). Basic research and practical problems: The promise of a "functional" personality and social psychology. *Personality and Social Psychology Bulletin, 19,* 251–264.

Snyder, M., & Ickes, W. (1985). Personality and social behavior. In G. Lindzey & E. Aronson (Eds.), *Handbook of social psychology* (3rd ed., Vol. 2, pp. 883–948). New York: Random House.

Thoits, P. A. (1986). Social support as coping assistance. *Journal of Consulting and Clinical Psychology, 54,* 416–423.

Veroff, J. (1983). Contextual determinants of personality. *Personality and Social Psychology Bulletin, 9,* 331–344.

Zirkel, S. (1992). Developing independence in a life transition: Investing the self in the concerns of the day. *Journal of Personality and Social Psychology, 62,* 506–521.

Zirkel, S., & Cantor, N. (1990). Personal construal of life tasks: Those who struggle for independence. *Journal of Personality and Social Psychology, 58,* 172–185.

R E A D I N G   6

The Dynamics of a Stressful Encounter

Susan Folkman, Richard S. Lazarus, Christine Dunkel-Schetter, Anita DeLongis
and Rand J. Gruen • University of California, Berkeley

Editors' Notes

The authors present a theory of the interrelations among appraisal, coping, and satisfactory outcomes in relation to a stressful encounter. Primary appraisal involves a person evaluating what is at stake in an encounter, such as whether there is potential harm or benefit to one's own self-esteem or to the well-being of a loved one. Secondary appraisal involves a person evaluating different coping options, such as changing the situation or accepting the situation. Following appraisal, different ways of coping with the demands of the situation given the person's resources are tried, such as engaging in planful problem-solving or distancing oneself from the situation. The outcomes of the encounters are evaluated by the individual as being satisfactory or not. The study examined the interrelations among these variables within each participant across several encounters in each person's life. Patterns were found such that a primary appraisal of a higher stake of some kind, such as concern for a loved one's well-being, or a secondary appraisal of a specific coping option, such as changing the situation, related to higher frequencies of specific ways of coping, such as planful problem-solving. In addition, higher frequencies of some ways of coping, such as planful problem-solving, were related to more satisfactory outcomes.

Discussion Questions

1. What are the self-regulatory functions of primary appraisal, secondary appraisal, and coping?
2. Provide an example of an interrelation between a primary appraisal, a way of coping, and a personal consequence.

Authors' Abstract

Despite the importance that is attributed to coping as a factor in psychological and somatic health outcomes, little is known about actual coping processes, the variables that influence them, and their relation to the outcomes of the stressful encounters people experience in their day-to-day lives. This study uses an intraindividual analysis of the interrelations among primary appraisal (what was at stake in the encounter), secondary appraisal (coping options), eight forms of problem- and emotion-focused coping and encounter outcomes in a sample of community-residing adults. Coping was strongly related to cognitive appraisal; the forms of coping that were used varied depending on what was at stake and the options for coping. Coping was also differentially related to satisfactory and unsatisfactory encounter outcomes. The findings clarify the functional relations among appraisal and coping variables and the outcomes of stressful encounters.

The recent burgeoning of research on coping is indicative of a growing conviction that coping is a major factor in the relation between stressful events and adaptational outcomes such as depression, psychological symptoms, and somatic illness (e.g., Andrews, Tennant, Hewson, & Vaillant, 1978; Baum, Fleming, & Singer, 1983; Billings & Moos, 1981, 1984; Collins, Baum, & Singer, 1983; Coyne, Aldwin, & Lazarus, 1981; Felton, Revenson, & Hinrichsen, 1984; Menaghan, 1982; Mitchell, Cronkite, & Moos, 1983; Pearlin & Schooler, 1978; Schaefer, 1983; Shinn, Rosario, Mørch, & Chestnut, 1984; Taylor, Wood, & Lichtman, 1983; Vaillant, 1977). This new body of research is characterized by an interest in the actual coping processes that people use to manage the demands of stressful events, as distinct from trait-oriented research, which focuses on personality dispositions from which coping processes are usually inferred, but not actually studied (e.g., Byrne, Steinberg, & Schwartz, 1968; Gaines, Smith, & Skolnick, 1977; Kobasa, Maddi, & Courington, 1981; Kobasa, Maddi, & Kahn, 1982).

A critical difference between the trait-oriented and the process-oriented approaches is the significance given to the psychological and environmental context in which coping takes place. In the trait-oriented approach, it is assumed that coping is primarily a property of the person, and variations in the stressful situation are of little importance. In contrast, the context is critical in the process-oriented approach because coping is assessed as a response to the psychological and environmental demands of specific stressful encounters. However, although coping processes are usually assessed contextually, with few exceptions (e.g., McCrae,

1984; Menaghan, 1982; Pearlin & Schooler, 1978; Stone & Neale, 1984), their impact tends to be evaluated without regard to their context. As a result, despite the increased attention that has been given to coping processes, there remains a lack of information about the contextual variables that influence them and the relation between coping processes and the outcomes of the specific stressful encounters in which they occur. This information is a prerequisite for understanding variations in coping processes and the mechanisms through which coping processes affect long-term outcomes.

This article reports an intraindividual approach to the problem in which each person's coping processes are examined across a variety of stressful encounters. Drawing on the cognitive-phenomenological theory of stress and coping described later, we have measured cognitive appraisal, coping, and encounter outcomes in order to understand the functional relations among these variables. The single stressful encounter and its immediate outcome is the focus of the analysis. Two other levels of analysis are examined in other reports. One report (Folkman, Lazarus, Gruen, & DeLongis, 1986) examined the relations among generalized person characteristics, appraisal and coping processes that are aggregated across encounters, and long-term outcomes. The other report will focus on the couple as the unit of analysis and will examine stress and coping processes within the dyad.

Stress and Coping Theory

This study is based on a theory of psychological stress and coping developed by Lazarus and his colleagues over a number of years (e.g., Coyne &

Lazarus, 1980; Lazarus, 1966, 1981; Lazarus, Averill, & Opton, 1970; Lazarus & DeLongis, 1983; Lazarus & Folkman, 1984a, 1984b; Lazarus, Kanner, & Folkman, 1980). The theory identifies two processes, cognitive appraisal and coping, as critical mediators of stressful person-environment relations and their immediate and long-range outcomes.

Cognitive appraisal is a process through which the person evaluates whether a particular encounter with the environment is relevant to his or her well-being, and if so, in what ways. In *primary appraisal*, the person evaluates whether he or she has anything at stake in this encounter. For example, Is there potential harm or benefit with respect to commitments, values, or goals? Is the health or well-being of a loved one at risk? Is there potential harm or benefit to self-esteem? In *secondary appraisal*, the person evaluates what if anything can be done to overcome or prevent harm or to improve the prospects for benefit. Various coping options are evaluated, such as altering the situation, accepting it, seeking more information, or holding back from acting impulsively and in a counterproductive way. Primary and secondary appraisals converge to determine whether the person-environment transaction is regarded as significant for well-being, and if so, whether it is primarily threatening (containing the possibility of harm or loss), or challenging (holding the possibility of mastery or benefit).

Coping is defined as the person's constantly changing cognitive and behavioral efforts to manage specific external and/or internal demands that are appraised as taxing or exceeding the person's resources (Lazarus & Folkman, 1984b). There are three key features of this definition. First, it is *process oriented*, meaning that it focuses on what the person actually thinks and does in a specific stressful encounter, and how this changes as the encounter unfolds. Our concern with the process of coping contrasts with trait approaches, which are concerned with what the person usually does, and hence emphasize stability rather than change. Second, we view coping as *contextual*, that is, influenced by the person's appraisal of the actual demands in the encounter and resources for managing them. The emphasis on context means that particular person and situation variables together shape coping efforts. Third, we make no a priori assumptions about what constitutes good or bad coping; coping is defined simply as a person's efforts to manage demands, whether or not the efforts are successful. This feature contrasts with animal models in which coping is defined as instrumental acts that control an aversive environment and, therefore, reduce arousal (cf. Ursin, 1980). It also contrasts with traditional ego-psychology conceptualizations that consider certain strategies inherently less desirable than others (e.g., Menninger, 1963) or that label a strategy as "coping" as opposed to defense only if it satisfies certain criteria such as adhering to reality (cf. Haan, 1977). Conceptualizations that define coping in terms of a value or outcome tend to create a tautology, whereby the coping process is confounded with the outcomes it is used to explain (see Folkman & Lazarus, 1980, 1985; Lazarus & Folkman, 1984a, 1984b).

Coping has two widely recognized major functions: regulating stressful emotions (emotion-focused coping) and altering the troubled person-environment relation causing the distress (problem-focused coping). Two previous studies have provided strong empirical support for the idea that coping usually includes both functions. Both forms of coping were represented in over 98% of the stressful encounters reported by middle-aged men and women (Folkman & Lazarus, 1980) and in an average of 96% of the self-reports of how college students coped with a stressful examination (Folkman & Lazarus, 1985).

The *immediate outcome* of an encounter refers to the person's judgment of the extent to which the encounter was resolved successfully. The overall judgment is based on the individual's values and goals, and his or her expectations concerning various aspects of the stressful encounter. For example, even though there has not been a resolution of the problem causing distress, an outcome can be evaluated favorably if the person feels that the demands of the encounter were managed as well as could be expected. Or, even though the problem causing distress may have been resolved, an outcome can be judged unfavorable if the resolution is inconsistent with other values and goals, less than what the person thought could be achieved, or creates additional conflicts in the person's social context.

Goals of This Study

The primary purpose of this study is to examine the functional relations among cognitive appraisal and coping processes and their short-term outcomes within stressful encounters. We use an intraindividual approach in order to compare the same person with himself or herself across five stressful encounters. This approach allows us to investigate how shifts away from the individual's typical style of appraisal and coping are related to each other and to the outcome of the stressful encounter. Most research on stress and coping addresses the different although related issue of the cumulative effects of particular styles of appraising and coping on indicators of psychological or somatic well-being. The latter calls for interindividual comparisons using scores that are aggregated over measurement occasions, or single scores that are assumed to represent a stable property of the person's appraisal and coping processes.

Intraindividual and interindividual comparisons address different questions and can lead to different conclusions about the same processes. A study of the effects of daily pleasant and unpleasant events on mood (Rehm, 1978) illustrates this possibility. Rehm found that there were no significant relations between the cumulative frequency of events and mood across 2 weeks when the subjects were compared to each other. However, when within-subjects comparisons were made, it was found that changes in both pleasant and unpleasant events were highly related to fluctuations in daily mood. What mattered was not the individual's overall level of stress compared to other individuals, but rather whether the individual had more or less stress than on previous days. It is possible that the apparent relations between appraisal and coping processes will likewise differ depending on whether they are examined within or across persons.

The present study addresses four specific questions. The first two concern the relations between primary and secondary appraisal and coping. In a previous study of coping in a community-residing sample (Folkman & Lazarus, 1980), we examined the relation between secondary appraisal and coping. Overall, problem-focused forms of coping were used more often in encounters that were appraised as changeable, and emotion-focused forms of coping in encounters appraised as unchangeable. However, we did not evaluate the relation between primary appraisal and coping. Our theory predicts a relation between primary appraisal and coping, but it does not make specific predictions about the relations between particular stakes and particular forms of problem- and emotion-focused coping.

A third question concerns the relation between coping and the short-term outcomes of stressful encounters. Our premise is that coping always involves multiple thoughts and acts, some of them oriented toward regulating emotional distress and others toward problem solving. However, our theory makes no specific predictions about the relations between problem- and emotion-focused coping and encounter outcomes.

Finally, if we ask about the relation between appraisal and coping and coping and encounter outcomes, we must address the subsidiary question of whether appraisal processes are also directly related to encounter outcomes. For example, encounters that involve threats to self-esteem or other personal vulnerabilities may be more difficult to resolve successfully than encounters in which the threat is less personal, such as when a goal at work is involved. And encounters that are appraised as unchangeable may be more difficult to resolve favorably than those appraised as changeable.

Method

SAMPLE

The sample consisted of 85 married couples living in Contra Costa County with at least one child at home. The sample was restricted to women between the ages of 35 and 45; their husbands, whose ages were not a criterion for eligibility, were between the ages of 26 and 54. In order to provide comparability with our previous community-residing sample (Folkman & Lazarus, 1980), the people selected for the study were Caucasian, primarily Protestant or Catholic, and had at least an 8th-grade education, an above-marginal family income ($18,000 for a family of four in 1981), and were not bedridden.

Qualified couples were identified through random-digit dialing. Prospective subjects received a letter explaining the study, then a telephone call from a project interviewer who answered questions and requested a home interview. Forty-six percent of the qualified couples who received letters agreed to be in the study. The acceptance rate was comparable to that of our previous field study, and not unexpected given that both members of the couple had to be willing to participate for 6 months. The mean age of the women was 39.6, and the mean age for men was 41.4. The mean number of years of education was 15.5, and the median family income was $45,000. Eighty-four percent of the men and 57% of the women were employed for pay. People who refused to be in the study were compared on all the above dimensions and differed significantly from those who participated only in years of education ($M = 14.3$). Ten couples dropped out of the study, an attrition rate of 11.8%. These couples were excluded from the analysis, yielding a final sample of 75 couples. Interviews were conducted in two 6-month waves from September 1981 through August 1982.

Procedures

Subjects were interviewed once a month for 6 months. Interviews were conducted at their homes, and husbands and wives were interviewed separately by different interviewers on the same day, and if possible, at the same time. The data reported here were gathered during the second through sixth interviews.

Measures

The data were gathered with a structured protocol used by the interviewer to elicit self-report information about the most stressful encounter the subject had experienced during the previous week. This study is based on the self-report interview data concerning primary appraisal, secondary appraisal, coping processes, and the outcome of the encounter.

Primary appraisal, which in this study refers to appraisals of what was at stake in a stressful encounter, was assessed with 13 items that described various stakes. The items were selected on the basis of a review of subjects' responses to open-ended questions in a previous study (cf. Folkman & Lazarus, 1980) and a review of the literature. Subjects indicated on a 5-point Likert scale (1 = *does not apply*; 5 = *applies a great deal*) the extent to which each stake was involved in the stressful encounter he or she was reporting.

The primary appraisal items were submitted to a principal factor analysis with oblique rotation. Five administrations for each of 150 subjects were entered, so that 750 observations were used in the factor analysis. Two factors were comprised of items that cohered both empirically and concep-

tually, and four additional items did not load on either factor. The first factor included items involving threats to self-esteem: the possibility of "losing the affection of someone important to you," "losing your self-respect," "appearing to be an uncaring person," "appearing unethical," "losing the approval or respect of someone important to you," and "appearing incompetent." The mean coefficient alpha of the five administrations for the self-esteem appraisal stakes was .78.

The second primary appraisal factor included items involving threats to a loved one's well-being: "harm to a loved one's health, safety, or physical well-being"; "a loved one having difficulty getting along in the world"; and "harm to a loved one's emotional well-being." The mean coefficient alpha for this scale for each of the five administrations was .76. The remaining items were the threat of "not achieving an important goal at your job or in your work"; "harm to your own health, safety, or physical well-being"; "a strain on your financial resources"; and "losing respect for someone else." These items were used individually in analysis and results based on them should be interpreted cautiously because of this. The intercorrelations among the stakes indices are shown in Table 1.

Secondary appraisal was assessed with four items that describe coping options The items were originally developed in accord with the theoretical model (Lazarus & Launier 1978), and they were used with a yes–no response format in a previous study (Folkman & Lazarus 1980). Subjects indicated on a 5-point Likert scale the extent to which the situation was one "that you could change or do something about," "that you had to accept," "in which you needed to know more before you could act," and "in which you had to hold yourself back from doing what you wanted to do." The intercorrelations among the indices of coping options are shown in Table 2.

TABLE 1. Stakes Indices: Intercorrelations Averaged Over Five Occasions

| Stakes | Index | | | | | |
	1	2	3	4	5	6
1. Own physical well-being	—	.14	.05	.13	.06	.22
2. Self-esteem		—	.23	.03	.29	.20
3. Goal at work			—	.31	.15	−.17
4. Financial strain				—	.12	.13
5. Lose respect for other					—	.11
6. Loved one's well-being						—

TABLE 2. Coping Options Indices: Intercorrelations Averaged Over Five Occasions

Coping option	Index			
	1	2	3	4
1. Could change	—	-.49	.14	-.10
2. Had to accept		—	.00	.01
3. Needed to know more			—	.09
4. Had to hold back				—

Coping was assessed with a revised version of the Ways of Coping (Folkman & Lazarus, 1985). The instrument contains 67 items that describe a broad range of cognitive and behavioral strategies people use to manage internal and/or external demands in specific stressful encounters. The strategies were originally drawn in part from a diverse literature (e.g., Mechanic, 1962; Sidle, Moos, Adams, & Cady, 1969; Weisman & Worden, 1976–1977) and constructed from our own theoretical framework (e.g., Lazarus & Launier, 1978). The original Ways of Coping (Folkman & Lazarus, 1980) contained 68 items that the subject indicated were or were not used in a specific stressful encounter. The revised version differs from the original in that redundant and unclear items were deleted or reworded; several items that were suggested by subjects in previous research were added (e.g., "I prayed," "I jogged or exercised," "I reminded myself how much worse things could be"); and the response format was changed from yes–no to a 4-point Likert scale (0 = *does not apply and/or not used*; 1 = *used somewhat*; 2 = *used quite a bit*, 3 = *used a great deal*).

As noted earlier, in the present study each subject was interviewed five times (months 2–6) about the most stressful encounter that had occurred during the 7 days prior to the interview. As a part of this interview, each subject filled out the revised Ways of Coping. The instructions were "Please read each item below and indicate, by circling the appropriate category, to what extent you used it *in the situation you have just described.*"

The Ways of Coping items were analyzed using alpha and principal factoring with oblique rotation. Oblique rotation was chosen because, from a theoretical perspective, we expect people to choose from a vast array of coping strategies rather than to use one set of strategies to the exclusion of others. Past research on coping supports this model (Folkman & Lazarus, 1980). Three separate factor analyses were completed using different strategies for combining person occasions, or observations. First, analyses were conducted on the entire 750 observations, 5 from each of 150 subjects, where each of the 5 concerned a different stressful encounter. Second, one stressful encounter per subject (*n* = 150) was random selected from the 750, equally representing each of the 5 time points. An additional sample of 150 stressful encounters was also randomly selected from the 750 total encounters without replacement of the prior 150 encounters, again equally representing each of the 5 time points.

The three factor analyses (using alpha and principal factoring) yielded very similar factor patterns. Thirty-seven items consistently loaded high on the same factor across all 3 analyses. Twenty-two items loaded on the same factor fairly consistently; 8 of these were eliminated on the basis of marginal factor loadings or lack of conceptual coherence with their scale. Seven items did not consistently load on any factor and were therefore eliminated. Because multiple factorings had been conducted, we had several estimates of each item's factor loading. A final principal factor analysis, calling for eight factors, was therefore performed on the 750 observations with the final 51 items in order to get an estimate of each item's factor loading.

The coping scales derived from the factor analytic procedures just described, their alphas, and factor loadings for the items are shown in Table 3. The eight scales accounted for 46.2% of the variance.

Confrontive coping (Scale 1) describes aggressive efforts to alter the situation (e.g., "stood my ground and fought for what I wanted," "tried to get the person responsible to change his or her mind"). It also suggests a degree of hostility (e.g., "I expressed anger to the person(s) who caused the problem") and risk-taking (e.g., "took a big chance or did something very risky," "I did something which I didn't think would work, but at least I was doing something").

Distancing (Scale 2) describes efforts to detach oneself (e.g., "didn't let it get to me—refused to think about it too much," "tried to forget the whole thing"). Another theme concerns creating a positive outlook (e.g., "made light of the situation; refused to get too serious about it," "looked for the silver lining—tried to look on the bright side of things").

Self-control (Scale 3) describes efforts to regulate one's own feelings (e.g., "I tried to keep my

TABLE 3. Coping Scales

Scale	Factor Loading	Scale	Factor Loading
Scale 1: Confrontive coping (α = .70)		45. Talked to someone about how I was feeling.	.57
46. Stood my ground and fought for what I wanted.	.70	18. Accepted sympathy and understanding from someone.	.56
7. Tried to get the person responsible to change his or her mind.	.62	22. I got professional help.	.45
17. I expressed anger to the person(s) who caused the problem.	.61		
28. I let my feelings out somehow.	.58	Scale 5: Accepting responsibility (α = .66)	
34. Took a big chance or did something very risky.	.32	9. Criticized or lectured myself.	.71
6. I did something which I didn't think would work, but at least I was doing something.	.30	29. Realized I brought the problem on myself.	.68
		51. I made a promise to myself that things would be different next time.	.49
Scale 2: Distancing (α = .61)		25. I apologized or did something to make up.	.39
44. Made light of the situation; refused to get too serious about it.	.55		
13. Went on as if nothing had happened.	.54	Scale 6: Escape–Avoidance (α = .72)	
41. Didn't let it get to me; refused to think about it too much.	.50	58. Wished that the situation would go away or somehow be over with.	.66
21. Tried to forget the whole thing.	.49	11. Hoped a miracle would happen.	.55
15. Looked for the silver lining, so to speak; tried to look on the bright side of things.	.34	59. Had fantasies about how things might turn out.	.54
12. Went along with fate; sometimes I just have bad luck.	.25	33. Tried to make myself feel better by eating, drinking, smoking, using drugs or medication, and so forth,	.49
		40. Avoided being with people in general.	.46
Scale 3: Self-controlling (α = .70)		50. Refused to believe that it had happened.	.42
14. I tried to keep my feelings to myself.	.55	47. Took it out on other people.	.40
43. Kept others from knowing how bad things were.	.46	16. Slept more than usual.	.36
10. Tried not to burn my bridges, but leave things open somewhat.	.40		
35. I tried not to act too hastily or follow my first hunch.	.40	Scale 7: Planful problem-solving (α = .68)	
54. I tried to keep my feelings from interfering with other things too much.	.37	49. I knew what had to be done, so I doubled my efforts to make things work.	.71
62. I went over in my mind what I would say or do.	.37	26. I made a plan of action and followed it.	.61
63. I thought about how a person I would admire would handle the situation and used that as a model.	.28	1. Just concentrated on what I had to do next—the next step.	.45
		39. Changed something so things would turn out all right.	.44
		48. Drew on my past experiences; I was in a similar position before.	.40
Scale 4: Seeking social support (α = .76)		52. Came up with a couple of different solutions to the problem.	.38
8. Talked to someone to find out more about the situation.	.73		
31. Talked to someone who could do something concrete about the problem.	.68	Scale 8: Positive reappraisal (α = .79)	
		23. Changed or grew as a person in a good way.	.79
42. I asked a relative or friend for advice.	.58	30. I came out of the experience better than when I went in.	.67
		36. Found new faith.	.64
		38. Rediscovered what is important in life.	.64
		60. I prayed.	.56
		56. I changed something and found myself.	.55
		20. I was inspired to do something creative.	.43

feelings to myself," "kept others from knowing how bad things were") and actions (e.g., "tried not to burn my bridges, but leave things open somewhat," "I tried not to act too hastily or follow my first hunch").

Seeking social support (Scale 4) describes efforts to seek informational support (e.g., "talked to someone to find out more about the situation"), tangible support (e.g., "talked to someone who could do something concrete about the problem"), and emotional support (e.g., "accepted sympathy and understanding from someone").

Accepting responsibility (Scale 5) acknowledges one's own role in the problem (e.g., "criticized or lectured myself," "realized I brought the problem on myself ") with a concomitant theme of trying to put things right (e.g., "I apologized or did something to make up," "I made a promise to myself that things would be different next time").

Escape-Avoidance (Scale 6) describes wishful thinking (e.g., "wished that the situation would go away or somehow be over with") and behavioral efforts to escape or avoid (e.g., "tried to make myself feel better by eating, drinking, smoking, using drugs or medication, etc."; "avoided being with people in general"; "slept more than usual"). These items, which suggest escape and avoidance, contrast with the items on the distancing scale, which suggest detachment.

Planful problem-solving (Scale 7) describes deliberate problem-focused efforts to alter the situation (e.g., "I knew what had to be done, so I doubled my efforts to make things work") coupled with an analytic approach to solving the problem (e.g., "I made a plan of action and followed it," "came up with a couple of different solutions to the problem").

Positive reappraisal (Scale 8) describes efforts to create positive meaning by focusing on personal growth (e.g., "changed or grew as a person in a good way," "I came out of the experience better than I went in") It also has a religious tone (e.g., "found new faith," "I prayed").

Scores were calculated by summing the ratings for each scale on each occasion. The average intercorrelations of the eight coping scales are shown in Table 4.

Five of the eight scales developed in this study are similar in content to those found in the analysis of our two previous data sets (Aldwin, Folkman, Schaefer, Coyne, & Lazarus, 1980; Folkman & Lazarus, 1985). Each of those analyses had a problem-focused scale that resembled planful problem-solving and confrontive coping, an escape–avoidance scale, an accepting responsibility scale (self-blame), a seeking social support scale, and a positive reappraisal scale. The emergence of similar coping scales in all three studies is especially noteworthy because there were substantial differences in populations and methods. In the Aldwin et al. (1980) analysis, for example, the sample was one hundred 45–64 year olds who indicated with a yes–no response (the original Ways of Coping) how they coped with a wide range of encounters they experienced in daily life. The sample for the Folkman and Lazarus (1985) study consisted of 108 students who completed the revised version of the Ways of Coping (used in the present study) with respect to one specific stresser, a midterm exam.

Each of the three studies also produced several unique factors. In the present study, for example, we identified a form of emotion-focused coping self-control, that was not defined in our previous research. In addition, the present analyses revealed a differentiation between two forms of problem-focused coping that was not apparent in the previous studies: confrontive coping, an aggressive form of problem-focused coping that is largely interpersonal; and planful problem-solving, which includes cool, deliberate strategies that are largely not interpersonal.

Outcomes were assessed only for those encounters the subject said were concluded as opposed to ongoing. Subjects were asked to select the item that best described the encounter outcome. Encounters that the subject said were "unresolved and worse," "not changed," or "resolved, but not to your

TABLE 4. Eight Coping Scales: Intercorrelations Averaged Over Five Occasions

Coping	Scale							
	1	2	3	4	5	6	7	8
1. Confrontive coping	—	.01	.36	.27	.26	.27	.28	.26
2. Distancing		—	.36	−.04	.27	.32	.09	.13
3. Self-controlling			—	.24	.30	.36	.37	.39
4. Seeking social support				—	.09	.23	.30	.32
5. Accepting responsibility					—	.39	.13	.18
6. Escape–Avoidance						—	.10	.23
7. Effortful, planful problem-solving							—	.39
8. Positive reappraisal								—

satisfaction" were defined as having unsatisfactory outcomes. Satisfactory outcomes were defined as "unresolved but improved," or "resolved to your satisfaction."[1]

Results

The results are presented in three sections. In the first section, we report the results of the analyses of the relations between appraisal and coping; in the second, the relation between coping and encounter outcomes; and in the third, the relation between appraisal and encounter outcomes.

APPRAISAL AND COPING

Primary appraisal and coping. The relation between the primary appraisal of stakes and coping was examined with six intraindividual multivariate analyses for repeated measures, one for each stake that was assessed. In each analysis the independent variable (the primary appraisal of one stake) was formed by aggregating the five encounters a subject reported into two groups according to whether they were above or below his or her own mean on that particular stake. The dependent variables consisted of the subject's mean score on each coping scale for those encounters that were above the mean on that particular stake, and mean coping scores for those that were below the mean. A multivariate analysis of variance for repeated measures was used to compare the coping scores in encounters that were above the mean on a particular stake with those that were below the mean.[2,3] The Ns in the analysis varied according to whether or not a subject rated a stake as applicable in at least one encounter. The results of the six analyses are shown in Table 5.

All six multivariate tests were significant. Relations between the two major primary appraisal indices, threat to self-esteem and threat to a loved one's well-being and coping scores, can be summarized as follows:

When threat to self-esteem was high, subjects used more confrontive coping, self-control coping, accepted more responsibility, and used more escape–avoidance compared to when threat to self-esteem was low; they also sought less social support. When a "loved one's well-being" was at stake, subjects used more confrontive and escape–avoidance coping and less planful problem-solving and distancing than when a loved one's well-being was not at stake.

The four single-item stakes not falling within the two factors just mentioned also had significant coping correlates. When "loss of respect for someone else" was threatened, confrontive coping and self-control were used more. In encounters involving a "goal at work," self-control and planful problem-solving were used more; when the stake was a strain on "financial resources," the dominant coping responses were confrontive coping and seeking social support. Finally, threats to "one's own physical health" were associated with more seeking of social support and escape–avoidance.

Whereas the results indicate a degree of specificity with regard to the relation between various stakes and coping, there were also some general trends. Although the majority of comparisons were nonsignificant, three strategies tended to be used more in high-stake conditions regardless of the stake involved: self-control, escape–avoidance, and seeking social support. In addition, one form of coping, positive reappraisal, was not related to any of the assessed stakes.

---

[1]The distinction between ongoing encounters and concluded encounters that were unresolved concerned the time frame of the encounter. For example, one subject reported a continuing conversation with her husband about the insecurity of his job. She labeled this as an ongoing stressful encounter. Another subject's stressful encounter concerned waiting for the results of his wife's laboratory tests following her recent hospitalization. The specific encounter was concluded when the results were reported to him, but the issue remained unresolved because no treatment was found for his wife's symptoms.

[2]For purposes of statistical analysis we treated our subjects as independent of their spouses. In so doing we may have overestimated the available degrees of freedom in those analyses that included both members of a couple. To examine

this possibility, we adjusted the degrees of freedom to reflect the N of couples in each analysis rather than the N of individuals. In no case did a relation that was previously significant ($p < .05$) become nonsignificant.

[3]A parallel set of analyses was conducted in which encounters were divided on the basis of the group mean rather than the individual's own mean. The findings were generally similar. All the multivariate F statistics remained significant at virtually the same level as in the analyses using the intraindividual mean. Of the 34 univariate comparisons that were significant using the intraindividual mean, 31 remained significant using the group mean. This suggests that as a whole, the sample was relatively homogeneous regarding the independent variables.

TABLE 5. Relation Between Primary Appraisal and Coping: Intraindividual Analysis

Univariate test	Coping Scale							
	1	2	3	4	5	6	7	8
Self-esteem stakes: Multivariate $F(8, 135) = 12.14, p < .0001$								
M Low	3.61	3.01	5.30	5.73	1.46	2.95	7.43	3.42
M High	4.56	3.08	6.60	4.85	2.58	3.67	7.26	3.81
F	16.81	.19	26.59	9.27	44.69	10.77	.37	3.16
p	.000	.659	.000	.003	.000	.001	.544	.078
Concern for loved one's well-being: Multivariate $F(8, 136) = 6.91, p < .001$								
M Low	3.68	3.31	5.86	5.37	1.81	2.81	7.67	3.40
M High	4.42	2.91	6.00	5.89	2.14	3.89	6.81	3.86
F	7.22	3.82	.28	2.21	3.80	20.04	9.95	2.89
p	.008	.053	.598	.139	.053	.000	.002	.091
Loss of respect for someone else: Multivariate $F(8,125) = 11.49, p < .001$								
M Low	3.31	3.09	5.43	5.34	1.99	3.14	7.28	3.69
M High	5.32	2.85	6.60	5.78	1.72	3.49	7.27	3.50
F	54.60	1.50	20.34	1.56	2.53	1.80	.01	.49
p	.000	.222	.000	.214	.114	.182	.741	.486
Goal at work: Multivariate $F(8, 108) = 5.78, p < .001$								
M Low	3.84	2.99	5.55	5.21	2.01	3.44	6.88	3.77
M High	3.90	3.33	6.49	5.52	1.84	3.40	8.51	3.66
F	.04	1.94	10.39	.75	.85	.02	35.57	.14
p	.841	.167	.002	.388	.360	.893	.000	.707
Strain on finances: Multivariate $F(8, 95) = 4.74, p < .001$								
M Low	4.18	3.25	5.92	5.05	1.95	3.33	7.28	3.72
M High	3.43	2.94	6.19	6.34	2.15	3.78	7.82	3.69
F	5.88	2.39	.70	10.40	.80	2.89	2.61	.01
p	.023	.125	.404	.002	.375	.092	.109	.918
Harm to own physical health: Multivariate $F(8, 86) = 3.83, p = .001$								
M Low	4.16	2.86	5.53	5.17	1.66	3.03	7.12	3.41
M High	3.97	3.25	5.77	6.17	1.96	4.35	7.55	3.64
F	.30	2.33	.46	6.35	2.77	21.14	1.65	.47
p	.585	.130	.499	.013	.100	.000	.202	.493

Note. 1 = confronting coping; 2 = distancing; 3 = self-controlling; 4 = seeking social support; 5 = accepting responsibility; 6 = escape–avoidance; 7 = planful problem solving; 8 = positive reappraisal.

Secondary appraisal and coping. The relation between secondary appraisal of coping options and coping processes was examined with four intraindividual multivariate analyses for repeated measures, one for each coping option. Using the same procedure described earlier, the independent variable (the secondary appraisal of one coping option) was formed by aggregating the five encounters a subject reported into two groups according to whether they were above or below his or her own mean on that particular coping option. The dependent variables consisted of the individual's means on each of the eight coping scales that were aggregated within each group. The results of the four analyses are shown in Table 6.

Subjects accepted more responsibility and used more confrontive coping, planful problem-solv-

ing, and positive reappraisal in encounters they appraised as changeable, and more distancing and escape–avoidance in encounters they appraised as having to be accepted. In encounters subjects appraised as requiring more information before they could act, they sought more social support, and used more self-control and planful problem-solving; and in encounters that subjects appraised as requiring that they hold back from doing what they wanted, they used more confrontive coping, self-control, and escape–avoidance.

COPING AND ENCOUNTER OUTCOMES

The concluded stressful encounters reported by each subject were grouped according to whether the outcome of each encounter was unsatisfactory or satisfactory. The mean for each of the eight coping scales was calculated within each of the two outcome groups, and a multivariate analysis of variance for repeated measures was used to determine whether there was a significant difference in coping between the two groups. The results are shown in Table 7.

The multivariate F statistic was significant. Satisfactory outcomes were characterized by higher levels of planful problem-solving ($p < .01$) and positive reappraisal ($p < .01$), and unsatisfactory outcomes by higher levels of confrontive coping ($p < .10$) and distancing ($p < .10$).

APPRAISAL AND ENCOUNTER OUTCOMES

As in the previous analysis, the independent variable was formed by aggregating each subject's concluded encounters into two groups according to whether the encounter had an unsatisfactory or satisfactory outcome. The relation between primary appraisal and encounter outcomes was examined by calculating a mean score for each of the six stakes indices within the two outcome groups, and testing whether there was a significant difference between the means of the two groups.

The multivariate F statistic was significant, indicating that there was a difference in stakes in encounters with unsatisfactory and satisfactory outcomes, $F(6, 77) = 2.74, p = .018$. The univariate tests revealed that the difference between the groups was due to a single stake, losing respect for someone else. Encounters with unsatisfactory outcomes were associated with more loss of respect than encounters with satisfactory outcomes ($M = 2.28$, 1.72, unsatisfactory and satisfactory outcomes, respectively, $p < .001$). There were no significant differences in any other stake between encounters with unsatisfactory and satisfactory outcomes.

The relation between secondary appraisal and encounter outcomes was examined by calculating scores for each of the four indices of coping options within the two outcome groups, and testing whether there was a significant difference between the means of the two groups. The multivariate F statistic was significant, indicating that there was a difference in the appraisal of coping options in encounters with satisfactory and unsatisfactory outcomes, $F(4, 80) = 5.65, p < .001$. The univariate test indicated that the difference between the groups was due to two coping options. Compared with unsatisfactory encounter outcomes, satisfac-

TABLE 6. Relation Between Secondary Appraisal and Coping: Intraindividual Analysis

Univariate test	Coping scale							
	1	2	3	4	5	6	7	8
Could change: Multivariate $F(8, 134) = 10.17, p < .0001$								
M Low	3.72	3.18	5.61	5.14	1.53	3.39	6.55	3.03
M High	4.39	2.94	5.84	5.53	2.36	2.86	8.07	3.93
F	5.88	1.87	.89	1.59	25.51	6.14	27.79	12.55
p	.017	.173	.346	.209	.000	.014	.000	.001
Had to accept: Multivariate $F(8, 133) = 5.60, p < .000$								
M Low	4.56	2.74	5.62	5.05	2.21	2.90	7.35	3.57
M High	3.53	3.22	5.73	5.56	1.64	3.44	7.16	3.51
F	12.68	5.49	.16	2.55	11.48	5.16	.43	.04
p	.001	.021	.685	.112	.001	.025	.512	.846
Need more information: Multivariate $F(8, 131) = 8.56, p < .0001$								
M Low	3.99	3.35	5.44	4.58	1.80	3.23	6.92	3.44
M High	4.00	2.71	6.30	6.69	2.09	3.30	7.78	3.67
F	.00	10.44	10.60	39.49	2.56	.09	9.27	.68
p	.977	.002	.001	<.0001	.112	.758	.003	.410
Had to hold back: Multivariate $F(8, 135) = 9.78, p < .001$								
M Low	3.16	3.20	5.03	5.21	1.91	2.78	7.13	3.65
M High	4.66	2.96	6.48	5.43	1.95	3.62	7.17	3.47
F	38.43	1.81	33.89	.47	.08	10.47	.02	.47
p	<.0001	.181	.000	.492	.778	.002	.885	.495

Note. 1 = confrontative coping; 2 = distancing; 3 = self-controlling; 4 = seeking social support; 5 = accepting responsibility; 6 = escape–avoidance; 7 = planful problem solving; 8 = positive reappraisal.

TABLE 7. Relation Between Coping and Encounter Outcomes: Intraindividual Analysis

Univariate tests	Unsatisfactory outcomes (*M*)	Satisfactory outcomes (*M*)	F	p
Coping scale				
1. Confrontive coping	3.98	3.31	3.34	.071
2. Distancing	3.35	2.78	3.38	.069
3. Self-controlling	5.98	5.36	2.53	.115
4. Seeking social support	4.71	5.16	1.22	.281
5. Accepting responsibility	1.92	1.65	1.10	.298
6. Escape–avoidance	2.86	2.64	.50	.482
7. Planful problem-solving	6.33	7.59	8.67	.004
8. Positive reappraisal	2.70	3.90	9.67	.003

Note. Multivariate $F(8, 76) = 4.64$, $p < .001$.

tory encounter outcomes were associated with higher levels of changeability ($M = 1.20$, 1.68, for unsatisfactory and satisfactory outcomes, respectively, $p = .006$) and lower levels of the need to hold back from doing what one wanted to ($M = 2.07$, 1.41, for unsatisfactory and satisfactory outcomes, respectively, $p < .001$). There was no relation between the remaining two coping options ("had to accept the situation" and "needed more information before acting") and encounter outcomes.

Discussion

The results of this intraindividual analysis indicate that the variables identified in our theoretical formulation play an important role in coping. Specifically, variability in coping is at least partially a function of people's judgments about what is at stake (primary appraisal) in specific stressful encounters and what they view as the options for coping (secondary appraisal). Further, the analysis points up important relations among appraisal, coping, and the outcomes of the stressful encounters in which these processes take place.

In assessing primary appraisal our goal was to tap physical, psychological, social, financial, and occupational stakes that people might have in encounters that are relevant to their well being. The results indicate that these stakes have a reasonable relation with the ways people cope.

Encounters that involved the two most reliably measured stakes—self-esteem and concern for a loved one's well being—resulted in coping patterns that overlapped to a degree. The overlap is due to the use of more confrontive coping and escape–avoidance in encounters that involved these

stakes. These seemingly contradictory forms of coping suggest that people might engage in a heated exchange and simultaneously wish they were somewhere else. Another possibility is that during the course of a stressful encounter, people might alternate the use of confrontive coping with escape–avoidance in a pattern of engagement, disengagement, and reengagement. As to differences in the patterns, people sought less social support in encounters that involved a threat to self-esteem than they did in encounters in which this stake was minimally involved, and they used significantly less planful problem-solving and distancing in encounters that involved a loved one's well-being than they did when this concern was low.

That people sought less social support in encounters that involved their self-esteem may have been due to shame or embarrassment. This possibility is consistent with Sarnoff and Zimbardo's (1961) finding that when threatened by the prospects of engaging in embarrassing behavior, subjects prefer to be alone rather than in the company of others. As for the lack of planful problem-solving and distancing in encounters that involved a loved one's well-being, it may be that such encounters are not amenable to rational problem-solving, and that when a loved one is involved, people cannot or do not wish to be emotionally detached.

The findings involving the four single-item measures of primary appraisal also contained interesting coping combinations. For example, people used more planful problem-solving and self-control in encounters that involved a goal at work. The use of planful problem-solving is consistent with our previous finding (Folkman & Lazarus, 1980) that problem-focused coping strategies are often used to deal with work-related stress. We speculated that emotional self-control might facilitate problem-solving, especially in work settings, where the culture emphasizes such control.

In addition, our subjects used more confrontive coping and self-control in encounters that threatened loss of respect for someone else. These forms of coping suggest that for some people, along with an impulse to confront, there is the simultaneous impulse to regulate assaultive statements and hostile feelings so that the situation does not get out of hand. The use of coping strategies that appear to have opposite purposes, as illustrated by the coping processes associated with threats to self-esteem, a loved one's well-being and respect for another, helps explain the moderate bivariate correlations among these coping variables, and highlights the need to consider the possibility that seemingly contradictory forms of coping can be mutually facilitative, depending on the nature of the threats and the manner in which an encounter unfolds over time. These findings highlight the need for microanalyses of coping processes (e.g., Folkman & Lazarus, 1985) in order to observe their interplay as a stressful encounter unfolds.

Based on our previous research on the relation between secondary appraisal (consisting of evaluations of coping resources, constraints, and options) and coping (Coyne et al., 1981; Folkman & Lazarus, 1980, 1985), we expected subjects to use more problem-focused forms of coping in encounters they appraised as changeable, and more emotion-focused forms of coping in situations where they saw few if any options for affecting the outcome. The findings from the present study are consistent with this expectation, and provide important elaboration concerning various forms of problem- and emotion-focused coping.

Four forms of coping were dominant in changeable encounters: confrontive coping, accepting responsibility, planful problem-solving, and positive reappraisal. The use of confrontive coping and planful problem-solving in changeable encounters is consistent with our two earlier sets of findings with community-residing adults (Folkman & Lazarus, 1980) and students (Folkman & Lazarus, 1985). In the latter study, problem-focused forms of coping were used more during the period of anticipation, when there was intensive preparation for a course examination, than during the waiting period after the exam and before grades were an-

nounced, when nothing could be done to change the outcome. Similarly, Bachrach (1983), who used a modified version of the Ways of Coping in a study of the ways community residents coped with the threat of a hazardous waste facility, found that people who thought something could be done about the situation used more problem-focused coping than people who appraised it as beyond their control.

Accepting responsibility and positive reappraisal were also used in changeable encounters. The items in the accepting responsibility coping scale include "criticized or lectured myself," "I made a promise to myself that things would be different next time," and "realized I brought the problem on myself." These items describe what Janoff-Bulman (1979) calls behavioral self-blame. Based on the findings of the present study, one might go a step further, and suggest that behavioral self-blame may even promote problem-focused efforts. For example, in Bulman and Wortman's (1977) study of victims of spinal cord injury, self-blame was correlated with effective adjustment. Bulman and Wortman suggested that if one accepts blame for bringing about stress, one may also know more clearly what to do about it, which may be the mechanism through which accepting blame (in our terms, accepting responsibility) sometimes promotes problem-focused coping.

In previous studies (Aldwin et al., 1980, Folkman & Lazarus, 1985), we found that problem-focused forms of coping and positive reappraisal were highly correlated. The consistency with which these forms of coping appear in combination across studies suggests that positive reappraisal may facilitate problem-focused forms of coping, or that there is something about the encounters in which people use problem-focused coping (such as a potential for being changed in a positive direction) that also elicits positive reappraisal.

The pattern of coping in encounters that subjects appraised as having to be accepted was strikingly different from the pattern in encounters that they appraised as changeable. In changeable encounters, subjects used coping strategies that kept them focused on the situation: they confronted, did planful problem-solving, accepted responsibility, and selectively attended to the positive aspects of the encounter. In contrast, when subjects appraised encounters as having to be accepted, they turned to distancing and escape-avoidance, which are forms of coping that allow the person not to focus on the troubling situation.

The appraisals that involved delaying or inhibiting action—needing more information before acting and having to hold back from acting—were both associated with efforts to exercise self-control. However, the use of self-control may serve different functions in the two kinds of encounters. In encounters where the subject needed more information, self-control seemed to facilitate problem-focused coping in that it was accompanied by seeking social support (which includes seeking advice) and planful problem-solving; in encounters where the subject had to hold back, self-control was accompanied by confrontive coping and escape–avoidance, which suggests that in these encounters self-control was used in an attempt to keep things from getting out of hand. Perhaps self-control processes are multidimensional and can be refined in future studies.

The assessment of encounter outcomes in this study included the subject's evaluation of whether there had been an improvement, no change, or a worsening of the problem, and whether or not he or she was satisfied with what had happened. These evaluations were collapsed into a dichotomous (satisfactory/unsatisfactory) variable. With few exceptions (e.g., Pearlin & Schooler, 1978), researchers have largely bypassed the question of short-term encounter outcomes in favor of long-term outcomes such as depression and somatic health status.

The assessment of encounter outcomes poses a number of difficult questions. For example, along what dimensions should encounter outcomes be assessed? We selected two dimensions, the problem causing distress and the subject's satisfaction with the outcome, which parallel the concepts of problem- and emotion-focused coping. Behavioral and psychophysiological dimensions could also be evaluated. Further, regardless of the dimension being evaluated, a retrospective account of an encounter's outcome may influence the report of appraisal and coping processes. It is clear that the development of a suitable approach to assessing encounter outcomes remains an unresolved and important measurement issue.

The overall relation between primary appraisal of stakes and encounter outcomes was weak. Encounters with unsatisfactory and satisfactory outcomes were distinguished by only one of the six stakes (losing respect for another).

The relation between secondary appraisal and encounter outcomes was stronger in that two of the four coping options (appraisals of changeability and having to hold back from acting) were related to encounter outcome. The results of this portion of the analysis bring up an intriguing question. How can it be that appraising a situation as changeable is associated with whether or not an encounter will have a satisfactory outcome, whereas appraising a situation as unchangeable, that is, as having to be accepted, is not? One possibility is that the appraisals of changeability and having to accept the situation may refer to different facets of a complex encounter (cf. Folkman, 1984), with the changeable facet mattering more in terms of the encounter's immediate outcome. Consider, for example, a disagreement between an employee and a supervisor. The employee may be able to change the supervisor's mind about an important decision, but not the supervisor's general decision-making style.

Encounters with unsatisfactory and satisfactory outcomes were also distinguished by coping. Unsatisfactory outcomes tended to be associated with confrontive coping, a form of problem-focused coping that includes strategies such as "stood my ground and fought for what I wanted" and "I expressed anger to the person(s) who caused the problem." These strategies may exacerbate rather than improve the situation. Satisfactory outcomes were associated with planful problem-solving, which includes strategies such as "I knew what had to be done, so I doubled my efforts to make things work," and "I made a plan of action and followed it." However, it is important not to assume that confrontive coping will always lead to unsatisfactory outcomes and that planful problem-solving will always lead to satisfactory ones. Whether or not a coping strategy results in positive outcomes depends on the demands and constraints of the context in which it is being used and the skill with which it is applied. In this study, the association between confrontive coping and unsatisfactory encounter outcomes may be due in part to the nature of the items on the confrontive coping scale, which may be biased in favor of unskillful forms of confrontation.

Distancing and positive reappraisal were emotion-focused forms of coping associated with unsatisfactory and satisfactory outcomes, respectively. These forms of coping could either be a cause or an effect of encounter outcomes. Distancing could cause an unfavorable outcome, for example, if people were to use this form of coping when they should instead be attending to the problem (e.g., Katz, Weiner, Gallagher, & Hellman, 1970). On the other hand, distancing may be an adaptive response to an outcome that is seen as negative and unalterable (e.g., Collins et al., 1983). Similarly, positive reappraisal could facilitate problem-focused coping as noted earlier, but it could also represent the reappraisal of a situation in which problem-focused coping has already been effective in producing a favorable outcome. This point is also made by Shinn et al. (1984), who point out in their study of job stress that palliative strategies, such as focusing on activities outside the job, may be reactions to high levels of stress and strain rather than their causes.

Conclusions

Four major issues are raised by this study concerning the relations among appraisal, coping, and encounter outcomes. The first issue concerns causality. It is tempting to infer that in general appraisal influences coping, and coping in turn influences encounter outcomes, which is what our theory suggests. However, the cross-sectional, retrospective design of this study does not allow us to evaluate these causal inferences. It is even possible that some of the obtained effects operate in the opposite direction. More likely, bidirectional relations exist among the variables. In addition to appraisal influencing coping, coping may influence the person's reappraisal of what is at stake and what the coping options are. Similarly, it is possible that certain forms of coping, such as positive reappraisal, may be influenced by the outcome of an encounter rather than vice versa. Questions about causality are especially important for deciding how to intervene in maladaptive appraisal-coping-encounter outcome sequences. This issue can only be addressed with a prospective design.

A second issue concerns microanalytic versus macroanalytic assessment techniques. For example, the measure of primary appraisal included relatively global items, such as concern with one's own physical well-being and a goal at work. The former could have involved very different threats, such as a threat to appearance, physical functioning, or even life. And a goal at work could have involved threats that ranged from problems with

meeting an immediate deadline to being reviewed for a major promotion. Similarly, the coping items, especially the problem-focused items, were somewhat general rather than highly situation-specific so that they would apply to a variety of situations. A nurse may have strategies for coping with work-related encounters that are very different from those of a salesman, and it is possible that these strategies are not captured in the items on the Ways of Coping. The choice in measurement is between having items that can be used with a variety of people in a variety of settings versus those that are richer in descriptive power, but limited to specific people in specific contexts (Folkman & Lazarus, 1981).

A third issue concerns method. In our research to date on appraisal and coping we have used the method of self-report to learn what subjects did, thought, and felt in the context of a particular stressful encounter. As we have pointed out (Folkman & Lazarus, 1985), the problem is not that self-report is inherently more fallible than other methods of inquiry—in fact, for certain kinds of psychological processes it may be the only way to obtain certain information—but rather that it ultimately requires verification by other methods such as observation of direct behavior and physiological assessment.

Finally, the results of this study support the importance of intraindividual analyses as a method of understanding the relations between the contextual features of specific stressful encounters and coping processes and the relations between these variables and short-term encounter outcomes. However, an understanding of the relations between coping processes and long-term adaptational outcomes, which is a major goal of stress and coping research, also requires an interindividual approach in which people are compared with each other with respect to the ways they cope with diverse stressful encounters over time (e.g., Folkman et al., 1986). Both intraindividual and interindividual approaches are needed to understand coping processes and the mechanisms through which they come to affect people's well-being over the long term.

REFERENCES

Aldwin, C., Folkman, S., Schaefer, C., Coyne, J. C., & Lazarus, R. S. (1980, August). *Ways of Coping: A process measure.* Paper presented at the meeting of the American Psychological Association, Montreal.

Andrews, G., Tennant, C., Hewson, D. M., & Vaillant, G. (1978). Life event stress, social support, coping style, and risk of psychological impairment. *Journal of Nervous and Mental Disease, 166,* 307–316.

Bachrach, K. M. (1983, August). *Coping with the threat of a hazardous waste facility.* Paper presented at the meeting of the American Psychological Association, Anaheim, CA.

Baum, A., Fleming, R. E., & Singer, J. E. (1983). Coping with technological disaster. *Journal of Social Issues, 3,* 117–138.

Billings, A. G., & Moos, R. H. (1981). The role of coping responses and social resources in attenuating the impact of stressful life events. *Journal of Behavioral Medicine, 4,* 139–157.

Billings, A. G., & Moos, R. H. (1984). Coping, stress, and social resources among adults with unipolar depression. *Journal of Personality and Social Psychology, 46,* 877–891.

Bulman, R. J., & Wortman, C. B. (1977). Attributions of blame and coping in the "real world": Severe accident victims react to their lot. *Journal of Personality and Social Psychology, 35,* 351–363.

Byrne, D., Steinberg, M. A., & Schwartz, M. S. (1968). Relationship between repression-sensitization and physical illness. *Journal of Abnormal Psychology, 73,* 154–155.

Collins, D. L., Baum, A., & Singer, J. E. (1983). Coping with chronic stress at Three Mile Island: Psychological and biochemical evidence. *Health Psychology, 2,* 149–166.

Coyne, J. C., Aldwin, C., & Lazarus, R. S. (1981). Depression and coping in stressful episodes. *Journal of Abnormal Psychology, 90,* 439–447.

Coyne, J. C., & Lazarus, R. S. (1980). Cognitive style, stress perception, and coping. In I. L. Kutash & L. B. Schlesinger (Eds.), *Handbook on stress and anxiety: Contemporary knowledge, theory and treatment* (pp. 144–158). San Francisco: Jossey-Bass.

Felton, B. J., Revenson, T. A., & Hinrichsen, G. A. (1984). Coping and adjustment in chronically ill adults. *Social Science and Medicine, 18,* 889–898.

Folkman S. (1984). Personal control and stress and coping processes: A theoretical analysis. *Journal of Personality and Social Psychology, 46,* 839–852.

Folkman, S., & Lazarus, R. S. (1980). An analysis of coping in a middle-aged community sample. *Journal of Health and Social Behavior, 21,* 219–239.

Folkman, S., & Lazarus, R. S. (1981). Reply to Shinn and Krantz. *Journal of Health and Social Behavior, 22,* 457–459.

Folkman, S., & Lazarus, R. S. (1985). If it changes it must be a process: Study of emotion and coping during three stages of a college examination. *Journal of Personality and Social Psychology, 48,* 150–170.

Folkman, S., Lazarus, R. S., Gruen, R. J., & DeLongis, A. (1986). Appraisal, coping, health status, and psychological symptoms. *Journal of Personality and Social Psychology, 50,* 571–579.

Gaines, L. L., Smith, B. D., & Skolnick, B. E. (1977). Psychological differentiation, event uncertainty, and heart rate. *Journal of Human Stress, 3,* 11–25.

Haan, N. (1977). *Coping and defending: Processes of self-environment organization.* New York: Academic Press .

Janoff-Bulman, R. (1979). Characterological versus behavioral self-blame: Inquiries into depression and rape. *Journal of Personality and Social Psychology, 37,* 1798–1809.

Katz, J. J., Weiner, H., Gallagher, T. G., & Hellman, L. (1970). Stress, distress, and ego defenses. *Archives of General Psychiatry, 23,* 131–142.

Kobasa, S. C., Maddi, S. R., & Courington, S. (1981). Personality and constitution as mediators in the stress-illness relationship. *Journal of Health and Social Behavior, 22,* 368–378.

Kobasa, S. C., Maddi, S. R., & Kahn, S. (1982). Hardiness and health: A prospective study. *Journal of Personality and Social Psychology, 42,* 168–177.

Lazarus, R. S. (1966). *Psychological stress and the coping process.* New York: McGraw-Hill.

Lazarus, R. S. (1981). The stress and coping paradigm. In C. Eisdorfer, D. Cohen, A. Kleinman, & P. Maxim (Eds.), *Models for clinical psychopathology* (pp. 177–214). New York: Spectrum.

Lazarus, R. S., Averill, J. R., & Opton, E. M., Jr. (1970). Toward a cognitive theory of emotions. In M. Arnold (Ed.), *Feelings and emotions* (pp. 207–232). New York: Academic Press.

Lazarus, R. S., & DeLongis, A. (1983). Psychological stress and coping in aging. *American Psychologist, 38,* 245–254.

Lazarus, R. S., & Folkman, S. (1984a). Coping and adaptation. In W. D. Gentry (Ed.), *The handbook of behavioral medicine* (pp. 282–325). New York: Guilford.

Lazarus, R. S., & Folkman, S. (1984b). *Stress, appraisal, and coping.* New York: Springer.

Lazarus, R. S., Kanner, A. D., & Folkman, S. (1980). Emotions: A cognitive-phenomenological analysis. In R. Plutchik & H. Kellerman (Eds.), *Theories of emotion* (pp. 189–217). New York: Academic Press.

Lazarus, R. S., & Launier, R. (1978). Stress-related transactions between person and environment. In L. A. Pervin & M. Lewis (Eds.), *Perspectives in interactional psychology* (pp. 287–327). New York: Plenum.

McCrae, R. R. (1984). Situational determinants of coping responses: Loss, threat and challenge. *Journal of Personality and Social Psychology, 46,* 919–928.

Mechanic, D. (1962). *Students under stress.* New York: The Free Press.

Menaghan, E. (1982). Measuring coping effectiveness: A panel analysis of marital problems and efforts. *Journal of Health and Social Behavior, 23,* 220–234.

Menninger, K. (1963). *The vital balance: The life process in mental health and illness.* New York: Viking.

Mitchell, R. E., Cronkite, R. C., & Moos, R. H. (1983). Stress, coping and depression among married couples. *Journal of Abnormal Psychology, 92,* 433–448.

Pearlin, L. I, & Schooler, C. (1978). The structure of coping. *Journal of Health and Social Behavior, 19,* 2–21.

Rehm, L. P. (1978). Mood, pleasant events, and unpleasant events: Two pilot studies. *Journal of Consulting and Clinical Psychology, 46,* 854–859.

Sarnoff, I., & Zimbardo, P. (1961). Anxiety, fear, and social affiliation. *Journal of Abnormal and Social Psychology, 62,* 356–363.

Schaefer, C. (1983). *The role of stress and coping in the occurrence of serious illness.* Unpublished doctoral dissertation, University of California, Berkeley.

Shinn, M., Rosario, M., Mørch, H., & Chestnut, D. E. (1984). Coping with job stress and burnout in the human services. *Journal of Personality and Social Psychology, 46,* 864–876.

Sidle, A., Moos, R. H., Adams, J., & Cady, P. (1969). Development of a coping scale. *Archives of General Psychiatry, 20,* 225–232.

Stone, A. A., & Neale, J. M. (1984). New measure of daily coping: Development and preliminary results. *Journal of Personalily and Social Psychology, 46,* 892–906.

Taylor, S., Wood, J. V., & Lichtman, R. R. (1983). It could be worse: Selective evaluation as a response to victimization. In R. Janoff-Bulman & I. H. Frieze (Eds.), Reactions to victimization. *Journal of Social Issues, 39*(2), 19–40.

Ursin, H. (1980). Personality, activation and somatic health. In S. Levine & H. Ursin (Eds.), *Coping and health* (NATO Conference Series III: Human Factors). New York: Plenum.

Vaillant, G. E. (1977). *Adaptation to life.* Boston: Little, Brown.

Weisman, A. D., & Worden, J. W. (1976–1977). The existential plight in cancer: Significance of the first 100 days. *International Journal of Psychiatry in Medicine, 7,* 1–15.

The Support of Autonomy and the Control of Behavior

Edward L. Deci and Richard M. Ryan
• Department of Psychology, University of Rochester

Editors' Notes

What is the role of autonomy in motivation and what conditions support it? Taking an organismic perspective, the authors propose that self-regulation of intentional behavior varies along a continuum from autonomy or self-determination to control or pressure. The more an intended behavior is autonomous, the more it is endorsed by the self as a whole and is experienced as emanating from one's own self, as an action for which one is responsible. Variability along this continuum occurs both across situations (or contexts) and across persons. There are both situational conditions and person conditions in which either autonomy or control is more likely to be experienced. Situational conditions that undermine autonomy include external rewards, deadlines, threats, and surveillance. Interpersonal feedback, including ever positive feedback, can be controlling as when suggesting what a person should do. Person conditions that undermine autonomy include public self-consciousness, a pressured and competitive orientation, and external locus of control. The authors also review evidence that greater autonomy has several motivational consequences, including greater interest in and enjoyment of tasks, less pressure and tension, and greater creativity and cognitive flexibility.

Discussion Questions

1. Describe the continuum from autonomy to control. Describe four situations that undermine autonomy.
2. Present evidence of three different motivational consequences of autonomy.

Authors' Abstract

In this article we suggest that events and contexts relevant to the initiation and regulation of intentional behavior can function either to support autonomy (i.e., to promote choice) or to control behavior (i.e., to pressure one toward specific outcomes). Research herein reviewed indicates that this distinction is relevant to specific external events and to general interpersonal contexts as well as to specific internal events and to general personality orientations. That is, the distinction is relevant whether one's analysis focuses on social psychological variables or on personality variables. The research review details those contextual and person factors that tend to promote autonomy and those that tend to control. Furthermore, it shows that autonomy support has generally been associated with more intrinsic motivation, greater interest, less pressure and tension, more creativity, more cognitive flexibility, better conceptual learning, a more positive emotional tone, higher self-esteem, more trust, greater persistence of behavior change, and better physical and psychological health than has control. Also, these results have converged across different assessment procedures, different research methods, and different subject populations. On the basis of these results, we present an organismic perspective in which we argue that the regulation of intentional behavior varies along a continuum from autonomous (i.e., self-determined) to controlled. The relation of this organismic perspective to historical developments in empirical psychology is discussed, with a particular emphasis on its implications for the study of social psychology and personality.

For several decades American psychology was dominated by associationist theories. Assuming that behavior is controlled by peripheral mechanisms, these theories held that the initiation of behavior is a function of stimulus inputs such as external contingencies of reinforcement (Skinner, 1953) or internal drive stimulations (Hull, 1943) and that the regulation of behavior is a function of associative bonds between inputs and behaviors that develop through reinforcement processes. With that general perspective, the central processing of information was not part of the explanatory system, so concepts such as intention were considered irrelevant to the determination of behavior.

During the 1950s and 1960s, associationist theories gave way to cognitive theories in which the processing of information was assumed to play an important role in the determination of behavior. On the basis of this assumption, the initiation of behavior was theorized to be a function of expectations about behavior-outcome contingencies and of the psychological value of outcomes (e.g., Atkinson, 1964; Tolman, 1959; Vroom, 1964), and the regulation of behavior was seen as a process of comparing one's current state to a standard (i.e., the desired outcome) and then acting to reduce the discrepancy (e.g., Kanfer, 1975; Miller, Galanter, & Pribram, 1960). Thus, the cognitive perspec-

tive shifted the focus of analysis from the effects of past consequences of behavior to expectations about future consequences of behavior. The concept of intentionality (Lewin, 1951) became important because behavior, whether implicitly or explicitly, was understood in terms of people's intentions to act in a way that would yield certain outcomes.

Within the concept of intentionality, however, a further distinction can usefully be made. Some intentional behaviors, we suggest, are initiated and regulated through choice as an expression of oneself, whereas other intentional behaviors are pressured and coerced by intrapsychic and environmental forces and thus do not represent true choice (Deci & Ryan, 1985). The former behaviors are characterized by autonomous initiation and regulation and are referred to as *self-determined*; the latter behaviors are characterized by heteronomous initiation and regulation and are referred to as *controlled*.[1]

We shall argue that the distinction between self-determined and controlled behaviors has ramifications for the quality of action and experience

---

[1]Like most dichotomies in psychology, being self-determined versus controlled is intended to describe a continuum. Behavior can thus be seen as being more or less self-determined.

and is relevant to the study of both social contexts and personality.

Intentionality and Autonomy

An intention is generally understood as a determination to engage in a particular behavior (Atkinson, 1964). In the cognitive theories of motivation and action (e.g., Heider, 1960; Lewin, 1951; Tolman, 1959), which have their roots in Gestalt psychology, having an intention implies personal causation and is equivalent to being motivated to act. Intentions are said to derive from one's desire to achieve positively valent outcomes or avoid negatively valent ones.

Using an intentional perspective, psychologists working in a neo-operant reinforcement tradition have emphasized that people's beliefs about whether certain behaviors are reliably related to desired outcomes are of central import. An abundance of research has shown, for example, that when a situation is structured so that outcomes are independent of behaviors (Seligman, 1975) or when people have a generalized belief that behaviors and outcomes are independent (Rotter, 1966), nonintentionality and maladaptation are likely to result. However, believing that behaviors are reliably related to outcomes is not enough to ensure a high level of motivation and adaptation. People must also believe that they are sufficiently competent to execute the requisite behaviors (e.g., Bandura, 1977). Indeed, the expectation of incompetence, like the expectation of behavior–outcome independence, has been shown to result in low motivation and maladaptation (Abramson, Seligman, & Teasdale, 1978). In sum, the cognitive perspective maintains that when people believe that desired outcomes will follow reliably from certain behaviors and that they are competent to execute those behaviors, they will display intentionality and experience personal causation (Heider, 1958).

Our organismic approach diverges from the cognitive approach by distinguishing between those intentional behaviors that are initiated and regulated autonomously and those that are controlled by intrapersonal or interpersonal forces. Whereas the cognitive approach equates the concepts of intention and choice (Lewin, 1951), the organismic approach reserves the concept of choice for those intentional behaviors that are autonomously

initiated and regulated, and it uses the concept of control for those intentional behaviors that are not autonomous. Thus, although having perceived control over outcomes (i.e., perceiving behavior–outcome dependence and competence) promotes intentionality, it does not ensure that the intentional behavior will be initiated and regulated autonomously.

The concept of autonomy is a theoretical rather than empirical one, though it has clear empirical consequences. Autonomy connotes an inner endorsement of one's actions, the sense that they emanate from oneself and are one's own. Autonomous action is thus chosen, but we use the term *choice* not as a cognitive concept, referring to decisions among behavioral options (e.g., Brehm & Brehm, 1981), but rather as an organismic concept anchored in the sense of a fuller, more integrated functioning. The more autonomous the behavior, the more it is endorsed by the whole self and is experienced as action for which one is responsible.

Let us clarify this point through some examples. First consider the behavior of an anorexic person abstaining from food. Clearly there is intentionality, yet the person would not appropriately be described as acting autonomously (or through choice), for the experience is one of compulsion (Strauss & Ryan, 1987). In a similar vein, the behavior of someone who is desperately seeking approval or avoiding guilt is intentional, but it is not autonomous. The person is compelled to engage in the behavior and would not experience a sense of choice. Finally, a person who follows a therapist's suggestion not out of an integrated understanding but rather out of deference to the therapist's authority is behaving intentionally, but until the action is self-initiated and grasped as one's own solution it would not be characterized as autonomous.

When autonomous, people experience themselves as initiators of their own behavior; they select desired outcomes and choose how to achieve them. Regulation through choice is characterized by flexibility and the absence of pressure. By contrast, being controlled is characterized by greater rigidity and the experience of having to do what one is doing. There is intention, but lacking is a true sense of choice. When controlled, people are, in the words of deCharms (1968), "pawns" to desired outcomes, even though they intend to achieve those outcomes.

Initiation and Regulation of Behavior

When someone engages in a behavior, there are generally aspects of the context that play a role in the initiation and regulation of that behavior. We have argued (Deci & Ryan, 1985) that these contextual factors do not, in a straightforward sense, determine the behavior. Instead, the person gives psychological meaning (what we call *functional significance*) to those contextual factors, and that meaning is the critical element in determination of the behavior.

Of central concern to the issue of autonomy and control in human behavior is whether people construe contexts as supporting their autonomy (i.e., encouraging them to make their own choices) or controlling their behavior (i.e., pressuring them toward particular outcomes). Thus, this review will consider varied social-contextual factors that have a functional significance of being either *autonomy supportive* or *controlling*[2] and it will relate each type of functional significance to the quality of people's experience and behavior. However, dispositional or person factors are also relevant to the study of autonomy and control. There are evident individual differences in the functional significance people give to contextual factors. Furthermore, individual difference measures of autonomy and control orientations have been used to predict people's experience and behavior directly, without reference to contextual factors. The current review is intended to give substance to the theoretical concepts of autonomy and control by examining research on both contextual and person factors that are relevant to that distinction. In addition, it will compare this organismic perspective to other perspectives within empirical psychology.

Contextual Factors

There are two broad sets of studies, generally considered to be in the province of social psychology, that focus on the autonomy supportive versus controlling distinction. The first set explored specific environmental events—things like task-contingent rewards, positive feedback, or imposed deadlines—that tend to promote either self-determined or controlled behaviors and the qualities associated with each. The second set of studies focused on interpersonal or social contexts, showing not only that general contexts can have either an autonomy-supportive or a controlling functional significance, but also that this varied functional significance has predictable effects on people's experience, attitudes, and behavior within those settings.

When the autonomy supportive versus controlling distinction was initially made (e.g., Deci & Ryan, 1980; Deci, Schwartz, Sheinman, & Ryan, 1981), it was hypothesized that autonomy-supportive events and contexts would maintain or enhance intrinsic motivation and that controlling events and contexts would undermine intrinsic motivation. Because intrinsic motivation has been so widely explored as the dependent variable in studies of autonomy-supportive versus controlling events and contexts, the effect of an event or context on intrinsic motivation can be used as one criterion for classifying whether that event or context tends to be experienced as autonomy supportive or controlling. Thus, within the reviews of research on external events and on interpersonal contexts, we will first present studies that used intrinsic motivation as a dependent variable, so as to specify the average functional significance of particular events or contexts. Then, within each of the two reviews, we will move on to studies that have explored the relation of those factors to other variables so as to explicate empirically the concomitants and consequences of self-determined versus controlled behavior.

External Events: Autonomy Supportive or Controlling

The term *event* refers to a specifiable occurrence or condition relevant to the initiation and regulation of behavior. The offer of a reward, for example, is an event, as is an instance of competence feedback, a demand, a deadline, and an opportunity for choice. The most frequently studied events have been rewards, though many others have also been explored. In this section, studies of the effects of various events on intrinsic motivation will be reviewed so as to allow each event to be classi-

---

[2]According to cognitive evaluation theory (Deci & Ryan, 1985b), inputs can also have an amotivating functional significance. These inputs signify or promote incompetence at reliably obtaining desired outcomes. They are not relevant to this discussion, however, as they promote nonintentional responding and impersonal causation.

fied as tending to be either autonomy supportive or controlling.

REWARDS

Dozens of studies have explored the effects of rewards on intrinsic motivation. These have included monetary payments (Deci, 1971), good-player awards (Lepper, Greene, & Nisbett, 1973), food (Ross, 1975), and prizes (Harackiewicz, 1979). In general, rewards have been found to undermine intrinsic motivation. When people received rewards for working on an interesting activity, they tended to display less interest in and willingness to work on that activity after termination of the rewards than did people who had worked on the activity without receiving a reward. This phenomenon, labeled the *undermining effect* (Deci & Ryan, 1980), has been most reliably obtained when rewards were expected (Lepper et al., 1973), salient (Ross, 1975), and contingent on task engagement (Ryan, Mims, & Koestner, 1983).

Ryan et al. (1983) pointed out that when rewards are differently structured, they have discernibly different effects. The authors provided a taxonomy of reward structures and related it to reward effects. Their review indicated that task-noncontingent rewards—those that are given independent of task engagement—were least likely to undermine intrinsic motivation because the reward is not given for doing the activity and thus is not salient as a control. Task-contingent rewards—those made contingent on doing the activity—have been consistently and reliably shown to undermine intrinsic motivation, presumably because their controlling function is salient. The effects of performance-contingent rewards—those given for attaining a specified level of good performance—are more complicated. Because they inherently provide positive competence feedback, the appropriate comparison condition is one that conveys the same feedback without a reward. When such comparisons have been made, performance-contingent rewards have generally been found to undermine intrinsic motivation, although they have sometimes been shown to maintain or enhance intrinsic motivation when the controlling aspect is minimized and competence cues are emphasized (Harackiewicz, Manderlink, & Sansone, 1984).

To summarize, many studies have shown that rewards, on average, undermine people's intrinsic motivation. It appears, therefore, that rewards tend to be experienced as controlling, which of course makes sense, as rewards are typically used to induce or pressure people to do things they would not freely do. When people behave in the presence of reward contingencies, the rewards tend to have a functional significance of control, thus representing an external event that restricts self-determination, although under certain circumstances they can be used to support self-determination.

THREATS AND DEADLINES

Using a modified avoidance conditioning paradigm, Deci and Cascio (1972) found that subjects who solved interesting puzzles to avoid an unpleasant noise demonstrated less subsequent intrinsic motivation for the activity than did subjects who solved the puzzles without the threat of noise. Amabile, DeJong, and Lepper (1976) found that the imposition of a deadline for the completion of an interesting activity also decreased subjects' intrinsic motivation for that activity. It appears, therefore, that these events, like rewards, tend to be experienced as controlling and thus to diminish people's self-determination.

EVALUATION AND SURVEILLANCE

Other experiments have indicated that the mere presence of a surveillant or evaluator, even without rewards or aversive consequences, can be detrimental to intrinsic motivation and thus, we suggest, to self-determination more generally. Lepper and Greene (1975), for example, found that surveillance by a video camera undermined the intrinsic motivation of children, and Plant and Ryan (1985) found the same result for college students. Pittman, Davey, Alafat, Wetherill, and Kramer (1980) reported that in-person surveillance also undermined intrinsic motivation.

Harackiewicz et al. (1984) found that subjects who were told that their activity would be evaluated displayed less subsequent intrinsic motivation than did subjects who were not told this, even though the evaluations were positive. Smith (1974) found the same results for intrinsic motivation to learn. Similarly, Benware and Deci (1984) and Maehr and Stallings (1972) have found that learning in order to be tested or externally evaluated has detrimental effects on intrinsic motivation for learning.

The effects of evaluation and surveillance are

not surprising, as both are integral to social control. These events tend to limit self-determination and thus reduce intrinsic motivation even when they are not accompanied by explicit rewards or punishments.

CHOICE

Autonomy-supportive events are defined as those that encourage the process of choice and the experience of autonomy. The one type of event that both fits the definition and has been shown, on average, to enhance intrinsic motivation is the opportunity to choose what to do.

Zuckerman, Porac, Lathin, Smith, and Deci (1978) found that when college student subjects were given a choice about which puzzles to work on and about how much time to allot to each, they were more intrinsically motivated during a subsequent period than were no-choice subjects in a yoked comparison group. The provision of choice enhanced their intrinsic motivation. Swann and Pittman (1977) reported similar results in an experiment with children.

POSITIVE FEEDBACK

The event of positive competence feedback has been widely studied as it relates to intrinsic motivation.[3] Several studies have found that it increased intrinsic motivation (Blanck, Reis, & Jackson, 1984; Boggiano & Ruble, 1979; Vallerand & Reid, 1984), although this has occurred only under certain circumstances (Fisher, 1978; Ryan, 1982) or for certain kinds of people (Boggiano & Barrett, 1985; Deci, Cascio, & Krusell, 1975; Kast, 1983). Taken together, the studies indicate that positive competence feedback neither supports autonomy nor controls behavior per se. It can enhance intrinsic motivation by affirming competence (e.g., Harackiewicz, Manderlink, & Sansone, in press) because intrinsic motivation is based in the need for competence as well as the need for self-determination, although it will do so only when the sense of competence is accompanied by the experience of self-determination (Fisher, 1978; Ryan, 1982).[4] But it can also undermine intrinsic motivation by being experienced as a form of interpersonal control (Ryan et al., 1983). The Harackiewicz, Abrahams, and Wageman (1987) article in this special section focuses on the issue of competence, whereas our article focuses on self-determination.

Effects and Correlates of Autonomy-Supportive Versus Controlling Events

The studies just reported used intrinsic motivation as the primary dependent variable and were used to help classify events as tending to be either autonomy supportive or controlling. It is interesting to note that more of the events manipulated in these experiments were experienced as controlling than as autonomy promoting. This makes sense, however, because autonomy must emanate from oneself and can therefore only be facilitated by contextual events, whereas control is something that can be done to people by contextual events and is therefore more easily evidenced. We shall now address additional effects of these autonomy-supportive versus controlling events to begin explicating the qualities of self-determined versus controlled behaviors.

INTEREST–ENJOYMENT

Along with the free-choice measure of intrinsic motivation, self-reports of interest are often obtained. Ryan et al. (1983) reported a correlation of .42 between the behavioral measure of intrinsic motivation and self-reports of interest, and Harackiewicz (1979) reported a correlation of .44 between intrinsic motivation and expressed enjoyment. Although research has not always found these strong correlations (see Ryan & Deci, 1986), self-reports of interest–enjoyment do appear to be related to intrinsic motivation. Furthermore, numerous studies that have not used the free-choice, behavioral measure have found that postexperimental interest–enjoyment is higher following autonomy-supportive events than following controlling events (e.g., Enzle & Ross, 1978).

CREATIVITY

Amabile (1979) reported that subjects who were told that their work would be evaluated produced artistic collages that were rated as less creative than

---

[3]Negative feedback has also been studied and has been found to reduce intrinsic motivation; however, we interpret these decreases as resulting from the feedback's being experienced as amotivating rather than controlling.

[4]In cognitive evaluation theory (Deci & Ryan, 1985), inputs that both affirm competence and promote self-determination are referred to as informational.

those produced by subjects who did not expect evaluations. Similar effects were found for surveillance (see Amabile, 1983). Furthermore, when children competed for a reward, they produced less creative collages than those produced in a noncompetitive condition (Amabile, 1982), and when children contracted for rewards they were also less creative (Amabile, Hennessey, & Grossman, 1986). Additionally, Kruglanski, Friedman, and Zeevi (1971) found that when subjects who wrote stories were rewarded with the opportunity to engage in an interesting activity in the future, their stories were judged to be less creative than the stories of subjects who were not rewarded. In sum, events that are typically controlling appear to affect creativity negatively, whereas events that are more autonomy supportive seem to promote creativity.

COGNITIVE ACTIVITY

Results similar to those for creativity have been reported for cognitive flexibility. McGraw and McCullers (1979) found that monetarily rewarded subjects had a more difficult time breaking set when doing Luchins-type (1942) water-jar problems than did nonrewarded subjects. Benware and Deci (1984) reported that evaluative tests impaired college students' conceptual learning in addition to undermining their intrinsic motivation. Grolnick and Ryan (1987) found impairments in conceptual learning of fifth-grade subjects who learned material under a controlling-evaluative condition rather than an autonomy-supportive one. It appears that when cognitive activity is controlled, it is more rigid and less conceptual, perhaps with a more narrow focus, than when it is self-determined.

EMOTIONAL TONE

Garbarino (1975) studied fifth- and sixth-grade girls who were rewarded with movie tickets for teaching younger girls how to do a sorting task. He reported that the rewarded tutors were more critical and demanding than were nonrewarded tutors. In a complementary study, children induced to interact with another child in order to play with a nice game had less positive impressions of that other child than did children who had not been focused on the incentive (Boggiano, Klinger, & Main, 1985). Controlling events, it seems, tend to induce a negative emotional tone and a less favorable view of others in that situation.

MAINTENANCE OF BEHAVIOR CHANGE

Rewards have also been studied as they relate to the persistence of behavior change following the termination of treatment conditions. A study by Dienstbier and Leak (1976) of a weight-loss program, for example, indicated that although rewards facilitated weight loss, their termination led to much of the lost weight's being regained.

When behavior is controlled by events such as rewards, the behavior tends to persist only so long as the controlling events are present. In terms of effective behavior change in therapeutic settings, the implication is that behavior change brought about through salient external controls is less likely to persist following the termination of treatment than is change that is brought about more autonomously. Behavior and personality change will be maintained and transferred, we have argued, when the change is experienced as autonomous or self-determined (Deci & Ryan, 1985).

To summarize, behavior undertaken when the functional significance of events is autonomy supportive has been related to greater interest, more creativity, more cognitive flexibility, better conceptual learning, a more positive emotional tone, and more persistent behavior change than has behavior undertaken when the functional significance of events is controlling. Thus far, research has related these motivationally relevant dependent variables primarily to the events of rewards and evaluation.

Interpersonal Contexts: Autonomy Supportive Versus Controlling

In the preceding discussion we described research on specific events relevant to the initiation and regulation of behavior. Numerous other studies have focused on interpersonal contexts rather than specific events. For example, in interpersonal situations the general ambience can tend either to support autonomy or to control behavior. We now turn to that research on interpersonal contexts. We begin, of course, with studies in which intrinsic motivation was the dependent measure, because those are the ones that we use to establish the usefulness of the distinction.

Studies of autonomy-supportive versus controlling contexts have been of two types. Some are correlational field studies in which the functional significance of the context is measured and related to motivationally relevant variables of people in those contexts. The others are laboratory experiments in which events such as rewards or feedback are administered within experimentally created autonomy-supportive versus controlling contexts.

GENERAL CONTEXTS

In one field study (Deci, Nezlek, & Sheinman, 1981), teachers and children in fourth- through sixth-grade classrooms were subjects. The researchers used a psychometric instrument to measure individual teachers' orientations toward supporting children's autonomy versus controlling children's behavior. They reasoned that teachers oriented toward supporting autonomy would tend to create a classroom context that promoted self-determination, whereas those oriented toward control would tend to create a controlling context for the children. The researchers then assessed the intrinsic motivation of children in the classrooms by using Harter's (1981) measure and found a strong positive correlation between teachers' autonomy support and children's intrinsic motivation. In another study, Deci, Schwartz, Sheinman, and Ryan (1981) analyzed changes in children's intrinsic motivation from the second day of school to the end of the second month. They found that children of autonomy-supportive teachers became more intrinsically motivated relative to children of control-oriented teachers.

EVENTS AND INTERPERSONAL CONTEXTS

Earlier, we saw that some events tend to be experienced as supporting self-determination and others tend to be experienced as controlling, and now we have seen that contexts can also be characterized as tending either to support autonomy or to control. A few studies have explored the effects of the same event in different experimentally created contexts.

In one study, Ryan et al. (1983) explored contextual influences on the effects of performance-contingent rewards: those rewards that people receive for attaining a specified level of good performance. Previous research had shown that these rewards generally undermined the intrinsic motivation of their recipients relative to that of subjects who received no rewards but got the same performance feedback that was inherent in the performance-contingent rewards. This means, in essence, that the reward itself tends to be controlling unless its evaluative component is removed (Harackiewicz et al., 1984). Furthermore, however, the positive feedback that is conveyed by the reward can enhance intrinsic motivation by affirming one's competence.

Ryan et al. argued that the effect of a performance-contingent reward could be significantly affected by the way it is conveyed, in other words, by the interpersonal context within which it is received. Two groups of college student subjects received performance-contingent rewards. Those in one group were told that they would receive a $3 reward if they "performed well," and those in the other group were told that they would receive a $3 reward if they "performed well, as you *should.*" Following each of three puzzles, subjects received positive feedback that was in line with the initial induction. For example, half were told, "You have done well," and the other half were told, "You have done well, just as you should." Then, at the end of the performance period, subjects were given the reward either "for doing well" or "for doing well and performing up to standards." It was expected, of course, that words like *should* and *standards* would serve to create a controlling context and lead the subjects to experience the rewards as controlling. Results revealed a significant difference between the intrinsic motivation of the two groups of subjects. Those who received rewards in an autonomy-supportive context were more intrinsically motivated than were those who received rewards in a controlling context. In other words, the interpersonal context within which the event (i.e., the reward) was administered affected the functional significance of the event.

The Ryan et al. (1983) results are consistent with others reported by Harackiewicz (1979), who also found significant differences between the intrinsic motivation of two groups of high school subjects receiving performance-contingent rewards. She had made one administration of the rewards less controlling by allowing subjects to self-monitor their performance against a table of norms, and these subjects were more intrinsically motivated than others who were not allowed to self-monitor.

In another study, Ryan (1982) argued that positive competence feedback, which is not inherently either autonomy supportive or controlling, will be differentially interpreted as autonomy promoting or controlling depending on the nature of the interpersonal context within which it is embedded. College student subjects received positive feedback, which either was made controlling through the use of additional words such as should (e.g., "Excellent, you did just as you should") or was noncontrolling. Again, results revealed that the subsequent intrinsic motivation of subjects who received positive feedback in an autonomy-supportive context was significantly greater than that of subjects who received it in a controlling context.

Finally, Koestner, Ryan, Bernieri, and Holt (1984) argued that it is even possible to constrain behavior in a way that will tend to be experienced as noncontrolling. In a field experiment with first- and second-grade children, limits were set regarding the children's being neat while painting a picture. Limits seem to be controlling by nature, yet they may be perceived as less controlling if they are set in a way that minimizes the use of control-related locution and acknowledges the probable conflict between what the limits require and what the person would want to do. The importance of the last point is that this acknowledgment conveys an appreciation of the perspective of the actor, thus decreasing his or her experience of being controlled. As expected, Koestner et al. found that children who received noncontrolling limits maintained their intrinsic motivation for painting (it did not differ from a no-limits comparison group), whereas those who received controlling limits showed significantly less intrinsic motivation.

Other Effects of Autonomy-Supportive Versus Controlling Contexts

The studies just reviewed all used the dependent variable of intrinsic motivation—assessed by the free-choice method, by self-reports of interest-enjoyment, or by Harter's (1981) questionnaire measure for children—to establish that the functional significance of interpersonal contexts can be either more autonomy supportive or more controlling. Numerous studies of autonomy-support-ive versus controlling contexts have used other dependent variables. Ryan et al. (1983), for example, also assessed experiences of pressure and tension and found, as one would expect from the definition of control, that subjects in a controlling context experienced greater pressure and tension than did those in a noncontrolling context.

SELF-ESTEEM, PERCEIVED COMPETENCE, AND AGGRESSION

In the classroom studies reported earlier, the children also completed Harter's (1982) measure of perceived cognitive competence and self-esteem. Deci, Nezlek, and Sheinman (1981) reported significant positive correlations between teachers' autonomy support and children's perceived cognitive competence and self-esteem. Furthermore, Deci, Schwartz, Sheinman, and Ryan (1981) reported that children in autonomy-supportive classrooms increased in perceived competence and self-esteem during the first 2 months of a school year relative to children in controlling classrooms. Finally, a study by Ryan and Grolnick (1986) found positive correlations between children's perceptions of the classroom as being autonomy supportive and their own perceived cognitive competence and self-esteem. With these three different research strategies, researchers found that when the interpersonal context of children's learning was autonomy supportive, the children perceived themselves to be more competent in their cognitive activity and felt better about themselves than when the context was controlling.

Ryan and Grolnick (1986) also had the children create stories about a neutral classroom scene using a projective technique. The researchers then rated the stories for thematic content. Results revealed that children who perceived their own classrooms to be autonomy promoting wrote about teachers who supported autonomy and children who were more self-determined, whereas children who perceived their classrooms to be controlling wrote stories with control themes. Furthermore, children who wrote about controlling classrooms projected more aggression into the classrooms than did children who portrayed the classroom as less controlling. Contrary to the common view that controls should be used to curb aggression, these results suggest that the aggression of children may be linked to their feeling controlled.

TRUST

Deci, Connell, and Ryan (1986) explored the relation between interpersonal contexts in work organizations and the attitudes and perceptions of employees in those environments. To do this, they developed a psychometric instrument to assess managers' orientations toward supporting autonomy versus controlling behavior. The instrument was conceptually analogous and structurally similar to the measure of teachers' orientations used by Deci, Schwartz, Sheinman, and Ryan (1981). The most salient finding in this study was that managers' orientations were strongly related to subordinates' level of trust. Subordinates with control-oriented managers had less trust in the corporation and its top management than did those with autonomy-supporting managers. This was particularly interesting because the data were collected in a large, geographically dispersed corporation, where most subjects had never met the corporate officers. Although the data were merely correlational, they suggest that the interpersonal context created by one's immediate manager may affect one's feelings and attitudes not only about the immediate environment but also about the whole organization.

CREATIVITY AND SPONTANEITY

Koestner et al. (1984) used Amabile's (1983) consensual assessment system to rate the paintings of 6- and 7-year-old children who had been given either autonomy-supportive or controlling limits. Results indicated that children who painted with autonomy-oriented limits were judged to have more creative and technically better paintings than were children who painted with controlling limits. The former children also showed greater spontaneity and less constriction in their paintings than did the latter. Whether an event itself or the context within which an event occurs tends to have a controlling functional significance, the behavior associated with it is likely to be less creative and more constricted. Creativity, it seems, is fostered by events and contexts that support autonomy.

PREFERENCE FOR CHOICE

In an experiment by Haddad (1982), 10- and 11-year-old children worked with age-appropriate anagrams. Half the children were given positive feedback with controlling locution, and half were given noncontrolling positive feedback. Subsequently, the children were told that they would be doing four more anagrams. Furthermore, they were told that they could select none, some, or all four of the ones they would work on and that the experimenter would select the rest. Results of the study indicated that when children had been controlled, they said they wanted to make fewer of the choices than when they had not, though this was primarily true for girls. It seems that the girls, when they were controlled, became more prone to allowing others to make their future choices for them.

BEHAVIOR

Deci, Spiegel, Ryan, Koestner, and Kauffman (1982) did a study of teaching behavior in which they created a more autonomy-supportive versus a more controlling context for subjects whose job it was to teach other subjects how to solve spatial relations puzzles. The controlling context was created by emphasizing to the teachers that it was their responsibility to see to it that their students performed up to high standards in the puzzle solving. This was expected to be experienced by the teachers as pressure toward particular outcomes and thus to have a functional significance of control.

The 20-min teaching sessions that followed were tape-recorded and subsequently analyzed by raters. The analyses revealed remarkable differences in the behavior of the two groups of teachers. Those who taught in a controlling context made about three times as many utterances, and many more of their utterances tended to be directives and to contain such controlling words or phrases as *should, have to, must,* and *ought to* than was the case for those who taught in a less controlling context. In addition, raters judged those who taught in the controlling context to be more controlling in their teaching behavior than those who taught in the less controlling context.

Teachers who had received the controlling induction proceeded from one puzzle to another, giving the solutions, as if rote memorization of solutions to specific problems was the route to learning problem solving. Teachers in the other group allowed their students to experiment with their own solutions. These teachers gave hints, but they seldom gave solutions. As a result of the different teaching, the students performed differently. Those with controlling teachers assembled twice as many puzzles as those with autonomy-supporting teachers, but they independently solved only one fifth as many puzzles.

In sum, the results suggest that when people are pressured to make others perform, they themselves tend to become more controlling. That in turn has negative consequences for the self-determination of people they relate to.

HEALTH

Langer and Rodin (1976) reported a study of the institutionalized aged in which an ambience that promoted self-determination—what we call an autonomy-supportive interpersonal context—was created for some of the residents. The intervention included a meeting devoted to discussing the residents' taking greater responsibility for themselves (vs. telling them that they would be well cared for by the staff), the opportunity to make choices about when they would attend a movie (vs. being assigned a time), and being given the gift of a plant that they were responsible to care for (vs. being given a plant that the staff would take care of for them).

Results of this study indicated that those elderly residents in the context that emphasized self-determination improved on both questionnaire and behavioral measures of well-being relative to those who lived in a context that did not. In an 18-month follow-up study, Rodin and Langer (1977) reported that there were still significant differences in well-being such that those residents whose self-determination had been supported were healthier than the other residents.

The Langer and Rodin study is often discussed as a study of control over outcomes; however, it went beyond merely providing control. The intervention not only gave residents control; it encouraged them to take initiative, to be more autonomous and self-determining. This can be contrasted with a study by Schulz (1976) in which elderly residents were given control over the hours they would be visited by volunteers in a visitation program. That intervention did not, however, encourage autonomous initiation and self-determination. The results did indicate short-term positive health effects for having control over outcomes, but a follow-up study (Schulz & Hanusa, 1978) showed

that after the visitation program was terminated, the subjects who had had control over outcomes evidenced significant declines in health. Apparently, it is only when people learn to experience their environment as supporting self-determination, only when they become more autonomous (rather than merely perceiving that they have control over outcomes), that there will be long-term positive effects on their health.

All of the research thus far reported has focused on the effects of inputs from the environment, whether specific events or interpersonal contexts. From these social psychological investigations, there is indication that when contextual factors function to support autonomy rather than to control, people tend to be more intrinsically motivated, more creative, more cognitively flexible, more trusting, more positive in emotional tone, and more healthy; they tend to have higher self-esteem, perceived competence, and preference for choice; their behavior tends to be appropriately persistent and to be less controlling; and they project less aggression. We turn now to studies that have focused on person variables rather than contextual variables: studies that are considered more in the province of personality.

Person Factors

Two sets of studies have focused on person factors. The first is composed of laboratory experiments on intrapersonal events or states—person processes such as ego involvement—that can be characterized as being either autonomy supportive or controlling. The second is composed of individual difference studies that focus primarily on causality orientations, which are people's tendencies to orient toward events and contexts that are autonomy supportive and those that are controlling.

Intrapersonal Events:
Autonomy Versus Control

Many of the inputs relevant to the initiation and regulation of behavior are intrapsychic and can be independent of external circumstances. Imagine, for example, a colleague who is lying on the beach with his or her mind idly wandering. An idea for a new experiment spontaneously occurs to the person, so with excitement he or she begins to design the experiment. The event that prompted the behavior was an internal, cognitive–affective event that could be characterized as autonomous. But one could easily imagine the person, while on vacation, designing an experiment out of an internal obligation, with the pressured feeling that he or she has to do an experiment to prove his or her worth. This event would also be intrapersonal, but it would be controlling. We predict that the consequences of these two types of internal events, which prompted the same overt behaviors, would be quite different and would have parallels to the consequences of the two types of external events.[5]

Although this hypothesis has received less empirical attention than the hypotheses discussed earlier, several studies have supported it. Ryan (1982) argued that the state of ego involvement as described by Sherif and Cantril (1947), a condition where people's self-esteem is hinged on performance, leads the people to pressure themselves in a way similar to the way external forces can pressure them. He suggested that this type of ego involvement is controlling and will thus undermine self-determination. In his study, college students worked on hidden-figures puzzles. Half of them were told that hidden-figures performance reflects creative intelligence and as such is used in some IQ tests. These subjects, being students in a competitive university, were expected to become quite ego involved and thus to be internally controlling. The other subjects were given a more task-involving induction, which was expected to initiate more autonomous self-regulation.

Results of this study supported the hypothesis. Those subjects who had been given the ego-involving induction displayed significantly less intrinsic motivation in a subsequent free-choice period than did those who had been given the task-involving induction. In addition, those subjects in the internally controlling (i.e., ego-involved) condition reported experiencing significantly greater pressure and tension than did those in the internally noncontrolling (i.e., task-involved) condition. It appears, therefore, that people can—and presumably do—pressure themselves in much the same way that they can be pressured by external events, and the results of controlling themselves in these ways are similar to the results of being externally controlled.

A follow-up study by Ryan and Deci (1986) used tape-recorded inductions of ego and task involvement to rule out the possibility of interper-

sonal control (e.g., the subject's trying to please the experimenter). The results replicated those of the Ryan (1982) experiment. Ego involvement in these studies refers to the induction of an inner, evaluative pressure. However, other researchers such as Sansone (1986) use ego involvement simply to mean that the value of an activity is highlighted for subjects, in which case it does not undermine intrinsic motivation.[6]

Plant and Ryan (1985) did a quite different study of internally controlling regulation and reported complementary results. In it they repeated the ego-involved/task-involved manipulation, again finding that ego involvement decreased intrinsic motivation, but they crossed this in a factorial design with three levels of self-consciousness. Using the concept of objective self-awareness introduced by Duval and Wicklund (1972), Plant and Ryan suggested that when people are objectively self-aware—aware of themselves as an object or as viewed by another—they are likely to regulate themselves controllingly (i.e., as if they were concerned about another's evaluation of them). Stated differently, objective self-awareness can constitute a kind of self-surveillance. Thus, Plant and Ryan (1985) hypothesized that the experimental treatments that have induced objective self-awareness would similarly induce internally controlling regulation and would therefore undermine intrinsic motivation. One third of the subjects worked in front of a mirror and one third worked in front of a video camera. The remaining third received no self-awareness induction. The self-awareness manipulations yielded a significant main effect, with the camera condition leading to the lowest level of intrinsic motivation and the mirror condition to the next lowest. Both self-consciousness groups differed significantly from the non-self-consciousness, comparison group.

Plant and Ryan (1985) had also premeasured subjects on public self-consciousness (Fenigstein, Scheier, & Buss, 1975), the dispositional tendency to view oneself as if through the eyes of another. They found that this variable was also negatively related to intrinsic motivation, presumably because

---

[5]Internal events can also be amotivating, though again they are not germane to the current discussion.

[6]Ryan (1982) suggested that the term *superego involvement* (rather than *ego involvement*) would in some ways be more accurately descriptive of the internal state that we assert is controlling.

the nature of one's self-focus is directly related to the relative autonomy of behavioral regulation, with public self-consciousness relating to a more controlling form of self-focus. The theoretical links between aspects of public self-consciousness, conformity, and social control await further explication.

Effects of Internal Events: Autonomy Versus Control

The consequences of autonomous versus internally controlled initiation and regulation have been less well explored, though we predict the same types of consequences as those reported for external initiation and regulation. Ryan (1982) found greater pressure and tension associated with internally controlling than with more autonomous self-regulation, and that parallels the Ryan et al. (1983) finding of greater pressure and tension associated with controllingly administered rewards than with noncontrolling rewards. We predict that such parallels would also appear for the other relevant dependent variables such as emotional tone and health. Indeed, it is possible that internally controlling regulation is involved in various stress-related syndromes.

Working in the area of achievement motivation, Nicholls (1984) recently suggested that there would be differences in the preferences and performance of task-involved versus ego-involved subjects. When task involved, he hypothesized, subjects will prefer moderately difficult tasks (ones that represent optimal challenges). When ego involved, however, subjects will focus on proving their competence (or not appearing incompetent), so they will select either very easy tasks that will allow them to succeed or very difficult tasks so they will have a good excuse for failing. Although Nicholls (1984) did not test these hypotheses directly, he reviewed studies that provide inferential support. For our purposes, the importance of the work is its suggestion that ego-involved subjects behave and attribute in a more defensive and self-aggrandizing way than do task-involved subjects. Being internally controlled leads subjects to focus on proving and defending themselves rather than engaging in activities for growth and challenge.

In sum, we have argued that the autonomy promoting versus controlling distinction is relevant to the categorization of intrapersonal events just as it is to the categorization of contextual events. When behavior is prompted by thoughts such as "I have to . . ." or "I should . . ." (what we call internally controlling events), the behavior is theorized to be less self-determined than when it is characterized by more autonomy-related thoughts such as "I'd find it valuable to . . ." or "I'd be interested in . . ." Accordingly, we predict that the qualities associated with external controlling events and with external autonomy-supportive events will also be associated with their intrapsychic counterparts. [. . .]

Self-Determined Versus Controlled Activity

The picture that emerges from this wide range of evidence is that when the functional significance of events or contexts is autonomy supportive, people initiate regulatory processes that are qualitatively different from those that are initiated when the functional significance of the events or context is controlling. Autonomy-supportive events and contexts facilitate self-determined or autonomous activity, which entails an inner endorsement of one's actions, a sense that they are emanating from oneself. Such activity is regulated more flexibility, with less tension and a more positive emotional tone, and this flexible use of information often results in greater creativity and conceptual understanding. When self-determined, people experience a greater sense of choice about their actions, and these actions are characterized by integration and an absence of conflict and pressure. Indeed, integration is the ultimate hallmark of autonomous regulation. By contrast, controlling events and contexts conduce toward compliance or defiance but not autonomy. Control, whether by external forces or by oneself, entails regulatory processes that are more rigid, involve greater pressure and tension and a more negative emotional tone, and result in learning that is more rote oriented and less integrated.

The Intrinsic–Extrinsic Metaphor

Intrinsically motivated behavior is by definition self-determined. It is done freely for the inherent satisfactions associated with certain activities and with undertaking optimal challenges. Many of the studies of self-determination have thus focused on intrinsic motivation. As a result, the self-determination versus control distinction has often been wrongly equated with the intrinsic versus extrinsic distinction. Even though intrinsically motivated behavior is the paradigmatic case of self-determination, it is not the only we of self-determined activity; extrinsically motivated behavior can also be self-determined.

Extrinsic motivation pertains to a wide variety of behaviors where the goals of action extend beyond those inherent in the activity itself. Persons can be described as extrinsically motivated whenever the goal of their behavior is separable from the activity itself, whether that goal be the avoidance of punishment or the pursuit of a valued outcome. Extrinsically motivated behavior is not necessarily either self-determined or controlled. One could willingly and freely pursue some extrinsic end (in which case it would be autonomous), or one could be pressured toward a goal (in which case it would be controlled).

This highlights an important definitional matter regarding intrinsic versus extrinsic motivation. What distinguishes the two is merely a teleological aspect, whether the behavior is done for its inherent satisfaction (intrinsic) or is done in order to obtain a separable goal. Although this distinction has historical and practical importance (see Deci & Ryan, 1985), it does not fully or adequately explicate the psychology of behavioral regulation because extrinsic or goal-oriented activity can vary considerably in terms of the degree to which it is autonomously regulated or controlled.

As an example, consider a person who derives considerable aesthetic pleasure from having a clean house but who does not enjoy the process of cleaning. If this person willingly chooses to clean the house, he or she would be self-determined in doing it. But the behavior would be extrinsic because it is instrumental to having a clean house, and the satisfaction is in the outcome rather than in the behavior itself. By contrast, consider another person who cleans because of a feeling that he or she has to, whether to get the approval of a business associate who will be visiting, to avoid guilt, or to satisfy a compulsion. In the case of this latter person, the extrinsically motivated behavior would be controlled.

In recent developmental work, Ryan, Connell, and Deci (1985) have outlined the processes through which children take on and eventually integrate extrinsic regulations so that initially external regulations can be the basis of self-deter-

mined functioning. The natural development of extrinsic motivation is described as a process of progressive internalization in which there is movement away from dependence on external prompts and controls toward greater self-regulation (Connell & Ryan, 1986; Ryan, Connell, & Grolnick, in press). This process involves identification with and integration of originally externally regulated action and results in more autonomous self-regulation. Work by Grolnick and Ryan (1986, 1987) and by Connell and Ryan (1986) indicates that the more extrinsic behavior is characterized by autonomy, the less it is accompanied by pressure and anxiety and the more it is associated with personal valuing of the goals involved.

Deci and Ryan (1985) have hypothesized that internalization and particularly identification are more likely to occur under autonomy-supportive than under controlling conditions. Two recent studies have provided initial support for this hypothesis. In the first, Grolnick and Ryan (1986) found that elementary-school children became more self-determined at extrinsically motivated activities with autonomy-supportive teachers than with controlling teachers. Furthermore, the researchers reported that children with autonomy-supportive parents were more self-determined in doing chores and homework than were children with controlling parents. Earlier research by Hoffman (1960) on moral behavior showed the complementary result that power-assertive (i.e., controlling) parenting styles were less effective for the internalization of moral behaviors than were styles more closely aligned to autonomy support.

In a second, experimental study (Eghrari & Deci, 1986), subjects engaged in an uninteresting computer-tracking task. Two groups of subjects received a rationale for doing the task and positive feedback about their performance on it. For one group the context was autonomy supportive, and for the other it was controlling. Results indicated that the autonomy-supportive context led to greater internalization of task value and greater persistence than did the controlling context and that internalization was positively correlated with experienced self-determination.

These studies suggest that extrinsically motivated behaviors can become self-determined through the process of integration and that the integrative process itself depends on the context's having an autonomy-supportive functional significance. In such cases the behavior is still extrinsically motivated, however, because the activity is still engaged in for reasons other than its inherent interest.

The Internal–External Metaphor

The internal-external distinction has been widely used in the past three decades in studies related to the regulation of behavior. Therefore, we shall briefly discuss its relevance to autonomy versus control. Basically, the metaphor has been used in two broad ways: to describe who or what is believed to control outcomes and to describe the experienced source of causality of one's behavior. Consider these in turn.

Rotter (1966) used the internal–external distinction to refer to expectations about control over reinforcements. One has an internal *locus of control* if one expects behaviors and reinforcements to be reliably related. Bandura (1977) added that expectations of competence are also necessary for internal control. The concept of internal control is therefore different from that of self-determination in two important ways. First, as we said earlier, expectations of behavior–outcome dependence and of competence promote intentional behavior, but they do not provide a basis of distinguishing between self-determined and controlled behaviors. Second, because the concept of locus of control was anchored to reinforcements, it failed to consider intrinsically motivated behaviors, which require no reinforcements.

Other work on internal–external control (e.g., Connell, 1985; Lefcourt, 1976) has used the term *perceived control over outcomes* (rather than locus of control of reinforcements). That work has included intrinsically motivated as well as reinforcement-dependent behaviors, but it too does not address whether the initiation and regulation of behavior is self-determined or controlled. Both self-determined and controlled behaviors can involve internal perceived control of outcomes.

The other way in which the internal–external metaphor has been used relates to the initiation and regulation of behavior. DeCharms (1968), elaborating on an earlier discussion by Heider (1958), spoke of an internal or an external *locus of causality* for behavior, pointing out that intrinsically motivated behavior has an internal locus of causality with the concomitant feeling of free choice, whereas extrinsically motivated behavior has an external locus of causality with the con-

comitant sense of dependence. We (Deci & Ryan, 1985) have modified the use of the locus of causality distinction to convey one's experience of whether a behavior is self-determined or controlled, namely whether one has a sense of "choice" versus "having to." Thus, the distinction does not strictly parallel the intrinsic–extrinsic distinction, nor does it refer to whether the initiating and regulatory factors are inside or outside the person. In motivational terms, factors inside the person are always involved in intentional behavior. However, all intentional behavior can be characterized as varying in the degree of relative autonomy, at one extreme having an external perceived locus of causality and at the other having an internal perceived locus of causality. For us, an internal perceived locus of causality describes the experience of an action's being one's own and being freely undertaken, whereas an external perceived locus of causality describes the experience of having to do something, of being compelled by heteronomous forces. Contextual factors as well as person factors can have either an autonomy-supportive or a controlling functional significance and can therefore promote either an internal or an external perceived locus of causality.

Weiner (1986, p. 46) has used the concepts internal–external control and internal–external causality interchangeably to refer to whether people attribute the cause of (i.e., the control over) outcomes such as successes or failures to factors such as effort that are inside the person (internal) or to factors such as luck that are outside the person (external). Therefore, Weiner's use of the locus of causality concept relates to the attributed causes of outcomes rather than to the experienced source of initiation and regulation of behavior, and it equates internal versus external causality with factors inside versus outside the person. Thus, his usage is consistent with the way the concept of internal–external control has traditionally been used, but it is inconsistent with our use of the concept of internal–external causality.

A straightforward and important implication of this discussion concerns what is typically referred to as the psychology of self-control (e.g., Bandura, 1977; Kanfer, 1975). A person can evidence self-control either through rigid, self-punitive methods or through more integrated, flexible methods. The former is herein categorized as internally controlling regulation and is exemplified by processes of introjection and ego involvement (Ryan, 1982;

Ryan, Connell, & Deci, 1985). The latter, more autonomous self-control can be described in terms of identification and integration of values and behavioral regulations. The clinical importance of this qualitative distinction has been treated elsewhere (Deci & Ryan, 1985).

Concluding Comments

In this article we have considered the implications of people's capacity to be autonomous and their vulnerability to being controlled. We have suggested that intentional behavior can be regulated in two qualitatively different ways: It can be flexibly and choicefully self-regulated or it can be controlled. Autonomous regulation is facilitated when events and contexts have an autonomy-supportive functional significance, and controlled regulation is promoted when events and contexts have a controlling functional significance.

When considered in terms of social psychology, the autonomy–control distinction is especially important in interpersonal situations involving power differentials: situations such as those of parent–child, teacher–student, manager–subordinate, or therapist–patient. Whether the basis of power (French & Raven, 1959) is rewards, force, position, expertise, or charisma, the person who is one down is particularly vulnerable to being controlled. An understanding of the autonomy–control issue can therefore clarify how authority relationships influence individuals' behavior, development, and experience. When considered in terms of personality psychology, the autonomy–control distinction is also very important for understanding behavior, development, and experience. It helps to clarify individual differences in selecting and responding to social situations, and it adds a qualitative dimension to the psychology of self-control.

The general framework offered herein thus highlights some ways in which the enigma of human choice and autonomy can be explored empirically to help explicate the dynamic interaction between persons and contexts.

REFERENCES

Abramson, L. Y., Seligman, M. E. P., & Teasdale, J. D. (1978). Learned helplessness in humans: Critique and reformulation. *Journal of Abnormal Psychology, 87,* 49–74.

Amabile, T. M. (1979). Effects of external evaluations on artistic creativity. *Journal of Personality and Social Psychology, 37,* 221–233.

Amabile, T. M. (1982). Children's artistic creativity: Detrimental effects of competition in a field setting. *Personality and Social Psychology Bulletin, 8,* 573–578.

Amabile, T. M. (1983). *The social psychology of creativity.* New York: Springer-Verlag.

Amabile, T. M., DeJong, W., & Lepper, M. R. (1976). Effects of externally imposed deadlines on subsequent intrinsic motivation. *Journal of Personality and Social Psychology, 34,* 92–98.

Amabile, T. M., Hennessey, B. A., & Grossman, B. S. (1986). Social influence on creativity: The effects of contracted-for rewards. *Journal of Personality and Social Psychology, 50,* 14–23.

Atkinson, J. W. (1964). *An introduction to motivation.* Princeton, NJ: Van Nostrand.

Bandura, A. (1977). Self-efficacy: Toward a unifying theory of behavioral change. *Psychological Review, 84,* 191–215.

Benware, C., & Deci, E. L. (1984). The quality of learning with an active versus passive motivational set. *American Educational Research Journal, 21,* 755–765.

Blanck, P. D., Reis, H. T, & Jackson, L. (1984). The effects of verbal reinforcements on intrinsic motivation for sex-linked tasks. *Sex Roles, 10,* 369–387.

Boggiano, A. K., & Barrett, M. (1985). Performance and motivational deficits of helplessness: The role of motivational orientations. *Journal of Personality and Social Psychology, 49,* 1753–1761.

Boggiano, A. K., Klinger, C. A., & Main, D. S. (1985). Enhancing interest in peer interaction: A developmental analysis. *Child Development, 57,* 852–861.

Boggiano, A. K., & Ruble, D. N. (1979). Competence and the overjustification effect: A developmental study. *Journal of Personality and Social Psychology, 37,* 1462–1468.

Brehm, S., & Brehm, J. W. (1981). *Psychological reactance: A theory of freedom and control.* New York: Academic Press.

Connell, J. P. (1985). A new multidimensional measure of children's perceptions of control. *Child Development, 6,* 281–293.

Connell, J. P., & Ryan, R. M. (1986). *Manual for the ASRQ: A theory and assessment of children's self-regulatory styles in the academic domain.* Unpublished manuscript, University of Rochester, Rochester, NY.

deCharms, R. (1968). *Personal causation: The internal affective determinants of behavior.* New York: Academic Press.

Deci, E. L. (1971). Effects of externally mediated rewards on intrinsic motivation. *Journal of Personality and Social Psychology, 18,* 105–115.

Deci, E. L., & Cascio, W. F. (1972, April). *Changes in intrinsic motivation as a junction of negative feedback and threats.* Paper presented at the meeting of the Eastern Psychological Association, Boston.

Deci, E. L., Cascio, W. F., & Krusell, J. (1975). Cognitive evaluation theory and some comments on the Calder, Staw critique. *Journal of Personality and Social Psychology, 31,* 81–85.

Deci, E. L., Connell, J. P., & Ryan, R. M. (1986). *Self-determination in a work organization.* Unpublished manuscript, University of Rochester, Rochester, NY.

Deci, E. L., Nezlek, J., & Sheinman, L. (1981). Characteristics of the rewarder and intrinsic motivation of the rewardee. *Journal of Personality and Social Psychology, 40,* 1–10.

Deci, E. L., & Ryan, R. M. (1980). The empirical exploration of intrinsically motivated processes. In L. Berkowitz (Ed.), *Advances in experimental social psychology* (Vol. 13, pp. 39–80). New York: Academic Press.

Deci, E. L., & Ryan, R. M. (1985). *Intrinsic motivation and self-determination in human behavior.* New York: Plenum Press.

Deci, E. L., Schwartz, A. J., Sheinman, L., & Ryan, R. M. (1981). An instrument to assess adults' orientations toward control versus autonomy with children. *Journal of Educational Psychology, 73,* 642–650.

Deci, E. L., Spiegel, N. H., Ryan, R. M., Koestner, R., & Kauffman, M. (1982). The effects of performance standards on teaching styles: The behavior of controlling teachers. *Journal of Educational Psychology, 74,* 852–859.

Dienstbier, R. A., & Leak, G. K. (1976, August). *Effects of monetary reward on maintenance of weight loss: An extension of the overjustification effect.* Paper presented at the annual convention of the American Psychological Association, Washington, DC.

Duval, S., & Wicklund, R. A. (1972). *A theory of objective self-awareness.* New York: Academic Press.

Eghrari, H., & Deci, E. L. (1986). *Facilitating internalization: The role of self-determination.* Unpublished manuscript, University of Rochester, Rochester, NY.

Enzle, M. E., & Ross, J. M. (1978). Increasing and decreasing intrinsic interest with contingent rewards: A test of cognitive evaluation theory. *Journal of Experimental Social Psychology, 14,* 588–597.

Fenigstein, A., Scheier, M. F., & Buss, A. H. (1975). Public and private self-consciousness: Assessment and theory. *Journal of Consulting and Clinical Psychology, 43,* 522–527.

Fisher, C. D. (1978). The effects of personal control, competence, and extrinsic reward systems on intrinsic motivation. *Organizational Behavior and Human Performance, 21,* 273–288.

French, J. R. P., & Raven, B. (1959). The bases of social power. In D. Cartwright (Ed.), *Studies in social power* (pp. 150–167). Ann Arbor: Institute for Social Research, University of Michigan.

Garbarino, J. (1975). The impact of anticipated reward upon cross-aged tutoring. *Journal of Personality and Social Psychology, 32,* 421–428.

Grolnick, W. S., & Ryan, R. M. (1986). *Parent styles associated with children's self-regulation and competence: A social contextual perspective.* Unpublished manuscript, University of Rochester, Rochester, NY.

Grolnick, W. S., & Ryan, R. M. (1987). Autonomy in children's learning: An experimental and individual difference investigation. *Journal of Personality and Social Psychology, 52,* 890–898.

Haddad, Y. S. (1982). *The effect of informational versus controlling verbal feedback on self-determination and preference for challenge.* Unpublished doctoral dissertation, University of Rochester, Rochester, NY.

Harackiewicz, J. (1979). The effects of reward contingency and performance feedback on intrinsic motivation. *Journal of Personality and Social Psychology, 37,* 1352–1363.

Harackiewicz, J., Abrahams, S., & Wageman, R. (1987). Performance evaluation and intrinsic motivation: The effects of evaluative focus, rewards, and achievement orientation. *Journal of Personality and Social Psychology, 53,* 1015–1023.

Harackiewicz, J., Manderlink, G., & Sansone, C. (1984). Rewarding pinball wizardry: Effects of evaluation and cue-valence on intrinsic interest. *Journal of Personality and Social Psychology, 47,* 287–300.

Harackiewicz, J., Manderlink, G., & Sansone, C. (in press). Competence processes and achievement motivation: Implications for intrinsic motivation. In A. K. Boggiano & T. S. Pittman (Eds.), *Achievement and motivation: A social-developmental perspective.* New York: Cambridge University Press.

Harter, S. (1981). A new self-report scale of intrinsic versus extrinsic orientation in the classroom: Motivational and informational components. *Developmental Psychology, 17,* 300–312.

Harter, S. (1982). The perceived competence scale for children. *Child Development, 53,* 87–97.

Heider, F. (1958). *The psychology of interpersonal relations.* New York: Wiley.

Heider, F. (1960). The Gestalt theory of motivation. In M. R. Jones (Ed.), *Nebraska Symposium on Motivation* (Vol. 8, pp. 145–172). Lincoln: University of Nebraska Press.

Hoffman, M. L. (1960). Power assertion by the parent and its impact on the child. *Child Development, 31,* 129–143.

Hull, C. L. (1943). *Principles of behavior: An introduction to behavior theory.* New York: Appleton-Century-Crofts.

Kanfer, F. H. (1975). Self-management methods. In F. H. Kanfer & A. P. Goldstein (Eds.), *Helping people change: A textbook of methods* (pp. 309–356). New York: Pergamon Press.

Kast, A. D. (1983). *Sex differences in intrinsic motivation: A developmental analysis of the effects of social rewards.* Unpublished doctoral dissertation, Fordham University, New York.

Koestner, R., Ryan, R. M., Bernieri, F., & Holt, K. (1984). Setting limits in children's behavior: The differential effects of controlling versus informational styles on intrinsic motivation and creativity. *Journal of Personality, 52,* 233–248.

Kruglanski, A. W., Friedman, I., & Zeevi, G. (1971). The effects of extrinsic incentive on some qualitative aspects of task performance. *Journal of Personality, 119,* 606–617.

Langer, E. J., & Rodin, J. (1976). The effects of choice and personal responsibility for the aged: A field experiment in an institutional setting. *Journal of Personality and Social Psychology, 34,* 191–198.

Lefcourt, H. (1976). *Locus of control.* Hillsdale, NJ: Erlbaum.

Lepper, M. R., & Greene, D. (1975). Turning play into work: Effects of adult surveillance and extrinsic rewards on children's intrinsic motivation. *Journal of Personality and Social Psychology, 31,* 479–486.

Lepper, M. R., Greene, D., & Nisbett, R. E. (1973). Undermining children's intrinsic interest with extrinsic rewards: A test of the "overjustification" hypothesis. *Journal of Personality and Social Psychology, 28,* 129–137.

Lewin, K. (1951). Intention, will, and need. In D. Rapaport (Ed.), *Organization and pathology of thought* (pp. 95–153). New York: Columbia University Press.

Luchins, A. S. (1942). Mechanization in problem solving: The effect of Einstellung. *Psychological Monographs, 54*(6, Whole No. 248).

Maehr, M. L., & Stallings, W. M. (1972). Freedom from external evaluation. *Child Development, 43,* 177–185.

McGraw, K. O., & McCullen, J. C. (1979). Evidence of a detrimental effect of extrinsic incentives on breaking a mental set. *Journal of Experimental Social Psychology, 15,* 285–294.

Miller, G. A., Galanter, E., & Pribram, K. H. (1960). *Plans and the structure of behavior.* New York: Holt.

Nicholls, J. G. (1984). Achievement motivation: Conceptions of ability, subjective experience, task choice, and performance. *Psychological Review, 91,* 328–346.

Pittman, R. S., Davey, M. E., Alafat, K. A., Wetherill, K. V., & Kramer, N. A. (1980). Informational versus controlling verbal rewards. *Personality and Social Psychology Bulletin, 6,* 228–233.

Plant, R., & Ryan, R. M. (1985). Intrinsic motivation and the effects of self-consciousness, self-awareness, and ego-involvement: An investigation of internally controlling styles. *Journal of Personality, 53,* 435–449.

Rodin, J., & Langer, E. J. (1977). Long-term effects of a control relevant intervention with the institutionalized aged. *Journal of Personality and Social Psychology, 35,* 897–902.

Ross, M. (1975). Salience of reward and intrinsic motivation. *Journal of Personality and Social Psychology, 32,* 245–254.

Rotter, J. B. (1966). Generalized expectancies for internal versus external control of reinforcement. *Psychological Monographs, 80*(1, Whole No. 609).

Ryan, R. M. (1982). Control and information in the intrapersonal sphere: An extension of cognitive evaluation theory. *Journal of Personality and Social Psychology, 43,* 450–461.

Ryan, R. M., Connell, J. P., & Deci, E. L. (1985). A motivational analysis of self-determination and self-regulation in education. In C. Ames & R. E. Ames (Eds.), *Research on motivation in education: The classroom milieu* (pp. 13–51). New York: Academic Press.

Ryan, R. M., Connell, J. P., & Grolnick, W. S. (in press). When achievement is not intrinsically motivated: A theory and assessment of self-regulation in school. In A. K. Boggiano & T. S. Pittman (Eds.), *Achievement and motivation: A social-developmental perspective.* Cambridge: Cambridge University Press.

Ryan, R. M., & Deci, E. L. (1986). *When free-choice behavior is not intrinsically motivated: Experiments on internally controlling regulation.* Unpublished manuscript, University of Rochester, Rochester, NY.

Ryan, R. M., & Grolnick, W. S. (1986). Origins and pawns in the classroom: Self-report and projective assessments of individual differences in children's perceptions. *Journal of Personality and Social Psychology, 50,* 550–558.

Ryan, R. M., Mims, V., & Koestner, R. (1983). Relation of reward contingency and interpersonal context to intrinsic motivation: A review and test using cognitive evaluation theory. *Journal of Personality and Social Psychology, 45,* 736–750.

Sansone, C. (1986). A question of competence: The effects of competence and task feedback on intrinsic interest. *Journal of Personality and Social Psychology, 5,* 918–931 .

Schulz, R. (1976). Effects of control and predictability on the physical and psychological well-being of the institutionalized aged. *Journal of Personality and Social Psychology, 33,* 563–573.

Schulz, R., & Hanusa, B. H. (1978). Long-term effects of control and predictability-enhancing interventions: Findings and ethical issues. *Journal of Personality and Social Psychology, 36,* 1194–1201.

Seligman, M. E. P. (1975). *Helplessness: On depression, development, and death.* San Francisco: Freeman.

Sherif, M., & Cantril, H. (1947). *The psychology of ego involvements, social attitudes and identifications.* New York: Wiley.

Skinner, B. F. (1953). *Science and human behavior.* New York: Macmillan.

Smith, W. E. (1974). *The effects of social and monetary rewards on intrinsic motivation.* Unpublished doctoral dissertation, Cornell University, Ithaca, NY.

Strauss, J., & Ryan, R. M. (1987). Autonomy disturbances in subtypes of anorexia nervosa. *Journal of Abnormal Psychology, 96,* 254–258.

Swann, W. B., & Pittman, T. S. (1977). Initiating play activity of children: The moderating influence of verbal cues on intrinsic motivation. *Child Development, 48,* 1128–1132.

Tolman, E. C. (1959). Principles of purposive behavior. In S. Koch (Ed.), *Psychology: A study of a science* (Vol. 2, pp. 92–157). New York: McGraw-Hill.

Vallerand, R. J., & Reid, G. (1984). On the causal effects of perceived competence on intrinsic motivation: A test of cognitive evaluation theory. *Journal of Sport Psychology, 6,* 94–102.

Vroom, V. H. (1964). *Work and motivation.* New York: Wiley.

Weiner, B. (1986). *An attributional theory of motivation and emotion.* New York: Spring-Verlag.

Zuckerman, M., Porac, J., Lathin, D., Smith, R., & Deci, E. L. (1978). On the importance of self-determination for intrinsically motivated behavior. *Personality and Social Psychology Bulletin, 4,* 443–446.

Bridging the Gap between Knowing and Doing

A simple way to think about motivation is as a state that bridges the gap between cognition and behavior; that is, the gap between knowing what is out there, and acting in order to get what one wants. Such a depiction may wrongly imply that knowing precedes wanting and that its formation does not require a motivational basis. In a sense, the situation appears to be quite the reverse. We do not seem to develop knowledge in a motivational vacuum but rather in the service of various wants to begin with. In other words, social and personality psychologists have stressed the functional or pragmatic nature of knowing. We are interested in some things and not others because they are useful to us in some way. (This point is emphatically made in the article by Fiske (1992) in the Suggested Readings section.)

Mischel and Shoda (1995) relate the interface of knowing and doing to one of the most fundamental questions of contemporary psychology: Is it possible to meaningfully talk of enduring personality dispositions given the considerable behavioral inconsistency in behavior that the same individual may exhibit in different situations? Mischel and Shoda offer an elegant solution to this problem— namely that behavior is consistent *within situations* but not *across situations*. The knowledge in this instance corresponds to individually perceived situational affordances and the actor's decision to act in a given way under given conditions. If those conditions are met, that is, if the situation affords a behavior, the behavior will be executed. Thus, in Mischel and Shoda's analysis an individual's knowledge of situational affordances gives rise to wants which in turn propel action.

But while knowing may occur in the service of wanting and doing, wanting itself is informed by knowing not only in the sense of selecting the appropriate means for goal attainment but of deciding what one's goals are in the first place. Commitment to a goal and taking action to attain it involves the determination of value and expectancy. The article by Ajzen and Fishbein (1970) in this section addresses the fundamental question of when a given behavior is likely to occur. The Ajzen and Fishbein (1970) notion is that the development of a behavioral intention, that is, the intention to perform the behavior, depends in part on the perceived consequences of the behavior (value) and the subjective likelihood that the behavior, indeed, will have these particular consequences.

The cognitive analysis of motivation in terms of expectancy and perceived value is also prominently featured in Atkinson's (1957) article on adjustment motives. In this article, the author analyzes individuals' behavior in achievement settings and derives it jointly from the person's dispositional achievement motives and the expectancy and incentive of goal-attainment as they are perceived in a given situation. According to Atkinson, in achievement settings the value of a success is directly proportional to the difficulty of attainment. It is the difficult tasks that are perceived as challenging and worthwhile, whereas the easy tasks are less valuable or challenging. Whereas the relation between value and difficulty may be particularly prominent in achievement settings, it does seem to exist in other domains as well, as illustrated by the economic principle of supply and demand where price (and hence value) is inversely related to availability (i.e., expectancy of attainment).

The information from which expectancies are formed is often provided "on line" as a function of our successes or failures en route to a goal. Such information attests to our self-efficacy in a given domain, telling us whether we are competent enough to attain our objectives. This topic is extensively dealt with by Bandura and Cervone (1983) in an article featured in the present section. These authors show that having an externally set goal is not enough to warrant effort expenditure on a task. To accept the goal as one's own, one needs to believe that one can readily attain it; that is, have enough positive feedback to develop a sense of self-efficacy in regard to the task.

A different perspective on the issue of feedback is provided in the article by Vallacher and Wegner (1987) that deals with the processes of labeling a given activity. Success feedback allows one to label the activity in terms of its underlying goal, or *why* the person is performing the activity, and hence to adopt a relatively abstract level of description. By contrast, failure at the activity focuses the individual's attention on *how* the activity is pursued leading to relatively concrete thinking about the activity. Thus, the very same activity can be thought about differently (see also Kruglanski, 1975) and in terms of different motivational constructs (namely as a goal and as a means). Vallacher and Wegener demonstrate that the level at which the activity is identified can have profound consequences for a variety of socially significant issues, such as performance under pressure, and the flexibility to change one's behavior.

REFERENCES

Ajzen, I., & Fishbein, M. (1970). The prediction of behavior from attitudinal and normative variables. *Journal of Experimental Social Psychology, 6,* 466–487.

Atkinson, J. W. (1957). Motivational determinants of risk-taking behavior. *Psychological Review, 64,* 369–372.

Bandura, A., & Cervone, D. (1983). Self-evaluative and self-efficacy mechanisms governing the motivational effects of goal systems. *Journal of Personality and Social Psychology, 45,* 1017–1028.

Fiske, S. T. (1992). Thinking is for doing: Portraits of social cognition from daguerreotype to laser photo. *Journal of Personality and Social Psychology, 63,* 877–889.

Kruglanski, A. W. (1975). The endogenous-exogeneous partition in attribution theory. *Psychological Review, 82,* 387–406.

Mischel, W., & Shoda, Y. (1995). A cognitive-affective system theory of personality: Reconceptualizing situations, dispositions, dynamics, and invariance in personality structure. *Psychological Review, 102,* 246–268.

Vallacher, R. R., & Wegner, D. M. (1987). What do people think they are doing?: Action identification and human behavior. *Psychological Review, 94,* 3–15.

Suggested Readings

Bargh, J. A., Chen, M., & Burrows, L. (1996). Automaticity of social behavior: Direct effects of trait construct and stereotype activation on action. *Journal of Personality and Social Psychology, 71,* 230–244.

Downey, G., Freitas, A. L., Michaelis, B., & Khouri, H. (1998). The self-fulfilling prophecy in close relationships: Rejection sensitivity and rejection by romantic partners. *Journal of Personality and Social Psychology, 75,* 545–560.

Fiske, S. T. (1992). Thinking is for doing: Portraits of social cognition from daguerreotype to laser photo. *Journal of Personality and Social Psychology, 63,* 877–889.

Klinger, E. (1975). Consequences of commitment to and disengagement from incentives. *Psychological Review, 82,* 1–25.

Sanbonmatsu, D. M., & Fazio, R. H. (1990). The role of attitudes in memory-based decision making. *Journal of Personality and Social Psychology, 59,* 614–622.

Taylor, S. E., & Schneider, S. K. (1989). Coping and the simulation of events. *Social Cognition, 7,* 174–194.

READING 8

A Cognitive-Affective System Theory of Personality: Reconceptualizing Situations, Dispositions, Dynamics, and Invariance in Personality Structure

Walter Mischel and Yuichi Shoda
• Department of Psychology, Columbia University

Editors' Notes

How can there be the kind of behavioral consistency postulated by the concept of personality when scientific studies of behavior have found that it is common for a person to behave differently in different situations? What does it mean to have control over one's behaviors if the behaviors are not consistent across different situations? The authors answer both questions by distinguishing between consistency as stability over time in the same situation and consistency as invariance across situations. They propose that personality is revealed in stable patterns of variability across situations. They discuss how cognitive–affective mediators, such as goal attainment, can account for these stable patterns and produce different behaviors in different situations in order to serve the same self-regulatory functions.

Discussion Questions

1. How does a cognitive–affective system theory of personality differ from a trait theory of personality in its conceptualization of behavioral consistency?

2. How can the same goal produce different behaviors in different situations?

Authors' Abstract

A theory was proposed to reconcile paradoxical findings on the invariance of personality and the variability of behavior across situations. For this purpose, individuals were assumed to differ in (a) the accessibility of cognitive–affective mediating units (such as encodings, expectancies and beliefs, affects, and goals) and (b) the organization of relationships through which these units interact with each other and with psychological features of situations. The theory accounts for individual differences in predictable patterns of variability across situations (e.g., *if* A *then* she X, but *if* B *then* she Y), as well as for overall average levels of behavior, as essential expressions or behavioral signatures of the same underlying personality system. Situations, personality dispositions, dynamics, and structure were reconceptualized from this perspective.

The construct of personality rests on the assumption that individuals are characterized by distinctive qualities that are relatively invariant across situations and over time. In a century of personality research, however, abundant evidence has documented that individual differences in social behaviors tend to be surprisingly variable across different situations. Although this finding has been interpreted as evidence against the utility of the personality construct, we show that it need not be and, on the contrary, that this variability reflects some of the essence of personality coherence. When personality is conceptualized as a stable system that mediates how the individual selects, construes, and processes social information and generates social behaviors, it becomes possible to account simultaneously for both the invariant qualities of the underlying personality and the predictable variability across situations in some of its characteristic behavioral expressions.

In this article, we begin with a review of recent empirical data demonstrating that individuals are characterized not only by stable individual differences in their overall levels of behavior, but also by distinctive and stable patterns of behavior variability across situations. These findings invite a new conception of personality in which such patterns of variability are seen not as mere "error" but also as reflecting essential expressions of the same underlying stable personality system that produces the individual's characteristic average levels of behavior. Toward that goal, we propose a cognitive–affective system theory of personality, drawing in part on the growing body of evidence and theorizing on individual differences in social and emotional information processing (e.g., as reviewed in Contrada, Leventhal, & O'Leary, 1990;

Dweck, 1991; Gollwitzer & Bargh, in press; Higgins, 1990, 1996; Higgins & Kruglanski, 1996; Markus 1977; Mischel, 1990, 1993; Pervin, 1990, 1994; Smith & Lazarus, 1990). Consistent with contemporary findings and theorizing on the biological bases of human information processing (e.g., Kandel & Schwartz, 1985), the theory assumes enduring individual differences in the features of situations that individuals select and the cognitive–affective mediating units (such as encodings and affects) that become activated, and that interact with and activate other mediating units (e.g., expectancies, goals, behavioral scripts and plans) in the personality system. This theory will be shown to take account of both the stability of the personality system and the variability of the individual's behaviors across situations in ways that reconcile numerous previously paradoxical findings and resolve basic controversies within personality and social psychology over many decades.

The Search for Personality Invariance

Conception of Personality in Terms of Behavioral Dispositions

In one long-standing tradition of personality psychology, individual differences in social behaviors have been conceptualized in terms of behavioral dispositions or traits that predispose individuals to engage in relevant behaviors. In its simplest form, dispositions and their behavioral expressions were assumed by definition to correspond directly: the more a person has a conscientious disposition, for example, the more conscientious the behavior will be. Figure 1 shows behavioral data typical of

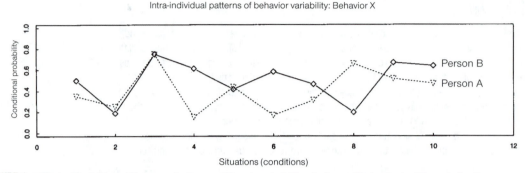

FIGURE 1 ■ Typical individual differences in the conditional probability of a type of behavior in different situations.

those found for any two individuals in a given domain of social behavior (e.g., friendliness) across different social situations. According to this model, dispositions determine the elevation of behavior in the profiles shown in Figure 1, and the variations of behavior across situations are irrelevant to personality.

Guided by this model, throughout the century researchers pursued cross-situational consistency as evidence for basic coherence in the underlying personality (behavioral) dispositions of individuals. In this search, cross-situational consistency in the expression of individual differences was defined as a relatively invariant rank-ordering of individuals across situations in their tendency to display trait-relevant behaviors and was measured with the cross-situational consistency correlation coefficient. The results in the search for this type of high cross-situational consistency were surprisingly discouraging from the start (e.g., Hartshorne & May, 1928; Mischel, 1968; Mischel & Peake, 1982; Newcomb, 1929; Peterson, 1968; Vernon, 1964). After years of study and discussion, the fact that the average cross-situational coefficients are typically low but nonzero is now widely accepted, although the interpretations continue to differ (e.g., Epstein, 1979; Mischel, 1984). Given such findings, the challenge has been to conceptualize and demonstrate the type of behavioral coherence that is produced by the invariant qualities within the person.

The most widely accepted current strategy within the behavioral disposition approach to personality is to acknowledge the importance of situations and the low cross-situational consistency in behavior generally found from situation to situation and then to aggregate the individual's behavior on a given dimension (e.g., "conscientiousness") over many different situations to estimate an overall "true score" (as discussed in Epstein, 1979, 1980; Mischel & Peake, 1982). This classic strategy, available ever since the Spearman–Brown formula predicted its effect at the turn of the century, recognizes that if the cross-situational consistency coefficients on average are above zero then the correlation between aggregate indexes can indeed be very high if enough situations are aggregated into the composite. Such correlations provide evidence that on average people differ significantly on a given dimension, demonstrating stable overall individual differences within virtually any domain of social behavior.

By averaging out variations across situations, however, this approach treats the variations in the individual's behavior across situations as unwanted or uninformative variance or as measurement error, and demonstrates that different people are in fact different on the whole with regard to the dimension. The approach is extremely useful for many goals, but its limits—as well as its strengths—are seen by analogy to meteorology, which studies systems that, like human behavior, seem unpredictable. No doubt overall climatic trends are useful to know, allowing, for example, the accurate prediction that in general, San Francisco is cooler and has higher precipitation than Los Angeles, and providing clues about the sources of such differences. If meteorologists were to focus only on the aggregate climatic trends however, they would constrain their understanding of the atmospheric processes that are responsible for the changing weather patterns and forgo the goal of more accurate specific prediction of weather. These limits notwithstanding, a current trend in the field seems to equate behavioral dispositions with the basic invariances of personality, with the personality construct, and indeed with the field of personality itself, as Pervin (1994) noted in a recent analysis.

Conception of Personality in Terms of Characteristic Mediating Processes

Throughout the history of the field, a second, fundamentally different, conception of personality invariance has construed personality as a system of mediating processes, conscious and unconscious, whose interactions are manifested in predictable patterns of situation–behavior relations. The relationship between the behavioral expressions and the underlying variables or processes is not necessarily one of direct correspondence. In these process conceptions, the personality assessor's task is to identify the meaningful patterns that characterize the person's behavior across seemingly diverse situations, and to discover the dynamics—the interactions among mediating process variables—that underlie that patterning and that can explain it.

Freud's psychodynamic theory was especially exciting exactly because it promised to offer such a conception in which the seeming inconsistencies and puzzling contradictions in behavior across situations would lose their mystery when their patterns of situation–behavior relations were seen, revealing the motivations and dynamics that underlie them. Although the empirical and methodological problems of Freud's theory became intractable for most psychologists, its appeal endured. It remained a vision and challenge for ultimately creating a dynamic mediating process theory that would capture the rich complexity and seeming contrariness of human behavior, not only in its abnormal manifestations but also in the ordinary situations of everyday life, not just for the exceptionally disturbed but for everyone. Freud's theory, of course, was only the first and boldest of process theories in what by now has become a long tradition, whose early pioneers include such figures as Henry Murray, Gardner Murphy, Kurt Lewin, and George Kelly.

In contemporary personality and social psychology, mediating process models have had a remarkable resurgence in the last two decades (see Cervone, 1991; Pervin, 1990). Although there are many differences among them in specific variables, they have family resemblance in their common focus on social cognitive mediating processes that underlie and motivate behavior. Many of these current process models use language and theoretical constructs that draw extensively on social, cognitive, and social learning theories and concepts, as well as on self theories and research (e.g., Bandura, 1982, 1986; Cantor, 1990; Dodge, 1986, 1993; Downey & Walker, 1989; Dweck & Leggett, 1988; Fiske & Taylor, 1991; Higgins, 1987; Kihlstrom & Cantor, 1984; Markus & Kitayama, 1991; Mischel, 1973, 1990; Scheier & Carver, 1988a; Shoda & Mischel, 1993). Most seem to be predominantly "social cognitive" in their preferred theoretical language, but they also are paying attention to the role of automatic and unconscious processing (e.g., Kihlstrom, 1987, 1990; Uleman & Bargh, 1989) and are concerned with the goals and motivations that underlie behavior (e.g., Gollwitzer & Bargh, in press; Pervin, 1989; Read & Miller, 1989).

Most important for the analysis of the nature of personality invariance and its behavioral expressions, process models seem to suggest that clues about the person's underlying qualities—the construals and goals, the motives and passions, that drive the individual—may be seen in when and where a type of behavior is manifested, not only in its overall frequency. If so, the patterns of situation–behavior relationships shown by a person might be a possible key to individuality and personality coherence, rather than an error source to be eliminated systematically.

Consider the differences between two people, A and B, whose behavior in a particular domain (e.g., their friendly behavior across situations), is shown in Figure 1. In the behavioral disposition view, the observed variability within each person on a dimension is seen as "error" and averaged out to get the best approximation of the underlying stable "true score." The goal is a single average summary score of the amount of the disposition each person has and the question simply becomes: Is A different overall in the level of aggressiveness than B? This question is important, and perhaps the best first one to ask, but it may be only the start of the analysis of personality invariance. It may also be its premature end if we ignore the profile information about where and when A and B differ in their unique pattern with regard to the particular dimension of behavior.

From the perspective of a process conception of personality one must ask: Are the individual's distinctive *if . . . then . . .* , situation–behavior relations within a particular domain of social behavior stable and meaningful? Granted that some of the variation in the individual's behavior across situations is random fluctuation (i.e., from unknown sources), is there a component that still may be enduring and reflective of underlying invariance? If the observed variability is simply "error," it needs to be removed; if it is potentially stable and meaningful, it may contain important clues about the underlying personality system, reflecting something of the essence of personality coherence and the system that produces it. Given these theoretical questions, it becomes necessary to determine empirically if distinctive and meaningful profiles of situation–behavior relations in fact characterize individual differences in the organization of social behavior as it occurs in vivo across everyday situations over an extended period of time.

Empirical Evidence for Intra–Individually Stable, If . . . Then . . . , Situation–Behavior Relations as Signatures of Personality

Data on the existence and meaningfulness of the hypothesized, stable *if . . . then . . .* , situation–behavior relations came from an extensive observational study conducted in a residential summer camp setting for children (Shoda, 1990; Shoda, Mischel, & Wright, 1989, 1993a, 1993b, 1994; Wright & Mischel, 1987, 1988). The first requirement in the field study undertaken was to identify the situations in which the behavior occurred (Shoda et al., 1994). In studies of the consistency of behavior across situations, the situations usually have been defined in nominal terms, as places and activities in the setting, for example, as woodworking activities, arithmetic tests, dining halls, or school playgrounds (e.g., Hartshorne & May, 1928; Newcomb, 1929). Individual differences in relation to such specific *nominal situations*, even if highly stable, necessarily would be of limited generalizability. On the other hand, if situations are redefined to capture their basic *psychological features*, then information about a person's behavior tendencies specific to those situations (Kelly, 1955; Mischel, 1973) might be used to predict behavior across a broad range of contexts that contain the same psychological features (Shoda et al., 1994). For example, situations that include criticism or lack of attention from a partner might be those in which individuals sensitive to rejection in

intimate relations become consistently more upset than others.

It was thus important to identify the relevant psychological features that occur within many nominal situations for the population studied, consisting of children ages 7 to 13, in this setting. A preliminary study identified the features of situations that seemed to be used spontaneously by the participants to characterize each other. Children and staff in the camp setting of the research were asked to characterize individuals who were prototype exemplars for the behavioral dimensions salient in the setting (Wright & Mischel, 1988). They were asked to tell "everything about [child], so I will know him as well as you do," and their descriptions were tape recorded and coded. The situational modifiers (e.g., "when someone teases him about his glasses"), which were used to qualify statements about the target's behaviors in these open-ended descriptions, were subjected to cluster analysis to identify commonly used features of such modifiers.

Two main constituent features in the encoding of interpersonal situations emerged: valence (positive vs. negative) of the interaction, and type of person (adult counselor vs. child peer) involved in the interaction. Examples of each combination of these features were selected to identify those that were psychologically salient within the setting (e.g., Susi, 1986; Wright & Mischel, 1988) that could be recorded objectively as they occurred and that were of potentially broad significance (i.e., that occurred often in many different nominal situations). The five interpersonal situations selected included three negative situations ("peer teased, provoked, or threatened"; "adult warned the child"; and "adult gave the child time out," i.e., prohibited the child from participating in the group activity for a certain amount of time), and two positive situations ("peer initiated positive social contact" and "adult praised the child verbally").

In the residential camp setting, the social behavior of participants was extensively observed on selected dimensions (e.g., verbal aggression, withdrawal, friendly, prosocial behavior) as it occurred in relation to each of the selected interpersonal situations (Shoda et al., 1989, 1993a, 1994). Briefly, participants were closely but unobtrusively observed in the course of the 6-week summer, with an average of 167 hours of observation per participant. Using this extensive data archive, the situation–behavior profiles of each of the participants were examined to test the hypothesis that these patterns of *if . . . then . . .* , situation–behavior relations reflect distinctive and stable characteristics of the person's behavior organization and not simply random fluctuations or "error." Specifically, for each person the stability of the profile of situation–behavior relationships was assessed. The frequencies of behavior were first converted to standardized scores within each situation to indicate the level of an individual's behavior in a situation relative to the normative levels in that situation. Each person's situation–behavior profile reflects how his or her pattern of variability across situations deviates from the normative pattern for the sample.

Figure 2 illustrates situation–behavior profiles of two children showing their verbally aggressive behavior across five types of situations sampled. On the vertical axis, the behaviors are shown in scores standardized with regard to the mean and standard deviation for each situation separately. Thus, 0 indicates that the probability for the behavior is at the normative (mean) level for that situation, whereas 1 and –1 indicate behavior probabilities that are 1 *SD* above or below the normative level within each situation, respectively. Standardization removes all the main effects of situations, so that the remaining intraindividual variance in the profile reflects the unique way in which the individual's behavior varies across the situations, above and beyond what is expected from the differences in the normative levels of behavior across situations. This type of data representation, which we refer to as *situation–behavior profiles*, shows how a particular individual's behavior pattern across the situations differs from the normative pattern of behavior variation across them (Shoda et al., 1994).

Note that if personality is conceptualized in terms of behavioral dispositions, the individual's variation in behavior across situations reflects differences among situations in people's typical levels of behavior (e.g., more cheerful at parties than at funerals), as well as the effects of measurement noise or random fluctuation. Therefore, when the data are standardized and rescaled relative to the typical level of behaviors expected in each situation, removing the main effects of situations, the remaining variation in an individual's behavior across situations should simply be "noise." Then,

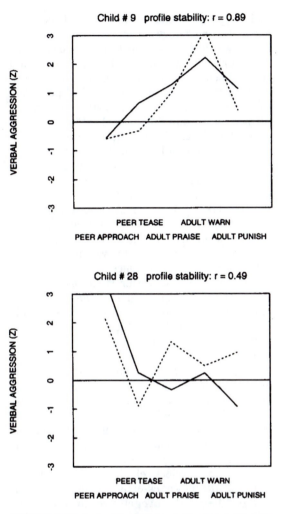

FIGURE 2 ■ Illustrative intra-individual, situational–behavior profiles for verbal aggression in relations to five situations in two time samples (solid and dotted lines). Data are shown in standardized scores (Z) relative to the normative levels of verbal aggression in each situation. (From Shoda, Mischel, & Wright, 1994, Figure 1, p. 678).

the mean stability of the intraindividual pattern of variation should be zero. On the other hand, if the observed situation–behavior profile reflects enduring qualities of the individual, it should show some significant stability despite the noise.

The two lines in the figure indicate the profiles based on two different, nonoverlapping, samples of situations in which the child encountered each type of psychological situation, shown as Time 1 and Time 2. To illustrate, Child 9 was more verbally aggressive than others (standardized score above 2.0 on average) when warned by an adult, but showed less aggression than others on average when approached positively by a peer (standard score of below 0). In contrast, Child 28 was most verbally aggressive when approached positively by a peer, but not particularly aggressive when warned by an adult (Shoda et al., 1994).

As these examples illustrate, the stability of intraindividual profiles varied from one individual to another and for different types of behavior. To test the overall hypothesis, the ipsatively computed profile stabilities for each individual were computed and the statistical significance of the group mean stability was tested (by t tests after Fisher's r-to-z transformation). The mean stability coefficients were .47 ($p < .01$) for verbal aggression, .41 ($p < .01$) for compliance, .28 ($p < .01$) for whining, and .19 ($p < .05$) for prosocial talk (Shoda et al., 1994).[1] Thus, overall, *if . . . then. . . .* , situation–behavior profiles were significantly stable over the course of the summer.

Compelling evidence for even subtler discriminativeness and stability of these behavioral coherences is seen in the intraindividual profiles among situations of the same valence. For each child, the stability of his or her pattern of behavior variability over the three negative situations was computed. Even though all three situations were negative in valence, and therefore the differences among them were subtler than among the five situations collectively, the mean profile stability coefficient was essentially as high as the stability of the profiles over all five situations. Specifically, they were .48 ($p < .01$) for verbal aggression, .32 ($p < .05$) for physical aggression, .45 ($p < .01$) for compliance, .08 ($p > .05$) for whining, and .20 ($p > .05$) for prosocial talk (Shoda et al., 1994). Thus for a significant portion of the children, in spite of the fact that all three of these situations were of negative valence, they still were psychologically distinct, and the child's aggressive and compliant responses to each situation were discriminative in ways that stably characterized him or her with a predictable *if . . . then . . .* pattern. It should be clear that these significant manifesta-

tions of behavioral coherence are obscured in the usual analyses of cross-situational consistency or by aggregating behaviors over different situations.

Recall that the conception of personality as behavioral dispositions implies that intraindividual variations in a type of behavior across situations (after the main effects of situations are removed by standardization) reflect only intrinsic unpredictability or measurement error. If that assumption were correct, the stability of the intraindividual pattern of variation should on average be zero. The overall findings are obviously inconsistent with this prediction and indicate that the situation–behavior profiles reflect a statistically significant, stable facet of individual differences in social behavior observed as it unfolds in vivo in everyday social situations. They are consistent with parallel findings showing significant amounts of variance attributable to Person × Situation interaction in analysis of variance studies, based on questionnaire responses (e.g., Endler & Hunt, 1969; Endler, Hunt, & Rosenstein, 1962; Endler & Magnusson, 1976; Magnusson & Endler, 1977). Furthermore, as shown elsewhere (Shoda, 1990), the degree that an individual is characterized by stable patterns of situation–behavior relations is negatively related to the level of overall cross-situational consistency that can be expected.

These profiles allow a glimpse of the essential configuration or pattern of behavior variation in relation to situations that is expressive of personality invariance but is completely bypassed in the traditional search for cross-situational consistency. Instead of searching for the traditional cross-situational consistency coefficient that has been pursued for most of the century (e.g., Hartshorne & May, 1928; Mischel, 1968; Newcomb, 1929; Peterson, 1968; Vernon, 1964), the findings of profile stability suggest that personality coherence must be reflected in the intraindividual stable pattern of variability. From this perspective, the explicit focus on the relationships between psychological features of situations and the individual's patterns of behavior variation across situations, rather than undermining the existence of personality, needs to become part of the conception of personality (e.g., Mischel, 1973, 1990; Shoda & Mischel, 1993; Shoda et al., 1994; Wright & Mischel, 1987). However, if situation units are defined in terms of features salient for the researcher but trivial for, or irrelevant to, the individuals studied, one cannot expect their behaviors

---

[1]Profile stability for physical aggression could not be computed by Shoda et al. (1994) because there were virtually no individual differences in physical aggression when "praised by an adult," and physical aggression was displayed only by one child in the entire summer in this situation.

to vary meaningfully across them, and the resulting pattern of behavior variation therefore would be unstable and meaningless. To discover the potentially predictable patterns of behavior variability that characterize individuals, a first step is to identify those features of situations that are meaningful to them and that engage their important psychological qualities (e.g., personal constructs and goals).

Revisiting the Classic Personality Paradox: The Behavioral Invariance of Those Who Perceive Themselves as Consistent

If stable situation–behavior patterns like these are meaningful reflections of personality invariance, they also may be related to self-perceptions about one's own consistency with regard to that behavior. To consider the relationship between the stability of the person–situation profile that characterizes an individual in a particular domain of behavior and the self-perception of consistency, we reexamined data that address the classic "personality paradox." It was noted two decades ago that on the one hand our intuitions convince us that people have broad behavioral dispositions that we see in the extensive consistency of their behaviors across situations, but on the other hand, the research results on cross-situational consistency in behavior persistently contradict this conviction (Bem & Allen, 1974). To resolve this dilemma and to show our intuitions are better than our research, Bem and Allen reasoned that because traditional nomothetic methodologies assume that all traits belong to all persons, the inconsistency of those for whom the trait is irrelevant will obscure the consistency of the subset of people for whom the trait is relevant. They therefore argued that a solution to the consistency problem requires first selecting on an a priori basis those persons who perceive themselves as consistent in the given disposition. We then should expect to find high cross-situational consistency in their behavior in that domain, but not in the behavior of those who see themselves as inconsistent with regard to it, or to whom it is irrelevant.

Initially, some encouraging support was obtained for this prediction (Bem & Allen, 1974). In a more comprehensive test in the Carleton College field study, behavior relevant to conscientiousness was observed in vivo over multiple situations and occasions (Mischel & Peake, 1982). Each of the 63 participating college students had been observed repeatedly in various situations on campus relevant to their conscientiousness in the college setting. The specific behaviors and contexts selected as relevant were supplied by undergraduates themselves in pretesting at the college. Conscientiousness was sampled in various situations such as in the classroom, in the dormitory, in the library, and the assessments occurred over repeated occasions in the course of the semester. It was found that actual consistency in their cross-situational behavior was not significantly greater for them than it was for those who perceived themselves as variable. (The same pattern was found in the Bem–Allen results, as well as in the Carleton data, as discussed in Mischel & Peake, 1982). Self-perceived consistency, however, was related to the temporal stability of their relevant behavior within particular types of situations.

For the present article, we reexamined those data to test the hypothesis that the students' self-perceptions of consistency will be related not only to the temporal stability of their behaviors within situations but also to the stability of their situation-behavior profiles. As the first set of two columns of Figure 3 show, and as Mischel and Peake (1982) reported, those who perceived themselves as con-

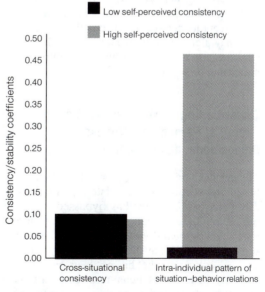

FIGURE 3 ■ Self-perceived consistency and the organization of behavior. Cross-situational consistency and the stability of person-situation profiles for people high versus low in perceived consistency in consciousness. (Based on data in Mischel and Peake, 1982, and reanalyses by Shoda, 1993.)

sistent (the first light column) did not show greater overall cross-situational consistency than those who did not. The second set of columns provides clear support for the hypothesis of coherence in terms of situation–behavior profiles: For individuals who perceived themselves as consistent, the average situation–behavior profile stability correlation was near .5, whereas it was trivial for those who saw themselves as inconsistent. Thus, the self-perception of consistency seems to be linked to stability in the situation–behavior profiles, and may be rooted in the personologically meaningful pattern of behavior variability that characterizes an individual. If so, the intuition of consistency is neither paradoxical nor illusory: it is based on behavioral consistency but not the sort for which the field was searching for so many years.

In sum, the finding of meaningful stable situation–behavior profiles indicates that there are characteristic intraindividual patterns in how individuals relate to different psychological conditions and that these patterns form a sort of behavioral signature that reflects personality coherence (Shoda et al., 1994). In retrospect, what seems remarkable is not so much that this type of behavioral signature of personality exists, but rather that it continues to be treated as error and eliminated by simply averaging behavior over diverse situations. Although such aggregation is widely seen as the way to capture personality, it actually removes data that may alert us to the person's most distinctive qualities and to his or her unique intraindividual patterning of social behavior.

Toward a Cognitive–Affective System Theory of Personality Processes, Dispositions, and Dynamics

The evidence reviewed suggests that the search for broad cross-situational consistency in individual differences in behavior has bypassed the stable intraindividual patternings of meaningful variability that mark the individual's distinctive behavior organization. The data demonstrate a type of personality coherence that has not been captured adequately in terms of behavioral dispositions. It cannot be dismissed as error and simply aggregated away without losing something of the essence of personality. It is consistent with other findings that have encouraged recent social cognitive analyses of the processes that underlie individual

differences (e.g., as reviewed in Gollwitzer & Bargh, in press; Higgins & Kruglanski, in press; Mischel, 1990; Pervin, 1990, 1994). Collectively, these developments call for a theory of a personality system that allows us to understand both the stable differences between people in their overall characteristic levels of different types of behavior and, concurrently, their stable profiles of situation–behavior variability.

Characteristics of the Theory

This theory incorporates into the conception of personality the role of situations, events, or contexts (Bandura, 1986; Mischel, 1968, 1973; Ross & Nisbett, 1991; Shoda et al., 1993b; Wright & Mischel, 1987). The concept of the situation, however, is not like the simple stimulus in early behaviorism that mechanically pulls responses from an organism's repertoire. Features of situations activate a set of internal reactions—not just cognitive but also affective—based on the individual's prior experience with those features (Mischel, 1973). These features of situations are encountered in the external environment but they also are generated in thought, planning, fantasy, and imagination (e.g., Antrobus, 1991; Gollwitzer, 1993; Klinger, 1977; Mischel, Shoda, & Rodriguez, 1989). They encompass not just social and interpersonal situations (as when lovers "reject" or peers "tease and provoke") but also intrapsychic situations, as in mood states (e.g., Isen, Niedenthal, & Cantor, 1992; Schwarz, 1990) and in the everyday stream of experience and feeling (e.g., Bolger & Eckenrode, 1991; Cantor & Blanton, in press; Emmons, 1991; Smith & Lazarus, 1990; Wright & Mischel, 1988).

Thus, what constitutes a situation in part depends on the perceiver's constructs and subjective maps, that is, on the acquired meaning of situational features for that person, rather than being defined exclusively by the observing scientist (e.g., Kelly, 1955; Medin, 1989; Mischel, 1973). In the proposed theory, individuals differ in how they selectively focus on different features of situations, how they categorize and encode them cognitively and emotionally, and how those encodings activate and interact with other cognitions and affects in the personality system. The theory views the person not as reacting passively to situations, nor as generating behavior impervious to their subtle features, but as active and goal-directed, constructing plans and self-generated changes, and in part creating the situations themselves. The organization of cognitions and affects in the system reflects the individual's total experience, and hence cognitive social learning history, but it is rooted in biological foundations and therefore also reflects genetic and constitutional variables such as temperament (e.g., Plomin, Owen, & McGuffin, 1994; Rothbart, Derryberry, & Posner, 1994; Wachs & King, 1994).

The theory deals with cognitive and emotional encoding of information at multiple levels of awareness and automaticity (e.g., Bargh, 1994; Kihlstrom, 1990). It encompasses not only social cognition but also the processes through which people transform their cognitions and affects into stable, meaningful patterns of social action in relationship to situations. Most important, the theory accounts both for individual differences in overall average levels of behavior and for stable *if . . . then . . .* profiles of behavior variability across situations, as essential expressions of the same underlying personality system. It will also be seen that this conception of personality allows resolution of the classically paradoxical findings on the consistency issue in personality psychology that have been debated for decades (e.g., Mischel, 1968, 1990; Newcomb, 1929; Pervin, 1994).

A Cognitive–Affective Personality System

The types of mental mediating units and information processing required by a model of personality responsive to the cognitive revolution in psychology were outlined a quarter of a century ago (Mischel, 1973). This "cognitive social learning reconceptualization of personality" proposed a set of person variables that "suggest useful ways of conceptualizing and studying specifically how persons mediate the impact of stimuli and generate distinctive complex molar behavior patterns" (Mischel, 1973, p. 265). The focus was on the psychological mediating processes underlying individual differences in social behavior, which were represented by five types of relatively stable person variables: the individual's encodings or construal (of self, other people, situations); expectancies (about outcomes and one's own efficacy); subjective values; competencies (for the construction and generation of social behavior); and self-regulatory strategies and plans in the pursuit of goals (Mischel, 1973).

FROM PERSON VARIABLES TO COGNITIVE–AFFECTIVE UNITS

In the years since that proposal, voluminous research has extended the understanding of basic types of cognitive–affective units that need to be hypothesized within the processing system of personality. For example, with regard to encoding, research has documented the importance of the representations of self and of the possible selves that people can imagine themselves to be (e.g., Bargh, 1982; Deci & Ryan, 1987; Dweck & Leggett, 1988; Griffin & Ross, 1991; Higgins, 1987; Markus, 1977; Markus & Kitayama, 1991; Markus & Nurius, 1986; Scheier & Carver, 1988b) as determinants of individual differences. Evidence for the significance of individuals' personal beliefs and expectancies about the self, as well as about outcomes, has now converged from diverse studies of self-efficacy, of attributional styles, of mastery, of perceived control, and of one's theories about self and the social world (e.g., reviewed in Mischel, 1993; Mischel, Cantor, & Feldman, in press).

It also has become clear that affects and emotions profoundly influence social information processing and coping behavior (e.g., Bower, 1981; Contrada et al., 1990; Foa & Kozak, 1986; Forgas, 1995; Smith & Lazarus, 1990; Zajonc, 1980), as well as self-regulation and the future-oriented pursuit of long-term goals (e.g., Mischel et al., 1989; Mischel et al., in press). It has long been emphasized that the processing of social information important to the person is intrinsically affect laden so that such cognitions as beliefs about the self and one's personal future are themselves "hot" and emotional (Mischel, 1973). Thus, person variables are inevitably closely connected with affective reactions. As Smith and Lazarus (1990) note, anything that implies important consequences, harmful or beneficial, for the individual can generate an emotional reaction. Likewise, people's decisions and behaviors do not merely reflect a simple arithmetic of expected utility calculations (e.g., Kahneman, Slovic, & Tversky, 1982; Kahneman & Snell, 1990). To illustrate, the influence of information about performance outcomes is mediated by the person's affective state. For example, when a person is experiencing a negative affective state and gets negative feedback about performance, an interaction may occur that virtually guarantees a pattern of self-defeating demoralization that goes greatly beyond the feedback information (Cervone, Kopp, Schaumann, & Scott, 1994; Wright & Mischel, 1982). Moreover, it can be argued that affective reactions depend on the cognitive structures through which they are interpreted and labeled and are inseparable from them (e.g., Beck, 1976; Schachter & Singer, 1962).

On the other hand, there now is considerable evidence that affective-evaluative reactions to situation features (such as faces) may occur virtually immediately and automatically (e.g., Murphy & Zajonc, 1993; Niedenthal, 1990) outside of awareness (Gollwitzer & Bargh, in press; Zajonc, 1980), and these preconscious emotional reactions may rapidly trigger closely associated cognitions and behaviors (Chaiken & Bargh, 1993). Furthermore, affect may be open to direct influences that range from such simple events as finding a coin on the street (e.g., Forgas, 1995; Isen et al., 1992; Schwarz, 1990) to chronic modification of mood states through psychopharmacological interventions. They may reflect long-standing individual differences (e.g., Fazio, Sanbonmatsu, Powell, & Kardes, 1986), which may be related to temperament and biological variables (Rothbart et al., 1994) and may have distinctive influences on information processing strategies (e.g., Epstein, 1994; Foa & Kozak, 1986). Finally, affective reactions also require distinctive measurement operations to monitor their psychophysiological components. It therefore should be of heuristic value at this point to call special attention to affects as key aspects of individual differences in social information processing that need to be incorporated as units of analysis in the personality system.

Table 1. Types of Cognitive-Affective Units in the Personality Mediating System

1. Encodings: Categories (constructs) for the self, people, events, and situations (external and internal).
2. Expectancies and Beliefs: About the social world, about outcomes for behavior in particular situations, about self-efficacy.
3. Affects: Feelings, emotions, and affective responses (including physiological reactions).
4. Goals and Values: Desirable outcomes and affective states; aversive outcomes and affective states; goals, values, and life projects.
5. Competencies and Self-regulatory Plans: Potential behaviors and scripts that one can do, and plans and strategies for organizing action and for affecting outcomes and one's own behavior and internal states.

Note. Based in part on Mischel (1973).

Individual differences in the meaning of a situation depend also on the goals and subjective values that people bring to it. Goals guide and structure the long-term projects people pursue and have become central in conceptions of the organization and motivation of behavior over time. Goals influence both the situations and outcomes individuals seek and create and their cognitive, affective, and behavioral reactions to them (e.g., Alexander & Higgins, 1993; Bargh & Gollwitzer, 1994; Cantor, 1993; Dweck, 1991; Gollwitzer, 1993; Higgins, 1996; Higgins & Kruglanski, 1996; Linville & Carlston, 1994; Linville & Clark, 1989; Markus, 1977; Martin & Tesser, 1989; Mischel, 1990, 1993; Pervin, 1989, 1990). Therefore, the individual's personal goals constitute another cognitive–affective unit that needs to be incorporated in the personality system. Finally, it is necessary to move beyond the social cognitions and feelings that are experienced to the social behavior and coping patterns they construct. This requires attention to their competencies, plans, and strategies for self-regulation at the action level, which also must be represented in the personality system (Gollwitzer, 1993; Kuhl & Beekman, 1985; Mischel et al., in press; Norem, 1989; Taylor & Schneider, 1989).

Cumulatively, these developments suggest a set of cognitive–affective units or mental representations in the personality system that are based in part on the previously proposed person variables as summarized in Table 1. Namely, affects and goals, as well as encodings, expectancies and beliefs, and competencies and self-regulatory plans and strategies, exemplify the types of units in the system that interact as the individual selects, interprets, and generates situations. The cognitive–affective units in the system are not isolated, static components. They are organized, for example, into subjective equivalence classes, as illustrated in theory and research on encoding, person prototypes, and personal constructs (e.g., Cantor & Mischel, 1977, 1979; Cantor, Mischel, & Schwartz, 1982; Forgas, 1983a, 1983b; Higgins, King, & Mavin, 1982; Kelly, 1955; Linville & Clark, 1989; Vallacher & Wegner, 1987). Some aspects of the organization of relations among the cognitions and affects, such as evaluative-affective associations and interconcept relations (e.g., Cantor & Kihlstrom, 1987; Murphy & Medin, 1985) are common among members of a culture, and others may be unique for an individual (e.g.,

Rosenberg & Jones, 1972). Whether common or unique, however, cognitive–affective representations are not unconnected discrete units that are simply elicited as "responses" in isolation: These cognitive representations and affective states interact dynamically and influence each other reciprocally, and it is the organization of the relationships among them that forms the core of the personality structure and that guides and constrains their impact, as discussed next.

INDIVIDUAL DIFFERENCES IN THE COGNITIVE–AFFECTIVE PERSONALITY SYSTEM

Most models of social information processing that have emerged in recent years share a common view of the nature of individual differences (e.g., Higgins, 1996; Higgins & Bargh, 1987): individuals differ stably in the chronic accessibility or activation levels of the particular mental representations available to them. For example, one person may easily access the representation of the "self as mother," but for another such self-encoding may be relatively inaccessible. Likewise, some individuals more readily encode ambiguous interpersonal situations as personal affronts and violations (e.g., Dodge, 1986) or focus on the potentially threatening, dangerous features (e.g., Miller & Mangan, 1983). Some may chronically experience such affective states as depression (e.g., Bargh & Tota, 1988; Nolen-Hoeksema, Parker, & Larson, 1994); others are prone to experience daily distress, irritability, and negative emotions (e.g., Eysenck & Eysenck, 1985) or differ stably in the goals and experiences that they value, fantasize about, and pursue most persistently (e.g., McClelland, 1985).

Thus, individual differences in chronic activation levels of cognitions and affects are basic for social cognitive theories of personality and social behavior, and the present theory begins with that foundation. In addition to such differences in chronic activation levels, however, the proposed theory also assumes stable individual differences in the distinctive organization of relationships among the cognitions and affects available in the system. This assumption is consistent with a new kind of revolution that has been occurring in cognitive and neuroscience in the last decade, which shifts from the serial, centralized processing that had been modeled after the architecture of traditional digital computers to a more parallel, dis-

tributed, and associative model. It was anticipated in Hebb's (1949) principle of contiguous activation among closely associated units and is more compatible with emerging models of the biological bases of human information processing. Although there are many specific versions within this direction, their theme is that the key to understanding human information processing lies in the organization of the relationships among the units. It is this pattern of relationships or associations, as well as the accessibility of the units, that is the essence of most (if not all) current models of cognition (e.g., Anderson, 1983; Rumelhart & McClelland, 1986) and of the brain (e.g., Churchland & Sejnowski, 1992; Crick & Koch, 1990; Edelman, 1987; Kandel & Hawkins, 1992).

ESSENTIALS OF THE PERSONALITY SYSTEM

Building on these contributions, we propose a unifying view of a personality system in which individuals are characterized both in terms of (a) the cognitions and affects that are available and accessible (Table 1), and (b) the distinctive organization of the interrelations among them and psychological features of situations. This organization guides and constrains the activation of the specific cognitions, affects, and potential behaviors when an individual processes situational features. It constitutes the basic structure of personality and reflects and underlies the individual's uniqueness. Within each individual, the organization of this system is assumed to be stable and unique. It reflects individual differences in the chronic availability and ease of activation of particular cognitions and affects and also in the organization of the relations among them.

A schematic, highly simplified illustration of such a personality system is in Figure 4. It shows that a personality system is characterized by the available cognitive and affective units (Table 1), organized in a distinctive network of interrelations. When certain configurations of situation features are experienced by an individual, a characteristic subset of cognitions and affects becomes activated through this distinctive network of connections in the encoding process. The figure indicates that within any individual a rich system of relationships among the cognitive and affective units guides and constrains further activation of other units throughout the network, ultimately activating plans, strategies, and potential behaviors in the

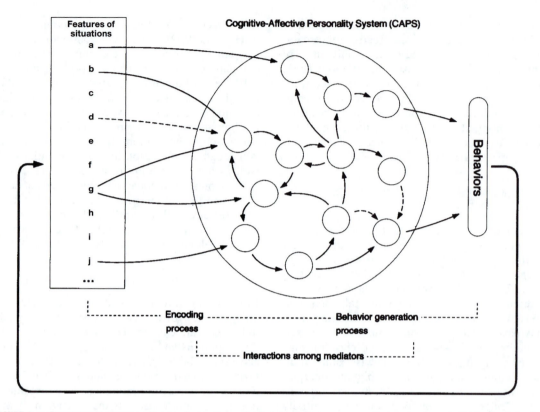

FIGURE 4 ■ Simplified illustration of types of cognitive–affective mediating processes that generate an individual's distinctive behavior patterns. Situational features are encoded by a given mediating unit, which activates specific subsets of other mediating units, generating distinctive cognition, affect, and behavior in response to different situations. Mediating units become activated in relation to some situation features, deactivated (inhibited) in relation to others, and are unaffected by the rest. The activated mediating units affect other mediating units through a stable network of relations that characterize an individual. The relation may be positive (solid line), which increases the activation, or negative (dashed line), which decreases the activation.

behavior generation process. The specific connections shown in this figure, chosen arbitrarily, illustrate that (a) there are many possible relations among the units but only some are functionally important; (b) units become activated in relation to situations and to other units in the personality system; (c) feedback activations occur that produce and sustain patterns of activation over time; and, most important, (d) units that become activated in the personality system activate other units through their distinctive organization in a network of relations, ultimately generating observable behaviors.

In this theory, the personality system is conceptualized at a highly abstract, psychological level of analysis. The theory is concerned with the relationships among relatively high level cognitive and

affective representations (see Table 1)—the macrostructure of personality units and molar level situations or stimuli—and not with the microstructures that might underlie them biologically. The "relations," "pathways," and connections among the units shown in Figure 4 describe functional relationships among these high-level cognitive and affective units and do not refer to physical connections in structure of the biological information processing system. The focus in the theory is on the relations among cognitions and affects in the system in terms of whether, and when, they become, in varying degrees, activated, deactivated, or are not influenced by each other. Furthermore, cognitive and affective units are shown by separate circles in the figure for the sake of simplicity, but these representations do not necessarily correspond to separate biological units. For example, different psychological units may be represented biologically by different patterns of activation of the same set of underlying biological units in a distributed, rather than local, representation (e.g., Hinton, McClelland, & Rumelhart, 1986).

To give a concrete example of such a system in action, suppose that while waiting for the results of medical tests, an individual scans for and focuses on a specific configuration of features in the situation, which activate the encoding that this is a health threat to the self, and concurrently trigger anxiety, which activates further scanning of and for those features, and simultaneously feeds back to reactivate the encoded health threat. The perceived threat activates the belief that this situation is uncontrollable, which triggers further anxiety and also negative outcome expectations. Both the negative expectancies and the anxiety concurrently activate defensive plans and scripts that generate a pattern of multiple behaviors at varying levels of strength. These events occur concurrently, in parallel activation within the system. The behaviors ultimately generated depend both on the situational features and on the organization of the network of cognitions and affects that become activated.

Individuals may differ characteristically in the thoughts and feelings that tend to be activated if particular configurations of features are present in situations, like those shown in the situation–behavior profiles of Figure 1. Each individual may be characterized by sets of such features, some common and some unique, that constitute the active psychological ingredients of situations: Their presence or absence in a given situation tends to influence that individual's cognitive and affective reactions in some potentially predictable ways. Cognitions and affects are activated not just by external features of situations, as when milk spilled on an adolescent in the cafeteria line is encoded as "being teased" (cf. Dodge, 1993), but also by feedback from cognitions and affects activated by internal events, such as the person's affective state and thoughts, for example, "when sad," "when lonely" (Wright & Mischel, 1988), and from imagined or anticipated situations and scripts (e.g., Cantor et al., 1982).

The activation of cognitions and affects also activates goals, behavioral scripts, and plans in the behavior generating process. The behaviors the person constructs may in turn affect the interpersonal environment and social ecology, which changes the situational features that are encountered subsequently in continuous transactions, indicated by the bold arrow in Figure 4 that connects the behavioral patterns constructed by the personality system back to the situations encountered.[2]

BEHAVIORAL EXPRESSIONS OF THE SYSTEM'S STABILITY: ELEVATION AND SHAPE OF *IF . . . THEN . . .* SITUATION–BEHAVIOR PROFILES

Given the assumptions of this theory, when an individual encounters situations that differ in their psychological features over time this type of personality system will generate distinctive *if . . . then . . .* , situation–behavior profiles of characteristic elevation and shape. To illustrate with a simple example, suppose that Person 1 tends to become irritated when she thinks she is being ignored, whereas Person 2 is happier when he is left alone, and even becomes irritated when people tell him personal stories. Suppose also that in Situation A people rarely initiate personal interactions whereas in Situation B such interactions are relatively frequent. Then Person 1 will become irritated in Situation A but not in Situation B; Person 2 will show the opposite *if . . . then . . .* pattern, irritated if B, but not if A. These affects further activate other cognitions and feelings in each situation, following the pathways of activation distinctive for each person. These individual differences reflect the particular acquired meanings of the situational features in terms of the cognitions and affects associated with them, so that even if both people are similar in their overall levels of "irritability" they will display distinctive, predictable patterns of behavioral variability in their *if . . . then . . .* signatures.

Like many personality models, this system generates variation in the individual's behavior across

---

[2] The activation pattern of the cognitive–affective units in the personality system, that is, the personality state, is never entirely the same across different occasions. For example, even when encountering the same person in the same office on different occasions, an individual's cognitive and affective state is not ever completely the same. That is, even if the external situation is identical, the internal, psychological situation will vary. Because the system's response is a function of the interaction between the external stimuli and the state of the personality system, the degree of predictability from external stimuli only is intrinsically limited.

different situations. Distinctive for the present model is that this variation across situations is neither entirely random, nor does it merely represent common differences in normative levels of social behavior in different situations shared by all individuals. Instead, the behavioral variation in relation to changing situations constitutes a potentially predictable and meaningful reflection of the personality system itself. It reflects at least in part the individual's selective and distinctive mapping of particular sets of situation features onto activated cognitions and affects and the distinctive organization through which they are interrelated and activate each other. Furthermore, although the activated cognitions, affects, and behaviors will change as the situation and its features change, their organization and the strengths of relations among them may remain essentially the same across situations. It is this assumption of stable individual differences in the organizations of the relations among cognitions and affects that leads the theory to expect characteristic, predictable patterns of variation in the individual's behavior across situations.

AN ILLUSTRATIVE COMPUTER SIMULATION

To show how the proposed personality system, even in extremely simplified form, could generate the types of behavior patterns predicted theoretically above, we constructed a computer simulation. In it hypothetical individuals differed stably in the connectivity and strengths of the activation networks, and we then "exposed" them to a set of hypothetical situations that differed in their features. We traced the activation of the mediating units to compute the expected behaviors of each individual in each situation. The activation networks implemented in the simulations are described in the Appendix, the set of network activation weights that uniquely characterized one of the hypothetical individuals in Table A1, and the features of situations are shown in Table A2.

The model implemented in the computer program produced stable patterns of intraindividual variability in behavior for most of the 100 simulated individuals. The stability of the intraindividual patterns of behavior variability was computed for each of the simulated individuals by exposing them to the 15 situations (Table A2), computing the expected activation patterns, and recording the predicted behavior. The average of these stability coefficients (computed using Fisher's r-to-z transformation) was 0.66, and 90 of the 100 hypothetical individuals had stability coefficients higher than 0.20. (Of course, the exact size of the coefficients, but not the sign, depends on the amount of intrinsic unpredictability of behavior modeled in the simulation and thus can be increased or decreased readily.) As also predicted mathematically (Bolger & Shilling, 1991; Shoda, 1990), the results confirmed that the type of mediating system simulated here generates intraindividual patterns of situation–behavior relations that show some significant stability. Essentially the same results can be produced with different summing functions, threshold functions, as well as different numbers of internal representations.

The computer simulations illustrate an important property of the type of mediating process model simulated: Individual differences in the patterns of activation pathways among the internal representations determine the relationship between the situation features and the observed behavioral outcomes from the system. The uniqueness of the individual's configuration of person variables is thus expressed in the uniqueness of the person–situation profiles generated.

It is also important to note that the expressions of the personality system are seen in the elevation as well as the shape of the situation–behavior profiles generated. As Figure A1 shows, the situation–behavior profiles of the hypothetical individuals differ not only in shape but also in elevation. Some individuals tended to be high and some low, resulting in average cross-situational consistency coefficients across the 15 situations that are positive and nonzero.

It is noteworthy that these stable individual differences in the elevation of the profiles were generated even though the simulation did not contain any unit that represented chronic individual differences in generalized behavioral dispositions independent of situation features: The only individual differences in the simulation were in the strength and sign of the individual connections among the mediating units and the degree to which they become activated in relation to each situation feature. The simulation thus shows that stable differences in the overall levels of behavior that characterize individuals can be produced by the hypothesized personality system without requiring the inclusion of mediating units that correspond directly to behavioral dispositions. [. . .]

RESOLVING THE CONSISTENCY ISSUE AND PERSON–SITUATION DEBATE

In the last three decades the field of personality has tried to reconcile the fact that the individual's behavior often is not consistent across situations, on the one hand, with the fundamental assumption and intuitive conviction that personality must be stable on the other hand (e.g., Bem & Allen, 1974; Krahe, 1990; Mischel, 1968; Moskowitz, 1982, 1994; Nisbett & Ross, 1980; Ross & Nisbett, 1991). The proposed theory dissolves this apparent dilemma because it considers the variability of behaviors within individuals across situations not as "error" nor as "due to situation rather than to the person," but as a meaningful reflection of the enduring personality system. It predicts that the person's behaviors in a domain will change from one situation to another—when the *if* changes, so will the *then*—even if the personality system were to remain entirely unchanged. The theory thus takes account both of the data on the variability of behavior and the intuitive conviction of the stability of personality and incorporates the former phenomenon into the conception of the latter. It resolves the person–situation debate, not merely by recognizing that person and situation are important, as has long been acknowledged, but by conceptualizing the personality system in ways that make variability of behavior across situations an essential aspect of its behavioral expression and underlying stability.

The theory also has important implications for the levels of behavioral consistency across situations that should be expected. To the degree that people are characterized by stable and distinctive patterns of variations in their behavior across situations, it will intrinsically limit the degree of cross-situational consistency that can be obtained, as has been demonstrated elsewhere (Shoda, 1990). Because intraindividual variability in behavior necessarily implies changes across situations in the person's rank ordering with respect to a behavior, it constrains the level of consistency, as traditionally defined, that one should expect theoretically. Consequently, researchers committed to demonstrating consistency in personality may do so more effectively by identifying the stable patterns of behavior variability that characterize an individual or a type, rather than pursuing higher cross-situational consistency coefficients.

Personality System, States, Dispositions, and Dynamics

This theory of personality coherence and its behavioral expressions requires a reexamination and redefinition of key concepts in the analysis of personality and individual differences. To recapitulate briefly, we have seen that in this theory the *personality system* refers to the cognitive–affective mediating units (Table 1) organized in a distinctive network of relations (Figure 4) that constitutes its structure. This system interacts with relevant psychological features of situations, generating the distinctive patterns of variability in social cognition, affect, and action across situations—the individual's personality signature—visible in stable, *if . . . then . . .*, situation–behavior profiles that have characteristic elevation and shape.

The *personality state* refers to the pattern of activation among cognitions and affects at a given time in this system. It thus depends on the particular context and the psychological situations experienced by the individual at that moment. The structure of the personality system can remain stable across situations, but the personality state changes readily when the situational features that are active change, or when they are alternatively encoded or cognitively and emotionally transformed (e.g., Mischel et al., 1989). [. . .]

INFERRING DYNAMICS FROM SITUATION–BEHAVIOR PROFILE PATTERNS

The specification of the diagnostic *if . . . then . . .* profiles that characterize exemplars of a hypothesized disposition constitutes one assessment task in research on dispositions from this perspective. It calls for measurement not only of characteristic mean levels of relevant behaviors but also of the distinctive behavioral signatures—the *if . . . then . . .* profiles that define the disposition. These distinctive *if . . . then . . .* patterns in turn provide clues to infer the hypothetical processing dynamics that generate them. Differences in these behavioral signatures of individuals observed in the research summarized in the first part of this article (Shoda et al., 1994) are illustrative. Compare, for example, the verbal aggression profile of two individuals (9 and 28), shown in Figure 2. Even if both persons have similarly elevated levels of overall verbal aggression, one is most aggressive when warned by counselors, whereas the other becomes most aggressive when peers try to approach him to make positive contact, suggesting that the profiles may reflect very different processing dynamics. By observing these situation–behavior patterns, perceivers, whether lay persons or professional observers, can more accurately predict the behaviors of the perceived presumably because context allows the underlying meanings and motivation to be inferred (Shoda et al., 1989).

The hypothesized personality system functions literally as a whole—a unique network of organized interconnections among cognitions and affects, not a set of separate, independent discrete variables, forces, factors, or tendencies. The challenge becomes to understand the psychological meaning of the organization of these relationships within the person, or the dispositional type, in terms of the goals, beliefs, and other mediating units hypothesized in Table 1. As Read, Jones, and Miller (1990) note, behavior organization becomes understandable in terms of the individual's model of goals, plans, resources, and beliefs. "Such a model is not a mere feature list, but is instead a model of how these components are related to one another" (Read et al., 1990, p. 1060). Thus, a person's seemingly inconsistent situation–behavior relations can become predictable manifestations of underlying personality dynamics if, for example, the goals served by the behaviors in particular situations are identified (e.g., Fein, Hilton, & Miller, 1990; Miller & Read, 1991). Current explorations of such cognitive–affective dynamics are abundant, for example, in studies of everyday personal projects (e.g., Cantor, 1993) and the goals, construals, and the personal theories that guide the individual in the coping and self-regulatory process (e.g., reviewed in Mischel et al., in press). They seek to clarify processing dynamics to answer questions such as: What goals are being pursued? Why does she do A in project X, but B in project Y? How are her self-encodings and theories of the self guiding her goal pursuits and constrain (or expand) her plans, for example, the choice of friends and partners? How do people's self-theories, for example, about the malleability of their own personality qualities and abilities (e.g., Dweck, Chiu, & Hong, in press), constrain and guide

their goals, judgements, feelings, and choices?

The theory's most basic assumption, namely that the personality system is not made up of a set of isolated tendencies, factors, or components, but consists of a psychologically meaningful organization of relationships among cognitions and affects (Table 1, Figure 4), has clear implications for the study of personality: The relationships among the person's important encodings, beliefs, and expectations (e.g., about the self), the enduring goals pursued, the key strategies used, and the affects experienced, all in relation to relevant features of situations, become the terrain the personologist needs to map. The ultimate goal becomes to articulate the psychological structure that underlies this organization within the personality system. The development of models to capture this organization becomes the theoretical challenge in the research agenda in particular content domains.

To apply the theory to a particular substantive domain one needs to identify the mental representations, and the interrelationships among them (i.e., their organization) in the processing system, that underlie the behavior of interest. To understand individual differences in dealing with information about personal risks for breast cancer, for example, one would identify common types of expectancies, affects, values, strategies, and other mediating units likely to become activated by such information, and their potential organization (Miller, Shoda, & Hurley, in press). The goal is to create a map of cognitions and affects like the one outlined in Figure 4 but with its empty circles filled in for that domain. Such a *cognitive–affective domain map* serves to limit for the researcher the range of cognitions and affects, and their potential organization, that need to be considered for the behaviors of interest. Guided by this domain map, research is then directed to identify the particular sets of relationships within the map that characterize an individual or a type of processing disposition. The results of such a strategy were discussed above in the examples of individuals who are rejection sensitive (Downey & Feldman, 1994), and are illustrated in detail for health-protective behavior elsewhere (Miller et al., in press).

INDIVIDUAL DIFFERENCES IN THE SITUATIONS SELECTED AND EXPERIENCED

Processing dynamics involve complex, multifaceted relationships and interactions that may operate at many levels of awareness, automaticity, and control. Although they are activated within the system, they are enacted or "played out" in social behavior in vivo as individuals interact with, select, and change their personal social world. The cognitive–affective dynamics activated within rejection sensitive individuals, for example, influence their own life situations by leading them to seek and select partners with distinctive qualities (e.g., who they believe will need them and will reassure them). By becoming coercive or violent when encountering cues that could be construed as rejection, however, they also create unsatisfying intimate relations in which they ultimately may become rejected (Downey & Feldman, 1994; Feldman & Downey, 1994). If the partner copes with violent behavior by becoming passive, withdrawn, and by appeasing the partner, these relationships may be maintained even after they become painful and destructive, especially when reinforced by tender reunions after violent fights. Because partners may be selected to obtain such qualities in the first place, these relationships can become difficult to terminate (e.g., Buss, 1987).

As a result of such interactions, stable individual differences may develop in the types of situations people typically experience. In that case it may be possible to characterize individuals in terms of the stable intraindividual profiles of types of situations that they encounter more or less than do relevant other people. For example, in a children's summer camp, one child may enduringly live in a world in which others interact with her more than with the average child, both in positive and negative encounters so that everything happens to her, making her world full of diverse situations: She is approached positively, praised, warned, teased. In contrast, another person may be characterized by living a relatively isolated life in which very little happens interpersonally, neither positively nor negatively. Another may be characterized by a situational profile distinguished by being bullied and tortured much more than others by peers but in which interactions with adults are conspicuously absent. Such profiles of situations typically encountered and their psychological features, if stable, would constitute an additional important facet of individual differences in contextual terms. These profiles can be informative not only about the characteristics of the social world but also about the dynamics of the individual.

To summarize, through the interactions of the personality system's structure with the features of situations that activate characteristic processing dynamics, individuals may select, seek, interpret, respond to, and generate stable social situations and experiences in patterns that are typical for them, ultimately in part shaping their own social environments (Patterson, 1976). These interactions seem to reflect two processes. They include selective exposure to (and construction of) particular types of situations as individuals construct their own life space, and also the individual's characteristic ways of reacting to those situations, cognitively, affectively, and behaviorally (Bolger & Schilling, 1991; Bolger & Zuckerman, 1994; Buss, 1987; Diener, Larsen, & Emmons, 1984; Emmons, Diener, & Larsen, 1986; Snyder & Ickes, 1985). As individuals form and pursue their personal projects, these person–context interactions progressively define and generate their unique trajectories—their personal vitae of experiences, relationships, and situations—that constitute their distinctive life course.

Implications for Person Perception, Development, Change, and Self-Regulation

IMPLICATIONS FOR THE PERCEIVER'S THEORIES OF PERSONALITY AND DISPOSITIONAL INFERENCES

It would be surprising if the processing dynamics and structure of personality were inferred only by professional psychologists and not also by lay perceivers in their intuitive theories of personality: At least some of the time, some perceivers surely try to infer the beliefs, goals, and affects of the people they want to understand to see how these qualities underlie their behavior (Shoda & Mischel, 1993). Given that the expressions of the personality system are reflected in the shape as well as in the elevation of the *if . . . then . . .* , situation–behavior profiles generated by the system, the perceiver (whether lay person or psychologist) needs such information to infer the underlying structure and dynamics and generate a theory about the person. In the relatively rare studies in which such data are made available to perceivers, they seem to be linked to the social perceptions and inferences that are formed and suggest the lay perceiver may be an intuitive interactionist at least some of the time (e.g., Chiu, 1994; Dweck, Hong, & Chiu,

1993; Kruglanski, 1989, 1990; Read & Miller, 1993; Shoda et al., 1994; Wright & Mischel, 1987, 1988).

If personality is tacitly equated with global behavioral dispositions, any variation in behavior within a domain across situations by definition becomes extraneous to personality, just as it is seen as "error" in personality research on consistency within that traditional perspective. The equation of personality with behavioral dispositions easily leads one to construe personality and situation as mutually exclusive and indeed opposing influences (as discussed in Shoda & Mischel, 1993). From that perspective, it makes sense to assume that perceivers dichotomize observed behavior into its situational versus dispositional components with the goal of partialling out the effect of the situation to discover the "true" score of the perceived. Then, however, the information on behavioral variability and *if . . . then . . .* , situation–behavior profiles that the present theory sees as an essential personality signature is considered as due to situations, and not reflective of personality. Because such information is assumed to be extraneous to personality it usually is not made available to the perceiver in research on personality inferences, and its potential role remains unexplored.

Such reasoning about personality inferences follows to the degree that in the culture and language the word "personality," as well as the concept, is simply synonymous with generalized behavior tendencies, usually described by adjectives. Although the semantic equation, personality = generalized behavior tendencies, is commonly made, intuitive perceivers are not necessarily limited to situation-free behavior tendencies when they try to understand other people and themselves. Goal-based inferences (Read et al., 1990), for example, may be found particularly when perceivers try to understand themselves and those they care about, or have an empathic orientation (e.g., Hoffman, Mischel, & Mazze, 1981), even if traits seem to be the preferred language for the psychology of the stranger (McAdams, 1994). The equation thus need not prevent researchers from investigating when and how the intuitive perceiver might make inferences about cognitive–affective dynamics and their nonobvious behavioral expressions and thus be guided by an intuitively interactionist theory of personality (e.g., Chiu, 1994; Dweck et al., in press; Shoda et al., 1989). To observe the effects of such implicit personality theories re-quires research paradigms that make available to the perceiver the situation–behavior relations that—in the present perspective—constitute the personality signatures of the perceived. [. . .]

Can Personality Psychology Pursue Its Two Goals Within a Unitary Framework?

Since the inception of the field, a major goal of personality psychology has been to characterize individuals in terms of stable qualities that remain invariant across situations and that are distinctive for the individual (e.g., Allport, 1937; Funder, 1991; Goldberg, 1993). Concurrently, in a second direction, other personality researchers have focused on the question "how does this person function?" and sought answers in terms of the psychological processes that underlie individual differences in social behavior and its variability across situations (e.g., Bandura, 1986; Cantor & Kihlstrom, 1987; Mischel, 1973; Pervin, 1990). Consequently, the study of individual differences has long been divided into two subdisciplines, pursuing two distinct sets of goals—either personality dispositions or personality processes—with different agendas often in seeming conflict with each other (Cervone, 1991; Cronbach, 1957, 1975: Mischel & Shoda, 1994). The present theory is an effort toward integrating the two disciplines to pursue both goals within the same conceptual framework.

Taken collectively, this cognitive–affective personality system (CAPS) theory provides a comprehensive unifying view that accounts for both the variability in the behavioral expressions of personality and the stability in the personality system that generates them. This is summarized in Figure 5, which shows the hypothesized cognitive–affective personality system in relation to the larger contexts in which it functions. Behaviorally, through its concurrent social information processing and interactions, the system generates characteristic, predictable patterns of variation as well as characteristic elevations in the individual's behavior across situations even if the system itself remains invariant. Developmentally, the organization of the relations among the cognitive–affective units reflects the individual's cognitive social learning history in interaction with the biological history, such as the temperamental and genetic–biochemical factors.

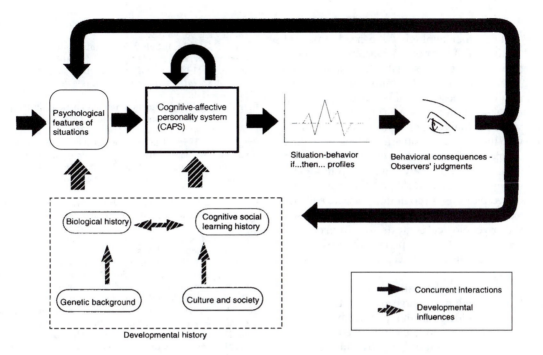

FIGURE 5 ■ The Cognitive–Affective Personality System (CAPS) in relation to concurrent interactions and developmental influences (see text).

The cognitive–affective personality system (CAPS) is activated in part in relation to psychological features of situations that are experienced at a given time. In part, it is continuously activated by its own internal feedback system through chronic activation of cognitions and affects and their interactions within the system, for example, in long-term planning and sustained goal pursuit, as well as in such activities as fantasy, ruminations, and daydreaming. The stable dispositional qualities of individuals are characterized in terms of the enduring structure of the organization among cognitive-affective mediating units (Table 1) in the personality system. This organization guides and constrains the activation of the specific cognitions, affects, and potential behaviors when an individual selects and acts on psychological features of situations. The functioning of the system is seen in the processing dynamics that are activated in relation to the situations experienced by the individual.

The system's characteristic processing dynamics in relation to the relevant features of situations generate diverse behaviors, some of which form situation–behavior profiles of variability that are distinctive in their shapes and elevations. These profiles constitute potential signatures of personality that are shared by individuals who have similar processing dispositions. To identify exemplars of a particular disposition requires specifying their characteristic situation–behavior profile shapes and elevations with regard to the situational features relevant or diagnostic for that disposition.

As Figure 5 also indicates, individuals' behaviors generate consequences that in turn affect the psychological features of situations that are subsequently encountered. They are encoded not only by psychologists who study them but also by other people who interact with them in vivo as well as by the individuals themselves. Such encodings, for example in the form of personality judgments in terms of traits, types, and prototypes, and the evaluations and reactions that they trigger, may themselves influence the situations to which the individual is subsequently exposed (e.g., by changing the feelings and behaviors of the interactants).

At the birth of the field, Gordon Allport's (1937) fundamental commitment was to show the importance of stable intraindividual patterns that characterize each person. The present theory was also designed with that goal. In his pioneering book, however, Allport also went on to decontextualize personality, contrasting the literary investigator who "develops his character within the stream of life" with the personologist who needs to avoid the "confusion of surrounding variables" and has to remove context to "fasten the personality *as-it-is* for analysis ..." (p. 61, emphasis added). In contrast, the proposed cognitive-affective system theory shares with Henry Murray (1938) the focus on the person's dynamic processes in interaction with the features of situations: It assumes that basic aspects of personality invariance become visible in the relations between the psychological features of the social world and the individual's distinctive patterns of cognition, affect, and behavior. In the theory, rather than being dismissed as noise, psychological contexts—far from obscuring personality—become part of the essence of coherence and the route to capturing the person's distinctiveness.

The two goals—dispositions and dynamics—that have so long been pursued separately do not require two fields from this perspective. In this theory, dispositions are conceptualized not in semantic terms but as processing structures characterized by stable cognitive–affective organizations in the processing system that become activated when the individual encounters relevant situational features. Over time and contexts they generate *if ... then ...*, situation–behavior relations that can be assessed as profiles that have characteristic elevations and shapes from which dispositional exemplars can be identified. Although the diverse *if ... then ...* patterns constructed by the system unfold seamlessly in vivo, one can focus on particular configurations that define a given processing disposition and isolate for attention those aspects of the system's structure and dynamics that are most germaine to it. Rather than dichotomizing personality research into the study of dispositions *or* processes, this theory allows one to pursue concurrently both personality dispositions and processes—structure and dynamics—as aspects of the same unitary system.

REFERENCES

Alexander, M. J., & Higgins, E. T. (1993). Emotional trade-offs of becoming a parent: How social roles influence self-discrepancy effects. *Journal of Personality and Social Psychology, 65,* 1259–1269.

Allport, G. W. (1937). *Personality: A psychological interpretation.* New York: Holt, Rinehart & Winston.

Anderson, J. R. (1983). *The architecture of cognition.* Cambridge, MA: Harvard University Press.

Antrobus, J. (1991). Dreaming: Cognitive processes during critical activation and high afferent thresholds. *Psychological Review, 98,* 96–121.

Bandura, A. (1982). Self-efficacy mechanisms in human agency. *American Psychologist, 37,* 122–147.

Bandura, A. (1986). *Social foundations of thought and action: A social cognitive theory.* Englewood Cliffs, NJ: Prentice Hall.

Bargh, J. A. (1982). Attention and automaticity in the processing of self-relevant information. *Journal of Personality and Social Psychology, 43,* 425–436.

Bargh, J. A. (1994). The four horsemen of automaticity: Intention, awareness, efficiency, and control as separate issues in social cognition. In R. S. Wyer & T. K. Srull (Eds.), *Handbook of social cognition* (2nd ed., Vol. 1, pp. 1–40). Hillsdale, NJ: Erlbaum.

Bargh, J. A., & Gollwitzer, P. (1994). Environmental control of goal-directed action: Automatic and strategic contingencies between situations and behavior. In *Nebraska Symposium on Motivation: Vol. 41* (pp. 71–124). Lincoln: University of Nebraska Press.

Bargh, J. A., & Tota, M. E. (1988). Context-dependent automatic processing in depression: Accessibility of negative constructs with regard to self but not others. *Journal of Personality and Social Psychology, 54,* 925–939.

Beck, A. T. (1976). *Cognitive therapy and the emotional disorders.* New York: International Universities Press.

Bem, D. J., & Allen, A. (1974). On predicting some of the people some of the time: The search for cross-situational consistencies in behavior. *Psychological Review, 81,* 506–520.

Bolger, N., & Eckenrode, J. (1991). Social relationships, personality, and anxiety during a major stressful event. *Journal of Personality and Social Psychology, 61,* 440–449.

Bolger, N., & Schilling, E. A. (1991). Personality and the problems of everyday life: The role of neuroticism in exposure and reactivity to daily stressors. *Journal of Personality, 59,* 355–386.

Bolger, N., & Zuckerman, A. (1994). *A framework for studying personality in the stress process.* Manuscript submitted for publication.

Bower, G. H. (1981). Mood and memory. *American Psychologist, 36,* 129–148.

Buss, D. M. (1987). Selections, evocation and manipulation. *Journal of Personality and Social Psychology, 53,* 1214–1221.

Cantor, N. (1990). From thought to behavior: "Having" and "doing" in the study of personality and cognition. *American Psychologist, 45,* 735–750.

Cantor, N. (1993, August). *Life task problem-solving: Situational affordances and personal needs.* Presidential address presented at the 101st Annual Convention of the American Psychological Association, Toronto, Canada.

Cantor, N., & Blanton, H. (in press). Effortful pursuit of personal goals in daily life. In J. A. Bargh & P. M. Gollwitzer (Eds.), *Thought, motivation, and action.* New York: Guilford Press.

Cantor, N., & Kihlstrom, J. E. (1987). *Personality and social intelligence.* Englewood Cliffs, NJ: Erlbaum.

Cantor, N., & Mischel, W. (1977). Traits as prototypes: Effects on recognition memory. *Journal of Personality and Social Psychology 35,* 38–48.

Cantor, N., & Mischel, W. (1979). Prototypes in person perception. In L. Berkowitz (Ed.), *Advances in experimental social psychology* (Vol. 2, pp. 3–52). New York: Academic Press.

Cantor, N., Mischel, W., & Schwartz, J. (1982). A prototype analysis of psychological situations. *Cognitive Psychology, 14,* 45–77.

Cervone, D. (1991). The two disciplines of personality psychology. Review of *Handbook of personality: Theory and research. Psychological Science, 2,* 371–377.

Cervone, D., Kopp, D. A., Schaumann, L., & Scott, W. D. (1994). Mood, self-efficacy, and performance standards: Lower moods induce higher standards for performance. *Journal of Personality and Social Psychology, 67,* 499–512.

Chaiken, S., & Bargh, J. A. (1993). Occurrence versus moderation of the automatic attitude activation effect: Reply to Fazio. *Journal of Personality and Social Psychology, 64,* 759–765.

Chiu, C. (1994). *Bases of categorization and person cognition.* Unpublished doctoral dissertation, Columbia University.

Chiu, C., Hong, Y., Mischel, W., & Shoda, Y. (in press). Discriminative facility in social competence behavior. *Social Cognition.*

Churchland, P. S., & Sejnowski, T. J. (1992). *The computational brain.* Cambridge, MA: MIT Press.

Contrada, R. J., Leventhal, H., & O'Leary, A. (1990). Personality and health. In L. A. Pervin (Ed.), *Handbook of personality: Theory and research* (pp. 638–699). New York: Guilford Press.

Crick, F., & Koch, C. (1990). Towards a neurobiological theory of consciousness. *Seminars in the Neurosciences, 2,* 263–275.

Cronbach, L. J. (1957). The two disciplines of scientific psychology. *American Psychologist, 12,* 671–684.

Cronbach, L. J. (1975). Beyond the two disciplines of scientific psychology. *American Psychologist, 30,* 116–127.

Deci, E. L., & Ryan, R. M. (1987). The support of autonomy and the control of behavior. *Journal of Personality and Social Psychology, 53,* 1024–1037.

Diener, E., Larson, R. J., & Emmons, R. A. (1984). Person × situation interactions: Choice of situations and congruence response models. *Journal of Personality and Social Psychology, 47,* 580–592.

Dodge, K. A. (1986). A social information processing model of social competence in children. In M. Perlmutter (Ed.), *The Minnesota symposium on child psychology* (Vol. 18, pp. 77–125). Hillsdale, NJ: Erlbaum.

Dodge, K. A. (1993). Social-cognitive mechanisms in the development of conduct disorder and depression. *Annual Review of Psychology, 44,* 559–584.

Downey, G., & Feldman, S. (1994). *Sensitivity to rejection and male violence in romantic relationships.* Manuscript submitted for publication.

Downey, G., & Walker, E. (1989). Social cognition and adjustment in children at risk for psychopathology. *Developmental Psychology, 25,* 835–845.

Dweck, C. S. (1991). Self-theories and goals: Their role in motivation, personality, and development. In R. A. Dienstbier (Ed.), *Nebraska Symposium on Motivation, 1990* (Vol. 38, pp. 199–235). Lincoln: University of Nebraska Press.

Dweck, C. S., Chiu, C., & Hong, Y. (in press). Implicit theories and their role in judgments and reactions: A world from two perspectives. *Psychological Inquiry.*

Dweck, C. S., Hong, Y., & Chiu, C. (1993). Implicit theories: Individual differences in the likelihood and meaning of dispositional inference. *Personality and Social Psychology Bulletin, 19,* 644–656.

Dweck, C. S., & Leggett, E. L. (1988). A social-cognitive approach to personality and motivation. *Psychological Review, 95,* 256–273.

Edelman, G. M. (1987). *Neural Darwinism.* New York: Basic Books.

Emmons, R. A. (1991). Personal strivings, daily life events, and psychological and physical well-being. *Journal of Personality, 59,* 453–472.

Emmons, R. A., Diener, E., & Larson, R. J. (1986). Choice and avoidance of everyday situations and affect congruence: Two models of reciprocal interactionism. *Journal of Personality and Social Psychology, 51,* 815–826.

Endler, N. S., & Hunt, J. (1969). Generalizability of contributions from sources of variance in the S–R inventories of anxiousness. *Journal of Personality, 37,* 1–24.

Endler, N. S., Hunt, J. M., & Rosenstein, A. J. (1962). An S–R inventory of anxiousness. *Psychological Monographs, 76* (No. 536).

Endler, N. S., & Magnusson, D. (1976). Toward an interactional psychology of personality. *Psychological Bulletin, 83,* 956–974.

Epstein, S. (1979). The stability of behavior: On predicting most of the people much of the time. *Journal of Personality and Social Psychology, 37,* 1097–1126.

Epstein, S. (1980). The stability of behavior: II. Implications for psychological research. *American Psychologist, 35,* 790–806.

Epstein, S. (1994). Integration of the cognitive and psychodynamic unconscious. *American Psychologist, 49,* 709–724.

Eysenck, H. J., & Eysenck, M. W. (1985). Personality and individual differences. New York: Plenum Press.

Fazio, R. H., Sanbonmatsu, D. M., Powell, M. C., & Kardes, F. R. (1986). On the automatic activation of attitudes. *Journal of Personality and Social Psychology, 50,* 229–238.

Fein, S., Hilton, J. L., & Miller, D. T. (1990). Suspicion of ulterior motivation and the correspondence bias. *Journal of Personality and Social Psychology, 58,* 753–764.

Feldman, S., & Downey, G. (1994). Rejection sensitivity as a mediator of the impact of childhood exposure to family violence on adult attachment behavior. *Development and Psychopathology, 6,* 231–247.

Fiske, S. T., & Taylor, S. E. (1991). *Social cognition* (2nd ed.). New York: McGraw-Hill.

Foa, E. B., & Kozak, M. J. (1986). Emotional processing of fear: Exposure to corrective information. *Psychological Bulletin, 99,* 20–35.

Forgas, J. P. (1983a). Episode cognition and personality: A multidimensional analysis. *Journal of Personality, 51,* 34–48.

Forgas, J. P. (1983b). Social skills and the perception of interaction episodes. *British Journal of Clinical Psychology, 22,* 195–207.

Forgas, J. P. (1995). Mood and judgment: The affect infusion model (AIM). *Psychological Bulletin, 117,* 39–66.

Funder, D. C. (1991). Global traits: A neo-Allportian approach to personality. *Psychological Science, 2,* 31–39.

Goldberg, L. R. (1993). The structure of phenotypic personality traits. *American Psychologist, 48,* 26–34.

Gollwitzer, P. M. (1993). Goal achievement: The role of intentions. In W. Stroebe & M. Hewstone (Eds.), *European review of social psychology* (Vol. 4, pp. 1–45). Chichester, England: Wiley & Sons.

Gollwitzer, P. M., & Bargh, J. A. (Eds.). (in press). *Action science: Linking cognition and motivation to action.* New York: Guilford Press.

Griffin, D. W., & Ross, L. (1991). Subjective construal, social inference, and human misunderstanding. *Advances in Experimental Social Psychology, 24,* 319–359.

Hartshorne, H., & May, A. (1928). *Studies in the nature of character: Vol. 1. Studies in deceit.* New York: Macmillan.

Hebb, D. O. (1949). *The organization of behavior.* New York: Wiley.

Higgins, E. T. (1987). Self-discrepancy: A theory relating self and affect. *Psychological Review, 94,* 319–340.

Higgins, E. T. (1990). Personality, social psychology, and person-situation relations: Standards and knowledge activation as a common language. In L. A. Pervin (Ed.), *Handbook of personality: Theory and research* (pp. 301–338). New York: Guilford Press.

Higgins, E. T. (1996). Knowledge activation: Accessibility, applicability, and salience. In E. T. Higgins & A. Kruglanski (Eds.), *Social psychology: Handbook of basic principles.* New York: Guilford Press.

Higgins, E. T., & Bargh, J. A. (1987). Social cognition and social perceptions. *Annual Review of Psychology, 38,* 369–425.

Higgins, E. T., King, G. A., & Mavin, G. H. (1982). Individual construct accessibility and subjective impressions and recall. *Journal of Personality and Social Psychology, 43,* 35–47.

Higgins, E. T., & Kruglanski, A. (Eds.). (1996). *Social psychology. Handbook of basic principles.* New York: Guilford.

Hinton, G. E., McClelland, J. L., & Rumelhart, D. E. (1986). Distributed representations. In D. E. Rumelhart & J. L. McClelland (Eds.), *Parallel distributed processing: Explorations in the microstructures of cognition: Vol. I. Foundations* (pp. 77–109). Cambridge, MA: MIT Press/Bradford Books.

Hoffman, C., Mischel, W., & Mazze, K. (1981). The role of purpose in the organization of information about behavior: Trait-based versus goal-based categories in person cognition. *Journal of Personality and Social Psychology, 40,* 211–225.

Isen, A. M., Niedenthal, P. M., & Cantor, N. (1992). An influence of positive affect on social categorization. *Motivation & Emotion, 16,* 65–78.

Kahneman, D., Slovic, P., & Tversky, A. (Eds.). (1982). *Judgment under uncertainty.* New York: Cambridge University Press.

Kahneman, D., & Snell, J. (1990). Predicting utility. In R. M. Hogarth (Ed.), *Insights in decision making: A tribute to Hillel J. Einhorn* (pp. 295-310). Chicago: University of Chicago Press.

Kandel, E. R., & Hawkins, R. D. (1992). The biological basis of learning and individuality. *Scientific American, 267,* 78–86.

Kandel, E. R., & Schwartz, J. H. (Eds.). (1985). *Principles of neural sciences* (2nd ed). New York: Elsevier Science.

Kelly, G. A. (1955). *The psychology of personal constructs* (Vols.1 and 2). New York: Norton.

Kihlstrom, J. F. (1987). The cognitive unconscious. *Science, 237,* 1445–1452.

Kihlstrom, J. F. (1990). The psychological unconscious. In L. A. Pervin (Ed.), *Handbook of personality: Theory and research* (pp. 445–464). New York: Guilford Press.

Kihlstrom, J. F., & Cantor, N. (1984). Mental representations of the self. In L. Berkowitz (Ed.), *Advances in experimental social psychology: Vol. 17. Theorizing in social psychology: Special topics* (pp. 240). New York: Academic Press.

Krahe, B. (1990). *Situation cognition and coherence in personality: An individual-centered approach.* Cambridge, England: Cambridge University Press.

Kruglanski, A. W. (1989). *Lay epistemics and human knowledge: Cognitive and motivational bases.* New York: Plenum Press.

Kruglanski, A. W. (1990). Lay epistemic theory in social-cognitive psychology. *Psychological Inquiry, 1,* 181–197.

Kuhl, J., & Beekman, J. (Eds.). (1985). *Action control: From cognition to behavior.* New York: Springer-Verlag.

Linville, P. W., & Carlston, D. E. (1994). Social cognition of the self. In P. G. Devine, D. L. Hamilton, & T. M. Ostrom (Eds.), *Social cognition: Its impact on social psychology.* New York: Academic Press.

Linville, P. W., & Clark, L. F. (1989). Can production systems cope with coping? *Social Cognition, 7,* 195–236.

Magnusson, D., & Endler, N. S. (Eds.). (1977). *Personality at the crossroads: Current issues in interactional psychology.* Hillsdale, NJ: Erlbaum.

Markus, H. (1977). Self-schemata and processing information about the self. *Journal of Personality and Social Psychology, 35,* 63–78.

Markus, H. R., & Kitayama, S. (1991). Culture and the self: Implications for cognition, emotion, and motivation. *Psychological Review, 98,* 224–253.

Markus, H., & Nurius, P. (1986). Possible selves. *American Psychologist, 41,* 954–969.

Martin, L., & Tesser, A. (1989). Toward a motivational and structural theory of ruminative thought. In J. Uleman & J. Bargh (Eds.), *Unintended thought* (pp. 307–327). New York: Guilford Press.

McAdams, D. P. (1994). A psychology of the stranger. *Psychological Inquiry, 5,* 145–148.

McClelland, D. C. (1985). How motives, skills, and values determine what people do. *American Psychologist, 40,* 812–825.

Medin, D. L. (1989). Concepts and conceptual structure. *American Psychologist, 44,* 1469–1481.

Miller, L. C., & Read, S. J. (1991). On the coherence of mental models of persons and relationships: A knowledge structure approach. In G. J. O. Fletcher & F. D. Fincham (Eds.), *Cognition in close relationships* (pp. 69–99). Hillsdale, NJ: Erlbaum.

Miller, S. M., & Mangan, C. E. (1983). Interacting effects of information and coping style in adapting to gynecologic stress: Should the doctor tell all? *Journal of Personality and Social Psychology, 45,* 223–236.

Miller, S. M., Shoda, Y., & Hurley, K. (in press). Applying cognitive social theory to health-protective behavior: Breast self-examination in cancer screening. *Psychological Bulletin.*

Mischel, W. (1968). *Personality and assessment.* New York: Wiley.

Mischel, W. (1973). Toward a cognitive social learning reconceptualization of personality. *Psychological Review, 80,* 252–283.

Mischel, W. (1984). On the predictability of behavior and the structure of personality. In R. A. Zucker, J. Aronoff, & A. I. Rabin (Eds.), *Personality and the prediction of behavior* (pp. 269–305). New York: Academic Press.

Mischel, W. (1990). Personality dispositions revisited and revised: A view after three decades. In L. A. Pervin (Ed.), *Handbook of personality: Theory and research* (pp. 111–134). New York: Guilford Press.

Mischel, W. (1993). *Introduction to personality* (5th ed.). Fort Worth, TX: Harcourt Brace Jovanovich.

Mischel, W., Cantor, N., & Feldman, S. (in press). Goal-directed self-regulation. In E. T. Higgins & A. Kruglanski (Eds.), *Social psychology: Basic principles.* New York: Guilford Press.

Mischel, W., & Peake, P. K. (1982). Beyond deja vu in the search for cross-situational consistency. *Psychological Review, 89,* 730–755.

Mischel, W., & Shoda, Y. (1994). Personality psychology has two goals: Must it be two fields? *Psychological Inquiry, 5,* 156–158.

Mischel, W., Shoda, Y., & Rodriguez, M. L. (1989). Delay of gratification in children. *Science, 244,* 933–938.

Moskowitz, D. S. (1982). Coherence and cross-situational generality in personality: A new analysis of old problems. *Journal of Personality and Social Psychology, 43,* 754–768.

Moskowitz, D. S. (1994). Cross-situational generality and the interpersonal circumplex. *Journal of Personality and Social Psychology, 66,* 921–933.

Murphy, G. L., & Medin, D. L. (1985). The role of theories in conceptual coherence. *Psychological Review, 92,* 289–316.

Murphy, S. T, & Zajonc, R. B. (1993). Affect, cognition, and awareness: Affective priming with optimal and suboptimal stimulus exposures. *Journal of Personality and Social Psychology, 64,* 723–739.

Murray, H. A. (1938). *Explorations in personality.* New York: Oxford University Press.

Newcomb, T. M. (1929). *Consistency of certain extrovert-introvert behavior patterns in 51 problem boys.* New York: Columbia University, Teachers College, Bureau of Publications.

Niedenthal, P. M. (1990). Implicit perception of affective information. *Journal of Experimental Social Psychology, 26,* 505–527.

Nisbett, R. E., & Ross, L. D. (1980). *Human inference: Strategies and shortcomings of social judgment.* Englewood Cliffs, NJ: Prentice Hall.

Nolen-Hoeksema, S., Parker, L. E., & Larson, J. (1994). Ruminative coping with depressed mood following loss. *Journal of Personality and Social Psychology, 67,* 92–104.

Norem, J. K. (1989). Cognitive strategies as personality: Effectiveness, specificity, flexibility, and change. In D. M. Buss & N. Cantor (Eds.), *Personality psychology: Recent trends and emerging issues* (pp. 45–60). New York: Springer-Verlag.

Patterson, G. R. (1976). The aggressive child: Victim and architect of a coercive system. In I. A. Hamerlynek, L. C. Handy, & E. J. Mash (Eds.), *Behavior modification and families: Vol. I. Theory and Research* (pp. 1–42). New York: Brunner/Mazel.

Pervin, L. A. (1989). Goal concepts: Themes, issues, and questions. In L. A. Pervin (Ed.), *Goal concepts in personality and social psychology* (pp. 473–479). Hillsdale, NJ: Erlbaum.

Pervin, L. A. (Ed.). (1990). *Handbook of personality: Theory and research.* New York: Guilford Press.

Pervin, L. A. (1994). A critical analysis of current trait theory. *Psychological Inquiry, 5,* 103–113.

Peterson, D. R. (1968). *The clinical study of social behavior.* New York: Appleton-Century-Crofts.

Plomin, R., Owen, M. J., & McGuffin, P. (1994). The genetic basis of complex human behaviors. *Science, 264,* 1733–1739.

Read, S. J., Jones, D. K., & Miller, L. C. (1990). Traits as goal-based categories: The importance of goals in the coherence of dispositional categories. *Journal of Personality and Social Psychology, 58,* 1048–1061.

Read, S. J., & Miller, L. C. (1989). The importance of goals in personality: Toward a coherent model of persons. In R. S. Wyer, Jr., & T. K. Srull (Eds.), *Advances in social cognition: Vol 2. Social intelligence and cognitive assessments of personality* (pp. 163–174). Hillsdale, NJ: Erlbaum.

Read, S. J., & Miller L. C. (1993). Rapist or "regular guy": Explanatory coherence in the construction of mental models of others. *Personality and Social Psychology Bulletin, 19,* 526–540.

Rosenberg, S., & Jones, R. (1972). A method for investigating and representing a person's implicit theory of personality. *Journal of Personality and Social Psychology, 22,* 372–386.

Ross, L., & Nisbett, R. E. (1991). *The person and the situation: Perspectives of social psychology.* New York: McGraw-Hill.

Rothbart, M. K., Derryberry, D., & Posner, M. I. (1994). Psychobiological approach to the development of temperament. In J. E. Bates & T. D. Wachs (Ed.), *Temperament: Individual differences at the interface of biology and behavior* (pp. 23–116). Washington, DC: American Psychological Association.

Rumelhart, D. E., & McClelland, J. L. (1986). *Parallel distributed processing: Explorations in the microstructure of cognition: Vol. I. Foundations.* Cambridge, MA: MIT Press/Bradford Books.

Schachter, S., & Singer, J. E. (1962). Cognitive, social and physiological determinants of emotional state. *Psychological Review, 69,* 379–399.

Scheier, M. F., & Carver, C. S. (1988a). Individual differences in self-concept and self-process. In D. M. Wegner & R. R. Vallacher (Eds.), *The self in social psychology.* New York: Oxford University Press.

Scheier, M. F., & Carver, C. S. (1988b). A model of behavioral self-regulation: Translating intention into action. In L. Berkowitz (Ed.), *Advances in experimental social psychology* (Vol. 21, pp. 322–343). San Diego, CA: Academic Press.

Schwarz, N. (1990). Feelings and information: Informational and motivational functions of affective states. In R. M. Sorrentino & E. T. Higgins (Eds.), *Handbook of motivation and cognition: Foundations of social behavior* (Vol. 2, pp. 527–561). New York: Guilford Press.

Shoda, Y. (1990). *Conditional analyses of personality coherence and dispositions.* Unpublished doctoral dissertation, Columbia University.

Shoda, Y., & Mischel, W. (1993). Cognitive social approach to dispositional inferences: What if the perceiver is a cognitive-social theorist? *Personality and Social Psychology Bulletin, 19,* 574–585.

Shoda, Y., Mischel, W., & Wright, J. C. (1989). Intuitive interactionism in person perception: Effects of situation-behavior relations on dispositional judgments. *Journal of Personality and Social Psychology, 56,* 41–53.

Shoda, Y., Mischel, W., & Wright, J. C. (1993a). Links between personality judgments and contextualized behavior patterns: Situation-behavior profiles of personality prototypes. *Social Cognition, 4,* 399–429.

Shoda, Y., Mischel, W., & Wright, J. C. (1993b). The role of situational demands and cognitive competencies in behavior organization and personality coherence. *Journal of Personality and Social Psychology, 65,* 1023–1035.

Shoda, Y., Mischel, W., & Wright, J. C. (1994). Intra-individual stability in the organization and patterning of behavior: Incorporating psychological situations into the idiographic analysis of personality. *Journal of Personality and Social Psychology, 67,* 674–687.

Smith, C. A., & Lazarus, R. S. (1990). Emotion and adaptation. In L. A. Pervin (Ed.), *Handbook of personality: Theory and research* (pp. 609–637). New York: Guilford Press.

Snyder, M., & Ickes, W. (1985). Personality and social behavior. In G. Lindzey & E. Aronson (Eds.), *Handbook of social psychology* (pp. 883–948). New York: Random House.

Susi, M. (1986). *Construct validation of the "competence-demand" hypothesis.* Unpublished master's thesis, Columbia University.

Taylor, S. E., & Schneider, S. K. (1989). Coping and the simulation of events. *Social Cognition, 7,* 174–194.

Uleman, J. S., & Bargh, J. A. (Eds.). (1989). *Unintended thought.* New York: Guilford Press.

Vallacher, R. R., & Wegner, D. M. (1987). What do people think they're doing? Action identification and human behavior. *Psychological Review, 94,* 3–15.

Vernon, P. E. (1964). *Personality assessment: A critical survey.* New York: Wiley.

Wachs, T. D., & King, B. (1994). Behavioral research in the brave new world of neuroscience: A guide to the biologically perplexed. In J. E. Bates & T. D. Wachs (Eds.), *Temperament: Individual differences at the interface of biology and behavior* (pp. 307–336). Washington, DC: American Psychological Association.

Wright, J. C., & Mischel, W. (1982). The influence of affect on cognitive social learning person variables. *Journal of Personality and Social Psychology, 43,* 901–914.

Wright, J. C., & Mischel, W. (1987). A conditional approach to dispositional constructs: The local predictability of social behavior. *Journal of Personality and Social Psychology, 53,* 1159–1177.

Wright, J. C., & Mischel, W. (1988). Conditional hedges and the intuitive psychology of traits. *Journal of Personality and Social Psychology, 55,* 454–469.

Zajonc, R. B. (1980). Feeling and thinking: Preferences need no inferences. *American Psychologist, 35,* 151–175.

Appendix   Details of the Simulation

To illustrate how individual differences in the behaviors are generated by the type of mediating processes shown in Figure 4, we created 100 hypothetical individuals who were assumed to have a common set of four mediating units that were potentially activated by a common set of six situation features. Individuals were assumed to differ in their sensitivity of each of these four units to each of the six features of situations. Each of these four mediating units in turn was assumed to activate, with varying connection weights, a fifth mediating unit representing the scripts for a potential behavior (which we labeled *friendly behavior*). Positive (excitatory) sensitivity and connection weight were assumed to increase the activation value of the recipient unit by the amount corresponding to the weight when the source unit was activated. Negative (inhibitory) connection weight was assumed to decrease the activation of the recipient unit when the source unit was activated. A connection weight of 0 was equivalent to having no connection. We assumed that all the positive and negative inputs into a mediating unit were simply summed, and the resultant activation value was 1 if the total activation was positive, and 0 if it was negative. (Different summing and threshold functions produced essentially the same overall results.)

Stable individual differences were implemented as differences between individuals in the connection weights. Individuals were assumed to vary in the strength and sign (excitatory vs inhibitory) of activation of their four mediating units in relation to each situation feature. They were also assumed to vary in the contribution of these mediating units, when they are activated, to the activation of the behavior script unit. These weights were randomly sampled from a normal distribution with a mean of 0 ($SD = 0.5$) to generate a different set of weights for each individual that once sampled stably charactaized the simulated individual. The weights for one of the simulated individuals ("Person 1" in Figure Al) are shown in Table Al. In the cognitive–affective system theory, the actual enactment of the behaviors is affected by the individual's self-regulatory strategies and competencies To allow for individual differences in this process as well as for momentary and unsystematic variations that affect the generation of actual behaviors, we added randomly generated perturbations (sampled from a normal distribution with a mean of 0 and standard deviation of 0.3) to the activation of the behavior units. The amount of random perturbations added also served to represent unpredictability intrinsic in the personality system and as a metric against which one on compare the effect of behavior variation across situations due to stable characteristics of the personality system. Thus, the magnitude of the coefficients obtained in this simulation is determined relative to the amount of random perturbation added.

To simulate the behaviors of these individuals in different situations, we constructed a hypothetical social world consisting of 15 situations. Each of the 15 situations had the features indicated in Table A2, representing all distinctive combinations of two (out of the total set of six) potential features. To determine if the model produced stable intraindividual patterns of behavior variability as observed empirically in the studies reviewed earlier, we "exposed" each computer model of a person to each of these situations. We repeated the procedure twice, producing two profiles for each individual. Illustrative profiles are shown in Figure Al, in which the profile from Time 1 is shown

by the solid line, and the profile from Time 2 is shown by the dotted line. Persons 1, 2, and 3 illustrate high profile stability, whereas 4, 5, and 6 illustrate low profile stability. Persons 1 and 4 illustrate relatively high mean levels, whereas Persons 3 and 6 illustrate relatively low mean levels.

Table A1. Activation Weights Characterizing the Simulated Person 1 Whose Behaviors are Shown in Figure A1

Situation feature	Mediating unit			
	1	2	3	4
1	−0.29	0.06	−0.56	0.24
2	−0.06	−0.62	−0.02	−0.14
3	0.31	−0.38	0.20	0.21
4	−0.05	−0.10	0.77	1.19
5	−0.42	1.28	0.10	−0.15
6	0.03	0.29	−0.12	1.06

Note. Mediating units 1 through 4 represent cognitions and affects that become activated in relation to situation features 1–6. Entries show the activation weights from each of situation features 1 through 6 to each of the four mediating units. Specifically, an entry in row *i* column *j* represents the activation contributed by situation feature *i* to mediating unit *j*. A fifth unit represented the behavioral scripts whose activation produces the behavior plotted in Figure A1. It is activated by mediating unites 1 through 4, with a set of activating weights characteristic for each person. For Person 1, they were .2, −.56, 1.07, and .55, respectively. The activation weights for persons 2–6 whose behaviors are plotted in Figure A1 are available on request.

Table A2. The Simulated Social World Consisting of 15 Situations in Which Each of 6 Features is Either Present (1) or Absent (0)

Situation	Feature					
	1	2	3	4	5	6
1	1	1	0	0	0	0
2	1	0	1	0	0	0
3	1	0	0	1	0	0
4	1	0	0	0	1	0
5	1	0	0	0	0	1
6	0	1	1	0	0	0
7	0	1	0	1	0	0
8	0	1	0	0	1	0
9	0	1	0	0	0	1
10	0	0	1	1	0	0
11	0	0	1	0	1	0
12	0	0	1	0	0	1
13	0	0	0	1	1	0
14	0	0	0	1	0	1
15	0	0	0	0	1	1

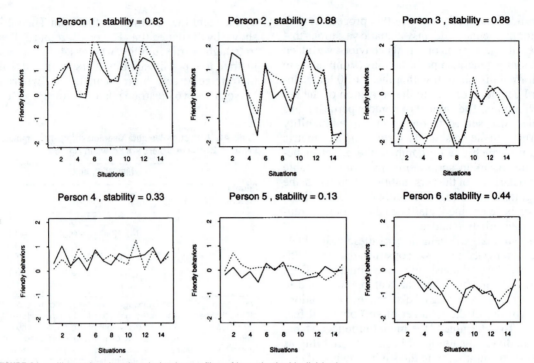

FIGURE A1 ■ Illustrative situation–behavior profiles of hypothetical individuals.

The Prediction of Behavior from Attitudinal and Normative Variables

Icek Ajzen and Martin Fishbein • Department of Psychology, University of Illinois

Editors' Notes

What variables predict social behavior? As a starting assumption, the authors propose that behavioral intentions mediate overt behavior. According to the model, individuals' intention to perform a given act in a given situation is a joint function of their attitude toward performing the act and their normative belief about how others think they should act in that situation. An individual's attitude toward performing the act is predicted by the product of the individual's beliefs about the desirability of each of the consequences of performing the act and the individual's evaluation of the likelihood of each consequence (its subjective probability). This product for attitude toward an act is a form of expectancy-value model. An individual's normative belief is multiplied by the individual's motivation to comply with that norm. This model was tested by examining the choices of participants in Prisoner's Dilemma games played in either a cooperative, competitive, or individualistic orientation. As predicted, the different forms of the games influenced the participants' attitudes and normative beliefs, which in turn mediated the participants' choices in the games.

Discussion Questions

1. Behavioral intentions are a joint function of what variables?
2. What is the role of expectancies in attitudes and normative beliefs?

Authors' Abstract

Fishbein's (1967) extension of Dulany's (1967) theory of propositional control was tested in the contest of the Prisoner's Dilemma (PD) game. The theory holds that a person's behavior (B) is a function of his behavioral intention (BI) which is determined by his attitude toward the act (A-act) and by his beliefs about the expectations of the other player, i.e., social normative beliefs (NBs). Two PD games differing in Cooperation Index (CI) were each played in a cooperative, a competitive, and an individualistic motivational orientation. CI and motivational orientations affected questionnaire measures of the theoretical constructs and game behavior as expected. Their influence on B was mediated by BI through A-act and NBs. BI correlated highly with B and was in turn accurately predicted from A-act and NBs in a multiple-regression equation. The relative importance of A-act and NBs in predicting BI and B varied as expected with the motivational orientation: in the cooperative condition norms were relatively more important; under competition more relative weight was placed on A-act.

This paper reports the results of an experiment designed to test the validity of a theoretical model of behavioral prediction recently presented by Fishbein (1967). The model can best be seen as an extension of Dulany's (1967) "theory of propositional control" to social behavior. Its use in the social area provides a test of the generality of the model which was developed initially in the framework of learning theory. While the original theory is almost identical to the present formulation, its constructs have been relabeled in an attempt to reveal their relations to more familiar social psychological concepts. In the process of translation some minor changes have occurred in the meaning of the constructs as well as in the ways in which they are measured. Nevertheless, all the predictions derived from the present model and tested in this experiment could have been derived just as well from the original formulation of the theory of propositional control. For a complete presentation of the relationships between Dulany's theory of propositional control and Fishbein's extension of it, cf. Fishbein (1967).

The immediate concern of the extended model, like that of the original formulation, is the prediction of behavioral intentions (BI) which are assumed to mediate overt behavior. According to the extended model, an individual's intention to perform a given act is a joint function of his attitude toward performing the act (A-act) and of his beliefs about what he is expected to do in that situation, i.e., his normative beliefs (NB). These normative beliefs are in turn multiplied by the individual's motivation to comply with the norms (Mc).

The two major components of the model are weighted for their importance in the prediction of behavioral intentions, as can be seen in the following algebraic expression:[1]

$$B \sim BI = [\text{A-act}]w_0 + [\text{NB (Mc)}]w_1$$

where B = overt behavior; BI = behavioral intention; A-act = attitude toward performing a given behavior in a given situation; NB normative beliefs; Mc = motivation to comply with the norms; w_0 and w_1 = empirically determined weights. The normative component of the model has not as yet been completely formalized. Most importantly, it refers to the individual's perception of the behaviors expected of him by relevant or significant others, called social normative beliefs (NBs). Of course, the potential reference groups or individuals whose expectations are perceived to be relevant, will vary with the behavioral situation. Thus, while in some instances the expectations of a person's friends or family may be most relevant, in others it may be the expectations of his supervisors or even the society at large which are most influential.

Elsewhere it was suggested (cf. Fishbein, 1967; Ajzen & Fishbein, 1969) that the normative component also included the individual's personal normative beliefs (NBp); i.e., his own beliefs as to what he should do in a given situation. It appears, however, that in many situations NBp may

---

[1] Ideally, the weights of the attitudinal and normative components should be established separately for each individual subject. However, in the absence of adequate methods for obtaining individual weights, they are obtained by a multiple-regression analysis, where A-act and NB(Mc) are used as the predictors, and BI is the criterion.

serve mainly as an alternative measure of behavioral intentions.[2] Since NBp is of no consequence for purposes of testing the hypotheses in the present study, it is not treated here as part of the theory and no further reference to it will be made. One other point needs to be mentioned regarding the motivation to comply (Mc). The measurement of this variable has repeatedly proved to be unsatisfactory (e.g., Ajzen & Fishbein, 1969). Research to date has indicated relatively little variance in this measure, and thus the results obtained with normative beliefs alone were as good or better than those obtained when NB was multiplied by Mc.[3]

Again, inclusion of the Mc measure is not crucial in the context of the present experiment. While Mc may still prove to be an important variable in some situations, it will not be considered in the present paper.

The inclusion of only social normative beliefs (NBs) and the deletion of the motivation to comply produces a somewhat simplified version of the theoretical model. This version can be expressed algebraically as follows :

$$B \sim BI = [A\text{-act}]w_0 + [NBs]w_1$$

The theory thus identifies three kinds of variables that function as the basic determinants of behavior: attitudes toward the performance of the behavior, normative beliefs, and the weights of these predictors. Any additional variable is held to influence BI only indirectly by influencing one or more of these determinants. Situational variables or personality characteristics will, therefore, influence a person's behavioral intentions (and thus his behavior) if, and only if, they are related to A-act, to NBs, or if they influence the relative weights that are placed on these predictors.

A-act, the attitude toward an act, deserves special attention. Consistent with the research of Peak (1935), Rosenberg (1956) and others, Fishbein (1963) has demonstrated that an individual's attitude toward any object can be predicted accurately from a knowledge of the person's beliefs about the object and the evaluative aspects of those beliefs. More specifically, attitude was found to be highly correlated with the sum of the beliefs, each multiplied by its respective evaluative aspect. When this formulation is applied to the attitude toward an act, rather than an object, the product involves beliefs about the consequences of performing the act (B_i) and the subjective evaluation

(a_i) of these consequences: A-act $= \Sigma B_i a_i$. It can be seen that A-act is concerned with a particular behavior in a given, well-defined situation. It should not be confused with the attitude toward an object, or class of objects, which has been of interest in most previous work on attitudes.

As mentioned earlier, the model's immediate concern is the prediction of behavioral intentions, A high correlation is assumed to exist between BI and actual behavior. The effects of the attitude toward the act and of normative beliefs on overt behavior are held to be mediated by BI. The prediction of behavioral intentions is, therefore, according to the theory, a necessary as well as sufficient condition for the prediction of overt behavior. Such an intimate relationship between BI and B will, of course, not unconditionally hold. Among other things, the more general the behavioral intention and the longer the time interval between the statement of intention and the actual behavior, the lower will the BI–B correlation tend to be. In attempting to predict behavior it is therefore the experimenter's responsibility to insure that the conditions under which BI is measured will be maximally conducive to a high correlation between BI and B.

It is interesting to note that Fishbein's (1967) conceptualization of attitude toward an act corresponds quite closely to a number of formulations proposed by other theorists. For example, Rotter's (1954) social learning theory maintains that the probability of the occurrence of a given behavior in a particular situation is determined by two variables: the subjectivity held probability (or expectance) that the behavior in question will be reinforced and the value of the reinforcer to the subject. Similarly, both Peak (1955) and Rosenberg (1956, 1965) view attitudes as a function of beliefs about the instrumentality of the object in obtaining goals and the value importance of those goals.

Also related to these notions is the SEU model of behavioral decision theory (cf. Edwards, 1954, 1961). Very briefly, this theory attempts to specify the subjective expected utilities (SEU) of a person's alternative actions. Different strategies for decision making may then be employed. The most

---

[2] In fact, a measure of NBp was also taken in the present study and the statistical analyses revealed that it was essentially equivalent to BI.

[3] In a more recent study, Ajzen (1969) demonstrated that more adequate measures of the motivation to comply can be obtained.

generally useful strategy is one that leads to the choice of the alternative which maximizes expected gain or minimizes expected loss. The SEU of a given alternative is a function of the subjective probability that certain outcomes will follow that act (SP_i) multiplied by the respective subjective values (or utilities) attached to these outcomes (U_i). The products are summed over all possible outcomes of the act: $SEU = \Sigma SP_i U_i$. The SEU maximization model predicts that behavioral alternative to occur for which SEU is maximal. It can be seen that SEU is closely related to the definition of attitude toward an act ($A\text{-act} = \Sigma B_i a_i$).[4] The difference between behavioral decision theory and the extended version of the theory of propositional control relates primarily to the sufficiency of SEU (or A-act) for the prediction of behavior. A decision theory approach leads to the conclusion that SEU is the ultimate antecedent and best predictor of behavior. In contrast, SEU (or A-act) is only one of the determinants of behavioral intentions, and hence of behavior proposed by Fishbein: A-act and normative beliefs (NBs) as well as their weights are expected to enter into the prediction of behavior.

The Experimental Situation

The situation selected for an evaluation of the present theory's usefulness was the two-person Prisoner's Dilemma (PD) game. In that game the players make repeated choices between two responses assumed to serve the motives of cooperation and competition. Following Rapoport and Chammah (1965) we may call the two alternative strategies "Cooperation" (C) and "Defection" (D). The combined choices of Player (P) and his Opponent (O) determine the payoff to each, as represented in Matrix 1 and subject to the following constraints (Scodel et al., 1959):

(1) $2\chi_1 > \chi_2 + \chi_3 > 2\chi_4$
(2) $\chi_3 > \chi_1$
(3) $\chi_3 > \chi_2$
(4) $\chi_4 > \chi_2$

	C_2	D_2
C_1	χ_1, χ_1	χ_2, χ_3
D_1	χ_3, χ_2	χ_4, χ_4

MATRIX 1

The first entry in each cell of the matrix is the payoff to the row player, the second entries are the payoffs to the column player.

Strategy D dominates Strategy C for both players and on the assumption that each subject plays rationally each is expected to defect. However, joint defection results in a payoff (χ_4) which is smaller than the payoff (χ_1) both players could secure by joint cooperation (Rapoport & Orwant, 1962). It appears, therefore, that in the PD game no unambiguous normative prescription of strategy choice is possible. The strategy that should be adopted from the standpoint of the individual player differs from joint strategy prescription (Rapoport & Chammah, 1965).

Experimental Design and Hypotheses

The main purpose of the experiment was to test several hypotheses derived from Fishbein's extension of Dulany's theory of propositional control in the contest of the PD game and to demonstrate the model's usefulness in the prediction of game behavior.

Since, as we have seen above, the first component of the model (i.e., A-act) is similar to SEU, the decision theory model was also subjected to a similar empirical test.[5] In order to do this, measures had to be obtained of the subjective probabilities of each of the game's four possible outcomes and of their utilities. It should be noted, however, that the measurement procedures used in the present experiment do not meet the requirements of a formal mathematical model. Thus, while our measures may provide adequate assessments of Fishbein's $\Sigma B_i a_i$ or some of the other social psychological formulations, they can at best be taken only as approximations of subjective expected utilities. For the sake of convenience, we shall nevertheless continue to refer to these measures as SEU.

It will be recalled that according to the theory of propositional control, the effects of external

---

[4] There are, however, some important differences between the two formulations which cannot be dealt with here in detail. For instance, beliefs about the probability of outcomes for A-act are measured on bipolar semantic differential scales ranging from −3 to +3 while SP in the SEU model ranges from 0–1. These measures may produce different results after multiplication with the outcome's utilities.

variables on game behavior are mediated by the model's theoretical constructs. That is, any external variable influencing A-act, NBs, or their weights will also be related to behavioral intentions and thus to game behavior. To test this hypothesis, as well as some additional hypotheses derived from the model, it was necessary to study the effects of a number of external variables on the model's theoretical constructs (i.e., on A-act, NBs, and BI) and to show that the latter were in turn related to the behavioral choices of the players. The choice of external variables was based on the investigation of these variables in previous studies on the Prisoner's Dilemma.

First, the effects of the subject's sex and their *F*-scores on the model's predictors as well as on game behavior were to be tested. Previous investigations of these variables (e. g., Rapoport & Chammah, 1965; Bixenstine, Potash, & Wilson, 1963; Bixenstine & Wilson, 1963; Pilisuk, Skolnik, & Overstreet, 1968 on sex; Deutsch, 1960b; Wrightsman, 1966; Driver, 1965 on the *F*-score) failed to demonstrate consistent effects on game behavior. According to the present theory, these variables are expected to be predictive of game behavior only to the extent that they are related to A-act, to NBs, or to the weights of these variables in the prediction of BI.

More important, however, were the effects of the following two experimental manipulations as variables external to the model.

MOTIVATIONAL ORIENTATION OF THE PLAYERS

The first experimental manipulation was an attempt to induce a certain motivational orientation in the players. By giving appropriate instructions in different experimental groups, Deutsch (1960a) succeeded in creating cooperative, competitive and individualistic motivational orientations in his subjects which were shown to be related to game behavior. The same experimental manipulation was applied in the present study. In the cooperative condition the group members were instructed to consider themselves to be partners. In the competitive condition they were told to do better than the other person. Players in the individualistic con-

dition were told to have no interest whatsoever in the fate of their partner. However, in all three conditions the players were also instructed to try and win as many points as they could for themselves, thereby introducing an element of conflict even in the cooperative motivational orientation groups.

It is expected that cooperative responses (as indicated by A-act, NBs, BI, and B) are most frequent in the cooperative motivational orientation, less so in the individualistic orientation, and least frequent in the competitive orientation.

THE "COOPERATION INDEX" OF THE PAYOFF MATRIX

Each pair of subjects played two Prisoner's Dilemma games with different payoff matrices. Rapoport and Chammah (1965) have shown that different payoff matrices tend to produce different amounts of cooperation. These investigators have developed certain indices of "cooperative advantage" which have been shown to be directly related to the proportion of cooperative choices in the games. The most generally useful index is the ratio $(x_1 - x_4)/(xx_3 - x_2)$ which has a range of 0 to 1 (see Matrix 1). This ratio has been called the "Cooperation Index" (CI) by Terhune (1968).

The two payoff matrices used in the present study had Cooperation Indices of .900 (Game 1) and .083 (Game 2). Game 1 was identical to the PD game first used by Deutsch (1960a).

	C_2	D_2		C_2	D_2
C_1	+9, +9	−10, + 10	C_1	+ 1, + 1	−12, +12
D_1	+10, −10	−9, −9	D_1	+ 12, −12	−1, −1
	Game 1			Game 2	

More cooperative responses (as evidenced in the measures of A-act, NBs, BI, and B) are predicted in Game 1 (CI = .90) than in Game 2 (CI = .083).

The remaining experimental hypotheses are directly related to the theoretical model and may be summarized as follows:

1. Game behavior is a function of behavioral intentions. Therefore, a high correlation is expected between BI and B.
2. Behavioral intentions are determined by A-act and by NBs. It is therefore predicted that a high

[5]Indeed, the authors were surprised that they were unable to find previous attempts to base prediction of game behavior in the PD on the SEU model.

multiple correlation will be found between these two predictors and BI.

The relative weights of A-act and NBs in predicting BI are expected to be contingent upon the motivational orientations of the players. The expectations of the other player (NBs) should be more important for the prediction of BI in the cooperative condition. The person's attitude toward the act, however, should carry more weight in the competitive condition. In the individualistic motivational orientation A-act and NBs should both carry some weight in the prediction of BI. These effects are expected to be particularly evident in the regression coefficients of A-act and NBs on behavioral intentions.

3. SEU is predicted to correlate with game behavior. That is, the subjective expected utility model is expected to be applicable to the prediction of behavior in PD games, under the various experimental conditions.

Since SEU is considered to be more or less equivalent to A-act, these two variables should be correlated.

4. As A-act (SEU) is only one of the predictors of behavioral intentions in Fishbein's model, it is hypothesized that the inclusion of NBs improves prediction of BI above the level obtained when using A-act (or SEU) alone, and BI is expected to be more highly related to game behavior than is SEU.

5. BI is the direct antecedent of overt behavior (B). This hypothesis has the following implications.

a. Holding BI constant should reduce to nonsignificance the partial correlations of overt behavior with A-act, with SEU, and with NBs.

b. In contrast, when SEU is held constant it is expected that a sizable correlation will remain between BI and B. This hypothesis follows from the theory where SEU is only one of the determinants of BI and of overt behavior.

c. The effects of the experimental manipulations and of the other external variables on game behavior should be substantially reduced when BI is treated as covariate (i.e., "held constant") in an analysis of covariance. Similarly, the effects of these variables on BI should diminish considerably when A-act and NBs are treated as two simultaneous covariates in an analysis of covariance.

6. A traditional attitude approach would predict that cooperation in the PD game is related to the attitude toward the other player (Ao). However, according to the present model, Ao will affect behavior only if it is related to one or more of the model's predictors. Since the relation between Ao and A-act or NBs is not expected to be very strong, it is also predicted that Ao correlates only slightly, if at all, with overt behavior. Thus, Ao is treated like any other external variable; its effect on BI and on B is expected to be mediated by A-act and NBs.

To summarize briefly then, the main purpose of the present experiment was to test the validity of Fishbein's extension of Dulany's theory of propositional control in a PD-type game situation. More specifically, it is hypothesized that an individual's performance of cooperative (or defective) behavior in the PD situation is a function of his intention to cooperate (BI) which is itself a function of (1) his attitude toward cooperating in the particular PD situation (A-act) and (2) his beliefs about what the other player expects him to do (NBs). Further, it is predicted that the individual's A-act is a part function of his beliefs about consequences of cooperating (SP_j) and his evaluations of these consequences (U_j).[6] In addition, it is hypothesized that any other variable (e.g., motivational orientation, Cooperation Index, sex, authoritarianism, or attitude toward the other player) can only influence BI (and thus behavior) indirectly, by influencing A-act, NBs, or the relative weight placed upon these two predictors.

Method

Subjects

The sample consisted of 96 undergraduate students at the University of Illinois, 48 males and 48 females. The players in a given game were always of the same sex. They were assigned at random to the experimental conditions; two groups were run simultaneously, but independent of each other.

Sixteen groups, eight male and eight female, were assigned to each of the three motivational conditions. Each group played both PD games; the

---

[6]In the present study, SEU is based only on a consideration of subjective probabilities and evaluations of outcomes as presented in the payoff matrix. Of course, the attitude toward cooperation is also influenced by perceived consequences of cooperation other than these payoffs. A measure of A-act will, therefore, tend to be more general than the measure of SEU, and the correlation between A-act and SEU will not be perfect.

order in which the games were played was counterbalanced within each motivational condition.

Procedure

The two players in the game were seated at opposite sides of a table, separated by a partition. They were not allowed to communicate in any manner. At the outset of the experiment they were given standard instructions describing the game and inducing one of the motivational orientations, cooperation, individualism, or competition. The instructions concerning the game were taken in large part from Rapoport and Chammah (1965, Appendix I). The motivational orientations were worded after Deutsch (1960a). The instructions were read from a recorded tape while the subjects followed them on a printed outline.

Each player had the payoff matrix for the given game in front of him as well as a "record sheet" on which he recorded his choice on each play of the game (i.e., cooperation or defection). After each trial the experimenter exposed a card to each player indicating his payoff, that is, the number of points he had gained or lost on that trial. In the cooperative and in the competitive conditions the subjects were also shown the payoffs to the other player, while in the individualistic condition they were shown only their own payoffs since here they were told to have no interest whatsoever in the fate of the other player. The payoffs were also recorded on the record sheets.

After receiving the instructions, the groups played their first game (either Game 1 or Game 2) for eight moves after which they were asked to fill out a questionnaire to be described below. They then played the game for 10 more moves. Between the first and the second game the subjects completed a 20-item *F* scale. The second game was then played for eight moves after which a questionnaire pertaining to this game was completed. Ten additional moves in the second game brought the experimental session to a close.

The last 10 moves in each game were taken as a measure of game behavior.

The Questionnaires

Cooperation and defection were called X and Y, respectively. The questionnaire items provided measures for the following experimental variables.

1. A-act, the attitude toward cooperation. A direct measure of attitude toward the act was based on the sum over four semantic differential scales with high loadings on the evaluative factor (cf. Osgood, Suci, & Tannenbaum, 1957), presented as follows:

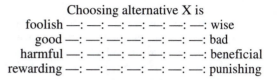

Choosing alternative X is

foolish —: —: —: —: —: —: —:	wise
good —: —: —: —: —: —: —:	bad
harmful —: —: —: —: —: —: —:	beneficial
rewarding —: —: —: —: —: —: —:	punishing

2. Subjective conditional probabilities, measured as follows: If I were to choose mainly X, my partner would choose ____ % X and ____ % Y.

3. Utilities of the payoffs. Each of the two possible outcomes of cooperation was followed by an evaluative semantic differential scale:
Example:

Obtaining the payoff (+ 9, + 9) is
good —: —: —: —: —: —: —: bad

4. SEU, the subjective expected utility of cooperation, was computed by multiplying the corresponding subjective probabilities and utilities and adding the two products: $SEU = \Sigma SP_iU_i$.

5. NBs, social normative beliefs. The perceived expectations of the other player were considered to be the relevant normative beliefs in tile experimental situation, and a measure was taken of these normative beliefs as follows.[7]

My partner expects me to choose ____ %X, and ____ %Y.

6. BI, the behavior intention, was measured as follows.

What are your intentions for this game?
I intend to choose ____ % X, and ____ % Y.

7. Ao, the attitude toward the other player, was measured by summing the five following evaluative semantic differential scales.

My partner is

wise —: —: —: —: —: —: —:	foolish
bad —: —: —: —: —: —: —:	good
sick —: —: —: —: —: —: —:	healthy
harmful —: —: —: —: —: —: —:	beneficial

[7]A measure was also taken of the perceived expectations of the experimenter (NB_E). Since the results obtained were similar to those using NBs and since NB_E was of less importance in the contest of the present experiment, only NBs was used as a measure of social normative beliefs.

The questionnaires administered in the two PD games were identical except for the outcomes of cooperation (i.e., the payoffs) that were evaluated.

Results

First, the possibility was examined that the introduction of questionnaires after the eighth move in each game has had a recognizable influence on behavior. The mean proportion of cooperative choices on moves 6 through 8 was compared with the mean on moves 9 through 11. In game 1 the two means were .531 and .542, respectively. In Game 2 the means were .375 and .399. Two-tailed t tests of the differences between these means were not significant ($t_{47} = -.131$ in Game 1 and $-.289$ in Game 2).

Effects of the Experimental Manipulations

Four-way analyses of variance were performed to examine the effects of the independent variables on the attitude toward the act (A-act), normative beliefs regarding the other player (NBs), subjective expected utilities (SEU), behavioral intentions (BI), and cooperative strategy choices on the last 10 moves (B). The four main effects in the analyses were: motivational orientations. Cooperation index (treated as a repeated measure since the same subjects played both games), the order in which the two games were played, and the sex of the players.[8]

Neither the game order nor the players' sex produced significant differences in the questionnaire responses or in overt behavior. The other two main effects, motivational orientation and Cooperation Index, were significant far beyond the .01 level, with mean differences in the hypothesized direc-

tions. As can be seen in Table 1, the cooperative motivational orientation produced the highest degree of cooperative responses while the competitive orientation produced least C responses. The degree of cooperation was intermediate in the individualistic condition. Also as expected, there were fewer cooperative responses in Game 2 than in Game 1. These effects could be observed in all dependent variables included in the analysis. (In Table 1 NBs, BI, and B are given in terms of percentages of cooperative choices).

The interaction between motivational orientation and CI was significant ($p < .01$) for A-act and B but not for the other dependent variables.

The one remaining independent variable, the subjects' F score, did not correlate significantly with any of the dependent variables (i.e., with A-act, SEU, NBs, BI, or B).

To summarize, the experimental manipulations were highly successful. Both the motivational orientations and the CI of the games strongly influenced questionnaire responses and game behavior in the expected directions. The sex and the F scores of the players were not significantly related to any of the dependent variables. Finally, the order in which the two games were played did not affect questionnaire responses or game behavior significantly.

The importance of these findings for the validity of the theoretical model is obvious. The effects of five different variables external to the model were tested. Whenever one of these variables was significantly related to the model's predictors (A-act and NBs) it also showed a significant relation with behavioral intentions and actual game behav-

[8]Since the responses of the two players in the game tend to lack independence, the means over the two players were used as dependent variables in the present analyses.

TABLE 1. Mean Questionnaire Responses and Game Behavior[a]

	Game 1 Motivational orientation			Game 2 Motivational orientation		
	Cooperation	Individualism	Competition	Cooperation	Individualism	Competion
A-act	21.84	16.84	13.69	22.16	11.72	9.91
SEU	5.97	4.10	2.51	5.08	2.81	1.80
NBs	83.97	51.19	39.88	73.22	37.56	24.66
BI	88.75	46.53	30.22	75.59	25.72	14.50
B	86.25	47.19	15.63	79.38	20.63	10.94

[a]The main effects of motivational orientation and Cooperation Index (Game No.) are significant ($p < .01$) in all analyses. Interaction effects are significant ($p < .01$) only for A-act and B.

ior. Sex, authoritarianism, and game order were unrelated to either A-act or NBs and, as expected, none of these variables influenced either BI or B.

In contrast to the significant effects of the experimental manipulations on the variables in the proposed model, Ao, the attitude toward the other player, was not affected significantly by any of the independent variables; no significant main effects or interactions were found for Ao.

Prediction of Game Behavior

Turning to the prediction of game behavior, Fishbein's extension of Dulany's model was found to be highly successful. As can be seen in Table 2, behavioral intentions were highly predictive of overt behavior in both games.

Table 2 also shows that, as expected, subjective expected utilities predicted game behavior with high accuracy. It should be noted, however, that in support of our hypothesis behavioral intentions were more closely related to game behavior than was SEU; the differences in the correlations are significant beyond the .01 level. In Table 2 it can also be seen that the correlations of A-act and NBs with game behavior are high and significant.

Also consistent with Fishbein's (1963) theory were the significant ($p < .01$) correlations found between SEU and A-act in both games (.633 in Game 1 and .672, in Game 2). Furthermore, A-act and SEU tended to stand in similar relations to the other variables in the study. Therefore, only A-act was used as the measure of the attitudinal component in the remaining analyses; similar results can be obtained by substituting SEU for A-act.

The prediction of behavioral intentions from A-act and NBs is presented in Table 3. Here the product-moment correlation coefficients of BI with A-act and with NBs are given as well as the standardized regression coefficients of the two predictors and their multiple correlation on BI. It can be seen that the experimental hypotheses were fully supported. First, the multiple correlations between the two predictors and behavioral intentions were high and significant in both PD games and in all three motivational conditions as well as over the total sample. Second, the inclusion of NBs greatly improved prediction of BI above the level obtained when only A-act was used. This is particularly obvious in the cooperative conditions of both games. However, as can be seen in Table 3, the regression coefficients of NBs on BI were signifi-

TABLE 2. Correlations of Proportion of Cooperative Choices on the Last 10 Moves (B) with BI, SEU, A-act, and NBs ($N = 96$)[a]

	Game 1	Game 2
BI–B	.847	.841
SEU–B	.704	.748
A-act–B	.631	.703
NBs–B	.685	.721

[a]All correlations are significant ($p < .01$).

cant under all conditions, providing evidence for the independent contribution of NBs to the prediction of BI. Third, as can best be seen in the regression coefficients, the relative importance of A-act and NBs in predicting BI varied as expected. A-act carried more weight than NBs in the competitive condition but less weight than NBs in the cooperative condition. As predicted, P's beliefs about the expectations of the other player (NBs) were clearly more important than was his own attitude in determining BI under a cooperative motivational orientation. However, when the orientation was competitive, the relative importance of A-act and NBs was reversed with A-act now being the more important determinant of BI.

The same pattern of results was observed when overt behavior (B) rather than BI was used as the criterion variable. However, as would be expected on the basis of the model, the correlations with game behavior are somewhat lower than those with BI (Table 4).

Of interest also are the correlations between the model's two predictors presented in Table 5. It can be seen that these correlations were significant in the individualistic and competitive conditions as well as for the total sample of subjects. In the cooperative condition, the correlations between A-act and NBs were not significant in either of the two games.

It should be noted that Dulany's (1967) theory of propositional control would lead us to expect at least some correlation between these two predictors since they are conceived to be partly determined by the same factor.[9]

---

[9]In Dulany's theory, the "cardinal rule" RHd (hypothesis of the distribution of reinforcement) enters twice into the equation for predicting behavioral intentions. RHd first multiplies RSv (the subjective value of a reinforcer); this product is A-act in the present formulation of the theory. RHd again appears in the equation as a multiplier of RHs (a hypothesis of the significance of a reinforcer) to produce BH—the behavioral hypothesis—in the present model NBs.

TABLE 3. Correlations, Regression Coefficients, and Multiple Correlations of A-act and NBs on BI

	Correlation coefficients		Regression coefficients		Multiple correla-tions
	A-act–BI	NBs–BI	A-act–BI	NBs–BI	
Game I					
Cooperation (N = 32)	.370*	.752**	.229	.707**	.785**
Individualism (N = 32)	.710**	.780**	.353*	.552**	.852**
Competition (N = 32)	.883**	.733**	.691**	.327**	.922**
Total (N = 96)	.754**	.838**	.378**	.601**	.888**
Game 2					
Cooperation (N = 32)	.253	.579**	.239	.573**	.626**
Individualism (N = 32)	.673**	.677**	.416**	.427**	.754**
Competition (N = 32)	.866**	.741**	.669**	.298**	.894**
Total (N = 96)	.735**	.786**	.405**	.539**	.849**

$* p < .05.$
$** p < .01.$

SEU Versus BI as Antecedents of Behavior

The comparison of SEU and BI as variables antecedent to game behavior provided substantial support for the hypothesis. As can be seen in Table 6, when BI was held constant the correlations of A-act, NBs, and SEU with overt behavior were substantially reduced, as compared with the correlations presented in Table 2. Indeed, all but one of the six partial correlations were nonsignificant. In contrast, when SEU was held constant all partial correlations remained significant beyond the .01 level.

More importantly, holding BI constant reduced to nonsignificance the correlations of SEU with overt behavior. But holding SEU constant left the correlations of BI with behavior high and significant. This finding indicates that BI, rather than SEU, is the variable that mediates between overt behavior and various antecedents. SEU may best be regarded as equivalent to A-act.

The intervening character of BI was at least partly supported in an analysis of covariance performed on the data.[10] Treating BI as the covariate eliminated the effect of the Cooperation Index on game behavior, and greatly reduced the influence

___

[10]The authors thank H. W. Norton for his assistance in the performance of the analyses of covariance.

TABLE 4. Correlations, Regression Coefficients, and Multiple Correlations of A-act and NBs on B

	Correlation coefficients		Regression coefficients		Multiple correla-tions
	A-act–BI	NBs–BI	A-act–BI	NBs–BI	
Game I					
Cooperation (N = 32)	.310	.482**	.223	.438**	.529**
Individualism (N = 32)	.465**	.477**	.270	.302	.519**
Competition (N = 32)	.773**	.576**	.664**	.186	.788**
Total (N = 96)	.631**	.685**	.331**	.478**	.732**
Game 2					
Cooperation (N = 32)	.272	.421*	.262	.415*	.496*
Individualism (N = 32)	.506**	.546**	.278	.379*	.590**
Competition (N = 32)	.734**	.655**	.535**	.300	.768**
Total (N = 96)	.703**	.721**	.419**	.464**	.793**

$* p < .05.$
$** p < .01.$

TABLE 5. Correlations Between A-act and NBs

	Game 1	Game 2
Cooperation ($N = 32$)	.199	.024
Individualism ($N = 32$)	.647*	.601*
Competition ($N = 32$)	.587*	.662*
Total ($N = 96$)	.627*	.614*

* $p < .01$.

TABLE 7. Means of Game Behavior Adjusted for Regression of BI on B[a]

	Game 1	Game 2
Cooperation	53.36	53.37
Individualism	50.86	35.12
Competition	32.14	35.63

[a] Only the main effect of motivation and the Motivation × Game interaction are significant ($p < .05$).

of motivational orientation, although the main effect of motivational orientation and the interaction remained significant at the .05 level. The differences between the cell means were considerably reduced after adjustment for regression of BI on B, as can be seen by comparing the adjusted cell means in Table 7 with the corresponding unadjusted means of game behavior presented in Table 1.[11]

To summarize, BI was found to mediate the effects of other variables on game behavior. When BI was statistically controlled, the correlations of A-act and of NBs with behavior were practically eliminated. Similarly, the effects of motivation and of CI on game behavior were substantially reduced by holding BI constant.

An additional analysis of covariance was performed to test the extent to which A-act and NBs mediated the effects of the experimental manipulations on behavioral intentions. When A-act and NBs were treated as simultaneous covariates, the main effects of motivational orientation and Cooperation Index were greatly attenuated. In fact, the effect of CI did not reach statistical significance nor was the interaction between the two factors significant. The effect of motivational orientation, although also strongly attenuated, remained significant ($F_{2, 45} = 4.80$; $p < .05$).

Overall, then, there was a strong tendency for the model's variables to mediate the effects of external factors on game behavior although in a few

cases some influence remained even after the appropriate theoretical constructs were statistically controlled.

Finally, as expected, the correlations between the attitude toward the other player (Ao) and game behavior were low. In Game 1 Ao correlated .256 with the proportion of cooperative choices on the last 10 trials ($p < .05$). In Game 2 the correlation between Ao and B was .091 (not significant).

In the light of the theoretical model employed these results are not surprising although they are contrary to widely held attitudinal theories. It will be recalled that Ao, like any other external variable, was expected to influence behavior only through its effects on the model's predictors. The correlations between Ao and A-act were .354 ($p < .01$) in Game 1 and .239 ($p < .05$) in Game 2. Ao correlated with NBs .262 ($p < .05$) and .015 (not significant) in the two games, respectively. Since these correlations were relatively low, the correlation of Ao with game behavior was also negligible.

Summary and Conclusion

The present results provide clear support for a variety of hypotheses derived from Fishbein's extension of Dulany's theory of propositional control. The cooperative behavior of players in two different Prisoner's Dilemma games were accurately predicted from expressed behavioral intentions (BI). These behavioral intentions were found

TABLE 6. Partial Correlations Between Game Behavior and A-act, NBs, BI, and SEU ($N = 96$)[a]

	BI held constant		SEU held constant	
	Game 1	Game 2	Game 1	Game 2
A-act–B	−.023	.233	.337	.408
NBs–B	−.083	.178	.368	.425
BI–B	—	—	.677	.596
SEU–B	.185	.175	—	—

[a] $r_{05} = .202$, $r_{01} = .262$.

[11]One possible explanation of the residual significant effects of the experimental manipulations may be suggested. According to Dulany's (1967) theory of propositional control, overt behavior is influenced not only by BI but also by habit (H). A voluntary response is expected to "habituate, to become automatic and involuntary as some function of number of voluntary executions of that response" (p. 352), and, to some extent, to influence behavior independently of BI. The effects of the experimental manipulations might have been reduced to nonsignificance had it been possible to hold H constant in addition to controlling for BI.

to mediate the effects of various other variables on game behavior. BI was found to be a function of both the attitude toward the act of cooperation (A-act) and of the perceived expectations of the other player (NBs). A high multiple correlation was obtained when A-act and NBs were used to predict BI. Also as expected A-act carried more weight than NBs in the multiple regression on BI as well as on game behavior under a competitive motivational orientation; the relative importance of A-act and NBs was reversed under a cooperative motivational orientation. A-act was shown to be roughly equivalent to the subjective expected utility (SEU) of cooperation, and a significant correlation between A-act and SEU was obtained. SEU also correlated highly with game behavior but, consistent with the theory, BI proved to be a better predictor than SEU. The effects of two experimental manipulations, the motivational orientation of the players, and the Cooperation Index of the game, were shown to be reflected not only in game behavior but in a similar manner also in the related questionnaire measures of the model's theoretical constructs. In contrast, the attitude toward the other player (Ao) was unaffected by these manipulations. This traditional attitude measure also failed to predict game behavior to any appreciable degree, just as it was relatively unrelated to any of the variables in the model.

In order to appreciate the importance of these findings it is necessary to understand some of the implications of the present theory. The model provides an explanation for, and an alternative to, the unsuccessful attempts in the past to base prediction of behavior vis-à-vis an object on the attitude toward that object (cf. Fishbein, 1967). According to the theory, Ao is often found to be unrelated to behavior because it fails to affect the predictors of behavior, A-act and NBs. The alternative, of course, is to measure A-act and NBs rather than Ao.

For the area of communication and persuasion this implies that the demonstration of attitude change as the result of a persuasive message is insufficient. Behavioral change is expected to be produced by changing BI, and this in turn depends on our ability to affect A-act, NBs, or their relative weights.

It is interesting to note that the present theory can also provide a bridge between the social psychological subareas of attitude and group dynamics which have traditionally taken separate paths.

A-act, of course, is closely related to attitude theory while social norms are an important variable in group dynamics. The present theory describes the interaction of these two variables in determining behavior.

While the importance of the present findings can hardly be refuted, the question may be raised as to the extent to which the obtained results could be due to demand characteristics of the situation (Orne, 1962), or to method variance. The argument of demand characteristics might be raised in particular with regard to the self reports of A-act, NBs, and BI. Under close investigation, however, this objection cannot be sustained. Although high intercorrelations among the different experimental variables might be accounted for by demand characteristics, the predicted and obtained complex pattern of interrelations must go beyond the insights into the experimental hypotheses that a subject can attain in the course of a 50-min experimental session. Thus, game behavior was found to be unrelated to the attitude toward the other player (Ao) while it was strongly related to A-act, NBs, and BI. It appears reasonable that under the operation of demand characteristics the hypothesis would be formed that a positive attitude toward the other player should be accompanied by cooperation with him. After all, similar hypotheses have frequently been suggested by more sophisticated social psychologists.

But more importantly, it appears completely implausible that the subjects were able to produce the predicted variations in the relative weights of A-act and NBs purely as the result of demand characteristics. In fact, a thorough understanding of the theoretical model is required in order to arrive at the correct hypotheses, and even this does not immediately suggest the exact questionnaire responses that have to be given in order to produce the desired results.

Thus, to propose the operation of demand characteristics as an alternative explanation of the obtained results appears unconvincing in the light of the intricate patterns of interrelations that were predicted and obtained in the present experiment.

It can, perhaps, be argued that some of the relations between the variables in the present study may be due to differential method variance. That is, social normative beliefs (NBs), behavioral intentions (BI), and game behavior (B) were all measured in a similar manner (i.e., as percentages) while the attitude toward cooperation (A-act) was measured on 7-point semantic differential scales. Thus, the interrelations of the first three variables (NBs, BI, and B) should be higher than their correlations with A-act.

But as the reader can verify for himself, this was not the case. Indeed, in the competitive motivational orientation A-act was more highly related to BI and to B than was NBs (see Tables 3 and 4).

Thus, differential method variance is also inadequate as an alternative explanation of the observed pattern of intercorrelations.

An issue of greater concern to the model is related to the expected correspondence between behavioral intentions and overt behavior. As stated in the description of the theory, a one-to-one relationship is expected if, and only if, BI is very specific to B and measured immediately preceding the performance of B. Requiring BI to be measured as close in time as possible to the performance of B is designed to insure that BI has not changed since it was measured; i.e., that no changes have occurred in either A-act or NBs, or in the weights of these predictors. For instance, in a social situation involving interaction between two or more persons A-act and NBs may change in the process of interaction itself. Thus, the behavioral intention measured at the beginning of interaction may differ greatly from that existing toward its end.

There is evidence in the present study, as well as in previous studies on the Prisoner's Dilemma (Rapoport and Chammah, 1965), that P's behavior changes with that of O. In particular, it appears that if one defects the other has but little choice and defects too. Correlations between the game behaviors of the two players are usually found to be high. In the present experiment these correlations were .919 in Game 1 and .885 in Game 2.[12]

The question may, therefore, be raised as to how it is at all possible to obtain high correlations between BI and game behavior if the latter changes in the process of interaction while the former is measured before the interaction takes place. The answer must be that, after eight moves of the game, P has formed relatively accurate hypotheses about O's future behavioral choices and these hypotheses are reflected in A-act, NBs, and thus in BI. Were the players now to change their game behavior drastically, the BI–B correlation would necessarily deteriorate.

It appears, therefore, that it may sometimes be insufficient to measure BI shortly before observing B in order to insure a high correlation between these two variables. Only if the situation under consideration allows P to form reasonably accurate expectations of his behavior's consequences (which may in part depend upon the behavior of another person) and of the social norms governing behavior in that situation will P be able to state a behavioral intention which will accurately predict his actual behavior. The eight preparatory moves in each game of the present experiment seem to have provided the opportunity for the development of an accurate perception of the situation.

Finally, a few additional words of caution are necessary. It was pointed out before that BI may not be the only variable influencing behavior. In footnote 12 "habit" was mentioned as a possible additional variable operating independently of BI.

Similarly, it may be proposed that a variable such as "feasibility" may also be necessary. That is, although the theory views BI as the immediate antecedent of behavior, it must be made clear that an intention is only an intention, and in many cases, it may not be possible for an individual to carry through his intentions because of various kinds of situational or interpersonal constraints. While problems of this kind can be avoided in the laboratory, it may be necessary to consider them in field situations. It is for this reason that earlier in the paper we made the statement that "it is the experimenter's responsibility to insure that the conditions under which BI is measured will be maximally conducive to a high correlation between BI and B."

Finally, just as there may be some restrictions vis-à-vis the BI–B relationship, a few additional words concerning the prediction of BI are also necessary. It has already been mentioned that there is still some question about the nature of the model's normative component. In particular, it may be necessary to consider personal normative beliefs in addition to social normative beliefs. Further, if social normative beliefs are considered, it is not clear whether the referent for the norm should be a "generalized other" (i.e., most people who are important to me expect me to . . .) or a specific other (i.e., my partner expects me to . . .) or a set of specific others (i.e., my family, my three

---

[12]These high correlations were the reason for using group means as dependent variables in the analyses of variables reported above.

closest friends, etc.). In addition, the relationship between an individual's belief that a "generalized other" expects him to behave in a given way and his beliefs that different specific others expect him to behave in given ways still has to be investigated and identified.

While a complete discussion of the many unresolved theoretical and methodological problems associated with the model and its applications is beyond the scope of the present paper, it should be clear that the present model, like most explanatory attempts, raises at least as many questions as it appears to answer. Our one hope is that these questions are interesting and relevant enough to stimulate additional research.

REFERENCES

Ajzen, I. (1969). *Prediction and change of behavior in the Prisoner's Dilemma.* Unpublished doctoral dissertation. Urbana, IL: University of Illinois Press.

Ajzen, I., & Fishbein, M. (1969). The prediction of behavioral intentions in a choice situation. *Journal of Experimental Social Psychology, 5,* 400–416.

Bixenstine, V. E., Potash, H. M., & Wilson, K. V. (1963). Effects of level of cooperative choice by the other player on choice in a Prisoner's Dilemma game: Part I. *Journal of Abnormal and Social Psychology, 66,* 308–313.

Bixenstine, V. E., & Wilson, K. V. (1963). Effects of level of cooperative choice by the other player on choices in a Prisoner's Dilemma game: Part II. *Journal of Abnormal and Social Psychology, 67,* 139–147.

Deutsch, M. (1960a). The effect of motivational orientation upon threat and suspicion. *Human Relations, 13,* 123–139.

Deutsch, M. (1960b). Trust, trustworthiness, and the F scale. *Journal of Abnormal and Social Psychology, 61,* 138–140.

Driver, M. J. (January 1965). A structural analysis of aggression, stress, and personality in an inter-nation simulation. Paper No. 97, Institute for Research in the Behavioral, Economic, and Management Sciences, Purdue University.

Dulany, D. E. (1967). Awareness, rules, and propositional control: A confrontation with S-R behavior theory. In D. Horton & T. Dixon (Eds.), *Verbal behavior and S-R behavior theory*. Englewood Cliffs, NJ: Prentice-Hall.

Edwards, W. (1954). The theory of decision making. *Psychological Bulletin, 51,* 380–418.

Edwards, W. (1961). Behavioral decision theory. *Annual Review of Psychology, 12,* 473–498.

Fishbein, M. (1963). An investigation of the relationships between beliefs about an object and the attitude toward that object. *Human Relations, 16,* 233–240.

Fishbein, M. (1967). Attitude and prediction of behavior. In M. Fishbein (Ed.), *Readings in attitude theory and measurement.* New York: Wiley.

Orne, M. T. (1962). On the social psychology of the psychological experiment: With particular reference to demand characteristics and their implications. *American Psychologist, 17,* 776–783.

Osgood, C. E., Suci, G. J., & Tannenbaum, P. H. (1957). The measurement of meaning. Urbana, IL: University of Illinois Press.

Peak, H. (1955). Attitude and motivation. In M. Jones (Ed.), *Nebraska symposium on motivation.* Lincoln: University of Nebraska Press.

Pilisuk, M., Skolnik, P., & Overstreet, E. (1968). Predicting cooperation from the two sexes in a conflict simulation. *Journal of Personality and Social Psychology, 10,* 35–43.

Rapoport, A., & Orwant, C. (1962). Experimental games: A review. *Behavioral Science, 7,* 137.

Rapoport, A., & Chammah, A. M. (1965). *Prisoner's Dilemma: A study on conflict and cooperation.* Ann Arbor: University of Michigan Press.

Rosenberg, M. J. (1956). Cognitive structure and attitudinal affect. *Journal of Abnormal and Social Psychology, 53,* 367–372.

Rosenberg, M. J. (1965). Inconsistency arousal and reduction in attitude change. In I. D. Steiner & M. Fishbein (Eds.), *Current Studies in Social Psychology.* New York: Holt, Rinehart & Winston.

Rotter, J. B. (1954). *Social learning and clinical psychology.* Englewood Cliffs, NJ: Prentice-Hall.

Scodel, A., Minas, J. S., Ratoosh, P., & Lipetz, M. (1959). Some descriptive aspects of two-person, non-zero-sum games I. *Journal of Conflict Resolution, 3,* 114–119.

Terhune, K. W. (1968). Motives, situation, and interpersonal conflict within Prisoner's Dilemma. *Journal of Personality and Social Psychology, 8,* Monograph supplement.

Wrightsman, L. S. (1966). Personality and attitudinal correlates of trusting and trustworthy behavior in a two-person game. *Journal of Personality and Social Psychology, 4,* 328–332.

Motivational Determinants of Risk-Taking Behavior

John W. Atkinson • Department of Psychology, University of Michigan

Editors' Notes

What is the relationship between achievement motivation and risk-taking behavior? Consistent with earlier expectancy-value models, it is proposed that the strength of the aroused motivation to achieve as shown in performance is a function of both a person's dispositional achievement motives and the expectancy and incentive of goal attainment that is aroused by situation cues. The author proposes that the pride incentive of success increases as the expectancy of success decreases, whereas the shame incentive of failure increases as the expectancy of success increases. He also proposes that individuals for whom the motive to achieve success is stronger than the motive to avoid failure will be motivated to approach an achievement task, whereas individuals for whom the motive to avoid failure is stronger than the motive to achieve success will be motivated to avoid an achievement task. These relations predict that when the expectancies of success and failure are the same (both .5), the achievement task will be most attractive for approach motivated individuals and least attractive for avoidance motivated individuals. Evidence is reported that supports both of these predictions.

Discussion Questions

1. How do expectancies influence approach and avoidance motivations in the theory of achievement motivation?
2. According to the theory of achievement motivation, when is an achievement task most attractive to someone whose motive to succeed is stronger than the motive to avoid failure, and why does the theory predict this?

There are two problems of behavior any theory of motivation must come to grips with. They may finally reduce to one; but it will simplify the exposition which follows to maintain the distinction in this paper. The first problem is to account for an individual's selection of one path of action among a set of possible alternatives. The second problem is to account for the amplitude or vigor of the action tendency once it is initiated, and for its tendency to persist for a time in a given direction. This paper will deal with these questions in a conceptual framework suggested by research which has used thematic apperception to assess individual differences that is the relationship between achievement motivation (Atkinson, 1954; McClelland, 1955; McClelland, Atkinson, Clark, & Lowell, 1953).

The problem of selection arises in experiments which allow the individual to choose a task among alternatives that differ in difficulty (level of aspiration). The problem of accounting for the vigor of response arises in studies which seek to relate individual differences in strength of motivation to the level of performance when response output at a particular task is the dependent variable. In treating these two problems, the discussion will be constantly focused on the relationship of achievement motivation to risk-taking behavior, an important association uncovered by McClelland (1955) in the investigation of the role of achievement motivation in entrepreneurial and economic development (McClelland, 1956).

Earlier studies have searched for a theoretical principle which would explain the relationship of strength of motive, as inferred from thematic apperception, to overt goal-directed performance. The effect of situation cues (e.g., of particular instructions) on this relationship was detected quite early (Atkinson, 1954), and subsequent experiments have suggested a theoretical formulation similar to that presented by Tolman (1955) and Rotter (1954). If has been proposed that *n* Achievement scores obtained from thematic apperception are indices of individual differences in the strength of achievement motive, conceived as ai relatively stable disposition to strive for achievement or success. This motive-disposition is presumed to be latent until aroused by situation cues which indicate that some performance will be instrumental to achievement. The strength of *aroused* motivation to achieve as manifested in performance has been viewed as a function of both the strength of motive and the *expectancy* of goal-attainment aroused by situation cues. This conception has provided a fairly adequate explanation of experimental results to date, and its implications have been tested (Atkinson, 1954; Atkinson & Reitman, 1956).

The similarity of this conception to the expectancy principle of performance developed by Tolman, which also takes account of the effects of a third variable, *incentive*, suggested the need for experiments to isolate the effects on motivation of variations in strength of expectancy of success and variations in the incentive value of particular accomplishments. The discussion which follows was prompted by the results of several exploratory experiments. It represents an attempt to state explicitly how individual differences in the strength of achievement-related motives influence behavior in competitive achievement situations. A theoretical model will be presented first, then a brief summary of some as yet unpublished experimental evidence will be introduced in order to call the reader's attention to the kinds of research problems it raises and the scope of its implications.

Three variables require definition and, ultimately, independent measurement. The three variables are *motive, expectancy,* and *incentive*. Two of these—expectancy and incentive—are similar to variables presented by Tolman (1955) and Rotter (1954). An expectancy is a cognitive anticipation, usually aroused by cues in a situation, that performance of some act will be followed by a particular consequence. The strength of an expectancy can be represented as the subjective probability of the consequence, given the act.

The incentive variable has been relatively ignored, or at best crudely defined, in most research. It represents the relative attractiveness of a specific goal that is offered in a situation, or the relative unattractiveness of an event that might occur as a consequence of some act. Incentives may be manipulated experimentally as, for example, when amount of food (reward) or amount of shock (punishment) is varied in research with animals.

The third variable in this triumvirate—motive— is here conceived differently than, for example, in the common conception of motivation as nondirective but energizing *drive* (Brown, 1953). A motive is conceived as a disposition to strive for a certain kind of satisfaction, as a capacity for satisfaction in the attainment of a certain class of incentives. The names given motives—such as achievement, affiliation, power—are really names of classes of incentives which produce essentially the same kind of experience of satisfaction: pride in accomplishment, or the sense of belonging and being warmly received by others, the feeling of being influential. McClelland (1951, pp. 341–352 and 441–458; McClelland, Atkinson, Clark, & Lowell, 1953) has presented arguments to support the conception of motives as relatively general and stable characteristics of the personality which have their origins in early childhood experience. The idea that a motive may be considered a *capacity for satisfaction* is suggested by Winterbottom's (McClelland, Atkinson, Clark, & Lowell, 1953; Winterbottom, 1952) finding that children who are strong in achievement motive are rated by teachers as deriving more pleasure from success that children who are weak in achievement motive.

The general aim of one class of motives, usually referred to as appetites or approach tendencies, is to maximize satisfaction of some kind. The achievement motive is considered a disposition to approach success.

The aim of another class of motives is to minimize pain. These have been called aversions, or avoidant tendencies. As avoidance motive represents the individual's capacity to experience pain in connection with certain kinds of negative consequences of acts. The motive to avoid failure is considered a disposition to avoid failure and/or a capacity for experiencing shame and humiliation of failure.

The Principle of Motivation

The strength of motivation to perform some act is assumed to be a multiplicative function of the strength of the motive, the expectancy (subjective probability) that the act will have as a consequence the attainment of an incentive, and the value of the incentive: Motivation = f (Motive × Expectancy × Incentive). This formulation corresponds to Tolman's (1955) analysis of performance except, perhaps, in the conception of a motive as a relatively stable disposition. When both motivation to approach and motivation to avoid are simultaneously aroused, the resultant motivation is the algebraic summation of approach and avoidance. The act which is performed among a set of alternatives is the act for which the resultant motivation is most positive. The magnitude of response and the persistence of behavior are functions of the strength of motivation to perform the act relative to the strength of motivation to perform competing acts.

Recent experiments (Atkinson & Reitman, 1956) have helped to clarify one problem concerning the relationship between measures of the strength of a particular motive (*n* Achievement) and performance. Performance is positively related to the strength of a particular motive only when an expectancy of satisfying that motive through performance has been aroused, and when expectancies of satisfying other motives through the same action have not been sufficiently aroused to confound the simple relationship. This is to say no more than that, when expectancies of attaining several different kinds of incentives are equally *salient* in a situation, the determination of motivation to perform an act is very complex. Performance is then overdetermined in the sense that its strength is now a function of the several different kinds of motivation which have been aroused. The *ideal situation* for showing the relationship between the strength of a particular motive and behavior is one in which the only *reason* for acting is to satisfy that motive.

The theoretical formulation which follows pertains to such an *ideal achievement-related situation,* which is at best only approximated in actual experimentation or in the normal course of everyday life. The discussion will deal only with the effects of the two motives, to achieve and to avoid failure, normally aroused whenever performance is likely to be evaluated against some standard of excellence.

Behavior Directed toward Achievement and Away from Failure

The problem of selection is confronted in the level-of-aspiration situation where the individual must choose among tasks which differ in degree of difficulty. The problem of accounting for the vigor of performance arises in the situation which will be referred to as *constrained performance*. Here there is no opportunity for the individual to choose his own task. He is simply given a task to perform. He must, of course, decide to perform the task rather than to leave the situation. There *is* a problem of selection. In referring to this situation as constrained performance, it is the writer's intention to deal only with those instances of behavior in which motivation for the alternative of leaving the situation is less positive or more negative than for performance of the task that is presented. Hence, the individual does perform the task that is given. The level of performance is the question of interest.

Elaboration of the implications of the multiplicative combination of motive, expectancy, and incentive, as proposed to account for strength of motivation, will be instructive if we can find some reasonable basis for assigning numbers to the different variables. The strength of expectancy can be represented as a subjective probability ranging from 0 to 1.00. But the problem of defining the positive incentive value of a particular accomplishment and the negative incentive value of a particular failure is a real stickler.

In past discussions of level of aspiration, Escalona and Festinger (see Lewin, Dembo, Festinger, & Sears, 1944) have assumed that, within limits, the attractiveness of success is a positive function of the difficulty of the task, and that the unattractiveness of failure is a negative function of difficulty, when the type of activity is held constant. The author will go a few steps farther with these ideas, and assume that degree of difficulty can be inferred from the subjective probability of success (P_s). The task an individual finds difficult is one for which his subjective probability of success (P_s) is very low. The task an individual finds easy is one for which his subjective probability of success (P_s) is very high. Now we are in a position to make simple assumptions about the incentive values of success or failure at a particular task. Let us assume that the incentive value of success (I_s) is a positive linear function of difficulty. If so, the value $1-P_s$ can represent I_s, the incentive value of success. When P_s is high (e.g., .90), an easy task, I_s is low (e.g., .10). When P_s is low (e.g., .10), a difficult task, I_s is high (e.g., .90). The negative incentive value of failure (I_f) can be taken as $-P_s$. When P_s is high (e.g., .90), as in

confronting a very easy task, the sense of humiliation accompanying failure is also very great (e.g., $-.90$). However, when P_s is low (e.g., .10), as in confronting a very difficult task, there is little embarrassment in failing (e.g., $-.10$). We assume, in other words, that the (negative) incentive value of failure (I_f) is a negative linear function of difficulty. It is of some importance to recognize the dependence of incentive values intrinsic to achievement and failure upon the subjective probability of success. One cannot anticipate the thrill of a great accomplishment if, as a matter of fact, one faces what seems a very easy task. Nor does an individual experience only a minor sense of pride after some extraordinary feat against what seemed to him overwhelming odds. The implications of the scheme which follows rest heavily upon the assumption of such a dependence.

In Table 1, values of 1 have been arbitrarily assigned to the achievement motive (M_s) and the motive to avoid failure (M_f). Table 1 contains the strength of motivation to approach success ($M_s \times P_s \times I_s$) and motivation to avoid failure ($M_f \times P_f \times I_f$) through performance of nine different tasks labeled A through I. The tasks differ in degree of difficulty as inferred from the subjective probability of success (P_s). The incentive values of success and failure at each of the tasks have been calculated directly from the assumptions that incentive value of success equals $1 - P_s$ and that incentive value of failure equals $-P_s$; and P_s and P_f are assumed to add to 1.00.

Table 1 may be considered an extension of ideas presented in the *resultant valence* theory of level of aspiration by Escalona and Festinger (Lewin, Dembo, Festinger, & Sears, 1944). The present formulation goes beyond their earlier proposals (a) in making specific assumptions regarding the in-

Table 1. Aroused Motivation to Achieve (Approach) and to Avoid Failure (Avoidance) as a Joint Function of Motive (*M*), Expectancy (*P*), and Incentive (*I*), Where $I_s = (1 - P_s)$ and $I_f = (-P_s)$

	Motivation to Achieve $M_s \times P_s \times I_s$ = Approach			Motivation to Avoid Failure $M_f \times P_f \times I_f$ = Avoidance			Resultant Motivation (Approach–Avoidance)
Task A	1	.10	.90	.09	1	.90	−.10	−.09	0
Task B	1	.20	.80	.16	1	.80	−.20	−.16	0
Task C	1	.30	.70	.21	1	.70	−.30	−.21	0
Task D	1	.40	.60	.24	1	.60	−.40	−.24	0
Task E	1	.50	.50	.25	1	.50	−.50	−.25	0
Task F	1	.60	.40	.24	1	.40	−.60	−.24	0
Task G	1	.70	.30	.21	1	.30	−.70	−.21	0
Task H	1	.80	.20	.16	1	.20	−.80	−.16	0
Task I	1	.90	.10	.09	1	.10	−.90	−.09	0

centive values of success and failure, and (b) in stating explicitly how individual differences in strength of achievement motive and motive to avoid failure influence motivation.[1]

When the achievement motive is stronger ($M_s > M_f$)

The right-hand column of Table 1 shows the resultant motivation for each of the tasks in this special case where achievement motive and motive to avoid failure are equal in strength. In every case there is an approach-avoidance conflict with resultant motivation equal to 0. This means that if the achievement motive were stronger than the motive to avoid failure—for example, if we assigned M_s a value of 2—the resultant motivation would become positive for each of the tasks and its magnitude would be the same as in the column labeled *Approach*. Let us therefore consider only the strength of approach motivation for each of the tasks, to see the implications of the model for the person in whom the need for achievement is stronger than his disposition to avoid failure.

One thing is immediately apparent. Motivation to achieve is strongest when uncertainty regarding the outcome is greatest, i.e., when P_s equals .50. If the individual were confronted with all of these tasks and were free to set his own goal, he should choose Task E where P_s is .50, for this is the point of maximum approach motivation. The strength of motivation to approach decreases as P_s increases from .50 to near certainty of success (P_s = .90) and it also decreases as P_s decreases from .50 to near certainty of failure (P_s = .10).

If this person were to be confronted with a single task in what is here called the constrained performance situation, we should expect him to manifest strongest motivation in the performance of a task of intermediate difficulty where P_s equals .50. If presented either more difficult tasks or easier tasks, the strength of motivation manifested in performance should be lower. The relationship between strength of motivation as expressed in performance level and expectancy of success at the task, in other words, should be described by a bell-shaped curve.

When the motive to avoid failure is stronger ($M_f > M_s$)

Let us now ignore the strength of approach motivation and tentatively assign it a value of 0, in or-

der to examine the implications of the model for any case in which the motive to avoid failure is the stronger motive. The resultant motivation for each task would then correspond to the values listed in the column labeled *Avoidance*.

What should we expect of the person in whom the disposition to avoid failure is stronger than the motive to achieve? It is apparent at once that the resultant motivation for every task would be negative for him. This person should want to avoid all of the tasks. Competitive achievement situations are unattractive to him. If, however, he is constrained (e.g., by social pressures) and asked to set his level of aspiration, he should *avoid* tasks of intermediate difficulty (P_s = .50) where the arousal of anxiety about failure is greatest. He should choose either the easiest (P_s = .90) or the most difficult task (P_s = .10). The strength of avoidant motivation is weakest at these two points.

In summary, the person in whom the achievement motive is stronger should set his level of aspiration in the intermediate zone where there is moderate risk. To the extent that he has any motive to avoid failure, this means that he will voluntarily choose activities that *maximize* his own anxiety about failure! On the other hand, the person in whom the motive to avoid failure is stronger should select either the easiest of the alternatives or should be extremely speculative and set his goal where there is virtually no chance for success. These are activities which *minimize* his anxiety about failure.

How does the more fearful person behave when offered only a specific task to perform? He can either perform the task or leave the field. If he chooses to leave the field, there is no problem. But if he is constrained, as he must be to remain in any competitive achievement situation, he will stay at the task and presumably work at it. But how hard will he work at it? He is motivated to avoid failure, and when constrained, there is only one path open to him to avoid failure—success at the task he is presented. So we expect him to manifest the

---

[1]In the resultant theory of level of aspiration, the resultant force (f^*) for a particular level of difficulty equals probability of success (P_s) times valence of success (Va_s) minus probability of failure (P_f) times valence of failure (Va_f). It is assumed that the valence of a goal [$Va(G)$] depends partly on the properties of the activity and specific goal (G) and partly on the state of need [$t(G)$] of the person, [$Va(G) = F(G, t(G))$] (Lewin, 1951, p. 273). In the present conception, the relative rewarding or punishing properties of specific goals (i.e., incentives) and the more general disposition of the person toward a class of incentives (i.e., his motive) are given independent status.

strength of his motivation to avoid failure in performance of the task. He, too, in other words, should *try hardest*[2] when P_s is .50 and less hard when the chance of winning is either greater or less. The 50–50 alternative is the last he would choose if allowed to set his own goal, but once constrained he must try hard to avoid the failure which threatens him. Not working at all will guarantee failure of the task. Hence, the thought of not working at all should produce even stronger avoidant motivation than that aroused by the task itself.

In other words, irrespective of whether the stronger motive is to achieve or to avoid failure, the strength of motivation to perform a task when no alternatives are offered and when the individual is constrained should be greatest when P_s is .50. This is the condition of greatest uncertainty regarding the outcome. But when there are alternatives which differ in difficulty, the choice of level of aspiration by persons more disposed to avoid failure is diametrically opposite to that of persons more disposed to seek success. The person more motivated to achieve should prefer a moderate risk. His level of aspiration will fall at the point where his positive motivation is strongest, at the point where the odds seem to be 50–50. The fearful person, on the other hand, must select a task even though all the alternatives are threatening to him. He prefers the least threatening of the available alternatives: either the task which is so easy he cannot fail, or the task which is so difficult that failure would be no cause for self-blame and embarrassment.

The tendency for anxious persons to set either extremely high or very low aspirations has been noted over and over again in the literature on level of aspiration (Lewin, Dembo, Festinger, & Sears, 1946). Typically, *groups* of persons for whom the inference of greater anxiety about failure seems justified on the basis of some personality assessment show a much greater variance in level of aspiration than persons whose motivation is inferred to be more normal or less anxious. When the details of behavior are examined, it turns out that they are setting their aspiration level either *defensively* high or *defensively* low.

Without further assumptions, the theory of motivation which has been presented when applied

[2]I do not mean to exclude the possibility that the very anxious person may suffer a performance decrement due to the arousal of some "task-irrelevant" avoidant responses, as proposed in the interpretation of research which has employed the Mandler-Sarason Measure of Test Anxiety (Mandler & Sarason, 1952).

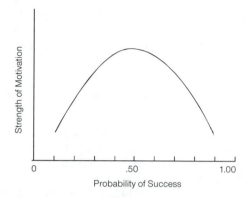

FIGURE 1 ■ Strength of motivation to achieve or to avoid failure as a function of the subjective probability of success, i.e., the difficulty of the task.

to competitive-achievement activity implies that the relationship of constrained performance to expectancy of goal-attainment should take the bell-shaped form shown in Figure 1, whether the predominant motive is to achieve or to avoid failure. Further, the theory leads to the prediction of exactly opposite patterns for setting the level of aspiration when the predominant motivation is approach and when it is avoidant, as shown in Figure 2.

Both of these hypotheses have been supported in recent experiments. The writer (Atkinson, in press) offered female college students a modest monetary prize for good performance at two 20-minute tasks. The probability of success was varied by instructions which informed the subject of the number of persons with whom she was in competition and the number of monetary prizes to be given. The stated probabilities were 1/20, 1/3, 1/2, and 3/4. The level of performance was higher at the intermediate probabilities than at the extremes for subjects having high thematic apperceptive *n* Achievement scores, and also for subjects who had low *n* Achievement scores, presumably a more fearful group.

McClelland (in press) has shown the diametrically opposite tendencies in choice of level of aspiration in studies of children in kindergarten and in the third grade. One of the original level-of-aspiration experiments, the ring-toss experiment, was repeated with five-year-olds, and a nonverbal index of the strength of achievement motive was employed. Children who were high in *n* Achievement more frequently set their level of aspiration in the intermediate range of difficulty. They took more shots from a modest distance. Children who were low in *n* Achievement showed a greater preponderance of choices at the extreme levels of difficulty. They more often stood right on top of the peg or stood so far away that success was virtually impossible. The same difference between high and low *n* Achievement groups was observed on another task with children in the third grade. McClelland views these results as consistent with his theoretical argument concerning the role of achievement-motivation in entrepreneurship and economic development (McClelland, 1955). He has called attention to the relationship between achievement motivation and an interest in enterprise which requires moderate or calculated risks, rather than very safe or highly speculative undertakings.

In an experiment designed for another purpose, Clark, Teevan, and Ricciuti (1956) have presented results with college students comparable to those of McClelland. Immediately before a final examination in a college course, students were asked a series of questions pertaining to grade expectations, affective reactions to grades, and the grades they would *settle for* if excused from taking the exam. A number of indices were derived from responses to these questions, by which the students were classified as: *hopeful of success*, i.e., if the *settle-for* grade was near the maximum grade the student thought he could possibly achieve; *fearful of failure*, i.e., if the *settle-for* grade was near the minimum grade the student thought he might possibly drop to; and *intermediate*, i.e., if the *settle-for* grade fell somewhere between these two extremes. Previously obtained *n* Achievement scores were significantly higher the *intermediate* group than for the two groups who set either extremely high or low levels of aspiration.

In terms of the model presented in Table 1, the two extreme patterns of aspirant behavior which are here designated *hope of success* and *fear of failure* are to be considered two *phenotypically* dissimilar alternatives that are *genotypically* similar. That is, they both function to avoid or reduce anxiety for the person in whom the motive to avoid failure is stronger than the motive to achieve.

A question may arise concerning the legitimacy of inferring relatively stronger motive to avoid failure from a low *n* Achievement score in thematic apperception. The inference seems justified on several counts. First, the kind of learning experience which is thought to contribute to the development of a positive motive to achieve (McClelland, Atkinson, Clark, & Lowell, 1953; Winterbottom, 1952) seems incompatible with the kind of experience which would contribute to the

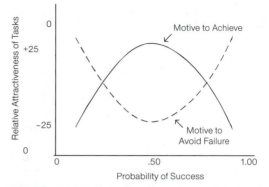

FIGURE 2 ■ Relative attractiveness of tasks which differ in subjective probability of success (i.e., in difficulty). The avoidance curve has been inverted to show that very difficult and very easy tasks arouse less fear of failure and hence are less unattractive than moderately difficult tasks.

development of an avoidant motive. In any specific early learning experience in which successful independent accomplishment is encouraged and rewarded, it seems impossible for incompetence, at the same time, to be punished. Second, even if it is assumed that high and low *n* Achievement groups may be equal in the disposition to be fearful of failure, the fact that one group does not show evidence of a strong motive to achieve (the group with low *n* Achievement scores) suggests that fear of failure should be *relatively* stronger in that group than in the group which does show evidence of strong *n* Achievement (high *n* Achievement scores). Finally, Raphelson (1956) has presented evidence that *n* Achievement, as measured in thematic apperception, is *negatively* related to both scores on the Mandler-Sarason Scale of Test Anxiety and a psychogalvanic index of manifest anxiety obtained in a test situation. Test anxiety scores and the psychogalvanic index of manifest anxiety were *positively* correlated, as they should be if each is an effective measure of fear aroused in a competitive situation.

Although a low *n* Achievement score can hardly be viewed as a direct index of the disposition to avoid failure, there seems good presumptive evidence that fear of failure is *relatively* stronger than the achievement motive in such a group. And this presumption is all the theory demands to explain the pattern of goal setting which focuses upon the extremes in the range of difficulty among persons low in *n* Achievement.

The details of the exploratory experiments suggest that one further assumption be made. In both experiments, the high *n* Achievement groups showed evidence of maximum motivation when the observed or stated probability of success was approximately .33. At this point, the high *n* Achievement group showed the highest level of constrained performance. And this point was most favored by the high *n* Achievement group in setting level of aspiration in the McClelland experiment. The assumption to be made seems a reasonable one: the relative strength of a motive influences the subjective probability of the consequence consistent with that motive—i.e., biases it upwards. In other words, the stronger the achievement motive relative to the motive to avoid failure, the higher the subjective probability of success, given stated odds. The stronger the motive to avoid failure relative to the achievement motive, the higher the subjective probability of failure, given stated odds or any other objective basis for inferring the strength of expectancy. Some evidence from two earlier studies is pertinent. When subjects stated the score that they *expected* to make on a test with very ambiguous or conflicting cues from past performance (McClelland, Atkinson, Clark, & Lowell, 1953, p. 247) or when faced with a novel task at which they had no experience (Pottharst, 1956), the stated level of *expectation* was positively related to *n* Achievement. The biasing effect of the motive on subjective probability should diminish with repeated learning experience in the specific situation.

When this assumption is made, the point of maximum motivation to achieve now occurs where the stated (objective) odds are somewhat *lower* than .50; and the point of maximum motivation to avoid failure occurs at a point somewhat higher than stated odds of .50, as shown in Figure 3. The implications of this assumption for constrained performance in somewhat novel situations are evident in the figure. When the achievement motive is stronger than the motive to avoid failure, there should be a tendency for stronger motivation to be expressed in performance when the objective odds are long, i.e., below .50. When the motive to avoid failure is stronger than the achievement motive, there should be greater motivation expressed when the objective odds are short, i.e., above .50.

The Effects of Success and Failure

Let us return to the model and ask, What are the effects of success and failure on the level of moti-

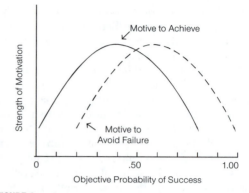

FIGURE 3 ■ Strength of motivation to achieve and to avoid failure as a function of the *objective* probability of success. It is assumed that the subjective probability of the consequence consistent with the stronger motive is biased upwards.

vation? We may refer back to Table 1 to answer this question. First, let us consider the effects of success or failure on the level of motivation in a person whose motive to achieve is stronger than his motive to avoid failure. In the usual level-of-aspiration situation, he should initially set his goal where P_s equals .50. In Table 1, this is Task E. If he succeeds at the task, P_s should increase. And, assuming that the effects of success and failure generalize to similar tasks, the P_s at Task D which was initially .40 should increase toward .50. On the next trial, P_s at Task E is now greater than .50, and P_s at Task D now approaches .50. The result of this change in P_s is diminished motivation to achieve at the old task, E, and increased motivation to achieve at Task D, *an objectively more difficult task*. The observed level of aspiration should increase in a step-like manner following success, because there has been a change in motivation.

A further implication of the change in strength of motivation produced by the experience of success is of great consequence: given a single, very difficult task (e.g., $P_s = .10$), the effect of continued success in repeated trials is first a gradual increase in motivation as P_s increases to .50, followed by a gradual decrease in motivation as P_s increases further to the point of certainty ($P_s = 1.00$). Ultimately, as P_s approaches 1.00, satiation or loss of interest should occur. The task no longer arouses any motivation at all. Why? Because the subjective probability of success is so high that the incentive value is virtually zero. Here is the clue to understanding how the achievement motive can remain insatiable while satiation can occur for a particular line of activity. The strength of motive can remain unchanged, but interest in a particular task can diminish completely. Hence, when free to choose, the person who is stronger in achievement motive should always look for new and more difficult tasks as he masters old problems. If constrained, the person with a strong achievement motive should experience a gradual loss of interest in his work. If the task is of intermediate difficulty to start with ($P_s =.50$), or is definitely easy ($P_s > .50$), his interest should begin to wane after the initial experience of success.

But what of the effect of failure on the person who is more highly motivated to achieve than to avoid failure? Once more we look at the *Approach* column of Table 1. If he has chosen Task E ($P_s = .50$) to start with and fails at it, the P_s is reduced. Continued failure will mean that soon Task F (formerly $P_s = .60$) will have a P_s near .50. He should shift his interest to this task, which was *objectively less difficult* in the initial ordering of tasks. This constitutes what has been called a lowering of the level of aspiration. He has moved to the easier task as a consequence of failure.

What is the effect of continued failure at a single task? If the initial task is one that appeared relatively easy to the subject (e.g., $P_s = .80$) and he fails, his motivation should increase! The P_s will drop toward .70, but the incentive value or attractiveness of the task will increase. Another failure should in crease his motivation even more. This will continue until the P_s has dropped to .50. Further failure should then lead to a gradual weakening of motivation as P_s decreases further. In other words, the tendency of persons who are relatively strong in achievement motive to persist at a task in the face of failure is probably attributable to the relatively high subjective probability of success, initially. Hence, failure has the effect of increasing the strength of their motivation, at least for a time. Ultimately, however, interest in the task will diminish if there is continued failure. If the initial task is perceived by the person as very difficult to start with ($P_s < .50$), motivation should begin to diminish with the first failure,

Let us now turn to the effect of success and failure on the motivation of the person who is more strongly disposed to be fearful of failure. If the person in whom the motive to avoid failure is stronger has chosen a very difficult task in setting his level of aspiration (e.g., Task A where $P_s = .10$) and succeeds, P_s increases and his motivation *to*

avoid the task is paradoxically increased! It would almost make sense for him deliberately to fail, in order to keep from being faced with a stronger threat on the second trial. Id there are more difficult alternatives, he should raise his level of aspiration to avoid anxiety! Fortunately for this person, his strategy (determined by the nature of his motivation) in choosing a very difficult task to start with protects him from this possibility, because P_s is so small that he will seldom face the paradoxical problem just described. If he fails at the most difficult task, as is likely, P_s decreases further, P_f increases further, and the aroused motivation to avoid failure is reduced. By continued failure he further reduced the amount of anxiety about failure that is aroused by this most difficult task. Hence, he should continue to set his level at this point. If he plays the game long enough and fails continuously, the probability of failure increases for all levels of difficulty. Sooner or later the minimal motivation to avoid failure at the most difficult task may be indistinguishable from the motivation to avoid failure at the next most difficult task. This may ultimately allow him to change his level of aspiration to a somewhat less difficult task without acting in gross contradiction to the proposed principle of motivation.

If our fearful subject has initially chosen the easiest task (Task I where $P_s = .90$) and if he fails, P_s decreases toward .80, and his motivation to avoid the task also increases. If there is no easier task, the most difficult task should now appear less *unattractive* to him, and he should jump from the easiest to the most difficult task. In other words, continued failure at a very easy task decreases P_s toward .50; and, as Table 1 shows, a change of this sort is accompanied by increased arousal of avoidant motivation. A wild and apparent irrational jump in level of aspiration from very easy to very difficult tasks, as a consequence of failure, might be mistakenly interpreted as a possible effort on the part of the subject to gain social approval by seeming to set high goals. The present model predicts this kind of activity without appealing to some extrinsic motive. It is part of the strategy of minimizing expected pain of failure after one has failed at the easiest task.

If our fear-disposed subject is successful at the most simple task, his P_s increases, his P_f decreases, and his motivation to avoid this task decreases. The task becomes less and less unpleasant. He should continue playing the game with less anxiety.

Table 1, when taken in its entirety, deals with the special case of the person on whom the two motives are exactly equal in strength. The implications are clear. In the constrained-performance situation, he should work hardest when the probability of success is .50, because motivation to achieve and motivation to avoid failure will summate in the constrained instrumental act which is at the same time the pathway toward success and away from failure. (This summation should also occur in the cases where one motive is stronger.) But in the level-of-aspiration setting where there is an opportunity for choice among alternatives, the avoidance motivation exactly cancels out the approach motivation. Hence, the resultant motivation for each of the alternatives is zero. His choice of level of aspiration cannot be predicted from variables intrinsic to the achievement-related nature of the task. If there is any orderly pattern in this conflicted person's level of aspiration, the explanation of it must be sought in extrinsic factors, e.g., *the desire to gain social approval.* Such a desire can also be conceptualized in terms of motive, expectancy, and incentive, and the total motivation for a particular task can then be attributed to both achievement-related motives and other kinds of motives engaged by the particular features of the situation.

In recent years there has been something of a rebirth of interest in the problems of level of aspiration, particularly in pathological groups. The tendency for anxious groups to show much greater variability in level of aspiration, setting their goals either very high or low relative to less anxious persons, was noted in early studies by Sears, Rotter, and others (Lewin, Dembo, Festinger, & Sears, 1944). Miller and Eysenck (1951), Himmelweit (1947), and Eysenck and Himmelweit (1946) have produced substantial evidence that persons with affective disorders (neurasthenia or dysthymia) typically set extremely high goals for themselves; hysterics, on the other hand, show a minimal level of aspiration, often setting their future goal even below the level of past performance. In all of these studies, normal control groups have fallen between these two extremes, as might be expected from the present model if *normals* are relatively more positive in their motivation in achievement-related situations.

In the work of Eysenck (1955) and his colleagues, both dysthymics and hysterics show greater *neuroticism* than normal subjects. Eysenck's interpretation of this factor as autonomic sensitivity is consistent with the implications of the present model, which attributes the setting of extremely high or low levels of aspiration to relatively strong motivation to avoid failure. A second factor, *extraversion-introversion*, discriminates the affective disorders and hysterics where the present model, dealing only with motives intrinsic to the competitive achievement situation, does not. An appeal to some other motivational difference, e.g., in strength of *n* Affiliation, might also predict the difference in pattern of level of aspiration.

Probability Preferences

The present analysis is relevant to another domain of current research interest, that specifically concerned with the measurement of subjective probability and utility. Edwards (1953, 1954) for example, has reported probability preferences among subjects offered alternative bets having the same expected value. We (Atkinson, Bastian, Earl, & Litwin, in preparation) have repeated the Edwards type experiment (e.g., 6/6 of winning 30¢ versus 1/6 of winning $1.80) with subjects having high and low *n* Achievement scores. The results show that persons high in *n* Achievement more often prefer intermediate probabilities (4/6, 3/6, 2/6) to extreme probabilities (6/6, 5/6, 1/6) than do persons low in *n* Achievement. What is more, the same differential preference for intermediate risk was shown by these *same* subjects when they were allowed to choose the distance from the target for their shots in a shuffleboard game. In other words, the incentive values of winning qua winning, and losing qua losing, presumably developed in achievement activities early in life, generalize to the gambling situation in which winning is really not contingent upon one's own skill and competence.

Social Mobility Aspirations

Finally, the present model may illuminate a number of interesting research possibilities having to do with social and occupational mobility. The ranking of occupations according to their prestige in Western societies clearly suggests that occupations accorded greater prestige are also more difficult to attain. A serious effort to measure the perceived probability of being able to attain certain levels on the occupational ladder should produce a high negative correlation with the usual ranking on prestige. If so, then the present model for level of aspiration, as well as its implications for persons who differ in achievement-related motives, can be applied to many of the sociological problems of mobility aspirations. A recent paper by Hyman (1953) has laid the groundwork for such an analysis.

Summary

A theoretical model is presented to explain how the motive to achieve and the motive to avoid failure influence behavior in any situation where performance is evaluated against some standard of excellence. A conception of motivation in which strength of motivation is a joint multiplicative function of motive expectancy (subjective probability), and incentive is offered to account for the selection of one task among alternatives which differ in difficulty (level of aspiration), and also to account for performance level when only one task is presented. It is assumed that the incentive value of success is a positive linear function of difficulty as inferred from the subjective probability of success; and negative incentive value of failure is assumed to be a negative linear function of difficulty. The major implications of the theory are (a) that performance level should be greatest when there is greatest uncertainty about the outcome, i.e., when subjective probability of success is .50, whether the motive to achieve or the motive to avoid failure is stronger within an individual; but (b) that persons in whom the achievement motive is stronger should prefer intermediate risk, while persons in whom the motive to avoid failure is stronger should avoid intermediate risk, preferring instead either very easy and safe undertakings *or* extremely difficult and speculative undertakings. Results of several experiments are cited, and the implications of the theoretical model for research on probability preferences in gambling and studies of social mobility aspirations are briefly discussed.

REFERENCES

Atkinson, J. W. (in press). Towards experimental analysis of human motivation in terms of motives, expectancies, and incentives. In *Motives in fantasy, action, and society*. Princeton, NJ: Van Nostrand Press.

Atkinson, J. W. (1954). Explorations using imaginative thought to assess the strength of human motives. In M. R. Jones (Ed.), *Nebraska symposium on motivation*. Lincoln, NE: University of Nebraska Press.

Atkinson, J. W., Bastian, J. R., Earl, R. W., & Litwin, G. H. (in preparation). The achievement motive, goal-setting, and the probability preferences.

Atkinson, J. W., & Reitman, W. R. (1956). Performance as a function of motive strength and expectancy of goal-attainment. *Journal of Abnormal Social Psychology, 53,* 361–366.

Brown, J. S. (1947). Problems presented by the concept of acquired drives. In *Current, theory and research in motivation*. Lincoln, NE: University of Nebraska Press.

Clark, R. A., Teevan, R., & Ricciuti, H. N. (1956). Hope of success and fear of failure as aspects of need for achievement. *Journal of Abnormal Social Psychology, 53,* 182–186.

Edwards, W. (1953). Probability preferences in gambling. *American Journal of Psychology, 66,* 349–364.

Edwards, W. (1954). The theory of decision making. *Psychological Bulletin, 51,* 380–417.

Eysenck, H. J. (1955). A dynamic theory of anxiety and hysteria. *J. ment. Sci., 101,* 28–51.

Eysenck, H. J., & Himmelweit, H. T. (1946). An experimental study of the reaction of neurotics to experiences of success and failure. *Journal of General Psychology, 35,* 59–75.

Himmelweit, H. T. (1953). A comparative study of the level of aspiration of normal and neurotic persons. *British Journal of Psychology, 37,* 41–59.

Hyman, H. H. (1953). The value systems of different classes: A social psychological contribution to the analysis of stratification. In R. Bendix & S. M. Lipset (Eds.), *Class, status, and power*. Glencoe, IL: Free Press.

Lewin, K. (1951). *Field theory in social science*. D. Cartwright (Ed.). New York: Harper Bros.

Lewin, K., Dembo, T., Festinger, L., & Sears, P. S. (1944). Level of aspiration. In J. McV. Hunt (Ed.), *Personality and the behavior disorders* (Vol. 1). New York: Ronald Press.

McClelland, D. C. (1951). *Personality*. New York: William Sloane Associates.

McClelland, D. C. (1955). Some social consequences of achievement motivation. In M. R. Jones (Ed.), *Nebraska symposium on motivation*. Lincoln, NE: University of Nebraska Press.

McClelland, D. C. (1956). *Interest in risky occupations among subjects with high achievement motivation*. Unpublished paper, Harvard University.

McClelland, D. C. (in press). Risk taking in children with high and low need for achievement. In *Motives in fantasy, action and society*. Princeton, NJ: Van Nostrand.

McClelland, D. C., Atkinson, J. W., Clark, R. A., & Lowell, E. L. (1953). *The achievement motive*. New York: Appleton-Century-Crofts.

Mandler, G., & Sarason, S. B. (1952). A study of anxiety and learning. *Journal of Abnormal Social Psychology, 16,* 115–118.

Miller, D. R. (1951). Responses of psychiatric patients to threat of failure. *Journal of Abnormal Social Psychology, 45,* 378–387.

Pottharst, B. C. (1956). *The achievement motive and level of aspiration after experimentally induced success and failure*. Unpublished dissertation, University of Michigan.

Raphelson, A. (1956). *Imaginative and direct verbal measures of anxiety related to physiological reactions in the competitive achievement situation*. Unpublished dissertation, University of Michigan.

Rotter, J. B. (1954). *Social leaning and clinical psychology*. New York: Prentice-Hall.

Tolman, E. C. (1955). Principles of performance. *Psychological Review, 62,* 315–326.

Winterbottom, M. R. (1952). *The relation of childhood training in independence to achievement motivation*. Unpublished doctor's dissertation, University of Michigan.

R E A D I N G   1 1

Self-Evaluative and Self-Efficacy Mechanisms Governing the Motivational Effects of Goal Systems

Albert Bandura and Daniel Cervone • Department of Psychology, Stanford University

Editors' Notes

The social learning analysis of motivation and performance postulates that internal comparison processes are critical to maintain motivation. Comparisons of performance to established standards provide information about one's capabilities to perform effectively (perceived self-efficacy) and feedback about how one is doing (self-evaluation of progress). Self-efficacy information is motivating through anticipated self-satisfactions from matching the standard in the future. Information about how one is doing is motivating from dissatisfactions with substandard performance in the past that provide incentives for increased effort in the future. A study was conducted that independently manipulated whether participants received an opportunity for goal-setting (establishing a standard to be met) and feedback about their performance on each trial. Compared to a control condition, only participants in the condition with both goal-setting and performance feedback showed increased effort on the task. The motivational increase was related to both perceived self-efficacy and self-evaluative satisfaction with progress.

Discussion Questions

1. What is self-efficacy and what is its relation to motivation?
2. What is the role of self-evaluative processes in motivation?

Authors' Abstract

The present research tested the hypothesis that self-evaluative and self-efficacy mechanisms mediate the effects of goal systems on performance motivation. These self-reactive influences are activated through cognitive comparison requiring both personal standards and knowledge of performance. Subjects performed a strenuous activity with either goals and performance feedback, goals alone, feedback alone, or without either factor. The condition combining performance information and a standard had a strong motivational impact, whereas neither goals alone nor feedback alone effected changes in motivation level. When both comparative factors were present, the evaluative and efficacy self-reactive influences predicted the magnitude of motivation enhancement. The higher the self-dissatisfaction with a substandard performance and the stronger the perceived self-efficacy for goal attainment, the greater was the subsequent intensification of effort. When one of the comparative factors was lacking, the self-reactive influences were differentially related to performance motivation, depending on the nature of the partial information and on the type of subjective comparative structure imposed on the activity.

The capability for intentional and purposive human action is rooted in cognitive activity. Social learning theory postulates two cognitively based mechanisms of motivation that serve such telic purposes. One mechanism operates anticipatorily through the exercise of forethought. By representing forseeable outcomes symbolically, future consequences can be converted into current motivators and regulators of behavior. The second major source of cognitive motivation derives from internal standards and self-evaluative reactions to one's performances (Bandura, 1977a).

The motivational effects of setting goals, which provides the standard against which performance is gauged, have been amply documented in different lines of research conducted under both controlled and naturalistic conditions. The evidence is relatively consistent in showing that explicit challenging goals enhance performance motivation (Locke, Shaw, Saari, & Latham, 1981). However, the psychological mechanisms through which personal standards create motivational effects and how these mechanisms govern motivation under different patterns of performance information have received less attention. It is to these issues that the present research addresses itself.

In the social learning analysis, self-motivation through performance standards operates largely through an internal comparison process (Bandura, 1978). When people commit themselves to explicit standards or goals, perceived negative discrepancies between what they do and what they seek to achieve creates self-dissatisfactions that serve as motivational inducements for enhanced effort. Both the anticipated self-satisfactions for matching accomplishments and the self-dissatisfactions with substandard performances provide incentives for heightened effort.

Performance motivation is not posited to be a monotonically increasing function of degree of perceived discrepancy. Performances that fall markedly short of standards are apt to give rise to discouragement and goal abandonment. Moderately discrepant performances, which leave construal of the standard as attainable (Atkinson, 1964; Locke, 1968), are likely to activate self-dissatisfactions that spur efforts to bring performance in line with valued standards. Attainments that match or surpass personal standards create self-satisfactions that serve as positive inducements for further pursuits.

Activation of self-evaluative processes through internal comparison requires both personal standards and knowledge of the level of one's performance. It follows from this formulation and Locke's goal theory (1968) that neither knowledge of performance without standards nor standards without knowledge of performance provides a basis for self-evaluative reactions and thus has little motivational impact. There is some empirical evidence to suggest that this is indeed the case (Becker, 1978; Strang, Lawrence, & Fowler, 1978). Simply adopting goals, whether easy or personally challenging ones, without knowing how one is doing seems to have no appreciable motivational effects.

Results of studies varying the properties of goals are also in accord with the postulated self-evaluative mechanisms (Bandura & Schunk, 1981;

Bandura & Simon, 1977; Locke, 1968; Steers & Porter, 1974). Explicitness, challengeability, and temporal proximity of subgoals and standards are conducive to enlisting self-reactive influence by specifying the amount and type of effort required to fulfill the goals. Such properties augment the motivational impact of goals. Empirical verification of the self-reactive causal link would provide a conceptual framework within which to analyze the features of goal systems that carry motivational potential.

The self-efficacy mechanism also plays a central role in human agency and self-motivation (Bandura, 1981, 1982). It is partly on the basis of self-percepts of efficacy that people choose what to do, how much effort to mobilize for given activities, and how long to persevere at them (Bandura, 1977b; Brown & Inouye, 1978; Schunk, 1981; Weinberg, Gould, & Jackson, 1979). Whether negative discrepancies between standards and performance are motivating or discouraging is likely to be influenced by people's perceptions of their efficacy to attain the standards they set for themselves. Those who have a low sense of self-efficacy may be easily discouraged by failure, whereas those who are assured of their capabilities for goal attainment intensify their efforts when their performances fall short and persist until they succeed.

The present research was primarily designed to test the notion that self-evaluative and self-efficacy mechanisms operate differentially in performance motivation, depending on the structure of comparative performance factors. The guiding conceptual scheme posits that both of these self-processes jointly regulate effort under conditions permitting cognitive comparison between a standard and knowledge of performance. To test this notion, conditions were created in which both comparative factors were present, one of the comparative factors was lacking, or both were absent. Subjects performed a strenuous physical activity on an ergometric device under conditions including either goals with performance feedback, goals alone, feedback alone, or without the presence of either factor. To equalize the constituent factors across subjects and treatment conditions, the goals involved a 40% increase in effortful performance and feedback of a 24% gain in performance. These values were selected to create a moderate negative discrepancy sufficient to activate self-dissatisfied reactions without unduly undermining self-percepts of efficacy for goal attainment. The

research of Atkinson (1964) and Locke (1968) indicates that a moderate discrepancy is well suited for this purpose. After the performance session in which the requisite goal and feedback conditions were created, subjects recorded their level of self-satisfaction with their performance and their perceived self-efficacy for goal attainment, whereupon their effortful performance was again measured.

By systematically varying the comparative factors and measuring the posited self-processes antecedently, the integrated design permits a dual level of verification of requisite conditions for motivational enhancement tied to mediating self-processes. It was predicted that subjects in the condition combining goals with performance feedback would display the highest gains in effortful performance. On the premise that self-evaluative and self-efficacy mechanisms are most consistently activated in the service of motivation only when goals and feedback information are both present, it was hypothesized that subjects receiving either goals or feedback alone would lack an essential comparative element and, hence, would not differ from those receiving neither of these factors.

As the primary test of the theory under examination, it was predicted that in the condition combining goals with feedback, the magnitude of performance gains would vary as a function of level of self-dissatisfaction and perceived self-efficacy for goal attainment. The higher the subjects' self-dissatisfaction, the more they would increase their performance to bring it in line with their standard. The higher their self-percepts of efficacy, the greater effort they would mount to attain their goal. Subjects who were self-dissatisfied with their substandard performance but judged themselves highly efficacious in attaining their goal would show the highest performance gains. In contrast, those who judged themselves inefficacious and were not unduly self-dissatisfied would mobilize the weakest effort. In conditions in which one or both comparative factors are lacking, the mediating mechanisms are likely to operate variably depending on what partial information is available and on subjective provision of the missing comparative factor.

Method

SUBJECTS

The subjects were 45 men and 45 women drawn from an introductory psychology course. Twenty subjects, equally divided by sex, were randomly assigned to each of four treatment conditions. Ten subjects were similarly assigned to a self-judgment control condition designed to determine whether recording one's self-satisfaction and self-percepts of efficacy, in itself, had any reactive effects on performance.

GENERAL PROCEDURE AND APPARATUS

The introductory instructions describing the nature of the study were identical for all subjects. The experiment was presented as part of a program of research ostensibly designed to identify performance tasks that might eventually prove useful for planning and evaluating postcoronary rehabilitation programs It was further explained that the information being gathered would not only aid development of diagnostic devices but also provide normative data on physical stamina at different age levels. The relation between cardiovascular fitness and performance on aerobic tasks was then described to lend further credibility to the activity.

The performance task apparatus was a Schwinn Air-Dyne ergometer in the form of an exercise device that uses a wind vane system to provide variable air resistance. In its modified form, the ergometer was operated by alternatively pulling and pushing two arm levers The exerted force rotated a wheel with fanlike wind vanes, creating resistance for the physical effort.

The ergometer task was chosen for a number of reasons. This effortful activity combined with the rationale was received with uniformly high credibility. It yielded a precise measure of performance effort with virtually no upper limit. Because it required considerable effort over extended periods, the task provided a stringent test of how the postulated determinants and mechanisms affect the mobilization and maintenance of performance motivation. Finally, the task itself provided little implicit feedback regarding performance level, which allowed for credible prearranged feedback. Because subjects could not easily discern quantitative variations in their physical output across sessions, goals and feedback information could be systematically varied without jeopardizing the perceived veridicality of the feedback.

The ergometer was connected by a cable to a work load indicator with an odometer in the adjoining room. The odometer readings were recorded at 1-minute intervals during the 5-minute sessions so as to capture any variations in performance during the session. To measure precisely the performance effort expended, the odometer readings were converted to kilopond meter units. Kilopond units are indices of work output that consider both the speed at which the ergometer is operated and the exponential increase in air resistance with increasing speed. The five sets of kilopond scores resulting from the five 1-minute intervals were summed to obtain a total performance score for each session.

Before starting the experiment, subjects completed a background questionnaire that asked about their age, sex, height, weight, and smoking habits. It was included both to add further credence to the prior instructions and to increase the naturalness of the assessment, in a later session, of self-reactions imbedded among filler items ostensibly tapping other aspects of physical status. They also filled out a physical-readiness questionnaire designed to exclude any subject for whom extended physical exertion would be medically contraindicated. Only one subject, who reported a history of cardiovascular problems, was excluded on this basis.

Subjects removed their watches to control for possible variations in the regulation of effort by checking the time elapsed. They were informed that each performance session would last 5 minutes but were not told how many sessions they would complete. The latter procedure was instituted to eliminate the possibility that subjects might intensify their performance in the third session if they knew it was their final effort.

The experimenter concluded the general instructions by explaining that he would be in the adjoining room tending to the recording instruments during each performance session. The subject would be signaled when to begin and end each session via an intercom system.

BASELINE PERFORMANCE SESSION

All subjects performed the ergometer task alone for a 5-minute baseline period. Pretesting indicated that a 5-minute session required substantial performance effort without being overly fatiguing.

Following the baseline assessment, subjects were randomly assigned within sex groupings to treatment conditions. The random order of assignment was devised for the entire sample at the outset of the study. After each subject completed the baseline session, the experimenter removed a cover card that revealed the condition to which the particular subject was assigned. Thus, the experimenter had no prior knowledge of the subjects' condition assignments during the baseline session.

GOAL SETTING AND FEEDBACK VARIATIONS

In conditions including goal setting subjects selected a goal for performance improvement in subsequent sessions. The experimenter explained that in coronary rehabilitation programs patients have goals for increasing their physical activity. These goals vary across cases. Therefore they would perform the ergometer task with goals to shed light on the effects of this goal variability.

Goals were not simply assigned to subjects. Rather, they ostensibly selected their own goal level. An apparent-choice procedure was used to increase subjects' sense of self-determination and commitment to the goal (Kiesler, 1971; Langer, 1975). They were told that to study goal levels representative of the range found in a rehabilitation program, they would choose one goal from among a wide range of goal levels. It was explained that in rehabilitation programs, goals are set based on the patient's current physical status. However, because this psychological information was not available for participants in the present study, there was no basis for assigning particular goals to particular subjects. Hence, subjects would simply select one from among a variety of goals.

Different goal levels representing percentage decrements and percentage improvements above baseline performance were printed on cards. After the full range of goal levels was inspected, the experimenter placed all the goal cards in a cloth bag attached to a wooden rim and handle, shook the bag and presented it to the subject, who selected a goal. Unbeknownst to the subject, the choice was prearranged to be a 40% increase in performance above baseline performance. This was achieved by flicking a hidden switch on the bottom of the handle, automatically switching compartments of the bag so that subjects were selecting their goals from a preloaded set of goal cards, all of which represented a 40% performance increase.

A 40% goal level was chosen for several reasons. It represented an attainable goal, a negative performance discrepancy from it would appear credible, and neither the goal nor the performance discrepancy was so high as to undermine perceived self-efficacy in attaining it.

Subjects in conditions that did not include goals received the identical information as did their goal-setting counterparts concerning how coronary rehabilitation patients strive for different goals of increased physical activity as part of their recovery program. They were all given the same information about goals and striving for performance improvement to equate the groups for the suggestion of increased effort. The experiment thus provided a clear test of the motivational contribution of actual goal adoption.

To control for any possible experimenter bias, all the information for creating the requisite conditions for the main phase of the experiment was presented remotely via a video system. The experimenter explained that he had to reset the recording instruments after the second session. Thus, the video system would be used to convey further information. Subjects then performed the ergometer task for 5 minutes alone in the room, whereupon they were instructed through the intercom to turn on the video terminal.

The performance feedback and goal-setting information was printed on subsets of cards that could be combined to include goals and feedback, goals alone, feedback alone, or neither. A camera in the adjoining room transmitted the relevant information to the video screen. In the feedback-alone conditions the sign read "Your performance score for the last session was _____ % _____ your first session." The experimenter wrote "24" and "above," respectively, in the blanks. This feedback information, independent of the subject's actual performance, was written in the blanks to avoid the impression that the feedback may have been prearranged. For subjects in goals-alone conditions, the sign read, "The goal you were aiming for is _____." The experimenter filled in "+40%." The above two subsigns were combined for subjects in the goals and feedback condition, informing them that they had attained a 24% increase in performance and were aiming for a 40% increase.

For subjects in all conditions the next sign that appeared on the screen instructed them to complete a questionnaire that was next to the video terminal.

MEASUREMENT OF SELF-EVALUATION AND PERCEIVED SELF-EFFICACY

The questionnaire contained the two measures of central interest: subjects' level of self-satisfaction with their performance and their perceived self-efficacy at reaching various performance attainments. These scales were embedded in a set of filler items (cast in the same format) measuring exercise routines and general physical status.

In measuring self-evaluative reactions subjects rated their self-reactions on a 25-point scale, ranging from "highly self-satisfied," through "neutral," to "highly self-dissatisfied." They first rated their level of self-satisfaction or dissatisfaction with their performance in the second session, which they had just completed. Subjects could be pleased with their prior progress but self-dissatisfied were they to achieve the same level of performance on their subsequent attempts. Hence, for the second rating, subjects rated how self-satisfied or self-dissatisfied they would be if they attained the same level of performance in the next session.

Subjects recorded their perceived self-efficacy for goal attainments on an efficacy scale that described 14 possible levels of performance attainments relative to the baseline level. The goal attainments varied in 10% intervals from a 50% decrement to an 80% increase above the baseline level. For each of the 14 performance levels, subjects rated the strength of their perceived efficacy that they could attain them on a 100-point scale, ranging in 10-unit intervals from "high uncertainty" to "intermediate values of certainty" to "complete certitude." The strength of subjects' perceived efficacy that they could achieve a 40% performance increase was the pertinent efficacy measure.

PERFORMANCE TEST

After the assessment of self-processes, subjects were instructed via the intercom to resume the ergometer task. They engaged in the effortful activity for 5 minutes, during which their performance was recorded.

At the conclusion of the formal experiment, subjects completed a questionnaire in which those in the goal conditions rated their perceptions of the attainability of a 40% increase in performance. Subjects in conditions without goals were asked if they had spontaneously set any performance goals for themselves and, if they had, to describe their goals. The groups did not differ on the earlier filler items on which they rated their physical stamina and the type and amount of physical activity they regularly perform each week.

Results

EFFECTS OF SELF-JUDGMENTS

To test for possible reactive effects of recording one's self-evaluative reactions and self-percepts of efficacy, the sample of 10 subjects randomly selected for this purpose performed with goals and feedback but did not record their self-evaluative reactions and self-percepts of efficacy. The questionnaire they completed contained only the filler items. Their performance was compared against that of subjects who also performed with goals and feedback after recording their self-satisfaction and perceived self-efficacy. The analysis revealed no significant difference between the groups in performance change, $t(28) = .70$. Nor did these two groups differ in how they responded to the postexperiment questionnaire. Recording self-judgments thus had no reactive effects.

INITIAL EFFECTS OF GOAL SETTING

As a first step toward creating the requisite treatment conditions, after the baseline performance half of the subjects received a goal of improving their performance by 40%. Subjects increased their performance level 42% without goals and 85% with goals. These performance changes were analyzed by a two-way analysis of variance with goals and sex as factors. To equalize variances, a square root transformation was performed on the scores. The analysis revealed a significant main effect for goals, $F(1, 76) = 16.26, p < .001$. As will be shown below, this initial gain carried over, but goals alone produced no further increment in performance motivation. Neither sex nor the interaction between sex and goals had any significant effect on change in performance.

At the end of the second performance session, the appropriate groups received performance feedback, all groups recorded their self-satisfaction and self-efficacy, and all groups then performed the effortful task again. In the second session the conditions comprising goals and feedback and feedback alone exist in name only. It is the performance of subjects in the final session, when all four treatment conditions were fully formed and operating, that bears on the major hypotheses, to which we turn next.

EFFECTS OF GOAL SETTING AND FEEDBACK ON EFFORTFUL PERFORMANCE

To test how the structure of comparative factors effects changes in level of motivation, the percentage increase in effortful performance above that of the second session was computed. In Figure 1 the mean percentage increases are plotted as a function of treatment conditions. Subjects who had the benefit of both goals and feedback more than doubled their performance over and above those subjects receiving either the goal alone, feedback alone, or neither factor.

Baseline performance levels could have influenced later performance change. An analysis of covariance was therefore computed, with treatment conditions and sex as factors and the first session performance as the covariate. A linear contrast showed that subjects in the condition combining goals with feedback outperformed those in the other conditions, $F(1, 71) = 18,42, p < .001$, which did not differ from each other. The same pattern of results is obtained if analysis of covariance is performed on performance scores in the third session, with performance in the second session serving as the covariate. Goals with feedback surpassed the other conditions, $F(1,71) = 5.59; p < .025$, which did not differ from each other. The analysis failed to yield any significant effects on performance change for sex either independently or in interaction with treatment conditions.

Mechanisms Governing Motivation Effects

Mean levels of perceived self-efficacy and self-evaluation in the various treatment conditions are presented in Table 1. The self-processes did not differ in mean level, but the condition combining a goal with feedback of a substandard gain substantially increased the variance of how self-satisfied subjects would be with a similar future performance as compared both to feedback alone, $F(19, 19) = 2.64, p < .05$, and to the control condition, $F(19, 19) = 2.15, p < .06$. However, as hypothesized, these self-processes relate to performance motivation in strikingly different ways when the requisite comparative factors are fully present than when they are present only partially or not at all.

Product-moment correlations were computed between the indices of the self-processes and percentage performance change. Degree of self-dissatisfaction with the preceding performance and self-dissatisfaction if the same level of performance was attained in the next session were each correlated with percentage of subsequent performance change. It is the predictiveness of the sec-

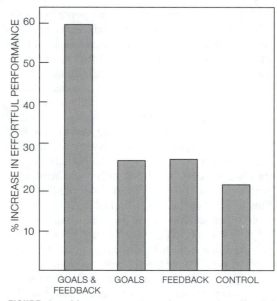

FIGURE 1 ■ Mean percentage increase in effortful performance under conditions varying in goals and performance feedback.

ond self-evaluative measure that is of greatest interest because it more closely reflects the future performance attainments subjects judge they must fulfill to feel self-satisfied. The role of perceived self-efficacy as a performance motivator was evaluated by correlating strength of perceived self-efficacy for a 40% goal attainment with percent of performance change. Correlational analyses were conducted separately for each of the four treatment conditions based upon 18 degrees of freedom for each group. The complete set of correlations is presented in Table 2.

Complete Comparative Factors (Goal Plus Feedback)

Social learning theory posits the dependable activation of self-evaluative mechanisms requires both goals and performance feedback. Correlational analyses conducted on data from the condition combining goals with feedback information indeed confirmed that self-dissatisfaction is predictive of performance change (Table 2). The more self-dissatisfied subjects were with the substandard performance they had just completed, the more they heightened their next performance ($r = .37, p = .05$). Level of self-dissatisfaction with the same

Table 1. Mean Levels of Perceived Self-Efficacy and Self-Evaluation in the Treatment Conditions

Self-process	Goal + feedback		Goal		Feedback		Control	
	M	SD	M	SD	M	SD	M	SD
Perceived self-efficacy	85.0	25.4	81.5	24.1	77.5	20.7	67.8	26.6
Self-dissatisfaction								
Prior performance	10.4	3.8	9.8	4.0	11.0	3.0	8.3	3.8
Future performance	10.1	5.9	9.8	4.5	9.6	3.6	8.6	4.0

substandard performance were it to occur on the next session was even more predictive of subsequent performance gains ($r = .51, p = .01$).

Perceived self-efficacy is also predictive of the performance changes exhibited by subjects who had the benefit of goals and feedback. The more self-efficacious they were that they could attain the 40% goal, the more highly they boosted their next performance ($r = .45, p < .025$). Correlations were also computed between performance effort and perceived self-efficacy to accomplish each of the 14 performance levels included in the efficacy scale. Subjects' perceived efficaciousness to attain the 40% goal exceeded the correlations at each of the 13 remaining levels, a pattern that is highly significant ($p < .001$), as estimated by binomial test). Self-satisfaction and percepts of self-efficacy were not significantly related in any of the conditions.

It is postulated that self-dissatisfaction and perceived self-efficacy jointly determine performance changes. To test this, indices of self-dissatisfaction with future substandard performance and perceived self-efficacy for goal attainment were converted to standardized T scores, combined, and correlated with performance change. This composite index of the mediating self-processes was highly predictive of subsequent performance change ($r = .63, p < .002$).

The joint operation of these two motivational self-processes in the condition combining an explicit goal with feedback is most graphically revealed by categorizing subjects in terms of whether they expressed self-dissatisfaction with future substandard performance and whether their perceived self-efficacy for goal attainment exceeded the 50% strength value. The mean percentage changes in performance as a function of varying combinations of these self-processes are presented in Figure 2. As may be seen in the left-hand panel, subjects who were both self-dissatisfied but highly self-efficacious displayed huge performance gains. The self-inefficacious but self-satisfied subjects manifested little performance change. If at least one of the two self-processes was strongly operative, subjects achieved moderate performance gains. Because the efficacious–dissatisfied and the inefficacious–satisfied subjects performed comparably, these two groups were combined to increase the subgroup size for statistical analysis. Even though the subgroups—formed by dichotomizing scores on the two self-processes—were small within this total sample of 20 subjects, the variations in effortful performance were significant, $F(2, 17) = 4.10, p < .04$.

These two self-processes even predict changes

Table 2. Relation of Self-Evaluation and Perceived Self-Efficacy to Effortful Performance Under Conditions in Which the Requisite Comparative Factors of a Goal System Are Present or Absent

Self-process	% change in effortful performance (Session 3 relative to Session 2)				% change in effortful performance (fifth minute relative to first minute of Session 3)			
	G + F	G	F	C	G + F	G	F	C
Perceived self-efficacy	.45**	.57***	−.32	−.09	.43**	.14	−.24	−.19
Self-dissatisfaction								
Prior performance	.37*	−.44*	−.18	.27	.36	.03	.08	.22
Future performance	.51**	−.24	−.59***	.24	.68****	−.20	−.03	.24

Note. G = goal; F = feedback; C = control.
* $p = .05$. ** $p < .03$. *** $p < .01$. **** $p < .001$.

in performance motivation over the course of the session. For this temporal analysis the difference in physical effort exerted between the first minute and the last minute of the final session was computed and correlated with the indexes of the self-processes (Table 2). Self-dissatisfaction with future substandard performance ($r = .68$, $p < .001$) and self-efficacy for goal attainment ($r = .43$, $p <.03$), both singly and in combination ($r = .72$, $p < .001$), predicted the degree of performance change over time.

As shown in the right-hand panel of Figure 2, the self-satisfied but self-efficacious subjects greatly accelerated their performance effort, those who were either self-dissatisfied or self-efficacious sustained their performance effort, and those who judged themselves inefficacious to fulfill the goal and were satisfied with a 24% future increase slackened their efforts and showed a substantial decline in performance by the end of the session. Because the means for the high-efficacy–low-dissatisfaction and the low-efficacy–high-dissatisfaction subgroups were virtually identical and the ns were small, these two subgroups were combined for the ANOVA. These differential patterns of motivational change are highly significant, $F(2, 17) = 14.73$, $p <.001$.

Of the subjects in the inefficacy-satisfied subgroup, 83% perceived the selected goal as virtually unattainable, whereas only 7% of the remaining subjects considered the goal beyond their reach. These differential perceptions of goal attainability, which can markedly affect goal adherence, are highly significant ($z = 3.45$, $p <.001$).

PARTIAL COMPARATIVE FACTORS

Subjects who performed with either goals alone or feedback alone lacked one of the critical elements to regulate their effort effectively through self-reactive influence unless they supplied the missing element subjectively. Correlational analyses indeed reveal that the constituent self-reactive influences operate differentially in performance motivation depending on which comparative factor is lacking.

Feedback-alone condition. Subjects in the feedback-alone condition were informed that they had improved by 24% but had no explicit goal to judge whether the gain was exemplary or insufficient. The extent to which they were self-satisfied with this performance gain was unrelated to subsequent

performance change, but the more satisfied they were with maintaining a similar future gain, the greater was their performance ($r = -.59$, $p < .01$, two-tailed). Enhanced effort is thus related to satisfaction under feedback of progress alone but to discontent when that same level of progress is viewed in relation to a seemingly difficult standard of a 40% gain.

When people engage in an ongoing activity and are periodically informed of their performance attainments, some spontaneously set goals for themselves (Bandura & Simon, 1977). In the feedback-alone condition 70% of the subjects indeed reported in the postexperiment questionnaire that they set performance standards for themselves on their own. Those who set no goals for themselves achieved no change (.4%), those who aimed to sustain their improvement realized a modest gain (27%), and those who set themselves the more demanding goal of bettering their improvement raised their level of performance substantially (40%). This pattern of differences is significant even with the limited sample size, $F(2, 16) = 3.51$, $p = .05$. In contrast, self-set goals had no effect on performance effort in the condition in which subjects received no performance feedback.

Whether knowledge of a 24% increase in performance is indicative of self-efficacy or self-inefficacy depends on what goals, if any, subjects set for themselves as suitable markers of capability. Because subjective goal setting varied widely, perceived self-efficacy for a 40% goal attainment bore no significant relation to performance change in the feedback-alone condition.

Goal-alone condition. In the goal-alone condition, subjects aimed for a 40% increase in performance but had no objective knowledge of how they were doing. The stronger the subjects' self-efficaciousness that they could attain such a goal, the greater was their performance change ($r = .57$, $p < .005$). The correlation of perceived self-efficacy to attain the 40% goal with performance effort was higher than the correlations at all but one (60% goal) of the 13 levels of goal attainment. This pattern is highly significant ($p < .002$, as estimated by the binomial test). In this condition, in which subjects had only their subjective performance impressions to go on, it was self-satisfaction with their imagined attainment that was related to subsequent performance change ($r = -.44$, $p < .05$, two-tailed), but degree of self-evaluation for a similar future performance was not.

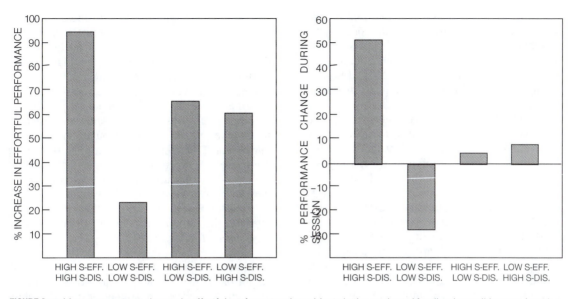

FIGURE 2 ■ Mean percentage change in effortful performance by subjects in the goals and feedback condition as a function of differential combinations of levels of self-dissatisfaction (S-DIS) and perceived self-efficacy (S-EFF) for goal attainment. (The left-hand panel shows the mean change for the entire session; the right-hand panel shows the mean change between the first and final minute of the session. The number of subjects in each of the four combinations of self-processes was as follows: High S-EFF–High S-DIS, 4; Low S-EFF–Low S-DIS, 6; High S-EFF–Low S-DIS, 6; Low S-EFF–High S-DIS, 4.)

NO COMPARATIVE FACTORS (NO GOAL, NO FEEDBACK)

In the condition in which subjects lacked both goals and knowledge of how they performed, they had little basis for either appraising or regulating their on-going performance effort. Self-processes were unrelated to performance change (see Figure 2).

Discussion

The findings of the present study support the theory that goal systems gain motivating power through self-evaluative and self-efficacy mechanisms activated by cognitive comparison. Goals enhanced performance effort only under conditions combining a personal standard with performance feedback of progress toward it. Neither goals alone nor performance feedback alone, both of which lack an essential comparative ingredient, effected change in motivational level. When first adopted, goals alone produced a performance gain that carried over, but they did not generate any further increments in motivation in the absence of performance knowledge. Although goals alone did not further augment performance motivation, persis-

tence of the initial boost enabled the subjects who performed with goals alone to surpass the controls. The pattern of results at the point at which all conditions were fully operative is consistent with Locke's goal theory (Locke et al., 1981).

Analysis of performance effort as a function of self-set standards under conditions of feedback alone is also in accord with the view that both performance knowledge and a standard of comparison are needed to produce motivational effects. For the most part, the self-prescribed goals were of a general sort and not unduly challenging. Nevertheless, participants who set no goals were outperformed by those who set themselves the goal of sustaining their performance gain, who, in turn, were outperformed by those who sought to better their past attainment. These goals were of a more qualitative sort of sustaining or surpassing one's prior accomplishments (e.g., "I want to do as well as the time before . . . do better than the previous session.") rather than stated in terms of explicit quantitative levels of performance change. Although such goals had motivating potential in the context of performance knowledge, the rise in performance effort for feedback with qualitative self-set standards was less than that for the same feedback with a challenging (40%) quantified standard. These findings are congruent with those of previous studies showing that explicit goals are more motivating than are general ones (Latham & Yukl, 1975; Locke, 1968). Self-set goals had no motivating potential without performance information in the control condition.

Results of the correlational analyses support the proposition that goal systems affect performance motivation in part through self-evaluative and self-efficacy mechanisms. Moreover, the findings shed interesting light on how these self-mechanisms operate in performance motivation when only partial comparative information is available. When performance information is combined with a standard of comparison, the higher the self-dissatisfaction with a substandard performance and the stronger the perceived self-efficacy for goal attainment, the greater is the subsequent intensification of effort. In a recently completed study employing a path analysis, Locke and his colleagues (Locke, Frederick, Lee, & Bobko, 1982) found that perceived self-efficacy affects the level of self-set goals, strength of goal commitment, and level of cognitive performance.

When one of the requisite comparative factors is lacking, the relation of self-reactive influences to performance motivation depends on the nature of the partial information provided or that performers fashion for themselves. Thus, in the condition providing only feedback, knowledge of a 24% gain in performance carried no absolute value. It represented a commendable accomplishment if judged against subjective modest aspirations but a failure if evaluated against subjectively invoked high standards. Subjects' reports of their self-set goals reveal that many of them either set no goals for themselves (45%) or aimed for the same level of performance gain (25%). For subjects in this condition, a 24% gain constituted positive or success feedback. The more pleased subjects were with sustaining this level of improvement, the more effortfully they behaved. In contrast, a 24% gain when one is aiming for a 40% increment constitutes negative or failure feedback. Discontent with the prospect of similar failure in the future spurred subjects to greater effort. Inverted meaning of the performance feedback thus produces inverse relations between self-evaluation and performance motivation.

The findings that self-evaluative reactions operated differently on motivation under varying comparative structures testify to the complexity of the relation between self-satisfaction and motivation. With goals and performance feedback, self-dissatisfaction affects effort (see also Locke, Cartledge, & Knerr, 1970), whereas with either goals alone or feedback alone, effort seems to be governed by level of self-satisfaction.

Variable self-prescribed standards similarly confer diverse self-efficacy value on the same performance gain. Subjects oriented toward sustaining their level of effortful performance are likely to raise their self-percepts of efficacy on learning that they surpassed their past achievements by 24%, whereas those who ask much of themselves might interpret the same performance gain as a sign of physical inefficacy. Perceived self-efficacy in attaining a 40% goal therefore bore no consistent relation to subsequent effort in the feedback-only condition. However, in the goal-alone condition, in which all performers aimed for the same challenging standard but had to guess how they were doing, the stronger their perceived self-efficaciousness for goal attainment and the more pleased they were with whatever they surmised their prior performance to be, the more they heightened their effort.

Self-reactive influences are least likely to be activated in any consistent way in different individuals by conditions providing neither evaluative standards, performance information, nor even distinct implicit feedback concerning the level of performance. Not surprisingly, the latter condition, which was devoid of information for monitoring, gauging, and regulating one's effort, yielded no significant correlates.

In the present study, predicted relations were tested under conditions in which performance was moderately discrepant from personal standards. The informative next stage for research is to clarify further the precise nature of the relation between self-percepts of efficacy, self-evaluation, and performance motivation when attainments diverge from personal standards across a wide range of positive and negative magnitudes. Recall that social learning theory postulates a linear positive function between perceived self-efficacy for goal attainment and effort but a nonlinear one between degree of goal discrepancy and effort, as mediated through self-evaluative reactions.

Theorists working within the framework of achievement motivation have addressed the issue of task difficulty mainly in terms of success expectancy and valuation of goal attainment (Atkinson & Raynor, 1974; Feather, 1982). Because these two factors are considered to be inversely related, performance is highest for tasks of moderate difficulty, although Heckhausen (1977) posits a somewhat lower success probability than does Atkinson as being maximally motivating. In the goal theory developed by Locke (1968), performance is linearly related to goal difficulty as long as performers continue to adhere to taxing goals. By expanding the self-process probes to include revision of goals, as well as perceived self-efficacy and self-satisfaction with prior and future attainments, the paradigm developed for the present experiment might help shed some additional empirical light on subprocesses mediating effort when attainments diverge from standards in degree and direction.

Performances that fall markedly short of standards are likely to be demotivating by undermining perceived self-efficacy. To the extent that performers judge the standard as exceeding their capabilities, they are apt to lower their standard and demand less of themselves. Such adjustments would lower effort and performance (Feather, 1982; Locke, 1 968). Of interest is the threshold strength value below which reduced self-efficaciousness results in goal abandonment. As already noted, moderately discrepant attainments heighten motivation to fulfill standards that appear attainable through extra effort. When dissatisfaction combines with self-efficaciousness, effort is mobilized to master the challenge. The third pattern of interest concerns attainments that either fall just short of challenging standards or exceed them. High accomplishments that strengthen perceived self-efficaciousness are likely to lead performers to raise their standards (Lewin, Dembo, Festinger, & Sears, 1944), thus creating new motivating discrepancies for themselves. Under the latter circumstance, the pattern of self-subprocess regulation of motivation would include satisfaction with prior attainments—but discontent with similar future ones—high self-efficaciousness, and raised aspirations.

Depending on their direction and magnitude, goal discrepancies can raise the motivational potential of one of the self-reactive factors while lowering the motivational potential of the other. Thus, large negative discrepancies increase self-dissatisfaction but lower perceived self-efficacy for goal attainment. However, a decrement in self-efficacy sufficient to prompt adoption of a lower standard would serve to moderate evaluative self-reactions. For example, when provided with feedback of a substandard performance, some of the subjects in the present study seemed to abandon their goal as unattainable and were no longer unduly self-dissatisfied with moderate progress. Smaller negative discrepancies reduce self-dissatisfaction but strengthen self-percepts of efficacy. Further research is needed to determine the relative susceptibility of these two self-reactive factors to failed efforts and how they may combine and compensate for each other as motivators of action.

Social learning theory distinguishes between the effects of strength of perceived self-efficacy on effort during learning and during execution of established skills (Bandura, 1982). In approaching learning tasks, persons who perceive themselves to be supremely self-efficacious in the undertaking may see little need to invest much preparatory effort in it (Salomon, in press). However, in applying acquired skills, strong belief in one's self-efficaciousness intensifies and sustains the effort needed to realize challenging goals, which are difficult to attain if one is plagued by self-doubts. In short, self-doubts create an impetus for learning but hinder adept use of established skills.

REFERENCES

Atkinson, J. W. (1964). *An introduction to motivation.* Princeton, NJ: Van Nostrand.

Atkinson, J. W., & Raynor, J. O. (1974). *Motivation and achievement.* Washington, DC: V. H. Winston.

Bandura, A. (1977a). *Social learning theory.* Englewood Cliffs, NJ: Prentice-Hall.

Bandura, A. (1977). Self-efficacy: Toward a unifying theory of behavioral change. *Psychological Review, 84,* 191–215.

Bandura, A. (1978). The self system in reciprocal determinism. *American Psychologist, 33,* 344–358.

Bandura, A. (1981). The self and mechanisms of agency. In J. Suls (Ed.), *Psychological perspectives on the self* (Vol. 1). Hillsdale, NJ: Erlbaum.

Bandura, A. (1982). Self-efficacy mechanism in human agency. *American Psychologist, 37,* 122–147.

Bandura, A., & Schunk, D. H. (1981). Cultivating competence, self-efficacy, and intrinsic interest through proximal self-motivation. *Journal of Personality and Social Psychology, 41,* 586–598.

Bandura, A., & Simon, K. M. (1977). The role of proximal intentions in self-regulation of refractory behavior. *Cognitive Therapy and Research, 1,* 177–193.

Becker, L. J. (1978). Joint effect of feedback and goal setting on performance: A field study of residential energy conservation. *Journal of Applied Psychology, 63,* 428–433.

Brown, I., Jr., & Inouye, D. K. (1978). Learned helplessness through modeling: The role of perceived similarity in competence. *Journal of Personality and Social Psychology, 36,* 900–908.

Feather, N. T. (Ed.). (1982). *Expectations and actions: Expectancy-value models in psychology.* Hillsdale, NJ: Erlbaum.

Heckhausen, H. (1977). Achievement motivation and its constructs: A cognitive model. *Motivation and Emotion, 1,* 283–329.

Kiesler, C. A. (1971). *The psychology of commitment: Experiments linking behavior to belief.* New York: Academic Press.

Langer, E. J. (1975). The illusion of control. *Journal of Personality and Social Psychology, 32,* 311–328.

Latham, G. P., & Yukl, G. A. (1975). A review of research on the application of goal setting in organizations. *Academy of Management Journal, 18,* 824–845.

Lewin, K., Dembo, T., Festinger, L., & Sears, P. S. (1944). Level of aspiration. In J. McV. Hunt (Ed.), *Personality and the behavior disorders* (Vol. 1). New York: Ronald Press.

Locke, E. A. (1968). Toward a theory of task motivation and incentives. *Organizational Behavior and Human Performance, 3,* 157–189.

Locke, E. A., Cartledge, N., & Knerr, C. S. (1970). Studies of the relationship between satisfaction, goal setting and performance. *Organizational Behavior and Human Performance, 5,* 135–158.

Locke, E. A., Frederick, E., Lee, C., & Bobko, P. (1982). The effects of self-efficacy, goals and task strategies on task performance. Unpublished manuscript, University of Maryland.

Locke, E. A., Shaw, K. N., Saari, L. M., & Latham, G. P. (1981). Goal setting and task performance: 1969–1980. *Psychological Bulletin, 90,* 125–152.

Salomon, G. (in press). Television is "easy" and print is "tough": The differential investment of mental effort in learning as a function of perceptions and attributions. *Journal of Educational Psychology.*

Schunk, D. H. (1981). Modeling and attributional effects of children's achievement: A self-efficacy analysis. *Journal of Educational Psychology, 73,* 93–105.

Steers, R. M., & Porter, L. W. (1974). The role of task-goal attributes in employee performance. *Psychological Bulletin, 81,* 434–452.

Strang, H. R., Lawrence, E. C., & Fowler, P. C. (1978). Effects of assigned goal level and knowledge of results on arithmetic computation: Laboratory study. *Journal of Applied Psychology, 63,* 446–450.

Weinberg, R. S., Gould, D., & Jackson, A. (1979). Expectations and performance: An empirical test of Bandura's self-efficacy theory. *Journal of Sport Psychology, 1,* 320–331.

What Do People Think They Are Doing?
Action Identification and Human Behavior

Robin R. Vallacher • Department of Psychology, Florida Atlantic University
Daniel M. Wegner • Department of Psychology, Trinity University

Editors' Notes

How do people's identifications of what they are doing influence what they do next? In their theory of action identification, the authors propose that any action can be identified at various levels, from low levels specifying how the action can be performed to high levels signifying the purpose or consequences of the action. Lower level identities support effective action procedures, whereas higher level identities increase understanding of the action. Lower identities are the means to higher identity ends. Three principles of the theory are: 1) an action is maintained with respect to its prepotent identity; 2) when both higher and lower level identities are available, there is a tendency for the higher one to become prepotent; and 3) when a prepotent identity is not maintaining an action, a lower level identity tends to become prepotent. Thus, the trade-off between effective action procedures and meaningful action moves identification to the highest level identity that maintains effective action. This theory helps to explain why social pressures to do well, which involve higher level identities, tend to facilitate performance on easy or familiar tasks but to impair performance on difficult or unfamiliar tasks. It also predicts that lower level self-identities are more likely than higher level self-identities to permit changes in self-perception.

Discussion Questions

1. What are the three basic principles of action identification theory?
2. How does action identification theory explain why social pressures to do well can help performance on easy tasks but hurt performance on difficult tasks?

Authors' Abstract

Issues in the cognitive representation and control of action are broached from the perspective of action identification theory. This theory holds that any action can be identified in many ways, ranging from low-level identities that specify how the action is performed to high-level identities that signify why or with what effect the action is performed. The level of identification most likely to be adopted by an actor is said to be dictated by processes reflecting a trade-off between concerns for comprehensive action understanding and effective action maintenance. This means that the actor is always sensitive to contextual cues to higher levels of identification but moves to lower levels of identification if the action proves difficult to maintain with higher level identities in mind. These respective processes are documented empirically as is their coordinated interplay in promoting a level of prepotent identification that matches the upper limits of the actor's capacity to perform the action. The implications of this analysis are developed for action stability, the psychology of performance impairment, personal versus situational causation, and the behavioral bases of self-understanding.

People always seem to be doing something. They also seem to be quite adept at identifying what they are doing. What is less clear is how these two observations relate to one another. The theory of action identification (Vallacher & Wegner, 1985; Wegner & Vallacher, 1986) is explicitly concerned with this issue. At the heart of the theory are three interacting processes that specify a causal interdependence between what people are doing and what they think they are doing. Through a delineation of these processes, we hope to reveal how action constrains one's identification of action and, in turn, how action identification exerts a selecting and guiding force in subsequent action. The proposed causal interdependence between action and action identification proves useful in understanding a host of issues in human psychology that center on the mental control of action. These issues are thus discussed in detail, with attention given in each case to the points of contact between our analysis and prior conceptualizations. We begin by reviewing the background and principles of the theory.

Cognition and Action

That people can think about what they do is hardly a controversial idea in psychology. The suggestion, however, that specifiable causal links exist between cognitive representations of action and overt behavior is greeted with skepticism in certain quarters. This skepticism is fueled in part by people's capacity for seemingly unbounded constructions of behavior. As philosophers have long noted, any segment of behavior can be consciously identified in many different ways (Anscombe, 1957; Austin, 1961; Danto, 1963; Goldman, 1970; Ryle, 1949; Wittgenstein, 1953). Something as simple as "meeting someone," for instance, could be recognized by anyone with an even mildly active mental life as "being social," "exchanging pleasantries," "learning about someone new," "revealing one's personality" or even "uttering words." But while representations of action admit to considerable variability and seem subject to noteworthy change from moment to moment, behavior seems to follow a more constrained path, often exhibiting a press toward completion in the face of situational forces, biological needs, and reinforcement contingencies. Thus, as interesting as cognitive representations may be in their own right, they are considered by many to operate independently of the causal mechanisms promoting overt action.

Many psychologists of course, balk at the notion that cognitive representations of action are mere epiphenomena, with no necessary mapping onto specific overt behavioral events. Those who have addressed this issue explicitly, however, commonly advocate only a limited perspective on the link between cognitive representations and overt behavior. Thus, some commentators have suggested that behavior dynamics are primary, with representations of action arising after the fact, or at best, concurrently with the action. This *reflective* connection ends explicit expression in such otherwise distinct theories as self-perception theory (Bem, 1972) and psychoanalysis (Freud, 1914/1960). In self-perception theory, the true cause of behavior is some stimulus in the action setting; if the actor does not recognize the stimulus as causal, he or she casts about for other likely causal candidates even inventing inner dispositions if a plausible external cause cannot be found. In classic Freudian theory, meanwhile, the true cause of action is some unconscious motive striving for expression in even the most mundane of everyday settings. Cognitive representations are said to arise after the fact in an attempt to justify or make sense of what was done. Because the true motive is too painful to acknowledge, moreover, the person's post hoc cognitions are, by definition, considered inaccurate.

Other systems stress what might be called the *intent* connection. In this perspective, cognitive representations of action function as templates for subsequent overt behavior. James's (1890) analysis of ideomotor action, for instance, holds that an idea of action tends to produce the action unless something intervenes to prevent it. This is readily apparent in the case of simple physical movements; to move a finger, one simply thinks about doing so. Not surprisingly, then, the intent connection provides a reasonable summary statement regarding contemporary work on the cognitive control of basic movements (e.g., Adams, 1971; Norman & Shallice, 1980; Rosenbaum, Kenny, & Derr, 1983; Schmidt, 1975). With respect to actions of significant duration or importance in people's lives, however, the role of cognitive representations of action in guiding action is less established. What little is known about the cognition-action link in the context of meaningful behavior has been inferred from work in cognitive behavior therapy (e.g., Meichenbaum, 1977); decision making (e.g., Kahneman, Slovic, & Tversky, 1982); and traditional social-psychological attitude research (e.g., Azjen & Fishbein, 1977). A direct analysis of how people think about their most far-reaching and consequential actions, and how such thoughts may affect the nature of these actions, is thus missing in contemporary psychology.

A compelling case can be made for both the reflective and intent connections. People do seem to develop representations of their action after the fact, but they also seem capable of planning and directing their action in accord with their cognitive representations. What is needed, then, is a system that provides for integration of these two prototypical cognition–action links, specifying the conditions under which one or the other is likely to occur. This is the task of action identification theory. The theory holds that the relationship between cognitive representations and overt behavior is not unidirectional, but cyclical. Through the intent connection, cognitive representations generate action, and through the reflective connection, new representations of what one is doing can emerge to set the stage for a revised intent connection. In this way, people sometimes are led to maintain a course of action over an extended period of time and on other occasions are led to show dramatic changes in behavior from one moment to the next.

Action Identification Theory

The essence of the theory is that the identification of one's action, though highly variable in principle, is ultimately constrained by reality. Through the interplay of three processes, each framed as a principle of the theory, people are said to gravitate toward an identification of action that proves effective in maintaining the action. In this section, we present these principles and show their coordinated operation in determining action identification. In the sections to follow, we develop specific determinants of action identification that derive from this analysis and develop the implications of the theory for recurring issues in psychology.

Levels of identification

Fundamental to the theory is the recognition that the various identifications for an action do not exist as a random assemblage of unrelated elements. Instead, act identities bear systematic relations to one another in an organized cognitive representation of the action—the action's *identity structure*. An identity structure is essentially a hierarchical arrangement of an action's various identities. Lower level identities in this hierarchy convey the details or specifics of the action and so indicate how the action is done. Higher level identities convey a more general understanding of the action, indicating why the action is done or what its effects and implications are. Relative to low-level identities, higher level identities tend to be less movement defined and more abstract and to provide a more comprehensive understanding of the action. Identification level is a relative concept, of course, and so whether a given act identity is considered a means or an end, a detail or an implication, depends on the act identity with which it is compared.

The distinction between relatively low- and high-level identities is communicated in everyday language when people indicate that one performs one act identity *by* performing another (Goldman, 1970). Thus, one sees if someone is home *by* pushing a doorbell, and one pushes a doorbell *by* moving a finger. Although these three act identities all pertain to the same act, they exist at different levels in a cognitive hierarchy by virtue of their perceived functional asymmetry. "Seeing if someone is home" occupies the highest level, "pushing a doorbell" the next highest, and "moving a finger" the lowest level. Our research has confirmed that people appreciate the notion of an asymmetric *by* relation and can use this relational property to distinguish among act identities (Vallacher, Wegner, Bordieri, & Wenzlaff, 1981).

Theoretical Principles

The differences between low- and high-level identities, when considered in conjunction with the three principles of the theory, indicate how the "uncertain act" is resolved realistically by people in everyday life. The first principle holds that *action is maintained with respect to its prepotent identity*. This principle acknowledges the mental control of action that is reflected in a broad spectrum of theoretical traditions (e.g. Carver & Scheier, 1981; James, 1890; Luria, 1961; Miller, Galanter, & Pribram, 1960; Powers, 1973; Schank & Abelson, 1977; Vygotsky, 1962). Thus, people have in mind a certain idea of what they are doing or want to do and use this prepotent identity as a frame of reference for implementing the action, monitoring its occurrence, and reflecting on its attainment. Because act identities exist at different levels, this principle also holds that people maintain action at different levels. A person may set out simply to "move a finger," for instance, and monitor subsequent action to see whether this intention has been fulfilled, or the person may set out to "dial the phone" (a higher level identity) or "call home" (a yet higher level identity), and monitor the attainment of whichever identity is prepotent.

This principle is useful for understanding instances of action stability, the maintenance of a given action over time and across circumstances.

Thus, as long as a particular act identity is prepotent, it provides direction for action in the service of identity attainment. Stability is an important and noteworthy feature of human action, of course, but so is the potential for change and apparent inconsistency. The second and third principles represent two basic processes underlying the manifestation of such change.

The second principle holds that *when both a lower and a higher level act identity are available, there is a tendency for the higher level identity to become prepotent*. The idea here is simply that people are always sensitive to the larger meanings, effects, and implications of what they are doing. This tendency is reflected, implicitly or explicitly, in a variety of psychological systems. Learning under reinforcement contingencies (e.g., Skinner, 1953), the mastery of skilled action (e.g., Bruner, 1970; Bryan & Harter, 1899; Kimble & Perlmuter, 1970), Gestalt principles of perception (e.g., Koffka, 1935), even the existentialists' focus on the "search for meaning" (e.g., Frankl, 1963)—all of these seemingly distinct dynamics have in common the notion that act representations expand to encompass broader effects and meanings. In learning a relatively basic act expands to incorporate the reinforcing effects of the act; in the development of mastery, discrete acts become automated and integrated into a larger action unit; in Gestalt psychology, parts become unified to produce a whole; and in existentialism, patterns discerned in distinct actions become the basis for new awareness of what one is doing and who one is.

Much of the research on action identification to date has focused on the emergence of higher level identities in accordance with the second principle (Wegner, Vallacher, Kiersted, & Dizadji, 1986; Wegner, Vallacher, Macomber, Wood, & Arps, 1984). This research confirms that any time a person has only a low-level understanding of what he or she is doing, there is a readiness to accept any higher identity made available by the context surrounding the action and that this emergent identity can promote wholly new courses of action. In a study by Wegner et al. (1986, Experiment 1), for instance, subjects who identified the act of "participating in an experiment" in terms of its details were found to be more susceptible to a suggestion that they were either "behaving altruistically" (e.g., helping the experimenter) or "behaving selfishly" (e.g., earning extra credits). These subjects, moreover, chose to participate in subsequent activities that were consistent with their emergent understanding. In another study (Wegner et al., 1986, Experiment 2), subjects were presented with bogus personality feedback indicating that they were either cooperative or competitive. In comparison with subjects who had initially described their behavior for analysis at a comprehensive (high) level, those who described their behavior at a detailed (low) level were more accepting of the feedback and more likely to volunteer for future activities consistent with the feedback.

If this were the only mechanism by which identifications of action showed change, people's mental life might indeed be one of fantasy, with little relation to overt behavior. Thus, a person could come to look upon "maintaining eye contact" as "winning trust," "throwing dice" as "winning money," or even "sitting with my legs crossed while watching TV" as "controlling the outcome of the Super Bowl." While these identities could well make sense at the time of their emergence, they may have a tenuous relation at best to any subsequent behavior, no matter how much the person thought he or she was enacting them. The accumulation of high-level identities through coincidence or chance, or through more standard avenues of emergence such as environmental cues and social feedback processes, could charge even the simplest act with unconstrained significance, leaving the actor "buried in thought" (Tolman, 1932) and allowing only occasional contact with the world of real behavior.

Action identification is brought back to reality through a process specified in the theory's third principle: *When an action cannot be maintained in terms of its prepotent identity, there is a tendency for a lower level identity to become prepotent.* The idea here is simply that people must sometimes concern themselves with the how-to aspects of action in order to perform the action. A person may set out to "change a light bulb," for instance, but unless that action is automated to an appreciable extent, he or she may have to consciously plan and monitor such things as "grasping the bulb at its widest point," "turning the bulb counterclockwise," and so forth. Even if the action has become automated through repeated experience, its details might still become prepotent if the action were to be disrupted by some means. The light bulb, for instance, may prove to be stuck in its socket, in which case the person might give conscious consideration to "grasping" and "turn-

ing" at the temporary expense of the higher level "changing" identity. In the attempt to maintain action under one identity, one must often abandon that identity in favor of more performable identities. So, although a person may be inclined to adopt any of a host of higher level identities for an action, these identities dissipate in short order if they prove to be ineffective guides to subsequent action. The potential for flights of fancy that is inherent in the second principle is unlikely to represent a serious problem for most people, then, because of the reality orientation inherent in the third principle.

Research to date has documented the potential for movement to lower levels of identification in the face of high-level disruption. In a study by Wegner et al. (1984, Experiment 2), for instance, experienced coffee drinkers were asked to drink coffee from one of two rather different cups—a normal cup and an unwieldly cup weighing approximately 0.5 kg. Upon completion of this act, subjects were asked to rate how well each of 30 identities for coffee drinking described what they had done. Subjects in the normal cup condition tended to give relatively strong endorsement to identities such as "getting energized" or "promoting my caffeine habit." Subjects in the unwieldly cup condition, for whom the act of drinking proved difficult to do, tended to give relatively strong endorsement to identities at a substantially lower level, such as "drinking a liquid," "swallowing" and "lifting a cup to my lips." Presumably these subjects could not "energize themselves" or "promote their caffeine habit" with only these identities in mind. Instead, to accomplish the act at all, they had to think about the mechanics of coffee drinking, and this low-level orientation became prepotent, temporarily at least, in lieu of their accustomed way of thinking about the act.

A similar effect was obtained by Wegner, Connally, Shearer, and Vallacher (1983) in a study involving the act of eating. All subjects were invited to "eat Cheetos." But whereas some subjects were to eat the Cheetos in the usual manner (with their hands), other subjects were asked to retrieve the Cheetos with a pair of chopsticks. This latter technique proved difficult to do, and when asked subsequently what they had done, subjects in the chopsticks condition tended to eschew identities like "eating," "reducing hunger," and "getting nutrition" in favor of lower level identities like "chewing," "swallowing," "putting food in my mouth," and "moving my hands." Subjects in the nonchop-sticks condition, meanwhile, gave weaker endorsement to these lower level identities and correspondingly stronger endorsement to the various higher level identities ("reducing hunger," "getting nutrition," etc.). As in the coffee drinking study, then, difficulty in enacting an action normally identified at high level promoted a movement to a lower level of identification.

The three principles of the theory work together in such a way that maintainable identifications of one's action ultimately develop. There is a constant press for higher level understanding and control of action, but this press is countermanded by movement to lower levels of identification when the higher level identities cannot be enacted automatically. Over time and repeated action, the oscillations reflected in this dynamic interplay begin to flatten out, and the person converges on an identity at a particular level that enables him or her to perform the action up to his or her capacity. For any given action performed by a particular person, then, the range of potential understanding is likely to be notably restricted in the service of effective action control.

Determinants of Identification Level

The principles of the theory suggest in a general way how people come to an unambiguous understanding of what they are doing. To enable predictions regarding specific instances of action identification, however, it is necessary to relate the processes outlined in the theory to factors amenable to operational definition. Three sets of such factors would seem to play especially pivotal roles in promoting unequivocal act knowledge: the context in which the action takes place, the action's difficulty, and the person's experience with the action. Each of these influences on prepotent identification is discussed in turn.

Action Context

Knowing only the physical movements involved in an action, it is difficult to know what was done. As Danto (1963) has observed, without knowledge of circumstances or events outside the action itself, one is left with only the most rudimentary of identities, or what he called a "basic act." It is through sensitivity to contextual cues that move-

ment becomes represented in terms of its causal effects, conventional interpretations, and the like. What appears to be the same action can therefore be identified in vastly different ways depending on the relative salience of various cues to identification provided by the action's context. "Solving a math puzzle," for instance, might be thought of primarily as "keeping track of numbers" or "making mental calculations" in one setting (e.g., the privacy of one's home) but as "showing my math skill" or "trying not to embarrass myself" in another (e.g., a testing situation).

Context often imparts a relatively high level of identification to action. It is difficult to look upon what one is doing as simply a set of movements when there are circumstantial and social cues as to the labels, effects, and implications of these movements. This idea, of course, is inherent in the second principle of the theory and has been confirmed in the research on action emergence alluded to earlier (Wegner et al., 1986; Wegner et al., 1984). Thus, unless one already has a clear sense of the larger meaning of what one is doing, there is a readiness to embrace new identifications of action provided by the context in which one is acting.

At the same time, certain kinds of contextual factors can move a person to relatively low levels of identification. Foremost among these factors are those that serve to disrupt action (e.g., Wegner et al., 1983; Wegner et al., 1984, Experiment 2). Thus, an awkward cup can make one think of the details associated with "drinking" and poor transmission quality during a phone call can change the prepotent identity of one's action from "exchanging gossip" to "making myself heard" or "speaking loudly and clearly." Beyond their potential for disrupting action, some situations offer ambiguous or inconsistent cues as to the meaning or effect of what one is doing. In social situations, for instance, it is often hard to discern whether one is creating a good or bad impression, demonstrating wit or poor taste, and so on. The only thing one knows for sure is that one is "talking," "gesturing" and the like. Uncertainty regarding the effects and implications of one's behavior is especially likely in novel settings lacking familiar cues to higher level meaning. A person in such a setting may be prone to accept any higher level identities made available, but until these identifies are provided the person is left with only a rudimentary sense of what he or she is doing. Finally, in some contexts a person may be asked to monitor the details of his or her behavior as it is being enacted and in this way experience a lower level of identification than would normally be the case (e.g, Wegner et al., 1986, Experiment 2; Wegner et al., 1984, Experiment 1).

Action Difficulty

Contextual cues to identities at different levels are probably present in the majority of everyday circumstances. The novelty of a particular setting could make one sensitive to the lower level features of what one is doing, for example, while the evaluative pressures in the setting might render higher level identities (e.g., "impress others," "show my skill") prepotent. For this reason, context alone is rarely an unambiguous guide to a person's prepotent level of identification. Our analysis suggests a far less equivocal guide to identification level—the action's personal level of difficulty.

Some things are harder to do than others. A person may set out to "push a doorbell," for example, and find that this identity is easily enacted. The person may then try to "sell a set of encyclopedias" to the person answering the doorbell—a somewhat more formidable task. As the action begins to unfold, the person finds it necessary to suspend the "selling" identity in favor of more specific identities such as "sounding sincere," "appearing respectful yet confident," and "raising the issue of responsible parenthood." Each of these identities, in turn, may prove somewhat difficult to maintain, in which case the person will probably begin to think in terms of yet lower level identities. "Sounding sincere," for example, may require "furrowing one's eyebrows," "making continuous eye contact," and "talking in a slow and deliberate tone of voice."

This example illustrates a very basic point: The more difficult or disruption-prone an action is under a given identity, the greater the likelihood that it will be enacted under a lower level identity. Disruption potential, in turn, is traceable to more specific aspects of action. Five aspects in particular seem important and so are likely to establish identification level prepotency. We refer to these key aspects of action as *maintenance indicators*, because they indicate the level at which an action should be identified for optimal performance. Thus, an action under a particular identity can be scaled with respect to its relative *difficulty of enactment, familiarity, complexity* (variety of means or subacts), *enactment time, and learning time* (amount of time it takes to learn to do the action well). Compared to the act of "selling encyclopedias" for instance, "pushing a doorbell" is relatively easy: familiar for most people, can be enacted in only a few ways, occupies a short interval of time, and takes little time to learn. An action should be identified at a relatively high as opposed to low level to the extent that it shares these indicator values; an action with indicator values at the opposite ends of these dimensions, meanwhile, is likely to be maintained with lower level identities in mind.

To see whether such relationships exist, Wegner and Vallacher (1983) arranged for a variety of everyday actions to be rated with respect to each of the five maintenance indicators and for these actions to be reidentified at either a lower or a higher level, according to the subjects' personal preference. A sample of 274 undergraduates (155 women, 119 men) was asked to choose low- versus high-level reidentifications for each of 25 actions.[1] These actions were chosen to represent a spectrum of the things people do in daily life and included such actions as "pushing a doorbell," "voting," "paying the rent," and "reading." Each was presented along with two alternative identities, one lower and one higher in level, and subjects were to indicate which alternative best expressed their personal understanding of the action. Because our concern centered on the level at which people would attempt to maintain a given action, we avoided high-level alternatives that were likely to be seen as unanticipated or unpleasant consequences of the action.

By tracking the proportion of high-level choices for a given action across subjects an average identification level value was obtained for the action (possible range = 0–1). These values were normally distributed, although the mean value was fairly high level (.66). Actions identified at a relatively low level included "having a cavity filled," "taking a test," and "resisting temptation." Actions identified at a relatively high level included "reading," "locking a door," and "pushing a doorbell."

Another sample (35 women, 15 men) was asked to rate the 25 action stems on 5-point scales for

---

[1]The action set was assembled initially for the construction of an instrument to assess individual differences in characteristic level of action identification (Vallacher, Wegner, & Cook, 1982).

difficulty, familiarity, complexity, enactment time, and learning time. We then intercorrelated all of the ratings with identification level across the 25 actions. Table 1 presents the results of this analysis. It is clear that an action's typical level of identification does indeed covary with each of the indicators. As predicted, an action was reidentified at a high rather than low level to the extent that it was seen as easy to do, familiar, performable in a few ways, short in duration, and requiring little time to learn well. Table 1 also reveals strong intercorrelations among the five indicators. Hence, they were summed (after reverse scoring familiarity) to create an overall index of maintenance difficulty. This index, which proved reliable (Cronbach's alpha = .83), was significantly correlated with identification level across the action set, $r(25) = -.39$, $p < .02$; overall, difficult-to-maintain actions were identified at lower levels.

These data should not be taken as evidence that for any action only one level of identification is likely to assume prepotence. Indeed, if that were the case, the "uncertain act" would not have emerged as a philosophical problem in the first place, nor would people be so adept at volunteering alternative depictions of what they are doing. There does seem to be something like a central tendency across actors in an action's identification level, a tendency that reflects a concomitant central tendency in the action's maintenance indicators. This much would be predicted by a categorical judgment model (e.g., Brown, 1958; Bosch, 1973, 1978). Against this normative backdrop, though, a certain degree of variability in both identification level and indicator values is to be expected. Thus, an action may be difficult in one setting or for one person but easy in another setting or for someone else, and these differences in personal act difficulty should be reflected in the respective identities that assume prepotence.

Action Experience

To a large extent, variability in an action's difficulty is determined by the person's degree of experience with the action. Several distinct traditions in psychology have converged on the notion that with increasing action experience there is a corresponding increase in action automaticity (e.g., Fitts & Posner, 1967; Kimble & Perlmuter, 1970; Langer, 1978; Weiss, 1939). Presumably as one gains familiarity with an action's lower level com-

TABLE 1. Intercorrelations of Maintenance Indicators and Identification Level

Variable	1	2	3	4	5
1. Difficulty	—				
2. Familiarity	-.53	—			
3. Complexity	.40	.21	—		
4. Enactment time	.77	-.25	.71	—	
5. Learning time	.85	-.37	.60	.91	—
6. Identification level	-.48	.29	-.20	-.26	-.27

Note. The correlations are computed across 25 actions and are based on the sample mean for each rating on each action. The mean rating across actions for each of the maintenance indicators is based on an *n* of 50; the mean identification level across actions is based on an *n* of 274.

ponents, these components become integrated or "chunked" into larger action units, and it is these larger units that become the basis for conscious control of the action. An accomplished pianist, for instance, does not give conscious consideration to finger movements, key selection, and pedal pushing (see, e.g., Sudnow, 1978). In short, with increments in action experience, there is an increment in action automaticity and personal ability, and a consequent reduction in the individual's personal difficulty in performing the action.

According to the theory, these changes should prompt corresponding changes in level of prepotent identification. Thus, when low-level identities are unfamiliar and relatively difficult to maintain, emergence to higher level identities is effectively blocked; the third principle (movement to lower level prepotence) in a sense holds sway over the second principle (movement to higher level prepotence). As the lower level identities become mastered with increasing experience, however, there is a readiness to appreciate higher level identities and attempt maintenance with respect to them; the second principle becomes ascendant over the third principle. As these high-level identities then become mastered, the person is in a position to maintain the action with respect to yet higher level identities, and so on, in a progression that leads to both greater proficiency and more comprehensive understanding of the action. No matter how proficient one is at an action, then, there is always a way to identify what one is doing so as to rekindle the challenge of effective maintenance.

The progression from low to high level identity prepotence with increments in action experience is demonstrated in an investigation by Vallacher,

Wegner, and Frederick (1981). We asked a group of subjects ($N = 116$) to tell us what they do when they engage in each of five distinct actions—tennis, karate, piano playing, writing, and the video game *Space Invaders*.[2] Action identification questionnaires were provided for this purpose, each consisting of 36–38 one-sentence descriptions of the action under consideration. Subjects were to rate (on 7-point scales) how well each identity statement described the action for them. Factor analyses of these ratings revealed a low-level factor for each action as well as several higher level factors. A low-level index was computed for each action that represented a subject's summed ratings of identities loading on the low-level factor relative to his or her summed ratings across all factors.

The low-level index was then correlated with a self-report measure of subjects' experience with the action. The correlations were negative for every action (rs ranged from –.17 to –.56), reaching statistical significance in three of the five cases. A similar pattern was observed when the low-level index was correlated with subjects' self-reported proficiency at the action (rs ranged from –.19 to –.45). So, for actions as diverse as video games and piano playing, there is a waning of low-level prepotence as the actor gains familiarity and proficiency with the action. In rendering actions progressively more familiar, more automatic, and otherwise easier to do, experience enables action to be understood in terms that transcend the action's mechanistic underpinnings and highlight instead its potential meanings, effects, and implications.

Identification Level and Behavior

The principles of the theory suggest that there is always conscious mental control of action. Across diverse domains of action, and despite wide natural variation in action context, action difficulty, and personal expertise, the immediate precursor to action is a mental representation of what one is doing. The representations that guide action, however, admit to considerable variation in their level of identification, and this variability has implications for the form that action control is likely to take. In this section, we outline the basic differences in action control associated with relatively low versus high levels of identification and develop the implications of these differences for the psychology of performance impairment, personal ver-

sus situational causation, and the relationship between self-concept and behavior.

Levels of Action Control

Variation in identification level holds two key implications for action control. The first concerns action stability. When an action is undertaken with only a relatively low-level identity in mind, there is a tendency to accept a higher level identity made available by the action's context, and this new understanding of what one is doing can serve to change dramatically the course of one's subsequent behavior. A person who is simply "riding a bike," for example, may come to look upon the action as "seeing the neighborhood," "unwinding from a hard day," or "getting exercise," depending on the contextual cues surrounding the act. Each of these higher level identities is associated with an array of lower level identities besides bike riding and so could transform the act entirely. "Seeing the neighborhood," for instance, might result in parking the bike and walking in order to at a better look; "unwinding" might lead the person home and to the liquor cabinet.

High-level identification, meanwhile, lends itself to action stability because it effectively shields the person against the emergence of alternative identities that could substantially change the nature of subsequent action. In essence, a person with a relatively high level understanding already knows what he or she is doing and thus is less primed to accept other understandings at the same level provided by the context surrounding the action. Such understanding allows people to maintain a course of action in the face of changing conditions and with the passage of time. The bike rider who is "getting exercise," for instance, is likely to persist in this action regardless of new possibilities for action that might become available.

The second implication of variation in identification level concerns action flexibility. When an

---

[2]The action identification tendencies of those who indicated they had never performed the action and of those who were in the initial stages of action involvement were also explored in this study. Because the perspectives of such outsiders and beginners are independent of the act maintenance considerations that influence prepotency on the part of act performers, the data relevant to these perspectives are not considered here. For a presentation and theoretical consideration of these data, see Vallacher and Wegner (1985, Chap. 7).

action is maintained at a relatively high level, its physical manifestation may appear to change markedly from one occasion to the next. The bike rider "getting exercise," for instance, may disembark from the bike to do something that looks quite different (e.g., jogging), although phenomenologically he or she is still doing the same thing. Lower level identities, on the other hand, come closer to specifying the physical movements involved in the action and so admit to far less variability in their mode of enactment. "Riding a bike" encompasses such lower level acts as speeding up, slowing down, and turning corners, for example, but unlike "getting exercise," it does not encompass getting off the bike to jog. Thus, with increments in identification level, there is a corresponding increase in the range of interchangeable means available for maintaining the action, and this imparts a noteworthy degree of flexibility to action.

When an action is controlled with respect to a relatively high-level identity, then, changes in its lower level manifestations over time do not necessarily signal inconsistency. Indeed, a certain amount of flexibility is often necessary to maintain a broadly conceived action. Consistency and flexibility, however, take on different meanings when viewed in terms of low-level action control. If consistency exists at all for an action identified at a low level, it is because of stable environmental cues that keep the person mindful of the task at hand. Flexibility, meanwhile, reflects impulsive emergence to new courses of action when the environmental cues change. An action controlled at a low level, then, cannot be consistent and flexible at the same time; which orientation predominates depends on the constancy of the action context.

Performance Impairment

In view of these differences between low- and high-level identification, it is tempting to view higher level states as preferable. High-level understanding seems to come closer to capturing the essence of knowing what one is doing and the stability and flexibility of action associated with the high-level state sound preferable to the inconsistency versus rigidity characterizing lower levels of identification. High levels of identification can prove to be a mixed blessing however. Particularly in contexts where behavior is highly scripted (Schank & Abelson, 1977), the inattention to de-

tail and nuance that comes with high-level action control can appear to be "mindless" rather than thoughtful (Langer, 1978). In terms of our account, of course, *mindless action* is a somewhat misleading term. The principles of the theory suggest that well-learned, automated acts are performed with a representation of the act in mind, just as difficult, unfamiliar acts are. If the person does not seem to know what he or she is doing—that is if he or she appears to be acting mindlessly—it is because the observer (or psychologist, for that matter) is identifying the action at a different level.

Nonetheless, it is possible for action control to be attempted at too high a level. Our data demonstrate, of course, that people tend to gravitate toward, a level of identification that is warranted by the action's difficulty (Wegner & Vallacher, 1983) and to embrace higher levels of identification only when their experience readies them for such understanding (Vallacher, Wegner, & Frederick, 1981). This tendency should not be taken to mean that people always think about what they are doing in the "right" way, however. People choke under pressure, suffer from evaluation apprehension, get distracted, lose concentration, revert to old habits, worry about failure, get overconfident, and in other ways manage to approach action with a dysfunctional mental set (e.g., Baumeister, 1984; Berlyne, 1963; Carver & Scheier, 1981; Norman & Shallice, 1980; Reason & Mycielska, 1982; Rosenberg, 1965; Sarason, 1972; Schwartz, 1982; Wine, 1971). The convergence on a maintainable identification level is clearly a delicate process, one that is sensitive to various forms of interference.

The potential for interference reflects the simple fact that an action's prepotent identity is shaped by the context in which the action occurs. Thus, an environmental press toward higher level identities for one's action could save to impair performance if the action's maintenance indicators warranted relatively low-level identification. The person might move to lower levels in accord with the third principle, but the cues to higher level meanings may not be sufficiently ignored to allow appropriate attention to detail. Indeed because the low-level state sensitizes one to higher level identities, the movement to low level in the face of high-level failure could ensure that the person would keep mindful of the disruptive higher level identities. In support of this reasoning, several lines of research have converged on the notion that social and environmental pressures to do well, engendered by such things as the promise of reward or threat of punishment, competition, audience evaluation, and the like, tend to facilitate performance on simple or well-learned tasks but to impair performance on difficult or unfamiliar tasks (e.g., Berlyne, 1963; Cofer & Appley, 1964; Fitts & Posner, 1967; Zajonc, 1965). Such factors are similar in that they emphasize the higher level meanings and effects of one's action.

At the same time, action control can be attempted at too low a level. Just as difficult or unfamiliar action can be impaired by high-level identities made available by the action's context, so too can easy or familiar action be disrupted when the context calls attention to the lower level aspects of one's action. Indeed, the idea that overlearned performance can be debilitated by explicit attention to mechanistic aspects of action represents another well-established empirical generalization regarding human performance (e.g., Bryan & Harter, 1899; Kimble & Perlmuter, 1970; Langer & Imber, 1979). Thus, for an expert typist, attention to key selection and finger movements can produce errors and disrupt rhythm, just as an experienced driver's attention to pedal pushing and steering wheel rotation can introduce awkwardness into driving. Not only are low-level identities unnecessary for easy-to-maintain action, then, but their prepotence can also serve to disintegrate an action normally integrated with respect to a higher level understanding. An action that flows smoothly when enacted at high level can become choppy when enacted at low level.

The context of action thus holds potential for impairing action performance, pulling the person away from an identification level determined by personal action difficulty. The manifestation of this potential, however, is probably tempered by people's self-selection of settings in which to act. The random assignment of people to conditions in psychological research provides valuable insight into the effects of audience pressure, competition, and the like on performance quality, of course, but it almost certainly overestimates the frequency of performance impairment in daily life. More often than not, people seek out new and more demanding contexts for action only when their experience and skill readies them for higher level challenges. Thus, whereas an inexperienced tennis player is likely to shy away from a tennis court surrounded by observers, a more proficient player might ac-

tively seek out a context that renders "demonstrating skill" or "impressing an audience" prepotent at the expense of more elementary act identities. More generally, when a given act identity becomes relatively easy to maintain, the person is in a preemergence state and thus is sensitive to new action contexts that would impart higher level understanding to the action. This sort of self-selection could ensure that most people will undertake action with respect to an optimal level of identification much of the time. [. . .]

Summary and Conclusions

Action identification theory is not the first perspective to propose explicit links between thinking and doing. Almost a century ago, James (1890) proposed that goal-directed physical movement is preceded by a mental representation of such movement. This emphasis on mental representations of action has provided the touchstone for virtually every perspective on mind and action advanced since James's time. It is common in this theoretical tradition to posit a hierarchy—or sometimes a heterarchy—of representations to account for complex goal-directed action (e.g, Carver & Scheier, 1981; Gallistel, 1980; Lashley, 1951; Miller, Galanter, & Pribram, 1960; Newell, 1978; Norman, 1981; Powers, 1973; Schank & Abelson, 1977). The action's goal or purpose is said to occupy the highest level in such hierarchies, whereas subordinate levels serve to subdivide this goal into progressively more concrete representations, until a level is reached that specifies the actual movements to be undertaken.

Like other approaches, action identification theory emphasizes the mental representation of action and the organization or such representations in a hierarchical structure. The principles of the theory, however, tend to spawn identity structures that lack the symmetry and closure normally associated with hierarchies. Principle 1 holds that people maintain action in accord with their prepotent identity for the action, Principle 2 holds that people embrace higher level identities when these become available, and Principle 3 holds that failure to maintain action under one identity will move people to a lower level of identification. The coordinated interplay of these principles promotes action understanding that is dynamic, self-correcting, and always open to change. Every time an action is performed, there is the potential for new act identities, higher or lower in level, to be incorporated into one's identity structure. Thus, as is common in hierarchical models, a given high-level identity can come to subsume a number of different lower level identities. But by the same token, the same low-level identity can, in different contexts, generate widely divergent higher level identities. These high-level identities, meanwhile, may be related to each other only by virtue of their mutual linkages to the lower level identity and thus will operate as independent meanings for the action. As a result, a person's identity structure for a domain of action is likely to be highly complex, consisting of multiple, overlapping hierarchies.

The complexity of identity structures imparts remarkable flexibility and individuality to the mental control of action. Indeed, without knowledge of a person's phenomenal organization of action, it may be difficult for an observer to determine whether the person is maintaining a particular course of action over time or, instead, is doing different things. Among those commentators who are sensitive to this feature of mental representations, the typical response has been to challenge the alleged lawfulness of human action (e.g., Gauld & Shotter, 1977; Gergen, 1978, 1985; Harré & Secord, 1972). In this view, not only can people identify their action in many different ways and thus chart idiosyncratic and flexible courses of action, the phenomenological nature of this process renders it opaque to traditional modes of scientific inquiry. After all, if action is open to different identifications, how can a researcher be sure that he or she has hit upon the "real" identity guiding a subject's behavior in an experimental setting? A discipline that cannot even come to agreement on its basic unit of analysis would seem to be a discipline based on shifting sands at best and, at worst, doomed to theoretical dead ends and contradictions.

The theory we have advanced attempts to reconcile the seeming conflict between unbounded consciousness on the one hand and bounded, lawful behavior on the other. Thus, although the identification of action appears to be open-ended, limited only by our constructive and labeling capacities, the particular identity that assumes prepotence is ultimately constrained by reality. Among the factors that restrict the range of viable identities are various contextual cues surrounding the action, the personal difficulty of the action,

and the person's experience with the action. Each of these determinants of identification level, in turn, can be cast in terms of yet more specific factors. Contextual cues, for example, include such things as situational novelty versus familiarity, audience presence versus absence, and the promise of rewards versus the threat of punishment. The degree of action difficulty, meanwhile, can be specified through knowledge of the action's maintenance indication (e.g., its unfamiliarity, complexity, and enactment time). And personal action experience can be gleaned from noting a person's history or involvement with the action. These factors operate in accordance with the three principles of the theory to dictate how a person will attempt to control action in a given circumstance.

The variation in prepotent identification level that results from the operation of these factors has extensive implications for important realms of personal functioning. Thus, a person controlling an act with relatively low-level identities in mind is prone toward inconsistent, perhaps even impulsive, behavior and is highly sensitive to social feedback and other contextual cues to higher level meaning. The person controlling action at a relatively high level, meanwhile, can behave flexibly with respect to lower level identities while maintaining a broader goal or purpose and is effectively shielded against new high-level identities afforded by the social and physical environment. Performance impairment also can be understood in terms of variation in identification level. An action is performed effectively to the extent that the person's prepotent level of identification is in line with the action's maintenance indicators.

Finally, we wish to emphasize that the dynamic, open-ended nature of action identification processes allows for marked changes in people's identity structures throughout their lives. Every time an action is undertaken, the identities made available by the action's context, the antecedent identity that set the action in motion, and other identities that exist in the person's accumulated identity structure, compete for prepotence. Only those identities that prove to be effective guides to action win this competition—and stand ready to provide direction for action in the future. Given the multiplicity of contexts in which people act and the likelihood that such contexts are encountered with different frequencies at different points in one's life, the repeated emergence of new act identities is an ever-present possibility. When all is said and done, perhaps the only enduring characteristic of a person's identity structure is its potential for change. Yet, no matter how idiosyncratic such changes are, they are ultimately driven by desires common to everyone—to know what one is doing and to do what one can.

REFERENCES

Adams, J. A. (1971). A closed-loop theory of motor learning. *Journal of Motor Behavior, 3,* 111–119.

Anscombe, G. E. M. (1957). *Intention.* Oxford, England: Blackwell.

Austin, J. L. (1961). *Philosophical papers.* London: Oxford University Press.

Azjen, I., & Fishbein, M. (1977). Attitude–behavior relations: A theoretical analysis and review of empirical research. *Psychological Bulletin, 81,* 888–918.

Baumeister, R. (1984). Choking under pressure: Self-consciousness and the paradoxical effects of incentives on skilled performance. *Journal of Personality and Social Psychology, 16,* 610–620.

Bem, D. J. (1972). Self-perception theory. In L. Berkowitz (Ed.), *Advances in experimental social psychology* (Vol. 6, pp. 1–62). New York: Academic Press.

Berlyne, D. E. (1963). Motivational problems raised by exploratory and epistemic behavior. In S. Koch (Ed.), *Psychology: A study of a science* (Vol. 5. pp. 284–364). New York: McGraw-Hill.

Brown, R. W. (1958). How shall a thing be called? *Psychological Review, 65,* 14–21.

Bruner, J. S. (1970). The growth and structure of skill. In K. Connolly (Ed.), *Mechanisms of motor skill development* (pp. 88–103). New York: Academic Press.

Bryan, W. L., & Harter, L. (1899). Studies on the telegraphic language: The acquisition of a hierarchy of habits. *Psychological Review, 6,* 345–378.

Carver, C. S., & Scheier, M. F. (1981). *Attention and self-regulation: A control therapy approach to human behavior.* New York: Springer-Verlag.

Cofer, C. N., & Appley, M. H. (1964). *Motivation: Theory and research.* New York: Wiley.

Danto, A. (1963). What we can do. *Journal of Philosophy, 10,* 435–445.

Fitts, P. M., & Posner, M. I. (1967). *Human performance.* Belmont, CA: Brooks/Cole.

Frankl, V. E. (1963). *Man's search for meaning.* New York: Washington Square Press.

Freud, S. (1960). *The psychopathology of everyday life.* New York: Norton. (Original work published 1914)

Gallistel, C. R. (1980). *The organization of action.* Hillsdale, NJ: Erlbaum.

Gauld, A., & Shotter, J. (1977). *Human action and its psychological investigation.* London: Routledge & Kegan Paul.

Gergen, K. J. (1978). Toward generative theory. *Journal of Personality and Social Psychology, 36,* 1344–1360.

Gergen, K. J. (1985). The social constructionist movement in modern psychology. *American Psychologist, 40,* 266–275.

Goldman, A. I. (1970). *A theory of human action.* Princeton, NJ: Princeton University Press.

Harré, R., & Secord, P. F. (1972). *The explanation of social behaviour.* Oxford England: Blackwell.

James, W. (1890). *Principles of psychology.* New York: Holt.

Kahneman, D., Slovic, P., & Tverky, A. (Eds.). (1982). *Judgment under uncertainty: Heuristics and biases.* New York: Cambridge University Press.

Kimble, G. A., & Perlmuter, L. C. (1970). The problem of volition. *Psychological Review, 77,* 361–384.

Koffka, K. (1935). *The principles of gestalt psychology.* New York: Harcourt.

Langer, E. J. (1978). Rethinking the role of thought in social interaction. In J. Harvey, W. Ickes, & R. F. Kidd (Eds.), *New directions in attribution research* (Vol. 2, pp. 35–58). Hillsdale, NJ: Erlbaum.

Langer, E. J., & Imber, L. G. (1979). When practice makes imperfect: Debilitating effects of overlearning. *Journal of Personality and Social Psychology, 37,* 2014–2024.

Lashley, K. (1951). The problem of serial order in behavior. In L. A. Jeffress (Ed.), *Cerebral mechanisms in behavior, the Hixon symposium* (pp. 112–136). New York: Wiley.

Luria, A. R. (1961). *The role of speech in the regulation of normal and abnormal behavior* (J. Tizard, Trans.). New York: Liveright.

Meichenbaum, D. (1977). *Cognitive-behavior modification.* New York: Plenum Press.

Miller, G. A., Galanter, E., & Pribram, K. H. (1960). *Plans and the structure of behavior.* New York: Holt.

Newell, K. M. (1978). Some issues on action plans In G. E. Stelmach (Ed.), *Information processing in motor control and learning* (pp. 41–54). New York: Academic Press.

Norman, D. A. (1981). Categorization of action slips. *Psychological Review, 88,* 1–15.

Norman, D. A., & Shallice, T. (1980). *Attention to action: Willed and automatic control behavior* (Tech. Rep. No. 8006). San Diego: Center for Human Information Processing, University of California.

Powers, W. T. (1973). *Behavior: The control of perception.* Chicago: Aldine.

Reason, J., & Mycielska, K. (1982). *Absent-minded? The psychology of mental lapses and everyday errors.* Englewood Cliffs: NJ: Prentice-Hall.

Rosch, E. H. (1973). Natural categories. *Cognitive psychology, 4,* 328–350.

Rosch, E. H. (1978). Principles of categorization. In E. Rosch & B. B. Lloyd (Eds.), *Cognition and categorization* (pp. 27–48). Hillsdale, NJ: Erlbaum.

Rosenbaum, D. A., Kenny, S. B., & Derr, M. A. (1983). Hierarchical control of rapid movement sequences. *Journal of Experimental Psychology: Human Perception and Performance 9,* 86–102.

Rosenberg, M. J. (1965). When dissonance fails: On eliminating evaluation apprehension from attitude measurement. *Journal of Personality and Social Psychology, 1,* 28–42.

Ryle, G. (1949). *The concept of mind.* London: Hutchinson.

Sarason, I. G. (1972). Experimental approaches to test anxiety: Attention and the uses of information. In C. D. Spielberger (Ed.), *Anxiety: Current trends in theory and research* (Vol. 2, 383–403). New York: Academic Press.

Schank, R. C., & Abelson, R. P. (1977). *Scripts, plans, goals, and understanding.* Hillsdale, NJ: Erlbaum.

Schmidt, R. (1975). A schema theory of discrete motor learning. *Psychological Review, 82,* 225–260.

Schwartz, B. (1982). Reinforcement-induced behavioral stereotypy: How not to teach people to discover rules. *Journal of Experimental Psychology: General, 111,* 23–59.

Skinner, B. F. (1953). *Science and human behavior.* New York: Macmillan.

Sudnow, D. (1978). *Ways of the hand.* New York: Harper & Row.

Tolman, E. C. (1932). *Purposive behavior in animals and men.* New York: Appleton-Century-Crofts.

Vallacher, R. R., & Wegner, D. M. (1985). *A theory of action identification.* Hillsdale, NJ: Erlbaum.

Vallacher, R. R., Wegner, D. M., Bordieri, J., & Wenzlaff, R. (1981). [Models of act identity structures]. Unpublished research data.

Vallacher, R. R., Wegner, D. M., & Cook, C. (1982). [Construction of the behavior identification form]. Unpublished research data.

Vallacher, R. R., Wegner, D. M., & Frederick, J. (1981). [Experience and the identification of action]. Unpublished research data

Vygotsky, L. S. (1962). *Thought and language.* Cambridge, MA: MIT Press.

Wegner, D. M., Connally, D., Shearer, D., & Vallacher, R. R. (1983). [Disruption and identifications of the act of eating]. Unpublished research data.

Wegner, D. M., & Vallacher, R. R. (1983). [Action identification level and maintenance indicator ratings]. Unpublished research data.

Wegner, D. M., & Vallacher, R. R. (1986). Action identification. In R. M. Sorrentino & E. T. Higgins (Eds.), *Handbook of motivation and cognition: Foundations of social behavior* (pp. 550–582). New York: Guilford.

Wegner, D. M., Vallacher, R. R., Kiersted, G., & Dizadji, D. (1986). Action identification in the emergence of social behavior. *Social Cognition, 4,* 18–38.

Wegner, D. M., Vallacher, R. R., Macomber, G., Wood, R., & Arps, K. (1984). The emergence of action. *Journal of Personality and Social Psychology, 46,* 269–279.

Weiss, P. (1939). *Principles of development.* New York: Holt.

Wine, J. D. (1971). Test anxiety and the direction of attention. *Psychological Bulletin, 76,* 92–104.

Wittgenstein, L. (1953). *Philosophical investigations.* Oxford, England: Blackwell.

Zajonc, R. B. (1965). Social facilitation. *Science, 149,* 269–274.

Getting What One Wants

The term motivation implies movement or motility, and a fundamental issue in motivational science is how such movement should be characterized. The most general answer to this question is that one moves toward, or approaches, desirable states of affairs or positive goals, and moves away from, or avoids, undesirable states of affairs or negative goals. However, theories of motivation have been able to considerably refine this basic conception. The article by Higgins (1997) reviews the historical thinking on approach and avoidance issues and proposes a theoretical distinction between promotion and prevention focus that determines the strategy that people use in approaching and avoiding desirable and undesirable states. The promotion strategy entails eagerly seeking matches to one's goals, and the prevention strategy involves vigilantly avoiding mismatches to one goals. These strategies have far-reaching implications for people's thoughts, memories, emotions, and actions.

Carver and Scheier (1990) describe the monitoring process that accompanies movement toward a goal. Specifically, one acts so as to remove the discrepancy between one's actual and desired states, and one's further actions depend on what kind of feedback one receives from previous actions. If the feedback is positive, one may be encouraged to go on, but what does one do when the feedback indicates that one hasn't made much headway? One may initially intensify one's efforts, but at some point the efforts might be reduced based on the metacognitive notion as to the very likelihood of goal attainment even under the greatest efforts, or the degree to which such efforts are warranted given the value of the goal.

In a paper included in this section, Gollwitzer et al. (1990) approach the movement issue from an entirely different perspective by asking whether it is continuous or discontinuous. They propose that it is discontinuous involving four distinct action phases each characterized by its own mindset aimed at meeting the specific demands dominant at the time. According to Gollwitzer et al. (1990), the action phases are the predecisional phase, postdecisional phase, actional phase, and postactional phase.

For social and personality psychologists the issue of motivation often arises when dealing with interactional and relational phenomena such as forming an impression of a person. Such seemingly straightforward processes can be quite complicated, often involving the contrasting goals of the perceiver and the target. The perceiver may have specific expectations of what the target will be like. The target knows what he or she is like, but that may not always coincide with what the perceiver expects. Moreover, both parties to the interaction are on the one hand motivated to verify their views, and on the other hand to get along with each other and keep him or her relatively satisfied. When the target's perceived identity is not what the perceiver expects these motivations may clash and the process of negotiation may ensue in which the target negotiates her or his perceived identity in the perceiver's eyes while also taking into account the perceiver's expectations. Also, to minimize conflict targets may seek social environments where the other persons share the targets' views of themself. In short, according to Swann (1987), the movement toward affirming who one is, or asserting one's social identity—though deceptively simple at first blush—is actually quite complex and possibly arduous.

REFERENCES

Carver, C. S., & Scheier, M. F. (1990). Origins and functions of positive and negative affect: A control-process view. *Psychological Review, 97,* 19–35.

Gollwitzer, P. M., Heckhausen, H., & Stellar, B. (1990). Deliberative vs. implemental mind-sets: Cognitive tuning toward congruous thoughts and information. *Journal of Personality and Social Psychology, 59,* 1119–1127.

Higgins, E. T. (1997). Beyond pleasure and pain. *American Psychologist, 52,* 1280–1300.

Swann, W. B., Jr. (1987). Identity negotiation: Where two roads meet. *Journal of Personality and Social Psychology, 53,* 1038–1051.

Suggested Readings

Baumeister, R. F., & Heatherton, T. F. (1996). Self-regulation failure: An overview. *Psychological Inquiry, 7,* 1–15.

Buss, D. M., & Schmitt, D. P. (1993). Sexual strategies theory: A contextual evolutionary analysis of human mating. *Psychological Review, 100,* 204–232.

Jones, E. E., & Berglas, S. (1978). Control of attributions about the self through self-handicapping strategies: The appeal of alcohol and the role of under-achievement. *Personality and Social Psychology Bulletin, 4,* 200–206.

Kelley, H. H. (1997). The "stimulus field" for interpersonal phenomenon: The source of language and thought about interpersonal events. *Personality and Social Psychology Review, 1,* 140–169.

Mischel, W., Shoda, Y., & Rodriguez, M. L. (1989). Delay of gratification in children. *Science, 244,* 933–938.

Snyder, M. (1974). The self-monitoring of expressive behavior. *Journal of Personality and Social Psychology, 30,* 526–537.

Trope, Y., & Bassok, M. (1983). Information gathering strategies in hypothesis testing. *Journal of Experimental Social Psychology, 19,* 560–576.

Beyond Pleasure and Pain

E. Tory Higgins • Department of Psychology, Columbia University

Editors' Notes

A classic principle of motivation is that people approach pleasure and avoid pain. The author proposes that a fuller understanding of approach–avoidance motivation requires identifying the principles that underlie the different ways that people approach pleasure and avoid pain. Both the principle of regulatory anticipation and the principle of regulatory reference distinguish between pleasant end-states to be approached and painful end-states to be avoided, with the former distinguishing between expecting positive versus negative outcomes and the latter distinguishing between regulating in reference to desired or undesired end-states independent of expected outcomes. In contrast to these principles' concern with end-states, the principle of regulatory focus concerns strategic means. A promotion focus on accomplishments and aspirations is distinguished from a prevention focus on safety and responsibilities. Evidence is presented that individuals with a promotion focus, whether as a person or situation variable, tend to use approach strategies for goal attainment whereas individuals with a prevention focus tend to use avoidance strategies for goal attainment. This difference in strategic means is shown to influence performance and decision making.

Discussion Questions

1. How does the principle of regulatory focus differ from the principles of regulatory anticipation and regulatory reference?
2. How does regulatory focus influence decision making?

Authors' Abstract

People approach pleasure and avoid pain. To discover the true nature of approach–avoidance motivation, psychologists need to move beyond this hedonic principle to the principles that underlie the different ways that it operates. One such principle is *regulatory focus*, which distinguishes self-regulation with a *promotion focus* (accomplishments and aspirations) from self-regulation with a *prevention focus* (safety and responsibilities). This principle is used to reconsider the fundamental nature of approach–avoidance, expectancy–value relations, and emotional and evaluative sensitivities. Both types of regulatory focus are applied to phenomena that have been treated in terms of either promotion (e.g., well-being) or prevention (e.g., cognitive dissonance). Then, regulatory focus is distinguished from r*egulatory anticipation* and *regulatory reference*, 2 other principles underlying the different ways that people approach pleasure and avoid pain.

It seems that our entire psychical activity is bent upon *procuring pleasure* and *avoiding pain*, that it is automatically regulated by the PLEASURE-PRINCIPLE. (Freud, 1920/1952, p. 365)

People are motivated to approach pleasure and avoid pain. From the ancient Greeks, through 17th- and 18th-century British philosophers, to 20th-century psychologists, this hedonic or pleasure principle has dominated scholars' understanding of people's motivation. It is the basic motivational assumption of theories across all areas of psychology, including theories of emotion in psychobiology (e.g., Gray, 1982), conditioning in animal learning (e.g., Mowrer, 1960; Thorndike, 1935), decision making in cognitive and organizational psychology (e.g., Dutton & Jackson. 1987; Edwards, 1955; Kahneman & Tversky, 1979), consistency in social psychology (e.g., Festinger, 1957: Heider, 1958), and achievement motivation in personality (e.g., Atkinson, 1964). Even when Freud (1920/1952) talked about the ego becoming controlled by the reality principle, and in this sense developing "beyond the pleasure principle," he made it clear that the reality principle "at bottom also seeks pleasure—although a delayed and diminished pleasure" (p. 365). Environmental demands simply modify the pleasure principle such that avoiding pain becomes almost equal in importance to gaining pleasure. Thus, Freud's proposal to move beyond the pleasure principle did not move beyond the hedonic principle of seeking pleasure and avoiding pain.

The problem with the hedonic principle is not that it is wrong but that psychologists have relied on it too heavily as an explanation for motivation. After many centuries, it continues to be the dominant way to conceptualize approach versus avoidance. This dominance has taken attention away from other approach–avoidance principles. Is people's entire psychical activity controlled by the hedonic principle, as Freud (1920/1952) wondered, or might there be other self-regulatory principles that underlie both its operation and other psychical activities? If there are, then psychologists' understanding of the hedonic principle itself would be increased by understanding more about these other principles. Moreover these other ways of conceptualizing approach versus avoidance could have implications beyond the hedonic principle. It's time for the study of motivation to move beyond the simple assertion of the hedonic principle that people approach pleasure and avoid pain. It's time to examine how people approach pleasure and avoid pain in substantially different strategic ways that have major consequences. It's time to move beyond the hedonic principle by studying the approach–avoidance principles that underlie it and have motivational significance in their own right.

This article begins by introducing the concept of *regulatory focus*, principle that underlies the hedonic principle but differs radically in its motivational consequences. I describe how viewing motivation from the perspective of regulatory focus sheds light on the fundamental nature of approach–avoidance, expectancy–value relations, and emotional and evaluative sensitivities. I discuss how relying on the hedonic principle alone constrains and limits research and theory development, and I provide examples of the potential benefits of considering both promotion and prevention when studying phenomena that have been considered mainly in terms of either promotion (e.g., well-being) or prevention (e.g., cognitive dissonance). I then distinguish regulatory focus from regulatory anticipation and regulatory reference, two other principles underlying how people approach pleasure and avoid pain. I briefly consider how a deeper understanding of these principles, alone and in combination with regulatory focus, might increase psychologists' understanding of approach–avoidance motivation still further beyond the hedonic principle.

Regulatory Focus as a Motivational Principle

The notion that people are motivated to approach pleasure and avoid pain is well accepted, but what exactly does this entail? The hedonic principle is often discussed as if it were unitary. There is more than one account of this principle in the psychological literature, however. By considering these different accounts, it is possible to identify distinct principles that underlie hedonic self-regulation.

One of the earliest uses of the hedonic principle was as a lawful description of orderly event patterns. Careful observations indicated that when a situated behavior produced pleasure it was more likely to be repeated in that situation, whereas when a behavior produced pain it was less likely to be repeated in that situation. These observed events led to summary statements like "pleasure stamps in" and "pain stamps out"' as Thorndike (1911) did in his law of effect. This postulated "hedonism of the past," whether confirmed as a law or not, provided a description of events rather than an understanding of underlying processes. Thorndike (1935) later dropped the pain-stamps-out notion, leaving just the pleasure-stamps-in description of how situated behaviors are strengthened. Around the same time, Skinner (1938) proposed the law that the occurrence of operant behaviors increases when they are followed by a reinforcer. This "pleasure principle" also basically describes a pattern of observed events.

There are other accounts of the hedonic principle that provide more than descriptions of observed-event patterns. These other accounts describe specific kinds of approach and avoidance processes that underlie the operation of the hedonic principle. I begin this article by discussing the new concept of regulatory focus as one such approach–avoidance principle. Later. I discuss the concepts of regulatory anticipation and regulatory reference, which have a longer history in psychology as approach–avoidance principles. Regulatory focus

receives the most attention in this article because its motivational consequences reveal most clearly why it is necessary to move beyond the hedonic principle in order to discover the true nature of approach–avoidance motivation.

My discussion of regulatory focus concentrates on self-regulation toward desired end-states because this is the kind of self-regulation that has been emphasized in the literature (see, e.g., Carver & Scheier, 1981, 1990; Gollwitzer & Bargh, 1996; Miller, Galanter, & Pribram, 1960; Pervin, 1989; von Bertalanffy, 1968; cf. Elliot & Church, 1997; Elliot & Harackiewicz, 1996). The critical characteristic of such self-regulation is its *approach motivation*, the attempt to reduce discrepancies between current states and desired end-states. Although animal learning–biological models (e.g., Gray, 1982; Hull, 1952; Konorski, 1967; Lang, 1995; Miller, 1944: Mower, 1960), cybernetic-control models (e.g., Carver & Scheier, 1990; Powers, 1973), and dynamic models (e.g., Atkinson, 1964; Lewin, 1935; McClelland, Atkinson, Clark, & Lowell, 1953) all distinguish approaching desired end-states from avoiding undesired end-states, they do not distinguish between different ways of approaching desired end-states. They also do not identify different types of desired end-states that relate to different means of approach. Indeed, influential models such as that proposed by Gray explicitly treat approaching "reward" and approaching "nonpunishment" as equivalent. In contrast, regulatory focus proposes that there are different ways of approaching different types of desired end-states.

The theory of self-regulatory focus begins by assuming that the hedonic principle should operate differently when serving fundamentally different needs, such as the distinct survival needs of nurturance (e.g., nourishment) and security (e.g., protection). Human survival requires adaptation to the surrounding environment, especially the social environment (see Buss, 1996). To obtain the nurturance and security that children need to survive, children must establish and maintain relationships with caretakers who provide them with nurturance and security by supporting, encouraging, protecting, and defending them (see Bowlby, 1969, 1973). To make these relationships work, children must learn how their appearance and behaviors influence caretakers' responses to them (see Bowlby, 1969; Cooley, 1902/1964: Mead, 1934; Sullivan, 1953). As the hedonic principle suggests, children must learn how to behave in order to approach pleasure and avoid pain. But what is learned about regulating pleasure and pain can be different for nurturance and security needs. Regulatory-focus theory proposes that nurturance-related regulation and security-related regulation differ in regulatory focus. Nurturance-related regulation involves a promotion focus, whereas security-related regulation involves a prevention focus.

In earlier articles on self-discrepancy theory (e.g., Higgins, 1987, 1989a), I described how certain modes of caretaker–child interaction increase the likelihood that children will acquire strong desired end-states. These desired end-states represent either their own or significant others' hopes, wishes, and aspirations for them (strong ideals) or their own or significant others' beliefs about their duties, obligations, and responsibilities (strong oughts). Regulatory-focus theory proposes that self-regulation in relation to strong ideals versus strong oughts differs in regulatory focus. Ideal self-regulation involves a promotion focus, whereas ought self-regulation involves a prevention focus. To illustrate the difference between these two types of regulatory focus, let us briefly consider how children's experiences of pleasure and pain and what they learn about self-regulation vary when their interactions with caretakers involve a promotion focus versus a prevention focus.

Consider first caretaker–child interactions that involve a promotion focus. The child experiences the pleasure of the presence of positive outcomes when caretakers, for example, hug and kiss the child for behaving in a desired manner, encourage the child to overcome difficulties, or set up opportunities for the child to engage in rewarding activities. The child experiences the pain of the absence of positive outcomes when caretakers, for example, end a meal when the child throws food, take away a toy when the child refuses to share it, stop a story when the child is not paying attention, or act disappointed when the child fails to fulfill their hopes for the child. Pleasure and pain from these interactions are experienced as the presence and the absence of positive outcomes, respectively. In both cases, the caretakers' message to the child is that what matters is attaining accomplishments or fulfilling hopes and aspirations, and it is communicated in reference to a state of the child that does or does not attain the desired end-state—either "this is what I would ideally like you to do" or "this is not what I would ideally like you

to do." The regulatory focus is one of promotion—a concern with advancement, growth, and accomplishment.

Consider next caretaker–child interactions that involve a prevention focus. The child experiences the pleasure of the absence of negative outcomes when caretakers, for example, childproof the house, train the child to be alert to potential dangers, or teach the child to "mind your manners." The child experiences the pain of the presence of negative outcomes when caretakers, for example, behave roughly with the child to get his or her attention, yell at the child when he or she doesn't listen, criticize the child for making a mistake, or punish the child for being irresponsible. Pleasure and pain from these interactions are experienced as the absence and the presence of negative outcomes, respectively. In both cases, the caretakers' message to the child is that what matters is insuring safety, being responsible, and meeting obligations, and it is communicated in reference to a state of the child that does or does not attain the desired end-state—either "this is what I believe you ought to do" or "this is not what I believe you ought to do." The regulatory focus is one of prevention—a concern with protection, safety, and responsibility.

These socialization differences illustrate how regulatory focus distinguishes between different kinds of self-regulation in relation to desired end-states. Children learn from interactions with their caretakers to regulate themselves in relation to promotion-focus ideals or in relation to prevention-focus oughts (see Higgins & Loeb, 1998). In later life phases, these significant others could be friends, spouses, coworkers, employers, or other persons rather than caretakers. More generally, regulatory-focus theory distinguishes between the following two kinds of desired end-states: (a) aspirations and accomplishments (promotion focus) and (b) responsibilities and safety (prevention focus).

Momentary situations are also capable of temporarily inducing either a promotion focus or a prevention focus. Just as the responses of caretakers to their children's actions communicate to the children about how to attain desired end-states, feedback from a boss to an employee or from a teacher to a student is a situation that can communicate gain–nongain information (promotion-related outcomes) or nonloss–loss information (prevention-related outcomes). Task instructions that present task contingency or "if–then" rules concerning which actions produce which consequences also can communicate either gain–nongain (promotion) or nonloss–loss (prevention) information. Thus, the concept of regulatory focus is broader than just socialization of strong promotion-focus ideals or prevention-focus oughts. Regulatory focus also can be induced temporarily in momentary situations.

People are motivated to approach desired end-states, which could be either promotion-focus aspirations and accomplishments or prevention-focus responsibilities and safety But within this general approach toward desired end-states, regulatory focus can induce either approach or avoidance strategic inclinations. Because a promotion focus involves a sensitivity to positive outcomes (their presence and absence), an inclination to approach matches to desired end-states is the natural strategy for promotion self-regulation. In contrast, because a prevention focus involves a sensitivity to negative outcomes (their absence and presence), an inclination to avoid mismatches to desired end-states is the natural strategy for prevention self-regulation (see Higgins, Roney, Crowe, & Hymes, 1994).

Figure 1 summarizes the different sets of psychological variables discussed thus far that have distinct relations to promotion focus and prevention focus (as well as some variables to be discussed later). On the input side (the left side of Figure 1), nurturance needs, strong ideals, and situations involving gain–nongain induce a promotion focus, whereas security needs, strong oughts, and situations involving nonloss–loss induce a prevention focus. On the output side (the right side of Figure 1), a promotion focus yields sensitivity to the presence or absence of positive outcomes and approach as strategic means, whereas a prevention focus yields sensitivity to the absence or presence of negative outcomes and avoidance as strategic means.

Regulatory focus is concerned with how people approach pleasure and avoid pain in different ways. It implies that differences in performance, emotions, decision making, and so on could occur as a function of regulatory focus independent of the hedonic principle per se. It even implies that some phenomena traditionally interpreted in hedonic terms might be reconceptualized in terms of regulatory focus. These implications are considered next.

When the Hedonic Principle Is Not Enough

This section reviews research on regulatory focus that examines a variety of psychological phenomena traditionally treated in hedonic terms. I begin with the phenomena of approach and avoidance that are central to the hedonic principle. Evidence is presented that promotion focus and prevention focus involve distinct approach–avoidance strategies, and these different ways of regulating pleasure and pain are shown to have important motivational consequences in their own right. Next, research on Expectancy × Value effects is described that has found different effects for promotion focus and prevention focus that cannot be explained in simple hedonic terms. The role of regulatory focus in emotional and evaluative sensitivities is then considered. Evidence is presented that people's emotional experiences of the objects and events in their lives involve different kinds of pleasure and different kinds of pain depending on their regulatory focus, a variability not covered by the hedonic principle.

Approach and Avoidance

The hedonic principle asserts that people approach pleasure and avoid pain. It is silent, however, on how people do this. But how people approach pleasure and avoid pain, what strategies they use, has important motivational consequences. This section reviews some of these consequences.

APPROACHING MATCHES VERSUS AVOIDING MISMATCHES AS STRATEGIC MEANS

Individuals can increase the likelihood that they will attain a desired endstate (i.e., reduce discrepancies) by either approaching matches or avoiding mismatches to that end-state. Higgins et al. (1994) tested the prediction that a strategic inclination to approach matches is more likely for promotion-focus regulation whereas a strategic inclination to avoid mismatches is more likely for prevention-focus regulation.

In one study (Higgins et al., 1994), undergraduate participants were asked to report on either how their hopes and goals had changed over time (priming promotion-focus ideals) or how their sense of duty and obligation had changed over time (priming prevention-focus oughts). A free-recall technique was used to reveal strategic inclinations (see

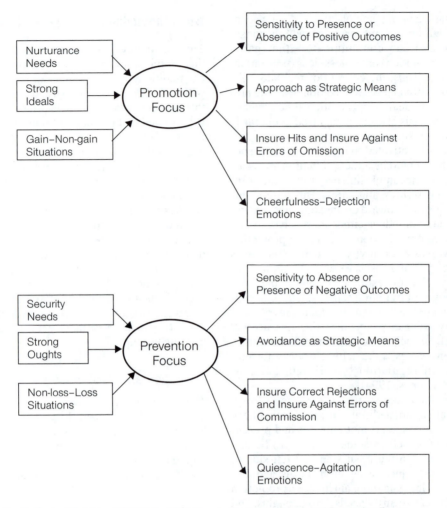

FIGURE 1 ■ Psychological Variables With Distinct Relations to Promotion Focus and Prevention Focus

also Higgins & Tykocinski, 1992). The participants read about several episodes that occurred over a few days in the life of another student. In each of the episodes, the target was trying to experience a desired end-state and used either the strategy of approaching a match or the strategy of avoiding a mismatch, as in the following examples: (a) "Because I wanted to be at school for the beginning of my 8:30 psychology class which is usually excellent, I woke up early this morning" (approaching a match to a desired end-state), and (b) "I wanted to take a class in photography at the community center, so I didn't register for a class in Spanish that was scheduled at the same time" (avoiding a mismatch to a desired end-state).

It was predicted that inducing either a promo-

tion focus or a prevention focus (operationalized by priming either ideals or oughts, respectively) would increase participants' inclinations for different regulatory strategies, which would be revealed by their recalling better those episodes that exemplified their strategic inclination. Consistent with this prediction, the participants remembered better the episodes exemplifying approaching a match to a desired end-state than those exemplifying avoiding a mismatch when a promotion focus versus a prevention focus was induced, whereas the reverse was true when a prevention focus versus a promotion focus was induced.

Higgins et al. (1994) also examined the possibility that individuals with chronic promotion focus versus prevention focus would use different strategies for friendship. An initial phase of the study elicited undergraduates' strategies for friendship and identified both tactics reflecting a strategy of approaching matches, such as "be supportive to your friends," and tactics reflecting a strategy of avoiding mismatches, such as "stay in touch and don't lose contact with friends." In the main phase of the study, participants were selected on the basis of their responses to the Selves Questionnaire. This questionnaire asks the respondent to list attributes for each of a number of different self-states, including the respondent's actual self and his or her ideals and oughts from different standpoints. It is administered in two sections, the first involving the respondent's own standpoint and the second involving the standpoints of the respondent's significant others (e.g., mother, father, best friend). The magnitude of self-discrepancy between the actual self and an end-state is calculated by summing the total number of mismatches and subtracting the total number of matches. The questionnaire responses were used to select participants with promotion-focus concerns (operationalized as participants with predominantly ideal discrepancies) and participants with prevention-focus concerns (operationalized as participants with predominantly ought discrepancies). The study found that, as predicted, friendship tactics reflecting a strategy of approaching matches were selected more by individuals with promotion-focus concerns whereas friendship tactics reflecting a strategy of avoiding mismatches were selected more by individuals with prevention-focus concerns.

The hedonic principle is totally silent about differences in strategic inclinations. The results of these studies indicate that it is important to distinguish between approach and avoidance strategies of attaining desired endstates because these strategies underlie what people consider significant in their lives. If so, then these different strategic inclinations also should influence the motivational significance of different incentives and performance means. This possibility is considered next.

APPROACH–AVOIDANCE AND STRATEGIC COMPATIBILITY

The literature reports inconsistent effects of incentives on performance (for a review, see Locke & Latham, 1990). One determinant of the perceived value of an incentive is its relevance to goal attainment (for a review, see Brendl & Higgins, 1996). Individuals with strong promotion goals are strategically inclined to approach matches to the goals. An incentive that is compatible with this strategic inclination should be perceived as more goal-relevant than one that is not. For individuals with strong prevention goals, however an incentive that is compatible with the strategic inclination to avoid mismatches to the goals should be perceived as more goal-relevant than one that is not. Shah, Higgins, and Friedman (1998) tested this hypothesis.

In Shah et al.'s (1998) study, the participants performed an anagrams task and were given the goal of identifying 90% of the possible words. The promotion framed condition emphasized the strategy of approaching a match to the goal by telling participants that they would earn an extra dollar (from $4 to $5) by finding 90% or more of the words. In contrast, the prevention framed condition emphasized the strategy of avoiding a mismatch to the goal by telling participants that they would avoid losing a dollar (keep their $5) by not missing more than 10% of the words. Shah et al. measured participants' strength of promotion focus and strength of prevention focus (operationalized in terms of the accessibility of their ideals and oughts, respectively). Consistent with previous work on attitude accessibility (see Bassili, 1995, 1996; Fazio, 1986, 1995), the accessibility of ideals and oughts was measured through participants' response latencies when answering questions on the computer about their ideals and oughts.

The prediction was that participants with a strong regulatory focus would perform better on the anagrams task when the strategic framing of the incentive was compatible with their chronic focus. This prediction was confirmed. As individuals' strength of promotion focus increased, performance was better with the framed incentive of approaching a match than avoiding a mismatch, and as individuals' strength of prevention focus increased performance was better with the framed incentive of avoiding a mismatch than approaching a match. These results suggest that strategic compatibility between incentives and people's goals increases motivation and performance. What about strategic compatibility between incentives, people's goals, and the strategic means by which the goals are attained? Shah et al. (1998) examined this issue in another study using the same basic paradigm.

Participants varying in promotion and prevention strength performed an anagrams task for a monetary incentive that was framed with either an approaching-a-match promotion focus or an avoiding-a-mismatch prevention focus. The anagrams were the same as those used in the first study but were divided into "red" and "green" subsets. The participants were told that when they found all the possible solutions for an anagram, they would gain a point if it was green and would not lose a point if it was red. Solving green anagrams (approaching a match) was compatible with a strong promotion focus, and solving red anagrams (avoiding a mismatch) was compatible with a strong prevention focus.

Shah et al. (1998) created a single variable representing the difference between participants' standardized ideal strength and standardized ought strength. They performed a median split on this difference variable, thus identifying a predominant ideal-strength group and a predominant ought-strength group. They found, as predicted, that strong promotion-focus individuals (predominant ideal strength) performed better than strong prevention-focus individuals (predominant ought strength) when working on the green anagrams in the promotion framing condition whereas strong prevention-focus individuals performed better than strong promotion-focus individuals when working on the red anagrams in the prevention framing condition.

These results suggest that motivation and performance are enhanced when the strategic nature of the means for attaining the goal is compatible with performers' regulatory focus while working on the task. Together, the results of both studies suggest that regulatory differences in strategic inclinations influence the impact of other motivational variables (i.e., incentives and means). To understand these effects, it is necessary to go beyond the hedonic principle that people approach desired end-states and recognize that they can do so by either approaching matches (promotion focus) or avoiding mismatches (prevention focus).

But this is not the end of the story. Bruner, Goodnow, and Austin (1956) noted years ago that a strategy "refers to a pattern of decisions in the acquisition, retention, and utilization of information that serves to meet certain objectives, i.e., to insure certain forms of outcome and to insure against certain others" (p. 54). Thus, not only can people strategically approach desired end-states by either approaching matches or avoiding mismatches, but both of these different strategies include tendencies to insure certain forms of outcome and insure against certain others. I now consider what these tendencies might be.

STRATEGIC TENDENCIES TO INSURE CERTAIN FORMS OF OUTCOME AND INSURE AGAINST CERTAIN OTHERS

Individuals in a promotion focus, who are strategically inclined to approach matches to desired end-states, should be eager to attain advancement and gains. In contrast, individuals in a prevention focus, who are strategically inclined to avoid mismatches to desired end-states, should be vigilant to insure safety and nonlosses. One would expect this difference in self-regulatory state to be related to differences in strategic tendencies. In signal-detection terms (e.g., Tanner & Swets, 1954; see also Trope & Liberman, 1996), individuals in a state of eagerness from a promotion focus should want, especially, to accomplish *hits* and to avoid errors of omission or *misses* (i.e., a loss of accomplishment). In contrast, individuals in a state of vigilance from a prevention focus should want, especially, to attain *correct rejections* and to avoid errors of commission or *false alarms* (i.e., making a mistake). Therefore, the strategic tendencies in a promotion focus should be to insure hits and insure against errors of omission, whereas in a prevention focus, they should be to insure correct rejections and insure against errors of commission (see Figure 1).

It should be noted that the promotion-focus tendency to insure against errors of omission is in the service of approaching matches and need not involve response suppression. A person in a promotion focus, for example, might persist on a difficult anagram rather than quitting to insure against omitting a possible word. Such persistence approaches a match to the goal of finding all solutions. It also should be noted that the prevention-focus tendency to insure correct rejections is in the service of avoiding mismatches. A person in a prevention focus, for example, might correctly reject a distractor in a recognition memory task by saying, "No, I haven't seen that word before." Such rejection avoids a mismatch to the goal of accuracy.

The difference between a promotion focus and a prevention focus in strategic tendencies has direct implications for the kind of decision making that has been examined in signal-detection tasks. In these tasks, a signal is either presented or not presented, and a respondent says either yes (a signal was detected) or no (no signal was detected). There are, therefore, four possible outcomes for a signal-detection trial: (a) a hit—saying yes when a signal was presented, (b) a miss—saying no when a signal was presented, (c) a false alarm—saying yes when there was no signal, and (d) a correct rejection—saying no when there was no signal. The strategic tendencies of individuals in a promotion focus are to insure hits and insure against errors of omission. These individuals, then, should want to insure hits (successfully recognizing a true target) and insure against misses (omitting a true target). They should try to recognize as many items as possible, producing an inclination to say yes (a risky bias). Individuals in a prevention focus in contrast, have strategic tendencies to insure comet rejections and insure against errors of commission and thus should want to insure correct rejections (successfully avoiding a false distractor) and insure against false alarms (failing to avoid a false distractor). They should try not to commit mistakes, producing an inclination to say no (a conservative bias).

A study by Crowe and Higgins (1997) tested these predictions. When the participants arrived for the study, they were told that they first would perform a recognition memory task and then would be assigned a second, final task. A liked and a disliked activity had been selected earlier for each participant to serve as the final task. There were four experimental framing conditions in which participants were told that which of the alternative final tasks they would work on at the end of the session depended on their performance on the initial recognition memory task. The relation between the initial memory task and the final task was described as contingent for everyone, but the framing varied in different conditions as a function of both regulatory focus (promotion vs. prevention) and valence (self-regulation working [pleasure] vs. self-regulation not working [pain]). Valence was included as a variable to test whether regulatory focus influences decision making beyond any simple hedonic effects of pleasure versus pain framing.

The participants were told that first they would be given a word recognition memory task. The instructions then varied across conditions: (a) promotion working—"if you do well on the word recognition memory task, you will get to do the [liked task] instead of the other task"; (b) promotion not working—"If you don't do well on the word recognition memory task you won't get to do the [liked task] but will have to do the other task instead"; (c) prevention working—"As long as you don't do poorly on the word recognition memory task you won't have to do the [disliked task] and will do the other task instead"; and (d) prevention not working—"If you do poorly on the word recognition memory task, you will have to do the [disliked task] instead of the other task." Crowe and Higgins (1997) found, as predicted, that participants in the promotion-focus condition had a risky bias of saying yes in the recognition memory task whereas participants in the prevention-focus condition had a conservative bias of saying no. Valence of framing had no effect whatsoever. Thus, regulatory focus had strategic consequences beyond the hedonic principle.

The difference in strategic tendencies between promotion and prevention focus also should produce differences in generating alternatives when problem solving. Some tasks, such as sorting, allow people to produce few or many alternatives without penalty. For example, one could use color as the criterion to son both fruits and vegetables, or one could use color for vegetables and shape for fruit. The only requirement is that the sorting criteria be consistent across all members within a category. Individuals in a vigilant state from a prevention focus want to avoid errors of commission and thus should be inclined to stick to or repeat a criterion across categories, thereby simplifying the task and reducing the likelihood of making mistakes. In contrast, individuals in an eager state from a promotion focus want to insure against omitting alternatives and thus should use alternative criteria across categories. The other prediction is that when sorting the members of a single category according to some criterion, individuals in a promotion focus should be motivated to generate many alternative subgroups to insure hits and insure against omissions. In contrast, individuals in a prevention focus should be motivated to generate few subgroups to simplify the task and avoid committing mistakes.

Using the same basic framing paradigm as in the recognition memory study. Crowe and Higgins (1997) examined the effects of regulatory focus on participants' sorting of fruits and vegetables.

They found, as predicted, that participants in the prevention-focus framing condition were more likely to repeat their sorting criteria across both fruits and vegetables than were participants in the promotion-focus framing condition. They also found that when sorting within a category, prevention-focus participants were more likely than promotion-focus participants to use the most extreme form of simplification in which category members are sorted into just two subgroups. "X" and "not X," in relation to a single alternative (e.g., "green" and "not green" vegetables). In this study as well, the effects of regulatory focus were independent of valence of framing (which itself had no effects).

The regulatory-focus difference in strategic tendencies also should produce differences in responding to difficulties during problem solving. When a task becomes difficult, promotion-focus individuals should be eager to find hits and insure against omitting any possible hits. In contrast, prevention-focus individuals should be vigilant against mistakes and insure against committing the error of producing them. When a task becomes difficult, then, one would expect promotion-focus individuals to persevere and prevention-focus individuals to quit more readily. Crowe and Higgins (1997) tested these predictions with three additional tasks.

One task was to solve anagrams. In this task, success at finding a word is a correct acceptance or hit, whereas failure to find a word is an error of omission. On this task, then, the promotion-focus individuals should be eager to find words (hits) and to avoid omitting any possible words. This should yield high persistence and a strong desire to find words following a failure to find any. In contrast, the prevention-focus individuals should be vigilant against nonwords and want to avoid committing the error of producing them. When individuals are experiencing difficulty, this orientation might motivate them to quit to avoid explicitly committing an error (see also Roney, Higgins, & Shah, 1995). The two other tasks were an especially difficult hidden figure in an embedded-figures task and a counting-backward task that had a difficult sequence following an easy sequence. As predicted, participants in the promotion-focus framing condition, as compared with those in the prevention-focus framing condition, solved more anagrams after experiencing difficulty on an unsolvable anagram persisted longer on the

especially difficult hidden figure, and performed better on the difficult counting-backward sequence. Once again, these effects of regulatory focus were independent of valence of framing (which itself had no effects).

The results of these studies by Crowe and Higgins (1997) highlight the need to go beyond the simple assertion of the hedonic principle that people approach pleasure and avoid pain. Not only can people generally approach desired end-states using different strategic means, but the promotion strategic inclination to approach matches involves tendencies to both insure hits and insure against errors of omission, and the prevention strategic inclination to avoid mismatches involves tendencies to both insure correct rejections and insure against errors of commission.

The next section considers how regulatory focus also can increase understanding of the nature of classic Expectancy × Value effects in motivation beyond the hedonic principle. I describe how expectancy and value can interact positively or negatively depending on regulatory focus, a finding that the hedonic principle does not predict.

Expectancy × Value Effects

Expectancy–value models of motivation assume not only that expectancy and value have an impact on goal commitment as independent variables but also that they combine multiplicatively (Lewin, Dembo, Festinger, & Sears, 1944; Tolman, 1955; Vroom, 1964; for a review, see Feather, 1982). The multiplicative assumption is that as either expectancy or value increases, the impact of the other variable on commitment increases. For example, it is assumed that the effect on goal commitment of higher likelihood of goal attainment is greater for goals of higher value. This assumption reflects the notion that the goal commitment involves a motivation to maximize the product of value and expectancy, as is evident in a positive interactive effect of value and expectancy. This maximization prediction is compatible with the hedonic or pleasure principle because it suggests that people are motivated to attain as much pleasure as possible.

Despite the almost universal belief in the positive interactive effect of value and expectancy, nor all studies have found this effect empirically (see Shah & Higgins, 1997b). Shah and Higgins proposed that differences in the regulatory focus of decision makers might underlie the inconsistent findings in the literature. They suggested that making a decision with a promotion focus is more likely to involve the motivation to maximize the product of value and expectancy. A promotion focus on goals as accomplishments should induce an approach-matches strategic inclination to pursue highly valued goals with the highest expected utility, which maximizes Value × Expectancy. Thus, the positive interactive effect of value and expectancy assumed by classic expectancy–value models should increase as promotion focus increases.

But what about a prevention focus? A prevention focus on goals as security or safety should induce an avoid-mismatches strategic inclination to avoid all unnecessary risks by striving to meet only responsibilities that an clearly necessary. This strategic inclination creates a different interactive relation between value and expectancy. As the value of a prevention goal increases, the goal becomes a necessity, like the moral duties of the Ten Commandments or the safety of one's child. When a goal becomes a necessity one must do whatever one can to attain it, regardless of the ease or likelihood of goal attainment. That is, expectancy information becomes less relevant as a prevention goal becomes more like a necessity. With prevention goals, motivation would still generally increase when the likelihood of goal attainment is higher but this increase would be smaller for high-value goals (i.e., necessities) than low-value goals. Thus, the second prediction was that the positive interactive effect of value and expectancy assumed by classic expectancy-value models would not be found as prevention focus increased. Specifically, as prevention focus increases, the interactive effect of value and expectancy should be negative.

These predictions were tested in both performance and decision-making tasks. As in Shah et al.'s (1998) studies, participants' chronic strengths of promotion and prevention focus were operationalized in terms of the accessibility of their ideals and oughts, respectively. The performance study involved solving anagrams. The participants gave subjective estimates of both the value of getting an extra dollar for succeeding at the task and the likelihood that they would succeed. The study found, as predicted, that as participants' promotion strength increased, the interactive effect of value and expectancy on performance was more positive. In contrast, as participants' prevention strength increased, the interactive effect of value and expectancy on performance was more negative.

The decision-making studies (Shah & Higgins, 1997b) involved undergraduates making decisions to take a class in their major or to take an entrance exam for graduate school. One study obtained measures of the participants' subjective estimates of value and expectancy, and other studies experimentally manipulated high and low levels of value and expectancy. One study involved comparing individuals who differed chronically in promotion strength and prevention strength, and other studies situationally induced regulatory focus using a framing procedure that emphasized approaching matches for the promotion focus and avoiding mismatches for the prevention focus. Together, these studies found, as predicted, that the interactive effect of value and expectancy was more positive when promotion focus was stronger but was more negative when prevention focus was stronger.

In one study (Shah & Higgins, 1997b), for example, participants were asked to evaluate the likelihood that they would take a course in their major. Both the value and the expectancy of doing well in the course were experimentally manipulated. High versus low expectancy of doing well in the course was manipulated by telling participants that 75% versus 25% of previous majors, respectively, received a grade of B or higher in the course. High versus low value of doing well in the course was manipulated by telling participants that 95% versus 51% of previous majors, respectively, were accepted into their honor society when they received a grade of B or higher in the course. Participants' chronic promotion strength and prevention strength also were measured. The contrast representing the Expectancy × Value effect on the decision to take the course was positive for individuals with a strong promotion focus but was negative for individuals with a strong prevention focus.

Together, the results of these studies demonstrate that even a motivational phenomenon considered to be as universal as the positive Expectancy × Value interaction depends on regulatory focus. Although the fact that a strong promotion focus can increase the maximizing, positive interaction is compatible with the pleasure principle, it is not obvious how this same principle could account for the fact that a strong prevention focus can make the interaction negative. Once again, there is a need to move beyond the hedonic principle to understand such phenomena. This is also true of the emotional and evaluative phenomena considered next.

Emotional and Evaluative Sensitivities

The hedonic principle implies that people experience pleasure when self-regulation works and they experience pain when it doesn't. It is silent, however, about the different kinds of pleasure or pain that people can experience. Why is it that failure makes some people sad and other people nervous? Regulatory focus goes beyond the hedonic principle in accounting for variability in people's emotional experiences, including variability in the quality and the intensity of people's emotions, and in their emotional responses to attitude objects. This section begins by illustrating that when self-regulation doesn't work, people experience different kinds of painful emotions depending on their regulatory focus. Then, evidence is presented for how strength of regulatory focus moderates the intensity of different kinds of pleasant and painful emotions. Finally, studies are reviewed that demonstrate how strength of regulatory focus underlies variability in people's evaluative sensitivities to attitude objects.

REGULATORY FOCUS UNDERLYING VARIABILITY IN PAINFUL EMOTIONS FROM SELF-DISCREPANCIES

A review of the psychological literature (see Higgins, 1987) revealed evidence that people experience dejection-related emotions, such as disappointment, dissatisfaction, or sadness, when they fail to attain their hopes or ideals whereas they experience agitation-related emotions, such as feeling uneasy, threatened, or afraid, when they fail to meet their obligations or responsibilities (e.g., Ausubel, 1955; Durkheim, 1951; Duval & Wicklund, 1972; Erikson, 1963; Freud, 1923/1961; Horney, 1950; James, 1890/1948; Kemper, 1978; Lazarus, 1968; Lewis, 1979; Piers & Singer, 1971; Rogers, 1961; Roseman, 1984; Roseman, Spindel, & Jose, 1990; Stein & Jewett, 1982; Sullivan, 1953; Wierzbicka, 1972). Such evidence suggests that discrepancies from promotion-focus ideals, which represent the absence of positive outcomes, produce different types of pain than discrepancies from prevention-focus oughts, which represent the presence of negative outcomes. This possibility

was directly investigated in a series of studies testing self-discrepancy theory (Higgins, 1987). Because these studies have been reviewed elsewhere (see Higgins, 1987, 1989b, 1998), only a few illustrative studies are described here.

An early study by Strauman and Higgins (1988) used a latent-variable analysis to test the hypothesis that promotion not working, as reflected in ideal discrepancies, predicts different emotional problems than prevention not working, as reflected in ought discrepancies. One month after filling out the Selves Questionnaire measure of self-discrepancies (see Strauman & Higgins, 1988), undergraduates filled out a battery of depression and social anxiety measures. Consistent with predictions, as the magnitude of participants' actual–ideal discrepancies increased, their suffering from depression symptoms increased, and as the magnitude of their actual–ought discrepancies increased, their suffering from social anxiety symptoms increased. Actual–ideal discrepancies were not related to social anxiety, and actual–ought discrepancies were not related to depression. Subsequent studies with clinically depressed and anxious persons also have generally found that depression is related to greater actual–ideal discrepancies whereas anxiety is related to greater actual–ought discrepancies (e.g., Scott & O'Hara, 1993; Strauman, 1989).

It also should be possible to have momentary effects on dejection and agitation emotions by temporarily increasing the strength of people's promotion-focus ideals or prevention-focus oughts. This hypothesis was tested in a study by Higgins, Bond, Klein, and Strauman (1986, Study 2) that situationally primed ideals and oughts. Undergraduate participants completed the Selves Questionnaire weeks before the experiment. Individuals with either both ideal and ought discrepancies or neither type of discrepancy were recruited for the study. Half of the participants had their ideals primed when they described their own and their parents' hopes and aspirations for them. The other half of the participants had their oughts primed when they described their own and their parents' beliefs about their duties and obligations. This priming had no effect on participants with neither type of discrepancy. But the participants with both types of discrepancy experienced an increase in dejection emotions when ideals were primed and an increase in agitation-related emotions when oughts were primed.

In a replication and extension of this study, Strauman and Higgins (1987) tested whether priming just a single attribute contained in participants' ideals or oughts would produce a dejection-related or agitation-related emotional syndrome, respectively (see also Strauman, 1990). Two types of individuals were selected to study—individuals with predominant actual–ideal discrepancies (i.e., individuals with relatively high actual–ideal discrepancies and relatively low actual–ought discrepancies) and individuals with predominant actual–ought discrepancies. Self-discrepancies were primed by asking each participant to complete the phrase "an X person ____" and selecting as "X" whichever trait represented a self-discrepancy for that participant. For each completed sentence, a participant's total verbalization time and skin-conductance amplitude were recorded. Measures of dejection and agitation emotions also were taken. As predicted, individuals with predominant actual–ideal discrepancies experienced a dejection-related syndrome from the priming (i.e., increased dejected mood, lowered standardized skin-conductance amplitude, decreased total verbalization time), whereas individuals with predominant actual–ought discrepancies experienced an agitation-related syndrome (i.e., increased agitated mood, raised standardized skin-conductance amplitude, increased total verbalization time).

STRENGTH OF REGULATORY FOCUS AS A MODERATOR OF EMOTIONAL INTENSITY

Regulatory focus clearly underlies the different kinds of pain that people experience from not attaining their goals. Other studies have shown that regulatory focus also underlies the different kinds of pleasure people experience from attaining their goals (see Higgins, Shah, & Friedman, 1997). Higgins et al. proposed that strength of regulatory focus also might moderate the intensity of people's pleasant and painful emotions. This proposal was consistent with earlier suggestions that goal strength (conceptualized as goal accessibility) might moderate the relation between goal attainment and emotional responses (see Clore, 1994; Frijda, 1996; Frijda, Ortony, Sonnemans, & Clore, 1992) and with evidence that attitude strength (operationalized as attitude accessibility) moderates the relation between attitudes and behavior (Fazio, 1986, 1995).

In a series of correlational studies, Higgins et

al. (1997) found that (a) the stronger the promotion focus (operationalized as highly accessible ideals), the stronger were the cheerfulness-related emotions experienced when promotion was working (actual–ideal congruency) and the stronger were the dejection-related emotions experienced when promotion was not working (actual–ideal discrepancy), and (b) the stronger the prevention focus (operationalized as highly accessible oughts), the stronger were the quiescence-related emotions experienced when prevention was working (actual–ought congruency) and the stronger were the agitation-related emotions experienced when prevention was not working (actual–ought discrepancy). These studies demonstrated that chronically strong promotion or prevention focus moderates the intensity of different types of pleasant and painful emotions (see Figure 1).

Higgins et al. (1997) hypothesized that similar effects should be obtained for situational variability in strength of regulatory focus. The task in their next study involved memorizing trigrams. As in Shah et al.'s (in press) studies, a framing paradigm was used to manipulate promotion-focus strength (i.e., emphasizing gains and nongains) and prevention-focus strength (i.e., emphasizing nonlosses and losses) while keeping constant both the criterion and consequences of success on the task. After completing the task, the participants were given false feedback that they had either succeeded or failed. It was predicted that feedback-consistent emotional change (i.e., increasing positive and decreasing negative emotions following success and decreasing positive and increasing negative emotions following failure) would be different in the two framing conditions. The study found, as predicted that feedback-consistent change on the cheerfulness–dejection dimension was greater for participants in the promotion framing condition than the prevention framing condition whereas feedback-consistent change on the quiescence–agitation dimension was greater for participants in the prevention framing condition than the promotion framing condition (see also Roney et al., 1995).

Taken together, the results of these studies demonstrate how regulatory focus goes beyond the hedonic principle by distinguishing between types of pleasant and painful emotions with respect to both quality and intensity. Regulatory focus also goes beyond the hedonic principle by providing an explanation for the variability in people's evaluative sensitivities to objects and events in the world. This issue is considered next.

STRENGTH OF REGULATORY FOCUS AND EVALUATIVE SENSITIVITY TO ATTITUDE OBJECTS

From the perspective of the hedonic principle alone, people have pleasant or painful responses to the objects and events in their lives. This simple binary description is captured in social psychology's classic distinction between liked and disliked attitude objects. But just as success and failure can produce different types of pleasure and different types of pain, respectively, so too can attitude objects produce different types of pleasant and painful responses. A liked object, such as a painting, might make one person happy and another person relaxed. A disliked object, such as a traffic jam, might make one person discouraged and another person tense. To capture such differences in emotional evaluations of attitude objects, it is necessary to go beyond the hedonic principle. Regulatory-focus strength is one variable that provides some insight into such differences.

To begin with, it should be noted that the significance of a particular emotional dimension for evaluation, such as the cheerfulness–dejection dimension, is independent of the extent to which pleasant versus painful emotions have been experienced in the past. Two persons with a strong promotion focus, for instance, might differ in their history of performance, with one experiencing primarily successes and cheerfulness and the other experiencing primarily failures and dejection. Although their specific emotional experiences differ, for both of these persons their evaluative sensitivity is to the cheerfulness–dejection significance of their personal qualities. Similarly, when evaluating other attitude objects, their sensitivity would be to the cheerfulness–dejection significance of an object (e.g., "How happy or sad does this object make me?"). In contrast, persons with a strong prevention focus would be sensitive to the quiescence–agitation significance of their personal qualities or the qualities of other attitude objects.

If one considers a dimension like cheerfulness–dejection as a bipolar construct, then this dimension is one way to construe the world of objects and events (see Kelly, 1955). Indeed, Kelly pointed out that both similarity and contrast are inherent in the same construct. A cheerful response is similar to other cheerful responses and contrasts with dejected responses. A dejected response is similar to other dejected responses and contrasts with cheerful responses. Thus, when objects and events are evaluated in terms of their cheerfulness–dejection significance, both cheerfulness and dejection are relevant to the construal even when the emotional experience is just feeling cheerful or just feeling dejected. Because of this, the cheerfulness–dejection dimension can have special significance for two persons with a strong promotion focus despite their having different histories of feeling cheerful or dejected. Similarly, the quiescence–agitation dimension of appraisal can have special significance for two persons with a strong prevention focus despite their having different histories of feeling quiescent or agitated.

Kelly (1955) also proposed that those ways of construing that are significant for a person increase that person's sensitivity to evaluating the world in relation to the construct. Similarly, Shah and Higgins (1997a) proposed that the more a particular emotional dimension is significant for a person, the more sensitive that person will be to evaluating the world along that dimension. Such sensitivity would be revealed in faster reaction times when reporting emotional experiences along that dimension. They predicted that stronger promotion focus (operationalized as highly accessible ideals) would be related to faster emotional evaluations along the cheerfulness–dejection dimension and stronger prevention focus (operationalized as highly accessible oughts) would be related to faster emotional evaluations along the quiescence-agitation dimension.

These predictions were tested in a series of studies by Shah and Higgins (1997a). The participants in every study made emotional appraisals on cheerfulness-related scales, dejection-related scales, quiescence-related scales, and agitation-related scales. In one set of studies, the participants reported how much they experienced each emotion, either during the study or during the previous week. In another set of studies, the participants emotionally evaluated positive and negative attitude objects that had been used in previous studies (e.g., Bargh, Chaiken, Govender, & Pratto, 1992). In each study, the analyses of reaction times statistically controlled for participants' ratings of the extent to which they experienced each emotion.

The results of these studies (Shah & Higgins, 1997a) strongly supported the predictions. In one study, for example, undergraduate participants were asked to rate how each word describing a positive object (e.g., music) or a negative object (e.g., guns) made them feel. For each participant, half of the positive object words were rated in relation to *happy* or *satisfying* and the other half in relation to *relaxed*; half of the negative object words were rated in relation to *sad* or *depressing* and the other half in relation to *tense* or *agitating*. Across the participants, each object word was rated on each emotional dimension an equal number of times. The study found that stronger promotion focus related to faster evaluations of the object words on the cheerfulness–dejection dimension whereas stronger prevention focus related to faster evaluations of the object words on the quiescence–agitation dimension. As in the other studies, this differential sensitivity (reflected in speed of responding) was independent of magnitude of evaluation (reflected in the extent ratings).

This section has reviewed research on approach and avoidance, Expectancy × Value effects, and emotional experiences and evaluations that was inspired by the concept of regulatory focus. Taken together this research demonstrates how psychologists' understanding of important phenomena can be enhanced by moving beyond the hedonic principle to consider processes that underlie the different ways that it operates. Thus, even for classic hedonic issues like the nature of approach and avoidance, the hedonic principle is not enough. The next, more speculative section of this article considers the possibility that there also might be cases where the hedonic principle is too much. Two questions are raised in that section. First, has theory development on some classic issues, such as the motivational effects of inconsistency or low self-esteem, been handicapped by limiting psychological concepts to simple pleasure–pain distinctions? Second, might at least some phenomena classically understood in hedonic terms have little to do, in fact, with pleasure and pain at all (or at least much less than commonly assumed)? These phenomena include the psychological effects of positive versus negative emotions and the psychological nature of threat versus opportunity and optimism versus pessimism.

When the Hedonic Principle Is Too Much

A disadvantage of a principle that is intuitively appealing and simple and that promises a wide range of applicability is that it tends to be used to understand phenomena with little questioning of its hidden assumptions. This is certainly true of the hedonic principle. Not only has its application been ubiquitous in psychology and other disciplines, but this has occurred with little consideration for the alternative ways in which it might operate. This is one sense in which the influence of the hedonic principle on theory development has been too much. To illustrate this point, let us consider what it would mean for studying some classic motivational issues if promotion and prevention were treated as alternative ways in which the hedonic principle operated.

When the Hedonic Principle Hinders Theory Development

It is remarkable how much psychological applications of the hedonic principle have been dominated by a prevention focus. Freud (1920/1952) conceptualized the production of pleasure and the avoidance of pain in terms of the lowering of tension. Conceptualizing pain in terms of tension and pleasure in terms of tension reduction has also been common in classic animal learning models (e.g., Hull, 1943), social psychological models (e.g., Festinger, 1957; Heider, 1958; Lewin, 1951), and personality models (e.g., Atkinson, 1964; Murray, 1938). Even in attachment theory, where Bowlby (1969, 1973) originally recognized security and nurturance as separate survival needs, concepts such as "safe haven," "secure base," and "fear of strangers" have received the most attention, and the classic attachment styles are called "secure," "anxious–avoidant," and "anxious–ambivalent."

Undoubtedly, this pervasive emphasis on prevention has influenced psychologists' observations and understanding of phenomena Freud (1917/1959), for example, described depression in terms of agitated-related symptoms rather than dejected-related symptoms. Such agitated symptoms would be consistent with the prevention focus of his ought-related theory of depression. Animal learning models have paid much more attention to negative reinforcement (i.e., the prevention pleasure of the absence of negative) than to positive punishment (i.e., the promotion pain of the absence of positive). Is this because negative reinforcement concerns tension reduction and involves a prevention focus, whereas positive punishment does not?

To illustrate this issue more fully, let us consider cognitive consistency models in social psychology as one example of how an emphasis on prevention focus might have constrained what was studied. Both of the most influential cognitive consistency models in social psychology, Festinger's (1957) cognitive dissonance theory and Heider's (1958) balance theory, postulated tension reduction as their underlying motivational principle. Did this prevention focus influence how these theories were developed? Might dissonance theory's prevention focus, for example, have inclined later models to emphasize individuals' feelings of responsibility for the negative consequences of their actions (e.g., Cooper & Fazio, 1984)?

It is possible that the prevention focus of dissonance and balance theory constrained which strategic resolutions to inconsistency received attention. In the classic dissonance paradigm of counterattitudinal advocacy, for example, the two resolutions that are emphasized are people rejecting responsibility for advocating the wrong position (e.g., by deciding they had no choice or derogating the experiment) and correcting what would be an error of commission by expressing a current attitude that is consistent with their advocated position. In contrast to these prevention strategies of weakening dissonant elements, a more promotion resolution would be to strengthen consonant elements, such as finding some positive consequence of one's actions, some silver lining. Similarly, Heider's (1958) resolutions for imbalance involved the prevention strategies of correcting mistaken beliefs and rejecting or denying associations, such as beginning to feel that some act is really not so bad or deciding that someone is not really responsible for his or her act. A more promotion resolution for imbalance, such as when two of one's close friends dislike each other might be to encourage and support them to get along better.

Concentrating on the hedonic principle rather than on the different ways that it operates is a shortcoming in theory development because alternative conceptualizations are overlooked. It can lead to an overemphasis on the prevention focus to the exclusion of promotion-focus possibilities, as just noted. It also can lead to an overemphasis on the promotion focus to the exclusion of prevention-focus possibilities. As one illustration, let us briefly consider the area of self-esteem. In contrast to the prevention focus of Freud (1917/1959), Rogers (1961) had a promotion focus. His concern with

actual–ideal congruencies and discrepancies inspired the next quarter century of investigating the pleasures and pains of high and low self-esteem, respectively. Once again, the field paid little attention to other principles that might underlie how self-esteem operates. In particular, psychologists remained content with conceptualizing self-esteem in terms of promotion focus with little consideration of alternatives.

An obvious alternative would be conceptualizing self-esteem in terms of prevention focus as well. If self-esteem is conceptualized as individuals' self-evaluations that they are failing to meet standards or attain goals that they or their significant others hold for them, then prevention-focus goats and standards are as relevant as promotion-focus goals and standards (see Higgins, 1996). Moreover, low self-esteem should then be predictive of agitation-related problems as well as dejection-related problems. In a similar way, psychologists study job satisfaction, marital satisfaction, life satisfaction, and so on, as if promotion working (satisfied, happy) or not working (dissatisfied, unhappy) is all that is relevant in these areas of life. Surely, prevention working (secure, relaxed) or not working (insecure, worried) is also relevant. After all, when people have problems at work, at home, and in other areas of their lives, they suffer from agitation-related distress as well as dejection-related distress.

Classic theories of cognitive consistency and well-being illustrate how psychologists' ability to address some basic issues has been handicapped by limiting psychological concepts to simple pleasure–pain distinctions. The hedonic principle is also too much when it is applied to phenomena that may have little to do with pleasure or pain at all. Illustrations of such overapplication are considered next.

When the Hedonic Principle Is Overapplied

Across all areas of psychology, there has been a fascination with the effects of positive and negative emotions. Most of the research questions have involved the simple distinction between the effects of good versus bad feelings. In social and cognitive psychology, for example, there has been an explosion of interest over the last decade in how good versus bad feelings influence cognition (for a recent review, see Schwarz & Clore, 1996). An early instance of this interest is the research on how positive versus negative moods influence memory (see, e.g., Bower, 1981; Isen, 1984). One especially influential conclusion from this research was that positively valenced material is more likely to be remembered in positive moods and negatively valenced material is more likely to be remembered in negative moods (see Schwarz & Clore, 1996). But are pleasure and pain really necessary for such memory effects to occur? Findings from a recent study suggest that they might not be.

Higgins and Tykocinski (1992) selected participants who had either a strong promotion focus (operationalized as predominant actual–ideal discrepancies) or a strong prevention focus (operationalized as predominant actual–ought discrepancies). All of the participants read about events in the life of another person that involved promotion working or not working (e.g., "I've been wanting to see this movie at the 8th Street theater for some time, so this evening I went there straight after school to find out that it's not showing anymore") and prevention working or not working (e.g., "I was stuck in the subway for 35 minutes with at least 15 sweating passengers breathing down my neck"). The study found that events involving promotion were remembered better by promotion-focus participants than prevention-focus participants, but the reverse was true for events involving prevention. Most important, this interaction was independent of participants' premood, postmood, or change in mood. Thus, pleasure or pain experiences during the study were not necessary for memory effects to occur. What influenced memory was the compatibility between participants' chronic regulatory focus and the regulatory focus of the events.

The results of this study (Higgins & Tykocinski, 1992) raise the possibility that previous mood and memory studies might not have depended on experiences of pleasure and pain. When these studies manipulated pleasure and pain with music, movies, gifts, or recollections of past experiences, might they have manipulated more than pleasure and pain? It is likely that regulatory focus was manipulated as well, and it is possible that inducing a promotion or prevention focus is critical for the memory effects to occur. Indeed, inducing a negative prevention focus might facilitate memory for fearful events but not for equally negative sad events, or inducing a promotion focus might facilitate memory for joyful events but not for

equally positive relaxing events (see Strauman, 1990). Rather than pleasure or pain being necessary for feelings to influence memory, what might be necessary is compatibility between a person's regulatory focus and the regulatory focus represented in the to-be-remembered events.

There has been a special fascination among psychologists, especially clinicians, with how anxiety influences cognition. One major conclusion is that anxiety has negative effects on creativity. When people experience high (vs. low) anxiety, for example, they produce fewer subgroups in a sorting task, which is said to reflect concrete rather than abstract thinking (e.g., Mikulincer, Kedem, & Paz, 1990). As described earlier, however, Crowe and Higgins (1997) found that individuals with a prevention focus produced fewer subgroups in a sorting task than did individuals with a promotion focus, and this effect was independent of the participants' feelings during the study. Rather than pleasure or pain being necessary for the sorting effects to occur, it was a prevention focus that produced fewer subgroupings. It should be noted in this regard that participants in the high-anxious group of previous studies (whether selected or induced) were likely to have been in a prevention focus.

The threat versus opportunity distinction in organizational psychology might be another case where the hedonic principle has been overapplied. Representing strategic issues as threats versus opportunities has been considered an important variable influencing decision makers' information processing and decisions. As Dutton and Jackson (1987) pointed out, a sense of importance and future is contained in both representations, but what differentiates them is that opportunity involves a positive situation in which gain is likely (and control is high) and threat involves a negative situation in which loss is likely (and control is low). This way of distinguishing between opportunity and threat potentially confounds the hedonic principle and regulatory focus. That is, opportunity is discussed as if it involved promotion working, and threat is discussed as if it involved prevention not working, thus confounding promotion versus prevention and pleasure versus pain.

By separating regulatory focus and the hedonic principle when studying threat versus opportunity, one might discover that there are significant independent effects of regulatory focus on decision makers' information processing and decisions.

Indeed, findings of regulatory-focus effects on decision making (e.g.. Crowe & Higgins, 1997; Shah & Higgins, 1997b) suggest that this is the case. It is important in this area to distinguish between the opportunity for accomplishment (promotion opportunity) and the opportunity for safety or security (prevention opportunity) and between the threat of nonfulfillment (promotion threat) and the threat of committing mistakes (prevention threat). With such distinctions, it would be possible to examine threat versus opportunity effects independent of the hedonic principle.

As a final example of potential overapplication of the hedonic principle, what exactly is meant by the familiar personality distinction between optimism and pessimism? Among personality psychologists, the dimension of optimism versus pessimism refers to the extent to which a person has favorable expectancies about attaining desired endstates (see, e.g., Carver, Reynolds, & Scheier, 1994; Norem & Cantor, 1986b; Norem & Illingworth, 1993). From this perspective, the critical difference between optimists and pessimists is that the former experience the pleasure of favorable expectancies whereas the latter experience the pain of unfavorable expectancies. Thus, the hedonic principle is critical to this distinction. Could optimism–pessimism be conceptualized in a manner that does not depend on the hedonic principle?

One possibility is that optimism involves a promotion focus whereas pessimism involves a prevention focus. From this perspective, hedonic experiences per se would no longer be critical to understanding the motivational consequences of optimism or pessimism. Instead, regulatory-focus differences in strategic inclinations would be critical. There is some support for this position in the literature. Both defensive pessimists and depressed pessimists experience the pain of anticipated failure (see Norem & Cantor, 1986b; Norem & Illingworth, 1993). The anxious affect of defensive pessimists suggests that they have a prevention focus. If they do, they should strategically insure against errors of commission. Indeed, the literature reports that defensive pessimists are vigilant in their efforts to avoid contemplated disaster, a strategy that reportedly works for them (see Norem & Cantor, 1986b; Norem & Illingworth, 1993). In contrast, the dejected affect of depressed pessimists suggests that they have a promotion focus. If they do, they should strategically insure against errors of omission. In fact, the strategies

of depressive pessimists include attempts to use others to obtain what they are missing, a strategy that reportedly doesn't work for them (see Coyne, Kahn, & Gotlib, 1987; Lewinsohn, 1974). Thus, the fact that defensive pessimists tend to perform well and depressive pessimists tend to perform poorly cannot be explained in terms of the hedonic principle, because both groups experience the pain of anticipating failure. It can be explained, however, in terms of differences in regulatory focus that produce different strategic inclinations that vary in effectiveness.

Beyond the Hedonic Principle to Its Ways of Operating

I began this article by asking whether there are implications of the different ways that hedonic regulation operates that are not captured by the hedonic principle itself. I proposed that it's time to examine principles of approach–avoidance orientation that underlie the hedonic principle and have motivational consequences in their own right. My review of some implications of regulatory focus suggests that it is fruitful to examine the unique consequences of the regulatory principles underlying hedonic regulation. Thus, it would be useful to consider additional principles of approach–avoidance orientation that underlie hedonic regulation, both independently and in combination with regulatory focus. This section considers two such principles—*regulatory anticipation* and *regulatory reference.*

Regulatory Anticipation

Freud (1920/1950) described motivation as a "hedonism of the future." In *Beyond the Pleasure Principle* (Freud, 1920/1950), he postulated that people go beyond total control of the "id" that wants to maximize pleasure with immediate gratification to regulating as well in terms of the "ego" or reality principle that avoids punishments from norm violations. For Freud, then, behavior and other psychical activities were driven by anticipations of pleasure to be approached (wishes) and anticipations of pain to be avoided (fears). Lewin (1935) described how the "prospect" of reward or punishment is involved in children learning to produce or suppress, respectively, certain specific behaviors (see also Rotter, 1954). In the area of animal learning, Mowrer (1960) proposed that the fundamental principle underlying motivated leaning was regulatory anticipation, specifically approaching hoped-for desired end-states and avoiding feared undesired end-states. Atkinson's (1964) personality model of achievement motivation also proposed a basic distinction between self-regulation in relation to "hope of success" versus "fear of failure," Wicker, Wiehe, Hagen, and Brown (1994) extended this notion by suggesting that approaching a goal because one anticipates positive affect from attaining it should be distinguished from approaching a goal because one anticipates negative affect from not attaining it. In cognitive psychology, Kahneman and Tversky's (1979) "prospect theory" distinguishes between mentally considering the possibility of experiencing pleasure (gains) versus the possibility of experiencing pain (losses).

Regulatory anticipation is not only an important principle underlying the operation of hedonic regulation but also one way in which the major psychological variable of expectancy influences human functioning. The variable of expectancy is one of the most important concepts in psychology (see Olson, Roese, & Zanna, 1996). It is a central variable in motivational theories in animal learning (e.g., Hull, 1952; Tolman, 1932), developmental psychology (e.g., Ford, 1987; Piaget, 1970), social psychology (e.g., Feather, 1966; Klinger, 1977; Lewin, 1951; Rosenthal & Jacobson, 1968), personality (e.g., Bandura, 1977a, 1986; Mischel, 1973), clinical psychology (e.g., Kelly, 1955; Norem & Cantor, 1986a; Rotter, 1954; Scheier & Carver, 1992), and other areas. Because regulatory anticipation is a specific case of expectancy functioning, knowing more about the variable of expectancy increases psychologists' understanding of regulatory anticipation. This, in turn, has implications beyond the hedonic principle itself. It is notable in this regard that processes basic to expectancies, such as knowledge accessibility (see Olson et al., 1996) or adaptation (e.g., Helson, 1964; Piaget, 1970), are not themselves hedonic in nature. Moreover, there are consequences of expectancy, such as the emotional effects of disconfirmation (e.g., Mandler, 1975), that are not implied in the hedonic principle.

One way to move beyond the hedonic principle, then, would be to learn more about the variable of expectancy. This presents a challenge of its own because expectancy itself has been used in more than one way as a motivational variable. Some psychologists use expectancy when studying events or outcomes that vary in their likelihood of occurrence (e.g., Ajzen & Fishbein, 1980). Other psychologists use expectancy when studying performances or goal attainments that vary in difficulty (e.g., Weiner et al., 1971). Still other psychologists use expectancy when studying value, and the claims about expectancy–value relations encompass notions that decreasing expectancy increases value (e.g., Atkinson, 1964), normal expectancy establishes neutral value (e.g., Kahneman & Miller, 1986), and smaller norm discrepancies are pleasant whereas larger ones are painful (e.g., McClelland et al., 1953).

Each of these different perspectives on expectancy tells something about motivation, even though their relation to the hedonic principle is not at ail clear, There are other self-regulatory models as well that include expectancy as a variable without linking it to hedonic regulation, such as models concerned with epistemic motivations (e.g., Gardner, Holzman, Klein, Linton, & Spence, 1959; Kruglanski, 1989; Lecky, 1961; Piaget, 1970; Snyder, 1984; Sorrentino & Short, 1986). To understand the motivational significance of expectancy, therefore, it is necessary to move beyond its role in hedonic regulation. In this way, the motivational significance of regulatory anticipation as a principle in its own right will become more evident.

Regulatory Reference

Consider two people who regard being in love as a desired end-state. One of them anticipates the pleasure of being in this state, whereas the other anticipates the pain of never being in this state. Now consider two other people for whom being alone is an undesired end-state. One of them anticipates the pain of forever being in this state, whereas the other anticipates the pleasure of never being in this state. The two who imagine being in love differ in their regulatory anticipation, as do the two who imagine being alone. But what about the difference between these pairs? Each pair has one person anticipating pleasure and another anticipating pain. Thus, the difference between the pairs does not concern anticipation per se. Rather, it concerns the difference between having a desired end-state versus an undesired end-state as the reference point for self-regulation.

This difference in regulatory reference is independent of whether pleasure or pain is anticipated. When people regulate in reference to desired or undesired end-states, they might anticipate pleasant or painful consequences or they might not. When they do anticipate consequences, they could anticipate the pleasure of either successful approach to desired end-states or successful avoidance of undesired end-states, and they could anticipate the pain of either failed approach to desired end-states or failed avoidance of undesired end-states. Regulatory reference and regulatory anticipation, then, are independent principles underlying hedonic regulation.

Distinguishing between self-regulation in relation to positive versus negative reference values also has a long history in psychology. Animal learning–biological models highlight the basic distinction between approaching desired end-states and avoiding undesired end-states (e.g., Gray, 1982; Hull, 1952; Konorski, 1967; Lang, 1995; Miller, 1944). Self theorists distinguish between good selves as positive reference values and bad selves as negative reference values (e.g., Erickson, 1963; Markus & Nurius, 1986; Sullivan, 1953). Social psychologists distinguish between positive reference groups and negative reference groups (e.g., Hyman, 1942; Kelley, 1952; Merton, 1957; Newcomb, 1950; Sherif & Sherif, 1964) and between positive and negative attitudes (e.g., Cacioppo & Berntson, 1994). Self-regulatory systems that have positive versus negative reference values also have been distinguished in cybernetic and control process models (e.g., Miller et al., 1960; Powers, 1973; Wiener, 1948).

Inspired by these latter models in particular, Carver and Scheier (1981, 1990) drew an especially clear distinction between self-regulatory systems that have positive versus negative reference values. A self-regulatory system with a positive reference value has a desired end-state as the reference point. The system is discrepancy-reducing and involves attempts to move one's (represented) current self-state as close as possible to the desired end-state. In contrast, a self-regulatory system with a negative reference value has an undesired end-state as the reference point. This system is discrepancy-amplifying and involves attempts to move the current self-state as far away as possible from the undesired end-state.

Like regulatory anticipation, regulatory reference is an important approach–avoidance principle underlying hedonic regulation, but it is not just this. Regulatory reference is one way in which the major psychological variable of standards influences human functioning. Like expectancy, the variable of standards is one of the most important concepts in psychology (see Higgins, 1990; Miller & Prentice, 1996). A *standard* is a criterion or rule established by experience, desires, or authority for the measure of quantity and extent or quality and value (Higgins, 1990). Self-regulation is influenced by both the standards that individuals chronically possess and the standards that are present in momentary situations.

As a criterion for measuring quantity and extent, the variable of standards has been a fundamental principle in theories of judgment in social psychology (e.g.. Festinger, 1954; Sherif & Hovland, 1961; Thibaut & Kelley, 1959), clinical psychology (e.g., Sarbin, Taft, & Bailey, 1960), and cognitive psychology (e.g., Helson, 1964; Tversky & Kahneman, 1974). The variable of standards (or reference points) as a criterion for measuring quality or value also has been a fundamental principle in theories of evaluation and goal-directed activity, including psychodynamic theories (e.g., Adler, 1929/1964; Freud, 1923/1961; Horney, 1950; Rogers, 1961), decision theories (e.g., Kahneman & Tversky, 1979), social learning theories (e.g., Bandura, 1977b; Bandura & Cervone, 1983; Kanfer & Hagerman, 1981; Kanfer & Karoly, 1972; Mischel, 1973; Rotter 1954), and social–personality theories (e.g., Duval & Wicklund, 1972; Ford, 1987; Lewin et al., 1944; McClelland et al., 1953).

Again, it is notable that there are processes involved in standard utilization, such as contextual salience, priming, and inferential processes (see Higgins, 1990; Miller & Prentice, 1996), that are separate from hedonic regulation. There are also consequences of standards that are not implied in the hedonic principle, such as memory effects from a change of standard (e.g., Higgins & Stangor, 1988). Thus, psychologists can move beyond the hedonic principle by increasing their understanding of standards in general and regulatory reference in particular. [. . .]

Regulatory focus, regulatory anticipation, and regulatory reference as distinct principles of approach–avoidance orientation have now been described. Table 1 provides a summary of the different ways these principles conceptualize approach versus avoidance. Regulatory anticipation concep-

TABLE 1. Self-Regulatory Principles of Approach–Avoidance Orientation

Self-regulatory principle	Avoidance orientation	Approach orientation
Regulatory anticipation	Avoid anticipated pain	Approach anticipated pleasure
Regulatory reference	Avoidance regulation in reference to undesired end-states	Approach regulation in reference to desired end-states
Regulatory focus	Prevention	Promotion
	Strategically avoid mismatches to desired end-states (and matches to undesired end-states)	Strategically approach matches to desired end-states (and mismatches to undesired end-states)
	Insure correct rejections	Insure hits
	Insure against errors of commission	Insure against errors of omission

tualizes approach versus avoidance in terms of anticipated consequences, distinguishing between approaching anticipated pleasure and avoiding anticipated pain. Regulatory reference conceptualizes approach versus avoidance in terms of movement in relation to reference points, distinguishing between approach regulation in reference to desired end-states (discrepancy-reducing) and avoidance regulation in reference to undesired end-states (discrepancy-amplifying). Regulatory focus conceptualizes approach versus avoidance in rams of strategic means for self-regulation, distinguishing between promotion-focus approach strategies (insuring hits and insuring against errors of omission) and prevention-focus avoidance strategies (insuring correct rejections and insuring against errors of commission).

Table 2 illustrates how these three approach–avoidance orientations combine together. Regulatory anticipation concerns anticipated consequences. It distinguishes between anticipating the pleasure of receiving an A (or avoiding receiving less than an A) and anticipating the pain of not receiving an A (or receiving less than an A). Regulatory reference concerns movement in relation to reference points. It distinguishes between approaching the desired end-state of receiving an A as a reference point and avoiding the undesired end-state of receiving less than an A as a reference point. Regulatory focus concerns strategic means for self-regulation. It distinguishes between promotion-focus approach strategies (e.g., pursuing means for advancement) regarding the accomplishment of receiving an A or the nonfulfillment of receiving less than an A and prevention-focus avoidance strategies (e.g., being careful) regarding the safety of receiving an A or the danger of receiving less than an A. [. . .]

Concluding Comment

What do I mean by going beyond the hedonic principle? One interpretation is that psychologists should not restrict themselves to this principle's simple assertion but should examine more fully

TABLE 2. Illustration of Different Approach–Avoidance Orientations

Regulatory focus and regulatory anticipation	Regulatory reference	
	Desired end-state reference point	Undesired end-state reference point
Promotion focus	Accomplishment	Nonfulfillment
Anticipate pleasure	I receive an A because I pursue so many means for advancement	I avoid receiving less than an A because I pursue enough means of advancement
Anticipate pain	I don't receive an A because I pursue too few means for advancement	I receive an A because I omit too many means for advancement
Prevention focus	Safety	Danger
Anticipate pleasure	I receive an A because I am so careful.	I avoid receiving an A because I am careful enough.
Anticipate pain	I don't receive an A because I am too careless.	I receive less than an A because I commit too many mistakes.

the different ways that people approach pleasure and avoid pain. I do, indeed, mean to suggest this. But I also mean to suggest something more. The subjective utility models are not just incomplete when they ignore the unpredicted negative interaction between expectancy and value for people in a prevention focus. A single emotional distress category that collapses mild depression and anxiety is not just too broad when these emotions, differing in regulatory focus, involve fundamentally different strategic motivation. Claims about biological underpinnings of emotion based on neuroimages of brain responses to pleasure and pain are not just overly general when they fail to distinguish among types of pleasure and types of pain. In such cases, the problem is not simply that psychologists overlook important distinctions by restricting themselves to the hedonic principle. The problem is that overreliance on the hedonic principle can yield misleading conclusions. To discover the true nature of approach–avoidance motivation, it is not simply desirable but essential to move beyond the hedonic principle to the principles underlying its operation.

REFERENCES

Adler, A. (1964). *Problems of neurosis.* New York: Harper & Row.

Azjen, I., & Fishbein, M. (1980). *Understanding attitudes and predicting social behavior.* Englewood Cliffs, NJ: Prentice Hall.

Ausubel, D. P. (1955). Relationships between shame and guilt in the socializing process. *Psychological Review, 62,* 378–390.

Bandura, A. (1977a). Self-efficacy: Toward a unifying theory of behavioral change. *Psychological Review, 84,* 191–215.

Bandura, A. (1977b). *Social learning theory.* Englewood Cliffs, NJ: Prentice Hall.

Bandura, A. (1986). *Social foundations of thought and action: A social cognitive theory.* Englewood Cliffs, NJ: Prentice Hall.

Bandura, A., & Cervone, D. (1983). Self-evaluative and self-efficacy mechanisms governing the motivational effects of goal systems. *Journal of Personality and Social Psychology, 45,* 1017–1028.

Bargh, J. A., Chaiken, S., Govender, R., & Pratto, F. (1992). The generality of the automatic attitude activation effect. *Journal of Personality and Social Psychology, 62,* 893–912.

Bassili, J. N. (1995). Response latency and the accessibility of voting intentions: What contributes to accessibility and how it affects vote choice. *Personality and Social Psychology Bulletin, 21,* 686–695.

Bassili, J. N. (1996). Meta-judgmental versus operative indexes of psychological attributes: The case of measures of attitude strength. *Journal of Personality and Social Psychology, 71,* 637–653.

Bower, G. H. (1981). Mood and memory. *American Psychologist, 16,* 129–148.

Bowlby, J. (1969). *Attachment (Attachment and loss,* Vol. 1). New York: Basic Rooks.

Bowlby, J. (1973). *Separation: Anxiety and anger (Attachment and loss,* Vol. 2). New York: Basic Books.

Brendl, C. M., & Higgins, E. T. (1996). Principles of judging valence: What makes events positive or negative? In M. P. Zanna (Ed.), *Advances in experimental social psychology* (Vol. 28, pp. 95–160). New York: Academic Press.

Bruner, J. S., Goodnow, J. J., & Austin, G. A. (1956). *A study of thinking.* New York: Wiley.

Buss, D. (1996). The evolutionary psychology of human social strategies. In E. T. Higgins & A. W. Kruglanski (Eds.), *Social psychology: Handbook of basic principles* (pp. 3–38). New York: Guilford Press.

Cacioppo, J. T., & Bentson, G. G. (1994). Relationship between attitudes and evaluative space: A critical review with emphasis on the separability of positive and negative substrates. *Psychological Bulletin, 115,* 401–423.

Carver, C. S., Reynolds, S. L., & Scheier, M. F. (1994). The possible selves of optimists and pessimists. *Journal of Research and Personality, 28,* 133–141.

Carver, C. S., & Scheier, M. F. (1981). *Attention and self-regulation: A control theory approach to human behavior.* New York: Springer-Verlag.

Carver, C. S., & Scheier, M. F. (1990). Principles of self-regulation: Action and emotion. In E. T. Higgins & R. M. Sorrentino (Eds.), *Handbook of motivation and cognition: Foundations of social behavior* (Vol. 2, pp. 3–52). New York: Guilford Press.

Clore, G. L. (1994). Why emotions vary in intensity. In P. Ekman & R. J. Davidson (Eds.), *The nature of emotion: Fundamental questions* (pp. 386–393). Oxford, England: Oxford University Press.

Cooley, C. H. (1964). *Human nature and the social order.* New York: Schoken Books. (Original work published 1902)

Cooper, J., & Fazio, R. H. (1984). A new look at dissonance theory. In L. Berkowitz (Ed.), *Advances in experimental social psychology* (Vol. 17, pp. 229–265). New York: Academic Press.

Coyne, J. C., Kahn, J., & Gotlib, I. H. (1987). Depression. In T. Jacobs (Ed.), *Family interaction and psychopathology: Theories, methods, and findings* (pp. 509–533). New York: Plenum Press.

Crowe, E., & Higgins, E. T. (1997). Regulatory focus and strategic inclinations: Promotions and prevention in decision-making. *Organizational Behavior and Human Decision Processes, 69,* 117–132.

Durkheim, E. (1951). *Suicide: A study in sociology.* New York: Free Press.

Dutton, J. E., & Jackson, S. E. (1987). Categorizing strategic issues: Links to organizational action. *Academy of Management Review, 12,* 76–90.

Duval, S., & Wicklund, R. A. (1972). *A theory of objective self-awareness.* New York: Academic Press.

Edwards, W. (1955). The prediction of decisions among bets. *Journal of Experimental Psychology, 51,* 201–214.

Elliot, A. J., & Church, M. A. (1997). A hierarchical model of approach and avoidance achievement motivation. *Journal of Personality and Social Psychology, 72,* 218–232.

Elliot, A. J., & Harackiewicz, J. M. (1996). Approach and avoidance achievement goals and intrinsic motivation: A mediational analysis. *Journal of Personality and Social Psychology, 70,* 461–475.

Erikson, E. H. (1963). *Childhood and society* (Rev. ed.). New York: Norton.

Fazio, R. H. (1986). How do attitudes guide behavior? In R. M. Sorrentino & E T. Higgins (Eds.), *Handbook of motivation and cognition: Foundations of social behavior* (Vol. 1, pp. 204–243). New York: Guilford Press.

Fazio, R. H. (1995). Attitudes as object-evaluation associations: Determinants, consequences, and correlates of attitude accessibility. In R. E. Petty & J. A. Krosnick (Eds.), *Attitude strength: Antecedents and consequences* (pp. 247–282). Mahwah, NJ: Erlbaum.

Feather, N. T. (1966). Effects of prior success and failure on expectations of success and subsequent performance. *Journal of Personality and Social Psychology, 3,* 287–298.

Feather, N. T. (1982). Actions in relation to expected consequences: An overview of a research program. In N. T. Feather (Ed.), *Expectations and actions: Expectancy-value models in psychology* (pp. 53–95). Hillsdale, NJ: Erlbaum.

Festinger, L. (1954). A theory of social comparison processes. *Human Relations, 1,* 117–140.

Festinger, L. (1957). *A theory of cognitive dissonance*. Evanston, IL: Row, Peterson.

Ford, D. H. (1987). *Humans as self-constructing living systems: A developmental perspective on behavior and personality*. Hillsdale, NJ: Erlbaum.

Freud, S. (1950). *Beyond the pleasure principle*. New York: Liveright. (Original work published 1920)

Freud, S. (1952). *A general introduction to psychoanalysis*. New York: Washington Square Press. (Original work published 1920)

Freud, S. (1959). Mourning and melancholia. In E. Jones (Ed.), *Sigmund Freud: Collected papers* (Vol. 4). New York: Basic Books. (Original work published 1917)

Freud, S. (1961). The ego and the id. In J. Strachey (Ed. & Trans.), *Standard edition of the complete psychological works of Sigmund Freud* (Vol. 19, pp. 3–66). London: Hogarth Press. (Original work published 1923)

Frijda, N. H. (1996). Passions: Emotion and socially consequential behavior. In R. D. Kavanaugh, B. Zimmerberg, & S. Fein (Eds.), *Emotion: Interdisciplinary perspectives* (pp. 1–27). Mahwah, NJ: Erlbaum.

Frijda, N. H., Ortony, A., Sonnemans, J., & Clore, G. (1992). The complexity of intensity. In M. Clark (Ed.), *Emotion: Review of personality and social psychology* (Vol. 13, pp. 60–89). Beverly Hills, CA: Sage.

Gardner, R. W., Holzman, P. S., Klein, G. S., Linton, H. B., & Spence, D. P. (1959). Cognitive control: A study of individual consistencies in cognitive behavior. In G. S. Klein (Ed.), *Psychological issues* (Pt. 4, pp. 1–18). New York: International Universities Press.

Gollwitzer, P. M., & Bargh, J. A. (Eds.). (1996). *The psychology of action: Linking cognition and motivation to behavior*. New York: Guilford Press.

Gray, J. A. (1982). *The neuropsychology of anxiety: An enquiry into the functions of the septo-hippocampal system*. New York: Oxford University Press.

Heider, F. (1958). *The psychology of interpersonal relations*. New York: Wiley.

Helson, H. (1964). Adaptation-level theory: An experimental and systemic approach to behavior. New York: Harper & Row.

Higgins, E. T. (1987). Self-discrepancy: A theory relating self and affect. *Psychological Review, 94,* 319–340.

Higgins, E. T. (1989a). Continuities and discontinuities in self-regulatory and self-evaluative processes: A developmental theory relating self and affect. *Journal of Personality, 57,* 407–444.

Higgins, E. T. (1989b). Self-discrepancy theory: What patterns of self-beliefs cause people to suffer? In L. Berkowitz (Ed.), *Advances in experimental and social psychology* (Vol. 22, pp. 93–136). New York: Academic Press.

Higgins, E. T. (1990). Personality, social psychology and person-situation relations: Standards and knowledge activation as a common language. In L. A. Pavin (Ed.), *Handbook of personality* (pp. 301–338). New York: Guilford Press.

Higgins, E. T. (1996). The "self digest": Self-knowledge serving self-regulatory functions. *Journal of Personality and Social Psychology, 71,* 1062–1083.

Higgins, E. T. (1998). Promotion and prevention: Regulatory focus as a motivational principle. In M. P. Zanna (Ed.), *Advances in experimental social psychology*. New York: Academic Press.

Higgins, E. T., Bond, R. N., Klein, R., & Strauman, T. (1986). Self-discrepancies and emotional vulnerability: How magnitude, accessibility, and type of discrepancy influence affect. *Journal of Personality and Social Psychology, 51,* 5–15.

Higgins, E. T., & Loeb, I. (1998). Development of regulatory focus: Promotion and prevention as ways of living. In J. Heckhausen & C. S. Dweck (Eds.), *Motivation and self-regulation across the life span*. New York: Cambridge University Press.

Higgins, E. T., Roney, C., Crowe, E., & Hymes, C. (1994). Ideal versus ought predilections for approach and avoidance: Distinct self-regulatory systems. *Journal of Personality and Social Psychology, 66,* 276–286.

Higgins, E. T., Shah, J., & Friedman, R. (1997). Emotional responses to goal attainment: Strength of regulatory focus as moderator. *Journal of Personality and Social Psychology, 72,* 515–525.

Higgins, E. T., & Stangor, C. (1988). A "change-of-standard" perspective on the relations among context, judgment, and memory. *Journal of Personality and Social Psychology, 5,* 181–192.

Higgins, E. T., & Tykocinski, O. (1992). Self-discrepancies and biographical memory: Personality and cognition at the level of psychological situation. *Personality and Social Psychology Bulletin, 18,* 527–532.

Horney, K. (1950). *Neurosis and human growth*. New York: Norton.

Hull, C. L. (1943). *Principles of behavior*. New York: Appleton-Century-Crofts.

Hull, C. L. (1952). *A behavior system: An introduction to behavior theory concerning the individual organism*. New Haven, CT: Yale University Press.

Hyman, H. H. (1942). The psychology of status. *Archives of Psychology, 269.*

Isen, A. M. (1984). Toward understanding the role of affect in cognition. In R. S. Wyer & F. K. Srull (Eds.), *Handbook of social cognition* (Vol. 3, pp. 179–236). Hillsdale, NJ: Erlbaum.

James, W. (1948). *Psychology*. New York: World Publishing. (Original work published 1890)

Kahneman, D., & Miller, D. T. (1986). Norm theory: Comparing reality to its alternatives. *Psychological Review, 93,* 136–153.

Kahneman, D., & Tversky, A. (1979). Prospect theory: An analysis of decision under risk. *Econometrica, 47,* 263–291.

Kanfer, F. H., & Hagerman, S. (1981). The role of self-regulation. In L. P. Rehm (Ed.), *Behavior therapy for depression* (pp. 143–179). New York: Academic Press.

Kanfer, F. H., & Karoly, P. (1972). Self-control: A behavioristic excursion into the lion's den. *Behavior Therapy, 3,* 398–416.

Kelley, H. H. (1952). Two functions of reference groups. In G. E. Swanson, T. M. Newcomb, & E. L. Hartley (Eds.), *Readings in social psychology* (2nd ed., pp. 410–450). New York: Holt, Rinehart & Winston.

Kelly, G. A. (1955). *The psychology of personal constructs.* New York: Norton.

Kemper, T. D. (1978). *A social interactional theory of emotions.* New York: Wiley.

Klinger, E. (1977). *Meaning and void.* Minneapolis: University of Minnesota Press.

Konorski, J. (1967). *Integrative activity of the brain: An interdisciplinary approach.* Chicago: University of Chicago Press.

Kruglanski, A. W. (1989). *Lay epistemics and human knowledge: Cognitive and motivational bases.* New York: Plenum Press.

Lang, P. J. (1995). The emotion probe: Studies of motivation and attention. *American Psychologist, 50,* 372–385.

Lazarus, A. A. (1968). Learning theory and the treatment of depression. *Behavior Research and Therapy, 6,* 83–89.

Lecky, P. (1961). *Self-consistency: A theory of personality.* New York: Shoe String Press.

Lewin, K. (1935). *A dynamic theory of personality.* New York: McGraw-Hill.

Lewin, K. (1951). *Field theory in social science.* New York: Harper.

Lewin, K., Dembo, T., Festinger, L, & Sears, P. S. (1944). Level of aspiration. In J. McV. Hunt (Ed.), *Personality and the behavior disorders* (Vol. 1, pp. 333–378). New York: Ronald Press.

Lewinsohn, P. M. (1974). A behavioral approach to depression. In R. J. Friedman & M. M. Katz (Eds.), *The psychology of depression: Contemporary theory and research* (pp. 157–185). Washington, DC: Winston.

Lewis, H. B. (1979). Shame in depression and hysteria. In C. E. Izard (Ed.), *Emotions in personality and psychopathology* (pp. 371–396). New York: Plenum Press.

Locke, E. A., & Latham, G. P. (1990). *A theory of goal setting and task performance.* Englewood Cliffs, NJ: Prentice Hall.

Mandler, G. (1975). *Mind and emotion.* New York: Wiley.

Markus, H., & Nurius, P. (1986). Possible selves. *American Psychologist, 41,* 954–969.

McClelland, D. C., Atkinson, J. W., Clark, R. A., & Lowell, E. L. (1953). *The achievement motive.* New York: Appleton-Century-Crofts.

Mead, G. H. (1934). *Mind, self, and society.* Chicago: University of Chicago Press.

Merton, R. K. (1957). *Social theory and social structure.* Glencoe, IL: Free Press.

Mikulincer, M., Kedem, P., & Paz, D. (1990). The impact of trait anxiety and situational stress on the categorization of natural objects. *Anxiety Research, 2,* 85–101.

Miller, D. T., & Prentice, D. A. (1996). The construction of social norms and standards. In E. T. Higgins & A. W. Kruglanski (Eds.), *Social psychology: Handbook of basic principles* (pp. 799–829). New York: Guilford Press.

Miller, G. A., Galanter, E., & Pribram, K. H. (1960). *Plans and the structure of behavior.* New York: Holt, Rinehart & Winston.

Miller, N. E. (1944). Experimental studies of conflict. In J. McV. Hunt (Ed.), *Personality and the behavior disorders* (Vol. 1, pp. 431–465). New York: Roland Press.

Mischel, W. (1973). Toward a cognitive social learning reconceptualization of personality. *Psychological Review, 80,* 252–283.

Mowrer, O. H. (1960). *Learning theory and behavior.* New York: Wiley.

Murray, H. A. (1938). *Exploration in personality.* New York: Oxford University Press.

Newcomb, T. M. (1950). *Social psychology.* New York: Dryden Press.

Norem, J. K., & Cantor, N. (1986a). Anticipatory and post hoc cushioning strategies: Optimism and defensive pessimism in "risky" situations. *Cognitive Therapy and Research, 10,* 347–362.

Norem, J. K.,& Cantor, N. (1986b). Defensive pessimism: Harnessing anxiety as motivation. *Journal of Personality and Social Psychology, 51,* 1208–1217.

Norem, J. K., & Illingworth, K. S. S. (1993). Strategy-dependent effects of reflecting on self and tasks: Some implications of optimism and defensive pessimism. *Journal of Personality and Social Psychology, 65,* 822–835.

Olson, J. M., Roese, N. J., & Zanna, M. P. (1996). Expectancies. In E. T. Higgins & A. W. Kruglanski (Eds.), *Social psychology: Handbook of basic principles* (pp. 211–238). New York: Guilford Press.

Pervin, L. A. (Ed.). (1989). *Goal concepts in personality and social psychology.* Hillsdale, NJ: Erlbaum.

Piaget, J. (1970). Piaget's theory. In P. H. Mussen (Ed.), *Carmichael's manual of child psychology* (3rd ed., Vol. 1, pp. 703–732). New York: Wiley.

Piers, G., & Singer, M. B. (1971). *Shame and guilt.* New York: Norton.

Powers, W. T. (1973). *Behavior: The control of perception.* Chicago: Aldine.

Rogers, C. R. (1961). *On becoming a person.* Boston: Houghton Mifflin.

Roney, C. J. R., Higgins, E. T., & Shah, J. (1995). Goals and framing: How outcome focus influences motivation and emotion. *Personality and Social Psychology Bulletin, 21,* 1151–1160.

Roseman, I. J. (1984). Cognitive determinants of emotion: A structural theory. *Review of Personality and Social Psychology, 5,* 11–36.

Roseman, I. J., Spindel, M. S., & Jose, P. E. (1990). Appraisals of emotion-eliciting events: Testing a theory of discrete emotions. *Journal of Personality and Social Psychology, 59,* 899–915.

Rosenthal, R., & Jacobson, L. (1968). *Pygmalion in the classroom: Teacher, expectancies and pupils' intellectual development.* New York: Holt, Rinehart & Winston.

Rotter, J. B. (1954). *Social learning and clinical psychology.* Englewood Cliffs, NJ: Prentice Hall.

Sarbin, T. R., Taft, R., & Bailey, D. E. (1960). *Clinical inference and cognitive theory.* New York: Holt, Rinehart & Winston.

Scheier, M. F., & Carver, C. S. (1992). Effects of optimism on psychological and physical well-being: Theoretical overview and empirical update. *Cognitive Therapy and Research, 16,* 201–228.

Schwarz, N., & Clore, G. L. (1996). Feelings and phenomenal experiences. In E. T. Higgins & A. W. Kruglanski (Eds.), *Social psychology: Handbook of basic principles* (pp. 433–465). New York: Guilford Press.

Scott, L., & O'Hara, M. W. (1993). Self-discrepancies in clinically anxious and depressed university students. *Journal of Abnormal Psychology, 102,* 282–287.

Shah, J., & Higgins, E. T. (1997a). *Emotional evaluations of self and other attitude objects: Distinct sensitivities from regulatory focus.* Unpublished manuscript.

Shah, J., & Higgins, E. T. (1997b). Expectancy × Value effects: Regulatory focus as determinant of magnitude and direction. *Journal of Personality and Social Psychology, 73,* 447–458.

Shah, J., Higgins, E. T., & Friedman, R. (1998). Performance incentives and means: How regulatory focus influences goal attainment. *Journal of Personality and Social Psychology, 74,* 285–293.

Sherif, M., & Hovland, C. I. (1961). *Social judgment: Assimilation and contrast effects in communications.* New Haven, CT: Yale University Press.

Sherif, M., & Sherif, C. W. (1964). *Reference groups.* New York: Harper.

Skinner, B. F. (1938). *The behavior of organisms: An experimental analysis.* New York: Appleton-Century-Crofts.

Snyder, M. (1984). When belief creates reality. In L. Berkowitz (Ed.), *Advances in experimental social psychology* (Vol. 18, pp. 248–306). New York: Academic Press.

Sorrentino, R. M., & Short, J. C. (1986). Uncertainty orientation, motivation, and cognition. In R. M. Sorrentino & E. T. Higgins (Eds.), *Handbook of motivation and cognition: Foundations of social behavior* (Vol. 1, pp. 379–403). New York: Guilford Press.

Stein, N. L., & Jewett, J. L. (1982). A conceptual analysis of the meaning of negative emotions: Implications for a theory of development. In C. E. Izard (Ed.), *Measuring emotions in infants and children* (pp. 401–443). New York: Cambridge University Press.

Strauman, T. J. (1989). Self-discrepancies in clinical depression and social phobia: Cognitive structures that underlie emotional disorders? *Journal of Abnormal Psychology, 98,* 14–22.

Strauman, T. J. (1990). Self-guides and emotionally significant childhood memories: A study of retrieval efficiency and incidental negative emotional content. *Journal of Personality and Social Psychology, 59,* 869–880.

Strauman, T. J., & Higgins, E. T. (1987). Automatic activation of self-discrepancies and emotional syndromes: When cognitive structures influence affect. *Journal of Personalty and Social Psychology, 53,* 1001–1014.

Strauman, T. J., & Higgins, E. T. (1988). Self-discrepancies as predictors of vulnerability to distinct syndromes of chronic emotional distress. *Journal of Personality, 56,* 685–707.

Sullivan, H. S. (1953). *The collected works of Harry Stack Sullivan, Vol. 1: The interpersonal theory of psychiatry* (H. S. Perry & M. L. Gawel, Eds.). New York: Norton.

Tanner, W. P., Jr., & Swets, J. A. (1954). A decision-making theory of visual detection. *Psychological Review, 61,* 401–409.

Thibault, J., & Kelley, H. H. (1959). *The social psychology of groups.* New York: Wiley.

Thorndike, E. L. (1911). *Animal intelligence.* New York: Macmillan.

Thorndike, E. L. (1935). *The psychology of wants, interests, and attitudes.* New York: Appleton-Century-Crofts.

Tolman, E. C. (1932). *Purposive behavior in animals and men.* New York: Appleton-Century-Crofts.

Tolman, E. C. (1955). Principles of performance. *Psychological Review, 62,* 315–326.

Trope, Y., & Liberman, A. (1996). Social hypothesis testing: Cognitive and motivational mechanisms. In E. T. Higgins & A. W. Kruglanski (Eds.), *Social psychology: Handbook of basic principles* (pp. 239–270). New York: Guilford Press.

Tversky, A., & Kahneman, D. (1974). Judgment under uncertainty: Heuristics and biases. *Science, 85,* 1124–1131.

von Bertalanffy, L. (1968). *General systems theory.* New York: Braziller.

Vroom, V. H. (1964). *Work and motivation.* New York: Wiley.

Weiner, B., Frieze, I., Kukla, A., Reed, L., Rest, S., & Rosenbaum, R. M. (1971). Perceiving the causes of success and failure. In E. E. Jones. D. E. Kanouse, H. H. Kelley, R. E. Nisbett, S. Valins, & B. Weiner (Eds.), *Attribution: Perceiving the causes of behavior* (pp. 95–120). Morristown, NJ: General Learning Press.

Wicker, F. W., Wiehe, J. A., Hagen, A. S., & Brown, G. (1994). From wishing to intending: Differences in salience of positive versus negative consequences. *Journal of Personality, 62,* 347–368.

Wiener, N. (1948). *Cybernetics: Control and communication in the animal and the machine.* Cambridge, MA: MIT Press.

Wierzbicka, A. (1972). *Semantic primitives.* Frankfurt, Germany: Athenaum.

Origins and Functions of Positive and Negative Affect: A Control-Process View

Charles S. Carver • Department of Psychology, University of Miami

Michael F. Scheier • Carnegie Mellon University

Editors' Notes

A control theory perspective is taken to consider how affect arises in the process of self-regulation. The basic construct of control theory is the discrepancy-reducing feedback loop. A perceived current state is compared to a reference value, such as a goal, and when a discrepancy is perceived between the current state and the reference value, a behavior is performed to reduce the discrepancy. Thus, feedback that a discrepancy exists between a current state and a desired end-state motivates discrepancy-reducing actions. In their approach to self-regulation, the authors supplement control theory with an expectancy-assessment process that is separate from the discrepancy-reduction process. In general, discrepancy-reducing attempts will be reduced to the extent that a person does not expect such attempts to be successful. A meta-monitoring system that checks the rate of discrepancy-reduction over time is proposed. It is postulated that feedback about the rate of discrepancy reduction rather than about the magnitude of discrepancy per se underlies people's affective experiences.

Discussion Questions

1. According to control theory, what processes underlie self-regulation?
2. What is meta-monitoring and what is its role in people's affective experiences?

Authors' Abstract

The question of how affect arises and what affect indicates is examined from a feedback-based viewpoint on self-regulation. Using the analogy of action control as the attempt to diminish distance to a goal, a second feedback system is postulated that senses and regulates the rate at which the action-guiding system is functioning. This second system is seen as responsible for affect. Implications of these assertions and issues that arise from them are addressed in the remainder of the article. Several issues relate to the emotion model itself; others concern the relation between negative emotion and disengagement from goals. Relations to 3 other emotion theories are also addressed. The authors conclude that this view on affect is a useful supplement to other theories and that the concept of emotion is easily assimilated to feedback models of self-regulation.

This article addresses the nature of certain aspects of emotion, as viewed from a control-theory perspective on behavior. This perspective focuses on the feedback-based processes through which people self-regulate their actions to minimize discrepancies between actual acts and desired or intended acts. In this article we consider what such a viewpoint on behavior may say about the nature of emotion (see also Simon, 1967). More specifically, we examine positive and negative affect, present a theory of how these feelings may arise, and consider how they function in human self-regulation.

We begin with a brief outline of a control-theory view on the organization of behavior, to provide a context for what follows.

Self-Regulation of Behavior

Control Processes and Self-Regulation

We construe intentional behavior as reflecting a process of feedback control (see, e.g., Carver, 1979; Carver & Scheier, 1981, 1982a, 1986a, in press; MacKay, 1963, 1966; Norman, 1981; Powers, 1973). When people move (physically or psychologically) toward goals, they manifest the functions of a negative (discrepancy reducing) feedback loop (see Figure 1). That is, people periodically note the qualities they are expressing in their behavior (an input function). They compare these perceptions with salient reference values—whatever goals are temporarily being used to guide behavior (a comparison process inherent in all feedback systems).[1] If the comparisons indicate discrepancies between reference value and present

state (i.e., between intended and actual qualities of behavior), people adjust behavior (the output function) so that it more closely approximates the reference value.

Taken as an organized system, these component functions act to "control" the quality that is sensed as input to the system. That is, when a feedback loop is functioning properly, it induces the sensed quality closer to the reference value. In terms of human behavior, the exercise of feedback control means that the person acts to minimize any discernible discrepancy between current actions and the behavioral reference value. To put it more simply, when people pay attention to what they are doing, they usually do what they intend to do, relatively accurately and thoroughly.

This brief description obviously omits a great deal that is important, and space limitations preclude treatment of all of the issues relevant to conceptualizing behavior. Two more sets of theoretical principles are needed, however, for us to address emotion and its role in self-regulation.

---

[1] A brief comment on our use of terms such as *reference value, standard,* and *goal*: We use these terms interchangeably here, despite the fact that they have slightly different connotations to many people. Reference values are qualities that are taken as guides, qualities to be approximated in one's actions. Although the word *standard* is often taken as implying social definitions of appropriateness, that is not meant here (see Carver & Scheier, 1985, for detail). The term *goal* often evokes an image of a "final state," but we do not mean to imply a static, statelike quality. People have many goals of continuous action—for example, the goal of being engaged in sailing or skiing or the goal of having a successful career. Indeed, most goals underlying behavior would seem to be of this sort. This emphasis on dynamic goals in self-regulation will become more obvious later in the article.

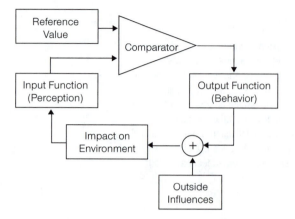

FIGURE 1 ■ Schematic depiction of a feedback loop, the basic unit of cybernetic control. (In such a loop a sensed value is compared to a reference value or standard, and adjustments are made, if necessary, to shift the sensed value in the direction of the standard.)

Hierarchical Organization of Behavior

One of these principles is the notion that behavior is organized hierarchically (e.g., Broadbent, 1977; Dawkins, 1976; Gallistel, 1980; Martin & Tesser, in press; Ortony, Clore, & Collins, 1988; Powers, 1973; Vallacher & Wegner, 1985, 1987). In control-process terms, the output of a superordinate feedback system (the system directing behavior at the level of present current concern—cf. Klinger, 1975; Shallice, 1978) is the resetting of reference values at the next lower level of abstraction (Figure 2). Powers (1973) argued that an identity between output at one level and resetting of standards at the next lower level is maintained from the level that is presently superordinate, down to the level of setting reference values for muscle tensions. Thus, the hierarchy creates the physical execution of whatever action is taking place.

We have adopted Powers's position as a conceptual heuristic, focusing on its implications at high levels of abstraction, the levels of our own interest (see Marken, 1986, and Rosenbaum, 1987, regarding the usefulness of similar notions at lower levels). The hierarchical organization in Figure 2 shows three high levels of control. At the highest level shown (labeled *system concepts*) are such values as the global sense of idealized self. Although self is not the only reference value at this level, it provides what may be the most intuitive illustration of the type of quality that occurs here,

and it may be the most frequently used value at this level. Other possibilities include the idealized sense of a relationship or of a society.

Reference values at this level are abstract and difficult to define. How do people minimize discrepancies between their behavior and such abstract qualities? What behavioral outputs are involved? The answer suggested by Powers (1973) is that the behavioral output of this high-order system consists of providing reference values at the next lower level, which he termed the level of *principle* control. Thus, people act to "be" who they think they want (or ought) to be by adopting any of the guiding principles that are implied by the idealized self to which they aspire. (The constituents of the idealized self to which the person aspires—and what principles are thereby implied—obviously will differ from person to person.)

Principles begin to provide some form for behavior. Principles are probably the most abstract aspects of behavior that have names in everyday language—for example, honesty, responsibility, and expedience. Principles are not specifications of acts but of qualities that can be manifest in many acts. People do not just go out and "do" honesty, or responsibility, or thrift. Rather, people manifest any one (or more) of these qualities while doing more concrete activities.

The concrete activities are termed *programs* (cf. Schank & Abelson's, 1977, discussion of scripts). Principles influence the program level by influencing what programs occur as potential reference values and by influencing choices made within programs. Programs of action are the sorts of activities that most people recognize more clearly as "behavior," although even programs are still relatively abstract. Going to the store, cooking dinner, writing a report—all these are programs.

Programs, in turn, are made up of movement *sequences*. One difference between programs and sequences is that programs involve choice points at which decisions must be made (ranging from trivial to important), whereas the constituents of a sequence are executed all-at-a-piece. When an action becomes sufficiently well learned that its enactment (once begun) is automatic rather than effortful (e.g., Shiffrin & Schneider, 1977), it can be thought of as having become a sequence rather than a program.

An important implication of the notion of hierarchical organization is that the higher one goes into this organization, the more fundamental to the

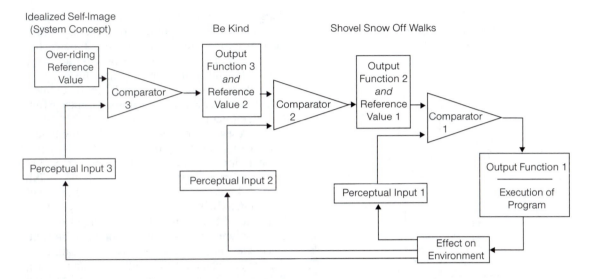

Idealized Self-Image (System Concept) | Be Kind | Shovel Snow Off Walks

FIGURE 2 ■ Three-level hierarchy of feedback loops showing the top three levels of control in the model proposed by Powers (1973) and illustrating the kinds of content that reference values at these three levels can assume. (This diagram portrays the behavior of someone who is presently attempting to conform to his ideal self-image, by using the principle of kindness to guide his actions, a principle that presently is being manifest through the program of shoveling snow from a neighbor's sidewalk.)

overriding sense of self are the qualities encountered. A second, related implication is that the importance of a reference value at a low level is at least partly a product of the degree to which its attainment contributes to success in the attempt to reduce discrepancies at higher levels.

A last point concerning the hierarchical model is that self-regulation does not inevitably require engaging the full hierarchy from the tap downward. We tentatively assume that whatever level of the hierarchy is temporarily focal is functionally superordinate at that moment, with self-regulation at any level higher suspended until attention is redirected toward reference values at the higher level. In practice, much of human behavior is probably self-regulated at the program level, with little or no consideration of values higher than that.

Difficulty, Disengagement, and Withdrawal

A final set of theoretical principles concerns the met that people are not always successful in attaining their goals. Sometimes the physical setting precludes intended acts. Sometimes personal inadequacies prevent people from accomplishing what they set out to do. Regardless of the source of the impediment, and regardless of the level of

abstraction at which it occurs (e.g., principle, program), there must be a way to construe the fact that people sometimes put aside their goals, aspirations, and intentions.

ASSESSING EXPECTANCIES

We believe that behavior proceeds smoothly until and unless people encounter impediments (Figure 3). When people encounter enough difficulty to disrupt their efforts, we assume that they step outside the behavioral stream momentarily and assess the likelihood that the desired outcome will occur, given further effort. Potential impediments to action that come to mind before action begins presumably act the same in this respect as do those confronted during the action.

This sequence of interruption and expectancy assessment can be initiated in several ways. The simplest initiator is frustration—existence of an obstacle to goal attainment, either external (impediments or constraints) or internal (deficits of skill, knowledge, or effort). Another major class of interrupters is anxiety, which is aroused in circumstances in which a contemplated or ongoing action is in some way threatening. Although other

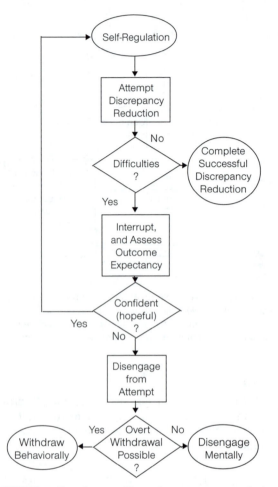

FIGURE 3 ■ Flow diagram of the various consequences that can follow when a person attempts to match his or her behavior to a standard of comparison. (Although self-regulation often proceeds unimpeded, discrepancy reduction efforts may be interrupted if difficulties or impediments are encountered, or anticipated. What follows this interruption is determined by the person's expectations about whether continued efforts will promote a good outcome.)

interrupters are certainly possible, most represent conditions that hamper or interfere with goal attainment.

The process of assessing outcome expectancy (whatever the interruptor) may make use of a wide variety of information pertaining to the situation and to internal qualities such as skill, anticipated effort, and available response options (cf. Lazarus, 1966). In many cases, however, expectancy assessment relies quite heavily on memories of prior experiences. Thus, a preexisting sense of confi-

dence or doubt with respect to some activity can be a particularly important determinant of situational expectancies. If the expectancies that emerge from this assessment process are sufficiently favorable, the person renews his or her efforts. If the expectancies are sufficiently unfavorable, however, the person begins to disengage from the attempt at goal attainment.

Our research on this rough dichotomy among responses to adversity occurred in the context of our explorations of the effects of self-directed attention (Carver, Blaney, & Scheier, 1979a, 1979b; Carver, Peterson, Follansbee, & Scheier, 1983; Carver & Scheier, 1981; Scheier & Carver, 1982). This line of thought has also been extended to certain problems in self-management, including both test anxiety and social anxiety (Carver et al., 1983; Carver & Scheier, 1984, 1986a, 1986b; Carver, Scheier, & Klahr, 1987; see also Burgio, Merluzzi, & Pryor, 1986; Galassi, Frierson, & Sharer, 1981; Rich & Woolever, 1988; Schlenker & Leary, 1982). These discussions all emphasize the idea that expectancies about one's eventual outcome are an important determinant of whether the person responds to adversity by continuing to exert effort at goal attainment or, instead, by disengaging from the attempt. This analysis has a good deal in common with other expectancy models of behavior (e.g., Abramson, Seligman, & Teasdale, 1978; Bandura, 1977, 1986; Kanfer & Hagerman, 1981, 1985; Rotter, 1954; Wortman & Brehm, 1975), although there are also differences among theories (for more detail, see Scheier & Carver, 1988).

EXPECTANCIES AND AFFECT

We have assumed for some time that the behavioral consequences of divergent outcome expectancies are paralleled by differences in affective experience (Carver, 1979), and research evidence tends to support this position (Carver & Scheier, 1982b; Andersen & Lyon, 1987; see also Weiner, 1982). When expectancies are favorable, people tend to have positive feelings, which are variously experienced as enthusiasm, hope, excitement, joy, or elation (cf. Stotland, 1969). When expectancies are unfavorable, people have negative feelings-anxiety, dysphoria, or despair. The specific tone of these feelings varies (in part) with the basis for the expectancies (Scheier & Carver, 1988). The latter is a theme that has been developed in much greater detail by Weiner (1982).

Limitation and Challenge

The preceding outline of the relations among expectancies, emotion, and behavior seems intuitively sensible to us. Making behavioral predictions from this aspect of the model has required (and continues to require) nothing more than the ideas in the preceding section. This outline has something of an ad hoc flavor to it, however, with a number of questions being left unasked and thus unanswered.

A fundamental question that is ignored in the preceding outline is how good and bad feelings come to arise while the person is engaged in goal-directed action. We are certainly not unique in having failed to ask this question. Indeed, it is remarkable how rarely anyone ever asks where affect comes from. Even information-processing theories touching on affect (which one might expect to be particularly attuned to this question) typically discuss only what happens once affect is already present. Discussions focus on the idea that affect is information that takes up space in working memory (Hamilton, 1983), information that may serve particularly important purposes in regulating motivation (Simon, 1967), and information that is encoded in long-term memory in much the same way as other information (Bower & Cohen, 1982). But where does it come from?

In the next section we examine this question. We do so by reconsidering, in somewhat different terms, the set of events we have just described. Nothing in the next section contradicts what we have already said, but our discussion takes a form that differs considerably from that of the preceding section.

A More Elaborated View: Meta-Monitoring and Emotion

We have characterized people's conscious self-regulation as a process of monitoring their present actions and comparing the qualities that they perceive therein with the reference values that presently are salient, making adjustments as necessary to render discrepancies minimal. In what follows, we will use the term *monitoring* to refer to this feedback process. As indicated earlier, we see this monitoring loop as fundamental to the control of intentional behavior.

We suggest, however, that there is also a sec-ond feedback process that (in a sense) builds on this one, in a fashion that is orthogonal to the hierarchical organization discussed earlier. This second function operates simultaneously with the monitoring function and in parallel to it, whenever monitoring is going on. The second feedback system serves what we will term a *meta-monitoring* function.

Discrepancy Reduction and Rate of Reduction

The most intuitive way to begin in describing this meta-monitoring function is to say that the meta loop is checking on how well the action loop is doing at reducing the behavioral discrepancies that the action loop is monitoring. More concretely, we propose that the perceptual input for the meta-monitoring loop is a representation of the *rate of discrepancy reduction in the behavioral (monitoring) system over time*. What is important to the meta loop is not merely whether discrepancies are being reduced at the level of the action leap, but how rapidly they are being reduced. If they are being reduced rapidly, the action loop's progress toward its goal (as perceived by the meta loop) is high. If they are being reduced slowly, the action leap's progress is lower. If they are not being reduced at all, the action loop's progress is zero. Any time discrepancies are enlarging at the level of action monitoring of course, the action loop's progress is inverse.[2]

Although it may be somewhat less intuitive than the foregoing, we find an analogy useful in describing the functioning of these two systems, an analogy that may also have more literal implications. Because action implies change between states, consider behavior to be analogous to distance (construed as a vector, because perception of one's action incorporates both the difference between successive states and also the direction of the difference). If the monitoring loop deals with distance and if (as we just asserted) the meta loop assesses the rate of progress of the monitoring loop, then the meta loop is dealing with the psychological equivalent of velocity (also directional). In mathematical terms, velocity is the first derivative of distance over time. To the extent that this physi-

---

[2]For convenience, we will treat as equivalent phrases such as *progress of the action loop* and *rate of discrepancy reduction in the action loop*.

cal analogy is meaningful, the perceptual input to the meta loop we are postulating presumably is the first derivative over time of the input information used by the action loop.

We propose that the meta-monitoring process functions as a feedback loop. It thus involves more than the mere sensing of the rate of discrepancy reduction in the action loop. This sensing constitutes an input function, but no more. As in any feedback system, this input is compared against a reference value (cf. Frijda, 1986, 1988). In this case, the reference value is an acceptable or desired rate of behavioral discrepancy reduction. As in other feedback systems, the comparison determines whether there is a discrepancy or deviation from the standard. If there is, an output function is engaged to reduce the discrepancy.

We suggest that the outcome of the comparison process that lies at the heart of this loop is manifest phenomenologically in two forms. The first is a hazy and nonverbal sense of outcome expectancy. The second is affect, a feeling quality, a sense of positiveness or negativeness.

When sensed progress in the action loop conforms to the desired rate of progress, the meta-monitoring system accordingly registers no discrepancy (see Table 1, Example 1). Given an absence of discrepancy at the meta level, affect is neutral. When the action loop is making continuous, steady progress toward reducing its own discrepancy, but its rate of discrepancy reduction is slower than the meta-monitoring system's reference value, a discrepancy exists for the meta loop (Table 1, Example 2). The result in this case should be a degree of doubt and negative affect, proportional to the size of this meta-level discrepancy When the rate of discrepancy reduction in the action loop is higher than the meta loop's reference

value (Table 1, Example 3), there is a positive discrepancy at the meta loop, an overshoot of the reference value that is reflected in confidence and in positive feelings.

It is clear that the two systems under discussion (monitoring and meta-monitoring) are related to each other, but we argue that only one of them has implications for affect. In all three cases shown in Table 1, the action loop is successfully reducing discrepancies. The fact that it is doing so does not, however, determine affect. Affect may be neutral, it may be positive, or it may even be negative (Examples 1, 2, and 3, respectively), depending on the adequacy of the *rate* of discrepancy reduction. Assessing the adequacy of the rate of operation of one system implies the use of a second system.

It is also important to note that the size of the discrepancy confronted by the action loop at any given point does not play an important role in the perceptual input to the meta loop. A large discrepancy—even a *very* large discrepancy—perceived at the level of the action loop can be associated with perceptions of either abundant or insufficient progress. This same discrepancy thus can be associated with either favorable or unfavorable expectancies and with either positive or negative affect. What matters with respect to the meta-monitoring system is solely whether the perceived *rate of progress* in the action system is adequate.

The same point can also be made of cases in which the behavioral discrepancy is relatively small. If the meta-monitoring system senses that there is an abundant rate of change toward discrepancy elimination, there should be positive affect and confidence. If it senses an inadequate rate of change, there should be negative affect and doubt.

Thus, ironically, it should be possible for a person who has a large discrepancy at the action loop

TABLE 1. Three Conditions of Behavior Over Time, How They Would be Construed at the Level of the Action Loop, How They Would Be Construed at the Level of the Meta-Monitoring Loop, and the Affect That Theoretically Would Be Experienced

Depiction of behavior	Action construal	Meta-loop construal	Affect
1. Progress toward goal, at a rate equal to the standard	Discrepancy reduction	No discrepancy	None
2. Progress toward goal, at a rate lower than the standard	Discrepancy reduction	Discrepancy	Negative
3. Progress toward goal, at a rate higher than the standard	Discrepancy reduction	Positive discrepancy	Positive

to feel more positively than a person who has a small discrepancy at the action loop, if the first person is perceiving a more acceptable rate of progress than the second person. In terms of the physical analogy, the first person is more distant from the goal, but is moving toward it with a higher velocity.

Just as the monitoring of action apparently can take any of several levels in a hierarchy of behavioral control as superordinate, so should the meta system be able to function at any of several levels. It seems likely, however, that discrepancies noted by the meta system have greater emotional impact when they concern a central element of self than when they bear only on a more peripheral goal (a program or a sequence of action). Sometimes a task failure has a big impact on one's feelings, sometimes not (cf. Dweck & Elliott, 1983; Dweck & Leggett, 1988; Elliott & Dweck, 1988; Hyland, 1987; Srull & Wyer, 1986). The difference between these cases would seem to be the level of abstraction at which the person is focusing. The consequences of meta-monitoring are more intense, or more impactful, at higher levels than at lower levels of the hierarchy (see also Frijda, 1988).

If the meta loop is truly a bidirectional feedback system, it follows that an overshoot of the reference value should lead to a self-corrective attempt to return to the reference value. To put it more concretely, this view argues that people who have exceeded the desired rate of progress are likely to slow their subsequent efforts. They are likely to coast for a while. The phenomenological result of this would be that the positive affect is not sustained for long.

It is important to recognize that we are not suggesting that affect is the controlled quality in this loop, but rate. Positive feelings reflect a positive discrepancy, which is good. To a system whose goal is controlling sensed rate, however, a discrepancy is a discrepancy and any sensed discrepancy should be reduced.

The existence of a natural tendency that has the effect of causing positive affect to be short-lived seems, at first glance, highly improbable. A plausible basis for such a tendency can be seen, however, in the idea that human behavior is hierarchically organized and involves multiple current concerns. That is, people typically are working toward several goals more or less simultaneously, and many lower level efforts contribute to minimizing discrepancies at high levels. To the extent that movement toward goal attainment is more rapid than expected in one domain, it permits the person to shift attention and effort toward goal strivings in another domain, at no cost. To continue the unnecessarily rapid pace in the first domain might increase positive affect with respect to that activity, but by diverting efforts from other goals, that action may create the potential for negative affect in other domains.

Changes in Rate and the Abruptness of Change

Although we have limited ourselves thus far to addressing various rates of progress toward action goals, it should be obvious that the rate of discrepancy reduction at the action loop can change. Changes in rate at the action loop are subjectively manifest, not as affect but as *change* of affect. Increases in rate are reflected in shifts toward more positive feelings, with the actual experience depending on the initial and final rates. When the change is from a rate far below the meta standard to a rate closer to the standard but still below it, affect should change from more negative to less negative. If the change is instead to a value that exceeds the meta standard, affect should change from negative to positive.

In the same manner, downward changes in sensed rate at the action loop are also reflected in affective shifts, with the quality of the experience again depending on the initial and final rates. When the change is from a rate that exceeds the meta standard to a rate below the standard, the affective change should be from positive to negative. When the change is from just below the standard to far below the standard, the affective change should be from mildly negative to very negative.

Shifts in rate of progress at the action loop can be gradual, or they can be more abrupt. The more abrupt an increase in the action loop's progress, the more the subjective experience incorporates a rush of exhilaration, reflecting the contrast between the more negative feelings and the more positive feelings (cf. the description of "sentimentality" by Frijda, 1988, p. 350). The more abrupt a slowing of the action loop's progress, the more the subjective experience should incorporate the well-known sinking feeling (de-exhilaration?) that reflects the contrast when feelings suddenly shift in a negative direction. Indeed, it seems reasonable to suggest that a discernible shift toward more negative feelings is often precisely the experience that causes people to interrupt ongoing action and consciously evaluate the probability of their eventual success.

We suggested earlier that the quality the meta loop senses as its input is analogous to the physical quality of velocity. Let us carry this analogy one step further. What we are addressing now is not velocity but change in velocity—acceleration. Acceleration is the second derivative of distance over time. Given that People apparently are equipped to sense these experiences, the analogy seems to suggest that some neural processor is computing a second derivative over time of the information input to the action loop. Does this imply the need to postulate a third layer of feedback control (complete with reference value and comparator)? Not necessarily. It is possible to sense a quality that is not involved in a feedback loop. In part because it is difficult for us to know what might be the implications of such a third layer of control, we are hesitant at this stage to assume its existence.

With respect to a final point, however, we are more confident. In the same way that distance and velocity are independent of each other, both are independent of acceleration. (An object moving 20 ft per second can be accelerating, decelerating, or its velocity can be constant; the same is true of an object moving 80 ft per second.) We suggest that the same independence exists on the other side of the analogy. We argued earlier that affect experienced is independent of the degree of discrepancy at the action level (Table 1). In the same fashion, we argue that the rush associated with acceleration is independent of the size of the discrepancy at the action level and also independent of the rate of discrepancy reduction at the action level.

As an example, a person with a large discrepancy at the action level will have positive affect if the rate of discrepancy reduction is greater than needed. This positive affect will be free of exhilaration if the rate of discrepancy reduction is constant. If the rate has suddenly shifted upward (to the same ending value), the positive feelings will be accompanied by a sense of exhilaration. [. . .]

Issues and Questions Within the Model

The preceding portrayal of what we have termed *meta-monitoring* raises a number of issues and

questions. Some of them pertain directly to the ideas that we have just outlined concerning the origins of positive and negative feelings. Others pertain more generally to the fit between this theory and other aspects of a control-process approach to behavioral self-regulation. Yet others pertain to relationships between this and other theories on emotion. These issues are addressed in the next three sections. We begin with issues that pertain directly to the emotion theory itself.

Reference Values Used in Meta-Monitoring

One important question is what reference value is being used by the meta-monitoring system. We assume that this system is capable of using widely varying definitions of adequate progress for the action loop. Sometimes the reference value is imposed from outside (as in tenure review decisions), sometimes it is self-imposed (as in someone who has a personal timetable for career development), and sometimes it derives from social comparison (as when people are in competition with each other). Sometimes the reference value is very demanding, sometimes it is less so.

As an example in which the meta standard is both stringent and externally imposed, consider the requirements of degree programs in medical or law school. In such cases, even continuous progress in an absolute sense (i.e., successful mastery of required material) is adequate only if it occurs at or above the rate required by the degree program. Thus, as the person attempts to attain the action goal of becoming a physician or a lawyer, the reference value for meta-monitoring will be a relatively stringent one.

How stringent a standard is used at the meta level has straightforward implications for the person's emotional life. If the pace of progress used as a reference point is too high, it will rarely be matched, even if (objectively) the person's rate of progress is extraordinarily high. In such a case, the person will experience negative affect often and positive affect rarely. If the pace of progress used as a reference point is low, the person's rate of behavioral discrepancy reduction will more frequently exceed it. In this case, the person will experience positive affect more often and negative affect more rarely.

What variables influence the stringency of the meta level standard being used? One important determinant is the extent to which there is time pressure on the activity being regulated, which varies greatly from one activity to another. Some actions are clearly time dependent ("Have that report on my desk by 5 o'clock"), others are more vaguely so (it's about the time of year to fertilize the lawn), and the time dependency is even hazier for others (I want to go to China some day; I'd like to have a boat before I get too old to enjoy it). When an activity has demanding time constraints, the meta-level reference value used necessarily is stringent. When there is a relative lack of time pressure, a relatively lax standard is more likely to be used.

Although time dependence is dearest in situations that require a rapid pace, there also appears to be a second sort of time dependence. This occurs for behavioral activities that people wish to have completed but have no desire to do (a common view of chores). Such goals are highly time dependent, in the sense that people wish their attainment to be instantaneous. Given this, the meta-level reference value must necessarily be at a very high level. Because the rate of progress therefore cannot meet the standard, positive affect is nearly impossible and aversiveness is almost inevitable when the activity is being engaged in. (On the other hand, the intensity of this affect is proportional to the importance of the activity, which is often relatively low.) This set of relations would seem to define the experience of drudgery.

Changing Meta-Level Standards

As noted in the preceding section, reference values for the meta loop differ across people and across categories of behavior. Reference values at the meta level can also shift as a result of time and experience (see also Lord & Hanges, 1987). To put it differently, as people accumulate more experience in a given domain, adjustments can occur in the pacing that they expect and demand of their efforts.

Sometimes the adjustment is downward. For example, a researcher experiencing difficulty in his attempt to be as productive as his colleagues may gradually adopt less stringent standards of pacing. One consequence of this is a more favorable balance of positive to negative affect across time (cf. Linsenmeier & Brickman, 1980). In other cases, the adjustment is upward. A person who gains work-related skills may undertake greater challenges, requiring quicker handling of each action unit. Upward adjustment has the side effect of decreasing the potential for positive affect and increasing the potential for negative affect.

This adjusting of meta-level reference values over the course of experience looks suspiciously like a self-corrective feedback process in its own right, as the person reacts to insufficient challenge by taking on a more demanding pace, and reacts to too much challenge by scaling back the criterion.[3] If a feedback process is responsible for changing standards at the meta level (or contributes to such changes), it is much slower acting than are those that are the focus of this article. Shifting the reference value downward is not the immediate response when the person has trouble keeping up with a demanding pace. First the person tries harder to keep up. Only more gradually, if the person cannot keep up, does the meta standard shift to accommodate. Similarly, an upward shift is not the immediate response when the person's rate of discrepancy reduction exceeds the standard. The more typical response is to coast for a while. Only when the overshoot is frequent does the standard shift to accommodate.

The idea that these changes are produced by a slow-acting feedback system may help to account for why it can be so difficult to shift meta standards voluntarily. That is, one can make a verbal change easily ("Stop being so demanding of yourself, and be more satisfied with what you are accomplishing"), but this sort of self-verbalization rarely takes effect immediately. If a true shift in standard relies on a slow-acting feedback loop, that would account for why subjective experience tends to lag behind the self-instruction.

It is of some interest that these patterns of shift in reference value (and the concomitant effects on affect) imply a mechanism within the organism that functions in such a way as to prevent the too-frequent occurrence of positive feeling, as well as the too-frequent occurrence of negative feeling. That is, the (bidirectional) shifting of the rate cri-

---

[3]A possibility that may be worth considering is that this shift of meta standard reflects the long-term consequences of the *opponent process* discussed by Solomon (1980). Solomon proposed the existence of a system that acts to dampen emotional reactions, in two senses: In the short term, the opponent process causes the affect evoked by a given event to return to neutral. In the longer term (after repeated experiences of similar events), the event comes to elicit less of an emotional response than it did at first. This latter effect seems comparable in some ways to the idea that there has been a shift in meta standard.

terion over time would tend to control pacing of behavior in such a way that affect continues to vary in both directions around neutral. We earlier suggested that the meta system does not function to maximize positive affect, in the same manner, an arrangement for changing meta-level reference values such as we are suggesting here would not work toward maximization of pleasure and minimization of pain. Rather, the affective consequence would be that the person experiences more or less the same range of variation in his or her affective experience over extended periods of time.

Time Frames for Input to Meta-Monitoring

Another question to be raised about the model concerns the span, of time over which the action loop's progress at discrepancy reduction is processed to form a perceptual input (a sensed rate) for the meta system. The time period across which information is merged may be brief or it may be quite long.[4] There seems to be nothing inherent in the meta-monitoring process per se that dictates whether it focuses on a short or a long time period. Whether input information is merged over a short or a long time period, however, can have important implications for the subjective experiences that result.

Consider the case of a person whose actions create gradual but erratic progress toward some goal (see Figure 4). If the input function to this person's meta-monitoring loop assesses rate of discrepancy reduction over a very short time frame, the person will be intermittently happy (periods A and C) and dysphoric (periods B and D). That is, the rate of progress exceeds the standard during

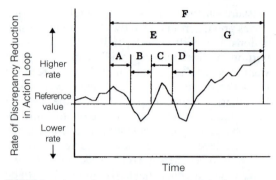

FIGURE 4 ■ Assessing rate of discrepancy reduction across different lengths of time can produce different patterns of emotional experience. (If assessment bears on brief time spans [periods A, B, C, and D], the experience is alternately positive feelings [A and C] versus negative feelings [B and D]. If assessed rate of discrepancy reduction is merged across a longer interval [E], experienced mood does not fluctuate. Assessing across too long a period, however [F], can be misleading because it can obscure meaningful changes that occur over a shorter term [G, compared with E].)

periods A and C (thus yielding positive affect) but falls short of the standard during period B and most of period D (thus yielding negative affect). If the person takes a longer view on the same set of events (i.e., merges across all of period E), the frequent deviations upward and downward from the standard will be blurred (in effect, averaged) in the derivation of perceptual input for the meta system. In the general case, this will produce affect (and a concomitant sense of expectancy) that is both more stable and more moderated. In the specific case of period E, the affect experienced will be near neutral, because the upward and downward deviations cancel each other out.

This reasoning might seem to argue that it is desirable to take the broader view of events. There is, however, a potential disadvantage of deriving input through the broader view. Merging data over a very long period can result in insensitivity to what are actually meaningful changes in the rate of discrepancy reduction at the action loop. Period G reflects considerably faster progress than took place across period E, but awareness of that shift in rate will be blunted if the input is merged across period F. Thus, taking too long a view in creating input for the meta system can be as bad as taking too short a view.

This general line of reasoning suggests a possible process basis for the fact that people seem

---

[4]We should distinguish between the matter under discussion here and other issues embedded in a growing literature on goal setting. One issue in goal setting concerns whether goals are close or distant in time (see Kirschenbaum, 1985, for a discussion of this and other variables). How distant a goal is in time, although important in its own right, is conceptually distinct from what we are discussing here. In general, assessment of progress toward any goal—whether close or distant—may still be made with respect to either a long or a short span of time and effort. Of course, with goals that are very close in time, one's freedom to assess over long time spans diminishes. Nor are we discussing the frequency with which a person "samples" perceptual input. That can also vary, from sampling often to sampling rarely. What is presently under discussion is the breadth of time (or the number of discrete bits of information) over which progress is merged to *form* a perceptual input.

naturally to differ in how variable their moods are (e.g., Diener, Larsen, Levine, & Emmons, 1985; Larsen, 1987; Wessman & Ricks, 1966). Perhaps these differences in emotional variability reflect default differences in the time spans merged for input by people's meta-monitoring systems.

Multiple Affects From a Single Event, and the Independence of Positive and Negative Affect

Our theoretical discussion was focused on the existence of one feeling at a time. Affect associated with goal-directed effort need not be purely positive or purely negative, however. A single event may produce both of these feelings, depending on how it is viewed in meta-monitoring.

Sometimes there is more than one view on an event, even with respect to a single goal (cf. Ortony et al., 1988, pp. 51–52). For example, it may happen that the experience of a failure yields the realization of how to attain future success. The failure is displeasing, but the insight is elating. Feelings from the event thus are mixed. Focusing more on the present failure to attain the goal (inadequate progress) will yield a greater sense of negative affect. Focusing more on the insight (progress toward future success) will yield a greater sense of positive affect. Both feelings, however, are produced by different aspects of the same outcome, and both can be felt at once (or as alternating time-shared experiences).

It is perhaps more common that an action or an outcome has implications for two distinct goals. The goals making up the hierarchy of a person's self-definition are not always perfectly compatible with each other, and occasionally two conflicting goals become salient at the same time (see also Emmons, 1986; Van Hook & Higgins, 1988). For example, the goal of career advancement and the goal of spending a lot of time with one's young children may both be desirable, but the 24-hr day imposes limitations on the time available for trying to attain them. Sometimes the actions that permit progress toward one goal (working extra hours at the office) simultaneously interfere with progress toward the other goal (spending time with one's children). To the extent that both goals remain salient, the result is mixed feelings. In this case, however, the two feeling qualities stem from meta-monitoring with respect to each of two distinct goals.

This line of discussion also suggests a perspective on the assertion, made frequently in recent years, that positive and negative affective experiences are not at opposite poles of a continuum but rather are independent (e.g., Diener & Emmons, 1984; Diener & Iran-Nejad, 1986; Warr, Barter, & Brownbridge, 1983; Watson & Tellegen, 1985; Zevon & Tellegen, 1982). This argument usually focuses on the experience of moods, not on the nature of affect.[5] As a statement about mood, the argument means in part that people's moods can incorporate mixed feelings. A mood can be partly good and partly bad, though only rarely are both of these feelings intense at the same time (Diener & Iran-Nejad, 1986).

This argument also means that knowing a person is not depressed does not make it reasonable to infer that the person is happy. Knowing a person is not happy does not make it reasonable to infer that the person feels bad. Sometimes people are affectively neutral. The relative independence of these qualities thus has important methodological implications. To know about both qualities in people's overall feelings, one must assess both (cf. Wortman & Silver, 1989).

Although these two qualities of mood have been observed to vary relatively independently, there has been very little discussion of why this is so. Diener and Iran-Nejad (1986) noted that their subjects sometimes reported moderate amounts of both positive and negative affect but did not speculate why. Watson and Tellegen (1985) noted the possibility that different parts of the brain might be involved in the two affect qualities, but did not address the question of why people might ever experience mixed feelings.

The preceding discussion suggests a very simple explanation for these findings. People often have many goals at once. A person who is making rapid progress on some current concerns and poor

---

[5]Careful examination of Watson and Tellegen's (1985) position on the structure of mood reveals, however, the involvement of another issue that is beyond the scope of this discussion. Specifically, their dimension of negative affect has heavy overtones of anxiety, rather than depression. Higgins (1987) has recently argued for the importance of a distinction between these two emotion qualities, and his argument seems to require distinctions beyond those we are making here (as does the Watson & Tellegen position). This distinction does not, however, detract in any way from the points we are making here. We address the Higgins (1987) model in more detail in a later section of the article.

progress on others should experience positive feelings with respect to the former and negative feelings with respect to the latter. This experience must be common, even in the course of a single day. The diversity of these "progress reports" from the meta-monitoring system should disrupt any inverse correlation between reports of having experienced positive affect and reports of having experienced negative affect in a given time span, particularly if that span is relatively long. As the time span narrows to a given "emotional" event, one would expect the independence of the two affects to diminish, because the person is more likely to be dealing with only one goal (and only one perspective on it) than would otherwise be the case. This is precisely what seems to happen (Diener & Iran-Nejad, 1986). [. . .]

Breadth of Intended Application

A final question to be raised about the model concerns its intended scope. Although most examples in this article come from domains of achievement and instrumental activity, this is not a theory of achievement-related affect. This analysis is intended to apply to all goal-directed behavior, including attempts to attain goals that are amorphous and poorly specified, and goals for which the idea of assessing the rate of progress toward discrepancy reduction might at first glance seem odd.

Human goals such as developing and maintaining a sound relationship, being a good mother or father, dealing honorably and pleasantly with acquaintances, seeing someone you care for be happy and fulfilled, having a full and rich life, and even becoming immersed in the fictional lives portrayed in a novel or film are fully amenable to analysis in these terms. These are all qualities of human experience toward which people attempt to move, goals that evolve or recur across time, as do most goals underlying human action. To the extent that progress toward goals such as these is taken by the person as important, to the extent that people are invested in experiencing these qualities in their lives sooner rather than later, the meta loop produces positive and negative feelings as progress is faster or slower than the standard being used. Sometimes pacing toward such goals matters little, but sometimes it matters a lot. In the latter circumstances, we suggest, these events are capable of producing affect.

Issues Relating Emotion to Disengagement

A second set of issues and questions emerges when one considers our viewpoint on affect in relation to the model of behavior with which we began this article. An important aspect of that model is the idea that if a person's expectancies of goal attainment are sufficiently unfavorable, the person may disengage from active pursuit of the goal (see also Klinger, 1975; Kukla, 1972; Wortman & Brehm, 1975). Thinking about disengagement and about the emotions that often surround it, raises several issues.

Hierarchical Organization Sometimes Creates an Inability to Disengage

One issue stems from the idea that behavior is hierarchically organized and that goals are increasingly important as one moves upward through the hierarchy. Presumably, in most cases disengagement from values low in the hierarchy of control is easy. Indeed, the nature of programs is such that disengagement from efforts at subgoals is quite common, even while the person continues to pursue the overall goal of the program (e.g., if you go to buy something and the store is closed for inventory, you are likely to head for another store rather than give up altogether).

Sometimes, however, lower order goals are more closely linked to values at a higher level. To disengage from lower level goals in this case enlarges discrepancies at higher levels. These higher order qualities are values that are important, even central, to one's life. One cannot disengage from them, or disregard them, or tolerate large discrepancies between those values and currently sensed reality, without substantially reorganizing one's value system (Carver & Scheier, 1986c; Kelly, 1955; Millar, Tesser, & Millar, 1988). In such a case, disengagement from concrete behavioral goals is quite difficult.

Now recall the affective consequences of being in this situation. The desire to disengage was prompted in the first place by unfavorable expectancies for discrepancy reduction. These expectancies are paralleled by negative affect. In this situation, then, the person is experiencing negative feelings (because of an inability to progress toward behavioral discrepancy reduction) and is unable to do anything about the feelings (because of an inability to give up the behavioral reference value). The person simply stews in the feelings that arise from irreconcilable discrepancies (see also Martin & Tesser, in press). In our view, this bind—being unable to let go of something that is unattainable—lies at the heart of exogenous depression (cf. Hyland, 1987; Klinger, 1975; Pyszczynski & Greenberg, 1987). It seems important to us to recognize that this bind often stems from the hierarchical nature of people's goal structures.

Disengagement Requires That There Be an Override Mechanism

The idea that people's efforts give way to disengagement from the goal as expectancies become more negative also raises a second issue. We believe that this characterization is reasonable as part of a model of motivated action. But there is a conceptual discontinuity between this idea and the feedback theories we have espoused regarding behavioral self-regulation and—now—affective experience.

Where in the model of affect is the mechanism to produce disengagement? We portrayed meta-monitoring as a feedback system in which discrepancies (inadequate progress) produce doubt and negative affect. Why should this system (and the corresponding behavioral monitoring system) not continue endlessly to attempt to reduce discrepancies, however ineffectively? Why should the negative affect not simply persist or intensify? What permits the person ever to disengage?

The answer has to be that in normal self-regulation there is an override that is capable of taking precedence over this feedback system and causing disengagement from the reference value currently being used to guide action. In the jargon of the computer field, there must be something akin to a *break* function, which permits ongoing action to be suspended or abandoned altogether. When disengagement is adaptive, it is so because it frees the system to take up other reference values and enables the person to turn to the pursuit of substitute or alternative goals. Such an override function has a critically important role in human self-regulation, inasmuch as there are any number of goals from which people simply must disengage, either temporarily or permanently (see Klinger, 1975, for a broader discussion of commitment to and disengagement from incentives).

Failure to override. Although it seems necessary to assume an override function in adaptive self-regulation, it should also be reemphasized that

disengagement does not always occur, even when the desire to disengage is there. As we noted just earlier, when the goal toward which the person is unable to make progress is central to that person's implicit definition of self, the person for that reason often cannot disengage from it. Disengagement from such a goal means disengagement from oneself. Such an inability to disengage, we said, yields depression.

Consistent with this general line of thought is a variety of evidence that the inability (or unwillingness) to disengage correlates with depression. Depression has been linked to behavioral indicators of failing to disengage mentally from experimentally created failures (Kuhl, 1984, 1985; Pyszczynski & Greenberg, 1985, 1987), to concurrent self-reports of a tendency to perseverate mentally on failure (Carver, La Voie, Kuhl, & Ganellen, 1988), and to ruminative thoughts during forced suspension of personally valued activities (Millar et al., 1988). Mental perseveration among depressed people is not limited to major life goals, but can occur even for transient and relatively trivial intentions (Kuhl & Helle, 1986). Thus, there is evidence that depression is bound up with a general failure to override and disengage. It is not clear why this should be so, but in some sense this failure seems to be at the core of the dynamics of depression (see also Klinger, 1975).

Discussion of this issue also raises a broader question. People clearly vary in how easily they put previously valued goals behind them and move on to new ones. This is true whether the goal has been removed permanently by some external event, for example, the death of a loved one (cf. Wortman & Silver, 1989), or whether the person has simply decided that the previously sought-after goal should no longer be pursued, as happens when people break off close relationships or give up previously desired careers. Some people disengage quickly and move on, experiencing relatively little distress; others take longer to disengage, and consequently (in our view) experience more negative affect. An important question would seem to be what makes people differ from each other in this way. [. . .]

Conclusion

In the preceding pages, we have tried to indicate some of the ways in which a control-process model of the self-regulation of behavior can incorporate assumptions about the nature and functions of certain qualities of emotion. We have attempted to specify how we think these affective qualities are created, and we have pointed to a link between them and another element that is important to self-regulation of action: expectancies. We have also tried to give a sense of how the model as a whole can provide a vehicle for conceptualizing some of the emotional difficulties that people periodically experience.

We obviously have not presented a comprehensive model of the nature of all emotional experiences (cf. Frijda, 1986; Leventhal, 1984). Nor have we catalogued the varieties of emotional experience (cf. Izard, 1977; Ortony et al., 1988; Plutchik, 1980; Tomkins, 1984). Doing so was not our intent. Our goal was less ambitious and more focused: To indicate how the nature of some emotions, as they are presently understood, seems compatible with the logic of control theory.

Our intent throughout this discussion was twofold. First, we wanted to contribute to an emerging line of argument that holds that the domain of human experience reflected in concepts such as *feeling* and *affect* is in no way inimical to information-processing or feedback models of thought and action. We believe that we have been able to address feeling states here in terms that do little or no violence either to feedback concepts or to intuitions and knowledge concerning the subjective experience of feeling states. To the extent we have done this successfully, our discussion contributes to this line of argument.

We have not, however, been entirely blind to broader concerns. To the contrary, we believe that our attempt to create a control-process account of affect has led us to conclusions that complement and supplement in useful ways other accounts of emotion. For example, we agree with Frijda (1988) that emotions arise in response to meaning structures of situations. In some sense, what we have tried to do here is to specify in generic terms what kinds of meaning structures—as inputs—may give rise to emotions. In brief, we assert that emotions intrinsically are related to goal values, and that they reflect differences between expected and experienced rates of movement toward (or away from) those goals. They represent an organismic monitoring of "how things are going" with respect to those values.

Clearly, others have been intuitively aware of

this quality of affect (see Frijda, 1988), but the importance of this aspect of the picture has rarely been emphasized. What we have done is simply to approach the subject from a somewhat different angle, which has served to make this aspect more salient. Independent of the origins of our effort (i.e., the desire to fit affect to control theory), we hope that others will find merit in the ideas developed here.

REFERENCES

Abramson, L. Y., Seligman, M. E. P, & Teasdale, J. D. (1978). Learned helplessness in humans: Critique and reformulation. *Journal of Abnormal Psychology, 87,* 49–74.

Andersen, S. M., & Lyon, J. E. (1987). Anticipating desired outcomes: The role of outcome certainty in the onset of depressive affect. *Journal of Experimental Social Psychology, 23,* 428–443.

Bandura, A. (1977). *Social learning theory.* Englewood Cliffs, NJ: Prentice-Hall.

Bandura, A. (1986). *Social foundations of thought and action: A social cognitive theory.* Englewood Cliffs, NJ: Prentice-Hall.

Bower, G. H., & Cohen, P. R. (1982). Emotional influences in memory and thinking: Data and theory. In M. S. Clark & S. T. Fiske (Eds.), *Affect and cognition: The 17th Annual Carnegie Symposium on Cognition* (pp. 291–331). Hillsdale, NJ: Erlbaum.

Broadbent, D. E. (1977). Levels, hierarchies, and the locus of control. *Quarterly Journal of Experimental Psychology, 29,* 181–201.

Burgio, K. L., Merluzzi, T. V., & Pryor, J. B. (1986). The effects of performance expectancy and self-focused attention on social interaction. *Journal of Personality and Social Psychology, 50,* 1216–1221.

Carver, C. S. (1979). A cybernetic model of self-attention processes. *Journal of Personality and Social Psychology, 37,* 1251–1281 .

Carver, C. S., Blaney, P. H., & Scheier, M. F. (1979a). Focus of attention, chronic expectancy, and responses to a feared stimulus. *Journal of Personality and Social Psychology, 37,* 1186–1195.

Carver, C. S., Blaney, P. H., & Scheier, M. F. (1979b). Reassertion and giving up: The interactive role of self-directed attention and outcome expectancy. *Journal of Personality and Social Psychology, 37,* 1859–1870.

Carver, C. S., La Voie, L., Kuhl, J., & Ganellen, R. J. (1988). Cognitive concomitants of depression: A further examination of the roles of generalization, high standards, and self-criticism. *Journal of Social and Clinical Psychology, 7,* 350–365.

Carver, C. S., Peterson, L. M., Follansbee, D. J., & Scheier, M. F. (1983). Effects of self-directed attention on performance and persistence among persons high and low in test anxiety. *Cognitive Therapy and Research, 7,* 333–354.

Carver, C. S., & Scheier, M. F. (1981). *Attention and self-regulation: A control-theory approach to human behavior.* New York: Springer-Verlag.

Carver, C. S., & Scheier, M. F. (1982a). Control theory: A useful conceptual framework for personality–social, clinical, and health psychology. *Psychological Bulletin, 92,* 111–135.

Carver, C. S., & Scheier, M. F. (1982b). Outcome expectancy, locus of attribution for expectancy, and self-directed attention as determinants of evaluations and performance. *Journal of Experimental Social Psychology, 18,* 184–200.

Carver, C. S., & Scheier, M. F. (1984). Self-focused attention in test anxiety: A general theory applied to a specific phenomenon. In H. M. van der Ploeg, R. Schwarzer, & C. D. Spielberger (Eds.), *Advances in test anxiety research* (Vol. 3, pp. 3–20). Hillsdale, NJ: Erlbaum.

Carver, C. S., & Scheier, M. F. (1985). Aspects of self, and the control of behavior. In B. R. Schlenker (Ed.), *The self and social life* (pp. 146–174). New York: McGraw-Hill.

Carver, C. S., & Scheier, M. F. (1986a). Functional and dysfunctional responses to anxiety: The interaction between expectancies and self-focused attention. In R. Schwarzer (Ed.), *Self-related cognitions in anxiety and motivation* (pp. 111–141). Hillsdale, NJ: Erlbaum.

Carver, C. S., & Scheier, M. F. (1986b). Analyzing shyness: A specific application of broader self-regulatory principles. In W. H. Jones, J. M. Cheek, & S. R. Briggs (Eds.), *Shyness: Perspectives on research and treatment* (pp. 173–185). New York: Plenum Press.

Carver, C. S., & Scheier, M. F. (1986c). Self and the control of behavior. In L. M. Hartman & K. R. Blankstein (Eds.), *Perception of self in emotional disorder and psychotherapy* (pp. 5–35). New York: Plenum Press.

Carver, C. S, & Scheier, M. F. (in press). Principles of self-regulation: Action and emotion. In R. Sorrentino & E. T. Higgins (Eds.), *Handbook of motivation and cognition* (Vol. 2). New York: Guilford.

Carver, C. S., Scheier, M. F., & Klahr, D. (1987). Further explorations of a control-process model of test anxiety. In R. Schwarzer, H. M. van der Ploeg, & C. D. Spielberger (Eds.), *Advances in test anxiety research* (Vol. 5, pp. 15–22). Lisse: Swets & Zeitlinger.

Clark, M. S., Milberg, S., & Ross, J. (1983). Arousal cues arousal-related material in memory: Implications for understanding effects of mood on memory. *Journal of Verbal Learning and Verbal Behavior, 22,* 633–649.

Dawkins, R. (1976). Hierarchical organisation: A candidate principle for ethology. In P. P. G. Bateson & R. A. Hinde (Eds.), *Growing points in ethology* (pp. 7–54). Cambridge, England: Cambridge University Press.

Diener, E., & Emmons, R. A. (1984). The independence of positive and negative affect. *Journal of Personality and Social Psychology, 47,* 1105–1117.

Diener, E., & Iran-Nejad, A. (1986). The relationship in experience between various types of affect. *Journal of Personality and Social Psychology, 50,* 1031–1038.

Diener, E., Larsen, R. J., Levine, S., & Emmons, R. A. (1985). Intensity and frequency: Dimensions underlying positive and negative affect. *Journal of Personality and Social Psychology, 48,* 1253–1265.

Dweck, C. S., & Elliott, E. S. (1983). Achievement motivation. In P. H. Mussen (Ed.), *Handbook of child psychology* (4th ed., pp. 643–691). New York: Wiley.

Dweck, C. S., & Leggett, E. L. (1988). A social–cognitive approach to motivation and personality. *Psychological Review, 95,* 256–273.

Elliott, E. S., & Dweck, C. S. (1988). Goals: An approach to motivation and achievement. *Journal of Personality and Social Psychology, 54,* 5–12.

Emmons, R. A. (1986). Personal strivings: An approach to personality and subjective well being. *Journal of Personality and Social Psychology, 51,* 1058–1068.

Frijda, N. H. (1986). *The emotions.* Cambridge, England: Cambridge University Press.

Frijda, N. H. (1988). The laws of emotion. *American Psychologist, 43,* 349–358.

Galassi, J. P., Frierson, H. T., Jr., & Sharer, R. (1981). Behavior of high, moderate, and low test anxious students during an actual test situation. *Journal of Consulting and Clinical Psychology, 49,* 51–62.

Gallistel, C. R. (1980). *The organization of action: A new synthesis.* Hillsdale, NJ: Erlbaum.

Hamilton, V. (1983). *The cognitive structures and processes of human motivation and personality.* Chichester, England: Wiley.

Higgins, E. T. (1987). Self-discrepancy: A theory relating self and affect. *Psychological Review, 94,* 319–340.

Hyland, M. (1987). Control theory interpretation of psychological mechanisms of depression: Comparison and integration of several theories. *Psychological Bulletin, 102,* 109–121.

Izard, C. E. (1977). *Human emotions.* New York: Plenum Press.

Kanfer, F. H., & Hagerman, S. (1981). The role of self-regulation. In L. P. Rehm (Ed.), *Behavior therapy for depression: Present status and future directions* (pp. 143–179). New York: Academic Press.

Kanfer, F. H., & Hagerman, S. (1985). Behavior therapy and the information processing paradigm. In S. Reiss & R. R. Bootsin (Eds.), *Theoretical issues in behavior therapy* (pp. 3–33). New York: Academic Press.

Kelly, G. A. (1955). *The psychology of personal constructs.* New York: Norton.

Kirschenbaum, D. S. (1985). Proximity and specificity of planning: A position paper. *Cognitive Therapy and Research, 9,* 489–506.

Klinger, E. (1975). Consequences of commitment to and disengagement from incentives. *Psychological Review, 82,* 1–25.

Kuhl, J. (1984). Volitional aspects of achievement motivation and learned helplessness: Toward a comprehensive theory of action control. In B. A. Maher (Ed.), *Progress in experimental personality research* (Vol. 13, pp. 99–170). New York: Academic Press.

Kuhl, J. (1985). Volitional mediators of cognition–behavior consistency: Self-regulatory processes and action versus state orientation. In J. Kuhl & J. Beckmann (Eds.), *Action control: From cognition to behavior* (pp. 101–128). New York: Springer-Verlag.

Kuhl, J., & Helle, P. (1986). Motivational and volitional determinants of depression: The degenerated-intention hypothesis. *Journal of Abnormal Psychology, 95,* 247–251.

Kukla, A. (1972). Foundations of an attributional theory of performance. *Psychological Review, 79,* 454–470.

Larsen, R. J. (1987). The stability of mood variability: A spectral analytic approach to daily mood assessments. *Journal of Personality and Social Psychology, 52,* 1195–1204.

Lazarus, R. S. (1966). *Psychological stress and the coping process.* New York: McGraw-Hill.

Leventhal, H. (1984). A perceptual-motor theory of emotion. In L. Perkowitz (Ed.), *Advances in experimental social psychology* (Vol. 17, pp. 117–182). New York: Academic Press.

Linsenmeier, J. A. W., & Brickman, P. (1980). *Expectations, performance, and satisfaction.* Unpublished manuscript.

Lord, R. G., & Hanges, P. J. (1987). A control system model of organizational motivation: Theoretical development and applied implications. *Behavioral Science, 32,* 161–178.

MacKay, D. M. (1963). Mindlike behavior in artifacts. In K. M. Sayre & F. J. Crosson (Eds.), *The modeling of mind: Computers and intelligence* (pp. 225–241). Notre Dame, IN: University of Notre Dame Press.

MacKay, D. M. (1966). Cerebral organization and the conscious control of action. In J. C. Eccles (Ed.), *Brain and conscious experience* (pp. 422–445). Berlin: Springer-Verlag.

Marken, R. S. (1986). Perceptual organization of behavior: A hierarchical control model of coordinated action. *Journal of Experimental Psychology: Human Perception and Performance, 12,* 267–276.

Martin, L., & Tesser, A. (in press). Toward a model of ruminative thought. In J. S. Uleman & J. A. Bargh (Eds.), *Unintended thought: The limits of awareness, intention, and control.* New York: Guilford.

Millar, K. U., Tesser, A., & Millar, M. G. (1988). The effects of a threatening life event on behavior sequences and intrusive thought: A self-disruption explanation. *Cognitive Therapy and Research, 12,* 441–458.

Norman, D. A. (1981). Categorization of action slips. *Psychological Review, 88,* 1–15.

Ortony, A., Clore, G. L., & Collins, A. (1988). *The cognitive structure of emotions.* Cambridge. England: Cambridge University Press.

Plutchik, R. (1980). *Emotion: A psychoevolutionary synthesis.* New York: Harper & Row.

Powers, W. T. (1973). *Behavior: The control of perception.* Chicago: Aldine.

Pyszczynski, T., & Greenberg, J. (1985). Depression and preference for self-focusing stimuli after success and failure. *Journal of Personality and Social Psychology, 49,* 1066–1075.

Prszczynski, T., & Greenberg, J. (1987). Self-regulatory perseveration and the depressive self-focusing style: A self-awareness theory of reactive depression. *Psychological Bulletin, 102,* 122–138.

Rich, A. R., & Woolever, D. K. (1988). Expectancy and self-focused attention: Experimental support for the self-regulation model of test anxiety. *Journal of Social and Clinical Psychology, 7,* 246–259.

Rosenbaum, D. A. (1987). Hierarchical organization of motor programs. In S. P. Wise (Ed.), *Higher brain functions: Recent explorations of the brain's emergent properties* (pp. 45–66). New York: Wiley.

Rotter, J. B. (1954). *Social learning and clinical psychology.* New York: Prentice-Hall.

Schank, R. C., & Abelson, R. P. (1977). *Scripts, plans, goals, and understanding.* Hillsdale, NJ: Erlbaum.

Scheier, M. F., & Carver, C. S. (1982). Cognition, affect, and self-regulation. In M. S. Clark & S. T. Fiske (Eds.), *Affect and cognition: The 17th Annual Carnegie Symposium on Cognition* (pp. 157–183). Hillsdale, NJ: Erlbaum.

Scheier, M. F., & Carver, C. S. (1988). A model of behavioral self-regulation: Translating intention into action. In L. Berkowitz (Ed.), *Advanced in experimental social psychol-ogy* (Vol. 21, pp. 303–346). New York: Academic Press.

Schlenker, B. R., & Leary, M. R. (1982). Social anxiety and self-presentation: A conceptualization and model. *Psychological Bulletin, 92,* 641–669.

Shallice, T. (1978). The dominant action system: An information-processing approach to consciousness. In K. S. Pope & J. L. Singer (Eds.), *The stream of consciousness: Scientific investigations into the flow of human experience* (pp. 117–157). New York: Wiley.

Shiffrin, R. M., & Schneider, W. (1977). Controlled and automatic human information processing: II. Perceptual learning, automatic attending, and a general theory. *Psychological Review, 84,* 127–190.

Simon, H. A. (1967). Motivational and emotional controls of cognition. *Psychological Review, 74,* 29–39.

Solomon, R. L. (1980). The opponent-process theory of acquired motivation: The costs of pleasure and the benefits of pain. *American Psychologist, 35,* 691–712.

Srull, T. K., & Wyer, R. S., Jr. (1986). The role of chronic and temporary goals in social information processing. In R. M. Sorrentino & E. T. Higgins (Eds.), *Handbook of motivation and cognition: Foundations of social behavior* (pp. 503–549). New York: Guilford.

Stotland, E. (1969). *The psychology of hope.* San Francisco: Jossey-Bass.

Tomkins, S. S. (1984). Affect theory. In K. R. Scherer & P. Ekman (Eds.), *Approaches to emotion.* Hillsdale, NJ: Erlbaum.

Vallacher, R. R., & Wegner, D. M. (1985). *A theory of action identification.* Hillsdale, NJ: Erlbaum.

Vallacher, R. R., & Wegner, D. M. (1987). What do people think they're doing? Action identification and human behavior. *Psychological Review, 94,* 3–15.

Van Hook, E., & Higgins, E. T. (1988). Self-related problems beyond the self-concept: Motivational consequences of discrepant self-guides. *Journal of Personality and Social Psychology, 55,* 625–633.

Warr, P., Barter, J., & Brownbridge, G. (1983). On the independence of positive and negative affect. *Journal of Personality and Social Psychology, 44,* 644–651.

Watson, D., & Tellegen, A. (1985). Toward a consensual structure of mood. *Psychological Bulletin, 9,* 219–235.

Weiner, B. (1982). The emotional consequences of causal ascriptions. In M. S. Clark & S. T. Fiske (Eds.), *Affect and cognition: The 17th Annual Carnegie Symposium on Cognition* (pp. 185–209). Hillsdale, NJ: Erlbaum.

Wessman, A. E., & Ricks, D. E. (1966). *Mood and personality.* New York: Holt, Rinehart & Winston.

Wortman, C. B., & Brehm, J. W. (1975). Responses to uncontrollable outcomes: An integration of reactance theory and the learned helplessness model. In L. Berkowitz (Ed.), *Advances in experimental social psychology* (Vol. 8, pp. 277–336). New York: Academic Press.

Wortman, C. B., & Silver, R. C. (1989). The myths of coping with loss. *Journal of Consulting and Clinical Psychology, 57,* 349–357.

Zevon, M. A., & Tellegen, A. (1982). The structure of mood change: An idiographic/nomothetic analysis. *Journal of Personality and Social Psychology, 43,* 111–122.

READING 15

Deliberative and Implemental Mind-Sets: Cognitive Tuning Toward Congruous Thoughts and Information

Peter M. Gollwitzer, Heinz Heckhausen and Birgit Steller
• Max-Planck-Institut, Federal Republic of Germany

Editors' Notes

Is a course of action continuous from its beginning to its end, or are there distinct phases of action regulation? If there are distinct phases, does a particular phase influence thought processes so as to better serve the function of that phase? The authors distinguish between four distinct and sequential action phases: 1) a predecisional phase in which potential goals are deliberated, and a decision to pursue one of them is made; 2) a postdecisional phase in which ways of implementing the goal are considered, and some means of goal attainment are selected; 3) an actional phase in which actions functioning as goal attainment means are initiated; and 4) a postactional phase in which outcomes of the initiated action are evaluated. The authors propose that each phase involves a distinct mind-set that tailors a person's cognitive processes to meet the task demands of that phase (cognitive tuning), thus enhancing task preparedness in each phase. This proposal is examined for the deliberative mind-set of the predecisional phase and the implemental mind-set of the postdecisional, but preactional, phase. As predicted, the studies found that thoughts congruent with deliberation were more likely when participants had a deliberative than an implemental mind-set, and thoughts congruent with implementation were more likely when participants had an implemental than a deliberative mind-set.

Discussion Questions

1. What is the difference between a deliberative mind-set and an implemental mind-set?
2. Describe evidence that a person's thoughts are tailored to meet the task demands of his or her current action phase.

Authors' Abstract

Study 1 established either deliberative mind-set by having subjects contemplate personal change decision or implemental mind-set by having subjects plan execution of intended personal project. Subjects were subsequently requested to continue beginnings of 3 fairy tales, each describing a main character with a decisional conflict. Analysis revealed that deliberative mind-set subjects ascribed more deliberative and less implementational efforts to main characters than implemental mind-set subjects. In Study 2, subjects were asked to choose between different test materials. Either before or after making their decision, subjects were given information on deliberative and implementational thoughts unrelated to their task at hand. When asked to recall these thoughts, predecisional subjects recalled more deliberative and less implementational thoughts, whereas for postdecisional subjects the reverse was true. These findings suggest that deliberative and implemental mind-sets tune thought production and information processing.

A course of action may be conceived rather narrowly as extending from its initiation (starting point) to its termination (end point). Alternatively, one may adopt a broader perspective that embraces the motivational origins of an action as the actual starting point and the individual's evaluative thoughts about the achieved action outcome as the final end point. In the present article, we take this broader perspective and segment the course of action into four distinct, sequential phases (Heckhausen, 1986).

The first segment is the *predecisional* phase, where potential action goals entailed by a person's many wants and wishes are deliberated. When a decision to pursue one of these goals is made, a transition to the *postdecisional* (preactional) phase takes place, where the individual becomes concerned with implementing the chosen goal. However, this phase ends and the *actional* phase starts when actions geared toward achieving the chosen goal are initiated. Once these actions have resulted in a particular outcome, the *postactional* phase is entered and the individual proceeds to evaluate the achieved outcome.

We postulate that each of these phases is accompanied by a distinct mind-set (Gollwitzer, 1990). Following the lead of the Würzburg School (Külpe, 1904; Marbe, 1901; Watt, 1905; for reviews, see Boring, 1950, pp. 401–406; Gibson, 1941; and Humphrey, 1951, pp. 30–131), we assume that the characteristics of each of these mind-sets are determined by the unique qualities of the different tasks to be solved within each phase. That is, the different mind-sets tailor a person's cognitive apparatus to meet phase-typical task demands, thus creating a special preparedness for solving these tasks. This preparedness should extend to a person's thought production, to the encoding and retrieval of information, and to the inferences drawn on the basis of this information. In this article, we explore the issue of mind-set congruous thought production as well as the encoding and retrieval of congruous information. As was done in a previous analysis of mind-set effects on a person's inferences (see Gollwitzer & Kinney, 1989, on illusion of control), we limit the analysis of cognitive tuning toward mind-set congruous thoughts and information to the *deliberative* mind-set of the predecisional phase and the *implemental* mind-set of the postdecisional, but preactional, phase.

What are the issues to which deliberative as compared with implemental mind-sets are attuned? To answer this question, one must consider the specific tasks that need to be tackled in the respective action phases. In the predecisional phase, people's task is to choose between action goals suggested by their wants and wishes. The likelihood of a "good" choice should be enhanced when the individual thoroughly ponders the attractiveness of the expected consequences (i.e., expected value) of these goals. Clearly, failing to think about the attractiveness of proximal and distant consequences will lead to problematic decisions associated with unexpected negative consequences. Accordingly, the deliberative mind-set should gear a person's thinking toward the expected values of potential action goals.

In the postdecisional (preactional) phase, however, people are confronted with quite a different task: The chosen goal awaits successful implementation. Postdecisional individuals should therefore benefit from an implemental mind-set that guides their thoughts toward the questions of *when, where,* and *how* to implement the chosen action goal. In this phase, thoughts about the goal's expected value should be distractive rather than useful, because they are not immediately related to implementational issues.

The classic definition of mind-set ("Einstellung") as advanced by the Würzburg School suggests that mind-set effects are based on cognitive precesses that promote solving the task that stimulated the rise of the mind-set. With respect to deliberative and implemental mind-sets, these maybe conceived of as cognitive procedures relating to how one chooses between various goal alternatives or to the planning of actions one must take in order to attain a chosen goal, respectively. A deliberative mind-set should, for instance, entail procedures of weighting pros and cons, whereas an implemental mind-set should entail procedures of timing and sequencing of goal-oriented actions.

As Smith and Branscombe (1987) pointed out in their procedural model of social inferences, cognitive procedures may transfer from a training (priming) task to a subsequent (test) task. If these procedures are sufficiently strengthened through intensive practice in the training task, and if there is overlap in the applicability of procedures, transfer is very likely. This model suggests he following test of the postulated effects of deliberative and implemental mind-sets: If we succeed in creating strong deliberative and implemental mind-sets by either having subjects intensively contemplate potential goals or plan the execution of a chosen project (training task), we should find the postulated mind-set effects in an unrelated subsequent task (test task). A prerequisite would be that the subsequent task allows for those cognitive procedures that were strengthened in the training task, that is, the cognitive procedures characteristic of a deliberative or implemental mind-set.

Experiment 1, testing the postulate of mind-set congruous thought production, was designed along this premise. Subjects' first task (training task) was to either thoroughly contemplate an unresolved decisional problem of their own (deliberative mind-set) or to make a detailed plan of how to pursue a pressing personal project (implemental mind-set). Then they were confronted with a second, allegedly unrelated task (test task) that requested the spontaneous production of ideas. Because these ideas could be deliberative or implementational in nature, we expected both de-

liberative and implemental mind-sets to guide thought production in a mind-set congruous direction.

The transfer assumption allowed us to go beyond a recent experiment reported by Heckhausen and Gollwitzer (1987), where the thoughts of deliberative and implemental mind-set subjects were sampled during the training task. In this study, the classification of the reported thoughts clearly evidenced cognitive tuning toward mind-set congruous thoughts. This study, however, lacks an unrelated test task, and therefore the results might be based on experimenter demands.

Experiment 1: Ascribing Deliberative and Implementational Efforts to Others

Asking subjects to deliberate unresolved personal problems that are pending a change decision should create strong deliberative mind-sets. Alternatively, asking subjects to plan the execution of chosen projects should evoke strong implemental mind-sets. Other experiments have indicated that deliberative and implemental mind-sets can reliably be produced through such a procedure (Gollwitzer, Heckhausen, & Ratajczak, 1990; Gollwitzer & Kinney, 1989). Accordingly, in the present experiment one third of the subjects were first asked to name an unresolved personal problem (e.g., Should I move from home? or Should I terminate my college education?) and then asked to contemplate whether or not to make a respective change decision. Another third of the subjects were to indicate a personal goal or project they planned to execute in the near future (e.g., moving from home or terminating one's college education) and then were to plan when, where, and how they wanted to accomplish it. The final third, a control group, were asked to passively view nature slides.

We tested whether deliberative and implemental mind-sets tune people's thought production in a mind-set congruous direction by asking subjects to fabricate ideas on an unrelated second task. To this end, we presented subjects with the beginnings of three fairy tales in which the main character of each story faced a different decisional conflict (e.g., a king had to go to war, but had nobody to whom he could entrust his young daughter). Subjects were asked to spontaneously compose the next three sentences for each of these fairy tales.

The mind-set congruency hypothesis implies

that deliberative efforts (i.e., contemplating possible goals) are most frequently ascribed to the main characters of the stories in the deliberative mind-set condition, less frequently in the control condition, and even less so in the implemental mind-set condition. In contrast, implementational efforts (i.e., executing a chosen solution to the conflict) should be most frequently ascribed in the implemental mind-set condition, less frequently in the control condition, and least frequently in the deliberative mind-set condition.

Method

SUBJECTS

The 97 participants were male students at the Ruhr-Universitat Bochum. Up to 4 subjects were invited to each experimental session and randomly assigned to one of three conditions. Subjects were recruited on the premise that they were willing to participate in two different studies, one on people's personal problems and projects, the other a test of their creativity. Subjects were separated by partitions, such that they could easily view the experimenter but none of the other participants. They were paid DM 10 (approximately $5.50) for participating.

DESIGN

Subjects in either a deliberative or implemental mind-set were asked to continue three different, incomplete fairy tales. Subjects' stories were analyzed with respect to whether deliberative or implementational efforts were ascribed to the main characters of the fairy tales. Subjects in the control condition passively viewed photographs of various outdoor scenes before receiving the fairy tales.

PROCEDURES

Cover story: The female experimenter explained that subjects would take part in two different experiments. In the first experiment, subjects would be requested to reflect on personal issues or on nature photographs. Subjects were told that this study was designed to answer the question of whether intense reflection on personal issues would help people act more effectively in everyday life. In the second experiment their cre-

ativity would be tested. For this purpose, three different creativity tasks would be used, all of which would request the spontaneous creation of ideas.

In order to ensure that subjects perceived the two experiments as unrelated, the format of the written materials was different in each study (e.g., typeface, color of paper, and writing style). In addition, the materials of each alleged experiment were distributed and collected separately.

Deliberative and implemental mind-set manipulation. Deliberative mind-set subjects were asked to weigh the pros and cons of making or not making a personal change decision. First, they had to indicate an unresolved personal problem (e.g., Should I switch my major?). Then they were to list both potential positive and negative, short-term and long-term consequences (i.e., to elaborate on the expected value). In contrast, implemental mind-set subjects were asked to plan the implementation of chosen personal projects. They were instructed to first name a personal project they intended to accomplish within the following 3 months (e.g., to move from home). Then they had to list the five most crucial implementational steps and commit themselves to when, where, and how to execute these steps.

As a manipulation check, both groups of subjects were then asked to fill out a final questionnaire consisting of the following items:

1. "On the line below, please indicate the point that best represents your distance from the act of change decision." (For this purpose, a horizontal line of 13 cm was provided. The starting point was labeled "far from having made a change decision," the 6.5-cm mark "act of change decision," and the end point "past having made a change decision.")
2. "How determined do you feel at this moment?"
3. "Do you feel that you have committed yourself to a certain implementational course of action?"
4. "Do you feel that you have committed yourself to make use of a certain occasion or opportunity to act?"

Items 2–4 were accompanied by unipolar 9-point answer scales ranging from *not at all* to *very.*

Control subjects. Subjects in the control condition received a booklet containing numerous black-and-white photographs depicting various nature scenes. Subjects were instructed to passively view the pictures for about 30 min (i.e., the amount of time deliberative and implemental subjects needed to complete their tasks). Thereafter, the alleged second experiment was started.

Dependent variable. The experimenter began the alleged second study by distributing three different fairy tales, the order of which was counterbalanced across conditions. Subjects received the following instructions:

All of these fairy tales end at a certain point in the plot. You are to fill in the next three sentences of each fairy tale. You should *not* write a "novel," and the fairy tales need not have an ending. When continuing the stories, give free rein to your fantasy and don't hesitate to write down your own creative thoughts, however unusual they may be. After you have finished the three sentences, please go on to the next fairy tale.

The first fairy tale read as follows:

Once upon a time there was a king who loved the queen dearly. When the queen died, he was left with his only daughter. The widowed king adored the little princess who grew up to be the most beautiful maiden that anyone had ever seen. When the princess turned 15, war broke out and her father had to go to battle. The king, however, did not know of anyone with whom he could entrust his daughter while he was away at war. The king....

The second fairy tale was about a king who had a huge forest by his castle. One day he had sent out a hunter into the forest who did not return. The two hunters he sent to look for the lost hunter also failed to return. The third fairy tale described a rather hedonistic tailor who had attended a christening party, out of town. Late at night and after a few drinks too many, he was on his way home and got lost in a dark forest. He suddenly found himself standing in front of a huge rock wall with a passage just large enough to permit a person to pass.

Thought production scoring. Subjects' stories were scored by two independent blind raters. The raters proceeded as follows: First, they underlined verbs relating to the main characters of the three fairy tales. Then, they classified the episodes denoted by these verbs with respect to whether the main character tackled the predecisional task of choosing between action goals or the postdecisional task of implementing a chosen action goal. For this purpose, a coding scheme was developed: two mutually exclusive categories are depicted in the Appendix. Each category could be

check-marked as often as necessary, depending on how many relevant episodes the subjects' stories contained. Eighty-one percent of the episodes could be placed into the categories provided by the coding scheme: the rest formed the category "unassignable episodes" (19%). Agreement between raters was determined by counting the number of "hits," defined as classifications on which the two raters agreed. Interrater reliability was high, with 91% of the ratings being hits.

Debriefing. When the subjects had finished working on the third fairy tale, the experiment was terminated and the subjects were debriefed. During the debriefing session, we probed whether subjects perceived the two experiments as related or not. As it turned out, subjects were only concerned with how well they had performed on the creativity task. None of the subjects raised the issue of the two experiments being potentially related or reported suspicions after being probed.

Results

EQUIVALENCE OF GROUPS

Deliberative and implemental mind-set subjects did not differ in the domains covered by their problems and projects, respectively. Unresolved personal problems (deliberative mind-set subjects) and personal projects (implemental mind-set subjects) were classified according to three different domains: career-related (42%), lifestyle-related (31%), and interpersonal (27%), the percentages being basically identical for both unresolved personal problems and personal projects.

The three groups of subjects also did not differ significantly in the number of words they wrote when continuing the three fairy tales: $M = 110.2$ for the deliberative mind-set group, $M = 112.5$ for the implemental mind-set group, and $M = 119.7$ for the control group, $F(2.84) = .52$, *ns.*

MANIPULATION CHECKS

Subjects had indicated their proximity (in time) to the act of making a change decision on a horizontal line. Nearly all (24 of 26) deliberative mind-set subjects indicated that they had not yet made the decision. The reverse was found for implemental mind-set subjects: 25 of 26 subjects indicated that they had already made the decision. In addition, deliberative mind-set subjects ($M =$

4.6) felt less determined than implemental mind-set subjects ($M = 8.2$), $F(1,50) = 50.8$. $p < .001$. Implemental mind-set subjects ($M = 7.6$) felt more committed to executing a certain implementational course of action than deliberative mind-set subjects ($M = 5.0$), $F(1,50) = 26.6$, $p < .001$: the same pattern held true for feelings of commitment with respect to making use of a certain occasion or opportunity to act ($M = 6.7$ vs. $M = 5.1$), $F(1.50) = 4.6$, $p < .04$.

DEPENDENT VARIABLES

To analyze subjects' stories, episodes ascribing deliberative efforts to the main characters (i.e., deliberating action goals and turning to others for advice) were added together to create a deliberative efforts index: actual acting on a chosen goal and thinking about the implementation of the chosen goal were added together to form an implementational efforts index (see Appendix). Scores on these indices were submitted to further analyses.

To test the hypothesis that ascribing deliberative and implementational efforts varies in a mind-set congruous direction, two one-way analyses of variance (ANOVAs) with linear contrast weights (see Rosenthal & Rosnow, 1985) were conducted. For ascribing deliberative efforts, these weights tested the hypothesis that the highest frequencies would be obtained among deliberative mind-set subjects, followed by control subjects and then implemental subjects: for implemental efforts, the highest frequencies would be observed among implementational mind-set subjects, followed by control subjects and then deliberative subjects. These analyses revealed that ascribing deliberative and implementational efforts significantly varies in a mind-set congruous direction, $F(1, 84) = 4.06$, $p < .025$ (one-tailed), and $F(1, 84) = 8.48$,

$p < .005$ (one-tailed), respectively. Pearson coefficients obtained by correlating ascribing deliberative and implementational efforts with the respective linear contrast coding of mind-set conditions underlined these results (see Table 1).

When the frequencies of ascribing deliberative and implementational efforts were submitted to an ANOVA with ascribed effort (deliberative vs. implementational) as a within-subjects variable and condition (deliberative, implemental, and control group) as a between-subjects variable, a significant main effect of ascribed effort emerged, $F(1, 84) = 322.5$, $p < .001$, which is qualified by the predicted interaction effect, $F(2, 84) = 4.65$, $p = .015$. We checked whether the pattern of data is different for each of the three fairy tales by computing a $3 \times 2 \times 3$ (Fairy Tale × Ascribed Effort × Condition) ANOVA. The significant Ascribed Effort × Condition interaction effect was *not* qualified by an interaction with fairy tale; that is, the three-way interaction did not reach significance ($F < 1.0$). In addition, the order in which the fairy tales were presented also failed to affect the critical interaction ($F < 1.0$). Finally, we explored how the episodes that could not be classified by our coding scheme were distributed across conditions. There were no significant differences among the conditions ($F < .25$).

Discussion

Subjects requested to ponder a personal problem in order to determine whether or not they should make a change decision fabricated fewer implementational and more deliberative ideas when writing a creative fairy tale than subjects who had been asked to plan the execution of a chosen personal goal. Deliberating and planning created distinct mind-sets that persisted even after subjects had turned to the subsequent task of writing cre-

Table 1. Mean Deliberative and Implementational Efforts Ascribed to the Main Character of the Three Fairy Tales

Type of ascribed efforts	F	r	Deliberative (n = 26)	Control (n = 35)	Implemental (n = 26)
			Mind-set conditions		
Deliberative	4.06*	.21*	1.00	0.71	0.38
Implementational	8.48**	.29**	5.81	6.94	7.85

Note. Means reflect the number of episodes in which subjects ascribed either deliberative or implementational efforts.

* $p \le .05$. ** $p \le .01$.

ative fairy tales. The ideas that spontaneously entered the subjects' minds when inventing their fairy tales corresponded to their deliberative or implemental mind-sets.

All groups of subjects imputed more implementational than deliberative efforts to the main characters of the fairy tales. Apparently, the task of writing creative endings to unfinished fairy tales predominantly relies on cognitive procedures characteristic of the implemental mind-set. As Rabkin (1979) and Rumelhart (1975, 1977) pointed out, fairy tales seem to follow a certain grammar. A "good" fairy tale is not complete until the problem faced by the main character is solved. Because such solutions commonly require the main character to take action, ascribing implementational efforts is more in the style of a good fairy tale. Still, despite few deliberative efforts ascribed overall, we observed the predicted mind-set congruency effect. However, the scarcity of ascribing deliberative efforts in the present study serves as a reminder that testing the postulated mind-set congruency effects through a subsequent (test) task has its limits. If working on a subsequent task does not allow for the cognitive procedures entailed by a deliberative or implemental mind-set (e.g., solving an arithmetic task), mind-set congruency effects cannot be observed.

Studies conducted on category accessibility effects on social judgments seem relevant to the paradigm used here (Higgins, Rholes, & Jones, 1977; Srull & Wyer, 1979). Assuming that social constructs (e.g., kindness) are stored in memory, these constructs were first primed by confronting subjects either with trait words closely related to the target construct (Higgins et al., 1977) or, descriptions of relevant behaviors (Srull & Wyer, 1979). Then, in a presumedly unrelated second experiment, subjects read descriptions of a target character who shows either ambivalent (Higgins et al., 1977) or vague (Srull & Wyer, 1979) indications of possessing the critical personal attribute. Finally, when subjects were asked to rate the target character, distortions in the direction of the primed category were observed. Both groups of researchers suggested that priming changes some property of the critical construct's representation in memory (i.e., activation or location in a storage bin, respectively) that makes it comparatively more accessible and more likely to be used in interpreting the behavior of the target person.

As in these priming experiments, subjects in

Experiment 1 were also exposed to ambiguous information about a target character (i.e., the main character of the open-ended fairy tales) in an alleged second experiment. However, the ambiguity is about the main character's course of action and not about a potential personality attribute. We believe that subjects' ascribing of deliberative or implementational efforts was affected by cognitive procedures (or productions: Anderson, 1983) that have been strengthened through prior deliberation and planning processes. The activation of declarative knowledge (specific episodic and general semantic) through the contents touched by subjects' deliberation and planning should have played a minor role. This assumption is supported by the fact that the observed mind-set effects were rather long-lived (one quarter to half an hour), whereas conceptual priming effects were generally extremely short-lived (a matter of seconds or a few minutes). As Smith and Branscombe (1987) demonstrated, studies on category accessibility effects only manage to produce long-lasting effects (several hours) when procedural strengthening is involved.

Experiment 2: Recalling Deliberative Versus Implementational Thoughts of Others

Experiment 1 demonstrated that deliberative and implemental mind-sets favor the production of congruous thoughts. This should facilitate the task of choosing between goal options and the task of implementing a chosen goal, respectively However, both of these tasks should also be facilitated by effective processing of task-relevant information. Therefore, one would expect that people in a deliberative mind-set show superior processing of information that speaks to the expected value of goal options, whereas people in an implemental mind-set should show superior processing of information that speaks to the issue of when, where, and how to execute goal-oriented behavior.

Our test of the superior processing of mind-set congruous information was also based on the transfer assumption of Smith and Branscombe's (1987) model of procedural strengthening and transfer. Instead of offering deliberative and implemental mind-set subjects information relevant to their decisional and implementational problem at hand, we offered information on other people's decisional and implementational problems. As this information could easily be identified as either expected value-related or implementation-related, we expected mind-set congruency effects with respect to subjects' recall of this information.

This information was depicted on eight pairs of slides. The first slide of each pair showed a person said to be experiencing a personal conflict of the following kind: Should I do *x* or not (e.g., sell my apartment)? The second slide presented four thoughts entertained by the person depicted on the first slide. Two of these thoughts were deliberative in nature, as they referred to the expected value of making a change decision. The other two thoughts were of an implementational nature, both addressing the issue of when (timing) and how (sequencing) to execute goal-oriented actions. When constructing these sentences, we used pilot subjects to establish that both types of information (expected value vs. implementation) were recalled about equally well.

A deliberative mind-set was established by asking subjects to contemplate the choice between one of two available creativity tests. An implemental mind-set was assumed for subjects who had just chosen between tests and were waiting to start working. A control group received and recalled the information without expecting to make a decision or to implement one already made.

Deliberative mind-set subjects should show superior recall of the expected value-related information, despite its being unrelated to the decision subjects were contemplating. Implemental mind-set subjects should show superior recall of the implementation-related information, despite its being unrelated to working on the chosen creativity test. Control subjects were expected to recall both expected value-related information and implementation-related information about equally well.

Method

SUBJECTS AND EQUIPMENT

The participants were 69 male students from the University of Munich. Two subjects were invited to each experimental session. They received DM 15 (approximately $8.00) for participation. A female experimenter ushered subjects into separate experimental cubicles where they received tape-recorded instructions through an intercom system. Each cubicle was equipped with a projection screen.

DESIGN

Subjects were randomly assigned to one of three conditions. In the deliberative mind-set condition, information on both expected values and implementational issues was received and recalled prior to making a choice between two available creativity tests. In the implemental mind-set condition, subjects received and recalled this information while waiting to begin working on their chosen creativity test. Finally, control subjects received and recalled this information without either expecting to make a choice or having made one.

PROCEDURE

Cover story: Subjects were told that two different personality traits, that is, social sensitivity and artistic creativity, would be assessed during the course of the experiment. The experimenter further explained that for measuring each of these traits two alternative test materials had been prepared. It was stated that subjects would be allowed to choose between test materials, because only if subjects chose the test material more appropriate for them personally would test scores reflect their "true" social or creative potential. The experimenter then distributed a short questionnaire consisting of the following items: (a) "How creative do you think you are" (b) "How confident are you that you are capable of creative achievements?" and (c) "How important is it for you to be a creative person?" Parallel questions were asked with respect to social sensitivity (All items were accompanied by 9-point answer scales ranging from *not at all* to *very*)

The first trait measured was *social sensitivity*: The experimenter presented subjects with short descriptions of two different interpersonal conflicts. Subjects were first asked to select the problem they personally found most engaging and then to suggest an appropriate solution to the conflict by writing a short essay Subjects were told that they would later receive feedback concerning the usefulness of their suggested solutions.

Then the experimenter turned to the presumed second part of the experiment, that is, assessing subjects' *artistic creativity*. She explained that subjects would create collages from material cut out of different newspapers. It was the subjects' task to select various elements (e.g., people, animals, and objects) needed to depict a certain theme provided by the experimenter. Finally, subjects should place the selected elements on a white sheet of paper and arrange them so that a creative picture emerged. When they had discovered the most appealing arrangement, they should glue the collage segments onto the white sheet of paper and then hand it to the experimenter.

Most important, however, two different sets of collage materials (black-and-white vs. color elements) would be available for this task. Subjects would be given a choice because they could reach their full creative potential only if they chose that set of elements they found personally most appealing. To help subjects choose properly, she would present four black-and-white as well as four color slides. She explained that these slides originated from a previous study on artistic creativity in which subjects had to invent the thoughts of people depicted on the slides. Subjects should view all of the slides carefully to determine which set of slides (color or black and white) would bring out their full creative potential.

However, subjects were instructed to refrain from making a choice of test material while viewing the slides. Impulsive choices, as well as choices based on initial preferences only were said to have proven problematic. Therefore, subjects should take their time, lean back, and ponder the best choice. In addition, shortly before viewing the sample pictures subjects were given false feedback with respect to the quality of their performance on the social sensitivity test. All subjects were told that if they had chosen the alternative test material, their score would have been higher than the rather modest score achieved. This feedback, as well as the instructions to refrain from impulse choices, was given for the sole purpose of stimulating intense deliberation.

Information materials. The sample pictures were grouped into eight pairs of slides. Each pair consisted of a first slide that pictured a person said to be pondering a decisional problem (e.g., an elderly lady). On the subsequent slide, subjects read that she was reflecting on the following decisional problem: Should I invite my grandchildren to stay at my house during the summer—or shouldn't I?

The slide also contained her thoughts on the expected value of a change decision: The first thought centered on possible positive consequences (i.e., *It would be good*, because they could help me keep up my garden): the second thought focused on possible negative consequences (i.e.,

It would be bad, because they might break my good china).

In addition, the slide depicted two thoughts related to the implementation of a potential change decision: One focused on the timing of a necessary implementational step (i.e., *If I decide yes, then* I won't talk to the kids *before* my daughter has agreed); the other thought mapped out the sequence of two further implementational steps (i.e., *If I decide yes, then I'll first* write my daughter and *then* I'll give her a call).

Altogether, eight different persons, each facing a specific decisional conflict, were presented (e.g., a young man who pondered the question of becoming a sculptor, a young lady who reflected on whether to quit her waitressing job, and a middle-aged man who deliberated whether or not to sell his condominium). Four slides depicting persons were in color, and four were in black and white. The verbal information was presented in the same format. The underlined parts of each sentence (see the example of the elderly lady above) remained analogous for each person and were written in black. The rest of the sentences were written in red.

Deliberative mind-set condition. Once subjects had viewed the eight pairs of slides, the experimenter told them that she would look for a second set of slides that might make it easier for subjects to make up their minds. While she was purportedly trying to set up this second set, subjects were to fill their time by working on a couple of tasks. Then the experimenter gave the instructions for a 5-min distracter (subjects counted the planes of several different geometrical figures drawn on a sheet of paper) and a subsequent recall test (as described below). When subjects were finished, the experimenter explained that she had failed to set up the additional set of slides. Therefore, subjects should make their decision based solely on viewing the original set of slides.

Implemental mind-set condition. Subjects were introduced to the choice option between two sets of collage materials and were instructed to deliberate on the question of which set of collage elements they found most appealing. After subjects had indicated their decision, the experimenter explained that it would take several minutes for her to bring the chosen collage elements to the subject's cubicle. In the meantime, the subjects would view slides and solve a number of different tasks. The eight pairs of slides were then presented: the origin of these slides was described to the subjects in the same words as in the deliberative mind-set condition. Following the distracter, subjects worked on the recall test.

Control condition. Control subjects were not made to either expect a decision between collage elements or work on a set of collage elements. They were shown the slides after being told solely about their origin. Finally, subjects' recall performance was assessed following the completion of the distracter task.

Recall procedure. Following the 5-min distracter task, subjects were again shown the eight slides depicting the persons said to be experiencing a decisional conflict. In addition, they were given a booklet consisting of eight pages, each one entitled with the deliberation problem of one of the eight characters pictured on the slides. Subjects found those parts of the sentences printed in black on the slides that presented the depicted persons' thoughts and were instructed to complete them (i.e., fill in the parts of the sentences printed in red on the original slides). For this recall procedure, the slides depicting the characters were shown in the order in which they were originally presented.

Postexperimental questionnaire and debriefing. Deliberative and implemental mind-set subjects were asked to complete a final questionnaire that contained the following items accompanied by 9-point answer scales ranging from *not at all* to *very:* (a) "How important is it for you to show a creative performance on the collage creativity test?" (b) "How difficult was the choice between the two sets of collage elements?" (c) "How important is it for you to work with the appropriate collage elements?" (d) "How certain are you that you picked the appropriate collage elements?" (e) "I generally prefer black-and-white pictures over color ones!" (*don't agree–agree*), and (f) "I generally prefer color pictures over black-and-white ones!" (*don't agree–agree*). After the subjects had completed this questionnaire, the experimenter debriefed them and paid them for their participation.

The debriefing was started by probing for suspicions. None of the subjects guessed our hypothesis. One subject (implemental mind-set) guessed that we were testing whether the information associated with the chosen type of material (black and white vs. color) is recalled better. The rest of the subjects took the incidental recall test as a check of whether they were good subjects who collaborated in an attentive and concentrated manner. As

in other studies using this paradigm (Heckhausen & Gollwitzer, 1986, 1987), subjects were primarily concerned with the upcoming creativity test, on which they wanted to give their best.

Results

EQUIVALENCE OF MIND-SET GROUPS

Subjects' answers on the preexperimental questionnaire did not differ between groups: There were no differences with respect to the belief in one's creativity (Ms = 5.65 vs. 5.66), the confidence in one's capability for creative achievements (Ms = 5.76 vs. 5.72), and the importance assigned to being a creative person (Ms = 6.94 vs. 6.67), all Fs < 1.0. The relatively high means (unipolar 9-point scales) indicate that the subjects valued being creative and were quite certain of their possessing this desirable trait.

Subjects' answers on the postexperimental questionnaire also did not indicate any differences. The importance (Ms = 4.89 vs. 5.17) and difficulty (Ms = 6.35 vs. 6.67) of succeeding in the collage creativity test were perceived as similar in both conditions, as was also the case for the perceived importance of making the correct choice (Ms = 5.53 vs. 5.17), all Fs < 1.0. These data suggest that deliberative and implemental subjects took the collage test as a valid means to demonstrate being creative, and that they felt making the correct choice would influence their performance on this test.

Although black-and-white elements were chosen more than twice as often as color collage elements (25 vs. 10), this ratio did not differ across conditions, χ^2 (1, N = 35) = .01, p = .91, nor did their general preference for black-and-white or for color collage elements (both Fs < 1.0).

DEPENDENT VARIABLES

Recall performance scores for expected value-related thoughts and implementation-related thoughts were determined by counting the respective thoughts that were recalled correctly. Deliberative mind-set subjects showed the predicted superior recall for expected value-related thoughts (M = 7.29) as compared with implementation-related thoughts (M = 4.88), t(16) = 2.25, p <.02 (one-tailed). Implemental mind-set subjects also evidenced mind-set congruous recall, recalling implementation-related thoughts (M = 8. 17) sig-

Table 2. Mean Recall of Information on Expected Value and Implementation

Mind-set condition	Type of information		
	Thoughts about expected value	Thoughts about implementation	Difference
Deliberative	7.29	4.88	2.41
Control	6.87	6.63	0.24
Implemental	6.11	8.17	−2.06

Note. Higher numbers indicate better recall performance.

nificantly better than expected value-related thoughts ($M = 6.11$), $t(17) = 2.02$, $p < .03$ (one-tailed). As expected, control subjects recalled expected value-related thoughts ($M = 6.88$) and implementation-related thoughts ($M = 6.63$) about equally well, $t(15) = .24$, *ns* (see Table 2).

To test the hypothesis that the recall performance for expected value-related and implementation-related information varies in a mind-set congruous direction, we conducted two separate one-way ANOVAs with linear contrast weights. With respect to the implementation-related information, the weights were set to test the hypothesis that its recall is highest for implemental mind-set subjects, followed by control subjects and then deliberative mind-set subjects. This analysis revealed a significant $F(1, 48) = 4.03$, $p = .025$ (one-tailed); the respective correlation coefficient is $r(51) = .28$, $p < .025$. For expected value-related information, the weights were set to test the hypothesis that this information is recalled best by deliberative mind-set subjects, followed by control subjects and then implemental mind-set subjects, $F(1, 48) = 1.02$, *ns*; $r(51) = .15$, $p = .15$.

Although these findings indicate that for expected value-related information there is comparatively less mind-set congruous recall than for implementation-related information, recall of expected value-related information and implementation-related information combined to produce strong mind-set congruous recall (as can be seen from the difference scores reported in Table 2). When this difference index is submitted to a one-way ANOVA with linear contrast weights, a highly significant $F(1,48) = 9.15$, $p < .003$ (one-tailed), emerges; the respective correlation coefficient is $r(51) = .41$, $p < .002$. This indicates that the superior recall for expected value-related information in the deliberative mind-set group was strongly reduced in the control group and reversed in the implemental mind-set group.

Discussion

Deliberative mind-set subjects recalled expected value-related information better than implementation-related information, whereas implemental mind-set subjects showed better recall of implementation-related information than of expected value-related information. This pattern of data supports our hypothesis of superior recall of mind-set congruous information. [. . .]

General Discussion

The tasks people face in the various action phases create distinct mind-sets that tune people toward congruous thoughts and information. This finding is important for any theorizing on the course of action; in particular, it speaks to the question of whether the course of action should be conceptualized as homogeneous or heterogeneous, that is, compartmentalized into a number of distinct, qualitatively different phases. Lewin (Lewin, Dembo, Festinger, & Sears, 1944) suggested that the realm of goal-oriented behavior entails at least two distinct phenomena—goal setting and goal striving. He believed that goal setting may be accounted for by expectancy × value theories, whereas different theories should be developed to account for goal striving. However, researchers interested in goal-oriented behavior did not develop distinct theories to account for goal striving: rather, they stretched expectancy × value notions, making them account for both goal setting and goal striving (e.g., Atkinson, 1957). This has been criticized on the grounds that the extended expectancy × value theories have only been very modestly successful in predicting vital aspects of goal performance (see Klinger, 1977, pp. 22–24, 329–330).

The present experiments support Lewin's contention that goal setting and goal striving differ in nature. Individuals deliberating action goals were tuned toward thoughts and information that were different from those of individuals planning the implementation of a chosen goal. In recent experiments, further differences were observed between deliberating and planning individuals with respect to the inferences they made on the basis of available information (Gollwitzer & Kinney 1989) and with respect to the absolute amount of available information they processed (Heckhausen & Gollwitzer, 1987, Study 2). These findings attest to differences in the natures of goal setting and goal striving; in addition, they bring to mind Lewin's claim that goal setting and goal striving deserve distinct theorizing.

REFERENCES

Anderson, J. R. (1983). *The architecture of cognition.* Cambridge, MA: Harvard University Press.

Atkinson, J. W. (1957). Motivational determinants of risk-taking behavior. *Psychological Review, 64,* 359–372.

Boring, E. G. (1950). *A history of experimental psychology.* New York: Appleton-Century-Crofts.

Gibson, J. J. (1941). A critical review of the concept of set in contemporary experimental psychology. *Psychological Bulletin, 38,* 781–817.

Gollwitzer, P. M. (1990). Action phases and mind-sets. In E. T. Higgins & R. M. Sorrentino (Eds.), *Handbook of motivation and cognition: Foundations of social behavior* (Vol. 2, pp. 53–92). New York: Guilford Press.

Gollwitzer, P. M., Heckhausen, H., & Ratajczak, H. (1990). From weighing to willing: Approaching a change decision through pre- or postdecisional mentation. *Organizational Behavior and Human Decision Processes, 45,* 41–65.

Gollwitzer, P. M., & Kinney, R. F. (1989). Effects of deliberative and implemental mind-sets on illusion of control. *Journal of Personality and Social Psychology, 56,* 531–542.

Heckhausen, H. (1986). Why some time out might benefit achievement motivation research. In J. H. L. van den Bercken, T. C. M. Bergen, & E. E. J. De Bruyn (Eds.), *Achievement and task motivation* (pp. 7–39). Lisse, The Netherlands: Swets & Zeitlinger.

Heckhausen, H., & Gollwitzer, P. M. (1986). Information processing before and after the formation of an intent. In F. Klix & H. Hagendorf (Eds.), *In memoriam Hermann Ebbinghaus: Symposium on the structure and function of human memory* (pp. 1071–1082). Amsterdam: Elsevier/North Holland.

Heckhausen, H., & Gollwitzer, P. M. (1987). Thought contents and cognitive functioning in motivational vs. volitional states of mind. *Motivation and Emotion, 11,* 101–120.

Higgins, E. T., Rholes, W. S., & Jones, C. R. (1977). Category accessibility and impression formation. *Journal of Experimental Social Psychology, 13,* 141–154.

Humphrey, G. (1951). *Thinking.* London: Methuen.

Klinger, E. (1977). *Meaning and void.* Minneapolis: University of Minnesota Press.

Külpe, O. (1904). Versuche über Abstraktion (Experiments on abstraction]. *Bericht über den I. Kongreß für Experimentelle Psychologie, 1,* 56–68.

Lewin, K., Dembo, T., Festinger, L. A., & Sears, P. S. (1944). Level of aspiration. In J. McV. Hunt (Ed.), *Personality and the behavior disorders* (Vol. 1, pp. 333–378). New York: Ronald.

Marbe, K. (1901). *Experimentell-psychologische Untersuchungen über das Urteil* [Experimental studies on judgment]. Leipzig: W. Engelmann.

Rabkin, E. S. (1979). *Fantastic worlds: Myths, tales, and stories.* Oxford, England: Oxford University Press.

Rosenthal, R., & Rosnow, R. L. (1985). *Contrast analysis: Focused comparisons in the analysis of variance.* New York: Cambridge University Press.

Rumelhart, D. E. (1975). Notes on a schema for stories. In D. G. Bobrow & A. M. Collins (Eds.), *Representation and understanding* (pp. 211–236). New York: Academic Press.

Rumelhart, D. E. (1977). Understanding and summarizing brief stories. In D. LaBerge & J. Samuels (Eds.), *Basic processes in reading and comprehension* (pp. 265–303). Hillsdale, NJ: Erlbaum.

Smith, E. R., & Branscombe, N. R. (1987). Procedurally mediated social inferences: The case of category accessibility effects. *Journal of Experimental Social Psychology, 23,* 361–382.

Srull, T. K., & Wyer, R. S. (1979). The role of category accessibility in the interpretation of information about persons: Some determinants and implications. *Journal of Personality and Social Psychology, 7,* 1660–1672.

Watt, H. J. (1905). Experimentelle Beiträge zu einer Theorie des Denkens [Experiments on a theory of thinking]. *Archiv für die gesamte Psychologie, 4,* 289–436.

Appendix
Coding Scheme for Subjects' Stories

Ascribing Deliberative Efforts to Main Character

Deliberation aimed at making a good decision: "The king racked his brains, wondering what to do. . . ."; "The king was thinking things over for many days and nights, weighing whether to stay at home. . . ."

Turning to others for advice and listening to their suggestions: "The king asked a monk to give him advice. . . ."; "The king listened to a fortune teller. . . ."

Ascribing Implementational Efforts to Main Character

Actual acting as a chosen goal: "The tailor forced himself through the rock passage. . . ."; "The king sent out more men to search the forest. . . ."; "The king ordered a trusted officer to stay at the castle and protect his daughter. . . ."

Thinking about the implementation of the chosen goal: "The king asked himself how could he find a trusted person who would stay home and protect his daughter. . . ."; "The tailor wondered how to climb up the steep wall. . . ."

Identity Negotiation: Where Two Roads Meet

William B. Swann, Jr. • Department of Psychology, University of Texas

Editors' Notes

When one person interacts with another, who determines how each person is perceived? Do the expectancies of each person as perceiver shape the target's behavior so as to confirm the perceiver's expectancies, or does the target shape the judgments of the perceiver to verify the target's own self-concept? The author proposes that both interpersonal forces can be at work, producing a negotiated social reality of what each person is like. Because stable self-conceptions function to organize experience, predict future events, and guide behavior, and because individuals may have negotiated their self-conceptions with significant others who now expect them to be maintained, people can resist changes in their self-conception and seek to maintain or verify them, even when a self-conception is negative. The author describes how selection of interaction partners, behavioral strategies during interaction, and display of identity cues can all be used to maintain self-conceptions. He suggests that most of such maintenance is done routinely as part of the natural flow of social interaction, but crises can also occur when individuals receive feedback that is discrepant from their self-conceptions. He also points out that self-conceptions can change when there is a major reorganization in a person's viewpoint and significant others support the new self-view, as can occur during therapy. Do individuals with negative self-conceptions really want negative feedback? The author suggests that self-verification and self-enhancement serve different cognitive and affective functions, respectively. Thus both motivations need to be considered, both separately and in interaction with one another.

Discussion Questions

1. Why are people motivated to verify their self-conceptions, and how do they do so?
2. When do the motivations for self-verification and self-enhancement come into conflict, and does one or the other dominate the reaction to the conflict?

Authors' Abstract

This article traces a program of research on the interplay between social thought and social interaction. Early investigations of the impact of perceivers' expectancies on the actions of target individuals illuminated the contribution of perceivers to the identity negotiation process but overlooked the role of targets. The research discussed here is based on the assumption that targets play an active role in the identity negotiation process. Specifically, just as perceivers strive to validate their expectancies, targets seek to verify their self-views. The nature and antecedents of the processes through which people verify their self-conceptions as well as the relationship of these activities to self-concept change and self-enhancement processes are discussed. This research suggests that perceivers and targets enter their interactions with independent and sometimes conflicting agendas that are resolved through a process of identity negotiation. The identity negotiation process therefore provides a theoretical context in which the interplay between other-perception and self-perception can be understood.

A little over a decade ago, Mark Snyder and I became interested in the self-fulfilling nature of social beliefs. We were particularly interested in *behavioral confirmation*, a process whereby the expectancies of some individuals (perceivers) channel social interaction so as to cause the behavior of other individuals (targets) to confirm perceivers' expectancies. In our research, for example, targets labeled as hostile grew aggressive, those believed to be extraverted became sociable, and those thought to be bright blossomed into star performers (e.g., Snyder & Swann, 1978a, 1978b; Swann & Snyder, 1980; for a review, see Snyder, 1984). On the basis of these and earlier findings (e.g., Jones & Panitch, 1971; Kelley & Stahelski, 1970; Rosenthal & Jacobson, 1968; Word, Zanna, & Cooper, 1974; Zanna & Pack, 1975), we concluded that there might exist a pervasive tendency for the beliefs of perceivers to shape the nature of social reality.

Yet the behavioral confirmation formulation seemed to illuminate only a portion of what was happening in our studies. True, most target individuals in our research did behaviorally confirm the expectancies of perceivers (see also Darley & Fazio, 1980; E. E. Jones, 1986; Miller & Turnbull, 1986). It was also true, however, that some targets vehemently resisted the labels with which they were tagged. Apparently, targets had their own ideas about themselves and social reality, and at least on occasion, they took active steps to ensure that perceivers shared those ideas. Social reality was not simply constructed by perceivers acting alone; it was negotiated by perceivers and targets acting together. It seemed crucial to learn more about the contribution of targets to the negotiation process.

This article offers one perspective on the role of targets in the identity negotiation process. The central notion is that targets want perceivers to see them as they see themselves, an idea that was advanced by Lecky (1945) and has since been elaborated by several others, most notably Carson (1969), Harvey, Hunt, and Schroder (1961), and especially Secord and Backman (1965). The self-verification formulation (Swann, 1983, 1985) represents a synthesis and extension of these earlier works.

One of my major objectives will be to identify various strategies of self-verification and the personal and situational factors that set them in motion. A second goal will be to consider two propositions that compete with various aspects of the self-verification formulation: the notion that self-concepts are highly malleable and the contention that people strive to enhance rather than maintain their self-views. A final goal will be to argue that the relative expansiveness of an identity negotiation framework makes it capable of offering insights into questions that cannot be understood from narrower perspectives. For this reason, I urge future researchers to adopt an identity negotiation framework. I begin with a discussion of the antecedents of the self and self-verification processes.

Self-Verification Processes

In the tradition of the symbolic interactionists (e.g., Cooley, 1902; Mead, 1934), I assume that people have a fundamental desire to know what to expect from their worlds. Toward this end, they observe their own behavior, the reactions of others to them, and the relation of their own performances to those of others; gradually, they translate these observations into self-conceptions.

As children gather more and more evidence on which to base their self-conceptions, they begin to work to confirm these conceptions. In part, such activity grows out of purely epistemic considerations. Studies of judgmental processes, for example, have indicated that people are more likely to seek and rely on evidence that confirms rather then disconfirms their hypotheses and beliefs, presumably because they find such confirmatory evidence to be particularly trustworthy, diagnostic, and easy to process (e.g., Bruner, Goodnow, & Austin, 1956; Klayman & Ha, 1987; Snyder & Swann, 1978b; Wason & Johnson-Laird, 1972). This suggests that there may be a fundamental, cognitively based tendency for people to regard information that confirms their self-conceptions as more diagnostic than information that disconfirms their self-conceptions. In support of this hypothesis, participants in a study by Swann and Read (1981a, Study 3) indicated that they could learn more about themselves by examining self-confirmatory information as compared with self-disconfirmatory information.

Even if people did not believe that self-confirmatory evidence was especially informative, they might still seek such evidence because it fosters a sense of existential security. That is, in a world in which one's surroundings, interaction partners, and rules governing survival may change rapidly, stable self-conceptions may play an important role in organizing experience, predicting future events, and guiding behavior (cf. Epstein, 1973; Lecky, 1945; Mead, 1934; Secord & Packman, 1965). Self-conceptions may therefore be construed as the lenses through which people view the world, the means whereby they define their existence and understand the world around them. Thus, substantial changes in self-conceptions may necessitate massive reorganization of the conceptual systems through which they make sense of their world.

People may also resist changes in their self-conceptions for pragmatic reasons. People who know that they lack particular abilities, for example, may resist changes in the associated self-conceptions lest they venture into situations in which they will fail miserably (e.g., Baumgardner & Brownlee, 1987). In addition, people may fear that marked changes in their self-views will sour their relationships, as their interaction partners typically expect them to honor the identities that they have negotiated with them earlier (Athay & Darley, 1981; Swann, 1984).

For these and other reasons, people are likely to think and behave in ways that promote the survival of their self-conceptions, regardless of whether the self-conception happens to be positive or negative. Although there are surely painful consequences associated with verifying negative self-conceptions, the foregoing analysis suggests that failing to verify them may have even more painful consequences both epistemically and pragmatically.

Recent research has supported the notion that people work to verify their self-conceptions by striving to acquire self-confirmatory feedback. For example, in a series of three studies, Swann and Read (1981b) found clear evidence of a preference for self-confirmatory feedback whether they examined the extent to which participants paid attention to such feedback, remembered it, or actively sought it. Three additional investigations by Swann and Read (1981a) showed that both men and women preferentially solicited self-confirmatory feedback pertaining to valenced as well as unvalenced self-concepts. Furthermore, people were undaunted in their quest for self-confirmatory feedback even when they had reason to believe that it would make them depressed (Swann, Krull, & Predmore, 1987) and even when they had to spend their personal funds to get it (Swann & Read, 1981a).

The specific strategies through which people verify their self-conceptions fall into two distinct classes. Within the first class are behavioral activities through which targets strive to control the reactions of perceivers. Specifically, targets work to create around themselves self-confirmatory *opportunity structures* (McCall & Simmons, 1966), that is, social environments that foster the survival of their self-views.

Within the second class of self-verification strategies are cognitive processes through which targets systematically distort their perceptions of social reality. In particular, targets process feedback from perceivers in ways that make perceivers' responses seem more supportive of their self-views than they actually are. I will now take a closer look at these strategies of self-verification.

Developing a Self-Confirmatory Opportunity Structure

For some years, biologists and ecologists have noticed that every living organism inhabits a niche or opportunity structure that routinely satisfies its needs and desires (cf. Clarke, 1954; Odum, 1963; Wilson, 1974). People are no exception to this rule. In fact, people seem to be particularly active in striving to ensure that their opportunity structures satisfy their desire for self-confirmatory feedback (e.g., McCall & Simmons, 1966).

In their quest for a self-confirmatory opportunity structure, people may use at least three strategies: They may strategically choose interaction partners and social settings, they may display identity cues, and they may adopt interaction strategies that evoke self-confirmatory responses.

Selective Interaction

For years, researchers have been intrigued with the notion that people seek out social contexts that will provide them with self-confirmatory feedback. Although it is very difficult to obtain definitive support for this hypothesis, several researchers have collected correlational evidence that is consistent with it. Pervin and Rubin (1967), for example, have found that students are less likely to drop out and are happier in college if it has qualities that are compatible with their self-views (see also Backman & Secord, 1962; Broxton, 1963; Newcomb, 1956).

My students and I have collected somewhat more direct evidence for the selective interaction hypothesis. For example, Swann and Pelham (1987, Study 1) found a highly reliable tendency for people to prefer their ideal friends and intimates to see them as they saw themselves ($Fs >$ 100). Thus, just as people who had positive self-conceptions preferred others to view them favorably, people who had negative conceptions of themselves preferred others to view them relatively unfavorably. A second series of investigations by Pelham and Swann (1987a) indicated that people's preferences for friends with either favorable or unfavorable appraisals were associated with the actual appraisals of their friends ($r = .65$), thus suggesting that people translate their desire for congruent relationship partners into actual selection of partners.

Further support for the selective interaction hypothesis comes from a field investigation of college roommates by Swann and Pelham (1987, Study 2). They discovered that individuals who found themselves in relationships in which their roommate's appraisal was incongruent with their self-conceptions were more likely to plan to change roommates than were those in congruent relationships. Moreover, this tendency was symmetrical with respect to self-esteem; people with negative self-conceptions were just as eager to flee from overly favorable roommates as people with positive self-conceptions were inclined to flee from overly unfavorable roommates.

These data therefore offer fairly clear evidence that people gravitate toward social relationships in which they are apt to receive self-confirmatory feedback. An important characteristic of this selective interaction strategy is that once people enter a particular social relationship or institution, forces such as legal contracts and inertia will tend to keep them there. Hence, the selective interaction strategy of self-verification tends to lock people into an interpersonal feedback system that will often be self-sustaining as well as self-verifying.

Displaying Identity Cues

Another way that people can succeed in laying claim to a particular identity is by looking the part. To be effective, identity cues must meet two criteria: They must be under the individual's control, and they must characteristically evoke desired responses from others.

People's physical appearance represents one class of identity cues. The clothes one wears, for example, can be used to tell others whether one is liberal or conservative, wealthy or destitute, easygoing or meticulous, prudish or promiscuous. Similarly, through the skillful use of cosmetics and wigs, people can project dramatically different identities to onlookers. Even body posture may be used to communicate various identities to others. Take, for example, the sex symbol who is forever striking a seductive pose or the aristocrat who never lets bearing belie his or her sense of dignity.

Given sufficient motivation, people may actually modify their body structure to convey particular identities to others. Self-perceived athletes, for example, may diet and lift weights to ensure that their physiques elicit the reactions they crave. Aging individuals who wish to retain their youthful appearance may take more drastic steps. With a little surgery, sagging breasts can regain their former stature, tummies can be tucked, and balding pates can go under cover again. And there is hope even for those who are wimpy about weights and squeamish about surgery, for they may accumulate and display various material possessions. The cars people drive, the homes they live in, the trophies they display in their den may all be used to tell others who they are and how they expect to be treated (cf. Goffman, 1959; Schlenker, 1980).

If physical appearances do not suffice, people may ensure that they are understood by relying on social conventions such as titles and occupational labels. In this way, people may ensure that before they even open their mouths, others know a great deal about the identities that they wish to assume.

Interaction Strategies

Even if people fail to acquire self-confirmatory feedback through selective interaction by displaying identity cues, they may still acquire such feedback by adopting appropriate interaction strategies. Swann and Read (1981b, Study 2), for example, had targets who perceived themselves as either likable or dislikable interact with perceivers. Some targets were led to suspect that the perceiver might like them; others learned that the perceiver might dislike them; still others learned nothing of the perceiver's evaluation of them.

There was an overall tendency for targets who perceived themselves as likable to elicit more favorable reactions than did targets who perceived themselves as dislikable. Moreover, this tendency was especially pronounced when targets suspected that perceivers' appraisals might disconfirm their self-conceptions. Just as targets who thought of themselves as likable and suspected that perceivers disliked them elicited the most favorable reactions, those who saw themselves as dislikable and suspected that perceivers liked them elicited the least favorable reactions. Therefore, targets were particularly inclined to elicit self-confirmatory feedback from perceivers when they suspected that perceivers' appraisals were incompatible with their self-views (cf. Hilton & Darley, 1985).

Swann and Hill (1982) obtained a similar pattern of results using another dimension of the self-concept (dominance) and a different procedural paradigm. Targets began by playing a game with a confederate in which each player alternately assumed the dominant "leader" role or the submissive "assistant" role. There was a break in the game, and the experimenter asked the players to decide who would like to be the leader for the next set of games. This signaled the confederate to deliver feedback to the target. In some conditions, the confederate indicated that the target seemed dominant and in other conditions asserted that the target seemed submissive.

If the feedback confirmed targets' self-conceptions, they more or less passively accepted the confederate's appraisal. If the feedback disconfirmed their self-conceptions, however, targets reacted quite vehemently, resisting the feedback and bending over backwards to demonstrate that they were not the persons the confederate made them out to be. Thus, self-conceived dominants who were labeled submissive became particularly dominant, and self-conceived submissives who were labeled dominant became especially submissive.

An interesting feature of the Swann and Hill study was that some people resisted the discrepant feedback more than others did. Swann and Ely (1984) speculated that such differences in resistance might reflect variability in the extent to which people were certain of their self-conceptions. They reasoned that as people become more certain of their self-conceptions, they will be more inclined to rely on these conceptions to organize their experiences, predict future events, and guide behavior. For this reason, the more certain people are of their self-conceptions, the more motivated they should be to defend them against threats.

To test this hypothesis, Swann and Ely (1984) had perceivers interview targets who were either certain or uncertain of their self-conceived extraversion. Perceivers were always provided with an expectancy about targets that was discrepant with the self-conceptions of targets. This created the potential for a battle of wills, with perceivers' experimentally manipulated beliefs vying against targets' chronic self-views. Consistent with earlier research by Snyder and Swann (1978b; see also Swann & Giuliano, in press), perceivers acted on their expectancies by encouraging targets to make self-discrepant statements. Targets who were low in self-certainty tended to answer in ways that confirmed perceivers' expectancies (but disconfirmed their own self-conceptions) when perceivers were highly certain of their expectancies. In contrast, targets who were high in self-certainty actively resisted perceivers' questions, eventually bringing perceivers to revise their expectancies in favor of targets' chronic self-views. Thus, when targets were high in self-certainty, self-verification "won" over behavioral confirmation in the battle of wills (for a discussion of other factors that influence the outcome of such battles, see Swann, 1984).

Together, our findings suggest that an important determinant of the outcome of the identity negotiation process is the efforts of targets to bring perceivers to see them as they see themselves. Nevertheless, as effective as such efforts may often be, people may sometimes fail to create a self-confirmatory opportunity structure through their behavioral self-verification strategies. When these self-verification strategies fail, the survival of people's self-views may hinge on the effectiveness of the three cognitive self-verification strategies described in the next section.

Seeing More Self-Confirmatory Evidence Than Actually Exists

When people encounter self-disconfirmatory feedback, it is not necessarily the end of the line for the self-conception in question. Researchers have shown that expectancies in general and self-conceptions in particular exert a powerful channeling influence on information processing (for reviews, see Higgins & Bargh, 1987; Kihlstrom & Cantor, 1984). This introduces the possibility that self-conceptions guide the processing of social feedback so as to promote their own survival.

Preferential Attention

To the extent that people are motivated to acquire self-confirmatory feedback, they should be especially attentive to it. A study by Swann and Read (1981b, Study 1) supported this hypothesis. Target individuals who perceived themselves as likable or dislikable learned that another person had evaluated them. Some targets were led to suspect that the other person had formed a favorable impression of them; others were led to suspect that the other person had formed an unfavorable impression of them. All were then given an opportunity to examine a series of statements that the other person had ostensibly made about them. These

statements were sufficiently vague and general so as to apply to anyone.

The results showed that targets spent more time scrutinizing the evaluative statements when they anticipated that the statements would confirm their self-conceptions. That is, just as people who saw themselves as likable spent more time scrutinizing the statements when they expected them to be favorable, those who saw themselves as dislikable spent more time scrutinizing the statements when they expected them to be unfavorable. Hence, it appears that people will be more attentive to social feedback if they suspect that it will confirm their chronic self-views.

Selective Encoding and Retrieval

Just as people may preferentially attend to self-confirmatory feedback, they may also encode and recall it preferentially. Crary (1966) and Silverman (1964), for example, reported that people recalled more incidental information about experimental tasks in which they received self-confirmatory rather than self-discrepant feedback.

Self-conceptions seem to channel the type as well as the amount of feedback that people recall. Swann and Read (1981b, Study 3) had participants who perceived themselves as likable or dislikable listen to another individual make a series of positive and negative statements about them. Some participants expected that the statements would be generally positive; others expected that the statements would be generally negative. After a brief delay, participants recalled as many of the statements as possible. Overall, those who saw themselves as likable remembered more positive statements and those who saw themselves as dislikable remembered more negative statements. In addition, this tendency to recall more self-confirmatory statements than self-disconfirmatory statements was greatest when individuals anticipated that their interaction partner's statements would confirm their self-conceptions.[1]

---

[1]These data may seem incompatible with Hastie and Kumar's (1979) contention that people are especially likely to recall expectancy-inconsistent evidence. Recent research, however, has suggested that Hastie and Kumar's findings were an artifact of a confound between set size and expectancy. Researchers who have avoided this confound (e.g., Bargh & Thein, 1985; Hemsley & Marmurek, 1982) have found that people preferentially recall information that confirms well-formed beliefs (for further details, see Higgins & Bargh, 1987).

Selective Interpretation

When people receive feedback, there are a number of questions they might ask themselves: Is the feedback valid? Is the source of feedback reliable and trustworthy? What implications does the feedback have in light of what I know about myself? The research literature suggests that people typically answer these questions in ways that promote the survival of their self-views.

At least three independent investigators have demonstrated that participants will endorse the validity of feedback only if it fits with their self-conceptions (Crary, 1966; Korman, 1968; Markus, 1977). Similarly, Shrauger and Lund (1975) reported that individuals expressed relatively more confidence in the perceptiveness of an evaluator when his or her impression confirmed their self-conceptions. Swann, Griffin, Predmore, and Gaines (1987) replicated this effect and also found that people tended to attribute self-confirmatory feedback to characteristics of themselves and self-disconfirmatory feedback to the source of the feedback.

Together, the attentional, encoding, retrieval, and interpretational processes described in this section may prove formidable adversaries for self-discrepant feedback. This may be one reason why people's self-conceptions sometimes conflict with the actual appraisals of others (e.g., Felson, 1981a, 1981b) and, more specifically, why people overestimate the extent to which the appraisals of their friends and acquaintances confirm their self-conceptions (Miyamoto & Dornbusch, 1956; Orpen & Bush, 1974; Sherwood, 1967; Walhood & Klopfer, 1971). The fact that these cognitive self-verification strategies can lead to such misconceptions suggests that it is important that they do not work *too* well, because they may blind targets to perceivers' actual appraisals of them. In fact, if targets' misconceptions are serious enough, perceivers may become sufficiently distraught that they withdraw from the identity negotiation process. [. . .]

Self-Verification and Self-Concept Change

Several theorists (e.g., Gergen, 1977; Tedeschi & Lindskold, 1976) have recently suggested that our self-conceptions and the identities we negotiate change very rapidly. These authors assume, as I do, that people base their self-conceptions on ob-servations of themselves and the reactions of others. They diverge from my viewpoint, however, in assuming that people place little weight on their personal histories in forming conceptions of self. Their viewpoint therefore suggests that the self is highly malleable, changing with every twitch of the social environment.

Advocates of the malleable-self viewpoint have buttressed their position with the results of laboratory investigations in which people have been shown to change their self-ratings in response to social feedback. Yet such evidence must be treated cautiously. For one thing, outside the laboratory, self-conceptions seem stubbornly resistant to change. Therapists, for example, often fail to alter the self-views of their clients, even after months of intensive therapy. In addition, longitudinal investigations (e.g., Block, 1981; Costa & McCrae, 1980) have shown that self-conceptions and related psychological structures remain stable over periods as long as 35 years. In light of these and similar data, several reviewers (Shrauger & Schoeneman, 1979; Wylie, 1979) have concluded that the results of laboratory investigators do not generalize to naturalistic settings.

Such lack of generalizability may stem from the fact that laboratory investigators commonly confront participants with self-discrepant feedback and then place them in interpersonal straitjackets. That is, in a typical study, the experimenter presents discrepant feedback to participants and then deprives them of opportunities to resist such feedback, opportunities that they ordinarily enjoy. Perhaps if participants were provided with opportunities to resist self-discrepant feedback, they would do so and consequently display minimal self-rating change.

Self-Generated Stability of Self Views

Research by Swann and Hill (1982) supports the notion that unconstrained individuals behave in ways that stabilize their self-views. As mentioned earlier, some targets in this study first received feedback from a confederate that disconfirmed their self-perceived dominance. Then, some targets had an opportunity to interact with the confederate; others received no such opportunity. Afterwards, all targets completed a measure of self-perceived dominance.

Targets in the interaction-opportunity conditions actively sought to undermine the feedback by behaving in a self-confirmatory manner. Furthermore, this opportunity to refute the feedback had important cognitive consequences: Those who had opportunity to interact with the source of the feedback displayed little self-rating change relative to those who were deprived of this opportunity. Therefore, if they could do so, targets actively sought to undermine self-discrepant feedback and consequently displayed little self-rating change.

The results of the Swann and Hill (1982) study suggest that people may change their self-ratings only when they receive self-discrepant feedback in highly structured situations in which they are unable to influence or resist the feedback they receive. Furthermore, even when people do receive discrepant feedback in highly structured situations, any changes produced there may be short-lived, because once they leave such situations they may return to self-confirmatory opportunity structures. Here, they will tend to receive feedback that will offset the effects of the self-discrepant feedback.

To test this reasoning, Swann and Predmore (1985) recruited pairs of individuals ("targets" and "intimates") who had been in intimate relationships for an average of 18 months. Some targets had positive self-views; others had negative self-views. Upon their arrival, targets and intimates were separated and intimates reported their perceptions of targets. Although intimates generally tended to see targets as targets saw themselves (r = .41), in some couples the amount of congruency was relatively high (congruent) and in others it was relatively low (incongruent).

After having targets complete a bogus Thematic Apperception Test (TAT), the experimenter ushered them into a room where either their intimate or a complete stranger was waiting. Shortly thereafter, the experimenter returned with the "results" of the TAT and delivered feedback that disconfirmed targets' self-views. The experimenter then left, leaving targets to interact with either their intimate or a stranger for 5 min. At the end of this period the experimenter returned to measure the final self-views of targets.

The results showed that congruent intimates insulated targets against the self-discrepant feedback, but interacting with a stranger did not. Incongruent intimates had some insulating influence on targets, although not as much as the congruent ones had, presumably because even incongruent intimates had appraisals of targets that were associated with targets' self-views. The really interesting finding, however, was that the congruent intimates of targets with low self-esteem were just as effective in insulating them against positive feedback as the congruent intimates of the targets with high self-esteem were in insulating them against negative feedback! These data therefore suggest that by entering particular social relationships, people enlist "accomplices" who assist them in their self-verification attempts by offering feedback that nullifies self-discrepant feedback. In this way, individuals in the person's opportunity structure may help stabilize their self-conceptions.

Considered together, these data suggest that it is inappropriate to assume that self-conceptions are frightfully frail cognitive structures that change at the drop of the hat. Yet if one accepts the notion that self-conceptions are highly stable, how should one characterize the self-rating changes that people display when they encounter discrepant feedback in laboratory settings? If such changes are not changes in self-conceptions, what are they?

The answer may reside in a consideration of the way self-knowledge is structured. Most self-theorists agree that self-knowledge is organized hierarchically, with global abstractions about the self at the top and highly specific, temporally or situationally bound information at the bottom (e.g., Epstein, 1973; Greenwald, 1981; Markus & Wurf, 1987; Vallacher & Wegner, 1985; cf. Jones & Gerard's, 1967, analysis of vertical attitude structure). Enduring shifts in self-views occur only when generalized, abstract self-conceptions change. In contrast, transitory fluctuations in self-views occur when specific, concrete self-images change. In some respects, then, a self-conception is analogous to a composite of all the frames in a motion picture film, whereas a self-image is analogous to a single frame in that film (e.g., Turner, 1968).

When Self-Concepts Change

The foregoing analysis suggests that for enduring changes in self-conceptions to occur, two things must happen. First, people must undergo a major reorganization in the way they view themselves. Second, people's interaction partners must begin providing them with feedback that supports the new self-view. Although the self-verification formulation suggests that both people and their interaction partners tend to resist such changes, this resistance is certainly not insurmountable.

Perhaps the most common chain of events that culminates in enduring self-concept change is for the community to recognize a change in the individual and adjust the way it treats him or her. Such community-initiated changes are usually precipitated by some fairly dramatic change in the individual's age, status, social role, or some combination of these factors. For example, when children become adolescents, when singles get married, or when graduate students become faculty members, they find that people suddenly begin to treat them differently. This causes them to modify their self-conceptions and identity negotiation activities accordingly.

Alternatively, people themselves may sometimes initiate a change in their self-views. For example, people with negative self-views may decide that such views prevent them from attaining some highly desirable goal. They may accordingly approach a therapist for help in modifying the undesirable self-view. A major difficulty that therapists sometimes encounter is that clients inexplicably resist efforts to change the self-view that caused them to seek therapy. Therapists and researchers, however, have begun to develop strategies for dealing with such resistance.

One way to handle resistance is to use it to facilitate the change process, a paradoxical strategy (cf. Watzlawick, Weakland, & Fisch, 1974). Consider that no matter how extreme people happen to be on a dimension, they are usually somewhat shy of the end point of that dimension. For example, most people with conservative sex role attitudes will feel that they have been misconstrued if someone asks them a question implying that they have extremely conservative attitudes, such as "Why do you think its a good idea to keep women barefoot and pregnant?" In response, they may try to distance themselves from the implications of the question by, for example, pointing out their few relatively liberal beliefs. The paradox is that such identity-protective activities may wind up changing their identities: After espousing relatively liberal beliefs, targets may reflect on their behavior and infer that they are actually more liberal than they once thought (e.g., Bem, 1972).

To test this reasoning, Swann, Pelham, and Chidester (in press) asked participants who were high or low in the certainty of their beliefs about sex roles a series of "superattitudinal" leading questions, that is, questions that encouraged them to make statements that were in the direction of

but slightly more extreme than their own viewpoints. As Swann and Ely (1984) found, those who were low in belief certainty displayed little resistance to the questions and changed their beliefs accordingly. In contrast, those high in belief certainty displayed considerable resistance to the questions, and as a result of such resistance, they displayed considerable belief change in the opposite direction! A follow-up study replicated the first and showed that paradoxical injunctions change people's positions on belief dimensions rather than merely changing their perception of the dimension. Together, this pair of studies suggests that although it may be very difficult to keep people who are high in belief certainty from resisting discrepant feedback, paradoxical strategies may effectively promote change among such individuals by turning such resistance activities against themselves.

The specific paradoxical strategy used by Swann, Pelham, and Chidester (in press) may be viewed as one of a broad class of strategies in which targets are mislabeled and find that, paradoxically, the only way to reaffirm their initial identity is to distance themselves from a caricature of that identity. One variant of the paradoxical approach was developed by reactance researchers (e.g., Brehm, 1966; Wicklund, 1974). Their approach was to encourage participants to endorse a self-consistent position (as compared with our tack of trying to bring participants to endorse a position that was slightly discrepant from their initial position). The key to the approach was encouraging participants to adopt this position in a manner so heavy-handed that participants' perceptions of autonomy were threatened. They reacted by reasserting their self-conceived autonomy in the only way available, that is, by distancing themselves from their initial position. In a sense, then, reactance processes can be understood as a special case of self-verification in which the threatened self-conception concerns the participant's general sense of autonomy (as opposed to his or her position on a belief dimension).

One general implication of this work is that if change agents use the right strategy, they can even change the self-views of targets who are high in self-certainty. But consider an important caveat. The strategies for changing self-views discussed thus far were designed to produce short-term changes in the self-views of targets. For change to be lasting, the social environment in which that target resides must support the new self-view, and research on selective interaction suggests that people tend to enter relationships with individuals who see them as they see themselves. This means that even if targets are amenable to changing their self-view, the change process may be undermined by the target's friends and intimates (e.g., Swann & Predmore, 1985).

Imagine, for example, a highly talented person who, for whatever reason (e.g., an abusive parent), has developed a negative view of herself or himself. A therapist may try to deal with this problem by establishing a supportive relationship with the client and encouraging him or her to focus on his or her many talents. Although this technique may produce momentary improvements in the client's self-view, such improvements may be completely undone when the client returns home to a spouse who showers him or her with abuse. Hence, once people establish relationships with partners who see them as they see themselves, these partners tend to reinforce the identities that have been negotiated, even if these identities are negative and at some level the person wishes to overcome them. It would seem then that people with negative self-views sometimes work both to maintain and to improve their self-views, at once pushing and pulling themselves into a standstill. One set of reasons why people might be ambivalent about their identities—the competing motives of self-verification and self-enhancement—will be considered next.

Self-Verification Versus Self-Enhancement

Surely the most provocative aspect of our findings is that they challenge one of psychology's most widely held theoretical viewpoints, self-enhancement theory (e.g., Baumeister, 1982; Greenwald, 1980; Jones, 1964; Jones, 1973; Kaplan, 1975; Taylor & Brown, in press; Tesser, 1985). This theory assumes that people have a powerful desire for positive feedback and that this desire exerts a potent influence on the identities they negotiate with their interaction partners.[2]

Our findings clearly challenge self-enhancement theory. It is not just that people with negative self-views fail to display the interest in acquiring favorable feedback that self-enhancement theory suggests they should; our findings show that such individuals actually prefer unfavorable to favorable feedback. That is, people with negative self-views seem to prefer and seek out unfavorable feedback (e.g., Swann, Pelham & Krull, 1987; Swann, Krull, & Predmore, 1987) and friends and intimates who think poorly of them (e.g., Pelham & Swann, 1987b; Swann & Pelham, 1987; Swann & Predmore, 1985). People with negative self-conceptions also adopt interaction strategies that tend to elicit unfavorable reactions, especially when they suspect that their partners view them positively (Swann & Read, 1981b, Study 2). Furthermore, should they somehow manage to elicit positive reactions, they may still maintain their self-views by failing to attend to and remember such reactions (Swann & Read, 1981a, Studies 1 and 3) or by dismissing such reactions as inaccurate (Swann, Griffin, Predmore, & Gaines, 1987).

Critics will surely counter such contentions by pointing to the large amount of evidence that seems to support self-enhancement theory (for reviews, see Jones, 1973; Shrauger, 1975). I suggest, however, that many alleged "self-enhancement effects" are actually self-verification effects in disguise. One reason for this is that most people develop highly positive conceptions of themselves.

The Ubiquity of Positive Self-Conceptions

My argument begins with some observations of the socialization process. As a rule, caretakers in our society are incredibly supportive of children, heaping on positive feedback at every turn (e.g., Fagot, 1978). Children, being rather naive in such matters, generally take such feedback to heart and develop remarkably positive self-views. They may then use these idealized conceptions of themselves to guide their subsequent behavioral and cognitive activities and gradually "edit" these conceptions as they acquire additional evidence (Turner, 1968).

---

[2]I refer to the weak form of self-enhancement theory here (which suggests that people with low and high self-esteem should be equally enamored with favorable feedback) instead of the strong form (which argues that people with low esteem should be more enamored with favorable feedback than should people with high esteem) because there is little sound support for the strong form. That is, most studies that have been taken as support for the strong form of self-enhancement are flawed (e.g., researchers generally manipulated rather than measured self-esteem). Moreover, recent research has consistently failed to support the strong form of the theory (e.g., Alloy & Abramson, 1979; Brown, 1986; Campbell, 1986; and the research reviewed in this article).

Although this editing process will generally promote more realistic self-views, several factors may lead people to maintain highly positive views of themselves. Caretakers, for example, may continue to be generous with positive feedback. In addition, children themselves may strive to be the wonderful human beings that their parents believe them to be by working to develop their strengths and avoiding contexts in which their weaknesses might become apparent.

Even people who fail to excel may encounter negative feedback only rarely. Blumberg (1972) and Tesser and Rosen (1975), for example, have shown that there exist social norms that discourage people from delivering direct negative feedback to others. So powerful are such norms that it is often impossible to tell that people dislike their interaction partners by listening to what they say to them. Only by looking at the paralinguistic content of their utterances (e.g., timing of utterances, tone of voice, etc.) is it sometimes possible to identify individuals who dislike their partners (e.g., DePaulo, Stone, & Lassiter, 1985; Mehrabian, 1972).

In short, people rarely develop self-views that are generally negative (e.g., Pelham & Swann, 1987b) because their social worlds rarely provide them with feedback that would sustain such views. This has several implications for assessing the relative merits of the self-enhancement and self-verification formulations. For example, the tendency for people with positive self-concepts to be over-represented in most samples means that it is futile to try to identify individuals who are low in self-esteem by using median split techniques (as many past researchers have done). We have found that to identify people who are truly low in self-esteem (i.e., who believe that they are below average), one must generally select individuals who score in the lower 10% to 30% of college student samples. This is not a minor methodological quibble; unless people designated as low in self-esteem are truly low in self-esteem, it is possible to mistake self-verification effects for self-enhancement effects. If, for example, individuals with high self-esteem are misclassified as having low self-esteem, it may appear that people with low self-esteem sought favorable feedback or resisted unfavorable feedback when, in reality, those with high self-esteem were responsible for such activity.

In addition, if most people have positive self-views, attempting to manipulate self-esteem by providing people with a dose or two of negative feedback (as many researchers have done) is not a viable way to compare the relative importance of self-verification and self-enhancement tendencies. Self-verification processes are presumably motivated by psychological investment borne out of considerable experience. Given that most people possess relatively positive self-views, presenting unfavorable feedback to unselected individuals might be likely to motivate them to verify their positive self-views (e.g., Swann & Read, 1981b); at any rate, it should not cause them to work to confirm negative self-views. The only individuals who should reliably work to verify their negative self-views are those who possess chronically negative self-views of which they are reasonably certain.

The Cognitive–Affective Crossfire

Lest I appear determined to reduce all self-enhancement effects to the status of epiphenomena or methodological artifacts, let me add an important caveat: Affective reactions to feedback generally conform to self-enhancement theory, and cognitive responses generally conform to self-verification theory (e.g., Shrauger, 1975). For example, Swann, Griffin, Predmore, and Gaines (1987) presented individuals who possessed either positive or negative self-concepts with either favorable or unfavorable social feedback. As the self-verification formulation would suggest, participants with negative self-concepts indicated that unfavorable feedback was more self-descriptive than favorable feedback. As self-enhancement theory would suggest, however, those who received unfavorable feedback were considerably more depressed, anxious, and hostile than were those who received favorable feedback. Swann, Krull, and Predmore (1987) provided further support for the independence of cognitive and affective responses. They found that the tendency for people with low self-esteem to actively solicit unfavorable feedback was independent of the negative affect introduced by previous doses of unfavorable feedback.

This research suggests that people who are low in self-esteem may be caught in a crossfire between their cognitions and affects: Even though they value unfavorable feedback on a cognitive level because of its apparent accuracy, they find it affectively abhorrent because of its damning implications. How then, should one answer the question "What do people with low self-esteem really want?" Part of the answer obviously depends on what one means by the word *want*. Evidence that people with low self-esteem seek unfavorable feedback (Swann, Krull, & Predmore, 1987; Swann & Read, 1981b, Study 1) obviously suggests that they want it in some sense of the word. Nevertheless, the fact that unfavorable feedback makes people miserable suggests that they would avoid it if possible.

Semantics aside, the real difficulty here may be that the question "What do people with low self-esteem really want?" is based on an erroneous assumption, the assumption of psychological unity. This assumption holds that a superordinate cognitive system directs all mental activity and resolves inconsistencies between thoughts, feelings, and actions. Several aspects of the Swann, Griffin, Predmore, and Gaines (1987) findings contradict the unity assumption. Most important, the overall pattern of data indicated that cognitive responses were based on the subjective veridicality of the stimuli, such as the extent to which the feedback was consistent with the person's self-views, and affective responses were based simply on whether the feedback was negative or positive.

What might account for this independence of cognitive and affective responses? Recent work by dual and multiple systems theorists (e.g., Epstein, 1984; Gazzaniga, 1985; Tomkins, 1981; Wilson, 1985; Zajonc, 1980, 1984) may be relevant here. This work suggests that the cognitive and affective systems perform very different tasks. The cognitive system seeks, classifies, and analyzes information in an attempt to maximize the subjective veridicality of the products of these operations. For example, when social feedback is received, it is first identified and then compared to information about the self stored in memory. If the feedback concurs with the information in memory (i.e., appears veridical), it is accepted and integrated with past knowledge.

The affective system, in contrast, enables the organism to respond quickly to events that pose an immediate threat to personal safety. This relatively primitive system apparently reacts on the basis of relatively gross discriminations (i.e., threatening vs. not threatening, favorable to self vs. unfavorable to self) and little or no analysis of the subjective veridicality of the stimuli. This system, then, trades precision for speed. It may not perform a highly sophisticated analysis of stimuli, but it reacts quickly.

Of course, believing that the affective system produces self-enhancement effects and the cognitive system independently produces self-verification effects still leaves many questions unanswered. For example, as there is obviously some interaction between the two systems, what is the nature of such interaction?

Eluding—and Failing to Elude—the Crossfire

Recent research by Swann, Pelham, and Krull (1987) offers some insight into how the cognitive and affective systems interact. Their central thesis was that people are motivated to avert conflicts between their cognitively based desire for self-verification and their affectively based desire for self-enhancement. Toward this end, people seek feedback that is both self-verifying and self-enhancing. They first showed that people's self-concepts are sufficiently differentiated that even those with very low global self-esteem (lowest 10%) believe that they possess a ray of hope, that is, a positive attribute that might serve as a source of pride and inspiration. They then asked if even people with globally negative self-views would seek verification for their positive attributes. They found that when people's information-seeking activities were relatively unconstrained, there was a tendency for them to sample feedback that would verify their positive attributes; when they were constrained to sample feedback pertaining to their negative attributes, however, people solicited unfavorable rather than favorable feedback. Moreover, people with low and high self-esteem were equally inclined to display this pattern of feedback seeking.

One implication of Swann, Pelham, and Krull's (1987) findings is that researchers should use measures of specific self-conceptions instead of or in addition to global measures of the self-concept. More generally, their data suggest that when they can, people try to avoid getting into cognitive–affective crossfires by striving to verify their positive attributes. Apparently, people want to know the truth about themselves, but there are many truths, and the truth people desire the most is the one that offers a ray of hope.

Although people may avoid crossfires when they can, it is important to remember that there are times when it is impossible to avoid such crossfires. In selecting a friend or intimate, for example, people with one or more negative self-conceptions may discover that it is impossible to locate someone who will verify both their positive and their negative attributes because halo biases (e.g., Chapman & Chapman, 1969; Hamilton & Gifford, 1976) tend to homogenize people's appraisals of one another. This means that sometimes individuals may be forced to choose between partners who are uniformly positive or uniformly negative toward them, a choice that places them in the middle of the cognitive–affective crossfire they wish to avoid.

How do people with negative self-views resolve this crossfire? It appears that they choose partners who have unfavorable appraisals of them. Swann and Pelham (1987), for example, found that people with negative as opposed to positive self-conceptions indicated that ideally, their friends and intimates should perceive them relatively unfavorably. Furthermore, a follow-up study indicated that roommates who possessed negative self-views planned to flee from relationships in which they were perceived favorably and remain in relationships in which they were perceived unfavorably!

At first blush, the results of the Swann and Pelham (1987) studies may seem to fly in the face of evidence indicating that even people with low self-esteem are more attracted to evaluators who have favorable appraisals of them (for recent reviews, see Berscheid, 1985; Huston & Levinger, 1978; Jones, 1973; Mettee & Aronson, 1974; Reis, 1985). Virtually all of the evidence suggesting that positivity is prepotent over congruency, however, has come from laboratory investigations in which participants' responses had few consequences. Clearly, it is one thing to express attraction for someone who seems to have an inappropriately favorable appraisal of oneself; it is quite another to pursue a relationship with such an individual (cf. Huston & Levinger, 1978), as doing so may bring on the undesired epistemic and pragmatic consequences associated with discrepant feedback.

It appears, then, that if people are forced into a crossfire between self-verification and self-enhancement, they will self-enhance only if they can avoid the aversive epistemic and pragmatic consequences associated with failure to self-verify (cf. Schlenker, 1980). In instances in which people must either self-verify or self-enhance, they will self-verify.

Summary and Implications

The basic argument here is that people are highly motivated to verify their self-conceptions, and this motivation shapes the nature of the identity negotiation process. Some strategies of self-verification are interpersonal, involving people's efforts to bring others to see them as they see themselves. Other strategies are intrapsychic, involving processes through which people see more self-confirmatory evidence than actually exists. Orthogonal to this distinction, some strategies are relatively automatic and effortless and others are conscious and effortful.

Although self-verification processes ordinarily tend to stabilize people's conceptions of themselves, under certain specifiable conditions they can actually be used to promote self-concept change. Self-concept change may be particularly desirable when people have negative self-conceptions, because such individuals are trapped in a crossfire between a cognitively based desire for self-verification and an affectively based desire for self-enhancement. Although people generally strive to avoid crossfires, at times they are unavoidable. When caught in such situations, people resolve them in favor of self-verification.

In emphasizing the contribution of targets to the process of identity negotiation, I do not wish to minimize the contribution of perceivers to this process. In fact, my use of the term *identity negotiation* in the title and throughout this article was intended to encourage researchers to consider simultaneously how the activities of both perceivers and targets are woven into the fabric of social interaction.

The concept of identity negotiation is based on the assumption that people enter their social interactions with certain goals in mind and try to establish mutual identities that enable them to attain these goals. A process of negotiation ensues and, if successful, a working consensus emerges that defines the identity that each person is to assume during the interaction. From then on, the interaction proceeds smoothly until the participants have achieved their goals or one partner decides not to honor the identity that he or she has negotiated (e.g., Goffman, 1959; McCall & Simmons, 1966; Stryker & Statham, 1985; Weinstein & Deutschberger, 1963).

A major advantage of the identity negotiation framework is that it explicitly acknowledges the influence of both personal characteristics (e.g., goals, agendas, and life histories) and social structural variables (e.g., norms, roles, and social conventions) on the nature and outcome of social interaction. This relatively expansive perspective may lead to insights that could not be reached from either a personological or a social perspective alone.

A case in point is the debate between advocates of self-enhancement and advocates of self-verification. Over the last three decades, dozens of psychologists have tested the hypothesis that people with negative self-conceptions are inclined to embrace unfavorable feedback. A common tactic has been to "lower people's self-conceptions" by providing them with negative feedback and to then observe their reactions to feedback. This approach ignores the fact that the vast majority of people enter the laboratory with well-articulated views of themselves: views that are liable to exert far more influence on reactions to unfavorable feedback than anything an experimenter could ethically do to them. In such instances the most appropriate research strategy is one based on an individual differences approach, that is, one that involves measuring rather than manipulating people's self-views.

Other research, such as work on the stability of self-conceptions, can benefit from a more social perspective. For example, many researchers have attempted to explain the tendency for people to maintain stable conceptions of themselves by referring to various biases in information processing. Although such biases are surely important, exclusive emphasis on such intrapsychic sources of stability in people's self-views leads researchers to overlook the contribution of people's social environments to the stability of their self-conceptions. That is, as the research in this article suggests, people may stabilize their self-conceptions by creating around themselves social environments that provide them with support for their self-conceptions. The stability inherent in these environments will in turn stabilize their self-views.

These are but two examples of the insights that can be gained from adopting an identity negotiation framework, a framework that embraces both personological and social influences on human behavior. Admittedly, one disadvantage associated with an identity negotiation framework is that it is inherently more complex than considering characteristics of people or of situations independently.

Yet I believe that the benefits to be gained from this approach far outweigh the costs. In fact, it is difficult to imagine how we can ever attain a full understanding of either other-perception or self-perception without understanding the process of identity negotiation, as this process may well be the major mechanism through which we come to understand ourselves and those around us.

REFERENCES

Alloy, L. B., & Abramson, L. Y. (1979). Judgments of contingency in depressed and non-depressed students: Sadder but wiser? *Journal of Experimental Psychology: General, 108,* 441–485.

Athay, M., & Darley, J. M. (1981). Toward an interaction centered theory of personality. In N. Cantor & J. F. Kihlstrom (Eds.), *Personality, cognition, and social interaction* (pp. 281–308). Hillsdale, NJ: Erlbaum.

Backman, C. W., & Secord, P. F. (1962). Liking, selective interaction, and misperception in congruent interpersonal relations. *Sociometry, 25,* 321–335.

Bargh, J. A., & Thein, R. D. (1985). Individual construct accessibility, person memory and the retail-judgment link: The case of information overload. *Journal of Personality and Social Psychology, 49,* 1129–1146.

Baumeister, R. F. (1982). A self-presentation of view of social phenomena. *Psychological Bulletin, 91,* 3–26.

Baumgardner, A. H., & Brownlee, E. A. (1987). Strategic failure in social interaction: Evidence for expectancy disconfirmation processes. *Journal of Personality and Social Psychology, 52,* 525–535.

Bem, D. J. (1972). Self-perception theory. In L. Berkowitz (Ed.), *Advances in experimental social psychology* (Vol. 6, pp. 1–62). New York: Academic Press.

Berscheid, E. (1985). Interpersonal attraction. In G. Lindzey & E. Aronson (Eds.), *Handbook of social psychology* (Vol. 2, pp. 413–484). New York: Random House.

Block, J. (1981). Some enduring and consequential structures of personality. In A. I. Rabin et al. (Eds.), *Further explorations in personality* (pp. 27–43). New York: Wiley.

Blumberg, H. H. (1972). Communication of interpersonal evaluations. *Journal of Personality and Social Psychology, 23,* 157–162.

Brehm, J. W. (1966). *A theory of psychological reactance.* New York: Academic Press.

Brown, J. D. (1986). Evaluations of self and others: Self-enhancement biases in social judgment. *Social Cognition, 4,* 353–376.

Broxton, J. A. (1963). A test of interpersonal attraction predictions derived from balance theory. *Journal of Abnormal and Social Psychology, 66,* 391–397.

Bruner, J. S., Goodnow, J. J., & Austin, G. A. (1956). *A study of thinking.* New York: Wiley.

Campbell, J. D. (1986). Similarity and uniqueness: The effects of attribute type, relevance, and individual differences in self-esteem and depression. *Journal of Personality and Social Psychology, 50,* 281–294.

Carson, R. C. (1969). *Interaction concepts of personality.* Chicago: Aldine.

Chapman, L. J., & Chapman, J. P. (1969). Illusory correlation as an obstacle to the use of valid psychodiagnostic signs. *Journal of Abnormal Psychology, 71,* 271–280.

Clarke, G. L. (1954). *Elements of ecology.* New York: Wiley.

Cooley, C. S. (1902). *Human nature and the social order.* New York: Scribner's.

Costa, B. T., Jr., & McCrae, R. R. (1980). Still stable after all these years: Personality as a key to some issues in adulthood and old age. In P. B. Baltes & O. G. Brim (Eds.), *Life span development and behavior* (Vol. 3, pp. 5–102). New York: Academic Press.

Crary, W. G. (1966). Reactions to incongruent self-experiences. *Journal of Consulting Psychology, 30,* 246–252.

Darley, J. M., & Fazio, R. H. (1980). Expectancy confirmation processes arising in the interaction sequence. *American Psychologist, 35,* 867–881.

DePaulo, B. M., Stone, J. I., & Lassiter, G. D. (1985). Deceiving and detecting deceit. In B. R. Schlenker (Ed.), *Self and social life* (pp. 323–370). New York: McGraw-Hill.

Epstein, S. (1973). The self-concept revisited: On a theory of a theory. *American Psychologist, 28,* 404–416.

Epstein, S. (1984). The self-concept: A review and proposal of an integrated theory of personality. In E. Staub (Ed.), *Personality: Basic issues and current research* (pp. 81–132). Englewood Cliffs, NJ: Prentice-Hall.

Fagot, B. I. (1978). The influence of child on parental reactions to toddler children. *Child Development, 49,* 459–465.

Felson, R. B. (1981a). Self and reflected appraisal among football players. *Social Psychology Quarterly, 44,* 116–126.

Felson, R. B. (1981b). Social sources of information in the development of the self. *Sociological Quarterly, 22,* 69–79.

Gazzaniga, M. S. (1985). *The social brain.* New York: Basic Books.

Gergen, K. J. (1977). The social construction of self-knowledge. In T. Mischel (Ed.), *The self: Psychological and philosophical issues* (pp. 139–169). Totowa, NJ: Rowman and Littlefield.

Goffman, E. (1959). *The presentation of self in everyday life.* New York: Anchor Books.

Greenwald, A. G. (1980). The totalitarian ego: Fabrication and revision of personal history. *American Psychologist, 35,* 603–618.

Greenwald, A. G. (1981). Self and memory. In G. H. Bower (Ed.), *Psychology of learning and motivation* (Vol. 15, pp. 201–236). New York: Academic Press.

Hamilton, D. L., & Gifford, R. K. (1976). Illusory correlation in interpersonal perception: A cognitive basis of stereotypic judgments. *Journal of Experimental Social Psychology, 12,* 392–407.

Harvey, O. J., Hunt, D. E., & Schroder, H. M. (1961). *Conceptual systems and personality organization.* New York: Wiley.

Hastie, R., & Kumar, P. (1979). Person memory: Personality traits as organizing principles in memory for behaviors. *Journal of Personality and Social Psychology, 37,* 25–38.

Hemsley, G. D., & Marmurek, H. C. (1982). Person memory: The processing of consistent and inconsistent person information. *Personality and Social Psychology Bulletin, 8,* 433–438.

Higgins, E. T., & Bargh, J. A. (1987). Social cognition and social perception. In M. R. Rosenzweig & L. W. Porter (Eds.), *Annual review of psychology* (Vol. 38, pp. 369–425). Palo Alto, CA: Annual Reviews.

Hilton, J. L., & Darley, J. M. (1985). Constructing other persons: A limit on the effect. *Journal of Experimental Social Psychology, 21,* 1–18.

Huston, T. L., & Levinger, G. (1978). Interpersonal attraction and relationships. In M. R. Rosenzweig & L. W. Porter (Eds.), *Annual review of psychology* (Vol. 29, pp. 115–156). Palo Alto, CA: Annual Reviews.

Jones, E. E. (1964). *Ingratiation.* New York: Appleton-Century-Crofts.

Jones, E. E. (1986). Interpreting interpersonal behavior. The effects of expectancies. *Science, 234,* 41–46.

Jones, E. E., & Gerard, H. B. (1967). *Foundations of social psychology.* New York: Wiley.

Jones, S. C. (1973). Self and interpersonal evaluations: Esteem theories versus consistency theories. *Psychological Bulletin, 79,* 185–199.

Jones, S. C., & Panitch, D. (1971). The self-fulfilling prophecy and interpersonal attraction. *Journal of Experimental Social Psychology, 7,* 356–366.

Kaplan, H. B. (1975). Prevalence to the self-esteem motive. In H. B. Kaplan (Ed.), *Self-attitudes and deviant behavior* (pp. 16–27). Pacific Palisades, CA: Goodyear.

Kelley, H. H., & Stahelski, A. J. (1970). The social interaction basis of cooperators' and competitors' beliefs about others. *Journal of Personality and Social Psychology, 16,* 66–91.

Kihlstrom, J. F., & Cantor, N. (1984). Mental representations of the self. In L. Berkowitz (Ed.), *Advances in experimental social psychology* (Vol. 12, pp. 1–47). New York: Academic Press.

Klayman, J., & Ha, Y-W. (1987). Confirmation, disconfirmation, and information in hypothesis testing. *Psychological Review, 94,* 211–228.

Korman, A. K. (1968). Task success, task popularity, and self-esteem as influences on task liking. *Journal of Applied Psychology, 35,* 484–490.

Lecky, P. (1945). *Self-consistency. A theory of personality.* New York: Island Press.

Markus, H. (1977). Self-schemas and processing information about the self. *Journal of Personality and Social Psychology, 35,* 63–78.

Markus, H., & Wurf, E. (1987). The dynamic self-concept: A social psychological perspective. In M. R. Rosenzweig & L. W. Porter (Eds.), *Annual review of psychology* (Vol. 38, pp. 299–337). Palo Alto, CA: Annual Reviews.

McCall, G. J., & Simmons, J. L. (1966). *Identities and interactions: An examination of human associations in everyday life.* New York: Free Press.

Mead, G. H. (1934). *Mind, self and society.* Chicago: University of Chicago Press.

Mehrabian, A. (1972). *Nonverbal communication.* Chicago: Aldine.

Mettee, D. R., & Aronson, E. (1974). Affective reactions to appraisal from others. In T. L. Huston (Ed.), *Foundations of interpersonal attraction.* New York: Academic Press.

Miller, D. T., & Turnbull, W. (1986). Expectancies and interpersonal processes. In M. R. Rosenzweig & L. W. Porter (Eds.), *Annual review of psychology* (Vol. 37, pp. 233–256). Palo Alto, CA: Annual Reviews.

Miyamoto, S. F., & Dornbusch, S. A. (1956). Test of the symbolic interactionist hypothesis of self-conception. *American Journal of Sociology, 61,* 399–403.

Newcomb, T. M. (1956). The prediction of interpersonal attraction. *American Psychologist, 11,* 575–586.

Odum, E. P. (1963). *Ecology.* New York: Holt, Rhinehart, and Winston.

Orpen, C., & Bush, R. (1974). The lack of congruence between self-concept and public image. *Journal of Social Psychology, 93,* 145–146.

Pelham, B., & Swann, W. B., Jr. (1987a). *Accuracy in friendship relationships.* Unpublished manuscript, University of Texas at Austin.

Pelham, B., & Swann, W. B., Jr. (1987b). *Self-esteem. Components and consequences.* Unpublished manuscript, University of Texas at Austin.

Pervin, L. A., & Rubin, D. B. (1967). Student dissatisfaction with college and the college dropout: A transactional approach. *Journal of Social Psychology, 72,* 285–295.

Reis, H. T. (1985). The role of the self in the imitation and course of social interaction. In W. Ickes (Ed.), *Compatible and incompatible relationships* (pp. 209–231). New York: Springer-Verlag.

Rosenthal, R., & Jacobson, L. (1968). *Pygmalion in the classroom. Teacher expectations and pupils' intellectual development.* New York: Holt, Rinehart & Winston.

Schlenker, B. R. (1980). *Impression management.* Belmont, CA: Wadsworth.

Secord, P. F., & Backman, C. W. (1965). An interpersonal approach to personality In B. Maher (Ed.), *Progress in experimental personality research* (Vol. 2, pp. 91–125). New York: Academic Press.

Sherwood, J. J. (1967). Self-identity and referent others. *Sociometry, 30,* 404–409.

Shrauger, J. S. (1975). Responses to evaluation as a function of initial self-perceptions. *Psychological Bulletin, 82,* 581–596.

Shrauger, J. S., & Lund, A. (1975). Self-evaluation and reactions to evaluations from others. *Journal of Personality, 43,* 94–108.

Shrauger, J. S., & Schoeneman, T. J. (1979). Symbolic interactionist view of self-concept: Through the looking glass darkly. *Psychological Bulletin, 86,* 549–573.

Silverman, I. (1964). Self-esteem and differential responsiveness to success and failure. *Journal of Social Psychology, 69,* 115–119.

Snyder, M. (1984). When belief creates reality. In L. Berkowitz (Ed.), *Advances in experimental social psychology* (Vol. 16, pp. 248–305). New York: Academic Press.

Snyder, M., & Swann, W. B., Jr. (1978a). Behavioral confirmation in social interaction: From social perception to social reality. *Journal of Experimental Social Psychology, 14,* 148–162.

Snyder, M., & Swann, W. B., Jr. (1978b). Hypothesis testing processes in social interaction. *Journal of Personality and Social Psychology, 36,* 1202–1212.

Stryker, S., & Statham, A. (1985). Symbolic interaction and role theory. In G. Lindzey & E. Aronson (Eds.), *Handbook of social psychology* (Vol. 2. pp. 311–378). Hillsdale, NJ: Random House.

Swann, W B., Jr. (1983). Self-verification: Bringing social reality into harmony with the self. In J. Suls & A. G. Greenwald (Eds.), *Social psychological perspectives on the self* (Vol. 2, pp. 33–66). Hillsdale, NJ: Erlbaum.

Swann, W. B., Jr. (1984). Quest for accuracy in person perception: A matter of pragmatics. *Psychological Review, 91,* 457–477.

Swann, W. B., Jr. (1985). The self as architect of social reality. In B. Schlenker (Ed.), *The self and social life* (pp. 100–125). New York: McGraw-Hill.

Swann, W. B., Jr., & Ely, R. J. (1984). A battle of wills: Self-verification versus behavioral confirmation. *Journal of Personality and Social Psychology, 46,* 1287–1302.

Swann, W. B., Jr., & Giuliano, T. (in press). Confirmatory search strategies in social interaction: When, how, why, and with what consequences. *Journal of Social and Clinical Psychology.*

Swann, W. B., Jr., Griffin, J. J., Jr., Predmore, S. C., & Gaines, B. (1987). Cognitive–affective crossfire: When self-consistency meets self-enhancement. *Journal of Personality and Social Psychology, 52,* 881–889.

Swann, W. B., Jr., & Hill, C. A. (1982). When our identities are mistaken: Reaffirming self-conceptions through social interaction. *Journal of Personality and Social Psychology 13,* 59–66.

Swann, W. B., Jr., Krull, D. S., & Predmore, S. C. (1987). *Seeking truth and reaping despair: Self-verification among people with negative self-views.* Manuscript submitted for publication.

Swann, W. B., Jr., & Pelham, B. W. (1987). *The social construction of identity: Self-verification through friend and intimate selection.* Manuscript submitted for publication.

Swann, W. B., Jr., Pelham, B. W., & Chidester, T. R. (in press). Change through paradox: Using self-verification to alter beliefs. *Journal of Personality and Social Psychology.*

Swann, W. B., Jr., Pelham, B. W., & Krull, D. S. (1987). *The ray of hope: Averting the conflict by avoiding the choice.* Manuscript submitted for publication.

Swann, W. B., Jr., & Predmore, S. C. (1985). Intimates as agents of social support: Sources of consolation or despair? *Journal of Personality and Social Psychology, 49,* 1609–1617.

Swann, W. B., Jr., & Read, S. J. (1981a). Acquiring self-knowledge: The search for feedback that fits. *Journal of Personality and Social Psychology, 41,* 1119–1128.

Swann, W. B., Jr., & Read, S. J. (1981b). Self-verification processes: How we sustain our self-conceptions. *Journal of Experimental Social Psychology, 17,* 351–372.

Swann, W. B., Jr., & Snyder, M. (1980). On translating beliefs into action: Theories of ability and their application in an instructional setting. *Journal of Personality and Social Psychology, 38,* 879–888.

Taylor, S. E., & Brown, J. D. (in press). Illusion and well being: Some social psychological contributions to a theory of mental health. *Psychological Bulletin.*

Tedeschi, J. T., & Lindskold, S. (1976). *Social psychology: Interdependence, interaction, and influence.* New York: Wiley.

Tesser, A. (1985, August). *Toward a self-evaluation maintenance model of social behavior.* Paper presented at the annual convention of the American Psychological Association, Los Angeles.

Tesser, A., & Rosen. S. (1975). The reluctance to transmit bad news. In L. Berkowitz (Ed.), *Advances in experimental social psychology* (Vol. 8, pp. 192–232). New York: Academic Press.

Tomkins, S. S. (1981). The quest for primary motives: Biography and autobiography of an idea. *Journal of Personality and Social Psychology, 11,* 306–329.

Turner, R. H. (1968). The self-conception in social interaction. In C. Gordon & K. G. Gergen (Eds.), *The self in social interaction* (pp. 93–106). New York: Wiley.

Vallacher, R. R., & Wegner, D. M. (1985). *Action identification theory*. Hillsdale, NJ: Erlbaum.

Walhood, D. S., & Klopfer, W. G. (1971). Congruence between self-concept and public image. *Journal of Consulting and Clinical Psychology, 37,* 148–150.

Wason, P. C., & Johnson-Laird, P. N. (1972). *Psychology or reasoning: Structure and content*. London: D. T. Batsford.

Watzlawick, P., Weakland, J. H., & Fisch, R. (1974). *Change: Principles of problem formation and problem resolution*. New York: Norton.

Weinstein, E., & Deutschberger, P. (1963). Some dimensions of alter-casting. *Sociometry, 26,* 454–466.

Wicklund, R. A. (1974). *Freedom and reactance*. Potomac, MD: Erlbaum.

Wilson, E. O. (1974). *Sociobiology: The new synthesis*. Cambridge: Harvard University Press.

Wilson, T. D. (1985). Strangers to ourselves: The origins and accuracy of beliefs about one's own mental states. In J. H. Harvey & G. Weary (Eds.), *Attribution in contemporary psychology* (pp. 9–36). New York: Academic Press.

Word, C. O., Zanna, M. P., & Cooper, J. (1974). The nonverbal mediation of self-fulfilling prophecy effects in interracial interaction. *Journal of Experimental Social Psychology, 10,* 109–120.

Wylie, R. (1979). *The self concept*. Lincoln: University of Nebraska Press.

Zajonc, R. B. (1980). Feeling and thinking: Preferences need no inferences. *American Psychologist, 35,* 151–175.

Zajonc, R. B. (1984). On the primacy of affect. *American Psychologist, 39,* 117–123.

Zanna, M. P., & Pack, S. J. (1975). On the self-fulfilling nature of apparent sex differences in behavior. *Journal of Experimental Social Psychology, 11,* 583–591.

INTRODUCTION TO PART 5

Knowing from Wanting

The notion that motivational factors may directionally influence what we know or believe on various topics has had a long and distinguished history in psychology. Freud's (1905/1953) fundamental notion of defense mechanisms embodies this idea in arguing that various deep-seated conflicts may affect our judgments, memories, and beliefs via such mechanisms as projection, sublimation, denial, or repression (see also A. Freud, 1937; Erdelyi, 1974; Klein, 1970). In social psychology, Festinger's dissonance theory (1957) and other cognitive consistency formulations inspired by Gestalt theoretic ideas (i.e., for a sourcebook see Abelson et al., 1968) convey a similar notion that a motivation (i.e., to have an internally coherent picture of reality) importantly affects how we think about various subjects, and that an introduction of a cognitive inconsistency into our belief system fosters cognitive activity that alters our beliefs in a consistency-restoring fashion.

But the notion that our beliefs are impacted and distorted by various motivational forces did not go unquestioned in social psychological research. In cleverly crafted critiques of the evidence for such a notion, some researchers raised the possibility that the seeming effects of motivation may be alternatively explained by purely cognitive or inferential mechanisms. Perhaps the most famous of such critiques was Daryl Bem's (1967) challenge of dissonance theory's account for why people subsequently express an attitude congruent with a position they agreed to advocate despite the fact that the advocated position contradicts the attitude they had expressed prior to their message. According to self-perception theory, to explain these phenomena one need not posit an aversive state of dissonance that motivates people to alter their attitudes. Instead, the theory proposes that people use inferential processes to determine the attitudinal significance of their actions.

303

As may often happen with scientific controversies, the controversy between dissonance and self-perception theories fueled important research designed to demarcate more precisely the theoretical domains of both theories from one another and sharpen our understanding of the processes involved. An early example of such work was the experiment by Zanna and Cooper (1974) in this section in which the aversive tension property of dissonance was explored. Aversive tension constitutes a uniquely motivational property that does not follow from the cool inferential processes; its presence and the role it plays in attitude inferences demonstrate that motivation does matter in at least some dissonance-related phenomena.

The notion that causal attribution may be affected by motivation (Kelley, 1967) has been questioned by Miller and Ross (1975). The motivational interpretation argues that attributions often are defensive and aimed at preserving one's positive sense of self. An example of such a process would be attributing one's success to one's ability and one's failure to such external factors as task difficulty. By contrast, one cognitive interpretation of such findings has been that because of a prior history of successes one may expect to succeed: attributing successes to oneself may reflect, therefore, the tendency to explain them in expectancy-consistent terms. Failures, by contrast, are not consistent with one's expectancy and hence have to be explained in alternative terms such as task difficulty. This argument and other critiques of the motivational hypotheses are systematically considered in Kunda's (1990) article in this section that concludes in favor of the notion that motivational effects do matter and that they do exert important influence on our judgments and beliefs.

Much of the work on motivated reasoning involved

directional motivations that propel one's cognitions toward specific desirable contents (e.g., that one is gifted, able, healthy, or loved). But humans possess also various nondirectional motivations related to the acquisition of knowledge per se, rather than a specific type of knowledge (see Kruglanski, 1989). One example of such a nondirectional motivation is reflected in individuals' orientations toward uncertainties in their environment. The theory of uncertainty orientation and some important research that it generated are reviewed in an article by Sorrentino, Bobocel, Gitta, Olson, & Hewitt (1988) included in this section. Sorrentino et al. (1988) propose that people vary in their motivation to engage in situations where uncertainty about the self or the world can be resolved through exploration (uncertainty-oriented persons) versus situations that directly promise certainty and hence do not require exploration (certainty-oriented individuals). This individual difference influences how information is processed and used as exemplified by the extent to which the quality of the arguments in a persuasive message is given more weight than the characteristics of the message source. Uncertainty orientation represents a nondirectional motivation because it is not biased in favor of specific contents of knowledge but rather refers to preferences among exploratory versus direct modes of uncertainty reduction.

Another nondirectional motivation that received research attention in recent years is the need for cognitive closure, defined as the desire to have clear and confident knowledge on a given topic and the eschewal of cognitive confusion and ambiguity. The need for closure, much like uncertainty orientation, is a dimension on which people may stably differ, but it also is a motivation arousable by various situational conditions, such as time-pressure, noise, and tedium, as well as by personal states such as fatigue or intoxication by alcohol. In an article by Kruglanski and Webster (1996) contained in this section, experimental evidence is examined for the effects of need for closure on a variety of cognitive and social phenomena such as impression formation, stereotyping, prejudice, interpersonal communication, attitudes toward deviates in one's group, and to other members of in- and outgroups. Kruglanski and Webster's (1996) theory explains these effects in terms of two fundamental tendencies fostered by the need for closure: the tendency to "seize" on highly accessible information and to "freeze" upon the judgments it implies; that is, ignore new or contradictory information once closure has been attained.

REFERENCES

Abelson, R. P., Aronson, E., McGuire, W. J., Newcomb, T. M., Rosenberg, M. J., & Tannenbaum, P. H. (Eds.). (1968). *Theories of cognitive consistency: A sourcebook.* Chicago: Rand McNally.

Bem, D. J. (1967). Self-perception: An alternative interpretation of cognitive dissonance phenomena. *Psychological Review, 74,* 183–200.

Erdelyi, M. H. (1974). A new look at the new look: Perceptual defense and vigilance. *Psychological Review, 81,* 1–25.

Festinger, L. (1957). *A theory of cognitive dissonance.* Evanston, IL: Row, Peterson.

Freud, A. (1937). *The ego and the mechanism of defense.* New York: International Universities.

Freud, S. (1953). Three essays on the theory of sexuality. *Standard Edition,* Volume 7. London: Hogarth Press. (Original work published 1905)

Kelley, H. H. (1967). Attribution theory in social psychology. In D. Levine (Ed.), *Nebraska Symposium on Motivation, 15,* 192–238.

Klein, G. S. (1970). *Perception, motives and personality.* New York: Knopf.

Kruglanski, A. W. (1989). *Lay epistemics and human knowledge: Cognitive and motivational bases.* New York: Plenum.

Kruglanski, A. W., & Webster, D. M. (1996). Motivated closing of the mind: "Seizing" and "freezing." *Psychological Review, 103,* 263–283.

Kunda, Z. (1990). The case for motivated reasoning. *Psychological Bulletin, 108,* 480–498.

Miller, D. T., & Ross, M. (1975). Self-serving biases in the attribution of causality: Fact or fiction? *Psychological Bulletin, 82,* 213–225.

Sorrentino, R. M., Bobocel, D. R., Gitta, M. Z., Olson, J. M., & Hewitt, E. L. (1988). Uncertainty orientation and persuasion: Individual differences in the effects of personal relevance on social judgments. *Journal of Personality and Social Psychology, 55,* 357–371.

Zanna, M. P., & Cooper, J. (1974). Dissonance and the pill: An attribution approach to studying the arousal properties of dissonance. *Journal of Personality and Social Psychology, 29,* 703–709.

Suggested Readings

Erdelyi, M. H. (1974). A new look at the new look: Perceptual defense and vigilance. *Psychological Review, 81,* 1–25.

Ross, M., & Sicoly, F. (1979). Egocentric biases in availability and attribution. *Journal of Personality and Social Psychology, 37,* 322–336.

Steele, C. M., & Liu, T. J. (1981). Making the dissonance act unreflective of the self: Dissonance avoidance and the expectancy of a value affirming response. *Personality and Social Psychology Bulletin, 45,* 5–19.

Wegner, D. M., Schneider, D. J., Carter, S., & White, T. (1987). Paradoxical effects of thought suppression. *Journal of Personality and Social Psychology, 53,* 5–13.

Dissonance and the Pill: An Attribution Approach to Studying the Arousal Properties of Dissonance

Mark P. Zanna and Joel Cooper • Department of Psychology, Princeton University

Editors' Notes

According to Festinger's (1957) theory of cognitive dissonance, the state of dissonance involves unpleasant tension that has drivelike properties. The authors designed a study to test whether this hypothesized state, rather than some alternative process such as self-perception, does indeed account for why counterattitudinal advocacy under high choice tends to produce attitude change consistent with the advocacy. As part of a supposedly unrelated study, the participants were told that a pill they took had no side effects or that it would either make them feel tense later or make them feel relaxed later. The participants then wrote a counterattitudinal essay under either high choice or low choice. According to dissonance theory, the participants should experience greater dissonance under high than low choice because the latter provides a justification for their behavior (a consonant cognition) whereas the former does not. But in the "tense" side effects condition, this tense state of dissonance can be attributed to the pill rather than to the counterattitudinal advocacy. This should reduce the motivation to deal with the tension through attitude change. In contrast, the tension from the counterattitudinal advocacy would supposedly be even greater were it not for the "relaxed" side effects, and this should increase the motivation to deal with this high tension through attitude change. These predictions based on conceptualizing dissonance as a drivelike state of tension were confirmed by the results of the study.

Discussion Questions

1. What is the motivational nature of the state of dissonance?
2. Counterattitudinal advocacy under high choice tends to produce attitude change consistent with the advocacy. Discuss evidence that this occurs because of the motivational nature of the state of dissonance.

Authors' Abstract

A study was designed to test the notion that dissonance has arousal properties. In a 2 × 3 design, experimental subjects were induced to write counterattitudinal essays under either high- or low-choice conditions. One third of the subjects were led to believe that a pill, which they had just taken in the context of a separate experiment, would lead them to feel tense. Another third were led to believe that the pill would cause them to feel relaxed. The final third expected the pill to have no side effects whatsoever. In this last condition, the results yielded the usual dissonance effect: High choice produced more attitude change in the direction of the essay than low choice. When subjects could attribute their arousal to the pill, this effect was virtually eliminated; when subjects felt they should have been relaxed by the pill, this effect was significantly enhanced. The implications of these results for Festinger's original statement that dissonance is a drivelike state were discussed.

In most investigations on the effects of cognitive dissonance, one can generally find terms like dissonance arousal, dissonance reduction, and tensions due to dissonance. These follow directly from Festinger's (1957) original statement of dissonance theory which indicated that dissonance has drivelike properties and is experienced as psychological discomfort or tension. Yet very few investigations have addressed themselves to the question of whether there actually is any arousal attached to the observed fact that inconsistency among cognitions often leads to efforts to reduce that inconsistency.

Perhaps spurred on by Bem's (1965) behavioristic explanation of dissonance results, Waterman and Katkin (1967) devised an ingenious paradigm to obtain some evidence for arousal. They argued that if dissonance is truly a drivelike state, then it should have energizing effects similar to other drive states such as hunger. Therefore, they first aroused dissonance by inducing subjects to write counterattitudinal essays and then had subjects learn either a simple or a complex assignment. Since Spence, Farber, and McFann (1956) had shown that high-drive states have an energizing effect upon dominant, well learned responses, Waterman and Katkin predicted enhanced learning of the simple task and diminished learning of the complex task by dissonance-aroused subjects. The results, however, provided only partial support for the hypotheses. Enhancement of simple learning was obtained, but there was no obtained interference with complex learning on the part of subjects who had gone through the dissonance procedure.

Subsequent experiments using this paradigm (Cottrell & Wack, 1967; Waterman, 1969) have tended to support the arousal notion—but not unequivocally. Moreover, as Pallak and Pittman (1972) have aptly pointed out, none of the earlier studies have obtained evidence that their dissonance-provoking procedures ever produced dissonance. That is, there is no evidence of dissonance-produced attitude change in any of those experiments. Of all of the research using this paradigm, only one of two recent experiments reported by Pallak and Pittman demonstrated both the attitude-change and learning-interference effects and then only in a complex learning situation.

In the present research, we would like to suggest a new approach to the study of arousal in dissonance. We take our lead from the work of Schachter and Singer (1962) who investigated the labeling of emotion. Those investigators reasoned that emotion was a combination of physiological arousal and cognitive labeling. They demonstrated that subjects who were aroused with epinephrine, but did not know the reason for that arousal, used external cues to label it as either anger or euphoria. Several years later, Ross, Rodin, and Zimbardo (1969) reasoned that subjects who were aroused by a given stimulus could reduce that arousal if they were able to attribute it to a different external cause. Specifically, they found that subjects who were frightened of electric shocks could reduce their fear and tolerate more shocks if they were able to attribute their naturally occurring arousal to the effects of a loud noise.

Finally, Storms and Nisbett (1970) suggested that subjects who were suffering from the arousal state of insomnia might find it easier to fall asleep if they were able to attribute their physiological arousal to some external agent—such as a pill. The investigators told a group of insomniacs that they were participating in a "drug and fantasy" experiment. They were instructed to take a pill prior to bedtime and were warned that the pill might cause them to feel tense, aroused, etc. Another group of insomniacs was told that the pill would have no side effects, while a third group believed that the pill would make them calm and relaxed. Storms and Nisbett reasoned that if insomniacs could attribute their arousal to the pill, they would find it easier to fall asleep, while subjects who believed they should experience relaxation might become more upset than ever when they found themselves as aroused as usual at bedtime. The results indicated that subjects given the "tension due to pill" label for their arousal actually fell asleep more quickly than control subjects who, in turn, fell asleep more quickly than subjects who believed they should be relaxed.

Now, if dissonance is arousing, it should be affected by the use of external labels in the same way as fear was for the Ross et al. (1969) subjects and insomnia was for Storms and Nisbett's (1970) subjects. If we can allow subjects, who have been aroused by dissonance, to attribute their arousal to an external agent, they should show less of a need to change their attitudes as a means of reducing dissonance.

Suppose that an individual is aroused by choosing to write an essay contrary to his belief. Festinger's theory leads us to believe that he will be in an uncomfortable tension state and will look for some means to reduce that tension; for example, he can change his opinion so as to eliminate the inconsistency. But suppose this individual had just taken a pill which he knew would cause tension and arousal. Then, after writing his essay, he would have an adequate (albeit, false) explanation for his tension. Attributing his tension to the pill, he would not have a need to change his opinion. Consequently, we would expect less opinion change from subjects exposed to a high dissonance manipulation if they could attribute their arousal to a pill than subjects who had no pill to which to attribute their arousal. Similarly, we would expect subjects whose inconsistent essay writing led to arousal *despite* their taking a pill which they believed would relax them to show more of a need to alter their opinion (cf. Storms & Nisbett, 1970).

To test these hypotheses, we established a 2 × 3 factorial design. Subjects wrote counterattitudinal essays under either high- or low-choice conditions. One third of all subjects were led to believe that a pill which they had just taken in the context of a separate experiment would lead them to feel tense. Another third were led to believe that the pill would cause them to feel relaxed. The final third expected that their pill would have no side effects whatsoever. A control condition, in which subjects simply indicated their attitude toward the experimental issue, was also run. If dissonance is truly arousing, then we predicted (a) a standard dissonance effect (i.e., more attitude change under high- than low-choice conditions) when the pill had no side effects, (b) a diminished dissonance effect when the pill provided a "tense" label, and (c) an enhanced dissonance effect when a "relaxed" label was provided.

Method

SUBJECTS

Seventy-seven freshmen males at Princeton University participated in a study on memory. They were each promised $1.50. Subjects were usually run in groups of 3 or 4. Seven subjects were not used in the analyses. Of these, 6 (comprising two groups) were omitted because at least 1 member of each group refused to take the drug. In addition, 1 subject indicated suspicion as a result of auditing a psychology course and having heard a description of a similar experiment.

PROCEDURE

Subjects arrived at a common experimental room where the experimenter began by explaining the alleged purpose of the experiment. She indicated that subjects were "asked to come here today to participate in an experiment on memory processes . . . " and that they would be given a drug in order to investigate its effects on short-term memory. After assuring subjects that "the drug is perfectly safe," the experimenter outlined the supposed design of the study by stating, "you will have two memory tasks to do: one prior to taking the drug, and the second one after its total absorption." Subjects were then taken to separate experimental cubicles where they performed the first memory task. A straightforward free-recall task was employed. Twelve nonsense words were presented consecutively on a common screen. Immediately after the last presentation, the subjects were asked to recall (in writing) as many words as they could.

Manipulation of drug side effect. Next, the experimenter entered each cubicle and gave each subject in turn a capsule and a glass of water. The capsule, in fact, contained powdered milk. In order to manipulate the potential side effect of the drug, the experimenter, blind to condition, gave each subject one of three drug consent forms to sign. In the arousal condition, the form stated:

> This M.C. 5771 capsule contains chemical elements that are more soluble than other parts of the compound. In this form of the drug these elements may produce a reaction of tenseness prior to the total absorption of the drug, 5 minutes after ingestion. This side effect will disappear within 30 minutes.

In the relaxation condition, the form was identical, except that "tenseness" was replaced with "relaxation." In the no-information condition the form merely stated that "the total absorption time of the drug is 30 minutes" and that "there are no side effects." Each group always contained at least one subject in each of the three drug side-effect conditions.

Manipulation of dissonance. After subjects had signed their consent forms and had ingested their capsules, the experimenter explained that "we now have 30 minutes before the second memory task" and that she had "another study going on, not about memory, but about opinion research."

Dissonance was manipulated by varying the degree of decision freedom which subjects were given to write an attitude-discrepant essay (Linder, Cooper, & Jones, 1967). In the high-choice (or high-dissonance) condition, therefore, the experimenter continued:

"I will leave it entirely up to you to decide if you would like to participate in it, but I would be very grateful if you would . . . "

In the low-choice (or low-dissonance) condition, she simply stated:

"During this wait, I am going to ask you to do a small task for this opinion research experiment."

In both conditions the experimenter continued by indicating that

> The issue of whether inflammatory speakers should be allowed to speak on a college campus often becomes a problem. . . . The Ivy League

Administrators Association is trying to formulate a standard policy on whether or not, and in what circumstances, inflammatory speakers should be allowed to speak on campus. . . . Past experience has indicated that one of the best ways to understand what the relevant arguments are on both sides of any issue is to ask people to write essays favoring one side of the issue. Therefore, what we would like you to do is to write the strongest, the most forceful essay that you can taking the position that inflammatory speakers should be banned from college campuses.

In the high-choice condition, the experimenter then secured each subject's verbal consent, adding after compliance, "Remember, you are under no obligation." All of the subjects agreed to write the essay.

In the control condition, subjects were recruited in an identical way as the experimental subjects but were not exposed to the experimental procedures. Instead, control subjects merely indicated their opinions on the attitudinal dependent measure to be described below.

Dependent measures. Subjects were given 10 minutes to complete the essay after which the experimenter collected the dependent measures. Subjects were first asked to indicate how they felt "right now" on a 31-point scale with endpoints labeled calm (1) and tense (31). Next, presumably for the Ivy League Administrators Association, subjects described their present feeling "about the adoption of a ban against inflammatory speakers on campus" on a 31-point scale with endpoints labeled strongly opposed (1) and strongly in favor (31). This served as the major dependent measure. Finally, to assess the effectiveness of the decision-freedom manipulation, subjects indicated "how free [they] felt to decline to participate in this Ivy League Administrators research project" on a 31-point scale with endpoints labeled for free at all (1) and extremely free (31).

After subjects competed these questions, they returned to the common experimental room and were debriefed with special emphasis placed in the fact that the ingested capsule was, in reality, a placebo.

Results

DECISION FREEDOM

Responses to the question designed to tap perceived freedom in writing the essay revealed that

TABLE 1. Mean of Subjects' Reported Tension

Decision freedom	Potential side effect of the drug		
	Arousal	None	Relaxation
High	19.60	17.90	9.90
Low	22.00	9.00	12.00

Note. Cell *n* = 10. The larger the mean, the more tense the response.

high-choice subjects reported more choice than low-choice subjects (X = 24.23 versus 11.33, respectively; F = 43.05, df = 1/54, $p < .001$). No other effects on the choice measure were significant. Apparently the decision-freedom manipulation was successful.

REPORTED TENSION

Subjects were also asked to indicate how tense or relaxed they felt immediately after having written their essays. The mean responses are presented in Table 1.

Analysis of variance indicated that only the main effect for the drug side effect (F = 10.32, df = 2/54, $p <.001$) and the interaction (F = 4.08, df = 2/54, $p < .05$) were significant. Subjects in the arousal condition reported being *more* tense than subjects on the no-infirmation condition ($\bar{x}$ = 20.80 versus 13.45, respectively; F = 10.63, df = 1/54, $p < .01$), while subjects in the relaxation condition reported being *less* tense than subjects in the no-information condition ($\bar{x}$ = 10.95 versus 13.45, respectively; F = 4.92, df = 1/54, $p < .05$). While this main effect indicate real differences, it seems as reasonable to conclude that it was a result of the demand characteristics of the situation.

More interesting is the interaction which can best be described as follows: High-choice subjects reported more tension than low-choice subjects (t = 2.79, $p < .01$), but only in the no-information condition; in the arousal and relaxation conditions, high-choice subjects reported trivially less tension than low-choice subjects ($t < 1$, in both cases).

This interaction is evidence in favor of viewing dissonance as an arousing state. When information was provided about the alleged side effect of the drug, subjects' self-reports tended to parrot the information provided. But when no information was provided, subjects reported being considerably more tense when dissonance was high rather than low.

ATTITUDE TOWARD THE SPEAKER BAN

The mean attitudes toward banning speakers on campus are presented in Table 2. Before describing the results in the experimental conditions, it should be noted that the mean attitude reported by the control subjects indicated that the essays which experimental subjects were induced to write were clearly attitude discrepant.

A 2 × 3 analysis of variance presented in Table 2 reveals that the predicted main effects and interaction were highly significant ($p < .001$, in each case). This overall analysis of variance, however, does not provide an exact test of the hypotheses. Comparison of individual conditions by the Newman-Keuls procedure indicated that the pattern of results conformed exactly to expectation. In the no-information condition, the standard dissonance effect was replicated: High-choice subjects agreed more with the position taken in their counterattitudinal essays than did low-choice subjects. In the arousal condition, this dissonance effect was virtually eliminated; in the relaxation condition, the effect was magnified.

Intracell correlations between the degree of attitude change and the magnitude of reported tension were also informative. All conditions revealed a positive correlation between tension and attitudes. However, the correlations were not significant in the four conditions in which information was provided regarding the alleged side effect of the pill. As we suggested previously, at least one factor in subjects' reports of tension in these conditions was probably the demand characteristic of parroting back the information that was just given to them. In the no-side-effects–low-choice condition, the reported tension was, as expected, quite low and the correlation with attitude change did not reach significance. However, when dissonance

TABLE 2. Mean of Subjects' Opinions toward Banning Speakers on Campus

Decision freedom	Potential side effect of the drug		
	Arousal	None	Relaxation
High	3.40_a	9.10_b	13.40_c
Low	3.50_a	4.50_a	4.70_a

Note. Cell *n* = 10. The larger the mean, the more agreement with the attitude-discrepant essay (Control group x = 2.30_a). Cells not sharing a common subscript differ at the .01 level by the Newman-Keuls procedure; cells showing a common subscript do not differ at the .05 level.

was high and no demand characteristics were present (no-side-effects–high-choice condition), the correlation between the magnitude of tension and the degree of opinion change was highly reliable ($r = .69$, $p < .05$).

Finally, two independent raters were asked to rate each essay in order to assess the possibility that differences in essay performance mediated the final attitude scores. The judges were asked to rate the essays on a 7-point scale according to their degree of "convincingness." The interjudge reliability was quite high ($r = .88$). No differences were found among conditions on the convincingness dimension nor were any differences revealed when the length of each essay was considered.

Discussion

The results of the experiment provide support for the notion that dissonance does indeed have arousal properties as Festinger (1957) originally suggested. High-dissonance subjects who could attribute their arousal to a pill showed less of a tendency to change their attitudes, while subjects in the high-dissonance–relaxation condition showed an increased need to deal with their arousal by changing their opinions. Under the low-dissonance conditions, the various side effects made virtually no difference.

Since previous dissonance research had focused mainly on the attitudinal effects which the drive state was supposed to produce, the way was paved for the appearance of alternative models of attitude change which could predict identical attitudinal results. First, Bem (1965) proposed that the results of previous dissonance experiments could be understood in terms of the mand–tact (Skinner, 1957) quality of the stimulus situation. Kelley (1967) then presented an attributional analysis that incorporated Bem's interpretation within a more general model of information processing. Like Bem, he proposed that dissonance results could be accounted for without recourse to assumptions about arousal or drives within the person. Rather, he viewed attitude change within the dissonance paradigm as a special case of an individual observing his own behavior and logically attributing an attitude to himself.

Research critical of Bem's analysis (Jones, Linder, Kiesler, Zanna, & Brehm, 1968) suggested that the way in which the behavioristic reinterpre-

TABLE 3. Summary of the Analysis of Variance of Subjects' Opinions toward Banning Speakers on Campus

Source	df	MS	F
Decision freedom (A)	1	290.40	40.73*
Side effect (B)	2	158.82	22.29*
A × B	2	96.95	13.60*
Error	54	7.13	

* $p < .001$.

tation of dissonance theory was stated could not account for all of the data predicted and obtained in dissonance experiments. Similarly, Cooper, Jones, and Tuller (1972) provided evidence which is at variance with Kelley's alternative based upon attribution theory. But because such criticisms do not provide data that bear on the internal process of dissonance arousal, they do not get at the heart of the argument.

However, the present results do combine with the earlier research using the Waterman and Katkin (1967) paradigm to provide support for the internal process of dissonance arousal. The results of the present investigation could only have been obtained if inconsistent cognitions produced at least the perception of arousal. While Bem's and Kelley's models may be considered useful heuristic devices and while they may accurately reflect the processes employed by observer subjects, the present results suggest that involved subjects do indeed perceive themselves to be aroused when participating in a counterattitudinal role-playing situation.

In our analysis of arousal in forced-compliance situations, we are not arguing against the veridicality of general attribution phenomena. To the contrary, attribution notions generated the present experiment. Following Storms and Nisbett (1970), for example, our arousal condition was intended to manipulate the perceived source of arousal; our relaxation condition, the perceived level of arousal. We have argued that subjects in the arousal condition mistakenly attributed their dissonance-produced arousal to a nonemotional, external agent (i.e., the pill) and, therefore, experienced less dissonance. Relaxation condition subjects, on the other hand, were assumed to make the mistaken attribution that they were more aroused than they really were and, therefore, to experience more dissonance. [. . .]

REFERENCE

Bem, D. J. (1965). An experimental analysis of self-persuasion. *Journal of Experimental Social Psychology, 1,* 199–218.

Cooper, J., Jones, E. E., & Tuller, S. M. (1972). Attribution, dissonance, and the illusion of uniqueness. *Journal of Experimental Social Psychology, 8,* 35–57.

Cottrell, N. B., & Wack, D. L. (1967). The energizing effect of cognitive dissonance on dominant and subordinate responses. *Journal of Personality and Social Psychology, 6,* 132–138.

Festinger, L. (1957). *A theory of cognitive dissonance.* Stanford, CA: Stanford University Press.

Jones, R. A., Linder, D. E., Kiesler, C. A., Zanna, M., & Brehm, J. W. (1968). Internal states or external stimuli: Observers' attitude judgments and the dissonance–self-persuasion controversy. *Journal of Experimental Social Psychology, 4,* 247–269.

Kelley, H. H. (1967). Attribution theory in social psychology. In D. Levine (Ed.), *Nebraska Symposium on Motivation: 1967.* Lincoln: University of Nebraska Press.

Linder, D. E., Cooper, J., & Jones, E. E. (1967). Decision freedom as a determinant of the role of incentive magnitude in attitude change. *Journal of Personality and Social Psychology, 6,* 245–254.

Pallak, M. S., & Pittman, T. S. (1972). General motivational effects of dissonance arousal. *Journal of Personality and Social Psychology, 21,* 349–358.

Ross, L., Rodin, J., & Zimbardo, P. G. (1969). Toward an attribution therapy: The reduction of fear through induced cognitive–motional misattribution. *Journal of Personality and Social Psychology, 12,* 279–288.

Schachter, S., & Singer, J. E. (1962). Cognitive, social, and physiological determinants of emotional state. *Psychological Review, 69,* 379–399.

Skinner, B. F. (1957). *Verbal behavior.* New York: Appleton-Century-Crofts.

Spence, K. W., Farber, I. E., & McFann, H. H. (1956). The relation of anxiety (drive) level to performance in competitional paired-associates learning. *Journal of Experimental Psychology, 52,* 296–305.

Storms, M. D., & Nisbett, R. E. (1970). Insomnia and the attribution process. *Journal of Personality and Social Psychology, 2,* 319–328.

Waterman, C. K. (1969). The facilitating and interfering effects of cognitive dissonance on simple and complex paired-associate learning tasks. *Journal of Experimental Social Psychology, 5,* 31–42.

Waterman, C. K., & Katkin, E. S. (1967). The energizing (dynamogenic) effect of cognitive dissonance on task performance. *Journal of Personality and Social Psychology, 6,* 126–131.

The Case for Motivated Reasoning

Ziva Kunda • Department of Psychology, Princeton University

Editors' Notes

Does motivation affect the way we reason and the judgments we form as a consequence of our reasoning? Following Freud's work, this assumption has been accepted unquestioningly in social and personality psychology and was illustrated empirically in work on cognitive dissonance, for example (Festinger, 1957), or on the "New Look" in perception (Erdelyi, 1974). However, in the late sixties and mid-seventies some social psychologists (in particular Bem, 1967; Miller & Ross, 1975) have advanced intriguing arguments where the evidence for putative motivational effects was susceptible to alternative interpretations in purely cognitive terms. This article reviews the evidence that has become available since the debate commenced. The author concludes that a case for motivated reasoning has been made, and that motivation biases the component cognitive processes that reasoning incorporates. Specifically, she cites evidence demonstrating how motivation affects the strategies people use for accessing, constructing, and evaluating beliefs. The author also argues that even though people are more likely to arrive at conclusions congruent with their motivations than at odds with their motivations, their ability to do so is limited by their ability to construct seemingly reasonable justifications for these conclusions.

Discussion Questions

1. What were some of the major cognitive reinterpretations of motivational effects? What evidence has since accumulated relevant to these reinterpretations?
2. If our motivation affects the conclusions we reach, why are people still disappointed, frustrated, and dejected? Why can't they just think what they like, that is, cognize in a manner congruent with their motivations?

Author's Abstract

It is proposed that motivation may affect reasoning through reliance on a biased set of cognitive processes—that is, strategies for accessing, constructing, and evaluating beliefs. The motivation to be accurate enhances use of those beliefs and strategies that are considered most appropriate, whereas the motivation to arrive at particular conclusions enhances use of those that are considered most likely to yield the desired conclusion. There is considerable evidence that people are more likely to arrive at conclusions that they want to arrive at, but their ability to do so is constrained by their ability to construct seemingly reasonable justifications for these conclusions. These ideas can account for a wide variety of research concerned with motivated reasoning.

The notion that goals or motives affect reasoning has a long and controversial history in social psychology. The propositions that motives may affect perceptions (Erdelyi, 1974), attitudes (Festinger, 1957), and attributions (Heider, 1958) have been put forth by some psychologists and challenged by others. Although early researchers and theorists took it for granted that motivation may cause people to make self-serving attributions and permit them to believe what they want to believe because they want to believe it, this view, and the research used to uphold it, came under concentrated criticism in the 1970s. The major and most damaging criticism of the motivational view was that all research purported to demonstrate motivated reasoning could be reinterpreted in entirely cognitive, nonmotivational terms (Miller & Ross, 1975; Nisbett & Ross, 1980). Thus people could draw self-serving conclusions not because they wanted to but because these conclusions seemed more plausible, given their prior beliefs and expectancies. Because both cognitive and motivational accounts could be generated for any empirical study, some theorists argued that the hot versus cold cognition controversy could not be solved, at least in the attribution paradigm (Ross & Fletcher, 1985; Tetlock & Levi, 1982).

One reason for the persistence of this controversy lies in the failure of researchers to explore the mechanisms underlying motivated reasoning. Recently, several authors have attempted to rectify this neglect (Kruglanski & Freund, 1983; Kunda, 1987; Pyszczynski & Greenberg, 1987; Sorrentino & Higgins, 1986). All these authors share a view of motivation as having its effects through cognitive processes: People rely on cognitive processes and representations to arrive at their desired conclusions, but motivation plays a role in determining which of these will be used on a given occasion.

Interestingly, this view of motivation as cognitively mediated has always been integral to the understanding of dissonance reduction phenomena, at least in theory. In the 1968 sourcebook on consistency theories, McGuire expressed regret that the dissonance ideas had not been used to shed light on cognitive processes. Abelson (1968) and Aronson (1968) both illustrated how this might be done, Abelson by outlining a series of cognitive microprocesses—that is, mechanisms that he argued could provide the vehicle for dissonance reduction—and Aronson by providing a detailed example of the cognitive processes that a smoker might engage in to dispel the notion that smoking might be harmful. Dissonance research, however, has not met this challenge, focusing as it has on the conditions that would give rise to dissonance rather than on mechanisms for reducing dissonance (for review, see Wicklund & Brehm, 1976).

In this article I explore the possibility that motivation may affect reasoning through reliance on a biased set of cognitive processes: strategies for accessing, constructing, and evaluating beliefs. I review a large and diverse body of research that has been concerned directly or indirectly with this issue and argue that the proposed mechanisms can account for all of it. By *motivation* I mean any wish, desire, or preference that concerns the outcome of a given reasoning task, and I do not attempt to address the thorny issue of just how such motives are represented. The discussion is restricted to cases in which motivation can be construed as affecting the process of reasoning: forming impressions, determining one's beliefs and attitudes, evaluating evidence, and making decisions. Studies in which motivation was viewed as regulating behavior and determining which people or information one would like to observe (e.g., Frey, 1986; Swann, 1983) are excluded unless the behavioral choices are viewed as indicative of biased reasoning.

The motivated reasoning phenomena under review fall into two major categories: those in which the motive is to arrive at an accurate conclusion, whatever it may be, and those in which the motive is to arrive at a particular, directional conclusion. The importance of this distinction has been stressed in the work of Kruglanski and his colleagues (Kruglanski, 1980; Kruglanski & Ajzen, 1983; Kruglanski & Klar, 1987; see also Chaiken, Liberman, & Eagly, 1989; Pyszczynski & Greenberg, 1987). The two categories are often discussed in the same breath because they are both indicative of motivated reasoning, but, as pointed out by Kruglanski and his colleagues, it is important to distinguish between them because there is no reason to believe that both involve the same kinds of mechanism. To foreshadow my conclusions, I argue that both kinds of goals affect reasoning by influencing the choice of beliefs and strategies applied to a given problem. But accuracy goals lead to the use of those beliefs and strategies that are considered most appropriate, whereas directional goals lead to the use of those that are considered most likely to yield the desired conclusion.

Reasoning Driven by Accuracy Goals

The work on accuracy-driven reasoning suggests that when people are motivated to be accurate, they expend more cognitive effort on issue-related reasoning, attend to relevant information more carefully, and process it more deeply, often using more complex rules. These ideas go back to Simon's (1957) notion of satisficing, according to which decision makers form aspirations as to how good an alternative they should find and terminate their search for alternatives as soon as they find one that meets that level. Stigler (1961) extended these ideas by pointing out that search strategies have costs that may be weighted against their utility. The implication is that people may focus not only on how good an outcome they desire but also, and sometimes predominantly, on how much cognitive effort they are willing to expend. In other words, people are aware of the effort–accuracy trade-off and select strategies by considering both their costs and their benefits (Beach & Mitchell, 1978; Payne, Bettman, & Johnson, 1988).

An experimental investigation by McAllister, Mitchell, and Beach (1979, Experiment 3) provides

some support for these ideas. They manipulated subjects' motivation to be accurate by informing them that the target task was highly important or by leading them to expect to defend their judgments to their peers. Subjects motivated to be more accurate in these ways chose more complex and time-consuming decision-making strategies. But inasmuch as subjects were explicitly provided with lists of strategies to choose from and with details about the probability that each strategy would be accurate, it is not obvious that people motivated to be accurate will choose more complex strategies spontaneously, in the absence of such information. More interesting, from my perspective, are those studies in which subjects' spontaneous selection of cognitive strategies was examined. The researchers who did this also extended these ideas from decision making, construed as choosing among options, to the more general process of forming judgments and beliefs.

In these studies, accuracy goals are typically created by increasing the stakes involved in making a wrong judgment or in drawing the wrong conclusion, without increasing the attractiveness of any particular conclusion. The key strategy used to demonstrate that accuracy motives lead to more deep and careful cognitive processing involves showing that manipulations designed to increase accuracy motives lead to an elimination or reduction of cognitive biases. Thus Kruglanski and Freund (1983; Freund, Kruglanski, & Shpitzajzen, 1985) showed that subjects motivated to be accurate (because they expected to be evaluated, expected to justify their judgments, expected their judgments to be made public, or expected their evaluations to affect the evaluated person's life) showed less of a primacy effect in impression formation, less tendency to use ethnic stereotypes in their evaluations of essay quality, and less anchoring when making probability judgments. Similarly, Tetlock (1983) showed that subjects motivated to be accurate (because they expected to justify their beliefs to others) showed less of a primacy effect in their judgments of guilt in a simulated murder trial.

Although these findings may be due to deeper and more careful processing, they may also result merely from a tendency to make more conservative, less extreme judgments in the presence of accuracy goals. A study by Tetlock (1985) ruled out the latter possibility. Subjects motivated to be accurate (because they expected to justify their beliefs to others) were less susceptible to the fundamental attribution error. In comparison with other subjects, accuracy-motivated subjects made less extreme dispositional attributions about a target person when they knew that the target person had little choice in deciding whether to engage in the observed behavior, but not when they knew that the target person had a high degree of choice. Because the less extreme judgments occurred only in the low-choice condition, they appear to be due to careful processing rather than to undifferentiated conservatism. Other researchers (Pittman & D'Agostino, 1985) have also found that need for accuracy (resulting from control deprivation) reduced the magnitude of the fundamental attribution error. Similarly, Kassin and Hochreich (1977) found that need for accuracy (aroused by instructions indicating that the task reflected an important ability or was important to the experimenter) decreased the tendency to attribute briefly described behaviors to the person.

The underlying assumption in these studies is that many biases and errors result from hasty reasoning; therefore, elimination of these biases indicates more careful thinking. This interpretation is supported by the finding that such biases are exaggerated when subjects are required to make judgments under time pressure—that is, when they are forced to be hasty (Freund et al., 1985; Kruglanski & Freund, 1983).[1] There is some evidence that the deeper processing appears to be triggered by accuracy goals rather than by self-presentational pressures, because accuracy-promoting manipulations reduce biases only when they are delivered before subjects' exposure to information. When they are delivered after subjects view the information but before they make their judgments, such manipulations have no impact on judgment (Tetlock, 1983, 1985). Thus the deeper processing results from accuracy motives that affect the initial encoding and processing of information.

More direct evidence that accuracy goals lead to more complex and elaborate reasoning comes from two studies in which the researchers attempted to examine thought processes directly, rather than infer them from their outcome, the judgment. Tetlock and Kim (1987) showed that subjects motivated to be accurate (because they expected to justify their beliefs to others) wrote more cognitively complex descriptions of persons whose responses to a personality test they had seen: They considered more alternatives and evaluated the persons from more perspectives, and they drew more connections among characteristics. Partly as a result of this increased complexity of processing, subjects motivated to be accurate were in fact more accurate than others in predicting the persons' responses on additional personality measures and were less overconfident about the correctness of their predictions.[2]

In a similar vein, Harkness, DeBono, and Borgida (1985) showed that subjects motivated to be accurate in their assessment of which factors affected a male target person's decisions about whether to date women (because the subjects expected to date him later and therefore presumably wanted to know what he was like) used more accurate and complex covariation detection strategies than did subjects who did not expect to date him.[3]

In sum, the case for accuracy-motivated reasoning appears quite strong. In the above studies subjects had no reason to prefer one conclusion or outcome over another; their sole goal was to be accurate. The evidence that people process information more carefully under such circumstances is considerable and persuasive. The bulk of this evidence is indirect; the greater complexity of processing is inferred from the fact that the judgments tended to be more accurate and to reflect less reliance on biased strategies or cognitive shortcuts. Although some of these findings may be due to

---

[1]Kruglanski and Freund (1983) theorize that this occurs because time pressure leads to the arousal of a need for structure—that is, the need to arrive at a conclusion, whatever it may be.

[2]A study by Sieber (1974) appears to show opposite results. Subjects motivated to be accurate were more overconfident than others in the correctness of their answers to an exam, which suggests less rather than more careful processing on their part. However, the imputation of different accuracy motives to the different groups in that study seems arbitrary. Sieber assumed that subjects who believed the exam to be their actual midterm exam were more motivated to be accurate than were subjects who believed that if they did well enough on the exam, they would receive an A, and if not, they would receive feedback and take another exam that would determine their grade. It seems just as likely, though, that the latter subjects were more motivated to be accurate than the former, in which case the results would be consistent with Tetlock and Kim's (1987) study.

[3]In this study, however, subjects motivated to be accurate may also be presumed to hold a directional goal: namely, they may want the target to like them and therefore to prefer women who possess their own characteristics. This possibility was not examined in this study, and so it is not known whether bias exists on top of the more detailed processing.

mere conservatism rather than to deeper processing, others may not. There also exists some more compelling, direct evidence that accuracy-motivated subjects use more complex strategies in their thinking. Taken together, the evidence is impressive in its diversity: Several different kinds of bias have been shown to be weakened in the presence of accuracy goals, and such findings have been obtained by different investigators working in diverse content areas and operationalizing the need for accuracy in a variety of different ways. It seems reasonable to conclude that people motivated to be accurate are more likely to access and use those rules and strategies for processing information that are deemed more appropriate.

One should not assume, however, that accuracy goals will always eliminate biases and improve reasoning. In several studies, incentives or admonitions to be accurate did not eliminate bias (Fischhoff, 1977; Kahneman & Tversky, 1972a; Lord, Lepper, & Preston, 1984; Tversky & Kahneman, 1973). For accuracy to reduce bias, it is crucial that subjects possess more appropriate reasoning strategies, view these as superior to other strategies, and be capable of accessing them at will. This is most probably not the case for the biases that have been resistant to accuracy manipulations: for example, biases resulting from using the availability heuristic and from the failure to use the law of large numbers in some situations, and the hindsight bias. One may even imagine that biases will sometimes be exacerbated and reasoning worsened in the presence of accuracy goals. This will occur if people erroneously believe faulty reasoning procedures to be best and are more likely to access these faulty procedures upon reflection. Indeed, it has been shown that subjects motivated to be accurate (because they expected to justify their judgments to others) were *more* susceptible than other subjects to the dilution effect—that is, were more likely to moderate their predictions about a target when given nondiagnostic information about that target—and this tendency appeared to have resulted from more complex processing of information (Tetlock & Boettger, 1989). Thus accuracy goals led to more complex processing, which in turn led to less rational judgment.

The notion that accuracy goals lead to more complex processing is compatible with and broader than Kruglanski and his colleagues' views on how accuracy goals affect reasoning (Kruglanski, 1980; Kruglanski & Ajzen, 1983). In their view, accuracy goals (or fear of invalidity, in their terminology) may delay the "freezing" of the process of generating and evaluating hypotheses; that is, they may delay the arrival at a conclusion. This delay results from a tendency to entertain a greater number of alternative hypotheses and to consider more evidence. Such lengthier processing is consistent with my view, but my view is broader in that it allows for the possibility that, in addition to increasing the quantity of processing, accuracy goals may also affect its quality, in that they may lead directly to the use of more complex inferential procedures.

The research just reviewed did not address the issue of what impact accuracy goals will have when they are accompanied by directional goals—that is, when the person also wants to arrive at a particular conclusion. I turn next to an examination of the effects of directional goals on reasoning.

Reasoning Driven by Directional Goals

Mechanisms for Motivated Directional Biases

As will become clear from the work reviewed in this section, an explanation for how directional goals affect reasoning has to account not only for the existence of motivated biases but also for the findings suggesting that such biases are not unconstrained: People do not seem to be at liberty to conclude whatever they want to conclude merely because they want to. Rather, I propose that people motivated to arrive at a particular conclusion attempt to be rational and to construct a justification of their desired conclusion that would persuade a dispassionate observer. They draw the desired conclusion only if they can muster up the evidence necessary to support it (cf. Darley & Gross, 1983). In other words, they maintain an "illusion of objectivity" (Pyszczynski & Greenberg, 1987; cf. Kruglanski, 1980). To this end, they search memory for those beliefs and rules that could support their desired conclusion. They may also creatively combine accessed knowledge to construct new beliefs that could logically support the desired conclusion. It is this process of memory search and belief construction that is biased by directional goals (cf. Greenwald, 1980). The objectivity of this justification construction process is illusory because people do not realize that the process is biased by their goals, that they are accessing only a subset of their relevant knowledge, that they would probably access different beliefs and rules in the presence of different directional goals, and that they might even be capable of justifying opposite conclusions on different occasions.

For example, people who want to believe that they will be academically successful may recall more of their past academic successes than of their failures. They may also use their world knowledge to construct new theories about how their particular personality traits may predispose them to academic success (Kunda, 1987). If they succeed in accessing and constructing appropriate beliefs, they may feel justified in concluding that they will be academically successful, not realizing that they also possess knowledge that could be used to support the opposite conclusion. The biasing role of goals is thus constrained by one's ability to construct a justification for the desired conclusion: People will come to believe what they want to believe only to the extent that reason permits. Often they will be forced to acknowledge and accept undesirable conclusions, as they appear to when confronted with strong arguments for undesired or counterattitudinal positions (Petty & Cacioppo, 1986).

The proposed mechanisms are based on the assumption that directional goals may influence which beliefs and rules are accessed and applied on a given occasion. This assumption seems reasonable because there is considerable evidence that people access different beliefs and rules on different occasions: They endorse different attitudes (Salancik & Conway, 1975; Snyder, 1982), express different self-concepts (Fazio, Effrein, & Falender, 1981), make different social judgments (Higgins & King, 1981), and use different statistical rules (Kunda & Nisbett, 1986; Nisbett, Krantz, Jepson, & Kunda, 1983). Although most relevant evidence shows that different knowledge structures are accessed because different external, contextual cues make them differentially salient, the work on the effects of accuracy goals on reasoning reviewed above suggests that people may also access different beliefs and strategies under the influence of different goals.

The proposed view has much in common with the models suggested by Kruglanski and his colleagues (Kruglanski, 1980; Kruglanski & Ajzen, 1983; Kruglanski & Klar, 1987) and by Pyszczynski and Greenberg (1987). In Kruglanski and his colleagues' view, as in mine, directional goals (or, in their terminology, the need for specific conclusions or structures) affect reasoning by affecting which information will be considered in the reasoning process. However, their view differs somewhat from mine in that their model implies that essentially the same sequence of reasoning will be followed in the presence of different goals but that the sequence will be arrested, or frozen, at different points in time, depending on one's goals. My view, in addition to allowing for the possibility that directional goals may lead to more or less lengthy processing under different circumstances, also allows for the possibility that different goals will lead directly to the consideration of different beliefs and rules.

Pyszczynski and Greenberg's (1987) model delineating the effects of the self-esteem motive on self-serving attributions is even closer in spirit to the current one. Pyszczynski and Greenberg likened the attribution process to a process of hypothesis generation and evaluation and proposed that motives may have an effect on any or all of the stages of the hypothesis-testing sequence—that is, on the generation and evaluation of hypotheses, of inference rules, and of evidence. My ideas are fully compatible with this view in that all the processes outlined by Pyszczynski and Greenberg may be regarded as resulting from a biased search through memory for relevant beliefs and rules. In this article I wish to extend these ideas by showing that such biased memory search is not restricted to the domain of self-serving attribution. Rather, it may take place under the influence of a broad variety of directional goals and in many reasoning tasks. Furthermore, by shifting the focus of discussion from the process of hypothesis testing to the process of justification construction, my view points to some novel implications of these ideas, particularly the notion that the biased memory search will result in the formation of additional biased beliefs and theories that are constructed so as to justify desired conclusions.

In the following section, I review evidence that directional goals bias reasoning. The studies reviewed came from diverse theoretical perspectives and focused on a variety of content areas. I argue that the biased memory search and belief construction mechanisms that I propose can account for all this research. Although few of the studies reviewed were explicitly concerned with the mechanisms underlying motivated reasoning, many provided indirect evidence for the proposed mechanisms and some provide more direct support for them. I first review evidence indicating that directional goals may bias the accessing and construction of beliefs about the self, other people, and events. Next, I review evidence that directional goals may bias use of inferential rules. Finally, I review evidence that directional goals may bias the evaluation of scientific evidence by biasing the selection of both beliefs and rules.

Biased Accessing of Beliefs

DISSONANCE RESEARCH

The most extensive evidence that directional goals may bias reasoning comes from work carried out in the dissonance tradition that has shown that people may bias their self-characterizations when motivated to do so. Most of the research designed to test this theory has been carried out within the induced compliance paradigm, in which people are induced to make statements or to perform behaviors that are counterattitudinal. Having done so, people typically then alter their attitudes to make them more consistent with their behavior (for an extensive review, see Wicklund & Brehm, 1976).

Why does counterattitudinal behavior lead to such attitude change? In its original formulation, dissonance theory proposed that holding two contradictory cognitions causes an unpleasant state of cognitive dissonance that a person strives to reduce by changing one or more of the relevant cognitions (Festinger, 1957). The cognitions "I believe X" and "I have stated or done not X" seem dissonant, and to reduce this dissonance, people change their beliefs so as to bring them into correspondence with their actions (Festinger & Carlsmith, 1959). Thus the general goal was presumed to be to reduce inconsistency among beliefs, and the subgoal of changing one's beliefs and endorsing particular attitudes was constructed as one means of doing so.

More recently, examination of the hundreds of empirical investigations within the induced compliance paradigm has led to a modification and restriction of the original theory. It is now believed that dissonance is aroused only when one freely chooses to engage in behavior that has foreseeable negative consequences (Cooper & Fazio, 1984). These conditions suggest that dissonance arousal requires a threat to the self: The cognition

that one has knowingly chosen to engage in a bad or foolish behavior is inconsistent with a self-image as a decent and intelligent person (Aronson, 1968; Greenwald & Ronis, 1978). This interpretation is strengthened by findings showing that dissonance reduction through attitude change is eliminated when one is given alternative means of boosting one's self-image (Steele & Liu, 1983). Subjects' goal in the typical dissonance experiment, then, is to disconfirm the view of themselves as bad or foolish, and the subgoal of changing one's attitudes is created to this end. Thus according to both the original and the modified versions of dissonance theory, people are motivated to believe that they hold a particular attitude. In other words, they hold directional goals.

This motivational account has been challenged by attempts to reinterpret the dissonance findings in nonmotivational terms. Bem (1972) argued that the findings could also result from self-perception: The subjects, who have limited direct access to their attitudes, may infer their attitudes from their behaviors. It has been shown, however, that self-perception cannot fully account for the phenomena, because attitude change in dissonance experiments requires the presence of arousal that cannot be misattributed to other sources (Zanna & Cooper, 1974; for review, see Cooper & Fazio, 1984). The crucial role of such arousal indicates that noncognitive processes are involved. The precise role of arousal in motivated reasoning is discussed in a later section. For now, the important point is that most theorists have accepted this as evidence that attitude change in dissonance experiments results, at least in part, from motivation.

But how does motivation lead to attitude change? The dissonance literature is, for the most part, mute on this question. The work has not been concerned with the processes leading from the arousal of dissonance motivation to attitude change, and it therefore offers little direct evidence about the nature of these processes. There is some indirect evidence, however, that attitude change results from a memory search among existing beliefs for evidence that one has the desired attitude. This evidence lies in the fact that attitude change appears to be constrained by preexisting beliefs and attitudes, which suggests that these are accessed in the process of constructing current attitudes. Dissonance clearly would be most effectively reduced if one were able to espouse an attitude that corresponds perfectly to one's behavior. Yet this is not always the case. In many dissonance experiments, the attitudes after performing the counterattitudinal behavior remain in opposition to the behavior.

For example, after endorsing a law limiting free speech, subjects were less opposed to the law than were control subjects, but they remained opposed to it (Linder, Cooper, & Jones, 1967). Similarly, after endorsing police brutality on campus, subjects were less opposed to such brutality than were control subjects but they remained opposed to it (Greenbaum & Zemach, 1972). Induced compliance studies in which subjects are led to describe boring tasks as enjoyable often do produce shifts from negative to positive task evaluations, but in these studies, initial attitudes are not very negative (e.g., −0.45 on a scale whose highest negative value was −5 in Festinger & Carlsmith's classic 1959 study), and postdissonance attitudes still seem considerably less positive than subjects' descriptions of the task as "very enjoyable . . . a lot of fun . . . very interesting . . . , intriguing . . . exciting," subjects rated the task as 1.35 on a scale whose highest positive value was 5 (Festinger & Carlsmith, 1959).

If we assume that subjects in these induced compliance studies were motivated to espouse attitudes corresponding to their dissonance-arousing behavior, it seems likely that in their attempt to do so, they accessed their initial attitudes and were constrained by them. However, they may have accessed a biased subset of these initial attitudes, which permitted them to shift their current attitudes somewhat in the desired direction. The constraints imposed by prior beliefs on attitude change imply that prior beliefs were accessed in the process of constructing current ones, and the directional shift in attitudes implies that only a biased subset of the relevant prior beliefs were accessed. Therefore, these data lend indirect support to the view that the postdissonance attitude is the end product of a biased search through existing knowledge structures for evidence that one holds the desired attitude. Such a biased search may yield an attitude that is somewhat more positive or somewhat more negative than the attitude that one would report in the absence of motivation, but it is unlikely to completely overturn existing attitudes. Apparently, people are not at liberty to espouse any attitude they want to; they can do so only within the limits imposed by their prior beliefs.

It is also possible that the constraints imposed

by prior knowledge reflect a process of anchoring and adjustment (Tversky & Kahneman, 1974). According to this view, the extremity of the behavior that subjects are induced to perform serves as an anchor, and the espoused attitudes are shifted toward it. However, it seems unlikely that anchoring alone can account for the obtained attitude change, because attitudes do not change when the same behaviors are performed under low-choice conditions. If one assumes that anchoring processes occur only in those conditions in which motivation is aroused, it is not clear how the anchoring account differs from the one proposed here. The mechanisms underlying anchoring phenomena are not well understood and may well involve a process of biased memory search and belief construction comparable with the one that I proposed.

The evidence that counterattitudinal behaviors will create dissonance only when they involve a threat to the self is considerable and compelling. But there is no reason to assume that such behaviors constitute the only source of dissonance or motivation to espouse particular conclusions. Indeed, it seems somewhat puzzling that, given the enormous breadth of the original theory, the research generated by it remained, for the most part, restricted to so narrow a domain. Much of the research to be reviewed in the next section was not carried out within the dissonance tradition, even though its findings could have been derived from that theory.

ADDITIONAL EVIDENCE OF BIASED SELF-CHARACTERIZATIONS

Several additional studies indicate that directional goals may bias people's construals of their attitudes, traits, and preferences. For the most part, these studies provide indirect evidence about the processes through which motivation affects self-characterizations, but several of them also provide more direct evidence that motivation may instigate biased memory search through relevant self-knowledge.

In a study providing indirect evidence for the biased memory search and construction model, Kunda and Sanitioso (1989) showed that subjects induced to theorize that a given trait (extraversion or introversion) was conducive to academic success came to view themselves as characterized by higher levels of that trait than did other subjects, presumably because they were motivated to view themselves as possessing success-promoting attributes. These changes in self-concepts were constrained by prior self-knowledge: The subjects, who were predominantly extraverted to begin with, viewed themselves as less extraverted when they believed introversion to be more desirable, but they still viewed themselves as extraverted. Further evidence for such constraints was found in a study in which experimenters preselected subjects who were extraverts or introverts and exposed them to similar manipulations (Sanitioso, Kunda, & Fong, 1990). Both groups viewed themselves as more extraverted when induced to believe that extraversion was beneficial than when induced to believe that introversion was beneficial. But in all conditions the extraverts still viewed themselves as considerably more extraverted than the introverts viewed themselves. In other words, the effects of the manipulation on self-concepts were constrained by prior self-knowledge. These constraints imply that motivated changes in self-concepts may result from a biased search through memory for evidence that one has the desired self-concept; the resulting self-concepts are constrained by the evidence accessed in this process.

Similar results were obtained by Dunning, Story, and Tan (1989), who exposed subjects to a training session that extolled the virtues of social skills and discounted the value of task skills for success in business; the subjects subsequently enhanced their self-ratings on social skills and deflated their self-ratings on task skills. Subjects given the opposite message changed their self-ratings in the opposite direction. Dunning et al. did not report the magnitude of pre- and postmanipulation self-ratings, but the small magnitude of change reported (the highest mean change obtained was 4.3 on a 100-point percentile score) implies that here, too, changes in self-ratings were constrained by prior self-knowledge.

More direct evidence for biased memory search was obtained by Sanitioso et al. (1990), who used a similar paradigm. In one study, subjects were asked to generate autobiographical memories reflecting their standing on the extraversion–introversion dimension. Subjects led to view introversion as desirable were more likely to generate introverted memories first and generated more introverted memories than did subjects led to view extraversion as more desirable. In another study, subjects led to view introversion as desirable were faster to generate autobiographical memories re-

flecting introversion and slower to generate memories reflecting extraversion than were subjects led to view extraversion as desirable. These studies both indicate that the accessibility of autobiographical memories reflecting a desired trait was enhanced, which suggests that the search for relevant memories was biased.

Additional direct evidence for biased memory search was obtained by Markus and Kunda (1986). Subjects were made to feel extremely unique or extremely ordinary. Both extremes were perceived as unpleasant by subjects, who could therefore be assumed to have been motivated to see themselves in the opposite light. Subjects were relatively faster to endorse as self-descriptive those adjectives reflecting the dimension opposite to the one that they had just experienced. Apparently they had accessed this knowledge in an attempt to convince themselves that they possessed the desired trait and, having accessed it, were able to endorse it more quickly.

Further direct evidence that directional goals may bias memory search comes from studies showing that directional goals may bias reconstruction of one's past behavior. Subjects led to believe that toothbrushing (Ross, McFarland, & Fletcher, 1981) or caffeine consumption (Sherman & Kunda, 1989) was bad for their health reported having performed those behaviors in the recent past less frequently than did subjects led to believe that the same behaviors were good for their health. These findings support the notion that directional goals may affect memory search for evidence of past behaviors that are consistent with goals (in this case, the goal is to believe that one's own behaviors were conducive to health). However, in both cases, past behaviors may have been inferred from the newly constructed beliefs about the positivity of the behavior in question. Thus subjects may have changed their attitudes without realizing that change had taken place and then inferred their behaviors from their new attitudes. This account seems plausible for Ross et al.'s study, in which the researchers made every effort to ensure that subjects would not realize that their attitudes had changed: Subjects who were asked to recall the frequency of their behaviors did so in the context of an allegedly different study and were never asked about their attitudes. But the account seems less plausible for Sherman and Kunda's study, in which no such effort was made.

Positive self-characterizations may be maintained not only by biased recall and construction of one's own traits and behaviors but also through biased construction of the traits. There is considerable evidence that people tend to view themselves as above average on many dimensions (e.g., Weinstein, 1980, 1982). Dunning, Meyerowitz, and Holzberg (1989) showed that this tendency is constrained by people's ability to construe traits in a self-serving manner. Thus people may all view themselves as above average in sensitivity only if they can each define sensitivity as consisting primarily of attributes on which they have high levels. In line with this reasoning, Dunning et al. showed that people are more likely to see themselves as above average on ambiguous traits that are open to multiple construals than they are on unambiguous traits, and even for ambiguous traits, the tendency is reduced when people are asked to use specific definitions of each trait in their judgments.

Another way of maintaining a positive view of oneself is through self-serving attribution of the causes of one's behavior. There is now considerable evidence that people tend to take credit for their successes and, to a lesser extent, that people tend to deny responsibility for failure. Because this line of work has been reviewed extensively elsewhere, I do not discuss it at length. In the most recent review, Pyszczynski and Greenberg (1987) argued, in line with my ideas, that directional goals play a role in producing this bias and that they do so by leading to biased reliance on cognitive processes.

The studies just cited show that motivation may bias self-characterizations and provide some evidence for the biased memory search and belief construction model of motivated reasoning. The following studies showing motivationally biased self-characterizations provide no evidence for these mechanisms, but they are all consistent with them.

McGuire (1960) showed that the perceived desirability of events may be biased by motivation. Subjects who were persuaded that some events were more likely to occur came to view these events as more desirable, presumably because they were motivated to view the future as pleasant. Subjects also enhanced the desirability of logically related beliefs that had not been specifically addressed by the manipulation, which suggests that they were attempting to construct a logically coherent pattern of beliefs.

Sherman and Gorkin (1980) demonstrated that behavior may sometimes cause attitudes to shift in a direction opposite to that corresponding to the behavior. Subjects whose failure to solve a trick word problem implied that they might be sexist came to view themselves as more strongly in favor of affirmative action than did controls. This suggests that they may have engaged in a memory search aimed at concluding that they were not sexist, though there is no evidence for this.

Tesser and his colleagues (Tesser, 1986; Tesser & Campbell, 1983) have based their work on the assumption that people are motivated to maintain positive self-evaluation and that they do so through social comparison processes. Self-evaluation is threatened when one is outperformed by similar others. To maintain positive evaluation in the face of such threats, people reduce the self-relevance of the activities in question. These studies do not seem to lend themselves to reinterpretation in cognitive terms, which suggests that the self-descriptions are biased by motivation. The mechanisms producing the bias have not been addressed in this research, but these findings are consistent with the view that changes may result from selective memory search for evidence that the activity in question is not important to the self.

In sum, there is considerable evidence that directional goals may bias people's self-conceptions as possessing various attitudes, traits, and histories. These motivated self-characterizations often appear to be constrained by prior self-knowledge, and these constraints provide indirect evidence that motivation biases self-conceptions by biasing the memory search for relevant information. There is also some direct evidence for this, coming from the biased content of reported memories and from the enhanced speed both of generating memories that are consistent with desired self-views and of endorsing desired self-conceptions.

BIASED BELIEFS ABOUT OTHERS

Evidence for the effect of directional goals on judgments about others comes from research involving a manipulation termed *outcome dependency*: Subjects expect their own outcomes to depend in some way on a target person. Such manipulations bias the perceptions of others in ways that are consistent with the biased memory search and belief construction model, though most studies provide no direct evidence for it.

Several studies indicate that people tend to see others as more likable if they expect to interact with them. In a study by Darley and Berscheid (1967), subjects who expected to hold intimate sexual discussions with one target person but not with another read personality descriptions of both. Subjects liked their expected partner better than they liked the other person, presumably because they wanted their partner to be likable. In a later study, Berscheid, Graziano, Monson, and Dermer (1976) employed a similar but more powerful manipulation in which subjects who expected to date one of three persons observed a taped discussion among the three. Once again, subjects liked the person whom they expected to date better than they liked the other persons. Ratings of the three persons' personalities were affected as well: Subjects rated their expected dates more extremely and positively on traits and were more confident of their ratings. Subjects also awarded more attention to their prospective dates and recalled more information about them than about other target persons, but the enhanced liking and trait ratings were not due to differential attention. One may understand these data by assuming that subjects had both a directional goal and an accuracy goal: They wanted their date to be nice so that the expected interactions would be pleasant, and they wanted to get a good idea of what the date was like so that they could better control and predict the interaction. The accuracy goal led to more intense processing, and the directional goal created bias.

A slightly different paradigm employed by Neuberg and Fiske (1987) also showed that outcome dependency enhances liking. In their studies, all subjects expected to interact with the target person, but half the subjects expected the reward that they would get for their own performance to depend on the target person's performance (outcome dependency), whereas half the subjects expected their own performance to be rewarded independently. All subjects observed written or videotaped self-descriptions allegedly produced by the target person. When the information contained in these self-descriptions was not inconsistent with subjects' expectations about the target person, subjects in the outcome-dependency condition attended to this information longer and, after exposure to this information, liked the target person better than did other subjects. Thus these subjects showed the same combination of more

intense processing and bias obtained in Berscheid et al.'s (1976) study, which suggests that they too may have held both accuracy and directional goals.[4]

One outcome-dependency study in which outcome-dependent subjects' did not enhance their liking for the target person sheds some light on the mechanisms through which the enhanced liking typically obtained in this paradigm occurs. Omoto and Borgida (1988) found that White men who expected to date a White woman did not rate her any more positively on dimensions including likability than did subjects who expected to interact with her only briefly.[5] One key difference between this study and the earlier ones lies in the quality of the information about the target person that was available to subjects. Unlike the rich and meaningful target information used in earlier studies, very impoverished materials consisting of, in the authors' words, "rather uninformative preference information" (about foods, color, etc.) were used in this study. The failure of outcome dependency to enhance subjects' liking of the target person in this study despite the finding that outcome-dependency subjects did appear to allocate more attention to the target information, supports the notion that directional goals will bias impressions only when the data are rich enough to permit one to construct a justification for the desired impression (cf. Darley & Gross, 1983). When attempts to justify desired impressions fail, the desired impressions will not be espoused.

A study by Klein and Kunda (1989) showed that evaluations of another person's abilities may also be biased by directional goals, and also provided some indirect evidence for the biased memory search and belief construction model. In this study all subjects were outcome dependent on the target person, but different groups of subjects were given opposite directional goals. All subjects expected to participate in a history trivia game, in which the target person was to be their partner or their opponent. After exposure to a sample of the target person's performance, in which he got a perfect score, subjects who expected the target to be their

---

[4]Neuberg and Fiske (1987) presented these findings as evidence for more accurate processing of the information about the target person, but this argument is difficult to maintain because the liking judgments made by outcome-dependent subjects were not sensitive to different levels of individuating information about the target.

partner (and therefore probably wanted him to have a high ability) judged him as better at history than did subjects who expected him to be their opponent (and who therefore probably wanted him to have low ability).

This study also provides some evidence for the underlying processes. First, subjects were clearly constrained by the nature of information they had received, inasmuch as even subjects expecting the target to be their opponent judged him as better than average, which indicates that they did not ignore the fact that he had performed very well. Second, changes in subjects' beliefs about the nature of the task reflect an attempt to construct reality so as to justify their evaluations of the target. If the target person's peers are good at the task, one may view his strong performance as less outstanding. Accordingly, subjects for whom the target person was an opponent, and who therefore wanted to disparage him, judged the average student to be better at the task than did subjects for whom the target person was their partner. If luck plays a big role in producing behavior, a strong performance is less likely to reflect ability. Accordingly, "opponent-target" subjects considered luck to play a larger role in producing behavior than did "partner-target" subjects.

In sum, research manipulating outcome dependency shows that directional goals may bias liking for a target person, as well as trait and ability evaluations of the target person. There is some indirect evidence that the biases are obtained through biased memory search, and all the findings are consistent with this view. There is also some evidence that outcome dependency may lead to more extensive processing of information, perhaps because the manipulations also arouse accuracy goals, but this extensive processing does not eliminate bias.

Indeed, it seems possible that accuracy goals, when paired with directional goals, will often enhance rather than reduce bias. This is because the more extensive processing caused by accuracy goals may facilitate the construction of justifications for desired conclusions. Thus people expecting to incur heavier costs if their desired beliefs turn out to be wrong may expend greater effort to justify these desired beliefs. This intuition runs counter to the common assumption that strong accuracy goals will minimize the impact of directional goals (e.g., Pyszczynski & Greenberg, 1987). To determine how these two kinds of goals interact with each other to affect reasoning, it is necessary to pit them against each other in the same study. To date, there has been no serious attempt to address this question empirically.[6]

A strength of the outcome-dependency paradigm is that none of the studies seem open to reinterpretation in purely cognitive terms: In all cases, subjects were randomly assigned to conditions, and the dependency manipulation had no additional informational value and could not be assumed to affect expectations in nonmotivational ways.

BIASED BELIEFS ABOUT EVENTS

There are several sources of evidence that directional goals may bias people's beliefs about the nature, the causes, and the likelihood of various events. Klein and Kunda's (1989) study indicated that the goal of disparaging or enhancing another's abilities at a given task may lead to changes in one's beliefs about the nature of that task. Theories about the causal determinants of events may also be influenced by goals. Kunda (1987) showed that people tend to believe that their own attributes are more conducive to marital happiness and to academic success than are other attributes. It is possible that people construct such beliefs by selectively accessing only information that is consistent with them, but there is no evidence for this. The motivational interpretation of this bias as resulting from people's wish to believe that they will experience desirable outcomes was strengthened by the finding that in the domain of academic success, the effect was not found for people for whom the outcome was not personally relevant.

Similarly, Dunning, Story, and Tan (1989) found that people view their strengths as more predictive of success than their weaknesses are. They showed that the self-ratings of management students on a variety of dimensions correlated positively with their beliefs about the importance of these dimensions for success as a business executive. They also found that undergraduates preselected because they had strong verbal and

---

[5]White men expecting to date a Black woman rated her less positively than did those expecting a brief interaction with her. But these effects may be due to differential willingness to express prejudice in the different conditions.

[6]Seemingly relevant studies in the self-serving attribution paradigm typically confound accuracy goals with self-presentational concerns.

weak math skills or strong math and weak verbal skills were more positive in their evaluations of prospective students who shared their strengths and weaknesses than of those with an opposing pattern of strengths and weaknesses. In both Kunda's (1987) and Dunning, Story, and Tan's (1989) studies, however, subjects were not randomly assigned to motivational conditions, and so the findings may also be due to different prior beliefs held by people with different attributes.

Directional goals may also bias the interpretation of athletic events. Gilovich (1983) showed that fans of a winning and a losing team are differentially affected when their attention is called to a fluke event that happened in the game and that may have determined its outcome. For fans of the losing team, the occurrence of such a fluke serves to restore their faith in their team and its ability and increases their belief in the likelihood that their team would win on a rematch. Fans of the winning team, on the other hand, are hardly affected by the fluke. This suggests that the fluke event is construed as having different meaning and implications by the different groups. Interestingly, in the absence of a fluke, fans of the losing team do lose faith in its talent, which suggests that their ability to maintain faith in their team's talent is constrained by their ability to construct an acceptable justification for such faith. They will not blindly expect their team to win despite a history of losses, but they will seize upon opportunities to explain its losses away. These data do not provide unambiguous support for the role of motivation in producing the biases because the biases may also have been due to differences in the prior beliefs held by fans of the two teams.

There is some evidence that people's evaluations of medical conditions may be biased by goals. In two studies (Ditto, Jemmott, & Darley, 1988; Jemmott, Ditto, & Croyle, 1986), subjects were given a laboratory test said to diagnose the presence of a potentially risky (fictitious) enzyme deficiency. In both studies, subjects diagnosed as having the deficiency rated it as less serious and health threatening and rated the diagnostic test as less accurate than did subjects diagnosed as not having it. These findings could result from a motivated attempt to minimize the likelihood that one has the disease and the danger involved in having it. However, the findings may also result from prior beliefs: College students tend to assume that they are and will be healthier than average (Weinstein,

1980). They therefore may infer that a test diagnosing deficiencies is invalid or that a deficiency that they have cannot be serious.

Several studies have shown that the perceived likelihood of an event may be biased by goals: More desirable events are perceived as more likely to occur. Marks (1951) asked children whether they expected to pick a picture card from a mixed pack. A higher proportion of subjects expected to draw a picture card when pictures were desirable (i.e., subjects expected to gain a point with each picture) than when pictures were undesirable (i.e., subjects expected to lose a point with each picture). This was true even though subjects knew the proportion of picture cards in each pack and were sensitive to it in their guesses, in that they were more likely to predict pictures for those packs that had higher proportions of pictures. Similar results have been found for adults asked to bet on the likelihood of drawing a marked card (Irwin, 1953; Irwin & Snodgrass, 1966) or to estimate the probability that different kinds of lights would flash (Pruitt & Hoge, 1965). Conceptually similar effects were found in two studies guided by dissonance theory. Subjects thought that they were more likely to be asked to take a test if they had invested or anticipated investing considerable effort in preparing for the test than if the effort had been or was expected to be minimal (Arrowood & Ross, 1966; Yaryan & Festinger, 1961).

How are these biased likelihood estimates produced? Because in most of these studies probability estimates were not measured directly, one possibility is that the bias affected not subjects' probability estimates, but rather the subjective interpretation of these estimates. Thus people may interpret their belief that an event has a 60% probability of happening to mean that the event is either slightly likely or somewhat likely to happen, depending on whether they want to view it as likely. Such an interpretation, in turn, may affect their willingness to assume and bet that the event will occur. This account gains support from Arrowood and Ross's (1966) finding that subjects in different conditions made different predictions, on a 6-point scale, about their own likelihood of taking the test even though their believed probabilities, expressed in percentage scores, that people in their experimental condition in general would take the test did not differ. This account suggests that the beliefs accessed and constructed to determine the subjective meaning of percentage scores may have been biased by directional goals.

A different account is needed to explain one study that did get an effect on probability estimates (Irwin & Snodgrass, 1966). This is the only study in which subjects were required to infer the probabilities that desired events would occur from a series of observations (these probabilities were given to subjects in the other studies). This is also the only study in which subjects' responses were not sensitive to actual probabilities: Higher probability estimates were given for events with lower actual probabilities. This suggests that in this case, desirability of particular events may have affected the process through which the frequency of events was detected. But there is no direct evidence for this possibility.

Biases in Selection of Statistical Heuristics

The evidence reviewed so far implies that directional goals may bias the selection and construction of beliefs about the self, other people, and the world—that is, the selection of declarative knowledge structures. The studies reviewed next imply that directional goals may also bias the selection of inferential rules—that is, procedural knowledge structures.

In two studies, researchers examined directly whether people with different directional goals use different statistical heuristics spontaneously. A study by Ginossar and Trope (1987) suggested that goals may affect the use of base rate information. Subjects read Kahneman and Tversky's (1972b) cab problem, in which a witness contends that the car involved in a hit-and-run accident was green. They received information about the likelihood that the witness was correct and about the prior probability that the car would be green (the base rate) and were asked to estimate the likelihood that the car was green. Subjects typically ignore the base rate when making such estimates. However, when asked to answer as though they were the lawyer for the green car company (a manipulation presumed to motivate subjects to conclude that the car was not green), subjects did use the base rate information and made considerably lower estimates when the base rate was low. The finding that only motivated subjects used base rate information suggests that motivated subjects conducted a biased search for an inferential rule that would yield their desired conclusion. It is also possible,

however, that those subjects conducted a more intense but essentially objective search for rules. This is because the pattern of results and the design do not permit assessment of whether all subjects pretending to be lawyers used the base rate or whether only subjects for whom use of base rate could promote their goals (i.e., subjects told that the prior probability was low) used it.

Research by Sanitioso and Kunda (in press) suggested that goals may affect the use of a variant of the law of large numbers. Subjects had to decide how many instances of athletic competitions they would want to observe before they predicted how the participating athletes would be ranked at the end of the season. Subjects were led to believe that the observation of each competition would require either high or low effort, and they were then asked to assess the predictability of the athletes' final scores either from a single competition or from an aggregate of competitions. Only subjects expecting evidence collection to be highly effortful accessed the aggregation principle—that is, believed that aggregates afforded greater predictability than did single instances. Because these high-effort subjects wanted to avoid collecting large samples, their goal was to conclude that they needed only small samples of competitions to arrive at reasonable levels of predictability. Their belief that predictability increased sharply with sample size could allow these subjects to arrive at that conclusion: As the increase of predictability with sample size becomes sharper, the size of the sample yielding a given level of predictability becomes smaller. Thus it appears that motivation may affect whether the aggregation principle will be accessed. But, once again, it is not clear whether high-effort subjects' use of the heuristic resulted from a more intense but essentially objective search for heuristics or whether it resulted from a biased search for a heuristic that would yield the desired conclusion. This is because the study did not permit assessment of the intensity of processing engaged in by low-effort subjects.

In sum, there is some evidence that directional goals may affect the use of statistical heuristics. Neither of the studies that demonstrated this directly are open to reinterpretation in cognitive terms because in both cases subjects were randomly assigned to conditions and the manipulations conveyed no information that could account for the results. In both cases subjects appeared to access rules only when these were conducive to their goals, which implies that subjects engaged in a biased search for rules. However, neither study ruled out the possibility that goals led to more intense and objective processing that just happened to yield helpful rules. To do this, it would be necessary to show that subjects with the same goals use a given rule when it is likely to support their goals but not when it is likely to thwart them, or to show that subjects with opposite goals use equally complex but different heuristics.

Biased Research Evaluation

The studies reviewed so far indicate that directional goals may bias the selection and construction of beliefs, as well as the selection of inferential rules. In studies concerning biased evaluation of scientific research, experimenters explore an arena for the biased selection of both types of knowledge structures. In the typical study, subjects are exposed to alleged scientific evidence whose conclusions are differentially acceptable to different subjects, and they are then asked for their reactions to this evidence. The typical finding is that subjects motivated to disbelieve the evidence are less likely to believe it, and there is some evidence that this outcome is mediated by differential processing of the information.

Wyer and Frey (1983) gave subjects success or failure feedback on an intelligence test and then exposed them to a report containing favorable and unfavorable information about intelligence tests. Afterwards, subjects receiving failure feedback judged intelligence tests to be less valid than did subjects receiving success feedback. Indirect evidence that this was mediated by failure subjects' attempts to refute the pro-test arguments is provided by the findings that they recalled more of these arguments, but there is no direct evidence for such attempts at refutation. More direct evidence that subjects are critical of research that they are motivated to disbelieve was found in a similar study by Pyszczynski, Greenberg, and Holt (1985). Subjects were given success or failure feedback on a social sensitivity test and then exposed to two studies, one concluding that the test's validity was high and another concluding that it was low. In comparison with failure subjects, success subjects judged the high-validity study to be more convincing and better conducted, and they judged the low-validity study to be less convincing and less well

conducted. Pyszczynski et al. did not attempt to assess what mediated subjects' evaluation of how well the research was conducted. In both their study and Wyer and Frey's, the reluctance to believe in the validity of tests indicating failure may have resulted from a nonmotivational inference: Subjects who believe themselves to have high levels of a certain ability are justified in doubting the validity of tests showing otherwise.

An early study by Kassarjian and Cohen (1965) showed that smokers were less persuaded than nonsmokers by the Surgeon General's report about the health risks of smoking, which suggests that people threatened by scientific evidence are motivated to disbelieve it. But here, too, prior beliefs may have been responsible for the phenomenon, inasmuch as smokers may have believed smoking to be less dangerous than did nonsmokers even before exposure to the report.

More recently, Kunda (1987) found similar results in studies in which she attempted to control for the possibility that the effects were mediated by prior beliefs rather than by motivation. Subjects read an article claiming that caffeine was risky for women. Women who were heavy caffeine consumers were less convinced by the article than were women who were low caffeine consumers. No such effects were found for men, who may be presumed to hold the same prior beliefs about caffeine held by women, and even women showed this pattern only when the health risks were said to be serious. Thus only subjects who stood to suffer serious personal implications if the article were true doubted its truth. This study provides a stronger case for the role of directional goals in biasing the evaluation of research.

The above studies all imply that subjects motivated to disbelieve evidence do so by recruiting those beliefs and inferential rules that could be used to criticize it. But none of them provided direct evidence for this. More direct evidence demonstrating that goals may bias the evaluation of scientific evidence comes from a study by Lord, Ross, and Lepper (1979). These authors preselected subjects who were for or against capital punishment and exposed them to two studies with different methodologies, one supporting and one opposing the conclusion that capital punishment deterred crime. Subjects were more critical of the research methods used in the study that disconfirmed their initial beliefs than they were of methods used in the study that confirmed their initial beliefs. The criticisms of the disconfirming study were based on reasons such as insufficient sample size, non-random sample selection, or absence of control for important variables; this suggests that subjects' differential evaluations of the two studies were based on what seemed to them a rational use of statistical heuristics but that the use of these heuristics was in fact dependent on the conclusions of the research, not on its methods. Having discounted the disconfirming study and embraced the confirming one, their attitudes, after exposure to the mixed evidence, became more polarized. Because subjects were given methodological criticisms and counterarguments, however, the study did not address whether people would spontaneously access differential heuristics. In fact, after exposure to a single study but before receiving the list of criticisms, all subjects were swayed by its conclusions, regardless of their initial attitudes. This suggests further that people attempt to be rational: They will believe undesirable evidence if they cannot refute it, but they will refute it if they can. Also although the differential evaluation of research obtained in this study may have been due to subjects' motivation to maintain their desired beliefs, it may also have been due to the fact that one of these studies may have seemed less plausible to them because of their prior beliefs.

Sherman and Kunda (1989) used a similar paradigm to gain insight into the process mediating differential evaluation of scientific evidence. Subjects read a detailed description of a study showing that caffeine either facilitated or hindered the progress of a serious disease. Subjects motivated to disbelieve the article (high caffeine consumers who read that caffeine facilitated disease, low caffeine consumers who read that caffeine hindered disease) were less persuaded by it. This effect seemed to be mediated by biased evaluation of the methods employed in the study because, when asked to list the methodological strengths of the research, threatened subjects spontaneously listed fewer such strengths than did nonthreatened subjects. Threatened subjects also rated the various methodological aspects of the study as less sound than did nonthreatened subjects. These included aspects pertaining to inferential rules such as those relating sample size to predictability, as well as to beliefs about issues such as the validity of self-reports or the prestige of research institutions. Of importance is that all subjects were also quite responsive to the differential strength of different

aspects of the method, which suggests that they were processing the evidence in depth. Threatened subjects did not deny that some aspects were strong, but they did not consider them to be as strong as did nonthreatened subjects. Thus bias was constrained by plausibility.

Taken together, these studies suggest that the evaluation of scientific evidence may be biased by whether people want to believe its conclusions. But people are not at liberty to believe anything they like; they are constrained by their prior beliefs about the acceptability of various procedures. These constraints provide indirect support for the biased memory search and belief construction model.

As a group, these studies are vulnerable to reinterpretation in terms of nonmotivational accounts. This is because the experimenters created different levels of motivation either by preselecting subjects presumed to have different goals, who therefore may also hold different prior beliefs, or by subjecting subjects to success or failure experiences that may be deemed differentially likely to reflect their abilities because of prior beliefs. But such nonmotivational mechanisms cannot fully account for these findings because the few researchers who attempted to rule out the role of prior beliefs obtained results similar to those of researchers who did not. [. . .]

Discussion

The case for directional motivated reasoning appears quite strong. Directional goals have been shown to affect people's attitudes, beliefs, and inferential strategies in a variety of domains and in studies conducted by numerous researchers in many paradigms. Some of these studies and paradigms are open to reinterpretation in nonmotivational terms, but many are not. Even in paradigms in which individual studies may reasonably be attributed to entirely cognitive processes, such as the dissonance paradigm, evidence indicating that arousal is crucial for motivated reasoning suggests that motivational factors are involved. The position that all self-serving biases are due to purely cognitive processes is therefore no longer tenable.

Cognitive interpretations for ambiguous phenomena were viewed by their proponents as preferable to motivational ones on the grounds of parsimony. The argument, which seemed persuasive at the time, was that because all extant evidence purporting to demonstrate motivational biases could be accounted for in terms of well-established cognitive processes, there was no need to infer the additional existence of motivational processes for which no independent evidence existed (Dawes, 1976, Miller & Ross, 1975; Nisbett & Ross, 1980). The evidence reviewed in this article suggests that psychologists are now' in a position to turn that argument on its head (cf. Showers & Cantor, 1985). A single motivational process for which unequivocal independent evidence now exists may be used to account for a wide diversity of phenomena. Many of these cannot be accounted for at all in nonmotivatienal terms. Accounting for the others in cognitive terms would require making a multitude of auxiliary assumptions that are special for each case, many of which have no empirical support. For example, cognitive accounts may require the assumption that people with different backgrounds differ in their prior beliefs about a particular issue when no evidence or plausible grounds for such differences exist. Thus, under the current state of knowledge, the motivational account appears to be more parsimonious and coherent than the purely cognitive one (Thagard, 1989).

The Mechanisms for Motivated Reasoning

Although cognitive processes cannot fully account for the existence of self-serving biases, it appears that they play a major role in producing these biases in that they provide the mechanisms through which motivation affects reasoning. Indeed, it is possible that motivation merely provides an initial trigger for the operation of cognitive processes that lead to the desired conclusions.

I have proposed that when one wants to draw a particular conclusion, one feels obligated to construct a justification for that conclusion that would be plausible to a dispassionate observer. In doing so, one accesses only a biased subset of the relevant beliefs and rules. The notion that motivated reasoning is mediated by biased memory search and belief construction can account for all of the phenomena reviewed earlier, but the evidence for this process is mostly indirect. The most prevalent form of indirect evidence lies in the constraints that prior knowledge imposes on motivational biases, a pervasive finding obtained in several paradigms. In the dissonance paradigm, prior attitudes

appear to constrain motivated shifts in postdissonance attitudes (e.g., Greenbaum & Zemach, 1972; Linder et al., 1967). Prior self-concepts similarly appear to constrain directional shifts toward desired selves (Kunda & Sanitioso, 1989; Sanitioso et al., 1990). Prior beliefs about how performance reflects ability appear to constrain motivated perceptions of the ability of a person (Klein & Kunda, 1989) or of a sports team (Gilovich, 1983). And prior beliefs about the strength of scientific methods appear to constrain motivated evaluations of scientific research (Sherman & Kunda, 1989). The existence of such constraints indicates that prior knowledge is accessed in the process of arriving at desired conclusions; the existence of bias implies that not all relevant prior knowledge is accessed.

Such constraints, however, do not necessarily reflect biased memory search and belief construction; they could also result from alternative processes. For example, the existence of constraints in the dissonance paradigm may reflect a compromise between a desire to espouse new attitudes and an opposing desire to maintain current ones (though the process of arriving at such a compromise may still be one of biased memory search). In the absence of measures indicating which prior beliefs have been accessed, the existence of constraints can provide only indirect evidence for the notion of biased memory search.

However, the interpretation of these constraints as reflecting biased memory search processes is strengthened by the existence of some more direct evidence for biased memory search. Three kinds of data are taken as evidence that directional goals bias the accessing of relevant knowledge structures. The first consists of cases in which subjects spontaneously listed different memories or beliefs under the influence of different directional goals. Thus subjects were more likely to list those autobiographical memories that were consistent with their currently desired self-concepts (Sanitioso et al., 1990); subjects reported performing behaviors more frequently in the past when these behaviors reflected their currently desired attitudes and beliefs (Ross et al., 1981; Sherman & Kunda, 1989); and subjects reported finding fewer methodological strengths in scientific studies when they were motivated to disbelieve the conclusions of these studies (Sherman & Kunda, 1989).

The second type of data providing relatively

direct evidence for biased memory search processes comes from studies in which experimenters found faster reaction times for generating and endorsing those memories and beliefs that could be used to justify desired conclusions. Such findings suggest that these memories and beliefs had become relatively more accessible to subjects. Thus subjects were faster to generate those autobiographical memories that were consistent with their currently desired self-concepts (Sanitioso et al., 1990), and subjects were faster to endorse as self-descriptive those traits reflecting currently desired self-concepts (Markus & Kunda, in press). In both the memory-listing and the reaction-time studies, subjects were typically asked to list, generate, or endorse specific memories or traits before they were asked about their current attitudes or beliefs. This is important because it reduces the plausibility of an alternative account for these findings: namely, that they result from post hoc attempts at justifying previously endorsed attitudes and beliefs.

The third type of evidence pointing to biased memory search comes from studies showing that people use different statistical heuristics in the presence of different goals. Thus subjects were more likely to use base rate information (Ginossar & Trope, 1987) and the law of large numbers (Sanitioso & Kunda, in press) when the use of these heuristics enabled them to draw desired conclusions.

These effects of directional goals on memory listing, on reaction time, and on rule use provide converging evidence for the notion that goals enhance the accessibility of those knowledge structures–memories, beliefs, and rules—that are consistent with desired conclusions. Such selective enhanced accessibility reflects a biased search through memory for relevant knowledge.

Even these relatively direct indications of goal-directed memory search may, however, be open to alternative interpretations because truly direct measures of cognitive processes are impossible. For example, the memory-listing findings may reflect a response bias rather than enhanced memory accessibility. Thus the enhanced tendency to report autobiographical memories that are consistent with currently desired self-concepts may have resulted from a desire to present oneself as possessing these self-concepts. And the reaction time findings may have resulted from affective interference with speed of processing rather than

from altered accessibility. However, neither of these alternative accounts provides a satisfactory explanation of the full range of findings. Thus self-presentational accounts do not provide a good explanation of reaction time findings, which are less likely to be under volitional control. And affective interference with speed of processing does not provide a good explanation for changes in overall levels of recall. Therefore, the presence of converging evidence from these different lines of work is best explained by the notion of biased memory search. Nevertheless, the evidence is as yet limited in its quantity and breadth. Thus the case for the biased accessing and construction model is by no means ironclad. But the evidence seems suggestive enough to justify concentrated efforts to strengthen the case.

If, as I propose, directional motivated reasoning results from a biased search through memory, it is still necessary to ask how the biased memory search comes about. One intriguing possibility is that the motive, or goal, merely leads people to ask themselves whether the conclusion that they desire is true; they ask themselves directional questions: "Do I support police intervention on campus?" "Am I extraverted?" "Is my date nice?" Standard hypothesis-testing processes, which have little to do with motivation, then take over and lead to the accessing of hypothesis-confirming information and thereby to the arrival at conclusions that are biased toward hypothesis confirmation and, inadvertently, toward goal satisfaction.

There is substantial evidence that in testing hypotheses, people tend to rely on a positive test strategy: They seek out instances in which the hypothesized property is known or expected to be present rather than absent (for review, see Klayman & Ha, 1987). In other words, people are biased toward seeking instances that are consistent with a hypothesis that they are testing rather than instances that are inconsistent with it. Such biases have been found in the solution of logic problems (Wason & Johnson-Laird, 1965), in attempts to discover the rules governing object categorization (Klayman & Ha, 1989), in the assessment of correlations (see Nisbett & Ross, 1980), and, of greatest relevance here, in the evaluation of people (Snyder & Cantor, 1979). In many cases this strategy is useful (Klayman & Ha, 1987), and it does not preclude sensitivity to the diagnosticity of instances (e.g., Skov & Sherman, 1986; Trope & Bassok, 1983). Nevertheless, under some circumstances, this strategy will lead to the favoring of hypothesis-confirming evidence. Thus if people possess mixed evidence that includes some instances that are consistent with the hypothesis and some that are inconsistent with it, their tendency to favor consistent instances will result in a hypothesis-confirmation bias. This is what happened in a study by Snyder and Cantor (1979) in which subjects read a rich account of a target person's behavior and then, several days later, were asked to judge, after first reporting all facts relevant to the judgment, whether the target person was suitable for a job requiring an extraverted or an introverted profile. Subjects were more likely to report facts supporting the hypothesis that the target person was suitable for the job they were asked about and judged the target person as more suitable for that job than did subjects who had judged suitability for the other job. Similar biased accessing of hypothesis-confirming evidence has been found for directional questions about the self (Sanitioso, 1989). Subjects who were asked whether they were extraverted recalled more extraverted material about themselves and judged themselves as more extraverted than did subjects who were asked whether they were introverted.

Further evidence indicating that such hypothesis-confirmation phenomena result from biased accessing of a subset of relevant knowledge comes from studies showing that the phenomenon is reduced or eliminated when subjects are encouraged to conduct more symmetrical memory searches. Subjects' confidence in the correctness of their responses to general knowledge questions is not affected when they are asked to provide reasons supporting their responses, which suggests that they do so spontaneously, even when not asked to; however, their confidence is reduced when they are asked to provide reasons contradicting their responses, which suggests that they do not engage in such hypothesis-disconfirming searches spontaneously (Koriat, Lichtenstein, & Fischhoff, 1980). Similarly, subjects' hindsight bias—that is, their belief that events that happened were bound to have happened—is not reduced when subjects are merely admonished to resist such bias, but it is reduced when subjects are asked to explain why opposite outcomes may have occurred, which suggests that subjects do not consider alternative hypotheses spontaneously (Fischhoff, 1977). In a similar vein, the tendency to evaluate research supporting counterattitudinal positions more harshly

(Lord et al., 1979) is not affected when subjects are told to be objective and unbiased, but it is eliminated when subjects are asked to consider what judgments they would have made had the study yielded opposite results (Lord et al., 1984).

Taken together, these findings imply that people are more likely to search spontaneously for hypothesis-consistent evidence than for inconsistent evidence. This seems to be the mechanism underlying hypothesis confirmation because hypothesis confirmation is eliminated when people are led to consider inconsistent evidence. It seems either that people are not aware of their tendency to favor hypothesis-consistent evidence of that, upon reflection, they judge this strategy to be acceptable, because accuracy goals alone do not reduce this bias.

Thus the tendency to confirm hypotheses appears to be due to a process of biased memory search that is comparable with the process instigated by directional goals. This parallel lends support to the notion that directional goals may affect reasoning by giving rise to directional hypotheses, which are then confirmed; if the motivation to arrive at particular conclusions leads people to ask themselves whether their desired conclusions are true, normal strategies of hypothesis-testing will favor confirmation of these desired conclusions in many cases. One implication of this account is that motivation will cause bias, but cognitive factors such as the available beliefs and rules will determine the magnitude of the bias.

In its strongest form, this account removes the motivational "engine" from the process of motivated reasoning, in that motivation is assumed to lead only to the posing of directional questions and to have no further effect on the process through which these questions are answered. If this were true, many of the distinctions between cognitive, expectancy-driven processes and motivated processes would break down. Both directional goals and "cold" expectancies may have their effects through the same hypothesis-confirmation process. The process through which the hypotheses embedded in the questions "Is my desired conclusion true?" and "Is my expected conclusion true?" are confirmed may be functionally equivalent. Indeed, there are some interesting parallels between motivated reasoning and expectancy confirmation that lend support to this notion. For example, Sherman and Kunda (1989) found that implausible evidence (namely, that caffeine may by good for one's health) was subjected to elaborate and critical scrutiny that was comparable to the scrutiny triggered by threatening evidence. Similarly, Neuberg and Fiske (1987) found that evidence inconsistent with expectations received increased attention comparable in magnitude to the increase caused by outcome dependency. Finally, Bem's (1972) findings that the beliefs of observers mirrored those of actors in dissonance experiments suggest that observers' expectations and actors' motivations may lead to similar processes.[7] These parallels between motivational processes and expectancy-confirmation processes suggest that rather than attempting to distinguish between the two, it may be more fruitful to focus attention on the mechanisms underlying both.

It is also possible, though, that the effects of motivation on reasoning may go beyond the mere posing of directional questions. For example, when motivation is involved, one may persist in asking one directional question after another (e.g., "Is the method used in this research faulty?" "Is the researcher incompetent?" "Are the results weak?"), thus exploring all possible avenues that may allow one to endorse the desired conclusion. It is also possible that in addition to posing directional questions, motivation leads to more intense searches for hypothesis-confirming evidence and, perhaps, to suppression of disconfirming evidence (cf. Pyszczynski & Greenberg, 1987). If motivation does have these additional effects on reasoning, the parallels between motivated reasoning and expectancy confirmations gain new meaning. They suggest that seemingly "cold" expectancies may in fact be imbued with motivation. The prospect of altering one's beliefs, especially those that are well established and long held, may be every bit as unpleasant as the undesired cognitions typically viewed as "hot." It was this intuition that led Festinger (1957) to describe the hypothetical situation of standing in the rain without getting wet as dissonance arousing.

It is difficult to tell, at this point, whether the effects of motivation on reasoning go beyond the posing of directional questions. It seems clear that the examples of motivational reasoning reviewed here could result merely from posing directional

questions. Further research is necessary to determine whether motivation plays an additional role.

Implications

Although the mechanisms underlying motivated reasoning are not yet fully understood, it is now clear that directional goals do affect reasoning. People are more likely to arrive at those conclusions that they want to arrive at. Whatever the mechanisms, the implications are serious and important. Taylor and Brown (1988) implied that motivated reasoning may be beneficial because the resulting illusions promote mental health; unrealistically positive views of oneself and the world are often adaptive. This seems true for illusory beliefs that do not serve as the basis for important action. But motivated illusions can be dangerous when they are used to guide behavior and decisions, especially in those cases in which objective reasoning could facilitate more adaptive behavior. For example, people who play down the seriousness of early symptoms of severe diseases such as skin cancer and people who see only weaknesses in research pointing to the dangers of drugs such as caffeine or of behaviors such as drunken driving may literally pay with their lives for their motivated reasoning. Hopefully, once the mechanisms producing such biases are fully understood, it will be possible to help people overcome them.

REFERENCES

Abelson, R. P. (1968). Psychological implication. In R. P. Abelson, E. Aronson, W. J. McGuire, T. M. Newcomb, M. J. Rosenberg, & P. H. Tannenbaum (Eds.), *Theories of cognitive consistency: A sourcebook* (pp. 112–139). Chicago: Rand McNally.

Aronson, E. (1968). Dissonance theory: Progress and problems. In R. P. Abelson, E. Aronson, W. J. McGuire, T. M. Newcomb, M. J. Rosenberg, & P. H. Tannenbaum (Eds.), *Theories of cognitive consistency: A sourcebook* (pp. 5–27). Chicago: Rand McNally.

Arrowood, A. J., & Ross, L. (1966). Anticipated effort and subjective probability. *Journal of Personality and Social Psychology, 4*, 57–64.

Beach, L. R, & Mitchell, T. R. (1978). A contingency model for the selection of decision strategies. *Academy of Management Review, 3*, 439–449.

Bem, D. J. (1972). Self-perception theory. In L. Berkowitz (Ed.), *Advances in experimental social psychology* (Vol. 6, pp. 1–63). New York: Academic Press.

Berscheid, E., Graziano, W., Monson, T., & Dermer, M. (1976). Outcome dependency: Attention, attribution, and attraction. *Journal of Personality and Social Psychology, 34*, 978–989.

---

[7] It is known that actors' responses are not due only to expectancies, because they occur only in the presence of arousal that cannot be attributed to other sources (Cooper & Fazio, 1984).

Chaiken, S., Liberman, A., & Eagly, A. H. (1989). Heuristics and systematic information processing within and beyond the persuasion context. In J. S. Uleman & J. A. Bargh (Eds.), *Unintended thought: Limits of awareness, intention, and control* (pp. 212–252). New York: Guilford Press.

Cooper, J., & Fazio, R. H. (1984). A new look at dissonance theory. In L. Berkowitz (Ed.), *Advances in experimental social psychology* (Vol. 17, pp. 229–266). New York: Academic Press.

Darley, J. M., & Berscheid, E. (1967). Increased liking as a result of anticipation of personal contact. *Human Relations, 20,* 29–40.

Darley, J. M., & Gross, P. H. (1983). A hypothesis-confirming bias in labeling effects. *Journal of Personality and Social Psychology, 44,* 20–33.

Dawes, R. M. (1976). Shallow psychology. In J. Carroll & J. Payne (Eds.), *Cognition and social behavior* (pp. 3–12). Hillsdale, NJ: Erlbaum.

Ditto, P. H., Jemmott, J. B., & Darley, J. M. (1988). Appraising the threat of illness: A mental representational approach. *Health Psychology, 7,* 183–201.

Dunning, D., Meyerowitz, J. A., & Holzberg, A. (1989). Ambiguity and self-evaluation: The role of idiosyncratic trait definitions in self-serving assessments of ability. *Journal of Personality and Social Psychology, 57,* 1082–1090.

Dunning, D., Story, A. L., & Tan, P. L. (1989). *The self as model of excellence in social evaluation.* Unpublished manuscript, Cornell University.

Erdelyi, M. H. (1974). A new look at the new look: Perceptual defence and vigilance. *Psychological Review, 81,* 1–25.

Fazio, R. H., Effrein, E. A., & Falender, V. J. (1981). Self-perception following social interaction. *Journal of Personality and Social Psychology, 41,* 232–242.

Festinger, L. (1957). *A theory of cognitive dissonance.* Stanford, CA: Stanford University Press.

Festinger, L., & Carlsmith, J. M. (1959). Cognitive consequences of forced compliance. *Journal of Abnormal and Social Psychology, 58,* 203–211.

Fischhoff, B. (1977). Perceived informativeness of facts. *Journal of Experimental Psychology: Human Perception and Performance, 3,* 349–358.

Freund, T., Kruglanski, A. W., & Shpitzajzen, A. (1985). The freezing and unfreezing of impressional primacy: Effects of the need for structure and the fear of invalidity. *Personality and Social Psychology Bulletin, 11,* 479–487.

Frey, D. (1986). Recent research on selective exposure. In L. Berkowitz (Ed.), *Advances in experimental social psychology* (Vol. 19, pp. 41–80). New York: Academic Press.

Gilovich, T. (1983). Biased evaluation and persistence in gambling. *Journal of Personality and Social Psychology, 44,* 1110–1126.

Ginossar, Z., & Trope, Y. (1987). Problem solving in judgment under uncertainty. *Journal of Personality and Social Psychology, 52,* 464–474.

Greenbaum, C. W., & Zemach, M. (1972). Role playing and change of attitude toward the police after a campus riot: Effects of situational demand and justification. *Human Relations, 25,* 87–99.

Greenwald, A. G. (1980). The totalitarian ego: Fabrication and revision of personal history. *American Psychologist, 35,* 603–618.

Greenwald, A. G., & Ronis, D. L. (1978). Twenty years of cognitive dissonance: Case study of the evolution of a theory. *Psychological Review, 85,* 53–57.

Harkness, A. R., DeBono, K. G., & Borgida, E. (1985). Personal involvement and strategies for making contingency judgments: A stake in the dating game makes a difference. *Journal of Personality and Social Psychology, 49,* 22–32.

Heider, F. (1958). *The psychology of interpersonal relations.* New York: Wiley.

Higgins, E. T., & King, G. A. (1981). Accessibility of social constructs: Information-processing consequences of individual and contextual variability. In N. Cantor & J. E. Kihlstrom (Eds.), *Personality, cognition, and social interaction* (pp. 69–121). Hillsdale, NJ: Erlbaum.

Irwin, F. W. (1953). Stated expectations as functions of probability and desirability of outcomes. *Journal of Personality, 21,* 329–335.

Irwin, F. W., & Snodgrass, J. G. (1966). Effects of independent and dependent outcomes on bets. *Journal of Experimental Psychology, 71,* 282–285.

Jemmott, J. B., Ditto, P. H., & Croyle, R. T. (1986). Judging health status: Effects of perceived prevalence and personal relevance. *Journal of Personality and Social Psychology, 50,* 899–905.

Kahneman, D., & Tversky, A. (1972a). Subjective probability: A judgment of representativeness. *Cognitive Psychology, 3,* 430–454.

Kahneman, D., & Tversky, A. (1972b). On prediction and judgment. *ORI Research Monograph, 12*(4).

Kassarjian, H. H., & Cohen, J. B. (1965). Cognitive dissonance and consumer behavior. *California Management Review, 8,* 55–64.

Kassin, S. M., & Hochreich, D. J. (1977). Instructional set: A neglected variable in attribution research? *Personality and Social Psychology Bulletin, 3,* 620–623.

Klayman, J., & Ha, Y.-W. (1987). Confirmation, disconfirmation, and information in hypothesis testing. *Psychological Review, 94,* 211–228.

Klayman, J., & Ha, Y.-W. (1989). Hypothesis testing in rule discovery: Strategy, structure, and content. *Journal of Experimental Psychology: Learning, Memory, and Cognition, 15,* 596–604.

Klein, W. M., & Kunda, Z. (1989, March). *Motivated person perception: Justifying desired conclusions.* Paper presented at the meeting of the Eastern Psychological Association, Boston.

Koriat, A., Lichtenstein, S., & Fischhoff, B. (1980). Reasons for confidence. *Journal of Experimental Psychology: Human Learning and Memory, 6,* 107–118.

Kruglanski, A. W. (1980). Lay epistemology process and contents. *Psychological Review, 87,* 70–87.

Kruglanski, A. W., & Ajzen, I. (1983). Bias and error in human judgment. *European Journal of Social Psychology, 13,* 1–44.

Kruglanski, A. W., & Freund, T. (1983). The freezing and unfreezing of lay-inferences: Effects on impressional primacy, ethnic stereotyping, and numerical anchoring. *Journal of Experimental Social Psychology, 19,* 448–468.

Kruglanski, A. W., & Klar, Y. (1987). A view from the bridge: Synthesizing the consistency and attribution paradigms from a lay epistemic perspective. *European Journal of Social Psychology, 17,* 211–241.

Kunda, Z. (1987). Motivation and inference: Self-serving generation and evaluation of evidence. *Journal of Personality and Social Psychology, 53,* 636–647.

Kunda, Z., & Nisbett, R. E. (1986). The psychometrics of everyday life. *Cognitive Psychology, 18,* 199–224.

Kunda, Z., & Sanitioso, R. (1989). Motivated changes in the self-concept. *Journal of Experimental Social Psychology, 25,* 272–285.

Linder, D. E., Cooper, J., & Jones, E. E. (1967). Decision freedom as a determinant of the role of incentive magnitude in attitude change. *Journal of Personality and Social Psychology, 6,* 245–254.

Lord, C. G, Lepper, M. R., & Preston, E. (1984). Considering the opposite: A corrective strategy for social judgment. *Journal of Personality and Social Psychology, 47,* 1231–1243.

Lord, C. G., Ross, L., & Lepper, M. R. (1979). Biased assimilation and attitude polarization: The effects of prior theories on subsequently considered evidence. *Journal of Personality and Social Psychology, 37,* 2098–2109.

Marks, R. W. (1951). The effects of probability, desirability, and "privilege" on the stated expectations of children. *Journal of Personality, 19,* 332–351.

Markus, H., & Kunda, Z. (1986). Stability and malleability of the self-concept. *Journal of Personality and Social Psychology, 51,* 858–866.

McAllister, D. W., Mitchell, T. R., & Beach, L. R. (1979). The contingency model for the selection of decision strategies: An empirical test of the effects of significance, accountability, and reversibility. *Organizational Behavior and Human Performance, 24,* 228–244.

McGuire, W. J. (1960). A syllogistic analysis of cognitive relationships. In M. J. Rosenberg, C. I. Hovland, W. J. McGuire, R. P. Abelson, & J. W. Brehm (Eds.), *Attitude organization and change* (pp. 65–111). New Haven, CT: Yale University Press.

McGuire, W. J. (1968). Theory of the structure of human thought. In R. P. Abelson, E. Aronson, W. J. McGuire, T. M. Newcomb, M. J. Rosenberg, & P. H. Tannenbaum (Eds.), *Theories of cognitive consistency: A sourcebook* (pp. 140–162). Chicago: Rand McNally.

Miller, D. T., & Ross, M. (1975). Self-serving biases in attribution of causality: Fact or fiction? *Psychological Bulletin, 82,* 213–225.

Neuberg, S. L., & Fiske, S. T. (1987). Motivational influences on impression formation: Dependency, accuracy-driven attention, and individuating information. *Journal of Personality and Social Psychology, 53,* 431–444.

Nisbett, R. E., Krantz, D. H., Jepson, C., & Kunda, Z. (1983). The use of statistical heuristics in everyday inductive reasoning. *Psychological Review, 90,* 339–363.

Nisbett, R. E., & Ross, L. (1980). *Human inference: Strategies and shortcomings of social judgement.* Englewood Cliffs, NJ: Prentice-Hall.

Omoto, A. M., & Borgida, E. (1988). Guess who might be coming for dinner?: Personal involvement and racial stereotyping. *Journal of Experimental Social Psychology, 24,* 571–593.

Payne, J. W., Bettman, J. R., & Johnson, E. J. (1988). Adaptive strategy selection in decision making. *Journal of Experimental Psychology: Learning, Memory and Cognition, 14,* 534–552.

Petty, R. E., & Cacioppo, J. T. (1986). The elaboration likelihood model of persuasion. In L. Berkowitz (Ed.), *Advances in experimental social psychology* (Vol. 19, pp. 123–203). New York: Academic Press.

Pittman, T. S., & D'Agostino, P. R. (1985). Motivation and attribution: The effects of control deprivation on subsequent information processing. In G. Weary & J. Harvey (Eds.), *Attribution: Basic issues and applications* (pp. 117–141). New York: Academic Press.

Pruitt, D. G, & Hoge, R. D. (1965). Strength of the relationship between the value of an event and its subjective probability as a function of method of measurement. *Journal of Experimental Psychology, 69,* 483–489.

Pyszczynski, T., & Greenberg, J. (1987). Toward an integration of cognitive and motivational perspectives on social inference: A biased hypothesis-testing model. In L. Berkowitz (Ed.), *Advances in experimental social psychology* (Vol. 20, pp. 297–340). New York: Academic Press.

Pyszczynski, T., Greenberg, J., & Holt, K. (1985). Maintaining consistency between self-serving beliefs and available data: A bias in information evaluation. *Personality and Social Psychology Bulletin, 11,* 179–190.

Ross, M., & Fletcher, G. J. O. (1985). Attribution and social perception. In G. Lindzey & E. Aronson (Eds.), *Handbook of social psychology* (pp. 73–122). New York: Random House.

Ross, M., McFarland, C., & Fletcher, G. J. O. (1981). The effect of attitude on recall of past histories. *Journal of Personality and Social Psychology, 10,* 627–634.

Salancik, G. R., & Conway, M. (1975). Attitude inference from salient and relevant cognitive content about behavior. *Journal of Personality and Social Psychology, 32,* 829–840.

Sanitioso, R. (1989). *Mechanisms for motivated changes in the self-concept.* Unpublished doctoral dissertation, Princeton University.

Sanitioso, R., & Kunda, Z. (in press). Ducking the collection of costly evidence: Motivated use of statistical heuristics. *Journal of Behavioral Decision Making.*

Sanitioso, R., Kunda, Z., & Fong, G. T. (1990). Motivated recruitment of autobiographical memory. *Journal of Personality and Social Psychology, 59,* 229–241.

Sherman, B. R., & Kunda, Z. (1989, June). *Motivated evaluation of scientific evidence.* Paper presented at the American Psychological Society convention, Arlington.

Sherman, S. J., & Gorkin, L. (1980). Attitude bolstering when behavior is inconsistent with central attitudes. *Journal of Experimental Social Psychology, 16,* 388–403.

Showers, C., & Cantor, N. (1985). Social cognition: A look at motivated strategies. *Annual Review of Psychology, 3,* 275–305.

Sieber, J. E. (1974). Effects of decision importance on ability to generate warranted subjective uncertainty. *Journal of Personality and Social Psychology, 30,* 688–694.

Simon, H. (1957). *Models of man: Social and rational.* New York: Wiley.

Skov, R. B., & Sherman, S. J. (1986). Information gathering processes: Diagnosticity, hypothesis-confirmatory strategies, and perceived hypothesis confirmation. *Journal of Experimental Social Psychology, 22,* 93–121.

Snyder, M. (1982). When believing means doing: Creating links between attitudes and behavior. In M. P. Zanna, E. T. Higgins, & C. P. Herman (Eds.), *Variability in social behavior: The Ontario Symposium* (Vol. 2, pp. 105–130). Hillsdale, NJ: Erlbaum.

Snyder, M., & Cantor, N. (1979). Testing hypotheses about other people: The use of historical knowledge. *Journal of Experimental Social Psychology, 15,* 330–342.

Sorrentino, R. M., & Higgins, E. T. (1986). Motivation and

cognition: Warming up to synergism. In R. M. Sorrentino & E. T. Higgins (Eds.), *Handbook of motivation and cognition: Foundations of social behavior* (pp. 3–19). New York: Guilford Press.

Steele, C. M., & Liu, T. J. (1983). Dissonance processes as self-affirmation. *Journal of Personality and Social Psychology, 45,* 5–19.

Stigler, G. J. (1961). The economics of information. *The Journal of Political Economy, 69,* 213–225.

Swann, W. B. (1983). Self-verification: Bringing social reality into harmony with the self. In J. Suls & A. G. Greenwald (Eds.), *Social psychological perspectives on the self* (Vol. 2, pp. 33–66). Hillsdale, NJ: Erlbaum.

Taylor, S. E., & Brown, J. D. (1988). Illusion and well-being: A social psychological perspective on mental health. *Psychological Bulletin, 103,*193–210.

Tesser, A. (1986). Some effects of self-evaluation maintenance on cognition and action. In R. M. Sorrentino & E. T. Higgins (Eds.), *The handbook of motivation and cognition: Foundations of social behavior* (pp. 435–464). New York: Guilford Press.

Tesser, A., & Campbell, J. (1983). Self-definition and self-evaluation maintenance. In J. Suls & A. Greenwald (Eds.), *Social psychological perspectives on the self* (Vol. 2, pp. 1–31). Hillsdale, NJ: Erlbaum.

Tetlock, P. E. (1983). Accountability and the perseverance of first impressions. *Social Psychology Quarterly, 46,* 285–292.

Tetlock, P. E. (1985). Accountability: A social check on the fundamental attribution error. *Social Psychology Quarterly, 48,* 227–236.

Tetlock, P. E., & Boettger, R. (1989). Accountability: A social magnifier of the dilution effect. *Journal of Personality and Social Psychology, 57,* 388–398.

Tetlock, P. E., & Kim, J. I. (1987). Accountability and judg-ment processes in a personality prediction task. *Journal of Personality and Social Psychology, 52,* 700–709.

Tetlock, P. E., & Levi, A. (1982). Attribution bias: On the inconclusiveness of the cognition–motivation debate. *Journal of Experimental Social Psychology, 18,* 68–88.

Thagard, P. (1989). Explanatory coherence. *The Behavioral and Brain Sciences, 12,* 435–467.

Trope, Y., & Bassok, M. (1983). Information-gathering strategies in hypothesis-testing. *Journal of Experimental Social Psychology, 19,* 560–576.

Tversky, A., & Kahneman, D. (1973). Availability: A heuristic for judging frequency and probability. *Cognitive Psychology, 5,* 207–232.

Tversky, A., & Kahneman, D. (1974). Judgment under uncertainty: Heuristics and biases. *Science, 185,* 1124–1131.

Wason, P. C., & Johnson-Laird, P. N. (1965). *Psychology of reasoning: Structure and content.* London: Batsford.

Weinstein, N. D. (1980). Unrealistic optimism about future life events. *Journal of Personality and Social Psychology, 39,* 806–820.

Weinstein, N. D. (1982). Unrealistic optimism about susceptibility to health problems. *Journal of Behavioral Medicine, 5,* 441–460.

Wicklund, R. A., & Brehm, J. W. (1976). *Perspectives on cognitive dissonance.* Hillsdale, NJ: Erlbaum.

Wyer, R. S., & Frey, D. (1983). The effects of feedback about self and others on the recall and judgments of feedback-relevant information. *Journal of Experimental and Social Psychology, 19,* 540–559.

Yaryan, R. B., & Festinger, L. (1961). Preparatory action and belief in the probable occurrence of future events. *Journal of Abnormal and Social Psychology, 63,* 603–606.

Zanna, M. P., & Cooper, J. (1974). Dissonance and the pill: An attributional approach to studying the arousal properties of dissonance. *Journal of Personality and Social Psychology, 29,* 703–709.

Uncertainty Orientation and Persuasion: Individual Differences in the Effects of Personal Relevance on Social Judgments

Richard M. Sorrentino • Department of Psychology, University of Western Ontario
D. Ramona Bobocel, Maria Z. Gitta and James M. Olson • Department of Psychology,
University of Western Ontario • Erin C. Hewitt • Department of Psychology, York University

Editors' Notes

How do individual differences in uncertainty orientation moderate the role of personal relevance in attitude change? Previous studies have found that the persuasive effectiveness of high quality arguments compared to positive source characteristics like high expertise is greater when the issue is more personally relevant to the message recipient. The authors hypothesize that this effect of personal relevance may be stronger for uncertainty-oriented persons than certainty-oriented persons. Uncertainty-oriented persons strongly engage situations in which uncertainty about the self or the world can be resolved through exploration. In contrast, certainty-oriented persons strongly engage situations involving certainty about the self or the world and avoid situations that threaten their certainty. A persuasive message is more likely to change what recipients know about themselves and the world when it concerns an issue of high than low personal relevance. Thus, persuasive issues of high relevance should engage uncertainty-oriented persons (who approach an opportunity to learn something new) more and engage certainty-oriented persons (who avoid possible challenges to their knowledge) less. To the extent that greater engagement increases the influence of argument quality compared to source characteristics, the typical finding in the persuasion literature is likely to be obtained for uncertainty-oriented persons but not for certainty-oriented persons. The results of the studies reported in this paper support these conclusions.

Discussion Questions

1. Which kinds of situations strongly engage uncertainty-oriented persons and certainty-oriented persons?
2. How do individual differences in uncertainty orientation moderate the role of issue relevance in the persuasive effectiveness of argument quality compared to source characteristics?

Authors' Abstract

In two studies we investigated the effects of personal relevance on attitude change as a function of one's uncertainty orientation. We predicted that, unlike uncertainty-oriented persons, high personal relevance would make certainty-oriented persons less careful or systematic in their processing of message arguments and more dependent on heuristic, or persuasion cues, than would low personal relevance. Results from both studies, within and across 2-week time periods, supported predictions. In Study 1, high personal relevance led to higher persuasiveness of two-sided communications and lower persuasiveness of one-sided communications than low personal relevance for uncertainty-oriented persons, but the reverse occurred for certainty-oriented persons. In Study 2, high personal relevance led to higher persuasive impact of strong arguments and lower impact for source expertise than did low personal relevance for uncertainty-oriented persons, but, again, the reverse occurred for certainty-oriented persons. We discuss implications for current theories.

Research in social psychology has identified two distinct styles of making social judgments. Sometimes perceivers carefully process available information and make rational judgments on the basis of the evidence. Anderson's (1974) information integration theory is one approach that conceptualizes decision makers in this fashion. At other times, however, perceivers rely on simple rules, or *heuristics*, that allow them to make judgments without much thought or effort. For example, Kahneman and Tversky (1973) identified several common errors in intuitive judgments that result from perceivers' instinctive use of simplifying assumptions (see also Nisbett & Ross, 1980; Sherman & Corty, 1984). Of course, these two styles actually represent the endpoints of a continuum of possible approaches to social judgments, ranging from mindful to mindless or from controlled to automatic processing (Langer, 1978; Schneider & Shiffrin, 1977).

Attitudes constitute one kind of social judgment. It may not be surprising, therefore, that attitude theorists have also proposed varying types of processing based on the amount of thought exerted by the perceiver. For example, Chaiken (1980) has distinguished between *systematic* attitude change, which results from active consideration of relevant arguments, and *heuristic* attitude change, which results from simple decision rules such as "I should agree with people I like." Similarly, Petty and Cacioppo (1981) have distinguished between persuasion via the *central route*, which is mediated by issue-relevant cognitions, and persuasion via the *peripheral route*, which is mediated by *persuasion cues* (external effects or simple assump-

tions that imply a particular attitudinal position). Clearly, systematic, or central, persuasion involves more effort and thought than does heuristic, or peripheral, persuasion.

Effects of Personal Relevance

In the social cognition literature, the variable of personal relevance, or involvement, has been suggested as a determinant of processing styles. Specifically, researchers have argued that perceivers process information in a more thoughtful or rational way when the issue is highly relevant to them than when the issue is low in personal relevance (see Fiske & Taylor, 1984; Langer, 1978; Nisbett & Ross, 1980). Attitude researchers have also been investigating personal relevance as a determinant of subjects' processing styles, hypothesizing that high relevance leads to more thinking about the issue or message. For example, Chaiken (1980) exposed subjects to a counterattitudinal message containing either two or six arguments, which allegedly came from either a likable or unlikable communicator. Some subjects expected to discuss the message topic at a future experimental session (high relevance), whereas other subjects expected to discuss a different topic (low relevance). In the high-relevance condition, subjects were more convinced by six than by two arguments, presumably because the additional information increased the cogency of the message, but the likability manipulation did not affect persuasion. In the low-relevance condition, communicator likability increased attitude change, presumably because this quality served as a judgmental heuristic, but the number of arguments in the message had no effect on subjects' opinions.

Petty, Cacioppo, and their colleagues have conducted several experiments showing that high relevance increases message-relevant thinking and thereby invokes the central route to persuasion (Petty & Cacioppo, 1979a, 1979b, 1984; Petty, Cacioppo, & Goldman, 1981). For example, Petty et al. (1981) exposed subjects to a counterattitudinal message containing either strong or weak arguments, which allegedly came from a source of either high or low expertise (source expertise was conceptualized as a possible persuasion cue). Personal relevance was manipulated by leading some subjects to believe that the recommendations in the message (advocating the institution of comprehensive examinations for senior undergraduates) were being considered for adoption at their own university in the following year, thus potentially affecting them directly; other subjects were told that the recommendations were being considered for adoption 10 years hence. In the high-relevance condition, strong arguments produced more attitude change than weak arguments, but source expertise did not affect persuasion. In the low-relevance condition, subjects were more persuaded by an expert than by a nonexpert source, but the quality of the arguments in the message did not affect subjects' attitudes.

Taken together, those experiments provide strong support for the plausible hypothesis that perceivers will process information more carefully, make more thoughtful judgments, and rely less on simple cues, or heuristics, when the issue is highly relevant than when the issue is low in personal relevance. As Petty et al. (1981) pointed out, evaluating the cogency of arguments and producing message-relevant cognitions is difficult work; presumably, people are willing to exert such effort only (or mostly) when the personal consequences of an issue are high.

An Individual Difference Perspective

Possible individual differences in the effects of personal relevance on processing styles have never been investigated to our knowledge. Cacioppo, Petty, and Morris (1983) did examine individual differences in the tendency to use central processing (this tendency was operationally defined as

subjects' responsiveness to a manipulation of argument quality) and found that subjects high in *need for cognition* manifested more central processing than subjects low on this dimension. Presumably though, individuals with both low and high need for cognition would be expected to manifest more thoughtful (central) processing as personal relevance increases.

In contrast, an individual difference dimension recently identified by Sorrentino, Short, and Raynor (1984) leads to the expectation that some persons may rely on heuristic devices more and on systematic processing less as relevance increases. This dimension is labelled *uncertainty orientation* and concerns individuals' approaches to uncertainty or ambiguity. Using earlier notions from Freud and Erikson (see Erikson, 1968) and Rokeach (1960), along with more recent notions concerning the interaction of motivation and cognition (see Sorrentino & Higgins, 1986), Sorrentino et al. (1984) proposed a hot to cold model of personality development concerning the way one adapts to new situations. This model assumes that uncertainty-oriented persons are those who have been rewarded for autonomous exploratory behavior. Such persons develop general schemas for situations that allow resolution of uncertainty about the self and the environment. When placed in these situations, they are affectively charged to resolve this uncertainty (Hoffman, 1986). Certainty-oriented persons, on the other hand, have not been rewarded for autonomous, exploratory behavior and in fact might have been punished for such behavior. Consequently, these persons gravitate toward and develop schemas for safe and familiar situations or schemas that do not require dealing with uncertain situations.[1] Hence, they are affectively charged by situations involving certainty about the self and the

---

[1] Evidence that uncertainty orientation may be thought of in terms of schemas comes from research by King and Sorrentino (in press) and from arguments by Sorrentino and Higgins (1986). King and Sorrentino found that uncertainty-oriented and certainty-oriented persons have greater recall of schematically relevant material and in fact distort ambiguous information in the direction of their respective schemas 2 weeks following presentation of that material. In addition, Sorrentino and Higgins argued that projective measures, as used in Studies 1 and 2 for one of the components of our measure of uncertainty orientation (see Method section), are actually measures of chronic construct or schema accessibility. That is, they access what is chronically available under neutral testing conditions.

environment. This reasoning leads to the general hypothesis that motivation will be aroused in situations relevant to one's uncertainty orientation. Thus, uncertainty-oriented persons should be more motivated in situations that involve uncertainty about the self or the environment, whereas certainty-oriented persons should be more motivated in situations that involve certainty about the self or the environment.

In their initial test of this hypothesis, Sorrentino et al. (1984) showed in three studies that for uncertainty-oriented persons, relevant sources of motivation (achievement-related motives) were most aroused in performance situations that contained uncertainty about the self or the environment. For certainty-oriented persons, the reverse occurred: Their achievement-related motives were most aroused in situations in which the uncertainty about the self or the environment was not at issue.

Although the research just discussed is not directly relevant to social influence implications of uncertainty orientation, two additional studies provide a direct link between research on achievement behavior and the role of personal relevance on persuasion. The first study (Sorrentino & Hewitt, 1984) tested directly whether there would be differences in the way uncertainty-oriented and certainty-oriented persons would approach information that was personally relevant. It was found, as predicted, that uncertainty-oriented persons chose to undertake activity that would resolve uncertainty about a new and potentially important ability, whereas certainty-oriented persons actually chose to undertake alternate activity that would tell them nothing new about this ability. Even more striking was the finding that it did not matter whether the information was likely to be positive (i.e., they were high in the ability) or negative (i.e., they were low in the ability). Regardless, uncertainty-oriented persons chose to find out in both conditions, certainty-oriented persons chose not to.

The second study (Sorrentino & Roney, 1986) demonstrated that the general hypothesis of Sorrentino and Short (1986)—motivational arousal will occur in situations relevant to one's uncertainty orientation—did apply directly to situations of high personal relevance. As expected, when presented with a task that was diagnostic or nondiagnostic of a new and potentially important ability, achievement-related motives of uncertainty-oriented persons were most aroused in the diagnostic task. For certainty-oriented persons, the

reverse occurred: Their achievement-related motives were most aroused in the nondiagnostic task.

The finding that uncertainty-oriented persons appear to be motivated by personally relevant information (i.e., the information is diagnostic about the self) and certainty-oriented persons by information that is not personally relevant (i.e., it does not tell them anything new about the self) has important implications for research on attitude change and persuasion. Uncertainty-oriented persons should tend to follow previous ideas related to the effects of personal relevance on information processing. They should be more motivated in situations of high than low personal relevance. Hence, they should be more likely to engage in systematic processing of information in the former situation but use heuristic cues in the latter situation. Paradoxically, certainty-oriented persons should be less likely to engage in systematic processing under high than low personal relevance. When the situation is of high personal relevance, they should in fact resort to heuristic information processing: allowing others to resolve the uncertainty for them rather than engage in uncertainty resolution themselves. Thus, they should be more receptive to clear and unequivocal solutions, source expertise, attractiveness, and so on, under high personal relevance than under low personal relevance.

Although the behavior we are predicting for certainty-oriented individuals may appear illogical, it is not necessarily so. Turning to powerful leaders, experts, or respected persons for advice are heuristics that everyone uses on occasion. To some individuals, these devices may appear to be even more appropriate for important than for trivial decisions. Thus, persuasion cues such as source attractiveness or expertise may, paradoxically, exert a greater impact on these individuals' attitudes when the issue is high rather than low in personal relevance. Similarly, when the issue does not arouse motivation for uncertainty-oriented persons (i.e., when it is not personally relevant), the very fact that it is not diagnostic about the self makes it schema relevant for certainty-oriented persons. Returning to the Sorrentino et al. (1984) research, certainty-oriented persons were most motivated in situations that others may deem to be trivial. A case in point is Study 3 of that research. There, grades in introductory psychology were significantly affected by motivational variables interacting with the perceived instrumentality of the course. The performance of uncertainty-oriented persons was most affected by achievement-related motives when they perceived the course to be relevant to their future careers. Paradoxically, but as predicted from our theoretical model, certainty-oriented persons were most affected by achievement-related motives when the course was perceived to be irrelevant to their future goals.

In sum, uncertainty-oriented persons are motivated by situations that allow them to resolve uncertainty about the self and the environment. A situation of high personal relevance should meet this condition, and they will engage in systematic processing of information. A situation of low personal relevance does not meet this condition, and they will engage in heuristic processing of information. Certainty-oriented persons are relatively more motivated by situations that do not involve uncertainty about the self and the environment than by those that do. Hence, they should be more likely to engage in systematic processing in situations of low personal relevance and heuristic processing in situations of high personal relevance.

In this article we report two studies designed to test the general hypothesis that high but not low personal relevance should differentially affect the processing of information as a function of individual differences in uncertainty orientation. In Study 1 we examined an issue that has been around for many years in the attitude literature: the relative effectiveness of one-sided versus two-sided communications. Predictions are based on the assumption that careful processing of information will make a two-sided communication more persuasive, whereas reliance on heuristic, or peripheral, cues will make a one-sided communication more persuasive. In Study 2 we manipulated heuristic versus systematic cues directly by varying the expertise of the source and the strength of the arguments.

Study 1: One-Sided Versus Two-Sided Communications

The number of sides of an issue presented in a persuasive message can affect the degree of active information processing required by the audience. By definition, one-sided messages do not require integration of conflicting views and do not introduce ambiguity about the correct position on the issue. Thus, recipients of such a message can, if they wish, engage in heuristic processing: they can

adopt the recommendations made by the communicator without investing much cognitive work. In contrast, two-sided messages introduce uncertainty or ambiguity into the issue and require active integration of inconsistent material. Thus, if a two-sided message is to be effective, recipients must be willing to process the arguments thoughtfully.

Consistent with this characterization of one-sided versus two-sided communications, several studies have shown that the target group's prior knowledge about the issue influences the effectiveness of each type of message. Specifically, one-sided messages are more effective when the audience is uninformed about the issue than when the audience is knowledgeable; whereas two-sided messages tend to persuade well-informed recipients more than individuals who are unfamiliar with the issue (see Chu, 1967; Hovland, Lumsdaine, & Sheffield, 1949). One interpretation of these findings is that knowledgeable recipients are able to process the two-sided arguments thoughtfully and resolve inconsistencies, whereas poorly informed individuals have difficulty integrating contradictory information. Along the same lines, Lumsdaine and Janis (1953) found that individuals who had been exposed to a two-sided message were better able to resist a subsequent influence attempt than individuals who had been exposed to a one-sided message. Presumably, the two-sided message stimulated more cognitive activity, thereby making subjects who were exposed to it (rather than the one-sided message) better equipped to counterargue persuasive attacks. Finally, in related research, it has been argued that when people are highly motivated (Petty & Cacioppo, 1981), they will search for counterarguments. Thus, it seems reasonable to argue that when people are motivated to systematically process information, they will be looking for counterarguments. Because a one-sided communication does not have counterarguments but a two-sided communication does, systematic processing of information should increase the persuasive impact of a two-sided communication and reduce the persuasive impact of a one-sided communication. After all, the former message would show the reader that the author did consider alternative arguments, whereas the latter would show that the author either did not consider them or in fact withheld them.

In this experiment, a one-sided or a two-sided counterattitudinal communication on an issue of high or low personal relevance was presented to uncertainty-oriented and certainty-oriented subjects. As explained previously, we postulated that when personal relevance increases, uncertainty-oriented individuals will become more careful and systematic, whereas certainty-oriented individuals will rely more on judgmental cues and heuristics. We also assume, on the basis of the studies reviewed earlier, that two-sided messages are effective to the extent that recipients are willing to process the arguments thoughtfully, whereas one-sided messages encourage or allow heuristic processing.

Hence, the predictions for the two-sided message in this study were that uncertainty-oriented subjects would be more persuaded under conditions of high relevance than low relevance, whereas certainty-oriented subjects would be less persuaded under high than low relevance.[2] The predictions for the one-sided message were exactly opposite to those for the two-sided message: Uncertainty-oriented subjects were expected to be less persuaded under high than low personal relevance, whereas certainty-oriented subjects were expected to be more persuaded under high than low relevance.

Thus, the predictions for Study 1 constituted a particular pattern of three-way interaction between uncertainty orientation, personal relevance, and one-sided versus two-sided messages, such that the effects of personal relevance on persuasion were expected to depend on both personality and message variables. We also examined the persistence of persuasion and possible changes over time in the pattern of results by obtaining a delayed attitude measure approximately 15 days after subjects' initial exposure to the message. Because the predicted three way interaction was based on assumptions about subjects' preferred processing styles, we thought that the anticipated differences would remain stable or perhaps become larger over time (see Cook & Flay, 1978, for a discussion of the variables affecting the persistence of attitude change). It seemed possible that as subjects' memory for the details of the message decayed, their attitudes would depend primarily on reconstructions of the material, which may exaggerate the initial differences (cf. Hennigan, Cook, & Gruder, 1982; Higgins & Rholes, 1978).

Two final comments about this experiment are necessary. First, the attitude topic selected for the study (the introduction or comprehensive examinations for senior undergraduates) was unfamiliar

to subjects. Consequently, the one-sided message was expected to be more effective overall than the two-sided message (see the previous discussion of Chu, 1967, and Hovland et al., 1949). Of course, the more complex predictions just articulated were also expected to hold, because they involved differences between high and low levels of personal relevance within message types and personality groups. Second, we measured the Cacioppo et al. (1983) personality variable of need for cognition. We assessed the relation of this measure to uncertainty orientation and examined its possible mediating role in the effects of personal relevance and one-sided versus two-sided messages on persuasion.

Method

SUBJECTS

Two hundred and eleven introductory psychology students at the University of Western Ontario received course credit for their participation in the experiment. The students were selected from participants in mass testing sessions held earlier in the year, during which the relevant personality measures had been administered. Of the 211 participants in the study, 38 could not be contacted for the delayed attitude measure, leaving a final sample of 173 (122 women and 51 men).

PERSONALITY ASSESSMENT

To measure uncertainty orientation, we used procedures similar to those used to asses achievement-related motives (see Atkinson & Feather, 1966). Frederick and Sorrentino (1977) developed a projective measure of n Uncertainty from which to infer the relevance of uncertain situations and adopted the Byrne and Lamberth (1971) measure of authoritarianism as a means to infer the rel-

---

[2]Pilot testing established that the recommendation in the messages was counterattitudinal when it was presented without any supportive arguments. Fifty-three subjects from the same population as the experimental subjects were asked to rate their favorability toward the introduction of comprehensive examinations for senior undergraduates. On a 7-point scale ranging from *very unfavorable* (1) to *very favorable* (7), subjects gave a mean response of 2.63. More recently a similar sample of subjects were again given this question to determine whether differences due to uncertainty orientation would be found. Uncertainty-oriented and certainty-oriented persons did not differ, $t(378) = 1.03$, *ns*.

evance of certain situations. The projective measure of *n* Uncertainty relies heavily in its conceptualization on Kagan's (1972) notions concerning modes of uncertainty resolution. It also uses a scoring system similar to those developed for *n* Achievement, *n* Affiliation, and *n* Power (see Atkinson, 1958). The acquiescence-free measure of authoritarianism (Byrne & Lamberth, 1971) is used to infer certainty orientation because persons who score high on this measure have an orientation toward familiar or certain situations (see Rokeach, 1960). Research indicates that compared with low authoritarians, high authoritarians are more intolerant of ambiguity (see Kirscht & Dillehay, 1967), have less experience with novel or uncertain situations (Kelman & Barclay, 1963), and show lower levels of integrative complexity for uncertain situations (Schroder, Driver, & Streufert, 1967).

Frederick and Sorrentino (1977) found that the *n* Uncertainty measure has interrater reliabilities above .90. Sorrentino (1977) obtained test–retest reliabilities above .90 for both male and female subjects on the Byrne and Lamberth (1971) measure of authoritarianism.

According to standard procedures (Atkinson, 1958, Appendix III), the projective measure of *n* Uncertainty was administered to subjects in the mass testing sessions. Sentence leads were used instead of pictures; this has been found to be a valid procedure to assess *n* Achievement (e.g., Raynor & Rubin, 1971) and, subsequently, *n* Uncertainty (Sorrentino & Hewitt, 1984; Sorrentino et al., 1984). Three sentences, numbered to correspond to three pictures in the Atkinson (1958, Appendix III) study, were presented to subjects in the following order: "two persons are working in a laboratory on a piece of equipment" (Picture 2), "a person is working with a typewriter and books" (Picture 48), and "several young people are sitting in a lounge talking" (Picture 86). We also administered a fourth sentence lead, constructed specifically to assess *n* Uncertainty: "a person is sitting wondering about what may happen." Stories written to the four leads were scored for uncertainty imagery and summed to form a total *n* Uncertainty score, in accordance with the manual developed by Frederick and Sorrentino (1977), by an expert scorer who correlated above .90 with the scoring of practice materials presented therein and with the scores assigned by another expert scorer. Sub-

jects then completed Byrne and Lamberth's (1971) acquiescence-free measure of authoritarianism and the shortened version of Cacioppo and Petty's (1982) Need for Cognition Scale.

A resultant measure of uncertainty was calculated for each subject who participated in the mass testing session by subtracting his or her standard score on authoritarianism from his or her standard score on *n* Uncertainty (as expected, the correlation between *n* Uncertainty and authoritarianism was close to zero, .01). A tertile split of these resultant scores was then performed, which yielded uncertainty-oriented mixed, and certainty-oriented groups. The subjects for this experiment were selected randomly from those who had participated in the mass testing, so that a full range of need for cognition scores would be represented. In the analyses involving uncertainty orientation, however, persons who scored moderately or mixed were excluded. This has been standard practice in our laboratory (Sorrentino & Hewitt, 1984; Sorrentino et al., 1984) and is also the norm in the achievement motivation area (e.g., Entin & Raynor, 1973; Karabenick & Youssef, 1968). Extreme-groups analyses are justified by evidence that moderate scores on motive measures are anomalous (see Sorrentino & Short, 1977). To maintain consistency in our approach to the data, the analyses involving need for cognition were also conducted by performing a tertile split of the scores and excluding the middle third.[3]

DESIGN AND PROCEDURE

The primary design of the study was a 2 (uncertainty orientation) × 2 (argument type) × 2 (personal relevance) × 2 (time) factorial, with repeated measures on the last variable. At Time 1, subjects were tested in noninteractive group sessions, ranging in size from 3 to 30, in which all experimental conditions were run simultaneously. On arrival, subjects received an envelope that contained a cover story, two essays, and two questionnaire booklets. The cover sheet stated the following:

> The purpose of the experiment today is to determine how you feel about various policy issues which are currently under consideration at the

---

[3]Analyses using a median split of the need for cognition scores produced similar results to those reported in Study 1 for the extreme-groups analyses.

University of Western Ontario.[4] Your task will involve reading two proposals which recommend different policy issues. The particular policy issues you will read about have been randomly chosen from a group of others all under consideration for institution at the University. We are interested in your feelings toward these issues.[5]

Subjects were instructed to read all of the sheets in the order given and were also told that when they finished reading the essays, they should respond to the appropriate questionnaire booklet. Subjects were told to return everything when they were done to the experimenter at the front of the room. When subjects brought the materials to the experimenter, they were informed that they would be debriefed by mail, ostensibly to permit data analyses prior to debriefing so that subjects could be given a fuller account of the study. In actuality, this was done to further assess attitudes at Time 2, 15–18 days following the experimental session. At that time, confederates of the experimenters contacted subjects by telephone. Subjects were told that the confederate was doing a class project for his or her journalism course and that the project dealt with assessing students' perceptions of university life. An item reassessing subjects' attitudes toward comprehensive examinations was among several questions asked.

EXPERIMENTAL CONDITIONS

Personal relevance. In the high-relevance conditions, subjects read that the proposed changes in academic policy (comprehensive examinations for seniors) were being considered for initiation in 1 or 2 years. In the low-relevance conditions, subjects read that the proposed changes in academic policy were being considered for initiation in 5–10 years. Subjects read the following, adapted from Petty and Cacioppo (1984):

The University Committee on Academic Policy has recently proposed several changes in academic policy to be instituted at the University of Western Ontario in (one or two/five to ten) years from now. The Committee functions as a primary advisory source to the president of Western on changes in academic policy that should be instituted at the University. One of the changes proposed to take place within (one or two/five to ten) years is the imposition of a requirement that seniors take a comprehensive exam in their area prior to gradu-

ation. The exam would be a test of what the student had learned after completing the major, and a certain score would be required if the student was to graduate. The material you will be reading is the summary section of the report written by the Committee which outlines the major reasons why the exam policy should begin in (one or two/five to ten) years from now. Please read the policy statement carefully, and respond to the questions about the policy statements which follow. (p. 73)

Argument type. For all subjects, the essay began as follows:

Proposed: Seniors at the University of Western Ontario should be required to take a comprehensive exam in their major area as a requirement for graduation. The exam would be a test of what the student had learned after completing the major, and a certain score would be required if the student was to graduate.

Following this statement, either a one- or a two-sided persuasive communication (of approximately 400 words) was presented. The one-sided message consisted of four of Petty and Cacioppo's (1984) strong arguments for the advocated viewpoint (e.g., graduate schools give preferential treatment to applicants from universities that have comprehensive examinations), without any mention of arguments for the opposing viewpoint. The two-sided message contained the same four strong arguments and two strong arguments against the institution of comprehensive examinations (e.g., it may be unfair to put so much emphasis on one examination). The two-sided message began with one argument in favor of examinations, then presented the two counterarguments, and closed with the three remaining arguments in favor of examina-

---

[4] We instructed subjects directly to evaluate the topic or message in this study rather than having them evaluate the author, in which case attitudes on the issue would have appeared to be a secondary concern of the research, as in Petty and Cacioppo (1984). This was done in an attempt to increase the probability that subjects would in fact search for and examine counterarguments. Fortunately, the results of this study are consistent with that aim. Unfortunately, however, this also led to an apparent anomaly between the two studies (see the General Discussion).

[5] In addition to the essay on comprehensive examinations, subjects read a proposal that recommended an increase in university tuition fees. This second essay was part of an unrelated experiment. The order of the two essays was counterbalanced across subjects. Preliminary analyses of the data showed no effects for order.

tions. This message concluded that the benefits outweigh the costs of examinations.

DEPENDENT MEASURES

Attitude measure at Time 1. Subjects' attitudes toward comprehensive examinations were assessed by five items, four of which were identical to those used by Petty and Cacioppo (1984, p. 73). Subjects were asked to respond to the phrase "Comprehensive exams are" on three 7-point semantic differential scales (good–bad, wise–foolish, and beneficial–harmful). Subjects were also asked to rate the following on a 7-point response scale (1 = *very unfavorable*, 7 = *very favorable*): "In general, how favorable or unfavorable are you toward instituting comprehensive exams for undergraduates?" Finally, subjects were asked, "Do you agree with the conclusions of the Committee?" (1 = *disagree strongly*, 7 = *agree strongly*). Answers to these five items correlated highly, ranging from .61 to .80 (*dfs* = 112), all *ps* < .001. Thus, responses were averaged for each subject to form an attitude index, similar to the procedure used by Petty and Cacioppo (1984).

The rating scales and averaging procedures that follow were replicated from Cacioppo et al. (1983).

Attitude measure at Time 2. When subjects were telephoned at Time 2, they were asked several questions about various issues, including the following item: "On a scale from 1 to 7, where 1 is undesirable and 7 is desirable, rate how you feel about the University making graduation for seniors contingent on the completion of comprehensive exams in the students' main area of study"

Other measures. In the questionnaire booklet following exposure to the message at Time 1, subjects were asked to evaluate the cogency of the essay on five 7-point scales (e.g., "To what extent do you feel the communication made its point effectively?"). The average of each subject's responses to these five questions served as a general index of message evaluation. Subjects also rated the message on three 7-point scales reflecting comprehensibility (e.g., "easy to understand/difficult to understand"), which were averaged to form an index of message comprehensibility. Two questions assessed on 7-point scales the degree of cognitive effort that subjects expended to understand the communication (e.g., "How much effort did you put into evaluating the communication?").

These items were averaged to serve as an index of cognitive effort. Finally, two 7-point items were averaged to measure the extent to which subjects felt the recommendation was personally important ("How likely do you believe it is that the University of Western Ontario will institute comprehensive exams for undergraduates?" and "How personally relevant or important did you find the policy recommendation?").

TREATMENT OF THE DATA

Subjects' attitudes measured at Time 1 and Time 2 were treated as a within-subjects variable in an analysis of variance (ANOVA), with uncertainty orientation, argument type, and personal relevance as between-subjects variables. A test of the hypothesis for the particular pattern of three-way interaction was conducted using a one-tailed *t* test based on the within-cell error term from the ANOVA (Winer, 1971). The hypothesis was also tested within Time 1 and within Time 2.

Results

TESTS OF THE HYPOTHESIS

Figure 1 shows the mean attitude scores for the Uncertainty Orientation × Argument Type × Personal Relevance design (excluding moderate scorers on uncertainty orientation, thereby involving 114 of the 173 subjects), at Time 1 (Figure 1A) and Time 2 (Figure 1B). The three-variable pattern of interaction was exactly as predicted at both time periods. That is, in spite of the finding that a one-sided communication appeared to be stronger overall than a two-sided communication (as we expected), this effect was diminished or overridden by the anticipated interaction with uncertainty orientation and personal relevance. For the uncertainty-oriented group, the two-sided message was more persuasive under high than low personal relevance, whereas a one-sided message became less persuasive under high than low personal relevance; for the certainty-oriented group, a two-sided message was actually more persuasive and a one-sided message less persuasive under low than high personal relevance. This predicted pattern of interaction was significant across time, $t(106) = 2.51$, $p < .01$, and significant or marginally significant at Time 1, $t(106) = 1.61$, $p < .06$, and at Time 2, $t(106) = 2.73$, $p < .005$.

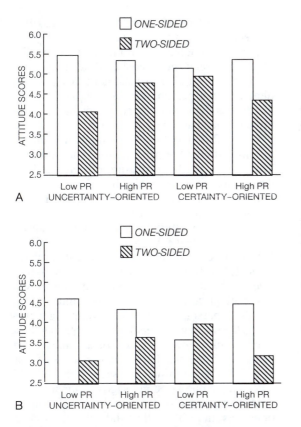

FIGURE 1 ■ (A) Mean attitude scores at Time 1 for Uncertainty Orientation × Personal Relevance (PR) × Argument Sides combinations. (B) Mean attitude scores at Time 2 for Uncertainty Orientation × Personal Relevance (PR) × Argument Sides combinations.

ANALYSIS OF VARIANCE

An Uncertainty Orientation × Argument Type × Personal Relevance × Time ANOVA with repeated measures on the last variable was conducted to test for overall effects on the attitude measure.[6] This analysis revealed a main effect for argument type, $F(1, 106) = 12.97, p < .001$, which indicated that the one-sided communication was more persuasive ($M = 4.79$) than the two-sided message ($M = 3.94$), as expected. There was also a significant Uncertainty Orientation × Argument Type × Personal Relevance interaction, $F(1, 106) = 6.31, p < .02$, illustrating the predicted pattern discussed earlier. Finally, a main effect for time revealed that the attitude measure taken at Time 1 ($M = 4.98$) yielded higher scores than the measure taken at

Time 2 ($M = 3.87$), $F(1, 106) = 81.98, p < .001.$[7] No other effects were reliable.

OTHER MEASURES

Analysis of the message evaluation measure yielded a main effect for argument type, $F(1, 101) = 4.99, p < .03$, which indicated that the one-sided message was evaluated more positively ($M = 5.07$) than the two-sided message ($M = 4.74$).[8]

A main effect for argument type was also revealed on the measure of personal relevance, $F(1, 104) = 8.31, p < .005$, which indicated that the one-sided message was rated as being more personally important or relevant ($M = 5.10$) than the two-sided message ($M = 4.46$). The measure of personal relevance did not yield a reliable main effect for the relevance manipulation, $F < 1$, although in retrospect the items might have been phrased improperly (this issue is discussed later).

No other effects were reliable in the analyses of the ancillary measures. Thus, the analyses of the message comprehensibility and cognitive effort measures revealed no significant effects. [. . .]

Discussion

The results of Study 1 confirmed the hypothesis that individual differences exist in the effects of personal relevance on social judgments. Specifically, the reliable ($p < .01$) three-way interaction of Uncertainty Orientation × Argument Type × Personal Relevance on the measure of attitudes toward comprehensive examinations supported the notion that as relevance increased, some individuals became more thoughtful and others relied more heavily on heuristics, or persuasion cues, in making their attitudinal judgments. Uncertainty-oriented subjects behaved like most attitude theorists appear to assume everyone behaves, being more influenced by the two-sided message and less influenced by the one-sided message under condi-

---

[6]A preliminary analysis was conducted to test for sex differences. Because the Gender × Argument Type × Personal Relevance × Time analysis revealed no main effects or interactions involving gender this factor was excluded from subsequent analyses.

[7]The attitude index at Time 1 correlated significantly with the attitude measure at Time 2, $r(112) = .60, p < .001$.

[8]As some subjects did not respond to all of the dependent measures, the degrees of freedom varied slightly across measures.

tions of high personal relevance than low personal relevance. Certainty-oriented subjects, however, demonstrated the opposite pattern of persuasion. Under conditions of high personal relevance, certainty-oriented individuals were less persuaded by the two-sided message and more persuaded by the one-sided message than under conditions of low relevance. Presumably certainty-oriented subjects are not motivated to think for themselves and therefore look for external guidance or cues on important issues; the one-sided message in this experiment provided a strong cue that the advocated position was valid, whereas the two-sided message introduced ambiguity. On the other hand, certainty-oriented persons are motivated to think for themselves, ironically, when the issue is not personally relevant.

This reasoning is supported by the main effect for argument type that was obtained on the message evaluation measure, which showed that subjects rated the one-sided message as being more effective than the two-sided message. For uncertainty-oriented subjects, the ambiguity inherent in the two-sided message presumably motivated more integrative thinking when the issue was personally relevant, thereby facilitating persuasion rather than inhibiting it. For certainty-oriented persons, this occurred when the issue was not personally relevant.

It is interesting that the predicted pattern of interaction on the attitude measures was statistically reliable 2 weeks following the experimental session ($p < .005$) but only marginally reliable at Time 1 ($p < .06$). Although the changes over time should be interpreted with caution, because the attitude measure had to be altered from Time 1 to Time 2 to camouflage the purpose of the telephone survey, it is tempting to speculate that the attitude effects partly depended on subjects' biased reconstructions of the message, which would enhance differences over time (see Higgins & Rholes, 1978). At the very least, the data from Time 2 show that the attitude effects, as a function of the three-variable pattern of interaction, were stable. The persistence of experimentally induced attitude change has concerned attitude theorists (cf. Cook & Flay, 1978; Higgins, Rhodewalt, & Zanna, 1979).

In this context, the greater effectiveness of the one-sided over the two-sided message deserves comment. This main effect presumably reflects that subjects had little prior knowledge relevant to the issue of comprehensive examinations in their se-

nior year (see Chu, 1967, and Hovland et al., 1949). Indeed, this is a nonissue at our university The important point, however is that the manipulation of personal relevance increased or decreased persuasion to each kind of message exactly as predicted within personality subgroups. Thus, the main effect for argument type did not interfere with the predicted pattern of persuasion.

It is unfortunate that the manipulation checks did not validate the personal relevance variable. That is, the ancillary measure of perceived relevance did not show a main effect for the manipulation of relevance. In retrospect, though, this null result may not be surprising. First, self-report measures of cognitive processes are often unsuccessful (cf. Nisbett & Wilson, 1977; Olson & Ross, 1985). More important, the relevance items asked subjects to estimate the likelihood of comprehensive examinations being adopted at their university, without any mention of time limits, and to rate how personally relevant or important they found the message. It seems reasonable that these items would show an effect for argument type, because the one-sided message was more persuasive than the two-sided message: Subjects who received the one-sided message presumably concluded that instituting comprehensive examinations was more likely than did subjects who received the two-sided message. Recall, however, that the manipulation of personal relevance consisted of different alleged time frames for adopting comprehensive examinations (1–2 vs. 5–10 years). A more appropriate check of this manipulation would have been to ask subjects to estimate the likelihood of comprehensive examinations being adopted while they were at the university. Petty and Cacioppo (1984) modified the likelihood item so that it included the time frame just mentioned and obtained a significant main effect for the identical manipulation of personal relevance as was used in this experiment. Thus, we are confident that our manipulation of relevance was effective but believe that the items designed to assess it were inadequate. This conclusion is supported by the finding that the relevance manipulation exerted its predicted effects on attitudes in this experiment and in the study by Petty and Cacioppo (1984). We return to this point later.

Study 1 demonstrated that need for cognition and uncertainty orientation are not isomorphic constructs, a point that was previously an open question (see Sorrentino et al., 1984). The correlation between the two measures was small, and they revealed different patterns of effects on the attitude measure. It appears that the key difference may be that whereas the need for cognition measure is a measure of motivation to think, uncertainty orientation is a measure of when to think. Certainty-oriented people appear to be thinking just as hard as uncertainty-oriented people given the right situation. In particular, uncertainty orientation interacted with personal relevance in such a way as to indicate that some individuals (certainty-oriented persons) became more dependent on heuristic cues as personal relevance increased. Need for cognition did not produce interaction effects that paralleled those for uncertainty orientation, which suggests that need for cognition may assess only individuals' motivation to process information carefully and may not tap the opposing inclination toward heuristic processing. Uncertainty orientation appears to have diagnostic power for identifying tendencies toward both systematic and heuristic processing in specific situations.

In summary, these results are encouraging as a first step toward extending individual differences in uncertainty orientation into the realm of social influence. One drawback remains, however. As stated previously, systematic versus heuristic processing was only inferred and was not directly manipulated in Study 1. It is possible, therefore, that something other than processing differences can account for our results. Although no alternative explanations are obvious, the disappointing results on the ancillary measures suggest that additional data are warranted. In particular, a study that directly manipulates systematic versus heuristic processing cues would lend credence to our position. This, then, was the purpose of Study 2.

Study 2: Strength of Arguments Versus Source Expertise

This study was based on the experiment by Petty et al. (1981) described in the introduction. Recall that in the high-relevance condition of the Petty et al. study, strong arguments produced more attitude change than weak arguments, but source expertise did not affect persuasion. In the low-relevance condition, subjects were more persuaded by an expert than by a nonexpert source, but the strength of the arguments did not affect subjects' attitudes. If uncertainty-oriented subjects are in fact

predisposed to systematic processing under high personal relevance, as suggested in Study 1, then they should behave much like the subjects in the Petty et al. study. Certainty-oriented subjects, however, should behave in the opposite manner. High personal relevance should actually accentuate heuristic processing of information, whereas low personal relevance should accentuate systematic processing of information. Hence, they will pay more attention to source expertise and less attention to strength of arguments under high than low personal relevance.

Method

Except for a shift in focus from the message to the communication in the initial instructions, as well as the new experimental manipulations of source expertise and argument strength (rather than one-sided vs. two-sided arguments), this study was similar to Study 1. Personal relevance was again manipulated by telling subjects that comprehensive examinations were being considered for implementation in either 1–2 or 5–10 years. The cover story was modified to replicate the one used by Petty and Cacioppo (1984). Rather than telling subjects that we wanted to measure their attitudes toward current university issues, subjects in this study were told the following:

> This study is concerned with first impressions. Research in psychology has shown that there are many sources of first impressions about people based on their looks, their voice, or their dress. The purpose of this study is to examine the process by which we make first impressions. What we would like you to do today is to read a sample of what someone else has written and to try to form an impression of that person. On the next page, you will find an essay someone has written. This person was asked to write an argument in favor of making comprehensive examinations mandatory for senior university undergraduates in the last year of their degree. This issue is a currently popular topic of debate among university administrators all over Canada. In fact, right now the President of the University of Western Ontario is considering the institution of comprehensive examinations for undergraduates. (p. 73)

SUBJECTS

Subjects were 237 male and female students recruited from a mass testing session based on their uncertainty orientation scores. Of these, 193 were contacted by phone for the follow-up attitude assessment 2 weeks after their participation in the experiment. The data from this study an from the latter group of subjects (results for all 237 subjects at Time 1 are isomorphic with those reported in this study).

SOURCE EXPERTISE

This manipulation was similar to that used by Petty et al. (1981), modified for a Canadian sample. In the instructions, and at the top of the arguments page, the expert source was identified as Dr. M. G. Richardson, Professor of Education, University of Toronto, Chairperson of the Ontario Commission of Higher Education. The nonexpert source was identified as M. G. Richardson, Grade 13 (secondary school) student.

ARGUMENT STRENGTH

Minor modifications to the arguments used in the Petty and Cacioppo (1984) study resulted in two messages, one consisting of six strong arguments in favor of comprehensive examinations (e.g., graduate schools give preferential treatment to applicants from universities that have comprehensive examinations) and the other consisting of six weak arguments in favor of comprehensive examinations (e.g., comprehensive exams prepare students for the cold realities of life).

DEPENDENT MEASURES

Items similar to those used in Study 1 were included in this experiment, together with several additional measures such as an improved manipulation check for the personal relevance variable (see the Manipulation Checks section). Also, immediately following their responses at Time 1, subjects were asked to list any thoughts they had about the communication or the communicator.

Results

TESTS OF HYPOTHESES

Figure 2 shows the mean attitude scores for the Uncertainty Orientation × Personal Relevance × Argument Strength interaction, and Figure 3 shows the mean attitude scores for the Uncertainty Ori-

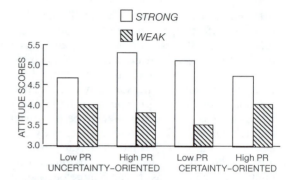

FIGURE 2 ■ Mean attitude scores for Uncertainty Orientation × Personal Relevance (PR) × Argument Strength combinations.

entation × Personal Relevance × Source Expertise interaction, collapsed across time. Note that results conform to predictions for both patterns of interaction. With regard to argument strength (Figure 2), personal relevance increased persuasion as a function of argument strength for uncertainty-oriented subjects, with strong versus weak arguments producing larger differences in attitude scores under high than low personal relevance. For the certainty-oriented group, the reverse occurred. Low relevance increased the impact of argument strength on persuasion, with strong versus weak arguments yielding larger differences under low than high personal relevance. Tests of this predicted three-variable pattern of interaction were significant across time, $t(177) = 8.98, p < .001$, and within Time 1, $t(177) = 1.75, p < .05$, and within Time 2, $t(177) = 2.20, p < .02$.

With regard to source expertise (Figure 2), although the expert source produced greater persuasion than the nonexpert source under low personal relevance for the uncertainty-oriented group, this difference was eliminated under high personal relevance, where the two means were identical. For the certainty-oriented group, personal relevance increased the persuasive impact of the expert source, as expected. In fact, under low personal relevance, there was a flip-flop as a function of source expertise, with the nonexpert source leading to greater persuasion than the expert source. Under high personal relevance, however, the expert source produced greater persuasion than the nonexpert source. Tests of this predicted three-variable pattern of interaction were also significant across time, $t(177) = 10.21, p < .001$, and within Time 1, $t(177) = 1.80$, $p < .05$, and within Time 2, $t(177) = 2.41$, $p < .01$.

ANALYSIS OF VARIANCE

An Uncertainty Orientation × Personal Relevance × Argument Strength × Source Expertise × Time analysis, with repeated measures on the last variable, was conducted to test for overall effects on the attitude measure. This analysis revealed a significant main effect for argument strength, $F(1, 177) = 35.32$, $p < .001$, with strong arguments leading to greater persuasion ($M = 5.03$) than weak arguments ($M = 3.91$). A significant effect for time was also found, $F(1, 177) = 65.26$, $p < .001$, with persuasion scores being higher at Time 1 ($M = 4.91$) than Time 2 ($M = 4.10$). Other reliable effects were an Uncertainty Orientation × Argument Strength × Time interaction, $F(1, 177) = 4.36$, $p < .04$; an Uncertainty Orientation × Personal Relevance × Argument Strength interaction, $F(1, 177) = 5.05$, $p < .03$; an Uncertainty Orientation × Personal Relevance × Source Expertise interaction, $F(1, 177) = 7.08$, $p < .01$; and a Personal Relevance × Argument Strength × Source Expertise interaction, $F(1, 177) = 4.24$, $p < .04$. Other than the main effect for time, the last interaction was the only significant effect not subsumed by the two patterns of interaction described earlier and shown in Figures 2 and 3. This last interaction is depicted in Table 1. It can be seen that in the expert condition, the impact of strength of arguments (strong vs. weak) is larger under high than low personal relevance. In the nonexpert condition, however, this pattern is reversed, with the difference due to strength of arguments being greater under low than high involvement.

MANIPULATION CHECKS

Personal relevance. Using a more precise measure of personal relevance than in Study 1, namely "If the University of Western Ontario institutes comprehensive exams, how long do you think it will be before they begin?", the manipulation check proved reliable, $F(1, 169) = 102.04$, $p < .001$. Mean estimates of 3.31 versus 6.09 years were found for subjects in the high and low personal relevance conditions, respectively. Another measure asked subjects how important the issue was to them. This item also showed a reliable ef-

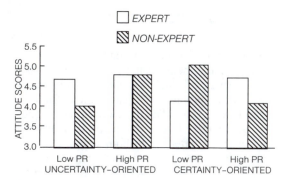

FIGURE 3 ▪ Mean attitude scores for Uncertainty Orientation × Personal Relevance (PR) × Source Expertise combinations.

fect of personal relevance, $F(1, 177) = 15.42$, $p < .001$, with subjects in the high-relevance condition rating the issue as being more important ($M = 5.03$) than subjects in the low-relevance condition ($M = 4.14$).

Argument strength. When asked to rate the strength of the arguments in the essay, subjects in the strong-arguments condition rated the arguments as being stronger ($M = 4.98$) than subjects in the weak-arguments condition ($M = 2.70$), $F(1, 174) = 139.75$, $p < .001$. Subjects in the former condition also rated the arguments as being more convincing ($M = 4.92$) than subjects in the latter condition ($M = 2.64$), $F(1, 174) = 107.08$, $p < .001$.

Source expertise. In reply to the question "To what extent do you think that the author is an expert in the topic written about?" subjects in the expert condition rated the person higher ($M = 3.97$) than subjects in the nonexpert condition ($M = 2.84$), $F(1, 174) = 33.10$, $p < .001$. On another item, subjects rated the author as being more knowledgeable in the expert than in the nonexpert condition ($Ms = 5.11$ vs. 4.57), $F(1, 177) = 10.21$, $p < .001$.

Table 1. Mean Attitude Scores for Source Expertise × Argument Strength × Personal Relevance (PR) Interaction

Argument strength	Expert source		Nonexpert source	
	Low PR	High PR	Low PR	High PR
Strong	4.70	5.85	5.12	4.88
n	23	26	27	27
Weak	4.16	3.83	3.66	4.02
n	20	22	23	25

ADDITIONAL EFFECTS ON MANIPULATION CHECKS

Several other effects were reliable on the personal relevance, argument strength, and source expertise measures, of which the following are interesting and interpretable. Basically, these findings, together with other data to be presented, suggest that both uncertainty-oriented and certainty-oriented subjects attended to both source expertise and argument strength but that only the latter subjects were willing to give the expert source the benefit of the doubt (i.e., uncertainty-oriented subjects tended to challenge the expert's opinion when arguments were weak). With regard to source expertise, for example, both groups of subjects rated the author as being more of an expert in the strong-arguments than in the weak-arguments condition. This difference was greater for the certainty-oriented group ($Ms = 4.24$ vs. 2.95) than the uncertainty-oriented group ($Ms = 4.20$ vs. 3.12), $F(1, 177) = 5.03$, $p < .03$. Interestingly, however, there was an Uncertainty Orientation × Argument Strength × Source Expertise interaction of borderline significance, $F(1, 177) = 3.61$, $p < .06$, on ratings of the author's knowledgeability. The source of this interaction was that certainty-oriented subjects in the expert-weak arguments condition maintained their belief that the communicator was knowledgeable (a mean of 4.80 as compared with 3.21, 3.63, and 3.28 in the other three weak-arguments conditions).

Turning to subjects' ratings of arguments, uncertainty-oriented persons rated the arguments as being stronger in the strong- than in the weak-arguments condition ($Ms = 4.98$ vs. 2.18), and this difference was greater than that for certainty-oriented persons ($Ms = 4.98$ vs. 3.36), $F(1, 174) = 11.41$, $p < .001$. This interaction, however, was subsumed by a reliable higher order interaction with source expertise, $F(1, 177) = 3.89$, $p < .05$. For the uncertainty-oriented group, the difference between strong and weak arguments was greater when the person was an expert ($Ms = 5.21$ vs. 2.09) than when the person was not an expert ($Ms = 4.76$ vs. 2.26). The reverse occurred for the certainty-oriented group, in which the difference between strong and weak arguments was greater in the non-expert condition ($Ms = 5.00$ vs. 3.00) than in the expert condition ($Ms = 4.95$ vs. 3.70).

THOUGHT-LISTING DATA

Subjects were asked to list on a separate page any thoughts or feelings that occurred to them as they read the essay. They were told that their thoughts could relate to the author, the essay, or neither and that they should feel free to list as many or as few responses as they wished but to number each separately. These thoughts were then coded according to the system advocated by Chaiken (1980) and Chaiken and Eagly (1983). Thoughts were divided into whether they were source or message related and further subdivided into whether they were positive, negative, or neutral. Intarater reliabilities on these six categories were high, ranging from .84 to 1.00. The ANOVAs on these measures yielded several lower order effects, but none that revealed much in relation to predicted effects. When regression analyses were used, however, to explore the relative abilities of thoughts about the message versus thoughts about the source to predict attitude scores, support for our hypothesis appeared on three of four comparisons. These results are presented in Table 2.

Negative thoughts about the source or message were subtracted from positive thoughts about the source or message, respectively. These differences scores were then submitted to a regression analysis on attitude scores. The larger the beta coefficient on attitude scores, the stronger was the relation between positive minus negative thoughts about the source (or message) and attitudes (see Chaiken, 1980). As can be seen from Table 2, results are consistent with the hypothesis in three of four comparisons. Under high personal relevance, the relation between thoughts about the message and attitudes was significant for uncertainty-ori-

Table 2. Beta Coefficients for Positive Minus Negative Thoughts About Source Versus Message on Attitude Scores

Condition	Source			Message		
	ß	t	p	ß	t	p
Uncertainty oriented						
High personal relevance	.18	1.59	ns	.53	4.69	.001
Low personal relevance	.14	< 1	ns	.25	1.75	.09
Certainty oriented						
High personal relevance	.41	2.81	.007	.10	< 1	ns
Low personal relevance	.17	1.22	ns	.44	3.20	.003

ented persons but not for certainty-oriented persons (.53 vs. .10). The reverse occurred for thoughts about the source. That is, under high personal relevance, the relation between thoughts about the source and attitudes was significant for certainty-oriented persons but not for uncertainty-oriented persons (.41 vs. .18). Under low personal relevance, the relation between thoughts about the message and attitudes was significant for certainty-oriented persons but not for uncertainty-oriented persons (.44 vs. .25). No significant relation was found between thoughts about the source and attitudes for either group under low personal relevance.

Consistent with our hypothesis, then, uncertainty-oriented people showed a stronger relation between their positive minus negative thoughts about the message and attitudes under high as opposed to low personal relevance, whereas the reverse occurred for certainty-oriented persons. Certainty-oriented persons also showed a stronger relation between positive minus negative thoughts about the source and attitudes under high as opposed to low personal relevance. Uncertainty-oriented persons, however, showed no reliable difference in their thoughts about the source and their attitudes in either condition.

OTHER DEPENDENT MEASURES

Several lower order effects were obtained on the other measures, but only one higher order effect was found. This was an Uncertainty Orientation × Personal Relevance × Source Expertise interaction on subjects' ratings of friendliness, $F(1, 176) = 4.35, p < .04$. Within the certainty-oriented group, under high personal relevance, the expert was rated as being friendlier than the nonexpert ($Ms = 4.86$ vs. 3.86), but under low personal relevance, the nonexpert was rated as being friendlier than the expert ($Ms = 5.05$ vs. 4.35). This pattern was less pronounced within the uncertainty-oriented group ($Ms = 4.33$ vs. 4.10, $Ms = 4.43$ vs. 4.17, respectively). [. . .]

General Discussion

In two experiments we obtained reliable persuasion effects that modify current assumptions about the impact of personal relevance on information processing. Generally, uncertainty-oriented sub-

jects behaved as current theorists might predict everyone behaves (e.g., Chaiken, 1980; Petty & Cacioppo, 1981, 1984). Thus, in Study 1, a one-sided communication became more persuasive and a two-sided communication less persuasive under high than low personal relevance. In Study 2, the difference in source expertise was smaller and the difference in argument strength greater in the high than low personal relevance condition. For the certainty-oriented group, heuristic processing appears to have occurred more and systematic processing less in the high- than low-relevance condition. Thus, subjects attended more to a two-sided than a one-sided communication under low than high personal relevance in Study 1, and they appeared to be more affected by argument strength and less affected by source expertise under low than high personal relevance in Study 2.

Personal relevance, then, does not appear to increase systematic processing for all persons. Rather, consistent with our general hypothesis (Sorrentino & Short, 1986), uncertainty-oriented persons are more motivated to engage in systematic processing when personal relevance increases, whereas certainty-oriented persons become more motivated when personal relevance decreases.

Although the behavior of the certainty-oriented person appears paradoxical, it is not inconsistent with our previous research on achievement behavior. Indeed, results of these two studies are consistent with these earlier findings. Certainty-oriented people simply do not like to figure things out for themselves when the situation implies uncertainty about the self or the environment. When forced into these situations, they rely on heuristics rather than use their own judgment. Uncertainty-oriented people, on the other hand, do like to figure things out for themselves when it involves uncertainty about the self or the environment. Indeed, one could argue that uncertainty-oriented people border on self-centeredness when it comes to the task at hand. If the task does not concern them, they simply rely on heuristics rather than think about the matter. This is, of course, a value statement. More appropriately, we could say that both uncertainty-oriented and certainty-oriented persons process information systematically when it is related to their self-schemas. Both groups resort to heuristic processing, at least with regard to an expert source and one-sided communications, when the situation is inconsistent with their uncertainty schemas.

As the careful reader might have noted, we used only one-sided communications in Study 2 because we replicated the procedures of Petty and Cacioppo (1984). Why, then, did personal relevance increase the persuasiveness of the strong-argument message for uncertainty-oriented subjects and decrease the persuasiveness of this message for certainty-oriented subjects (opposite to the effects for the one-sided communication in Study 1)? We believe that the answer may lie in one or both of the following differences between the two studies. First, Study 1 had only four strong arguments, whereas Study 2 had six. With fewer arguments in Study 1, subjects might have been prompted to search for more alternatives, whereas six arguments might have lessened this demand. A second and perhaps more interesting difference is that in Study 1 subjects were directed to the message itself (they were asked their opinions about the issue), whereas in Study 2 subjects were asked to give their opinions about the author, with the message being only incidental. Perhaps when subjects were directed to the message itself, systematic processing of information led them to search for counterarguments, which produced an increase in the persuasiveness of a two-sided message and a decrease in the persuasiveness of a one-sided message. However, when subjects were asked to evaluate the author rather than the message, systematic processing of information might have led merely to an examination of the strength of the arguments and not to a search for counterarguments. In cognitive terms, the two studies might have activated different schemas for message evaluation versus author evaluation. In Cantor and Mischel's (1977) terms, for example, message evaluation might have activated a script for a good message, whereas author evaluation might have activated a prototype for a good author. Consequently, Study 1 led subjects to determine the adequacy of the message itself, whereas Study 2 led subjects to determine the ability of the author to present a reasonable case. Indeed, the author might not have been expected to present counterarguments but only to come up with a good set of strong arguments. This could also explain the apparent liking heuristic in Study 2. We would expect subjects to pay closer attention to the author, given activation of a prototype for author evaluation. Thus, liking might have played a more important role, paradoxically, when systematic processing occurred.

Although examining how people process infor-

mation when directed to the message itself versus the source of the message would seem to be an interesting topic in its own right, we could unfortunately find no research that bears directly on this issue. To the extent that message evaluation script versus author evaluation prototypes may affect information processing, however, it would seem that this is an important future issue for investigators in this area. At present, we are not aware of any research in this area that directly seeks the recipient's opinion as the ostensible purpose of the study. This would seem to be a rich area for subsequent research. [. . .]

REFERENCES

Anderson, N. H. (1974). Cognitive algebra: Integration theory applied to social attribution. In L. Berkowitz (Ed.), *Advances in experimental social psychology* (Vol. 7, pp. 1–101). New York: Academic Press.

Atkinson, J. W. (Ed.). (1958). *Motives in fantasy, action, and society.* Princeton, NJ: Van Nostrand.

Atkinson, J. W., & Feather, N. T. (Eds.). (1966). *A theory of achievement motivation.* New York: Wiley.

Byrne, D., & Lamberth, J. (1971). The effect of erotic stimuli on sex arousal, evaluative responses, and subsequent behavior. *Technical Reports of the Commission on Obscenity and Pornography* (Vol. 8). Washington, DC: U.S. Government Printing Office.

Cacioppo, J. T., & Petty, R. E. (1982). The need for cognition. *Journal of Personality and Social Psychology, 42,* 116–131.

Cacioppo, J. T., Petty, R. E., & Morris, K. J. (1983). Effects of need for cognition on message evaluation, recall, and persuasion. *Journal of Personality and Social Psychology, 45,* 805–818.

Cantor, N., & Mischel, W. (1977). Traits as prototypes: Effects of recognition on memory. *Journal of Personality and Social Psychology, 35,* 38–48.

Chaiken, S. (1980). Heuristic versus systematic information processing and the use of source versus message cues in persuasion. *Journal of Personality and Social Psychology, 9,* 752–766.

Chaiken, S., & Eagly, A. H. (1983). Communication modality as a determinant of persuasion: The role of communicator salience. *Journal of Personality and Social Psychology, 45,* 241–256.

Chu, G. C. (1967). Prior familiarity, perceived bias, and one-sided versus two-sided communications. *Journal of Experimental Social Psychology, 3,* 243–254.

Cook, T. D., & Flay, B. R. (1978). The temporal persistence of experimentally induced attitude change: An evaluative review. In L. Berkowitz (Ed.), *Advances in experimental social psychology* (Vol. 11, pp. 2–57). New York: Academic Press.

Entin, E. C., & Raynor, J. O. (1973). Effects of contingent future orientation and achievement motivation on performance in two kinds of tasks. *Journal of Experimental Research in Personality, 6,* 314–320.

Erikson, E. (1968). *Identity, youth, and crisis.* New York: Norton.

Fiske, S. T, & Taylor, S. E. (1984). *Social cognition.* Reading, MA: Addison-Wesley.

Frederick, J. E.. & Sorrentino, R. M. (1977). *A scoring manual for the motive to master uncertainty* (Research Bulletin No. 410). London, Ontario, Canada: University of Western Ontario.

Hennigan, K. M., Cook, T. D., & Gruder, C. L. (1982). Cognitive tuning set, source credibility, and the temporal persistence of attitude change. *Journal of Personality and Social Psychology, 42,* 412–425.

Higgins, E. T., Rhodewalt, E., & Zanna, M. P. (1979). Dissonance motivation: Its nature, persistence, and reinstatement. *Journal of Experimental Social Psychology, 15,* 16–34.

Higgins, E. T., & Rholes, W. S. (1978). "Saying is believing": Effects of message modification on memory and liking for the person described. *Journal of Experimental Social Psychology, 14,* 363–378.

Hoffman, M. L. (1986). Affect, cognition, and motivation. In R. M. Sorrentino & E. T. Higgins (Eds.), *The handbook of motivation and cognition: Foundations of social behavior* (pp. 244–280). New York: Guilford Press.

Hovland, C. I., Lumsdaine, A. A., & Sheffield, F. D. (1949). *Experiments on mass communication* (pp. 201–227). Princeton, NJ: Princeton University Press.

Kagan, J. (1972). Motives and development. *Journal of Personality and Social Psychology, 22,* 51–66.

Kahneman, D., & Tversky, A. (1973). On the psychology of prediction. *Psychological Review, 80,* 237–251.

Karabenick, S. A., & Yousseff, Z. I. (1968). Performance as a function of achievement motive level and perceived difficulty. *Journal of Personality and Social Psychology, 10,* 414–419.

Kelman, K. C., & Barclay, J. (1963). The F scale as a measure of breadth and perspective. *Journal of Abnormal and Social Psychology, 67,* 608–615.

King, G. A., & Sorrentino, R. M. (in press). Category accessibility and uncertainty orientation: Recall and memory of ambiguous and unambiguous trait descriptors. *Social Cognition: A Journal of Social, Personality, and Developmental Psychology.*

Kirscht, J., & Dillehay, R. (1967). *Dimensions of authoritarianism.* Lexington: University of Kentucky Press.

Langer, E. J. (1978). Rethinking the role of thought in social interaction. In J. H. Harvey, W. J. Ickes, & R. F. Kidd (Eds.), *New directions in attribution research* (Vol. 2, pp. 35–58). Hillsdale, NJ: Erlbaum.

Lumsdaine, A. A., & Janis, I. L. (1953). Resistance to "counterpropaganda" produced by one-sided and two-sided "propaganda" presentations. *Public Opinion Quarterly, 17,* 311–318.

Nisbett, R. E., & Ross, L. (1980). *Human inference: Strategies and shortcomings of social judgment.* Englewood Cliffs, NJ: Prentice-Hall.

Nisbett, R. E., & Wilson, T. D. (1977). Telling more than we can know: Verbal reports on mental processes. *Psychological Review, 84,* 231–259.

Olson, J. M., & Ross, M. (1985). Attribution research: Past contributions, current trends, and future prospects. In J. H. Harvey & G. Weary (Eds.), *Attribution: Basic issues and applications* (pp. 283–311). New York: Academic Press.

Petty, R. E., & Cacioppo, J. T. (1979a). Effects of forewarning of persuasive intent and involvement on cognitive responses and persuasion. *Personality and Social Psychology Bulletin, 5,* 173–176.

Petty, R. E., & Cacioppo, J. T. (1979b). Issue involvement can increase or decrease persuasion by enhancing message-relevant cognitive responses. *Journal of Personality and Social Psychology, 37,* 1915–1926.

Petty, R. E., & Cacioppo, J. T. (1981). *Attitudes and persuasion: Classic and contemporary approaches.* Dubuque, IA: Wm. C. Brown.

Petty, R. E., & Cacioppo, J. T. (1984). The effects of involvement on responses to argument quantity and quality: Central and peripheral routes to persuasion. *Journal of Personality and Social Psychology, 46,* 69–81.

Petty, R. E., Cacioppo, J. T., & Goldman, R. (1981). Personal involvement as a determinant of argument-based persuasion. *Journal of Personality and Social Psychology, 41,* 847–855.

Raynor, J. O., & Rubin, I. S. (1971). Effects of achievement motivation and future orientation on level of performance. *Journal of Personality and Social Psychology, 17,* 36–41.

Rokeach, M. (1960). *The open and closed mind: Investigations into the nature of belief systems and personality systems.* New York: Basic Books.

Schneider, W., & Shriffin, R. M. (1977). Controlled and automatic information processing: I. Detection, search, and attention. *Psychological Review, 84,* 1–66.

Schroder, H. M., Driver, M. J., & Streufert, S. (1967). *Human information processing.* New York: Holt, Rinehart & Winston.

Sherman, S. J., & Corty, E. (1984). Cognitive heuristics. In R. S. Wyer & T. K. Srull (Eds.), *Handbook of social cognition* (Vol. 1, pp. 189–286). Hillsdale, NJ: Erlbaum.

Sorrentino, R. M. (1977). [Test–retest reliabilities of authoritarianism scores]. Unpublished raw data.

Sorrentino, R. M., & Hewitt, E. C. (1984). The uncertainty-reducing properties of achievement tasks revisited. *Journal of Personality and Social Psychology, 47,* 884–899.

Sorrentino, R. M., & Higgins, E. T. (Eds.). (1986). *The handbook of motivation and cognition: Foundations of social behavior.* New York: Guilford press.

Sorrentino, R. M., & Roney, C. J. R. (1986). Uncertainty orientation, achievement-related motives, and task diagnosticity as determinants of task performance. *Social Cognition: A Journal of Social, Personality, and Developmental Psychology, 4,* 420–436.

Sorrentino, R. M., & Short, J. C. (1977). The case of the mysterious moderates: Why motives sometimes fail to predict behavior. *Journal of Personality and Social Psychology, 35,* 478–484.

Sorrentino, R. M., & Short, J. C. (1986). Uncertainty orientation, motivation, and cognition. In R. M. Sorrentino & E. T. Higgins (Eds.), *The handbook of motivation and cognition: Foundations of social behavior* (pp. 379–403). New York: Guilford Press.

Sorrentino, R. M., Short, J. C., & Raynor, J. O. (1984). Uncertainty orientation: Implications for affective and cognitive views of achievement behavior. *Journal of Personality and Social Psychology, 46,* 189–206.

Winer, B. (1971). *Statistical principles in experimental design* (2nd ed.). New York: McGraw-Hill.

READING 20

Motivated Closing of the Mind: "Seizing" and "Freezing"

Arie W. Kruglanski • **Department of Psychology, University of Maryland**
Donna M. Webster • **Department of Psychology, University of Florida**

Editors' Notes

The need for nonspecific closure is a desire for any answer, any knowledge on an issue as long as it is definite. The state of having a need for nonspecific closure can be an individual difference variable—some people are chronically in this state more than others—or it can be situationally induced. Individuals in this state tend to seek answers urgently, "seizing" on whatever answers are available, and tend to maintain permanently whatever answers they have by "freezing" on them. This seizing and freezing has various psychological effects. Greater need for nonspecific closure relates to a lesser extent of information processing, a lesser extent of hypothesis generation, greater judgmental confidence, and greater utilization of early, versus later, cues. These relations in turn have implications for important social psychological phenomena, including the process of hypothesis-testing, primacy-recency effects in impression formation, construct accessibility effects, use of stereotypes in judgment, and negative responses to out-group members and deviate in-group members.

Discussion Questions

1. Describe the need for nonspecific closure.
2. Describe evidence of the effect of need for closure on the use of stereotypes in judgment and responses to deviate out-group members.

Authors' Abstract

A theoretical framework is outlined in which the key construct is the need for (nonspecific) cognitive closure. The need for closure is a desire for definite knowledge on some issue. It represents a dimension of stable individual differences as well as a situationally evocable state. The need for closure has widely ramifying consequences for social–cognitive phenomena at the intrapersonal, interpersonal, and group levels of analysis. Those consequences derive from 2 general tendencies, those of urgency and permanence. The urgency tendency represents an individual's inclination to attain closure as soon as possible, and the permanence tendency represents an individual's inclination to maintain it for as long as possible. Empirical evidence for present theory attests to diverse need for closure effects on fundamental social psychological phenomena, including impression formation, stereotyping, attribution, persuasion, group decision making, and language use in intergroup contexts.

The construction of new knowledge is a pervasive human pursuit for both individuals and collectives. From relatively simple activities such as crossing a busy road to highly complex endeavors such as launching a space shuttle, new knowledge is indispensable for secure decisions and reasoned actions. The knowledge-construction process is often involved and intricate. It draws on background notions activated from memory and local information from the immediate context. It entails the extensive testing of hypotheses and the piecing of isolated cognitive bits into coherent wholes. It integrates inchoate sensations with articulate thoughts, detects meaningful signals in seas of ambient noise, and more.

Two aspects of knowledge construction are of present interest: its motivated nature and its social character. That knowledge construction has a motivational base should come as no particular surprise. The host of effortful activities it comprises pose considerable demands on resource allocation; hence, it may well require motivation to get under way. Specifically, individuals may desire knowledge on some topics and not others, and they may delimit their constructive endeavors to those particular domains. But what kind of a motivational variable is the "desire for knowledge"? At least two answers readily suggest themselves: Knowledge could be desired because it conveys welcome news in regard to a given concern or because it conveys any definite news (whether welcome or unwelcome) in instances in which such information is required for some purpose. For instance, a mother may desire to know that her child did well on the Scholastic Aptitude Test (SAT) so that she may send her or him to a selective college, whereas

the college admissions officer may desire to simply know how well or poorly the child did so that he or she may make the appropriate admission decision. The former type of desire has been referred to as the need for a specific closure, and the latter has been referred to as the need for a nonspecific closure. The need for a specific closure implies the desirability of a particular answer to a question (e.g., that one's child did well on the SAT), whereas the need for a nonspecific closure implies the desirability of any answer as long as it is definite (Kruglanski, 1989, 1990a, 1990b). Various needs for specific closure have received considerable emphasis in the social cognition literature (e.g., for reviews, see Kruglanski, in press; Kunda, 1990). The need for nonspecific closure has attracted much less attention. A major purpose of this article is to redress this imbalance by focusing on the latter type of desire.

In addition to its motivated nature, the knowledge-construction process is suffused with social significance. First, various social entities (other persons, groups, or social categories) are often the objects of knowledge-construction endeavors. In other words, constructive efforts are frequently meant to yield socially relevant knowledge. Furthermore, other people may often supply the informational means whereby constructive ends are attained. They may provide social comparison information (Festinger, 1954) or feedback pertinent to self-verification or self-enhancement motives (Swann, 1990). They may supply consensus information in instances in which consensus is desired, confirm one's favorite hypotheses, or bear witness to one's efficacy and control. Of course, people might impede rather than facilitate the attainment of desired knowledge and be occasionally the bearers of "bad news." Even then, however, they remain motivationally relevant to one's epistemic purposes as potential sources of pertinent information. An important objective of the present article is, therefore, to flesh out the social psychological significance of knowledge-construction processes, particularly as these processes relate to the need for (nonspecific) closure.

In what follows, up present theory and research elucidating the nature of this need, its antecedent conditions, and its consequences. Essentially, we hope to demonstrate that the need for closure exerts a broad range of effects on the knowledge-construction process and hence, indirectly, on a wide range of related social psychological phenomena at the intrapersonal, interpersonal, and group levels of analysis.

The Need for Closure

The need for cognitive closure refers to individuals' desire for a firm answer to a question and an aversion toward ambiguity. As used here, the term *need* is meant to denote a motivated tendency or proclivity rather than a tissue deficit (for a similar usage, see Cacioppo & Petty, 1982). We assume that the need for cognitive closure is akin to a person's goal (Pervin, 1989). As such, it may prompt activities aimed at the attainment of closure, bias the individual's choices and preferences toward closure-bound pursuits, and induce negative affect when closure is threatened or undermined and positive affect when it is facilitated or attained.

A Motivational Continuum in Regard to Closure

We assume that the motivation toward closure varies along a continuum anchored at one end with a strong need for closure and at the other end with a strong need to avoid closure. Closure, in other words, may not be desired universally. Although in some circumstances people may strive to attain it, in other situations they may actively avoid it or exhibit little preference for it over ambiguity. Individuals at the need for closure end of the continuum may display considerable cognitive impatience or impulsivity: They may "leap" to judgment on the basis of inconclusive evidence and exhibit

rigidity of thought and reluctance to entertain views different from their own. At the opposite end of the continuum, denoting a high need to avoid closure, people may savor uncertainty and be reluctant to commit to a definite opinion. In those circumstances, individuals may suspend judgment and be quick to engender alternatives to any emergent view.

Effects of the motivation for closure are assumed to be monotonic along the continuum. By this assumption, the motivational effects should be directionally similar for any pair of points on the continuum: A higher (vs. lower) degree of the need for closure should effect a higher or lower degree of some phenomenon, irrespective of the points' specific locations. Thus, comparing low and high need for closure conditions should yield effects directionally similar to those involved in comparing high and low need to avoid closure conditions. Evidence reviewed in subsequent sections consistently supports this assumption.

Antecedents of the Motivation Toward Closure

What conditions may induce a given motivation toward closure? According to the present analysis, these may be conditions that highlight the perceived benefits or desirability of closure or of the absence of closure (see also Kruglanski, in press). For instance, a potential benefit of closure may be the ability to act or decide in time for meeting an important deadline. Thus, the need for closure should be heightened under time pressure. An alternative benefit of closure is removal of the necessity for further information processing; if so, need for closure should be heightened under conditions that render processing difficult, laborious, or aversive. Some such conditions (e.g., environmental noise) may reside in the exogenous context of processing, whereas others (e.g., tedium and dullness of a cognitive task) may relate to endogenous aspects of processing (Kruglanski, 1975). Yet other conditions may stem from the perceiver's organismic state. For instance, people may find processing particularly arduous when in a state of fatigue. Accordingly, need for closure should be heightened under noise, when the task is unpleasant or dull, or when the individual is fatigued. It should also be heightened when closure is valued by significant others, because possessing closure may promise to earn their esteem and appreciation. Finally, it should be heightened, simply, when judgment on some topic is required (as compared with cases in which the individual feels free to remain opinionless).

The need for closure may be lowered and that to avoid closure heightened by conditions that highlight the costs of closure and the benefits of openness. In some situations, closure costs may be made salient by "fear of invalidity," or a gnawing concern about a costly judgmental mistake (e.g., when the perceiver is "outcome dependent" on the target; cf. Fiske & Neuberg, 1990). Under these conditions, people may desire to suspend judgment or avoid premature closure. This may seem to imply that validity concerns are necessarily at odds with those of closure. Obviously, however, no one would consciously adopt a closure she or he judged invalid. In fact, the very notion of subjective knowledge connotes the joint sense of closure and validity. To know, for example, that Washington, D.C., is the capital of the United States is at once to have closure on the topic and to believe it to be true. This logic notwithstanding, psychological concerns for closure and validity may arise fairly independently of each other; more important, they may pull information processing in diametrically opposed directions.

When closure concerns loom large, for example, individuals may perform closure-promoting activities without sacrificing their sense of validity. They may generate fewer competing hypotheses or suppress attention to information inconsistent with their, hypotheses. Both processes may promote a sense of valid closure uncontested by alternative interpretations or inconsistent evidence. By contrast, when validity concerns are salient, people may engage in a thorough and extensive information search and generate multiple alternative interpretations to account for known facts. To wit, they may process information in exactly the opposite manner to that observed under a heightened need for closure. In fact, when validity represents the overriding concern, individuals may be motivated to postpone closure and, in extreme cases, to avoid it altogether. This is not inevitable, however: If a particular closure appears valid beyond the shadow of a doubt (e.g., because of the impeccable credibility of its source), the fear of invalidity may increase the tendency to embrace it rather than prompting its avoidance or postponement. Thus, closure avoidance should be conceptually

distinguished from the fear of invalidity. Although closure avoidance may be often induced by such fear, this may not hold invariably.

The need to avoid (or postpone) closure may arise for alternative reasons, such as when the judgmental task is intrinsically enjoyable and interesting (relative to possible alternative pursuits) and closure threatens to terminate this pleasant activity. Finally, as noted earlier, individuals may exhibit stable personal differences in the degree to which they value closure. Such differences may spring from various sources, such as cultural norms (Hofstede, 1980) or personal socialization histories that place a premium on confidence and "know-how." Accordingly, we have recently developed a measure of individual differences in need for closure and established its reliability and validity (Webster & Kruglanski, 1994).

A major upshot of the foregoing analysis is that the need for closure may be operationally defined in a broad variety of ways. If our theory is correct, such diverse operationalizations should prove functionally equivalent in regard to theoretically relevant phenomena. Specific evidence for such an equivalence is examined subsequently.

Consequences of the Need for Closure: The Urgency and Permanence Tendencies

The motivation toward cognitive closure may affect the way individuals process information en route to the formation, alteration, or dissolution of knowledge. Because such processes are typically embedded in social-interaction contexts, they may significantly affect the way a person thinks about, feels about, acts toward, and even talks about others.

What form might such effects assume? We posit two general tendencies that need for closure may instill: the *urgency tendency* and the *permanence tendency*. The urgency tendency refers to the inclination to "seize" on closure quickly. People under a heightened need for closure may perceive that they desire closure immediately. Any further postponement of closure is experienced as bothersome, and the individual's overriding sense is that he or she simply cannot wait.

The permanence tendency refers to the desire to perpetuate closure, giving rise to the dual inclination (a) to preserve, or "freeze" on, past knowledge and (b) to safeguard future knowledge. Individuals under a heightened need for closure may thus desire an enduring closure and, in extreme cases, abhor losing closure ever again. The urgency and permanence notions both rest on the assumption that people under a heightened need for closure experience its absence as aversive. They may, therefore, wish to terminate this unpleasant state quickly (the urgency tendency) and keep it from recurring (the permanence tendency).

The abstract tendencies toward urgency and permanence may translate into a variety of concrete social psychological phenomena. Specifically, people under a heightened need for closure may seize on information appearing early in a sequence and freeze on it, becoming impervious to subsequent data. Such seizing and freezing trends may affect information processing and, indirectly, the multiple social psychological phenomena information processing may mediate.

Extent of Information Processing

Because of the tendency to seize on early information and immediately freeze, people under a heightened need for closure may process less information before committing to a judgment and generate fewer competing hypotheses to account for the available data. Paradoxically, they may feel more assured of those judgments, even though they are less grounded in thorough exploration. Specifically, the less competing hypotheses a person might entertain, the more confidence he or she may have in those hypotheses (Kelley, 1971) simply because fewer alternatives to a given judgment may appear plausible, enhancing the individual's confidence in those that are.

Cue Utilization

A straightforward implication of our seizing and freezing postulate is that people under a heightened need for closure should bar their judgments predominantly on early or preexisting cues rather than on later information. As a concrete implication, people under a high (vs. low) need for closure should often exhibit stronger primacy effects in impression formation (Asch, 1946). Furthermore, individuals under a heightened need for closure should rely more on stereotypes than on case-specific or individuating information simply because stereotypes represent preexisting knowledge structures, ready to be used momentarily, whereas individuating information may require

extensive further processing. The tendency, based on need for closure, to overutilize early cues implies a disposition to keep one's estimates close to initial anchors rather than correct them in light of subsequent evidence (Tversky & Kahneman, 1974). A similar tendency induced by a heightened need for closure may augment the assimilation of judgments to semantic primes (Higgins, Rholes, & Jones, 1977). The rationale for these predictions is straightforward: Anchors as well as primes define initial bases for a judgment and should be seized and frozen on under a heightened need for closure.

The Quest for Epistemic Permanence: Consensus and Consistency Strivings

Once a person under a heightened need for closure has managed to formulate a belief and freeze on it, he or she may tend to preserve it for future reference. This is what our permanence notion implies. Such a tendency may manifest itself in a preference for consensual opinions that are unlikely to be challenged and potentially undermined by significant others. As a corollary, people high in need for closure should prefer to associate with similar-minded others, feel positively disposed toward group members who facilitate consensus, and feel negatively disposed toward dissenters or opinion deviates who jeopardize consensus.

Beyond the consensus bias, permanence strivings might induce a bias toward consistency, expressed as a preference for general knowledge applicable across situations over situationally restricted knowledge. Among other things, such a preference may manifest itself in the way people use language in social contexts. Specifically, they may exhibit, under a heightened need for closure, an increased tendency to use trait terms or abstract category labels in describing others, simply because these terms and labels connote trans-situational stability (e.g., to say someone is intelligent or friendly means she or he would behave intelligently or in a friendly manner across numerous specific instances).

Separating Seizing From Freezing: The Point of Belief Crystallization

According to the present theory, a demarcation point separating seizing phenomena from those of freezing is the juncture during which a belief crystallizes and turns from hesitant conjecture to a subjectively firm "fact." Before that point, it should be possible to observe pure seizing, manifest, for example, in quickened pace and enhanced volume of the informational search under a heightened need for closure. As an additional implication, seizing should dispose people to be relatively open to persuasion attempts because such attempts promise to furnish the coveted closure. Subsequent to crystallization, by contrast, it should be possible to witness freezing manifest as a reluctance to continue information processing or a resistance to persuasive arguments aimed at undermining one's current closure and effecting cognitive change. The notion that the predecision action phase is characterized by cognitive openness (the deliberation mind-set) and that the postdecision phase is characterized by narrow restrictiveness (the implementation mind-set) was stressed also by Gollwitzer (1990).

In summary, our theory (a) views the need for closure as a desire for confident knowledge, (b) suggests that motivation toward closure varies along a continuum from a strong need for closure to a strong need to avoid closure, (c) views the need for closure both as an individual-differences variable and as a situationally inducible state prompted by the perceived benefits or costs of lacking closure, and (d) implies that need for closure may affect how an individual thinks, feels, acts toward and speaks about socially significant others. The empirical evidence for the present theory is reviewed in subsequent sections of this article. First, however, we consider its conceptual predecessors and examine its relation to those earlier notions. We ultimately argue that, commonalities with alternative formulations notwithstanding, the need for closure construct is unique and fundamentally different from previous relevant notions in its essence, antecedent conditions, and consequences. [. . .]

Empirical Evidence

Seizing and Freezing Effects

Earlier we posited two general tendencies that need for closure may instigate: the urgency tendency of seizing on judgmentally relevant cues and the permanence tendency of freezing on judgments the cues imply. Operating jointly, the seizing and freezing sequence may produce a broad range of judg-

mental effects observable under a heightened need for closure.

EXTENT OF INFORMATION PROCESSING

At a minimum, the seizing and freezing mechanism implies a reduced extent of information processing under a heightened need for closure. The speeded-up reliance on early cues implied by seizing and the truncation of further exploration due to freezing suggest that individuals under a high (vs. low) need for closure should consider less evidence before forming a judgment. In an experiment relevant to this proposition, Mayseless and Kruglanski (1987, Study 2) had participants perform a tachistoscopic recognition task of identifying barely visible digits on a screen. As a means of arousing the need for closure, participants were told that forming unambiguous, clear-cut opinions is positively correlated with high mental concentration and intelligence. This manipulation was designed to enhance the perceived value (or benefit) of closure and, hence, to increase the need for closure. Note that stating that unambiguous or clearcut opinions are valuable does not, in itself, demand briefer information processing. To the contrary, it seems more reasonable to assume that the arrival at clarity and the dispelling of ambiguity would require, if anything, more rather than less extensive processing. The present seizing and freezing notion implies the opposite, of course.

As a means of inducing the need to avoid closure, participants were given accuracy instructions and promised extra experimental credit for correctly identifying 9 of 10 digits. A neutral control condition was also included in which no motivational induction took place. Participants were allowed to operate the tachistoscope an unlimited number of times. As predicted, their extent of informational search (number of times they operated the tachistoscope) was lowest in the need for closure condition, intermediate in the control condition, and highest in the need to avoid closure condition.

HYPOTHESIS GENERATION

In addition to a reduced extent of processing "external" stimulus information, the seizing and freezing notions imply that, under heightened need for closure, there will be a parallel reduction in "internal" hypothesis generation. Presumably those two processes are intimately linked: Examination of external information may suggest new, internally formed hypotheses, the testing of which may require, in turn, further processing of external information. Need for closure effects on hypothesis generation were specifically addressed in another experiment conducted by Mayseless and Kruglanski (1987, Study 3). Participants were shown enlarged photographs of parts of common objects (e.g., a comb, a toothbrush, and a nail). These photos were taken from unusual angles, masking the objects' actual nature. On each trial, participants were urged to list the maximal number of hypotheses concerning an object's identity and ultimately chose the identity most likely to be correct. As in the study mentioned earlier (Mayseless & Kruglanski, 1987, Study 2), need for closure was induced by informing participants that clear-cut opinions relate to mental concentration and intelligence. Again, this, in and of itself, should not artificially "demand" a curtailment of hypothesis generation. Rather, an emphasis on clarity and intelligence may demand increased hypothesis generation, contrary to the present prediction.

To induce the need to avoid closure, the instructions noted a correlation between the desirable mental qualities and correct visual recognition. As in the previous study, a neutral control condition devoid of a motivational induction was included. The results showed, as predicted, that participants in the need to avoid closure condition generated the largest number of hypotheses, followed by participants in the control condition; participants in the need for closure condition produced the fewest hypotheses.

SUBJECTIVE CONFIDENCE

An interesting corollary to the notion that individuals under a high (vs. low) need for closure generate fewer hypotheses is that they will be quicker to attain high judgmental confidence. This implication follows from Kelley's (1971) discounting principle, whereby reduction in the number of alternative hypotheses should boost an individual's confidence in each hypothesis. Relevant to this prediction, in the tachistoxopic recognition study conducted by Mayseless and Kruglanski (1987, Study 2), participants' confidence in their initial hypotheses and the magnitude of confidence shifts (upward or downward) occasioned by each successive stimulus presentation were significantly lower in the need to avoid closure condition than in the need for closure condition, with the control condition falling in the middle.

Elevated confidence of participants under heightened need for closure has been replicated in several studies using widely divergent methods, such as ambient noise (Kruglanski & Webster, 1991; Kruglanski, Webster, & Klem, 1993), dullness of the task (Webster, 1993), and time pressure (Kruglanski & Webster, 1991), of inducing this motivation. Identical results were obtained when need for closure was assessed via our individual-differences measure (Webster & Kruglanski, 1994) rather than manipulated situationally.

Elevated confidence under a heightened need for closure is striking against the backdrop of reduced information processing under those very circumstances. This finding is incongruous with the common presumption that attainment of secure views requires more rather than less extensive processing, and it defines an "unfounded confidence" paradox under a heightened need for closure.

SEEKING DIAGNOSTIC OR PROTOTYPICAL INFORMATION

Restriction of hypothesis generation under a heightened need for closure (Mayseless & Kruglanski, 1987, Study 3) should, finally, affect not only the amount of information sought by hypothesis-testing participants but also the type of information sought. Specifically, under high need for closure, participants may seek prototypical information about a category, whereas, under high need to avoid closure, they might instead seek diagnostic information (Trope & Bassok, 1983) capable of discriminating among different categories. Consider an interviewer testing the focal hypothesis that an interviewee is a painter. Under a high need for closure, this individual may refrain from generating specific competing alternatives to this hypothesis and search for information capable of demarcating it from the diffuse nonpainter hypothesis. Such information may pertain to features prototypical of painters (e.g., "bohemian" life-style or artistic ability). The case may be very different, however, if the individual's need to avoid closure was aroused. This might motivate her or him to be sensitive to possible specific alternatives to the hypothesis, such as that the interviewee is an architect. If so, the interviewer might specifically seek information diagnostic in regard to the painter-architect pair: Artistic ability is presumably shared by painters and architects alike and hence is nondiagnostic, whereas bohemian life-style is diagnostic because it may principally characterize painters but not architects. In research designed to investigate these possibilities (Kruglanski & Mayseless, 1988), we asked participants to evaluate whether a target belonged to a given professional category, subtly hinting at a competing alternative possibility. As expected, individuals under a high need for closure, manipulated through implied time pressure, sought more prototypical information than diagnostic information, whereas those under need to avoid closure, manipulated through instilled fear of invalidity, sought more diagnostic information capable of differentiating between the competing alternatives.

EARLY-CUE UTILIZATION

Perhaps the broadest implication of the seizing and freezing mechanism is that under a high (vs. low) need for closure, individuals tend to base their final judgments on early cues. Because of the urgency tendency, such cues should be quickly utilized to form an initial judgment (seizing), and, because of the permanence tendency, such a judgment should tend to stay fixed (freezing) rather than be altered in light of subsequent evidence. This fundamental process may underlie a diverse array of phenomena that, at first glance, might appear unrelated.

Impressional-primacy effects. An obvious such phenomenon is the impressional "primacy effect" (Asch, 1946; Luchins, 1957), that is, the tendency to base impressions of a social target more on information presented early versus late in a sequence. If primacy effects are an instance of the seizing and freezing process, they should be appropriately magnified under high need for closure and attenuated under high need to avoid closure. This prediction has received support in several studies differing in the ways in which needs for closure or closure avoidance were operationalized. Specifically, need for closure has been variously operationalized in terms of scores on the Need for Closure Scale (Webster & Kruglanski, 1994), time pressure (Freund, Kruglanski, & Schpitzajzen, 1985; Heaton & Kruglanski, 1991; Kruglanski & Freund, 1983), instructions to form an overall

evaluative judgment of the target (vs. separately evaluating each of his or her characteristics; Freund et al., 1985), and degree of mental fatigue (Webster, Richter, & Kruglanski, 1995). Need to avoid closure has been operationalized in terms of evaluation apprehension (Freund et al., 1985; Kruglanski & Freund, 1983) or potential costs to the evaluation target (in the case of a participant's mistake; Freund et al., 1985). As predicted, in all of these studies, the magnitude of primacy effects varied positively with need for closure and negatively with need to avoid closure.

Note, however, that in the research described thus far, it was relatively easy for participants to downplay the late appearing evidence if motivated to do so. It is quite possible that if the late evidence is particularly compelling and participants high in need for closure are pressured to seriously consider it, they may change their mind more abruptly and completely than those low in need for closure, manifesting a recency effect. In dynamic systems terms (Vallacher & Nowak, in press), need for closure could serve as a "control parameter," effecting quick gravitation to "attractors" representing conclusions implied by the early and late appearing evidence.

Anchoring effects. A different instance of early cue utilization may underlie the "anchoring" effect discovered by Tversky and Kahneman (1974). Consider a probability-estimation task (cf. Bar-Hillel, 1973) in which participants assess the probability of compound conjunctive or disjunctive events. Participants typically use the probability of the simple constituent events as an anchor and then adjust. When the adjustment is insufficient, they should therefore overestimate the probability of conjunctive events (calculation of which involves the multiplication of fractions) and underestimate the probability of disjunctive events (calculation of which involves the addition of fractions). If anchoring represents a special case of cue utilization, it should be appropriately affected by the need for closure. Consistent with this notion, participants' tendency to overestimate the likelihood of conjunctive events and underestimate that of disjunctive events increased under need for closure manipulated via time pressure and decreased under need to avoid closure manipulated by evaluation apprehension (Kruglanski & Freund, 1983, Study 2).

The correspondence bias. The correspondence bias in person perception (Jones, 1979) is among the most persistently studied phenomena in social cognition (see discussion by Trope & Higgins, 1993). It is, therefore, of considerable interest that it too may represent a special case of early-cue utilization and be appropriately influenced by the need for closure. The correspondence bias refers to a perceiver tendency to overascribe actors' behavior to personal inclinations, even in the presence of situational pressures that in and of themselves should be capable of eliciting the behavior. In an original demonstration of this phenomenon, Jones and Harris (1967) presented participants with essays allegedly written by a person given either a free choice or no choice in the matter of doing so. In both cases, that is, even when the writer was denied choice, participants assumed that his or her attitude was largely congruent with the essay content.

Different theorists (Gilbert, Pelham, & Krull, 1988; Jones, 1979; Quattrone, 1982) have implied that the underlying mechanism for the correspondence bias could involve the anchoring and insufficient adjustment process discussed earlier. Thus, when participants come to judge the writer's attitude, the most salient evidence is the very behavior that took place. Often, the earliest hypothesis this suggests is that the behavior faithfully mirrored the writer's attitude. This attitude-correspondence hypothesis may pop to mind spontaneously or "automatically" and serve as an initial anchor to be subsequently adjusted via a "controlled" cognitive process during which further relevant evidence (e.g., concerning pertinent situational constraints) is considered.

Such controlled adjustment, however, may require substantial cognitive effort. For instance, Gilbert et al. (1988) found that when perceivers were cognitively busy, the correspondence bias was enhanced. This may mean that the increased effort required by the adjustment process was more than the participants were willing to put out, which suggests that motivational considerations may indeed enter into the correspondence bias. Research by Tetlock (e.g., 1985) supports this possibility. He found that such bias was markedly reduced when participants were made to feel accountable for their judgments. Presumably, manipulation of accountability motivated participants to process information in a more discriminating manner, affording a more adequate adjustment of the initial bias.

The preceding findings are consistent with the notion that, as with the primacy or anchoring effect, the correspondence bias represents an over-utilization of early cues. If so, the correspondence bias too should be appropriately affected by the need for closure. In a recent set of studies, Webster (1993) tested this proposition, manipulating the need for closure via task attractiveness. Her underlying assumption was that when an activity is attractive or intrinsically motivated (e.g., Deci & Ryan, 1985; Higgins & Trope, 1990; Kruglanski, 1975), this should induce the motivation to extensively explore it (Berlyne, 1960) and, hence, to avoid premature closure. By contrast, when an activity is extrinsically motivated, the motivation may be to reach closure quickly so as to reach the exogenous reward without delay.

An attitude-attribution task was used in which a target made a speech critical of student-exchange programs under free-choice or no-choice conditions. As a means of portraying this task as unattractive, the task participants expected to perform subsequently (the watching of comedy videos) promised to be particularly attractive. This was assumed to render relatively unappealing or subjectively costly the current, duller task and hence to elevate the need for closure.

As a means of portraying the same task as attractive, the subsequent task promised to be particularly unattractive (watching a video of a statistics lecture). This was assumed to render the current task subjectively appealing and hence to lower the need for closure. Finally in a third, control condition, the subsequent task was portrayed as largely similar to the current one (also involving attitude attributions), lending it intermediate appeal. Manipulation checks confirmed that the experimental manipulations produced the corresponding differences in need for cognitive closure. Most important, the correspondence bias in the no-choice condition was affected by the need for closure in the predicted manner: Substantial correspondence bias was already present in the control condition (replicating prior research), and such bias was significantly enhanced in the unattractive task condition and completely eliminated in the attractive task condition.

The same pattern of results was obtained in Webster's second study, in which need for closure was assessed via the Need for Closure Scale (Webster & Kruglanski, 1994). Finally, when the initial cues implied a situational rather than a personal attribution, the results of the previous two studies were completely reversed. The tendency to overascribe the essay to the writer's attitude was reduced under a high need for closure (manipulated via task attractiveness) and enhanced under a low need for closure, both as compared with the control condition. This last finding is particularly significant because it demonstrates that need for closure effects are content free and depend on the order in which cues are received rather than on their specific substance (e.g., implying a personal or a situational attribution).

Stereotypic judgments. From a social psychological perspective, some particularly interesting sources of early cues are previously formed stereotypes, prejudices or attitudes readily accessible in memory. Such preexisting knowledge structures may preempt the use of case-specific (or individuating) information in the forming of social judgments. The present seizing and freezing mechanism suggests that such preemption should be particularly likely under a heightened need for closure, simply because extensive processing of case-specific information may substantially postpone closure. In an early demonstration of those effects, Kruglanski and Freund (1983, Study 3) found that ethnic stereotypes of Ashkenazi and Sephardi Jews influenced grade assignments for a literary composition more in conditions likely to elevate the graders' need for closure (time pressure, lack of accountability, or both) than in conditions likely to reduce it (accountability and no time pressure). Time pressure also increased the degree to which preexisting prejudice against women in management versus individuating information about specific applicants' qualifications tended to affect discrimination toward female versus male candidates (Jamieson & Zanna, 1989).

Construct accessibility effects. A key assumption in predicting more pronounced judgmental influence of stereotypes under a high (vs. low) need for closure is that such stereotypes are highly accessible in memory. Such accessible guides to judgment should be seized and frozen on under a heightened need for closure. A direct test of this assumption was recently carried out by Ford and Kruglanski (1995), who used a priming paradigm developed by Higgins et al. (1977). In the context of an allegedly unrelated memory experiment, participants were primed by either the negatively valenced adjective *reckless* or the positively valenced adjective *adventurous*. They were subsequently presented a passage about Donald that

was ambiguous with respect to the adventurous–reckless pair. Participants' task was to characterize Donald using a single word. In this situation, participants high in dispositional need for closure (Webster & Kruglanski, 1994) exhibited stronger assimilation of judgment to prime than participants low in this need. That is, participants high (vs. low) in need for closure tended more to characterize Donald in terms suggesting recklessness in the negative prime condition and adventurousness in the positive prime condition. An independently executed study by Thompson, Roman, Moscovitz, Chaiken, and Bargh (1994), using a different method of priming (the scrambled sentence technique) and of assessing need for closure (Neuberg & Newsom's, 1993, Personal Need for Structure Scale), yielded the same results. Participants high in need for structure–closure exhibited greater assimilation of their judgments to primed constructs than participants low in this need. Finally, both Ford and Kruglanski (1995) and Thompson et al. (1994) succeeded in significantly reducing the assimilation-to-prime effect under accuracy instructions (i.e., in conditions likely to reduce participants' need for closure).

Isolating the Urgency and Permanence Effects

Whereas the seizing and freezing research described earlier examined the joint workings of the urgency and permanence tendencies, further studies have aimed at separating their effects. In the next section, we examine work pertaining to permanence phenomena as such, followed by research on the boundary conditions for urgency versus permanence effects.

Consensus and Consistency Biases

As already noted, the permanence tendency involves the desire to maintain closure over time. The freezing phenomenon represents one manifestation of such a desire: Once closure has been attained, confronting it with new information might risk its subsequent dissolution. Freezing may be understood as an attempt to forestall this possibility. However, the permanence tendency may manifest itself in other ways as well, specifically in a bias toward consensual judgments unlikely to be contested by significant others. Furthermore, it may promote a preference for abstract judgments connoting transsituational consistency, and in this sense permanence, of knowledge.

CONSENSUS

An indication that need for closure may enhance the desire for consensus appeared in a pair of studies conducted by Kruglanski et al. (1993). In this research, the participant acted as a juror whose task was to discuss a legal case with another juror. Half of the participants received prior information allowing them to form a fairly confident opinion about the case. The remaining participants received no prior information, forestalling secure opinion formation. The need for closure was either manipulated via noise produced by a computer printer (Kruglanski et al., 1993, Study 2) or assessed via the Need for Closure Scale (Study 3). In both cases, participants under a high need for closure professed greater desire to agree with the other juror (i.e., to attain consensus) than did participants under a low need for closure. Of even greater interest, the specific manner in which participants tended to deal with their desire for consensus varied as function of the informational conditions: When presence of an information base led participants to crystallize a prior opinion, they professed a preference for an easily persuadable partner. Presumably, such a partner could be readily won over to the participant's side, affording consensus via what Festinger (1950) called the "change other" strategy. By contrast, when absence of an informational base kept participants from crystallizing a prior opinion, they professed a significant preference for a persuasive partner. Presumably, such a partner could readily convince the participant to adopt a given view, hence forging consensus by what Festinger (1950) called the "change self" strategy. These findings, too, emerged regardless of whether need for closure was operationalized via ambient noise or scores on the Need for Closure Scale.

REJECTION OF OPINION DEVIATES

When both the "change other" and "change self" strategies fail, however, there may exist a third possible way of attaining consensus in a group. It consists of "rejecting the deviate" and thus achieving consensus in a group by excluding the dissenters (Festinger, 1950; Schachter, 1951). If the permanence tendency fosters a quest for consensus and if, under the appropriate conditions, this encourages the rejection of deviates, heightening group members' need for closure should yield evidence of enhanced "rejectionism." This prediction was investigated in a series of experiments by Kruglanski and Webster (1991).

In their first study, need for closure was operationally defined via time pressure or temporal proximity of attitude assessment to the group-decision deadline. Our assumption has been that when the deadline is relatively remote, group members' predominant concern might be to safeguard the quality of their decision. This may induce a need to avoid premature closure and increase the tolerance for ambiguity induced by dissenting views. With the deadline approaching, however, the implied time pressure may induce an overriding need for closure. This may reduce group members' tolerance for dissent and increase their tendency to reject the deviates.

In a field experiment designed to test those ideas (Kruglanski & Webster, 1991, Study 1), groups of Tel Aviv (boy and girl) scouts were presented with a decision of choosing a location for their annual "working camp" of 2 weeks' duration. Two choices of kibbutz settlements were presented. One was an affluent, centrally located kibbutz (Naan) amply endowed with such accoutrements as swimming pools, tennis courts, and color TVs. The other choice was a fledgling borderline kibbutz (Ktora) in the Judean desert lacking at the time even such basic amenities as in-house bathrooms.

Despite what to some might appear the obvious choice, the idealistically inspired scouts predominantly preferred the rugged, little settlement over its lush alternative. This fact was well known to the investigation and was treated as the group's consensual opinion. To introduce our deviancy manipulation, we asked one member in each group (known to occupy a median sociometric standing) to argue for either the consensual choice (the conformist role) or the unpopular alternative (the deviant role) and to do so either early on in the deliberation process or late, near the putative deadline.

Actually, there existed three experimental conditions related to the timing of opinion expression. In the *objectively early* condition, the confederate announced her or his (conforming or deviant) opinion near the commencement of discussion. In the *objectively late* condition, he or she did so near the expected deadline. In the *subjectively early* condition, she or he did so at the same actual time as in the objectively late condition; because the deadline was appropriately postponed, however, the participant believed that he or she had as much discussion time remaining as did others in the subjectively early condition.

The available evidence confirmed that participants' need for closure was proportionate to the discussion time they believed they had at their disposal. Specifically, participants' differentiation between attractiveness of the two choice alternatives was significantly lower in the early conditions (objective as well as subjective) than in the (objectively) late condition. This suggests that participants were more open-minded to both alternatives when they perceived little (vs. a great deal of) time pressure to make up their mind. Those findings were paralleled by expressed confidence in the attractiveness ratings, which was significantly higher at the late versus the early (objective and subjective) points. Both findings support the notion that time pressure, induced by perceived proximity of the deadline, contributed in the expected manner to need for closure arousal.

The main dependent variable of interest was an evaluative shift toward the confederate in the deviant and conformist roles. Results are depicted in Figure 1. As can be seen, the evaluative shifts toward the conformist were negligible and did not appreciably vary as a function of timing. The shifts toward the deviant exhibited a strikingly different pattern. They were progressively more negative as the expected deadline drew near.

We (Kruglanski & Webster, 1991, Study 2) conceptually replicated this experiment, manipulating need for closure via ambient noise. Groups of University of Maryland students were instructed to discuss to consensus compulsory drug testing for campus athletes. Students were preselected to be in favor of such testing. Two members of each group were confederates, whose behavior during the discussion was systematically varied as function of our experimental manipulations. One confederate enacted a conformist's role and expressed opinions consistent with the expected consensus (i.e., in favor of drug testing). The other confederate enacted a deviant's role and expressed opinions at odds with the expected consensus (arguing against drug testing). As a means of controlling for possible effects due to the confederates' personalities, the conformist and deviant roles were rotated across the experimental sessions.

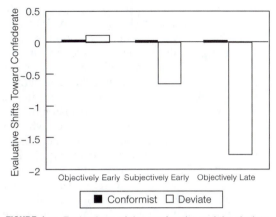

FIGURE 1 ■ Evaluations of the conformist and the deviate at different degrees of proximity to the group-decision deadline.

As in the Kruglanski et al. (1993) research described earlier, the noise was produced via a computer printer. We assumed that in a noisy environment, information processing would be more laborious, and hence subjectively costly, and that this would heighten participants' need for closure, leading to greater rejection of the deviate.

If participants in the noise (vs. no-noise) condition experience a higher need for closure, they may experience greater subjective confidence in their opinion. This turned out to be the case, although the difference was statistically borderline ($p < .13$). Of greater interest, the deviant was evaluated more negatively ($p < .001$) under noise than under no noise (see Table 1). Although the conformist was evaluated somewhat more positively under noise (vs. no noise), this difference was not significant.

To examine the possible alternative interpretation that derogation of the deviant under noise stemmed from the irritability that noise might have

TABLE 1. Mean Evaluations of the Deviate and the Conformist as a Function of Environmental Noise

Confederate's opinion	Noise	No noise
Deviant	8.12	14.87
Conformist	15.75	14.68

Note. Adapted from "Group Members' Reactions to Opinion Deviates and Conformists at Varying Degrees of Proximity to Decision Deadline and of Environmental Noise," by A. W. Kruglanski and D. M. Webster, 1991, *Journal of Personality and Social Psychology, 61,* p. 216. Copyright 1991 by the American Psychological Association.

induced rather than the need for closure, we replicated our experiment (Kruglanski & Webster, 1991, Study 3) with a single exception, participants in one condition were provided an alternative way of safeguarding collective closure: the possibility of formally excluding the deviant from decision making. Specifically, participants in this condition were allowed to form a decision by majority rather than by consensus. To see whether the noise manipulation induced differences in the need for closure, we looked again at participants' expressed confidence in their opinion. As expected, the confidence ratings were significantly higher ($p < .015$) under noise than under no noise. Of greater interest, the only condition in which the deviant was downgraded was the noise-consensus cell (see Table 2). Thus, it appears that noise-induced irritability may not have accounted for derogation of the deviant. The deviant would have been upsetting enough to foster rejection only when he or she may have undermined the other members' sense of closure by constituting a dissenting voice in a significant reference group.

Additional evidence that rejection is not merely the consequence of noise-related irritability is the finding described subsequently, that the conformist might be actually evaluated more positively under noise (vs. no noise). The reason this may not have been apparent in the research described thus far is that, in those experiments, the conformist merely reiterated the normative opinion, and hence her or his statements may have lacked saliency. As a means of overcoming this problem, in our last study (Kruglanski & Webster, 1991, Study 4), the conformist was made to assume a leader's role (including initiation of conversations with the deviate and issuing of repeated reminders to the group of the consensus objective). In this study, too, participants under noise (vs. no noise) reported

TABLE 2. Mean Evaluations of the Deviate and the Conformist as a Function of Environmental Noise and Group-Decision Rule

Confederate's opinion	Consensus rule		Majority rule	
	Noise	No noise	Noise	No Noise
Deviant	11.87	21.07	18.67	20.00
Conformist	20.75	22.36	20.58	20.50

Note. Adapted from "Group Members' Reactions to Opinion Deviates and Conformists at Varying Degrees of Proximity to Decision Deadline and of Environmental Noise," by A. W. Kruglanski and D. M. Webster, 1991, *Journal of Personality and Social Psychology, 61*, p. 221. Copyright 1991 by the American Psychological Association.

higher judgmental confidence ($p < .01$). More important, whereas the deviant continued to be downgraded more ($p < .0001$) under noise (vs. no noise), the conformist was actually applauded more ($p < .01$) in this condition. Taken as a body, then, the reviewed findings support the notion that need for closure increases participants' desire for consensus and that this may lead to derogating those who hinder consensus and countenancing those who facilitate it.

Need for Closure-Based Permanence Seeking and Linguistic Abstraction Biases

If need for closure induces the tendency to seek permanent knowledge and avoid the recurrence of ambiguity, such a need should also foster bias toward general, transitionally stable knowledge. Accordingly, people under a heightened need for closure should prefer abstract descriptions and category labels over concrete (and hence situationally specific) ones.

GLOBAL ATTRIBUTIONS FOR FAILURE

Consistent with this reasoning, Mikulincer, Yinon, and Kabili (1991) found in one study, that "need for structure" assessed via a questionnaire (Naccarato, Thompson, & Parker, 1986), a notion highly akin to the need for closure, was positively correlated with stable and global self-attributions for failure assessed by the Attributional Style Questionnaire (Seligman, Abramson, Semmel, & von Baeyer, 1979). By contrast, an individual-differences measure of the "fear of invalidity" (Naccarato et al., 1986), assumed to often foster a need to avoid closure, was associated with the tendency to make specific (vs. global) attributions for failure.

In a second study conducted by Mikulincer et al. (1991), failure was induced experimentally via unsolvable problems. Here, too, participants who reported a high need for structure and a low fear of invalidity attributed failure on the problems to more global causes than did other types of participants. Furthermore, failure impaired subsequent performance on a different task for participants high in need for structure but not for those low in need for structure. Finally, in their third experiment, Mikulincer et al. (1991) varied the need for structure experimentally. Specifically, this need was induced by leading participants to believe that the research examined their ability to create "firm beliefs." Fear of invalidity was induced by telling participants that the purpose of the research was to examine their ability to make "correct judgments" about their performance. It was found that participants exposed to failure feedback exhibited performance deficits on a subsequent, unrelated task in the need for structure condition but not in the fear of invalidity condition. These results were interpreted to mean that need for structure–closure induces a globalized belief about one's low abilities that may translate, in turn, into subsequent performance deficits.

USE OF TRAIT LABELS IN COMMUNICATION

Whereas Mikulincer et al. (1991) referred to globality of beliefs about the self, a recent experiment by Boudreau, Baron, and Oliver (1992) pertained to the tendency to use global trait labels in descriptions of others. Specifically, Boudreau et al. (1992) found that an expectation to communicate impressions of a target to an expert (a clinical psychology graduate student) suppressed the proportion of traits used by college students in their person descriptions. By contrast, an expectation to communicate to a fifth grader increased the proportion of trait labels in such descriptions. Boudreau et al. interpreted these results in terms of an increased fear of invalidity (and hence lowered need for closure) when confrontation with an expert is expected and an increased need for structure–closure when a confrontation with "inferiors" (presumably less capable of drawing definite conclusions about the target on their own) is expected.

NEED FOR CLOSURE AND THE LINGUISTIC INTERGROUP BIAS

Maass and her colleagues demonstrated, in a series of studies (for a review, see Maass & Arcuri, 1992), that positive in-group and negative out-group behaviors are often described in relatively abstract terms, implying that such behaviors are associated with constant characteristics of the actor. By contrast, negative in-group and positive out-group behaviors tend to be described in relatively concrete terms, restricting the behaviors to the specific situation and affording little generalization. These phenomena have been collectively referred to as the linguistic intergroup bias. Research aimed at uncovering the underlying mechanism of the linguistic intergroup bias has obtained evidence for expectancy-based as well as motivational explanations. According to the expectancy explanation, the general stereotype of the in-group is positive and that of the out-group is negative. Thus, positive behaviors of the in-group and negative behaviors of the out-group are consistent with the abstract stereotype and, hence, could be assimilated thereto. By contrast, negative in-group and positive out-group behaviors are inconsistent with the corresponding stereotypes. Instead, they tend to be viewed as unique and described in their own, concrete terms.

The motivational explanation has been phrased in terms of in-group protection. As Maass and Arcuri (in press) put it:

> Assuming that concrete descriptions dissociate the actor from the act, whereas abstract descriptions imply that the behavior reflects a stable and enduring property of the actor, one may argue that the linguistic intergroup bias helps to portray the ingroup in a favorable light while derogating the outgroup. (p. 29)

According to the present analysis, the need for closure may constitute another motivational factor with consequences for the linguistic abstraction level at which in-group and out-group behaviors are described. Of even greater interest, those consequences may constitute a joint function of strivings for transsituational consistency and consensus that the permanence tendency based on need for closure may foster. As noted earlier, strivings for transsituational consistency should increase the abstraction level of linguistic descriptions. This tendency should apply across the board (i.e., for positive and negative behaviors of in-groups as well as out-groups). On the other hand, the permanence tendency should also enhance the striving for in-group consensus and lend the in-group particular attractiveness as a source of motivational gratification (i.e., of consensus strivings). This may increase the motivation for in-group protectiveness.

Consider how inclinations toward abstraction and in-group protectiveness may interact. With respect to positive in-group behaviors and negative out-group behaviors, those inclinations should work in concert and converge on the same outcome: enhanced abstraction level of the linguistic descriptions. However, in the case of negative in-group behaviors and positive outgroup behaviors, those inclinations should clash: The in-group protectiveness tendency should effect a reduced abstraction level, whereas the abstraction tendency should effect an increased abstraction level. In short, it is possible to predict that individuals with a high (vs. low) need for closure will adopt a higher level of linguistic abstraction when describing positive behaviors of in-group members and negative behaviors of outgroup members. The differences due to need for closure should be reduced if not completely eliminated for negative behaviors of in-group members and positive behaviors of outgroup members. These notions were examined in a recent study by Webster, Kruglanski, and Pattison (1995, Study 1).

In this research, the in-group versus out-group status of a given person was operationally defined in terms of a controversial issue, endorsement of the pro-choice or pro-life stand on abortion. At the beginning of the semester, students in an introductory psychology course at the University of Florida filled out, as part of a "mass testing" procedure, several personality measures, including the Need for Closure Scale (Webster & Kruglanski, 1994). Individuals with scores in the upper 25% of the distribution were labeled the high need for closure group, and those in the lower 25% of the distribution were labeled the low need for closure group.

The experimental sessions commenced several weeks later. The study was introduced as an investigation of impression formation. Participants were asked to fill out a questionnaire in which they provided general information about their attitudes on various issues. Embedded in this questionnaire was an item concerning the respondent's stand on abortion ("I consider myself pro-choice/ pro-life"). In addition, participants were asked to provide, to the best of their ability, transcripts of two conversations during which they persuaded another person of something. This information, in a condensed form, was presumably to be handed to another participant as a basis for impression formation about the information provider.

The participant also was asked to form an impression of another target (called Pat) on the basis of similar materials. The two conversations Pat had allegedly provided were used to manipulate the valence of the target's behavior. A positive behavior referred to an instance in which Pat selflessly persuaded a peer to accept monetary assistance, and a negative behavior referred to an instance in which Pat persuaded a friend to cheat. Participants

also learned of Pat's stance on the pro-choice–pro-life issue. After reviewing the information, participants were asked to describe, in their own words, Pat's behavior relevant to the two conversations. This constituted the main dependent variable of the research.

The design of the experiment was a $2 \times 2 \times 2$ factorial; dispositional need for closure (high vs. low) and target's group status (in-group vs. outgroup) were between-subjects variables, and target behavior (positive vs. negative) was a within-subject variable. Participants' descriptions of Pat's behaviors were analyzed via a method developed by Semin and Fiedler (1988) in which a distinction is drawn among four levels of abstraction in interpersonal terms. The most concrete terms are descriptive action verbs (e.g., "A hits B") providing objective descriptions of specific, observable events. Next in level of abstraction are interpretive action verbs that refer to larger classes of behavior (e.g., "A hurts B"), although they clearly refer to a specific behavioral instance. Even more abstract are state verbs (e.g., "A hates B") depicting enduring psychological states that apply beyond specific situations, even though they maintain a reference to a specific person (B in this case). Finally, the most abstract terms are adjectives (e.g., "A is aggressive") in that they generalize beyond a specific situation, object, or behavior.

For each phrase in the participant's descriptions, language abstraction was coded by two raters (the interrater agreement level was .89). The abstraction score was computed by a simple monotonic scheme involving the numbers 1, 2, 3, and 4 to weigh the frequency of the four respective linguistic categories. Thus, descriptive action verbs were given the weight of 1; interpretive action verbs, 2; state verbs, 3; and adjectives, 4. The resulting score was akin to an ordinal scale indicating the degree of abstractness involved in language use.

Appropriate manipulation checks indicated that participants high versus low in the dispositional need for closure exhibited the expected differences on our state-like indicators of this motivation. Thus, those high in the dispositional need for closure expressed greater confidence in their impressions of Pat than those low in the dispositional need for closure; also, they reported that forming an impression of Pat required less thought and that the impression formation task was easier. A composite index of these statelike manifestations of the need for closure yielded the expected effect of our individual-differences measure of this motivation ($p < .01$). In other words, high scorers on the Need for Closure Scale manifested, in the specific experimental situation, a response pattern assumed to be indicative of an "acute" need for closure state. The in-group–out-group manipulation also appeared to work; participants perceived the in-group target as more similar to themselves than the outgroup target ($p < .04$). The critical abstraction data are displayed in Table 3. An analysis of variance performed on these results yielded a significant main effect of the need for closure variable ($p < .01$) qualified by a significant ($p < .05$) three-way interaction among need for closure, target's group status, and behavior positivity.

Specifically, participants high (vs. low) in need for closure generally adapted a higher abstraction level ($p < .0001$) in their descriptions. However, as predicted, this difference was significant only for positive behaviors of the in-group member ($p < .05$) and negative behaviors of the out-group member ($p < .05$). The difference was much reduced and nonsignificant for negative behaviors of the in-group member and positive behaviors of the out-group member.

The foregoing data pattern is consistent with our hypothesis that the permanence tendency induced by a heightened need for closure produces both a general inclination toward linguistic abstraction and a more specific inclination toward in-group protectionism. Those inclinations may work in concert for positive behaviors of the in-group and negative behaviors of the outgroup, leading to a pronounced difference in the abstraction level adopted by participants high versus low in need for closure. The same inclinations may be in conflict, however, for negative behaviors of the in-group and positive behaviors of the out-group, reducing the difference in abstraction level adopted by participants high versus low in need for closure with respect to those behavioral categories.

In an additional experiment, we (Webster, Kruglanski, & Pattison, 1995, Study 2) used an identical task and procedure but operationalized need for closure via ambient noise. Appropriate manipulation checks indeed attested that noise heightened the need for closure in the expected ways. Participants in the noisy condition, in comparison with those in the quiet condition, reported higher confidence in their judgments and reported that the task required less thought and was easier. A composite index based on those items yielded a

TABLE 3. Language Abstractness as a Function of Need for Closure, In Group–Out-Group Status, and Behavior Valence

	Behavior valence			
	Positive		Negative	
Need for closure	In-group	Out-group	In-group	Out-group
High	3.46_a	2.37_b	2.72_b	3.49_a
Low	2.49_b	2.04_b	2.13_b	2.51_b

Note. The higher the figure, the higher the level of abstraction. Means with different subscripts differ significantly at $p < .05$. Adapted from *Motivated Language Use in Intergroup Contexts: Need for Closure Effects on the Linguistic Intergroup Bias,* by D. M. Webster, A. W. Kruglanski, and D. S. Pattison, 1995, Experiment 1, p. 32, unpublished manuscript, University of Florida.

significant main effect of noise ($p < .05$). The target's in-group versus out-group status also produced the expected differences in that participants perceived the out-group target as less similar to themselves than the in-group target ($p < .01$). The linguistic abstraction data are summarized in Table 4.

As predicted, participants under noise adopted a generally higher abstraction level in their descriptions than participants in the quiet environment. This difference was significant only for positive behaviors of the in-group member and negative behaviors of the out-group member ($p < .01$ in both cases). The abstraction-level difference proved nonsignificant for negative behaviors of the in-group member and positive behaviors of the out-group member, however. These data closely replicated those of the previous study in which need for closure was operationalized as an individual-differences variable rather than manipulated via noise.

Boundary Conditions of Urgency Versus Permanence Effects

Research described thus far addressed the joint operation of the urgency and permanence tendencies (reflected in the seizing and freezing phenomena) and the separate effects of the permanence tendency promoting strivings for consensus and consistency. It is of interest to consider now the separate effects of the urgency tendency and, more important perhaps, the boundary conditions separating its applicability domain from that of the permanence tendency. In other words, the question is, When are need for closure effects mediated by the urgency tendency, and when are they

TABLE 4. Linguistic Abstractions as a Function of Behavior Valence, Target Group Membership, and Environmental Noise

	Positive behavior						Negative behavior					
	In-group member			Out-group member			In-group member			Out-group member		
Environment	Abstraction level	s	n	Abstraction level	s	n	Abstraction level	s	n	Abstraction level	s	n
Noisy	3.521$_a$	.743	16	2.654$_b$	.661	13	2.493$_b$	.940	16	3.526$_a$	.775	13
Quiet	2.700$_b$	.798	13	2.462$_b$	.794	15	2.322$_b$	.876	13	2.600$_b$	.784	15

Note. The higher the figure, the higher the level of linguistic abstraction. Means with different subscripts differ significantly at $p < .05$. s = linguistic abstraction index (adapted from Semin and Fiedler, 1988). Adapted from *Motivated Language Use in Intergroup Contexts: Need for Closure Effects on the Linguistic Intergroup Bias,* by D. M. Webster, A. W. Kruglanski, and D. S. Pattison, 1995, Experiment 2, p. 33, unpublished manuscript, University of Florida.

mediated by the permanence tendency? As noted earlier, we assume that a relevant boundary condition here is the moment of belief crystallization, that is, the juncture during which an opinion is solidified. Heightened need for closure during the precrystallization phase should intensify seizing: At that knowledge-formation stage, high need for closure signifies a discrepancy between actual and desired states (of lacking closure on the one hand and wanting it on the other). This state of affairs should potentiate urgent seizing geared to remove the discrepancy. After crystallization, however, a heightened need for closure should intensify freezing. At that stage, the need for closure is gratified, and hence there is no discrepancy between actual and desired states. The higher the need for closure, the more psychologically important such gratification and the stronger the tendency to perpetuate it or lend it permanence via freezing.

INTERACTIVE EFFECTS OF NEED FOR CLOSURE AND INITIAL CONFIDENCE ON SOCIAL INFORMATION SEEKING

One way in which the precrystallization and postcrystallization periods may be differentiated from each other is in terms of judgmental confidence: Before crystallization, individuals' confidence in a judgment should be relatively low, whereas, after crystallization, it should be higher by comparison. Furthermore, seizing may be distinguished from freezing by the intensity and extent of the informational search. During the seizing phase, the individual may search for information rather energetically and voluminously. By contrast, during the freezing phase, she or he may be reluctant to consider new information and, if at all, do so sparingly and hesitantly.

Those notions were tested in two experiments by Kruglanski, Peri, and Zakai (1991). Participants were presented with five series of drawings. All series contained either two or four standard drawings on a given topic (a man, woman, or tree), each drawn by a different person, and a criterion drawing on a different topic (invariably a house) drawn by one of the individuals who had prepared the standard drawings. Participants' task was to identify, for each series, the particular standard drawing of the person responsible for the criterion drawing. The time allotted was 3 min. Participants stated their interim judgment after 1 min and, during the remaining 2 min, were allowed to engage in an information search concerning alleged other participants' responses. This was accomplished by having participants turn over some (or all) of the standard drawings, which bore on their backs the percentages of previous participants choosing them as the correct answers.

Initial confidence was manipulated via the number of choice alternatives presented to participants. In the high confidence condition, participants chose from among two standard drawings; in the low confidence condition, they chose from among four drawings. Appropriate checks verified that this confidence manipulation had the intended effect.

The two studies differed in how they manipulated the need for closure. Our pilot research suggested that the novel experimental task was somewhat confusing to participants, introducing a relatively high base level of the need for closure. Rather than attempting to further elevate it via experimental manipulations, we therefore decided to lower it instead in some conditions. In one study we did so by providing participants with clear criteria for assessing the drawings' similarity (the drawing's size and location on the page, its linear quality, its degree of elaboration, and the presence–absence of a depth dimension). In the second study,

TABLE 5. Mean Numbers of Drawings Turned Over and Latency of Turning Over the First Drawing

	Confidence level			
	High		Low	
Need for closure	Mean no. of drawings turned over	Latency of turning over first drawing	Mean no. of drawings turned over	Latency of turning over first drawing
	Experiment 1			
High	2.62	65.11	3.60	39.79
Low	3.94	37.01	3.00	47.84
	Experiment 2			
High	2.60	60.39	3.52	33.67
Low	4.37	19.47	2.82	49.01

Note. From "Interactive Effects of Need for Closure and Initial Confidence on Social Information Seeking," by A. W. Kruglanski, N. Peri, and D. Zakai, 1991, *Social Cognition, 9*, pp. 136 and 137. Copyright 1991 by Guilford Publications, Inc. Adapted with permission.

we did so via a fear of invalidity induction whereby mistaken judgments were to be punished by a loss of points.

Two aspects of the information search were of interest: (a) the alacrity with which participants commenced it and (b) its overall extent, that is, the number of drawings participants turned over. If low confidence typifies the precrystallization phase and high confidence typifies the postcrystallization phase, and if, moreover, the need for closure produces seizing in the former phase and freezing in the latter, need for closure should exert opposite effects on the dependent variables at the two confidence levels. In the low confidence condition, high versus low need for closure should induce seizing manifest in a relatively hurried commencement of the informational search and its relatively ample extent. By contrast, in the high confidence condition, high versus low need for closure should induce freezing manifest via relatively retarded commencement and sparse extent of the informational search. As Table 5 indicates, that is exactly what happened. Thus, initial confidence may constitute a boundary condition separating the urgency tendency underlying seizing from the permanence tendency underlying freezing.

Motivated Reactions to Persuasion in the Presence or Absence of Prior Information

The dramatically disparate effects of need for closure on information processing in the precrystallization versus postcrystallization phases should have intriguing implications for the persuasion process: In the precrystallization phase, heightened need for closure may enhance individuals' tendency to accept persuasion, whereas, in the postcrystallization phase, it may enhance their tendency to resist persuasion. Specifically, the discrepancy under a heightened need for closure between actual and desired states before crystallization should induce the tendency to urgently remove it. A persuasive communication offers a means of doing so; hence, it should be quickly accepted. By contrast, in the postcrystallization phase, an absence of discrepancy between the desire for closure and its possession should induce the tendency to maintain this pleasing state in relative permanence. This should induce a resistance to persuasion because it requires at least a temporary unfreezing of one's mind.

These notions were examined in the research by Kruglanski et al. (1993, Studies 2 and 3) referred to earlier. Dyads were formed consisting of a naive participant and a confederate. The experiment was portrayed as a psychological investigation of legal juries. A participant and a confederate were presented with the essentials of a legal case (a civil suit against an airline company by a lumber company). For half of the participants, the materials included a "legal analysis" affording the formation of a definite opinion favoring the defendant or the plaintiff. The remaining participants received no such analysis, and hence they lacked an informational base for a confident opinion.

The presence or absence of an opinion base was

crossed orthogonally with need for closure, manipulated via environmental noise produced by a rackety computer printer. Participants read the case materials, recorded their opinion (or hunch) concerning the appropriate verdict, and confronted a confederate who argued for the opposite verdict. The results supported our theoretical analysis. In the absence of the legal analysis assumed to prevent the development of a confident opinion (representing the precrystallization phase), participants evinced greater persuadability under noise than under no noise. Specifically, they tended more to change their prediscussion verdicts and spent less time arguing with the confederate in the noisy versus the quiet condition. Precisely the opposite happened when participants were given the legal analysis affording a crystallized opinion. In this condition, participants under noise (vs. no noise) evinced less persuadability. They shifted less in their verdicts and spent more time arguing with the confederate. The relevant data are summarized in Table 6.

This experiment was conceptually replicated with scores on the Need for Closure Scale as a way of operationalizing need for closure. The same data pattern was reproduced: Participants high (vs. low) in need for closure, as assessed by our scale, were more readily persuaded in instances in which absence of prior information presumably prevented them from crystallizing an opinion and were less readily persuaded in instances in which prior information made such crystallization possible (see Table 7).

THE "FIGHT RATHER THAN SWITCH" PARADOX

Note that, in both of our studies, freezing on a prior

TABLE 6. Mean Prediscussion to Postdiscussion Verdict Shifts and Time Spent in Discussion as a Function of Environmental Noise and Informational Base

	Noise		No noise	
Informational base	Verdict shift	Time spent in discussion (min)	Verdict shift	Time spent in discussion (min)
Present	1.48	6.99	3.04	6.25
Absent	4.64	3.89	3.23	5.67

Note. The higher the figures, the greater the shifts from initial to final verdict. Adapted from "Motivated Resistance and Openness to Persuasion in the Presence or Absence of Prior Information," by A. W. Kruglanski, D. M. Webster, and A. Klem, 1993, *Journal of Personality and Social Psychology; 65,* p. 866. Copyright 1993 by the American Psychological Association.

TABLE 7. Mean Prediscussion to Postdiscussion Verdict Shifts and Time Spent in Discussion as a Function of Dispositional Need for Closure and Informational Base

	Dispositional need for closure			
	High		Low	
Informational base	Verdict shift	Time spent in discussion (min)	Verdict shift	Time spent in discussion (min)
Present	1.50	7.32	3.46	5.60
Absent	4.10	4.20	2.30	6.47

Note. The higher the figures, the greater the shifts from initial to final verdict. Adapted from "Motivated Resistance and Openness to Persuasion in the Presence or Absence of Prior Information," by A. W. Kruglanski, D. M. Webster, and A. Klem, 1993, *Journal of Personality and Social Psychology, 65,* p. 870. Copyright 1993 by the American Psychological Association.

opinion under a heightened need for closure led to considerable arguing with a different-minded person. Such a tendency to "fight rather than switch" under a heightened need for closure could be paradoxical and potentially dysfunctional from the individual's own perspective. For instance, an individual who craves closure so as not to expend energy on laborious information processing (e.g., under noise) ends up expending considerable energy, in fact, on heated argument. Apparently, then, even though the goal of closure may have originally evolved on the basis of rational (energy saving) considerations, once in place it may acquire functional autonomy from those incipient considerations and prompt activities that may, ironically, defeat them.

General Discussion

Theoretical Convergence

If knowledge construction constitutes a pervasive cognitive activity typically occurring in social contexts, an epistemic motivation of key relevance to such activity should have significant consequences for diverse aspects and domains of social cognition. We have outlined a conceptual framework in which the need for (nonspecific) cognitive closure is identified as one such epistemic motivation and reviewed empirical evidence converging on a broad range of social–cognitive phenomena affected by that need.

We have defined need for closure as a desire for definite knowledge on some issue and the eschewal of confusion and ambiguity. It is assumed to represent a relatively stable dimension of individual differences as well as a situationally inducible state influenced by perceived benefits of closure (or costs of lacking it). Finally, need for closure is presumed to exert its effects via two general tendencies: the urgency tendency, reflecting the inclination to attain closure as quickly as possible, and the permanence tendency, reflecting the tendency to maintain it for as long as possible.

Jointly, the urgency and permanence tendencies may produce the inclinations to seize and then freeze on early judgmental cues. A seizing and freezing sequence under heightened need for closure may (a) reduce the extent of information processing and hypothesis generation (Mayseless & Kruglanski, 1987); (b) elevate judgmental confidence (e.g., Kruglanski & Webster, 1991; Kruglanski et al., 1993; Mayseless & Kruglanski. 1987; Webster & Kruglanski, 1994); (c) focus the information search on prototypical rather than diagnostic evidence (Kruglanski & Mayseless, 1988); (d) effect the use of early cues giving rise to impressional primacy, anchoring effects, or stereotypic judgments (Freund et al., 1985; Heaton & Kruglanski, 1991; Jamieson & Zanna, 1989; Kruglanski & Freund, 1983; Webster & Kruglanski, 1994); (e) induce the tendency to exhibit correspondence or overattribution biases (Webster, 1993); and (f) increase the tendency to assimilate judgments to primed constructs (Ford & Kruglanski, 1995; Thompson et al., 1994).

Beyond the promotion of epistemic freezing, the permanence tendency under a heightened need for closure may effect a preference for consensual knowledge unlikely to be challenged by significant others and a preference for consistent knowledge generalizable across specific situations. The greater predilection for consensus under high (vs. low) need for closure has been shown to be manifest in (a) an increased preference for a persuadable partner by participants who are high (vs. low) in need for closure and who have a prior opinion base, (b) an increased preference for a persuasive partner by participants who are high (vs. low) in need for closure and who do not have a prior opinion base (Kruglanski, Webster, & Klem, 1993), (c) rejection of opinion deviates, and (d) countenance accorded to salient conformists (Kruglanski & Webster, 1991).

The greater predilection for transsituational consistency in knowledge exhibited by participants under high (vs. low) need for closure has been shown to be manifest in the tendency to (a) as-

cribe failures to global (vs. specific) self-characteristics (Mikulincer et al., 1991), (b) communicate social knowledge using abstract trait labels (Boudreau et al., 1992), and (c) use abstract linguistic descriptions (Webster, Kruglanski, & Pattison, 1995) in reference to positive in-group behaviors and negative out-group behaviors, consistent with the linguistic intergroup bias (Maass & Arcuri, 1992). Also as predicted, these differences in abstraction were largely absent in reference to positive out-group and negative in-group behaviors. In accordance with the theory, the quest for in-group consensus due to the permanence tendency may inspire stronger in-group favoritism and protectionism under a heightened need for closure. This may instill the inclination to concretize (and hence situationally restrict) negative in-group behaviors and positive outgroup behaviors, contrary to the general preference for abstraction associated with permanence strivings under a heightened need for closure.

A significant boundary condition separating the effects of seizing from those of freezing has been hypothesized to reside at the point of belief crystallization. Before that juncture, need for closure is assumed to augment seizing; subsequent to that juncture, it is assumed to enhance freezing. Consistent with these notions, participants under a high (vs. low) need for closure have been shown to exhibit shorter latencies of information seeking and more ample information seeking when their initial confidence in a hypothesis is low (assumed to represent a precrystallization seizing) and longer latencies and sparser information seeking when their initial confidence is high (assumed to represent postcrystallization freezing; Kruglanski et al., 1991). Similarly, participants under a high need for closure have been shown to be more accepting of persuasion in conditions preventing the formation of a confident opinion (representing precrystallization seizing) and more resistant to persuasion in conditions affording the formation of an opinion (representing postcrystallization freezing; Kruglanski et al., 1993). [. . .]

REFERENCES

Asch, S. E. (1946). Forming impressions of personality. *Journal of Abnormal and Social Psychology, 41,* 258–290.

Bar-Hillel, M. (1973). On the subjective probability of compound events. *Organizational Behavior and Human Performance, 9,* 396–406.

Berlyne, D. E. (1960). *Conflict, arousal and curiosity.* New York: McGraw-Hill.

Boudreau, L. A., Baron, R., & Oliver, P. V. (1992). Effects of expected communication target expertise and timing of set on trait use in person description. *Personality and Social Psychology, Bulletin, 18,* 447–452.

Cacioppo, J. T., & Petty, R. E. (1982). The need for cognition. *Journal of Personality and Social Psychology, 42,* 116–131.

Deci, E. L., & Ryan, R. M. (1985). *Intrinsic motivation and self-determination in human behavior.* New York: Plenum.

Festinger, L. (1950). Informal social communication. *Psychological Review, 57,* 271–282.

Festinger, L. (1954). A theory of social comparison processes. *Human Relations, 7,* 117–140.

Fiske, S. T., & Neuberg, S. L. (1990). A continuum of impression formation, from category-based to individuating processes: Influences of information and motivation on attention and interpretation. In M. P. Zanna (Ed.), *Advances in experimental social psychology* (Vol. 23, pp. 1–74). New York: Academic Press.

Ford, T. E., & Kruglanski, A. W. (1995). Effects of epistemic motivations on the use of accessible constructs in social judgment. *Personality and Social Psychology Bulletin, 21,* 950–962.

Freund, T., Kruglanski, A. W., & Schpitzajzen, A. (1985). The freezing and unfreezing of impressional primacy: Effects of the need for structure and the fear of invalidity. *Personality and Social Psychology Bulletin, 11,* 479–487.

Gilbert, D. T., Pelham, B. W., & Krull, D. S. (1988). On cognitive busyness: When person perceivers meet persons perceived. *Journal of Personality and Social Psychology, 54,* 733–740.

Gollwitzer, P. M. (1990). Action phases and mind-sets. In E. T. Higgins & R. M. Sorrentino (Eds.), *Handbook of motivation and cognition. Foundations of social behavior* (Vol. 2, pp. 5–92). New York: Guilford Press.

Heaton, A., & Kruglanski, A. W. (1991). Person perception by introverts and extraverts under time pressure: Need for closure effects. *Personality and Social Psychology Bulletin, 17,* 161–165.

Heider, F. (1958). *The psychology of interpersonal relations.* New York: Wiley.

Higgins, E. T., Rholes, W. S., & Jones, C. R. (1977). Category accessibility and impression formation. *Journal of Experimental Social Psychology, 13,* 141–154.

Higgins, E. T., & Trope, Y. (1990). Activity engagement theory: Implications of multiply identifiable input for intrinsic motivation. In E. T. Higgins & R. M. Sorrentino (Eds.), *Handbook of motivation and cognition: Foundations of social behavior* (Vol. 2, pp. 229–264). New York: Guilford Press.

Hofstede, G. (1980). *Culture's consequences: International differences in work-related values.* Beverly Hills, CA: Sage.

Jamieson, D. W., & Zanna, M. P. (1989). Need for structure in attitude formation and expression. In A. Pratkanis, S. Breckler, & A. G. Greenwald (Eds.), *Attitude structure and function* (pp. 46–68). Hillsdale, NJ: Erlbaum.

Jones, E. E. (1979). The rocky road from acts to dispositions. *American Psychologist, 34,* 107–117.

Jones, E. E., & Harris, V. A. (1967). The attribution of attitudes. *Journal of Experimental Social Psychology, 3,* 1–24.

Kelley, H. H. (1971). Attribution in social interaction. In E. E. Jones, D. E. Kanause, H. H. Kelley, R. E. Nisbett, S.

Valins, & B. Weiner (Eds.), *Attribution: Perceiving the causes of behavior* (pp. 1–26). Morristown, NJ: General Learning Press.

Kruglanski, A. W. (1975). The endogenous-exogenous partition in attribution theory. *Psychological Review, 82,* 387–406.

Kruglanski, A. W. (1989). *Lay epistemics and human knowledge: Cognitive and motivational bases.* New York: Plenum.

Kruglanski, A. W. (1990a). Lay epistemic theory in social cognitive psychology. *Psychological Inquiry, 1,* 181–197.

Kruglanski, A. W. (1990b). Motivations for judging and knowing: Implications for causal attribution. In E. T. Higgins & R. M. Sorrentino (Eds.), *Handbook of motivation and cognition: Foundations of social behavior* (Vol. 2, pp. 333–368). New York: Guilford Press.

Kruglanski, A. W. (in press). Motivated social cognition: Principles of the interface. In E. T. Higgins & A. W. Kruglanski (Eds.), *Social psychology: A handbook of basic principles.* New York: Guilford Press.

Kruglanski, A. W., & Freund, T. (1983). The freezing and unfreezing of lay-inferences: Effects on impressional primacy, ethnic stereotyping and numerical anchoring. *Journal of Experimental Social Psychology, 19,* 448–468.

Kruglanski, A. W., & Mayseless, O. (1988). Contextual effects in hypothesis testing: The role of competing alternatives and epistemic motivations. *Social Cognition, 6,* 1–21.

Kruglanski, A. W., Peri, N., & Zakai, D. (1991). Interactive effects of need for closure and initial confidence on social information seeking. *Social Cognition, 9,* 127–148.

Kruglanski, A. W., & Webster, D. M. (1991). Group members' reactions to opinion deviates and conformists at varying degrees of proximity to decision deadline and of environmental noise. *Journal of Personality and Social Psychology, 61,* 212–225.

Kruglanski, A. W., Webster, D. M., & Klem, A. (1993). Motivated resistance and openness to persuasion in the presence or absence of prior information. *Journal of Personality and Social Psychology, 65,* 861–876.

Kunda, Z. (1990). The case for motivated reasoning. *Psychological Bulletin, 106,* 480–498.

Luchins, A. S. (1957). Primacy-recency in impression formation. In C. I. Hovland (Ed.), *The order of presentation in persuasion* (pp. 33–61). New Haven, CT: Yale University Press.

Maass, A., & Arcuri, L. (1992). The role of language in the persistence of stereotypes. In G. Semin & K. Fiedler (Eds.), *Language, interaction and social cognition* (pp. 129–143). Newbury Park, CA: Sage.

Maass, A., & Arcuri, L. (in press). Language and stereotyping. In N. Macrae, M. Hewstone, & C. Stangor (Eds.), *The foundations of stereotypes and stereotyping.* New York: Guilford Press.

Mayseless, O., & Kruglanski, A. W. (1987). What makes you so sure? Effects of epistemic motivations on judgmental confidence. *Organizational Behavior and Human Decision Processes, 39,* 162–183.

Mikulincer, M., Yinon, A., & Kabili, D. (1991). Epistemic needs and learned helplessness. *European Journal of Personality, 5,* 249–258.

Naccarato, M. F., Thompson, M. M., & Parker, K. (1986). *Update on the development of the need for structure and fear of invalidity scales.* Unpublished manuscript.

Neuberg, S. L., & Newsom, J. (1993). Individual differences in chronic motivation to simplify: Personal need for structure and social-cognitive processing. *Journal of Personality and Social Psychology, 65,* 113–131.

Pervin, L. A. (Ed.). (1989). *Cool concepts in personality and social psychology.* Hillsdale. NJ: Erlbaum.

Quattrone, G. A. (1982). Overattribution and unit formation: When behavior engulfs the person. *Journal of Personality and Social Psychology, 14,* 593–607.

Schachter, S. (1951). Deviation, rejection and communication. *Journal of Abnormal and Social Psychology, 46,* 190–207.

Seligman, M. E. P., Abramson, L. Y., Semmel, A., & von Baeyer, C. (1979). Depressive attributional style. *Journal of Abnormal Psychology, 88,* 242–247.

Semin, G. R., & Fiedler, K. (1988). The cognitive functions of linguistic categories in describing persons: Social cognition and language. *Journal of Personality and Social Psychology, 54,* 558–568.

Swann, W. B., Jr. (1990). To be known or to be adored? The interplay of self enhancement and self-verification. In E. T. Higgins & R. M. Sorrentino (Eds.), *Handbook of motivation and cognition: Foundations of social behavior* (Vol. 2, pp. 408–448). New York: Guilford Press.

Tetlock, P. E. (1985). Accountability: A social check on the fundamental attribution error. *Social Psychology Quarterly, 48,* 227–236.

Thompson, E. P., Roman, R. J., Moscovitz, G. B., Chaiken, S., & Bargh, J. A. (1994). Accuracy motivation attenuates covert priming: The systematic reprocessing of social information. *Journal of Personality and Social Psychology, 66,* 474–489.

Trope, Y., & Bassok, M. (1983). Information gathering strategies in hypothesis testing. *Journal of Experimental Social Psychology, 19,* 560–576.

Trope, Y., & Higgins, E. T. (1993). The "what," "when" and "how" of dispositional inference: New answers and new questions. *Personality and Social Psychology Bulletin, 19,* 493–500.

Tversky, A., & Kahneman, D. (1974). Judgment under uncertainty: Heuristics and biases. *Science, 185,* 1124–1131.

Vallacher, R. R., & Nowak, A. (in press). The emergence of dynamical social psychology. *Psychological Inquiry.*

Webster, D. M. (1993). Motivated augmentation and reduction of the overattribution bias. *Journal of Personality and Social Psychology, 65,* 261–271.

Webster, D. M., & Kruglanski, A. W. (1994). Individual differences in need for cognitive closure. *Journal of Personality and Social Psychology, 67,* 1049–1062.

Webster, D. M., Kruglanski, A. W., & Pattison, D. S. (1995). *Motivated language use in intergroup contexts: Need for closure effects on the linguistic intergroup bias.* Unpublished manuscript, University of Florida, Gainesville.

Webster, D. M., Richter, L., & Kruglanski, A. W. (1995). *On leaping to conclusions when feeling tired: Mental fatigue effects on impressional primacy.* Unpublished manuscript, University of Maryland, College Park.

Wanting from Knowing

As noted earlier, the relations between wanting and knowing are fully bi-directional: not only does wanting affect knowing, but knowing affects wanting as well. People learn about how the world works and this determines their motivated strivings. In other words, they possess (subjective) knowledge about possible future events and outcome contingencies, and they know pretty well how they feel about things. In Part 3 we already discussed how perceived expectancies and values affect the attainment of goals. However, the effects of knowledge on motivation are more general than that. Primarily, an individual's motivation depends on attributions that he or she has made about the outcomes of past behaviors. Attribution of a failure to a lack of effort, for example, may motivate the individual to expend greater effort in order to attain the desired objective. Attribution of the same failure to a lack of ability, by contrast, may dispose the individual to give up on the goal in question. The relations among outcome-attribution, motivation, and affect are explored in the paper by Weiner and Kukla (1970) featured in the present section.

The patterns of causal attributions that people make for their failures or successes may derive from their lay theories about various psychological phenomena (Heider, 1958). For example, people can have different theories about the nature of human intelligence. They may believe that intelligence is a controllable and increasable quality; that is, subscribe to an incremental theory of intelligence. Alternatively, they may believe that intelligence constitutes a fixed and uncontrollable trait; that is, they may subscribe to an entity theory of intelligence. The theory of intelligence to which people subscribe can have important motivational consequences mediated by their attributions of failures and successes. Those with an entity perspective may view failures as evidence of their low ability;

this may arouse considerable negative affect and motivate the individuals in question to give up on a task. By contrast, individuals with an incremental perspective may see failure outcomes as malleable, and hence increase their efforts or seek alternative strategies so that their goal might be attained. The paper by Dweck and Leggett (1988) featured in this section explores the relations between incremental and entity theories and persons' experiences and actions in achievement settings.

The papers discussed so far have dealt with the motivational consequences of attributing performance outcomes; that is, successes or failures on tasks. Yet, other types of attribution, too, can have significant motivational effects. An intriguing case concerns the attribution and potential misattribution of physiological arousal (Schachter & Singer, 1962). Arousal is an integral part of motivational states. One is typically aroused, or excited, when strongly motivated to attain some goal; for example, when one is in the presence of a person whom one wants to impress, or when confronted with a danger that one wants to avoid. However, arousal or excitation might also occur for entirely nonmotivational reasons. For instance, it could be the results of a chemical one has ingested (e.g., caffeine or alcohol) or constitute the product of a strenuous physical activity. The interesting phenomenon in this connection is that persons often are unaware of the true origin of their arousal, and hence can misattribute it to a motivation that is evoked in a given situational context.

In the last paper featured in this section, Zillmann, Johnson, and Day (1974) propose an excitation-transfer theory where excitation or arousal decays slowly, so the residual excitation from a prior activity can combine with the excitatory response to a subsequent activity. Because people tend to attribute their current excitation level to the current activity, their emotional response to the current activity will be intensified. Zillmann et al. (1974) demonstrate that the motivation to respond to a provocation with aggression is greater following an exercise-produced arousal if the latter is misattributed to one's response to the provocation.

REFERENCES

Dweck, C. S., & Leggett, E. L. (1988). A social cognitive approach to motivation and personality. *Psychological Reviews, 95,* 256–273.

Heider, F. (1958). *The psychology of interpersonal relations.* New York: Wiley.

Schachter, S., & Singer, J. E. (1962). Cognitive, social and physiological determinants of emotional state. *Psychological Review, 69,* 379–399.

Weiner, B., & Kukla, A. (1970). An attributional analysis of achievement motivation. *Journal of Personality and Social Psychology, 15,* 1–20.

Zillmann, D., Johnson, R. C., & Day, K. D. (1974). Attribution of apparent arousal and proficiency of recovery from sympathetic activation affecting excitation transfer to aggressive behavior. *Journal of Experimental Social Psychology, 10,* 503–515.

Suggested Readings

Andersen, S. M., Reznik, I., & Manzella, L. M. (1996). Eliciting facial affect, motivation, and expectancies in transference: Significant-other representations in social relations. *Journal of Personality and Social Psychology, 71,* 1108–1129.

Bem, D. J. (1967). Self-perception: An alternative interpretation of cognitive dissonance phenomena. *Psychological Review, 74,* 183–200.

Higgins, E. T., Trope, Y., & Kwon, J. (1999). Augmentation and undermining from combining activities: The role of choice in activity engagement theory. *Journal of Experimental Social Psychology, 35,* 285–307.

Lepper, M. R., Greene, D., & Nisbett, R. E. (1973). Undermining children's intrinsic interest with extrinsic reward: a test of the overjustification hypothesis. *Journal of Personality and Social Psychology, 28,* 129–137.

Schachter, S., & Singer, J. E. (1962). Cognitive, social and physiological determinants of emotional state. *Psychological Review, 69,* 379–399.

Weary, G., Elbin, S. D., & Hill, M. G. (1987). Attribution and social comparison processes in depression. *Journal of Personality and Social Psychology, 52,* 605–610.

Zajonc, R. B. (1980). Feeling and thinking: Preferences need no inferences. *American Psychologist, 35,* 151–175.

READING 21

An Attributional Analysis of Achievement Motivation

Bernard Weiner and Andy Kukla • Department of Psychology, University of California

Editors' Notes

The authors propose that causal attributions mediate between individuals' level of achievement motivation and their performance. Success could be attributed to high effort or high ability and failure could be attributed to low effort or low ability. Do these alternative attributions influence the evaluations of the performance outcomes by self and others? The results of one set of studies indicate that attributions of high effort generally yield more positive evaluations by self or others than attributions of high ability. For a task in which performance could be attributed to either luck or skill, another study found that participants with high achievement motivation were more likely to attribute their success on the task to high skill and their failure on the task to low effort than participants with low achievement motivation. A final study found that internal attributions for success increased as the task became more difficult, and internal attributions for failure increased as the task became easier. An attributional analysis of achievement motivation suggests that individuals high (versus low) in achievement motivation: 1) have stronger motivation to approach achievement tasks because they are more likely to attribute success to themselves, which increases their pride in success, 2) persist more after failure because they are more likely to attribute it to lack of effort, and 3) prefer tasks of intermediate difficulty because performance on such tasks (whether success or failure) is more likely to be attributed internally than externally, thus providing more information about the self.

Discussion Questions

1. How do attributions of ability versus effort influence evaluations of self and others?
2. According to an attributional analysis, why do individuals high in achievement motivation prefer tasks of intermediate difficulty?

Authors' Abstract

Six experiments are reported which relate achievement motivation to causal ascription. The first three experiments revealed that the evaluation of achievement-related outcomes is positively related to the amount of expended effort, but inversely related to level of ability. Evaluative differences between social classes (Experiment II), and disparities between self- and other-judgments (Experiment III) also were examined. In Experiments IV and V individual differences in locus of causality were related to level of achievement needs. The results of these investigations indicate that individuals high in resultant achievement motivation are more likely to take personal responsibility for success than individuals low in achievement motivation. Clear differences in perceived responsibility for failure were not exhibited between the two motive groups. Finally, in Experiment VI risk-preference behavior and Atkinson's theory of achievement motivation were construed in attribution theory language. It was contended that cognitions about causality mediate between level of achievement needs and performance.

The relationship between causal ascription and achievement motivation is examined in this study. The reported experiments were guided by two distinguishable, albeit overlapping, approaches to the study of psychological causation. One approach, based primarily on the writings of social psychologists such as Heider (1958), Jones and Davis (1965), and Kelley (1967), emphasizes the environmental factors or stimulus conditions which affect the formation of attributions. Frequently, these psychologists have been concerned with the processes which influence interpersonal perception; that is, attributions about others generally are dependent variables. The second approach, which is exemplified in the work of Crandall and her colleagues (Crandall, Katkovsky, & Crandall, 1965; Crandall, Katkovsky, & Preston, 1962) and Rotter (1966), focuses upon the relationship between individual differences in perceived personal causation, or "internal versus external" control of events, and a variety of behavioral consequents. That is, attribution or self-perception is considered to be an independent variable. Both the social psychological and individual difference attempts to study attribution, or the use of causal ascription as a dependent or independent variable, are employed here to provide insights concerning the determinants of achievement-related strivings.

Structure of Attributions and Achievement Evaluation

In his "naive analysis of action," Heider (1958) specified two factors which in part determine the

outcome of an event. One variable he labeled "power"; included under this heading are personal characteristics such as ability, intelligence, etc., which indicate whether a goal "can" be attained. The second determinant of action identified by Heider was motivation, or "trying." Heider postulated that both "can" and "try" are necessary to reach a desired goal.

The intuitively reasonable dichotomy between ability (can) and motivation (try) has proven useful in the analysis of many aspects of behavior. For example, Schmitt (1964) demonstrated that the invocation of moral obligation is contingent upon a deficiency in the try rather than can behavioral determinant. Schmitt's study revealed that subjects rarely invoke moral obligations when, for example, a hypothetical individual does not repay a debt because he is unable yet willing to do so. Yet moral codes frequently were designated as broken when the debt was not repaid when the lendee was monetarily able, but unwilling, to return the money. Correspondingly, a recent survey (Tietze & Lewit, 1969) has revealed that abortions sought when a child is merely not wanted are less likely to be condoned than those undertaken because the family also is financially incapable of support. (See Maselli & Altrocchi, 1969, for a more detailed discussion of the relationship between perceived causality and moral judgment.)

A similar elemental analysis into can and try components of achievement-related behavior is undertaken in the initial three investigations reported in this article. Success at an achievement goal may be attributed to unusual effort and/or special ability, while failure might indicate a lack of motivation and/or ability. The experiments examine whether these disparate patterns of perceived causality affect subsequent evaluations (rewards or punishments, and pride or shame) of achievement activities.

Experiment I

Method

Twenty paid male students enrolled at the University of California, Los Angeles, participated in a "simulated teaching" experiment. The subjects were told, in part:

> Assume for a moment that you are a teacher in a grade-school classroom. You have given an exam and now must convey some feedback to the pupils. You know each student's ability [Yes or No], and the effort which each has expended [Yes or No]. And you know the outcome of their exams [Excellent, Fair, Borderline, Moderate Failure, or Clear Failure]. The feedback which you dispense is in the form of stars: gold stars are a reward, and red stars a punishment. You can give 1–5 gold stars, 1–5 red stars, or neither gold nor red stars. A student never receives both gold and red stars.

Each subject then evaluated all 20 (2 Ability × 2 Effort × 5 Outcome) experimental conditions. Four different randomized orders of experimental conditions were used.

Results

Figure 1 shows the mean reward and punishment administered in the five outcome conditions to the four hypothetical pupil groups—ability and motivation (AM); ability and no motivation (A – M); no ability and motivation (– AM); and neither ability nor motivation (– A – M). The figure indicates that the amount of reward and punishment was directly related to the exam outcome (0; $F = 108.22$, $df = 4/76$, $p < .001$). Further, Figure 1 reveals that the two groups motivated to perform were rewarded more, and punished less, than the two groups which did not expend effort ($F = 25.43$, $df = 1/19$, $p < .001$). In addition, students with less

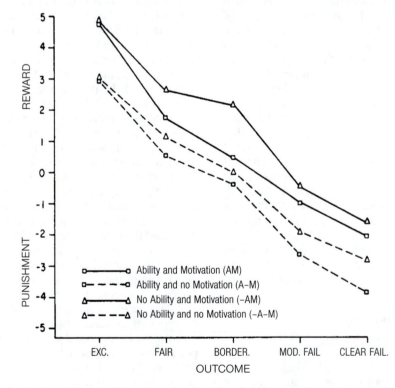

FIGURE 1 ■ Evaluation (reward and punishment) as a function of pupil ability, motivation, and examination outcome (relatively upper-class college sample).

ability received more positive and less negative feedback than the high ability students ($F = 24.10$, $df = 1/19$, $p < .001$). Additional inspection of the figure indicates that among the motivated (M) groups, low ability (– A) pupils were evaluated more favorably than high ability (A) pupils ($t = 5.55$, $df = 19$, $p < .001$). Similarly, among the nonmotivated (–M) groups, –A pupils again received more favorable evaluations than the A pupils ($t = 2.71$, $df = 19$, $p < .02$). Correspondingly, within both the A and –A groups, evaluation of the M group exceeded that of the –M group (respectively, $t = 4.36$, $df = 19$, $p < .001$; $t = 4.79$, $df = 19$, $p < .001$). Further data analysis also indicates that there was a O × A × M interaction ($F = 3.36$, $df = 4/76$, $p < .05$). That is, among the M groups, the difference in reward for success between the A and –A groups was greater than the difference in punishment for failure. Conversely, among the –M soups, the disparity in punishment for failure between the A and –A groups was greater than the inequality in reward.

One further finding is that over all conditions there was a tendency toward greater reward than punishment; 18 of the 20 subjects dispensed more gold than red stars ($p < .001$).

Discussion

The results revealed that within this simulation setting, both motivation and ability influence the appraisal of achievement behavior. Yet the try and can behavioral determinants acted in a diverse manner: *high* motivation and *low* ability both resulted in augmented performance evaluation. The complex interactions within the data suggest the cognitions which might be mediating these cultural biases, or achievement value systems. One prevalent cultural belief is that the individual who is able to overcome personal handicaps and avoid failure is especially worthy of praise. This would account for the results indicating that –AM pupils particularly received more positive feedback for success or borderline performance than the AM pupils. Another frequently expressed belief is that the individual who fails because he does not attempt to realize his potential is to be reproached, as though it were immoral not to utilize one's capacities. Hence, the A – M group would be expected to receive more negative feedback for failure than the –A –M group. (Perhaps the reader will be disconcerted with the knowledge that there

are adverse consequences of possessing ability. However, high ability people are more likely to meet with success, and can capitalize on the outcome source of rewards.)

There are numerous interpretations of the additional finding that there is a tendency to distribute more reward than punishment. The subjects in this study might intuitively have understood what psychologists also have contended—that rewards are a more effective and efficient method of behavioral control than punishments (see Ring & Kelley, 1963). On the other hand, the greater use of reward might respect a generalized defensive operation elicited in the valuation of failure. This interpretation will be discussed again later.

TEACHER EXPECTANCY AND PERFORMANCE

A recent study which has generated much interest and speculation (Rosenthal & Jacobson, 1968) involved the arousal of false teacher expectations concerning the abilities of certain students. Teachers were told that a selected subset of students, who actually had been chosen randomly, would exhibit unusual intellectual growth. Subsequent testing of these students allegedly revealed that they did display greater intellectual development than control students not paired with the fraudulent expectancies.

The teacher behaviors which gave rise to these stated intellectual gains is yet unknown. Heider's analysis, considered in conjunction with the present study, does provide some plausible explanations. The false information given to the teachers conveyed that the selected students had special abilities. Therefore, poor scholastic performance among this group could reasonably be attributed to a lack of motivation.

Attributing failure to motivational deficits has a number of consequents. The data presented here demonstrate that the high ability children mould be castigated more for any failures. Perhaps differential punishment indirectly led to enhanced intellectual growth. Alternately, it is possible that attributing failure to motivation, rather than to a lack of ability, facilitates subsequent achievement strivings. Attributing failure to a lack of ability implies that success is not possible in the future, while attributions to insufficient effort intimate that instrumental action can be undertaken which will lead to goal attainment. (Of course, such an explanation assumes that the children introject the ascriptions of their teachers.) In sum, the intent of these interpretations is to convey that false ability expectancies have implications for teacher attributions concerning the causes of success and failure, and these attributions conceivably can influence subsequent performance.

Experiment II

Method

Experiment II repeated the procedure outlined in the initial study. Subjects were 18 male high school students from a lower-lower- and lower-middle-class community. Hence, the experiment examined the generality of the value systems expressed by the relatively middle- and upper-class college students participating in Experiment I.

Results

Figure 2 shows that there again were significant evaluative main effects attributable to outcome and motivation (respectively, $F = 92.42$, $df = 4/68$, $p < .001$; $F = 35.25$, $df = 1/17$, $p < .001$); the main effect of ability did not approach significance ($F < 1$).

Further analysis reveals that within both the A and −A groups the M pupils received higher evaluations than the −M pupils (respectively, $t = 4.40$, $df = 17$, $p < .001$, $t = 6.84$, $df = 17$, $p < .001$). The O × A × M interaction displayed in the initial experiment was not exhibited ($F < 1$). However, again the majority of the subjects (12 of the 18) dispensed more reward than punishment.

Discussion

The pattern of results revealed that the lower-class sample in this experiment placed as great a value on outcome, and a relatively greater positive appraisal for motivation, than did the comparatively upper-class sample in the initial study. In addition, motivation had a much greater influence on evaluation than did ability (see Jones & deCharms, 1957). Perhaps it is rational to be influenced differentially by the try and can determinants of behavior. Ability is a dispositional or invariant property of the individual; it remains relatively constant over time. On the other hand, effort presumably can be altered, and therefore may be influenced by contingent rewards and punishments. If this lower-class group is sensitized to, or persuaded by, the "deficient motivation" attribution which

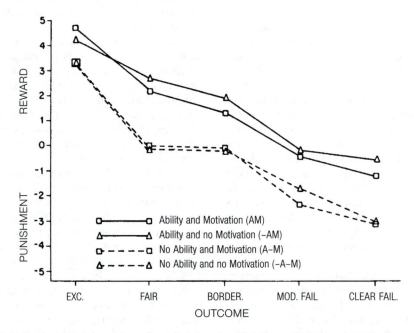

FIGURE 2 ■ Evaluation (reward and punishment) as a function of pupil ability, motivation, and examination outcome (relatively lower-class high school sample).

often is used to characterize them, then they might be likely to attend to the try determinant when evaluating the behavior of others. However, clearly more data are needed before the evaluative differences displayed by the two samples can be reasonably discussed.

Experiment III

Method

Experiment III introduced two additional variables for study. First, the subjects were female student teachers, rather than the college and high school male students used in Experiments I and II. The change in subject population provided an opportunity to examine again the generality of the functions observed in the prior two studies. Further, this subject population is more likely to reveal information about behaviors which might be exhibited in actual classroom situations. Secondly, a new experimental condition was introduced. One group of subjects ($n = 47$) received the same general instructions as the subjects in the prior two experiments, although they were allowed to give 1–10 gold or red stars as reward or punishment. A second group ($n = 41$) was instructed to estimate how much pride or shame they personally would experience in the various experimental conditions. A 10-point scale also was used to represent positive and negative affect.

Results and Discussion

The pattern of results in the evaluation condition is consistent with that obtained in the prior two experiments, and will merely be summarized here. There again are significant main effects due to outcome and motivation (respectively, $F = 309.21$, $df = 4/184$, $p < .001$; $F = 101.92$, $df = 1/46$, $p < .001$). While ability once more had a significant effect ($F = 17.42$, $df = 1/46$, $p < .001$), as in Experiment I, its magnitude was not as great as that of motivation. Again within both the A and –A groups, M pupils were evaluated more highly than the –M pupils (respectively, $t = 8.76$, $df = 46$, $p < .001$; $t = 9.57$, $df = 46$, $p < .001$). Similarly, within the M and –M groups there was greater evaluation of the –A than A hypothetical students (respectively, $t = 6.61$, $df = 46$, $p < .001$; $t = 2.02$, $df = 46$, $p < .05$). The O × A × M interaction did not approach significance ($F < 1$). In addition, the vast

majority of the student-teachers (39 of 47, $p < .001$) allocated more rewards than punishments.

In sum, across three subject groups there were significant main effects of outcome and motivation, and a trend toward a main effect of ability which was of lesser magnitude than that of motivation. The relative strength and consistency of these findings suggest that intense and widely held beliefs within this culture are being expressed in this simulation experiment.

Analysis of the introspective reports concerning pride and shame tell a similar story, yet yield additional information (see Figure 3). As in the prior analysis, there were significant main effects due to outcome, motivation, and ability (respectively, $F = 180.32$, $df = 4/160$, $p < .001$; $F = 42.52$, $df = 1/40$, $p < .001$; $F = 87.31$, $df = 1/40$, $p < .001$). There were also highly significant differences ($t < .001$) between the various ability and motivational groups. However, in contrast with the evaluate-other data, the introspective reports concerning self-punishment (shame) indicate that shame primarily is experienced when failure occurs given ability ($t = 5.92$, $df = 46$, $p < .001$), while effort has a secondary, although quite significant, influence on punishment ($t = 3.43$, $df = 46$, $p < .001$).

Thus far the evaluate-others and self-affect conditions have been examined independently, and some similar and contrasting inferences drawn from these data. But the individual reward and punishment functions of the four hypothetical pupil groups have not been compared between the affect and evaluation conditions. Direct comparisons between these two experimental conditions are vulnerable because one must impose rather questionable assumptions concerning the comparability of the scales and the underlying dimensions. However, the individual comparisons (see Figure 4) do provide food for thought, and actually may reflect the true state of affairs.

Figure 4 shows the magnitude of the reward-punishment and pride-shame ratings in the four ability-motivation groupings. The figure indicates that the amount of reported pride associated with extreme success is identical with the magnitude of external reward in all four comparisons. That this is not merely a ceiling effect is shown in the nonmotivated group comparisons. But the degree of pride for moderate success, and the degree of shame given any failure, consistently are less favorable than the magnitude of the external evaluation. If these comparisons are appropriate, then

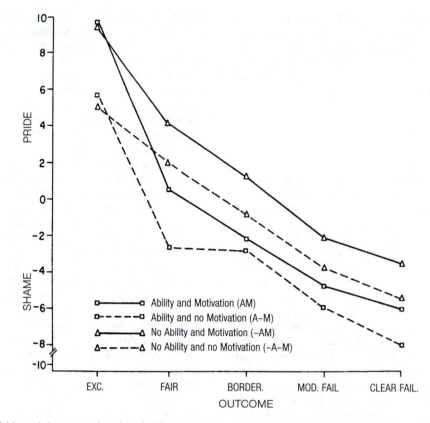

FIGURE 3 ■ Pride and shame as a function of ability, motivation, and examination outcome.

the negative affect given unfavorable outcomes is more severe than others may think it ought to be. Indeed, the superego appears to be a harsh master. Further, the possibility exists that external punishment for failure really has little negative reinforcement value in achievement-related contexts, for one's internalized self-punishment system is probably more salient, more efficient, and more cruel. It is of interest to note that 69 of 85 subjects (81%) in the three experiments dispensed more reward than punishment over all conditions, while only 16 of 41 subjects (39%) reported that they felt more overall pride than shame ($z_{diff} = 4.65, p < .001$).

FURTHER IMPLICATIONS FOR THE STUDY OF ACHIEVEMENT MOTIVATION

The results concerning the differential determinants of pride and shame have important implications for current conceptions of achievement motivation. Atkinson (1964) has contended that the

achievement motive represents a capacity to experience pride in the attainment of achievement-related goals. Yet the present data indicate that pride in successful accomplishment primarily is a function of perceived effort. Further, effort is an internal causal attribute. Therefore, an individual high in achievement motivation might be conceptualized as one who has the capacity to attribute success to internal determinants. That is, the achievement motive could be considered a complex cognitive system in which self-attributions for success play a vital role (see Heckhausen, 1967). [. . .]

Experiment V

The experiments reported thus far have not included any direct behavioral measures in support of their conclusions. Experiments I–III involved role-playing situations, while Experiment IV related data of various self-report assessment instru-

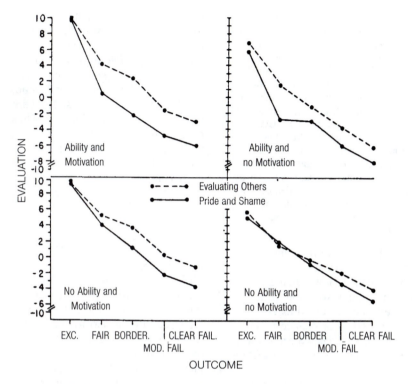

FIGURE 4 ■ Comparisons of self- and other-evaluation within the four hypothetical ability and motivation groups.

ments. In Experiment V behavioral evidence gathered in a "real" situation is finally presented.

Experiment V was guided by the prior results indicating that individuals high in achievement motivation tend to attribute success to themselves, rather than to external sources. An alternate statement of this relationship is that individuals high in achievement motivation perceive successful outcomes as determined by skill or effort, rather than luck. On the other hand, individuals low in achievement motivation relatively tend to attribute success to external factors. That is, the data intimate that they are inclined to perceive positive outcomes as determined by chance or fate. In Experiment V these relations were examined by employing an ambiguous task in which performance might be perceived as determined by either luck or skill. Task perception was then related to achievement outcome and level of achievement-related needs. The study also allowed further investigation of the yet undetermined association between causal ascription and achievement motivation given an unsuccessful outcome.

Procedure

Subjects were 71 males enrolled in introductory psychology and required to participate in psychological experiments. The study was conducted on nine occasions with groups varying in size from 7 to 10.

The subjects were first given a modified version of the self-report measure of resultant achievement motivation described in Experiment IV (Mehrabian, 1969). They were then read the following task instructions:

> I have in front of me a list of 50 numbers, either 0 or 1, in an order which is unknown to you. Your task is to guess whether the next number on my list is either 0 or 1. You will write down your guess on the answer sheet which I have passed out, and then I will tell you what the number actually was. If your guess is correct, place a check on the line next to it. You will then be asked to make your next guess, and so on until all 50 guesses have been completed. Now this is a test of your *synthetic* as opposed to your *analytic* ability. By this we mean that there is no one definite pattern, like

010101, that you could easily detect and get all the answers correct from then on. But the list also is not random. Instead there are certain general trends and tendencies in the list—perhaps a greater frequency of one kind of pattern over another. To the extent that you can become sensitive to those tendencies, you can make your score come out consistently above chance. Of course, your score also will be heavily influenced by luck. Even if you learn just exactly as much about the patterns as we expect, you could get a much higher total score just by being lucky in your guessing. Similarly, your score could be much lower just because of bad luck. To get a really accurate idea of just where you stood, you would have to take the test a number of times so that the good and bad luck would average out.

The list of 0s and 1s read to the subjects was randomly constructed, so that the outcome was determined solely by chance. However, the instructions created an ambiguous situation which allowed performance to be perceived as either attributable to skill and effort or chance (also see Jenkins & Ward, 1965). Subjects were allowed 15 seconds to make each guess, with the correct answer read after each trial.

Upon completion of the task, subjects added up their total number of correct responses. They were then instructed to estimate how many points of that total were due to "skill rather than lucky guessing." In addition, they were asked to estimate "what score [they] would expect to obtain if [they] performed the task again, using a new set of 0s and 1s, but with the same general trends and tendencies." Finally, the subjects also were instructed to judge "how hard [they] had tried to succeed at the task," and to indicate their answer on a 10-point scale anchored at the extremes ("I did not try at all" and "I tried as hard as I possibly could"). Thus, the dependent measures included estimation of task skill, future performance expectation, and perceived expended effort.

COMPOSITION OF THE SUBGROUPS

The 71 subjects were divided at the median into high-(H) and low-(L) achievement-oriented groups. They were further placed into success (Su), failure (Fa), and intermediate (In) conditions on the basis of their performance. The Su condition was defined as a score in the upper one-third of the total distribution of scores obtained on the guessing task, while the Fa condition comprised subjects falling in the lower one-third of the outcome distribution. This resulted in scores of 27 or

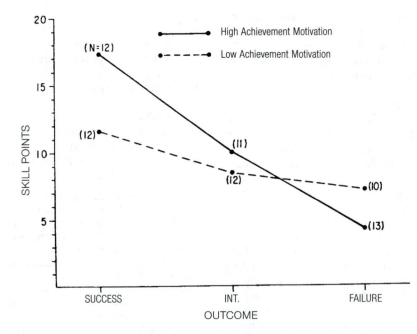

FIGURE 5 ■ Number of skill points ascribed as a function of motive classification and task performance.

more included within the Su condition, and scores of 24 or less included within the Fa condition. Within each of the three conditions there were no significant differences between the scores obtained by the H and L groups.

Results

SKILL POINTS

The mean number of points ascribed to skill in the six experimental groups is shown in Figure 6. The figure indicates that the number of skill points increased directly with total score ($F = 16.28$, $df = 2/65$, $p < .001$; see Jenkins & Ward, 1965). Of greater importance in the present context was the visible interaction between task outcome and level of achievement needs ($F = 3.92$, $df = 2/65$, $p < .05$). The H subjects in the Su condition attributed more skill points to themselves than the L subjects ($t = 2.12$, $df = 21$, $p < .05$). On the other hand, in the Fa condition L subjects assigned themselves more skill points than the H subjects ($t = 1.82$, $df = 21$, $p < .10$), although this difference failed to reach an acceptable significance level. Further comparisons of the data within the motive groups and between conditions indicate that H subjects clearly differentiated the number of skill points which they took credit for in the Su and Fa conditions ($t = 5.88$, $df = 23$, $p < .001$). However, among the L subjects the difference in perceived skill between the two experimental conditions, while approaching significance ($t = 1.90$, $df = 21$, $p < .10$), was not as marked.

EXPECTED RETEST SCORE

The expected retest performance increased directly with the level of original performance ($F = 2.43$, $df = 2/65$, $p < .10$; see Table 4). However, neither the level of achievement motivation, nor the Motivation × Outcome interaction, significantly predicted task expectancy (respectively, $F = 1.70$, $df = 1/65$, $p < .20$; $F < 1$).

While in the Su condition mean expected retest scores of the H and L subjects were not significantly different with a parametric analysis ($t = 1.52$, $df = 23$, $p < .20$), nonparametric analysis of these data showed that 9 of the 12 H subjects expected to improve on the subsequent trials, while only 2 of the 13 L subjects believed that they would attain a better score on the next series ($p < .01$, Fisher

Table 1. Mean Expected Retest Score and Effort Ratings in the Success, Intermediate, and Failure Conditions among Subjects Classified as High or Low in Resultant Achievement Motivation

Experimental condition	Retest score		Perceived effort	
	High achieve-ment	Low achieve-ment	High achieve-ment	Low achieve-ment
Success	30.33	28.39	8.25	7.69
Intermediate	29.50	28.09	7.42	6.73
Failure	27.08	27.60	5.31	7.10

exact test). Differences in retest expectation did not approach significance within the Fa ($t < 1$) or In ($t = 1.18$, $df = 21$, $p < .20$) conditions.

EFFORT

Ratings of effort systematically varied as a function of the outcome of the task ($F = 5.58$, $df = 2/65$, $p < .01$; see Table 4). Subjects tended to believe that they tried harder after having experienced success than failure. The reader should note that this Effort × Outcome association appeared even though performance objectively was determined only by chance. There was again no main effect due to level of achievement-related needs ($F < 1$). There was, however, a significant interaction between level of achievement motivation and task outcome ($F = 3.42$, $df = 2/65$, $p < .05$). Although H subjects did not state that they tried significantly harder than the L subjects in the Su or In conditions ($t < 1$), they did rate their effort significantly lower than the L subjects within the Fa condition ($t = 2.53$, $df = 21$, $p < .05$). Further analysis of these data revealed that L subjects perceived little difference between their effort in the two extreme conditions ($t < 1$), whereas H subjects believed that they tried significantly harder in the Su than in the Fa condition ($t = 4.44$, $df = 23$, $p < .001$).

Discussion

The data again support the hypothesis that individuals high in achievement motivation are more internal with respect to success, that is, perceive they have more ability and expend more effort, than subjects low in achievement motivation. The positive recency effect which is exhibited by subjects high in level of achievement needs, or their expected increment in performance following success, and the negative recency effect which characterizes subjects low in achievement motivation, or their expected decrements in performance after success, support the notion that the motive groups relatively attribute positive achievement results to different sources. The data indicate that the high-achievement group perceives the task outcome as primarily determined by skill, and hence is likely to believe that success in this situation is internally controlled. The negative recency effect displayed by subjects in the L group reveals that they perceived success to be strongly influenced by good luck, or externally controlled.

Although significant differences between the motive groups were not observed in the Fa condition, the general pattern of results do lend themselves to a plausible interpretation. It can be contended that the fewer skill points which the H subjects attributed to themselves after failure suggests that they were prone to perceive the failed task as determined primarily by fate rather than by skill. On the other hand, the greater skill points allocated by the L than H group given failure suggests that the L subjects may have been more likely to hold themselves responsible for the poor level of performance, inasmuch as the outcome was internally controlled. In sum, the data in the Su and Fa conditions may be interpreted as supporting the interaction hypothesis proposed earlier. [. . .]

A Theory of Achievement Motivation

An approach-avoidance conflict model for achievement-oriented behavior formulated by Atkinson (1957, 1964) includes three determinants of approach behavior: the motive for success (M_s), probability of success (P_s), and the incentive value of success (I_s). In a similar manner, the achievement avoidance tendency in Atkinson's model also is comprised of three components: the motive to avoid failure (M_{AF}), probability of failure (P_f), and the incentive value of failure ($-I_f$). Experiments IV and V provided evidence that the cognitive mediator of M_s is an internal attribution for success. Experiment VI attempts to demonstrate that the four environmental components of the approach and avoidance tendencies, P_s and I_s, and P_f and $-I_f$, also can be conceptualized with the language of attribution theory.

Within Atkinson's (1957) model of the determinants of achievement-related behavior, the incentive value of success and probability of success are inversely related. That is, pride in accomplishment is believed to be limited when the task is perceived as easy, and relatively intense when the task is perceived as difficult. Similarly, the incentive value of failure and probability of failure are conceived to be inversely related. The degree of shame experienced following nonattainment of an achievement-related goal is believed to be minimal when the task is perceived as difficult, and great when the task is easy. The relationship between affect and probability also can be accounted for by attributional processes. According to Kelley (1967), the allocation of causality is guided by an examination of "variations in effect [p. 194]." Given an easy task, the majority of individuals undertaking that task succeed. Correspondingly, most of the individuals attempting an objectively difficult task fail. Hence, the modal success and failure performance outcomes may primarily be attributed to external factors (the task), rather than to internal sources (the individuals). It can therefore be contended that little pride is experienced in successful performance of an easy task, or little shame in unsuccessful performance at a different task, because the ascription of causality tends to be external rather than internal. On the other hand, perhaps success at a difficult task, or failure at an easy task, primarily will be ascribed to the individuals undertaking the task. This would result in relatively great pride or shame, given respective success or failure outcomes.

The above analysis leads to the hypothesis that P_s and internal attribution will be linearly related within success and failure outcome conditions. Experiment VI investigated whether individuals can utilize task difficulty information to make inferences about casualty, and examined the function relating probability to attribution in success and failure situations.

Experiment VI

Method

The experiment was administered in group form to two psychology classes. Thirty male and 46 female students participated as subjects. The following instructions were read to the classes:

You will be given some information about a series of individuals in various situations, and asked to make judgments about certain aspects of their performance. The first column on the paper which you have tells the percentage of a group that has succeeded at a certain task. The second column tells whether the particular person under consideration has succeeded or failed at that task. In the last column you are asked to judge to what extent the person's success or failure was or was not due to his own effort or ability.

Each subject then rated the locus of causality for nine success and nine failure conditions. The to-be-judged situations indicated, for example, that Individual A succeeded at a task which 90% of the group solved, failed a task which 5% of the group solved, etc. Judgments were made on a Likert-type scale anchored at both ends with the following descriptions: "Performance due to ability or effort of the person" versus "Performance not due to ability or effort of the person." The stated group success (P_s) norms for both the success and failure outcomes were .99, .95, .90, .70, .50, .30, .10, .05, and .01. There were four P_s and outcome orders. The positions of the internal-external anchors were randomized over the 18 judgments (9

P_s levels × 2 outcomes). For scoring purposes the scale was subdivided into 17 equal 1/4-inch line segments, and assigned the corresponding scores of 1–17.

Results

Figure 6 shows the internal attribution scores in the success and failure conditions. For both success and failure outcomes the relationship between P_s and attribution was clearly linear ($p < .0001$). The internal attribution for success increased as the task became more difficult, while the internal attribution for failure increased as the task became easier. There also was greater internal attribution for success than for failure ($F = 6.67$, $df = 1/148$, $p < .05$.

Discussion

The results demonstrate that within the range of task difficulty encountered in most situations, judged self-attribution for success is inversely related to P_s, while personal ascription for failure is positively related to P_s. It was suggested previously that the degree of self-attribution for success and

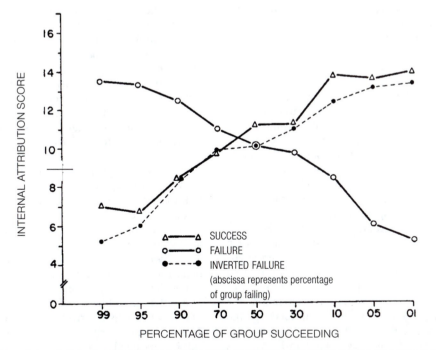

FIGURE 6 ■ Mean internal attribution scores for success and failure outcome conditions as a function of task difficulty.

failure influences the positive and negative incentive values of the goal. It is therefore contended that one experiences more pride (I_s) given success at a difficult task because there is greater self-attribution for success at low P_s tasks. Similarly, it is suggested that more shame ($-I_f$) is experienced given failure at an easy task because there is greater selfattribution for failure at high P_s tasks. It also is interesting to note, as Hoppe (1931) previously demonstrated, that there is a tendency to react defensively to failure by ascribing the cause as external to the individual. This occurred despite the lack of personal participation on the part of the rater.

The present experimental demonstration may have been somewhat contrived in that it "forced" attributions to be related to task outcome and P_s level. Yet very similar information is conveyed in many investigations of achievement motivation. Often experimental studies manipulating success and failure employ false norms to establish an initial P_s level. The experimenter states, for example, that "__% of the other students are able to solve this problem" (see Feather, 1961; Weiner, 1970). It is suggested that in these experiments the subjects covertly make attributional inferences on the bases of the normative data and their performance outcomes. It is further contended that these cognitions systematically influence subsequent (predicted) performance.

ATTRIBUTIONAL CONFLICT

The data presented in this article indicate that the assignment of responsibility is an extremely complex behavioral act. Task difficulty, results of the action, individual differences, perceptions of motivation and ability, and undoubtedly many other factors contribute to the final attribution. It is likely that at times an underlying individual difference in attributional tendency will be at variance with the allocation of responsibility which is generated by the stimulus situation (Watson & Baumel, 1967). For example, consider a situation in which an individual high in resultant achievement motivation succeeds (internal attribution) at an easy task (external attribution situation). Perhaps notions of balance might be helpful in explaining the resolution of such attributional conflicts (e.g., the task is then perceived as more difficult than it really is). The development of a model which specifies how opposing attributions are integrated remains a difficult and important problem.

RISK PREFERENCE

Perhaps the most well-documented finding emerging from Atkinson's conception of achievement motivation is that individuals high in achievement needs prefer tasks of intermediate difficulty, while the low-motive group tends to select tasks which are relatively easy or relatively difficult (see Atkinson, 1964; Weiner, 1970). A task of intermediate difficulty connotes that approximately one-half of the individuals undertaking the activity succeed, while the other half fail. Hence, individual success or failure primarily yields information about the capabilities of the person performing the task. On the other hand, success at an easy task, or failure at a difficult task (which me the modal experiences at such activities), primarily gives rise to information concerning the characteristics of the task, rather than to knowledge about the person attempting the task (see Experiment VI). It is therefore suggested that individuals high in achievement motivation select tasks of intermediate difficulty because such tasks have the greatest informational (rather than hedonic or consummatory) value. On the other hand, individuals low in achievement motivation prefer to avoid information concerning their relative abilities, and select activities which result in task attributions. This argument finds support in data indicating that high-achievement-oriented individuals prefer occupations which can be evaluated and which provide informational feedback (see McClelland, 1961).

In sum, an attributional analysis of achievement motivation leads to the following suppositions :

1. Individuals high in achievement motivation are more likely to approach achievement-related activities than those low in this motivational disposition because they tend to ascribe success to themselves, and hence experience greater reward for goal attainment.
2. Individuals high in achievement motivation persist longer given failure than those low in this motivational tendency because they are more likely to ascribe the failure to a lack of effort, and less likely to attribute failure to a deficiency in ability. This pattern of attribution is hypothesized to result in continued goal activity.

3. Individuals high in achievement motivation choose tasks of intermediate difficulty with greater frequency than individuals low in achievement motivation because performance at those tasks is more likely to yield information about one's capabilities than selection of tasks which are very easy or extremely difficult.

REFERENCES

Atkinson, J. W. (1957). Motivational determinants of risk-taking behavior. *Psychological Review, 64,* 359–372.

Atkinson, J. W. (1964). *An introduction to motivation.* Princeton, NJ: Van Nostrand.

Crandall, V. C., Katkovsky, W., & Crandall, V. J. (1965). Children's beliefs in their own control of reinforcements in intellectual-academic achievement situations. *Child Development, 36,* 91–109.

Crandall, V. C., Katkovsky, W., & Preston, A. (1962). Motivational and ability determinants of young children's intellectual achievement behaviors. *Child Development, 33,* 643–661.

Feather, N. T. (1961). The relationship of persistence at a task to expectation of success and achievement-related motives. *Journal of Abnormal and Social Psychology, 63,* 552–561.

Heckhausen, H. (1967). *The anatomy of achievement motivation.* New York: Academic Press.

Heider, F. (1958). *The psychology of interpersonal relations.* New York: Wiley.

Hoppe, F. (1931). *Erfolg und Misserfolg. Psychologische Forschung, 14,* 1–62.

Jenkins, H. M., & Ward, W. C. (1965). Judgment of contingency between responses and outcome. *Psychological Monographs, 79*(1, Whole No. 594).

Jones, E. E., & Davis, K. E. (1965). From acts to dispositions. In L. Berkowitz (Ed.), *Advances in experimental social psychology.* Vol. 2. New York: Academic Press.

Jones, E. E., & deCharms, R. (1957). Changes in social perception as a function of the personal relevance of behavior. *Sociometry, 20,* 75–85.

Kelley, H. H. (1967). Attribution theory in social psychology. *Nebraska Symposium on Motivation, 15,* 192–240.

Maselli, M. D., & Altrocchi, J. (1969). Attribution of intent. *Psychological Bulletin, 71,* 445–454.

McClelland, D. C. (1961). *The achieving society.* Princeton, NJ: Van Nostrand.

Mehrabian, A. (1969). Measures of achieving tendency. *Educational and Psychological Measurement, 29,* 445–451.

Ring, K., & Kelley, H. H. (1963). A comparison of augmentation and reduction as modes of influence. *Journal of Abnormal and Social Psychology, 66,* 95–102.

Rosenthal, R., & Jacobsen, L. F. (1968). Teacher expectations for the disadvantaged. *Scientific American, 218,* 19–23.

Rotter, J. B. (1966). Generalized expectancies for internal versus external control of reinforcement. *Psychological Monographs, 80*(1, Whole No. 609).

Schmitt, D. R. (1964). The invocation of moral obligation. *Sociometry, 21,* 299–310.

Tietze, C., & Lewit, S. (1969). Abortion. *Scientific American, 220,* 21–27.

Watson, D., & Baumal, E. (1967). Effects of locus of control and expectation of future control upon present performance. *Journal of Personality and Social Psychology, 6,* 212–215.

Weiner, B. (1970). New conceptions in the study of achievement motivation. In B. Maher (Ed.), *Progress in experimental personality research,* Vol. 5. New York: Academic Press.

A Social-Cognitive Approach to Motivation and Personality

Carol S. Dweck • Department of Psychology, University of Illinois
Ellen L. Leggett • Harvard University

Editors' Notes

The authors propose that individual differences in goals and beliefs about social reality contribute to individual differences in adaptive behavior. This general proposal is illustrated in the domains of intellectual achievement and morality. In the domain of intellectual achievement, for example, a performance goal concerned with positive evaluations of one's competence is distinguished from a learning goal concerned with increasing one's competence. An entity theory that intelligence is a fixed and uncontrollable trait is distinguished from an incremental theory that intelligence is a controllable and increasable quality. Evidence is presented that possessing an entity theory relates to having a performance goal orientation that then relates to a maladaptive helpless pattern of behavior. In contrast, possessing an incremental theory relates to having a learning goal orientation that then relates to an adaptive mastery pattern of behavior. This paper illustrates the interrelations among goals, implicit theories, and self-regulatory effectiveness.

Discussion Questions

1. How can theories of social reality influence people's goals?
2. Which theory of intelligence and which achievement goal orientation relate to maladaptive achievement behaviors? Explain these relations.

Authors' Abstract

Past work has documented and described major patterns of adaptive and maladaptive behavior: the mastery-oriented and the helpless patterns. In this article, we present a research-based model that accounts for these patterns in terms of underlying psychological processes. The model specifies how individuals' implicit theories orient them toward particular goals and how these goals set up the different patterns. Indeed, we show how each feature (cognitive, affective, and behavioral) of the adaptive and maladaptive patterns can be seen to follow directly from different goals. We then examine the generality of the model and use it to illuminate phenomena in a wide variety of domains. Finally, we place the model in its broadest context and examine its implications for our understanding of motivational and personality processes.

The task for investigators of motivation and personality is to identify major patterns of behavior and link them to underlying psychological processes. In this article we (a) describe a research-based model that accounts for major patterns of behavior, (b) examine the generality of this model—its utility for understanding domains beyond the ones in which it was originally developed, and (c) explore the broader implications of the model for motivational and personality processes.

Toward this end, we begin by describing two major patterns of cognition–affect–behavior that we identified in our early work: the maladaptive "helpless" response and the more adaptive "mastery-oriented" response (Diener & Dweck, 1978, 1980; Dweck, 1975; Dweck & Reppucci, 1973).[1] The helpless pattern, as will be seen, is characterized by an avoidance of challenge and a deterioration of performance in the face of obstacles. The mastery-oriented pattern, in contrast, involves the seeking of challenging tasks and the maintenance of effective striving under failure.

Most interesting, our research with children has demonstrated that those who avoid challenge and show impairment in the face of difficulty are initially equal in ability to those who seek challenge and show persistence. Indeed some of the brightest, most skilled individuals exhibit the maladaptive pattern. Thus it cannot be said that it is simply those with weak skills or histories of failure who (appropriately) avoid difficult tasks or whose skills prove fragile in the face of difficulty. The puzzle, then, was why individuals of equal ability would show such marked performance differences in response to challenge. Even more puzzling was the

fact that those most concerned with their ability, as the helpless children seemed to be, behaved in ways that impaired its functioning and limited its growth.

Our efforts to explain this phenomenon led us to the more general conceptualization of *goals* (Dweck & Elliott, 1983). We proposed that the goals individuals are pursuing create the framework within which they interpret and react to events. Specifically, in the domain of intellectual achievement, we identified two classes of goals: *performance* goals (in which individuals are concerned with gaining favorable judgments of their competence) and *learning* goals (in which individuals are concerned with increasing their competence). We then tested and supported the hypothesis that these different goals foster the different response patterns—that a focus on performance goals (competence judgments) creates a vulnerability to the helpless pattern, whereas the pursuit of learning goals (competence enhancement) in the same situation promotes the mastery-oriented pattern (Elliott & Dweck, in press; Farrell & Dweck, 1985; Leggett & Dweck, 1986).

The question that remained, however, was why individuals in the same situation would pursue such different goals. This led us to the more general conceptualization of individuals' *implicit theories*. Here, we tested the hypothesis that different theories about oneself, by generating different con-

---

[1]The term *helpless* was adapted from the animal work of Seligman, Maier, and Solomon (1971). At the time of our initial work (Dweck & Reppucci, 1973), only animal work on helplessness had been conducted. See the section on control formulations (The Attributional Approach) for a discussion of how our current approach differs from other approaches to human helplessness.

cerns, would orient individuals toward the different goals. Specifically, we showed that conceiving of one's intelligence as a fixed entity was associated with adopting the performance goal of documenting that entity, whereas conceiving of intelligence as a malleable quality was associated with the learning goal of developing that quality (Bandura & Dweck, 1985[2]; Dweck, Tenney, & Dinces, 1982; Leggett, 1985). Thus we will present a model in which individuals' goals set up their pattern of responding, and these goals, in turn, are fostered by individuals' self-conceptions.

The model represents an approach to motivation in that it is built around goals and goal-oriented behavior. At the same time, it represents an approach to personality in that it identifies individual differences in beliefs and values that appear to generate individual differences in behavior. The model may also be said to represent a social–cognitive approach to motivation and personality in that it (a) seeks to illuminate specific, moment-to-moment psychological mediators of behavior and (b) assigns a central role to interpretive processes in the generation of affect and the mediation of behavior.

Having arrived at this more general conceptualization, we asked a number of questions about the range of phenomena that the model could potentially explain. In this article we examine the degree to which the model can be used to organize and illuminate a variety of phenomena beyond those it was developed to explain, to generate new hypotheses about personality–motivational phenomena, and to shed light on more general issues in the study of personality and motivation.

In these next sections, for clarity, we start with the response patterns and work up to the goals and implicit theories that appear to foster them. We also begin with the domain of intellectual achievement, where the patterns were established and the model has been most extensively researched, and then move to the domain of social interactions, where evidence for the model is growing.

Maladaptive Versus Adaptive Patterns: Cognitive, Affective, and Behavioral Components

Why are the helpless and the mastery-oriented patterns considered to be maladaptive and adaptive, respectively and why are they important? The

helpless response as a characteristic style can be considered maladaptive because challenge and obstacles are inherent in most important pursuits. Indeed, one might ask, what valued long-term goal (e.g., pertaining to one's work, one's relationships, or one's moral strivings) does not at some point pose risks, throw up barriers, present dilemmas? A response pattern that deters individuals from confronting obstacles or that prevents them from functioning effectively in the face of difficulty must ultimately limit their attainments.

The mastery-oriented pattern involves the seeking of challenging tasks and the generation of effective strategies in the face of obstacles. As a characteristic style, this enjoyment of challenge and willingness to sustain engagement with difficult tasks appears to be an adaptive stance toward valued goals. Of course, individuals need to be able to gauge when tasks *should* be avoided or abandoned (see Janoff-Bulman & Brickman, 1981); nonetheless, the ability to maintain a commitment to valued goals through periods of difficulty must maximize attainments in the long run.

As we have noted, the helpless and the mastery-oriented patterns are two distinct, coherent patterns, with striking differences in the cognitions, affect, and behavior that characterize each. Because these patterns lie at the heart of our model, we shall describe them in some detail. In doing so we draw primarily on a series of studies conducted by Diener and Dweck (1978, 1980), in which the patterns were first extensively analyzed and in which the cognitive, affective, and behavioral components of the pattern were first conceptualized as interrelated aspects of a continuous process. A brief outline of their basic method will provide a context for the findings. In these studies, participants (late grade-school age children) who were likely to display the helpless or mastery-oriented patterns were identified by their responses to an attributional measure.[3] They worked on a concept

---

[2]This study has been cited in previous works as M. Bandura & Dweck (1981, unpublished manuscript). It was the first of our studies on implicit theories of intelligence.

[3]This classification was made on the basis of our earlier research (Dweck, 1975; Dweck & Reppucci, 1973), linking children's performance following failure to their attributions for failure on the Intellectual Achievement Responsibility Scale (Crandall, Katkovsky, & Crandall, 1965). However, our concern here was with revealing the entire pattern of cognition, affect, and behavior over time, and it was an empirical question what role attributions would play in these patterns.

formation task, successfully solving the first eight problems, but failing to solve the next four problems (which were somewhat too difficult for children their age to solve in the allotted number of trials). Of interest here were the changes in cognition, affect, and behavior as the subjects went from success to failure.

To capture the timing and the nature of these changes, several procedures were used. First, after the sixth success problem, subjects were requested to verbalize aloud what they were thinking and feeling as they worked on the problems (Diener & Dweck, 1978, Study 2). They were given license to hold forth on any topic they wished—relevant or irrelevant to the task—and they did so at length. Second, the problems were constructed so that children's hypothesis-testing strategies could be continuously monitored, and thus changes in the sophistication of the strategies could be detected (Diener & Dweck, 1978, Studies 1 & 2; 1980). Third, specific measures, such as predictions of future performance, were taken before and after failure (Diener & Dweck, 1980).

All children attained effective problem-solving strategies on the success problems, with training aids being given when necessary. Moreover, there was no difference in the strategy level attained by the helpless and mastery-oriented children on the success problems or in the ease with which they attained that level. (Indeed, whenever any difference emerged, it was the helpless children who appeared slightly more proficient.) In addition, the verbalizations of both groups on the success problems showed them to be equally interested in and engaged with the task. However, with the onset of failure, two distinct patterns rapidly emerged.

First helpless children quickly began to report negative self-cognitions. Specifically, they began to attribute their failures to personal inadequacy, spontaneously citing deficient intelligence, memory, or problem-solving ability as the reasons for their failure. This was accompanied by a striking absence of any positive prognosis and occurred despite the fact that only moments before, their ability had yielded consistent success.

Second, helpless children began to express pronounced negative affect. Specifically, they reported such things as an aversion to the task, boredom with the problems, or anxiety over their performance—again, despite the fact that shortly before they had been quite pleased with the task and situation.

Third, more than two thirds of the helpless children (but virtually none of the mastery-oriented ones) engaged in task-irrelevant verbalizations, usually of diversionary or self-aggrandizing nature. For example, some attempted to alter the rules of the task, some spoke of talents in other domains, and some boasted of unusual wealth and possessions, presumably in an attempt to direct attention away from their present performance and toward more successful endeavors or praiseworthy attributes. Thus, instead of concentrating their resources on attaining success they attempted to bolster their image in other ways.

And finally, also in line with the negative cognitions and negative affect, the helpless children showed marked decrements in performance across the failure trials. Specifically, more than two thirds of them showed a clear decline in the level of their problem-solving strategy under failure and over 60% lapsed into ineffective strategies—strategies that were characteristic of preschoolers and that would never yield a solution (even if sufficient trials for solution had been permitted on those problems). Thus although all of the helpless children had demonstrated their ability to employ mature and useful strategies on the task, a sizable number were no longer doing so.

In short, helpless children viewed their difficulties as failures, as indicative of low ability, and as insurmountable. They appeared to view further effort as futile and, perhaps, as their defensive maneuvers suggest, as further documentation of their inadequate ability.

In striking contrast, the mastery-oriented children, when confronted with the difficult problems, did not begin to offer attributions for their failure. Indeed, they did not appear to think they were failing. Rather than viewing unsolved problems as failures that reflected on their ability, they appeared to view the unsolved problems as challenges to be mastered through effort. Toward that end, they engaged in extensive solution-oriented self-instruction and self-monitoring. Interestingly, their self-instructions and self-monitoring referred to both the cognitive and motivational aspects of the task at hand. That is, in addition to planning specific hypothesis-testing strategies and monitoring their outcomes, they also instructed themselves to exert effort or to concentrate and then monitored their level of effort or attention.

Also in contrast to the helpless children, the mastery-oriented children appeared to maintain an unflagging optimism that their efforts would be fruitful. For example, the mastery-oriented children said such things as "I did it before, I can do it again" or even "I'm sure I have it now." Nearly two thirds of them spontaneously offered statements of positive prognosis.

In keeping with their optimistic stance, the mastery-oriented children maintained their positive affect toward the task, and some even showed heightened positive affect with the advent of the difficult problems. As noted by Diener and Dweck (1978), one boy, soon after the failure problems began, pulled up his chair, rubbed his hands together, smacked his lips, and exclaimed, "I love a challenge!" Another boy, also upon confronting the failure problems, regarded the experimenter and stated in a pleased tone of voice, "You know, I was *hoping* this would be informative." Thus, the mastery-oriented children not only believed they could surmount obstacles and reach a solution, but some even relished the opportunity to do so.

Finally, the positive cognitions and affect were reflected in the problem-solving performance of the mastery-oriented children. In contrast to the helpless children, who showed marked decrements in their level of problem-solving strategy, 80% of the mastery-oriented children succeeded in maintaining their problem-solving strategies at or above prefailure levels, with over 25% increasing the level of their strategy. That is, these children actually taught themselves new, more sophisticated hypothesis-testing strategies over the four failure trials.

In short, in the face of failure, helpless children exhibited negative self-cognitions, negative affect, and impaired performance, whereas mastery-oriented children exhibited constructive self-instructions and self-monitoring, a positive prognosis, positive affect, and effective problem-solving strategies. Despite the fact that they had received identical tasks and earned identical task outcomes, helpless and mastery-oriented children processed and responded to the situation in entirely different ways.

Although these patterns were first identified in research with children, they have been well documented in adults as well (see, e.g., Brunson & Matthews, 1981). Moreover, although the patterns were first investigated in laboratory settings, they have been shown to operate in natural settings. A study by Licht and Dweck (1984) provides a clear demonstration. In this study, children were taught new material (the principles of operant condition-

ing) in their classrooms by means of programmed instruction booklets. For all children, an irrelevant passage (on imitation) was inserted near the beginning of their instructional booklet. For half of the children, this passage, although irrelevant to the principles to be learned, was clear and straightforward. For the other half, the passage was rather tortuous and confusing. The question was whether helpless and mastery-oriented children (as defined in this study by their attributional tendencies) would show differential mastery of the material in the no-confusion and confusion conditions; that is, whether difficulty in the irrelevant passage would impair helpless children's subsequent learning.

Mastery of the material was assessed by means of a seven-question mastery test that asked subjects to employ the principles they had just learned. Any child who failed to answer the seven questions correctly was given a review booklet followed by another mastery test. In all, children were given as many as four opportunities to demonstrate mastery.

The results showed that in the no-confusion condition, the mastery-oriented and helpless children were equally likely to master the material: 68.4% of the mastery-oriented children and 76.6% of the helpless ones reached the mastery criterion, again demonstrating no difference in ability between the groups. However, in the confusion condition a clear difference emerged. As before, most of the mastery-oriented children, 71.9%, reached the learning criterion. In contrast, only 34.6% of the helpless children in the confusion condition ever mastered the material. Thus with "real" material in a real-world setting, the mastery-oriented and helpless patterns were shown to be associated with effective versus ineffective functioning in the face of difficulty.

To conclude, the Diener and Dweck research suggests that whereas helpless individuals appear to focus on their ability and its adequacy (or inadequacy), mastery-oriented ones appear to focus on mastery through strategy and effort; whereas helpless individuals appear to view challenging problems as a threat to their self-esteem, mastery-oriented ones appear to view them as opportunities for learning something new.

Goals

In view of these entirely different ways of perceiving identical situations, Elliott and Dweck

(1988) hypothesized that helpless and mastery-oriented individuals might be pursuing very different goals. That is, their different perceptions and reactions might be a result of their different aims or purposes in the situation. Helpless children, they suggested, might be pursuing *performance* goals, in which they seek to establish the adequacy of their ability and to avoid giving evidence of its inadequacy. In other words, they may view achievement situations as tests or measures of competence and may seek, in these situations, to be judged competent and not incompetent. Mastery-oriented individuals, in contrast, might be pursuing *learning* goals. They may tend to view achievement situations as opportunities to increase their competence and may pursue, in these situations, the goal of acquiring new skills or extending their mastery. Thus, in challenging achievement situations, helpless children might be pursuing the performance goal of *proving* their ability, whereas the mastery-oriented children might be pursuing the learning goal of *improving* their ability. It might be these different goals, Elliott and Dweck reasoned, that set up the patterns of cognition, affect, and behavior.

To test the hypothesis that goals generate the helpless and mastery-oriented responses, Elliott and Dweck experimentally induced performance or learning goals and examined the pattern of cognition, affect, and behavior that followed from each goal. The question of interest was whether the performance goal, with its emphasis on measuring ability, would create a greater vulnerability to the helpless pattern, whereas the learning goal, with its emphasis on acquiring ability, would create a greater tendency to display the mastery-oriented pattern. More specifically, as shown in Table 1, they hypothesized that when individuals held a

performance goal and had a low assessment of their present ability level, they would display the helpless pattern in the face of failure. That is, concern with one's ability combined with doubts about its adequacy should create the negative ability attributions, negative affect, and performance deterioration characteristic of helplessness.

In contrast, it was hypothesized that when individuals held a learning goal, they would display the mastery-oriented pattern, even when they assessed their present ability level to be low. That is, when individuals are seeking to increase their ability, the adequacy of their present level of ability should not be a deterrent to their pursuit of their goal and could even be seen as providing an additional reason to pursue the goal.

Briefly then, Elliott and Dweck simultaneously manipulated subjects' (a) goals (by orienting them more toward evaluations of ability or more toward the value of the skill to be learned) and (b) assessments of their present ability level (via feedback on a pretest). To test the effect of the goal-orienting manipulation on subjects' actual goal choices, children were then asked to choose one task from an array of tasks that embodied either a learning or a performance goal. The learning goal task was described as enabling skill acquisition, but as entailing a high risk of a negative ability judgment. In contrast, the performance goal options allowed children to obtain a favorable ability judgment (by succeeding on a difficult task) or to avoid an unfavorable judgment (by succeeding on an easier task), but did not afford any opportunity for learning. Following this choice, all children were given the Diener and Dweck concept-formation task. (Children had in fact been asked to make several task selections so that the Diener and Dweck task—described as moderately difficult—could be

TABLE 1. Theories, Goals and Behavior Patterns in Achievement Situations

Theory of intelligence	Goal orientation	Perceived present ability	Behavior pattern
Entity (Intelligence is fixed)	Performance (Goal is to gain positive judgments/avoid negative judgments of competence)	High	Mastery oriented (Seek challenge; high persistence)
		Low	Helpless (Avoid challenge; low persistence)
Incremental (Intelligence is malleable)	Learning (Goal is to increase competence)	High or low	Mastery oriented (Seek challenge that fosters learning; high persistence)

presented to them as consonant with their choice. Thus it would not appear that the wishes of some children were granted and others denied.) As in the Diener and Dweck research, children were requested to verbalize as they worked on the problems, and verbalizations and strategies were monitored and categorized.

The results showed the predicted relations. When children were oriented toward skill acquisition, their assessment of their present ability was largely irrelevant: They chose the challenging learning task and displayed a mastery-oriented pattern. In contrast, when children were oriented toward evaluation, the task they adopted and the achievement pattern they displayed (mastery-oriented or helpless) were highly dependent on their perceived ability. Children who perceived their ability to be high selected the challenging performance tasks that would allow them to obtain judgments of competence, whereas children who perceived their ability to be low selected easier tasks that would permit them to avoid judgments of incompetence. Note that the great majority of children in the evaluation-oriented condition sacrificed altogether the opportunity for new learning that involved a display of errors or confusion.

What was most striking was the degree to which the manipulations created the entire constellation of performance, cognition, and affect characteristic of the naturally occurring achievement patterns. For example, children who were given a performance orientation and low ability pretest feedback showed the same attributions, negative affect, and strategy deterioration that characterized the helpless children in our earlier studies (Diener & Dweck, 1978, 1980).

Research from other laboratories is yielding similar findings. For example, in a study by Ames (1984), different goal structures (competitive vs. individualistic) were instituted by orienting subjects either toward evaluation of their ability relative to a peer or toward improvement of their ability over time. The results showed that subjects in the competitive (performance goal) condition were significantly more likely than those in the individualistic (learning goal) condition to focus on ability attributions, whereas those in the individualistic condition were significantly more likely to focus on self-instructions (with ability attributions being their least frequent category of achievement cognition). Ames interpreted these findings as suggesting that the different goal structures elicit the helpless and mastery-oriented achievement cognitions described by Diener and Dweck.

Studies by Bandura and Dweck (1985) and by Leggett and Dweck (1986), in which individuals' existing goal preferences were measured (rather than manipulated) have provided further confirmation for the hypothesis that performance goals are associated with a vulnerability to challenge avoidance, as well as to negative ability attributions, negative affect, and low persistence in the face of difficulty. In contrast, learning goals again were found to be associated with challenge seeking (despite low confidence in ability), as well as with an effort/strategy focus, positive affect, and high persistence under difficulty.

Moreover, a recent study by Farrell and Dweck (1985) provides evidence that individuals' goal preferences predict patterns of learning in real-world settings. One of the hallmarks of effective learning is the tendency to apply or transfer what one has learned to novel tasks that embody similar underlying principles. Farrell and Dweck (1985) examined the relation between children's goal orientations and transfer of learning. As a week-long unit in their regular science classes, eighth-grade children were taught one of three scientific principles by means of self-instructional booklets. They were then tested for their generalization of this learning to tasks involving the two (conceptually related) principles that had not been taught. The results showed that children who had learning goals for the unit, compared to those who had performance goals, (a) attained significantly higher scores on the transfer test (this was true for children who had high and low pretest scores); (b) produced about 50% more work on their transfer tests, suggesting that they were more active in the transfer process; and (c) produced more rule-generated answers on the test even when they failed to reach the transfer criterion, again suggesting a more active stance toward learning and mastery opportunities.

Although we have been emphasizing the vulnerability created by an orientation toward performance goals over learning goals, it is essential to note that there are also adaptive performance concerns. It is often important for individuals to evaluate their abilities or to gain positive judgments of their competence. Indeed, sometimes this may be a prerequisite to the successful pursuit of learning goals: Obtaining an objective diagnosis of strengths and weaknesses may be a necessary step in the learning process, and earning the positive judgment of those who control important resources may be a necessary step in one's pursuit of skills and knowledge. Thus adaptive individuals effectively coordinate performance and learning goals. It is when an overconcern with proving their adequacy (to themselves or others) leads individuals to ignore, avoid, or abandon potentially valuable learning opportunities that problems arise.

It is also important to reiterate that when confidence in ability is high, performance goals can produce mastery-oriented behavior, and they have undoubtedly fueled many great achievements. However, it is equally important to reiterate that high confidence is necessary within a performance goal to support a mastery orientation but, as we will show, high confidence may be difficult to sustain within a performance goal. Learning goals, as the research indicates, tend to make individuals less vulnerable to the effects of fluctuations in confidence.

How Goals Create Patterns

What are the mechanisms through which the different goals produce their associated patterns of cognition, affect, and behavior? Why and how do they lead to such different patterns? Evidence increasingly suggests that the goal an individual is pursuing creates a framework for interpreting and responding to events that occur. Thus the same event may have an entirely different meaning and impact if it occurs within the context of a learning versus a performance goal. In this section, we propose what the different frameworks established by the two goals might be and build a case for how the observed cognitive, affective, and behavioral patterns follow from these frameworks.

COGNITIONS

How might the different goal frameworks set up the different cognitions in the face of failure? Individuals adapting different goals can be seen as approaching a situation with different concerns, asking different questions, and seeking different information (see, e.g., Dweck & Elliott, 1983). For each individual, the data in the situation are interpreted in light of their focal concern and provide information relevant to their question.

Within a performance goal, individuals are concerned with measuring their ability and with an-

swering the question, Is my ability adequate or inadequate? Within such a framework, outcomes will be a chief source of information relevant to this concern and thus failure outcomes may readily elicit the helpless attribution that ability is inadequate.

In contrast, learning goals create a concern with increasing one's ability and extending one's mastery and would lead individuals to pose the question, What is the best way to increase my ability or achieve mastery? Here, then, outcomes would provide information about whether one is pursuing an optimal course and, if not, what else might be necessary. Failure would simply mean that the current strategy may be insufficient to the task and may require upgrading or revision. The self-instructions and self-monitoring of the mastery-oriented children can therefore be seen as a direct implementation of this information in pursuit of future goal success. Thus the attributions of the helpless children and the self-instructions of the mastery-oriented children in response to failure may be viewed as natural outgrowths of their goals.

Recent research (Leggett & Dweck, 1986) has shown that another potentially informative event— one's input or effort expenditure—will also be interpreted in line with the differing goal concerns: as an indicant of ability versus a means of achieving learning or mastery. Leggett and Dweck measured eighth graders' goal preferences and devised a questionnaire to assess their interpretation of effort information. The results clearly indicated that those with performance goals used effort as an index of high or low ability. Specifically, they viewed effort and ability as inversely related: High effort (resulting in either success or failure) implies low ability, and low effort (resulting in success) implies high ability. These children endorsed items such as "If you have to work hard at some problems, you're probably not very good at them" or "You only know you're good at something when it comes easily to you." In essence then, children with performance goals use an inference rule that says effort per se—even when it accompanies success—signifies a lack of ability.

In contrast, those with learning goals were more likely to view effort as a means or strategy for activating or manifesting their ability for mastery. Here effort and ability are seen as *positively related*: Greater effort activates and makes manifest more ability. These children endorsed items such as "[Even] when you're very good at something, working hard allows you to really understand it" or "When something comes easily to you, you don't know how good you are at it." Thus, within a learning goal, high effort would represent a mastery strategy and would signify that one was harnessing one's resources for mastery.

In short, children with different goals appear to use very different inference rules to process effort information (cf. Jagacinski & Nicholls, 1983; Surber, 1984). This research suggests how use of the *inverse* rule by individuals with performance goals can contribute to their helpless pattern of attributing high effort failures to low ability (and of doubting their ability after high effort *success*; see Diener & Dweck, 1980). It also shows, in contrast, how use of the *positive* rule by those with learning goals can contribute to their mastery-oriented tendency to focus on effort when challenged.[4]

In summary, performance goals create a context in which outcomes (such as failures) and input (such as high effort) are interpreted in terms of their implications for ability and its adequacy. In contrast, learning goals create a context in which the same outcomes and input provide information about the effectiveness of one's learning and mastery strategies.

AFFECT

How would the different goal frameworks result in different affective reactions to challenge or setbacks? Within a performance goal, experiencing failure or effort exertion warns of a low-ability judgment and thus poses a threat to self-esteem. Such a threat might first engender anxiety (Sarason, 1975; Wine, 1971), and then, if the negative judgment appears increasingly likely, depressed affect (Seligman, Abramson, Semmel, & von Baeyer, 1979) and a sense of shame (Sohn, 1977; Weiner & Graham, 1984) may set in. Alternatively, individuals could adopt a more defensive, self-protective posture, devaluing the task and expressing boredom or disdain toward it (Tesser & Campbell, 1983; cf. Berglas & Jones, 1978). All of these emotions-anxiety, depressed affect, boredom, defiance—were apparent among the helpless subjects in the Diener and Dweck (1978, 1980) studies as failures accrued.

Within a learning goal, however, the occurrence of failure simply signals that the task will require more effort and ingenuity for mastery. This cre-

ates, for some, the opportunity for a more satisfying mastery experience, producing the heightened positive affect noted earlier. In addition, the continued belief that success can occur through effort will engender determination—and indeed in many of our studies, mastery-oriented children (whether instructed to verbalize or not) have issued battle cries or vows of victory.

Finally for individuals with learning goals, exerting effort in the service of learning or mastery may bring intrinsic rewards, pleasure, or pride (Deci & Ryan, 1980; Lepper, 1981). Whereas within performance goals high effort may engender anxiety, and high-effort progress or mastery is a mixed blessing within a learning goal high-effort mastery may often be precisely what is sought. Indeed, in the study by Bandura and Dweck (1985), children with learning goals reported that they would feel bored or disappointed with a low-effort success. (Children with performance goals reported that they would feel proud or relieved about a low-effort success.) Similarly Ames, Ames, and Felker (1977) found that within an individualistic (learning goal) structure, children's pride in their performance was related to the degree of effort they perceived themselves to have exerted. This was true in both the success and the failure conditions, indicating that within a learning goal, effort per se can be a source of pride.

In summary, because of their different meanings in the context of the two goals, events that produce negative or depressed affect within one goal may produce positive affect and heightened engagement within the other.

BEHAVIOR

How would the goal-related differences in cognition and affect create different behavior? First, they would influence task choices. The ideal task within each goal would be a task that maximized goal

---

[4]In this study, junior high school students (l4 years old) were chosen as subjects because developmental evidence suggests that children are not able to reason reliably about effort and ability in inverse relation to each other until after 10 or 11 years of age (e.g., Nicholls, 1978). We thus asked, once children are able to use either rule, which rule do they use? However, the developmental evidence raises the additional possibility that some aspects of our model may not be fully in place until the later grade school years. For this reason we are conducting research (Cain & Dweck, 1987) that traces the development of the theories of intelligence and the theory–goal–behavior linkages across the grade school years.

success and positive affect or minimized goal failure and negative affect, or both (see Dweck & Elliott, 1983).

Within a performance goal the ideal task would be one that maximized positive judgments and pride in ability, while minimizing negative judgments, anxiety, and shame. For performance-oriented individuals with Low confidence in their ability, challenging tasks (those requiring high effort and having uncertain outcome) would promise aversive experiences: high anxiety, expected negative judgments, and loss of esteem. These individuals would thus orient themselves toward easy tasks, ones that minimized negative outcomes and affect, even though such tasks would preclude the possibility of positive judgments.

Performance-oriented individuals with high confidence, although more challenge seeking, would nonetheless avoid challenge when the threat of performance failure existed. And indeed, these individuals are found to sacrifice learning opportunities that pose the risk of errors and difficulty (Bandura & Dweck, 1985; Elliott & Dweck, 1988).

The ideal task within a learning goal, however, would be one that maximized the growth of ability and the pride and pleasure of mastery, quite apart from how one's abilities are showing up at any given moment. Indeed, Bandura and Dweck (1985) found that their learning-oriented children with low confidence were the most likely of any group to seek a challenging learning opportunity even though it carried the risk of negative ability judgments. Moreover, within a learning goal, there

is no need to withdraw from a task that proves to be unexpectedly difficult, because a failure episode or the exertion of high effort does not engender cognitive or affective distress. Instead one would expect withdrawal from a task that became useless or boring, even if it continued to promise favorable ability judgments (see Bandura & Dweck, 1985).

In addition to influencing task choice, goal-related cognitive and affective factors will influence the quality of performance in the face of failure. We note that there are at least five separate cognitive and affective factors that would impair performance for performance-oriented individuals but that would sustain or facilitate performance for learning-oriented individuals. These factors are shown in Table 2.

First, within a performance goal an attribution of failure to a lack of ability suggests that given one's incompetence at the task, further effort may not be useful in bringing about success (see, e.g., Dweck & Reppucci, 1973; Weiner, 1972). A second factor that may prompt a slackening of effort arises from the use of the inverse rule: a belief that greater effort further confirms the low ability judgment.

It is critical to note that the inverse rule sets up a conflict between the effort that is necessary for mastery of a challenging task and the goal of obtaining a high ability judgment. Ironically, what is required to do well at the task and what it takes to attain the performance goal may come into conflict such that when effort is most needed, it may be most likely to be defensively withheld (see

TABLE 2. Cognitive and Affective Mechanisms of Debilitation and Facilitation in the Face of Difficulty

Performance goal: Debilitating factors	Learning goal: Facilitating factors
1. Loss of belief in efficacy of effort, given given low ability attribution	Continued belief in efficacy of effort: Effort self-instruction instead of low ability attribution; positive rule emphasizes utility of effort
2. Defensive withdrawal of effort: Effort confirms low ability judgment; inverse rule creates conflict between task requirements and goal	No defense required: Effort is consonant with task requirements and goal
3. Attention divided between goal (worry about outcome) and task (strategy formulation and execution)	Undivided, intensified attention to task that directly serves goal
4. Negative affect can interfere with concentration or can prompt withdrawal	Affect channeled into task
5. Few intrinsic rewards from effort (or high effort progress) to sustain process	Continuous intrinsic rewards for meeting challenge with effort

Covington & Omelich, 1979; Frankl & Snyder, 1978).

Next, anxiety over goal failure (both the cognitive worry component and the aversive affective component) may divide attention, inspire escape wishes, and interfere with concentration and effective strategy deployment (see Carver, Peterson, Follansbee, & Scheier, 1983; Sarason, 1980; Sarason & Mandler, 1952; Spielberger, 1958; Wine, 1971). Finally, the absence of intrinsic rewards from goal-oriented effort or high-effort progress would remove an important means of sustaining the process in the face of difficulty (Deci & Ryan, 1980; Lepper, 1981).

Looking at the analogous factors within a learning goal, we can see first that failure, rather than signaling low ability, provides a cue to escalate effort. Moreover, the positive inference rule reinforces the utility of effort: Effort mobilizes one's ability for task mastery. Second, there is no conflict between the effort requirements of the task and the requirements of the goal, for effort is at once the means of mastering the task and the means of maximizing goal attainment. Next, the affect generated by failure (e.g., heightened interest or determination) is consonant with task requirements and may promote an intensification of concentration. Finally, the intrinsic rewards that accompany the meeting of challenge with effort and the attainment of progress through effort will provide additional impetus to performance.

In summary, the performance goal focuses the individual on judgments of ability and can set in motion cognitive and affective processes that render that individual vulnerable to maladaptive behavior patterns, whereas the learning goal creates a focus on increasing ability and sets in motion cognitive and affective processes that promote adaptive challenge seeking persistence, and sustained performance in the face of difficulty. Indeed, the goal framework may tie together and organize various constructs in the literature that have been proposed to account for performance impairment or enhancement, including attributional patterns, defensive strategies, self versus task focus, ego versus task involvement, evaluation anxiety, and intrinsic motivation. That is, the present conceptualization may provide a way to illuminate the origins and dynamics of these processes within a single system.

Implicit Theories of Intelligence

What leads individuals to favor performance goals over learning goals or vice versa? Why do some individuals focus on the adequacy of their ability whereas others focus on the development of their ability? Our recent work shows that a consistent predictor of children's goal orientation is their "theory of intelligence," that is, their implicit conception about the nature of ability (cf. Goodnow, 1980; Nicholls, 1984; Sternberg, Conway, Ketron, & Bernstein, 1981; Wellman, 1985; Yussen & Kane, 1985). Some children favor what we have termed an *incremental* theory of intelligence: They believe that intelligence is a malleable, increasable, controllable quality. Others lean more toward an *entity* theory of intelligence: They believe that intelligence is a fixed or uncontrollable trait. Our research consistently indicates that children who believe intelligence is increasable pursue the learning goal of increasing their competence, whereas those who believe intelligence is a fixed entity are more likely to pursue the performance goal of securing positive judgments of that entity or preventing negative judgments of it (see Table 1).

For example, in a study with late grade-school-age children, Bandura and Dweck (1985) found that children who endorsed the incremental theory (e.g., "Smartness is something you can increase as much as you want to") were significantly more likely to adopt learning goals on an experimental task than were children who endorsed the entity theory (e.g., "You can learn new things, but how smart you are stays pretty much the same"). Similar findings were obtained in a classroom setting (see Dweck & Bempechat, 1983): Incremental theorists were significantly more likely than en-

TABLE 3. Percentage of Subjects With Each Theory of Intelligence Selecting Each Achievement Goal

Theory of intelligence	Goal choice		
	Performance goal (avoid challenge)	Performance goal (seek challenge)	Learning goal (seek challenge)
Entity theory (n = 22)	50.0	31.8	18.2
Incremental theory (n = 41)	9.8	29.3	60.9

tity theorists to report a preference for classroom tasks that embodied learning goals ("Hard, new, and different so I could try to learn from them") versus performance goals ("Fun and easy to do, so I wouldn't have to worry about mistakes"; "Like things I'm good at so I can feel smart").

In a recent study, Leggett (1985) revised the theories of intelligence assessment and examined the relation between theories of intelligence and goal choice in a junior high school sample. As shown in Table 3, children's theories of intelligence were again reliable predictors of their goal choice. The challenge-seeking performance goal ("I'd like problems that are hard enough to show that I'm smart") and the challenge-avoidant performance goal ("I'd like problems that aren't too hard, so I don't get many wrong" or "I'd like problems that are fairly easy, so I'll do well") are presented separately in Table 3 to emphasize the degree to which the incremental and entity theories are differentially.

To illuminate the causal relationship between implicit theories and goal choice, Dweck, Tenney, and Dinces (1982) experimentally manipulated children's theories of intelligence and then assessed their goal choice on an upcoming task. In their study, children were oriented toward either an entity or incremental theory by means of reading passages that portrayed the intelligence of notable individuals (Albert Einstein, Helen Keller, and the child Rubik's Cube champion) as either a fixed, inborn trait or an acquirable quality. The structure, content, tone, and interest value of the two passages were highly similar, except that they presented and illustrated different definitions of smartness. Great we was taken to avoid attaching any goals to these theories, that is, to avoid any mention or implication of learning versus performance goals.

The passage on intelligence was embedded in a series of three short, interesting reading passages, all concerning "things that psychologists study" (imprinting, intelligence, dreams). As a rationale for reading these passages, children were asked to indicate after each one whether they would like to know more about this topic. As a rationale for their subsequent goal choice, children were told that psychologists also study how people think, form concepts, and solve intellectual problems. They were then asked to select from a list of different types of problems (each embodying a different goal choice) the type of problem they would like to work on when the experimenters returned. The results showed that the experimental manipulation of theory affected children's goal choices in the predicted direction: Subjects who had read the incremental passage were significantly more likely to adapt learning goals for the upcoming task than were those who had read the entity passage. This study, then, by (temporarily) orienting children toward a particular theory of intelligence, provided support for a causal relationship between implicit theories and goal choice.

Taken together, the research indicates that an incremental theory of intelligence is more consistently associated with adaptive motivational patterns. In this context, it is interesting to note (along with Covington, 1983, and Gould, 1981) that Alfred Binet, the inventor of the IQ test, was clearly an incremental theorist. He believed that not only specific skills, but also basic capacity for learning were enhanced through his training procedures:

> It is in this practical sense, the only one accessible to us, that we say that the intelligence of these children has been increased. We have increased what constitutes the intelligence of a pupil: the capacity to learn and to assimilate instruction. (Binet 1909/1973, p. 104)

It is therefore a particular irony that the assessment tool he developed within an incremental theory and learning goal framework has been widely interpreted within an entity theory and performance goal framework as a measure of a stable quality. As Dweck and Elliott (1983) pointed out, perhaps the most appropriate view represents an integration of both entity and incremental theories, that is, a recognition of present differences in relative ability but an emphasis on individual growth in ability (see also Nicholls, 1984).[5]

In summary, implicit beliefs about ability pre-

---

[5]For research purposes we have treated theory of intelligence as a dichotomous variable, and in some studies (where the measure has permitted it) we have in fact obtained bimodal distributions of theory scores. However, it is of great interest to us to determine more precisely the exact nature of individuals' theories (e.g., whether there are quantitatively or qualitatively different versions of both theories, or whether some individuals hold blends of the two theories), and this research is currently underway (Henderson, Cain, & Dweck, 1987).

dict whether individuals will be oriented toward developing their ability or toward documenting the adequacy of their ability. As such, these theories may be at the root of adaptive and maladaptive patterns. Indeed it may be the adherence to an underlying entity theory that makes performance goals potentially maladaptive, for within an entity theory individuals are not simply judging a momentary level of ability. Rather, they may be judging what they perceive to be an important and permanent personal attribute. Thus, an entity theory may place one's intelligence on the line in evaluative situations, magnifying the meaning and impact of negative judgments.

Generalization of the Model to Other Domains

Does the Formulation Have Generality?

The research we have reviewed indicates that the theory–goal–behavior formulation illuminates behavior patterns in achievement situations, but does it also illuminate behavior patterns in other major domains, such as social situations or moral situations? Do individuals hold theories about the malleability of their social and moral attributes, such as their personality or their moral character? Do these theories orient them toward different goals (to document vs. develop these attributes)? Finally, do these goals generate different behavior patterns?

Note that achievement situations are particularly suitable for developing and testing motivational models. Researchers can readily establish convincing and compelling situations that afford a high degree of control and precision. For example, achievement situations allow for standardization of tasks and feedback across individuals. They also allow one to separate ability or skill factors from motivational factors—to control for the former and investigate the latter. Finally, the moment-to-moment impact of motivational factors on cognitive performance can be precisely monitored in both laboratory and field settings. However, it is then important to examine the generality of the models developed in this context.

In this section we review research evidence that suggests that the motivational formulation developed in achievement situations can illuminate behavior in social relationships as well. Following this, we evaluate the applicability of the formulation to still other domains, reviewing relevant evidence when it is available and proposing relevant research when it is not.

Social Domain

As shown in Table 4, the model applied to the social domain would predict that (a) there are adaptive mastery-oriented and maladaptive helpless responses to difficulty (rejection, conflict) in social situations, (b) these reflect the social goal the individual is pursuing in that situation, and (c) the goal is linked to the individual's theory of his or her attributes as fixed entities or malleable qualities. What is the evidence for the model?

First, Goetz and Dweck (1980) documented helpless and mastery-oriented responses to social rejection that are clearly analogous to those found by Diener and Dweck (1978, 1980) in achievement settings. To tap children's attributions for social rejection, Goetz and Dweck developed a questionnaire depicting a series of hypothetical social situations involving rejection. For each situation, children were asked to evaluate different reasons the rejection might have occurred. Both the situations and their causes were based on those

Table 4. Model of Social Motivation

Theory	Goal orientation	Behavior pattern
Entity (Social/personality attributes are fixed traits)	Performance (Goal is to gain positive judgments/avoid negative judgments of social attributes)	Helpless (Avoid risk; low persistence)
Incremental (Social/personality attributes are malleable qualities)	Learning/development (Goal is to increase social competence, develop relationships)	Mastery oriented (Seek challenge; high persistence)

Note. Predicted interaction of goal with confidence level (depicted in Table 1) is omitted here for simplicity.

most frequently generated by children in pilot interviews, for example, "Suppose you move to a new neighborhood. A girl/boy you meet does not like you very much. Why would this happen to you?" The reasons offered included such factors as personal social incompetence, a negative characteristic of the rejector, the chance mood of the rejector, or a misunderstanding.

Within the 3-week period following the administration of this attribution questionnaire, each subject was seen individually in a situation that posed the possibility of rejection from a peer and that allowed assessment of changes in strategies in the face of rejection. Specifically, children tried out for a pen pal club by communicating their sample getting-to-know-you letter to a peer evaluator who represented the pen pal acceptance committee. The evaluator initially expressed uncertainty about admitting the child into the club, but allowed the child the opportunity to compose a second letter and attempt to obtain a positive decision. The pre- and postrejection letters were then coded and assessed for change. The major measure of adaptive change was the amount of new information the child introduced into the second letter.

As in the achievement research, children were initially classified into groups on the basis of their attributions. Those blaming personal social incompetence for rejection were predicted to show the helpless pattern, whereas those attributing rejection to the other factors were predicted to display a more mastery-oriented pattern. Also as in the achievement research, children falling into the different groups did not differ in their skill at the task, as evidenced by their performance prior to failure. That is, children in different groups showed no differences in the length or quality of the first letter they produced. However, clear differences emerged in the letter that followed rejection.

First, children making the incompetence attribution were far more likely than others to show complete disruption of performance following rejection. Approximately 39% of the children in this group showed withdrawal (initial refusal to try again after rejection) or perseveration (verbatim repetition of the first unsuccessful message). Few children in other groups showed this degree of disruption. Second, looking at the amount of new information contained in the second message, Goetz and Dweck found that children making the incompetence attribution showed the least message change of any group. Thus, the results directly

parallel the Diener and Dweck findings that helpless children are less likely than others to formulate new strategies in the face of difficulty and are more likely than others to repeat ineffective strategies or to abandon effective strategies entirely.

Looking at the specific content of the second message, another striking parallel to the Diener and Dweck results was apparent. Children making the incompetence attribution were more likely to engage in defensive self-aggrandizement than were children in the other groups. Specifically, they boasted in their postrejection message about their popularity in other contexts, even though they were not more popular than children in the other groups (as assessed by classroom sociometric ratings). In summary, this research provides clear evidence for the impact of motivational patterns in social situations.

Do children's social goals predict their motivational patterns? Although there is as yet no direct evidence linking goals to specific behavior patterns, Renshaw and Asher (1983) and Taylor and Asher (1984a, 1984b, 1985) have begun to link the goals children pursue in social situations to their sociometric status (i.e., their popularity with peers). They have devised a variety of means for tapping children's goals—having the child respond to hypothetical conflicts with a peer and probing for the goal of the child's actions (Renshaw & Asher, 1983) or having the child complete a questionnaire on which various goals are pitted against each other (e.g., Taylor & Asher, 1984b).

The consistent finding is that children of low sociometric status are more likely to formulate or endorse "avoidance" goals—performance goals in which the concerns center around avoiding negative outcomes. Indeed, on Taylor and Asher's questionnaire measure (which included concerns about social rejection, as well as about skill-related failures in a game-playing context), children of low sociometric status were more concerned than other children with avoiding both negative social outcomes and negative game-related achievement outcomes. Taylor and Asher suggested that this preoccupation with negative outcomes may be in part responsible for the lower popularity of these children. However, as they acknowledge, further research is necessary to establish more clearly the direction of causality between goals and sociometric status and determine more precisely the specific ways in which goals may affect social behavior to produce sociometric differences.

These issues can be directly addressed in studies that manipulate goals and then assess the quality and success of subsequent peer interactions. Another strategy for addressing the second issue (although it does not establish causal direction) is to measure children's goals and then examine important aspects of their social behavior, such as their response to conflict or rejection. One such study is currently underway in our laboratory. Olshefsky, Erdley and Dweck, (1987), using the Goetz and Dweck (1980) paradigm, are assessing children's goals in the pen pal acquaintanceship task: Is a given child pursuing predominantly a performance goal (hoping to win positive judgments and validation of his or her likeability, or avoid negative judgments and rejection), or is that child focusing on a learning/development goal (hoping to develop a new relationship, expand social horizons and social experiences, master a new social task)?[6] It is hypothesized that the two goals will be differentially associated with the helpless and the mastery-oriented response to rejection found by Goetz and Dweck; specifically, the performance goal (particularly when combined with low confidence) will be most predictive of the helpless pattern, and the learning/development goal (even when accompanied by low confidence) will be predictive of the mastery-oriented pattern.

In the Olshefsky et al. study and in another study as well (Benenson, 1987), we are testing the hypothesis that children's implicit theories of their social attributes predict their social goals. Olshefsky et al., as well as Benenson, have developed questionnaires assessing whether children believe their personality or their likeability to be a fixed, uncontrollable characteristic or a malleable, acquirable one. For example, Olshefsky et al. have asked children to indicate the degree to which they agree with statements such as "You have a certain personality and there isn't much you can do to change it." In both cases, pilot results have revealed clear individual differences in whether children subscribe to the entity or incremental theory of their social attributes, and it is hypothesized that, as in achievement situations, these theories will predict the goals they adopt and pursue.

In summary, past research has established the existence of helpless and mastery-oriented patterns of response to social rejection and has suggested a link between children's goals in social situations and the success of their social interactions. Current research is aimed at fleshing out and testing

precisely the larger model of social motivation in which implicit theories predict social goals and social goals provide the framework for social behavior.

Morality and Other Attributes of the Self

As a final example, the same conceptualization may be applied to the moral domain to illuminate the reasons or purposes for which individuals (at any stage of moral development) engage in moral actions. As before, the model would suggest that some people tend to engage in moral actions in order to prove to themselves and others that they are moral individuals (performance goals), whereas other people might tend to pursue courses of action that would develop their moral understanding or that would allow them to master a morally difficult situation according to some standard (learning goals). It would be predicted, as well, that performance goals would create a vulnerability to risk avoidance (e.g., conformity) and low persistence in situations that contained the threat of negative moral judgments, whereas learning goals would better arm the individual to withstand conflict with or disapproval from others (see Rest, 1983, for a discussion of the need to consider motivational variables in the prediction of moral behavior).

Also as before, the model would predict that different "theories of morality" would be associated with the different goals. Those who believe that their goodness or moral character is a fixed trait would orient toward documenting that trait, whereas those who believe it is a malleable quality would orient toward developing and exercising that quality.

Thus far, we have developed a motivational model and examined its applicability to major attributes of the self: intellectual competence, social competence, and, very briefly, morality. However, it may be possible to generalize the model to any attribute of the self. Bempechat and Dweck (1985) sampled a variety of personal attributes (intelligence, morality, physical skills, and physical attractiveness) and found that each was seen by

---

[6]The learning goal in the social domain will include not only developing one's own social skills, but also developing relationships between oneself and others. It might thus be more accurate to call it a "development" goal.

some children as quite malleable ("You can get more and more _____ all the time") but by others as more fixed ("You're a certain amount _____, and how _____ you are stays pretty much the same").[7] The further prediction, of course, is that for any personal attribute that the individual values, viewing it as a fixed trait will lead to a desire to document the adequacy of that trait, whereas viewing it as a malleable quality will foster a desire to develop that quality.

Theories and Goals: Two Types of Self-Concept, Two Sources of Self-Esteem

The two theories about one's personal attributes may be seen as fundamentally different ways of conceptualizing the self. That is, entity and incremental theories represent two different forms of self-concept. Within a generalized entity theory, the self would be conceptualized as a collection of fixed traits that can be measured and evaluated. Within an incremental theory, the self would be seen as a system of malleable qualities that is evolving over time through the individual's efforts.

As a consequence of the different self-concepts, the processes that generate and maintain self-esteem (i.e., feelings of satisfaction with one's attributes) will differ (see Damon & Hart, 1982, for a discussion of the important distinction between self-concept and self-esteem). Indeed, the different goals allied with each theory may be seen as the means of generating self-esteem within that self-concept. For the entity theorist, self-esteem will be fed by performance goals. Outcomes indicating the adequacy of one's attributes will raise and maintain self-esteem. However, for the incremental theorist, self-esteem will be acquired and experienced via learning goals. Pursuit of, progress on, and mastery of challenging and valued tasks will raise and maintain self-esteem.

Data collected by Elliott and Dweck (see Dweck & Bempechat, 1983) provide support for this suggestion. Following an assessment of their theories of intelligence, children were asked to describe when they felt smart in school, that is, when they experienced high self-esteem with regard to their intelligence. They were told "Sometimes kids feel smart in school, sometimes not. When do you feel smart?" In line with prediction, children who had endorsed an entity theory reported that they felt smart when their schoolwork was error free

("When I don't do mistakes"), when their work surpassed that of their peers ("When I turn in my papers first"), or when the work was easy for them ("When I get easy work"). In sharp contrast, children with an incremental theory reported that they felt smart when they worked on hard tasks and when they personally mastered these challenges ("When I don't know how to do it and it's pretty hard and I figure it out without anyone telling me"; "When I'm doing school work because I want to learn how to get smart"; "When I'm reading a hard book"). Thus children with different theories reported experiencing high self-esteem under essentially opposite conditions, but these were conditions that represented the goals that accompany their theories.

In summary, it is proposed that the theories and their allied goals can be seen as two distinct "self-systems": two forms of self-concept with two different sources of self-esteem. These notions may provide one way of thinking specifically and concretely about the global construct self-concept, of theoretically linking self-concept to self-esteem, and of placing both within a system that predicts patterns of behavior.

In the context of the entity versus the incremental self-systems, it is interesting to consider that different personality theories have focused primarily on one or the other. For example, Freud's psychodynamic theory depicts essentially an entity self-system (e.g., Freud, 1923/1960, 1933/1964), in which the judging superego continually assesses the adequacy of the ego and the various defenses are set up to deflect information that is threatening to the ego. Surprisingly, there appear to be no direct mechanisms within his system for generating goals oriented toward growth (see White, 1960).[8] In contrast, and in reaction to Freud, theorists like Jung (1933) and White (1959) have de-

---

[7]Many children held the same theory across attributes, although others held different ones for different attributes. However, for purposes of clarity and simplicity in subsequent sections, we will often speak as though individuals held the same theory across attributes.

[8]Although Freud was a therapist and therefore believed in the possibility of personal change, his therapy remained within the entity selfsystem. The aim was to repair the maladaptive patterns of cognition, affect, and behavior that arise within that system (such as overly harsh self-judgments, excessive anxiety, and the overuse of defenses and their behavioral sequelae), and thereby promote efficient functioning of that system. His vision of therapy did not encompass change toward a different (incremental) mode of functioning.

scribed self-systems built around the impetus toward growth and development (see also Adler, 1927; Erikson, 1959; Rapaport, 1951). Clearly, a comprehensive theory of personality must take account of both systems.

Generalization of the Model Beyond the Self

Thus far we have discussed individuals' implicit theories about the mutability of self-attributes. But now we ask whether individuals hold implicit theories about the mutability of attributes of things outside of themselves: characteristics of other people, places, things, or the world in general (see Epstein, 1980, Janoff-Bulman, 1985, and Lerner, 1980, for related discussions of "world" beliefs). Here an entity theory would assert that people, places, things, and the world in general are what they are and there is little one can do to alter them. An incremental theory would propose that desirable qualities can be cultivated: People can be made more competent, institutions can be made more responsible, the environment can be made more healthful, the world can be made more just. We suggest that mutability or controllability is a dimension along which important things—be they internal or external, abstract or concrete—are categorized. We further suggest that the way something is categorized has important consequences for the way it is treated: Fixed or uncontrollable things that are important will tend to be monitored, measured, and judged, whereas controllable things that are important will tend to be acted on and developed.

The idea that mutability is a central dimension in terms of which things are conceptualized receives indirect support from a great variety of sources. Philosophers, anthropologists, historians of science, linguists, and psychologists have documented historical changes and cultural differences in whether people and things tend to be viewed in terms of fixed entities or malleable processes.

For example, Whitehead (l938) contrasted in detail scientific theories and philosophical systems that presuppose a world of static objects versus dynamic, evolving processes. Moreover, he details the consequences of each for the way in which one conducts scientific inquiry, that is, whether one focuses on measuring the entities or on understanding and influencing the processes.

Heller (1967/1981) contrasted pre- and post-Renaissance thought and proposed that the true revolution of the Renaissance was a revolution in the conception of persons. "During antiquity, a static conception of man prevailed: his potentialities were circumscribed both in his social and individual life. . . . With the Renaissance a dynamic concept of man appears" (p. 1). And with this dynamic conception of individuals, argued Heller, came the idea of development, whereby individuals can form and shape their own natures.

Furthermore, some linguists have suggested that different languages may embody, and different cultural–linguistic groups may favor, one mode of thought over the other. For example, Bloom, in his book *The Linguistic Shaping of Thought* (1981), developed the position that the English language, in contrast to the Chinese language, "entifies" properties of people and things. The English language, for instance, consistently takes adjectives that describe a person's action or way of behaving and creates nouns that accord this property a separate reality of its own. This entification, Bloom contended, is not simply a different way of expressing something, but rather reflects and perpetuates a different way of thinking about it (see Langer, 1982, for related arguments).

Finally, it has just come to our attention that Piaget, in his last book (Piaget & Garcia, 1983, currently being translated into English by J. Easley), modified his stage theory of cognitive development to include "conceptions of the world" similar to the ones we have described here. In this book, Piaget discussed at length how in addition to universal logical structures, the individual "possesses a conception of the world which controls his assimilation of any and every experience." In particular, he contrasted the conception of the world as fundamentally static (the Aristotelian view) with the conception of the world as being in a constant state of becoming and suggested how these ideologies can generate different interpretive frameworks for experience.

In summary, thinking in terms of relatively static, reified entities versus thinking in terms of dynamic, malleable processes can be seen as two alternative ways of conceptualizing many phenomena, with science and culture perhaps fostering particular views of particular phenomena at certain times.

Table 5 presents our model generalized to attributes external to the self (properties of people,

TABLE 5. Generalization of Model to External Attributes

Theory	Goal orientation	Predicted pattern
Entity (Attributes of people and world are fixed or uncontrollable)	Judgment (Goal is to make positive or negative judgment of attributes)	Behavior: Low initiation of and persistence toward change Cognition: Rigid, over-simplified thinking Affect: Evaluative affect such as contempt
Incremental (Attributes of people and world are malleable)	Development (Goal is to understand and improve attributes)	Behavior: Mastery-oriented goal pursuit Cognition: Process analysis Affect: Empathy

places, things, phenomena, or the world). In this model, an entity theory predisposes the individual to adopt "judgment" goals. That is, when individuals believe that important external attributes are fixed or uncontrollable, they will tend to measure and evaluate those attributes in order to know what to expect: Is this person competent/trustworthy or not? Is this institution fair or not? Is the world benign or not? Judgment goals can be seen as the general case of performance goals: An attribute is being judged on the basis of a sample of actions or outcomes.

What patterns should follow from an entity theory of external attributes? An entity theory of external attributes, by its very nature, should inhibit the initiation and pursuit of change, even when an external attribute is judged negatively and improvement is seen as desirable.[9] Individuals holding entity theories of external attributes and pursuing judgment goals might also display a tendency to derive oversimplified, all-or-nothing characterizations from a small sample of actions or outcomes. Believing others to possess fixed attributes that are positive or negative, adequate or inadequate, they may view actions and outcomes as providing a reading of those attributes. For example, just as some individuals with an entity theory of intelligence and performance goals were found to infer a lack of ability from a few failures (without considering such factors as task difficulty and without giving themselves the time and leeway to improve with experience), so individuals with an entity theory of others and judgment goals may ascribe to others broad traits like dishonesty, untrustworthiness, or incompetence on the basis

of isolated pieces of evidence (perhaps without considering situational factors or taking the perspective of the individual in the situation).

In contrast, when individuals hold an incremental theory of important external attributes (*and* view the attributes as being in need of improvement), then, we predict, they will tend to adopt "development" goals toward those attributes. Development goals can be viewed as the general case of learning goals: Improvement of valued attributes or mastery of valued tasks or situations is sought. For example, individuals may seek to increase the competence, sensitivity, or morality of another person, an institution, or a society. They may seek to tackle and rectify a problematic situation in their environment. As such, development goals should have all the characteristics described for learning goals, including a focus on process and a mastery-oriented response to difficulty.

One can also make predictions about the affect that might follow from the different theories and goals. For example, within an entity theory, a negative judgment of another's qualities (as permanently inferior) may well lead to contempt for that individual. In contrast, within an incremental theory, the observation of inadequate performance or deficient behavior may lead to compassion or empathy for the individual (Hoffman, 1978).

Erdley and Dweck (1987) are currently testing these hypotheses. They have suggested that an entity theory about others' traits—the belief that

---

[9]Entity theorists may attempt to punish, restrain, exploit, or control those they judge to be evil or inferior, but they will not engage in ameliorative measures vis-à-vis the negative attribute.

people or groups of people have unalterable positive or negative qualities—may lie at the heart of stereotypes and prejudices, and they have predicted that individuals who hold entity theories of others will be more susceptible to forming stereotypes of others, distorting information in terms of stereotypes, acting on stereotypes, and maintaining stereotypes in the face of counter information. In contrast, it is predicted that individuals who hold an incremental theory of others, because they do not see others in terms of fixed traits, should be more sensitive to situational factors that can account for a person's negative behavior (cf. Jones & Nisbett, 1972). They should also be more likely to take account of subsequent behavior that contradicts the initial negative behavior, and finally, they should be more willing to engage in behavior that will facilitate desired change in the other person.

To summarize the overall formulation thus far, it is proposed that individuals identify valued attributes or characteristics of themselves, others, and the world; that they have implicit theories about the controllability of those attributes; and that they adopt particular goals (judgment or development goals) with respect to those attributes.

We might also note that individuals will vary in the extent to which they pursue goals relating to the self versus other people versus the world. This will depend on where they place their values, that is, on the extent to which they value attributes in these different spheres. For example, among individuals with generalized incremental theories, some may prize self-attributes most highly and strive to develop their own qualities; others may focus on attributes of others, striving to teach new skills, perform psychotherapy, or cure physical illnesses; still others may focus on the societal level, striving to increase human rights or promote world peace. In our experimental situations thus far, we have constrained individuals' goal choices to "within-attribute" choices—to learning/development versus performance/judgment goals with respect to a given characteristic of the self or another person. However, it should be possible to construct situations that present between-attribute goal choices and to predict individuals' goals by measuring the relative values they place on the different attributes and the theories they hold of those attributes. In this way, we can gain a fuller picture of these motivational processes in less constrained settings. [. . .]

Implications for Personality and Motivation

The current formulation, which began with patterns of cognition, affect, and behavior and then traced these patterns to underlying psychological processes, has implications for a number of theoretical issues in personality and motivation.

One class of issues concerns the role of situational versus dispositional factors in determining behavior (see Bem & Allen, 1974; Bem & Funder, 1978; and Mischel & Peake, 1982, for discussions of this issue). Dispositional approaches have had wide appeal because we know that people confronting the same situation react differently (and often, it seems, characteristically). Situational approaches have also had appeal in that many situations appear to constrain or compel behavior. Perhaps the widest appeal has been enjoyed by the interactionist (Disposition × Situation) position because it grants the contribution of both types of variables and thereby promises a more complete story (see Buss, 1977; Diener, Larsen, & Emmons, 1984; and Endler, 1983, for reviews).

But how should we conceptualize dispositions? Does the existence of dispositions imply, as some have argued, that an individual's behavior should be similar across diverse situations? How should we think about situations? And how do dispositional and situational factors combine to produce behavior?

First, our research has clearly shown that both situational variables and dispositional variables play important roles in producing behavior. We have experimentally induced goals and behavior patterns by manipulating situational variables (Dweck, Davidson, Nelson, & Enna, 1978; Elliott & Dweck, 1988), but we have also predicted goal choice and behavior patterns by measuring existing dispositional variables (e.g., implicit theories: Bandura & Dweck, 1985; Leggett, 1985). A view that integrates these findings is one in which dispositions are seen as individual difference variables that determine the a priori probability of adopting a particular goal and displaying a particular behavior pattern, and situational factors are seen as potentially altering these probabilities.

In other words, we suggest that person–situation interactions are best understood in probabilistic terms, with the situation potentially altering the probability that a predisposing tendency will prevail. Let us assume that in a situation affording a choice between a performance goal and a learning goal, an individual brings to the situation a predisposition of a certain strength to favor one goal or the other. Where the situation offers no cue favoring either, the predisposition should hold sway. If, on the other hand, the situation offers strong cues in favor of either (appreciably increasing its salience or value), predispositions should be overridden and greater homogeneity among individuals will result. The stronger a predisposition, the less likely it is to be overriden by situational cues or the stronger will be the situational cues necessary to override it. Analogously, the weaker the predisposition, the more easily it can be altered by situational cues. Thus although we grant an important role to dispositional variables, this view of how situational cues and dispositional tendencies combine would lead one not to expect behavioral consistency across situations when the strength of the relevant situational cues varies across these situations.

Another factor that would work against finding behavioral consistency across situations is the fact that different goals may be available in different situations. Consider three situations: one affords a choice of intellectual achievement goals (learning or performance), the second affords a choice of these achievement goals along with social goals, and the third affords a choice of achievement goals along with social goals and moral goals. By measuring for each individual, the relative value of intellectual, social, and moral attributes, as well as the theory attached to each (entity or incremental), one can begin to predict the goal that will be pursued in each situation. In some cases, it will be the same goal across situations; in other cases it may be a different one in each. In the latter case, little behavioral resemblance would be expected across situations. In fact, marked contradictions in behavior might emerge as the individual pursued different goals. A person might cheat in the first situation in order to obtain a high grade and be judged intelligent, but might be honest and altruistic in the latter two situations in order to be judged favorably on social and moral attributes.

In short, the power of personality theories and dispositional variables lies in their ability to predict what behavior will be displayed in various situations, not in their prediction that the same behavior will be displayed across these situations. [. . .]

Summary and Conclusion

We began by documenting patterns of cognition–affect–behavior that have profound effects on adaptive functioning. We then asked questions about the underlying motivational and personality variables that give rise to these response patterns, first demonstrating the role of learning and performance goals in producing the patterns and then linking these goals to individuals' implicit theories of their attributes.

Next we examined the generalizability of the model to a variety of self-attributes. We suggested that each implicit theory could be seen as a different form of self-concept and that its allied goal could be seen as the way of generating and maintaining self-esteem within that self-concept. Finally, we proposed that the model could be extended to attributes outside of the self, hypothesizing that individuals hold implicit theories about the characteristics of other people, places, and things, and that these theories will predict the goals they adopt vis-à-vis these external variables.

In this context, we examined the relation of our model to other current formulations and developed the implications of our approach for contemporary issues in motivation and personality. In closing, we would like to highlight what we believe to be the central aspect of our model: its depiction of the manner in which underlying personality variables can translate into dynamic motivational processes to produce major patterns of cognition, affect, and behavior. Although much model-testing and model-building research remains to be done, the existing work lends encouraging support to the present model. It suggests that this model may be useful for both tying together existing lines of research and generating new lines of research in the future.

REFERENCES

Adler, A. (1927). *The practice and theory of individual psychology.* New York: Harcourt, Brace & World.

Ames, C. (1984). Achievement attributions and self-instructions under competitive and individualistic goal structures. *Journal of Educational Psychology, 76,* 478–487.

Ames, C., Ames, R., & Felker, D. W. (1977). Effects of competitive reward structure and valence of outcome on children's achievement attributions. *Journal of Educational Psychology, 69,* 1–8.

Bandura, M., & Dweck, C. S. (1985). *The relationship of conceptions of intelligence and achievement goals to achievement-related cognition, affect and behavior.* Manuscript submitted for publication.

Bem, D., & Allen, A. (1974). Predicting some of the people some of the time: The search for cross-situational consistencies in behavior. *Psychological Review, 81,* 506–520.

Bem, D., & Funder, D. (1978). Predicting more of the people more of the time: Assessing the personality of situations. *Psychological Review, 85,* 485–501.

Bempechat, J., & Dweck, C. S. (1985). *Children's conceptions of self-attributes.* Unpublished manuscript.

Benenson, J. (1987). [Children's implicit theories and goals in their friendships]. Unpublished raw data.

Berglas, S., & Jones, E. (1978). Drug choice as a self-handicapping strategy in response to non-contingent success. *Journal of Personality and Social Psychology, 36,* 405–417.

Binet, A. (1973). *Les idees modernes sur les enfants* [Modern ideas on children]. Paris: Flamarion. (Original work published 1909)

Bloom, A. (1981). *The linguistic shaping of thought.* Hillsdale, NJ: Erlbaum.

Brunson, B., & Matthews, K. (1981). The Type-A coronary-prone behavior pattern and reactions to uncontrollable stress: An analysis of performance strategies, affect, and attributions during failure. *Journal of Personality and Social Psychology, 40,* 906–918.

Buss, A. (1977). The trait–situation controversy and the concept of interaction. *Personality and Social Psychology Bulletin, 3,* 196–201.

Cain, K., & Dweck, C. S. (1987). [The development of children's theories of intelligence]. Unpublished raw data.

Carver, C. S., Peterson, L. M., Follansbee, D. J., & Scheier, M. F. (1983). Effects of self-directed attention on performance and persistence among persons high and low in test anxiety. *Cognitive Therapy and Research, 7,* 333–354.

Covington, M. V. (1983). Strategic thinking and the fear of failure. In J. Sigal, S. Chipman, & R. Glaser (Eds.), *Thinking and learning skills: Relating instruction to research* (Vol. 2, pp. 389–416). Hillsdale, NJ: Erlbaum.

Covington, M. V., & Omelich, C. (1979). Effort: The double-edged sword in school achievement. *Journal of Educational Psychology, 71,* 169–182.

Crandall, V. C., Katkovsky, W., & Crandall, V. J. (1965). Childrens' beliefs in their own control of reinforcement in intellectual–academic situations. *Child Development, 36,* 91–109.

Damon, W., & Hart, D. (1982). The development of self-understanding from infancy through adolescence. *Child Development, 53,* 841–864.

Deci, E. L., & Ryan, R. M. (1980). The empirical exploration of intrinsic motivational processes. In L. Berkowitz, (Ed.), *Advances in experimental social psychology* (Vol. 13, pp. 39–80). New York: Academic Press.

Diener, C. I., & Dweck, C. S. (1978). An analysis of learned helplessness: Continuous changes in performance, strategy and achievement cognitions following failure. *Journal of Personality and Social Psychology, 36,* 451–462.

Diener, C. I., & Dweck, C. S. (1980). An analysis of learned helplessness: II. The processing of success. *Journal of Personality and Social Psychology, 39,* 940–952.

Diener, E., Larsen, R., & Emmons, R. (1984). Person × Situation interactions: Choice of situations and congruence response models. *Journal of Personality and Social Psychology, 47,* 580–592.

Dweck, C. S. (1975). The role of expectations and attributions in the alleviation of learned helplessness. *Journal of Personality and Social Psychology, 31,* 674–685.

Dweck, C. S., & Bempechat, J. (1983). Children's theories of intelligence. In S. Paris, G. Olsen, & H. Stevenson (Eds.), *Learning and motivation in the classroom* (pp. 239–256). Hillsdale, NJ: Erlbaum.

Dweck, C. S., Davidson, W., Nelson, S., & Enna, B. (1978). Sex differences in learned helplessness: II. The contingencies of evaluative feedback in the classroom and III. An experimental analysis. *Developmental Psychology, 14,* 268–276.

Dweck, C. S., & Elliott, E. S. (1983). Achievement motivation. In P H. Mussen (Gen. Ed.) & E. M. Hetherington (Vol. Ed.), *Handbook of child psychology: Vol. IV. Social and personality development* (pp. 643–691). New York: Wiley.

Dweck, C. S., & Reppucci, N. D. (1973). Learned helplessness and reinforcement responsibility in children. *Journal of Personality and Social Psychology, 25,* 109–116.

Dweck, C. S., Tenney, Y., & Dinces, N. (1982). [Implicit theories of intelligence as determinants of achievement goal choice]. Unpublished raw data.

Elliott, E. S., & Dweck, C. S. (1988). Goals: An approach to motivation and achievement. *Journal of Personality and Social Psychology, 54,* 5–12.

Endler, N. (1983). Interactionism: A personality model, but not yet a theory. In R. A. Dienstbier (Ed.), *Nebraska Symposium on Motivation* (pp. 155–200). Lincoln: University of Nebraska Press.

Epstein, S. (1980). The self-concept: A review and the proposal of an integrated theory of personality. In E. Straub (Ed.), *Personality: Basic aspects and current research* (pp. 81–131). Englewood Cliffs, NJ: Prentice-Hall.

Erdley, C. A., & Dweck, C. S. (1987). [Implicit personality theories: Effects on social judgment]. Unpublished raw data.

Erikson, E. H. (1959). Identity and the life cycle. *Psychological Issues, 1,* 1–171.

Farrell, E., & Dweck, C. S. (1985). *The role of motivational processes in transfer of learning.* Manuscript submitted for publication.

Frankl, A., & Snyder, M. (1978). Poor performance following unsolvable problems: Learned helplessness or egotism? *Journal of Personality and Social Psychology, 36,* 1415–1423.

Freud, S. (1960). *The ego and the id.* (J. Riviere, Trans.). New York: W. W. Norton. (Original work published 1923)

Freud, S. (1964). New introductory lectures on psychoanalysis. (J. Stachey, Trans.). New York: W. W. Norton. (Original work published 1933)

Goetz, T. E., & Dweck, C. S. (1980). Learned helplessness in social situations. *Journal of Personality and Social Psychology, 39,* 249–255.

Goodnow, J. J. (1980). Everyday concepts of intelligence and its development. In N. Warren (Ed), *Studies in cross-cultural psychology* (Vol. 2, pp. 191–219). Oxford, England: Pergamon Press.

Gould, S. J. (1981). *The mismeasure of man.* New York: W. W. Norton.

Heller, A. (1981). *Renaissance man* (R. Allen, Trans.). New York: Schocken. (Original work published 1967)

Henderson, V., Cain, K., & Dweck, C. S. (1987). [Theories of intelligence and their dimensions]. Unpublished raw data.

Hoffman, M. (1978). Empathy, its development and prosocial implications. In C. B. Keasey (Ed.), *Nebraska Symposium on Motivation* (pp. 169–218). Lincoln: University of Nebraska Press.

Jagacinski, C., & Nicholls, J. (1983, March). *Concepts of ability*. Paper presented at the annual meeting of the American Educational Research Association, New York, NY.

Janoff-Bulman, R. (1985, March). *Understanding people in terms of their assumptive worlds*. Paper presented at the Boston University Symposium on the Interdisciplinary Study of Personality, Boston.

Janoff-Bulman, R., & Brickman, P. (1981). Expectations and what people learn from failure. In N. T. Feather (Ed.), *Expectancy, incentive, and action* (pp. 207–237). Hillsdale, NJ: Erlbaum.

Jones, E. E., & Nisbett, R. E. (1972). The actor and the observer: Divergent perceptions of the causes of behavior. In E. E. Jones, D. E. Kanouse, H. H. Kelley, R. E. Nisbett, S. Valins, & B. Weiner (Ed.), *Attribution: Perceiving the causes of behavior* (pp. 79–94). Morristown, NJ: General Learning Press.

Jung, C. (1933). *Modern man in search of a soul*. New York: Harcourt, Brace & World.

Langer, S. K. (1982). *Mind: An essay on human feeling, Vol. III*. Baltimore: Johns Hopkins University Press.

Leggett, E. L. (1985, March). *Children's entity and incremental theories of intelligence: Relationships to achievement behavior*. Paper presented at the annual meeting of the Eastern Psychological Association, Boston.

Leggett, E. L., & Dweck, C. S. (1986). *Goals and inference rules: Sources of causal judgments*. Manuscript submitted for publication.

Lepper, M. (1981). Intrinsic and extrinsic motivation in children: Detrimental effects of superfluous social controls. In W. W Collins (Ed.), *Minnesota Symposium on Child Psychology* (Vol. 14, pp. 155–214). Hillsdale, NJ: Erlbaum.

Lerner, M. (1980). *The belief in a just world: A fundamental delusion*. New York: Plenum Press.

Licht, B. G., & Dweck, C. S. (1984). Determinants of academic achievement: The interaction of children's achievement orientations with skill area. *Developmental Psychology, 20,* 628–636.

Mischel, W., & Peake, P. K. (1982). Beyond deja-vu in the search for cross-situational consistency. *Psychological Review, 89,* 730–755.

Nicholls, J. G. (1978). The development of the concepts of effort and ability, perception of academic attainment, and the understanding that difficult tasks require more ability. *Child Development, 49,* 800–814.

Nicholls, J. G. (1984). Achievement motivation: Conceptions of ability, subjective experience, task choice, and performance. *Psychological Review, 91,* 328–346.

Olshefsky, L. M., Erdley, C. A., & Dweck, C. S. (1987). [Self-conceptions and goals in social situations]. Unpublished raw data.

Piaget, J., & Garcia, R. (1983). *Psychogenese et l'histoire des sciences* [Psychogenesis and the history of the sciences]. Paris: Ramarion.

Rapaport, D. (1951). *Organization and pathology of thought: Selected sources*. New York: Columbia University Press.

Renshaw, P. D., & Asher, S. R. (1983). Children's goals and strategies for social interaction. *Merill-Palmer Quarterly, 29,* 353–374.

Rest, J. R. (1983). Morality. In P. H. Mussen (Gen. Ed.) & J. H. Flavell & E. M. Markman (Vol. Eds), *Handbook of child psychology: Vol. III. Cognitive development* (pp. 556–629). New York: Wiley.

Sarason, I. G. (1975). Anxiety and self-preoccupation. In I. G. Samson & C. D. Spielberger (Eds.), *Stress and anxiety* (Vol. 2, pp. 27–44). Washington, DC: Hemisphere.

Sarason, I. G. (1980). *Test anxiety: Theory research, and applications*. Hilldale, NJ: Erlbaum.

Attribution of Apparent Arousal and Proficiency of Recovery from Sympathetic Activation Affecting Excitation Transfer to Aggressive Behavior

Dolf Zillmann • Institute for Communication Research, Indiana University
Rolland C. Johnson and Kenneth D. Day • Indiana University

Editors' Notes

Can arousal from one activity spill over to another activity? If so, what is the role of attribution in such spillovers? Excitation-transfer theory proposes that because excitation decays slowly, residual excitation from a prior activity can combine inseparably with the excitatory response to a subsequent activity, and because people tend to attribute their current excitation level to the current activity, their emotional responses to the current activity will be intensified. This theory was tested in a study relating excitation from strenuous exercise to aggressive responses to a provocation. All the participants were first provoked by someone. Following this, they engaged in a bicycle riding exercise. They were then given an opportunity to retaliate against the person who provoked them. When the exercise occurred immediately before the opportunity to retaliate, the earlier provocation did not increase retaliation, presumably because the participants' high excitation could be attributed to the immediately preceding exercise. In contrast, when there was a six minute period of sitting in a chair between the exercise and the opportunity to retaliate, the earlier provocation did increase retaliation for the less physically fit participants who were most likely to have residual excitation from the exercise when given the opportunity to retaliate.

Discussion Questions

1. Describe the excitation-transfer theory.
2. Provide evidence that excitation from one activity can intensify emotional responses in a subsequent activity and that attribution plays a role in such spillover.

Authors' Abstract

In a pretest, subjects' proficiency to recover from sympathetic arousal induced by strenuous exercise was assessed. The results were used to determine conditions of high, intermediate, and low recovery proficiency (fitness). After an assessment of subjects' unprovoked aggressiveness, subjects were aggressively provoked. Within proficiency blocks, they were then given one of two treatments, (a) sitting followed by exercising (no decay) or (b) exercising followed by sitting (partial decay), and were thereafter provided with an opportunity to retaliate against their tormentor. Under conditions of no decay, in which the high levels of arousal experienced were attributable to exertion, the provocation treatment failed to increase aggressiveness significantly, and there were no differences in aggressiveness in the various proficiency conditions in spite of differentiations in the magnitude of prevailing excitatory residues. Under partial decay, in the absence of cues linking arousal to exertion, the magnitude of residual arousal did affect aggressive behavior: In the conditions of intermediate and low recovery proficiency, aggressiveness increased significantly with provocation and was more pronounced than in the condition of high proficiency (best fitness); in the condition of low proficiency (least fitness) aggressiveness was higher than in the condition of intermediate proficiency, but not reliably so.

It has been demonstrated that under conditions of prior provocation, residual portions of an excitatory response induced by strenuous exercise can markedly facilitate aggression (Zillmann, Katcher, & Milavsky, 1972). Similarly, it has been observed that such residues can intensify the experience of anger and thereby facilitate retaliatory aggression after arousal has subsided (Zillmann & Bryant, in press). These findings were interpreted as consistent with expectations derived from excitation-transfer theory (cf. Zillmann, 1972). It was assumed that essential elements of exertion-induced excitation, known to decay rather slowly, combine inseparably with the excitatory response to stimuli to which the organism is subsequently exposed. Involving the two-factor theory of emotion (cf. Schachter, 1964, 1970), it was proposed that, to the extent that residual excitation from prior activities is transferred into subsequent behavior, the individual experiences any emotional state more intensely because he causally attributes his acute excitation to the stimuli in his immediate environment. Clearly then, the intensification of emotional states and dependent behaviors is seen as resulting from the causal misattribution of potentially unrelated excitatory residues.

The misattribution of residual excitation should not be seen as occurring by necessity, however. Transfer effects, it would appear, can be impaired and possibly prevented by the presence of extero- and interoceptive feedback of the excitation asso-

ciated with the initial emotional experience. It may be assumed that the individual who has attributed his excitatory response to a particular inducer is provided, for some time, with apparent cues indicative of his dependent state of arousal. This is not to say that he receives highly specific, reliable feedback, but rather that he may notice, e.g., a shiver or tremble in a state of acute anxiety, erection in a state of sexual arousal, flushing in a state of euphoria or rage, or heart pounding after exertion. Based on this assumption of the involvement of feedback, it is proposed that the individual is unlikely to reattribute or misattribute residual excitation to alternative, subsequently provided potential inducers of emotional responses as long as he has apparent cries of the state of arousal which he linked to particular prior inducers. Thus, during this feedback period, transfer should not be expected.

This proposition has been tested recently (Cantor, Zillmann, & Bryant, in press). The time periods of actual and perceived recovery from elevated exertion-induced excitation were determined in a pretest to ascertain three distinct phases: a first one, in which excitation was measured to be elevated and in which, through the perception of apparent cues, it was recognized by the subject as still being elevated; a second one, in which measured excitation was still elevated, but was no longer recognized as elevated; and a final one, in which recovery was measured to be achieved and recognized as completed. In the main experiment, subjects were exposed to moderately explicit, erotic film segments during the first, second, or third recovery phase. They were instructed to report the degree to which they perceived themselves to be sexually aroused by these segments. With the data deriving from the final-phase condition serving as a control (no residual excitation), it was expected that sexual arousal, combining with residues from exertion, would be overexperienced only in the second-phase condition and that in the first-phase condition, although residues were more substantial, the attribution of prevailing excitation, to exertion could only hamper feelings of sexual arousal. The findings were entirely consistent with these expectations.

Applied to the facilitation of aggression via transferred excitation, these findings have implications of interest. Counter to the popular notion that excitation, conceived of as generalized drive or energy, will enhance any and every response the individual is called upon to perform, it must be expected that, since residual excitation presumably becomes less pronounced as apparent cues vanish, predisposed aggression will be intensified to a greater extent by smaller, but more readily misattributable excitatory residues.

The present investigation sought to establish that the intensification of aggressive behavior by excitation transfer call be impaired and prevented by the presence of apparent cues associated with prior arousal. In earlier transfer studies (e.g., Zillmann, 1971; Zillmann et al., 1972), the problem of apparent cues was circumvented by delaying the performance of aggressive activities with instructions lasting at least one minute. In the present study, a delay condition was maintained, and a no-delay condition was added to accomplish an absence vs. presence variation of apparent cues.

A second goal of this investigation was to establish a relationship between a basic physical capability of a person, the proficiency to recover physiologically from exertion, and the degree to which he is susceptible to aggression-intensifying transfer effects. The reasoning on recovery proficiency simply takes transfer theory, modified to accommodate the problem of apparent cues, and applies it to individual differences.

1. Given a situation in which (a) an individual appraises, assimilates, and responds to emotion-inducing stimuli, (b) he experiences a level of sympathetic arousal that is still elevated from prior stimulation, and (c) he is not provided with apparent extero- and/or interoceptive cues which would indicate that his arousal results from this prior stimulation, excitatory residues from prior arousal will combine inseparably with the excitatory response to present stimuli and intensify emotional behavior.

2. Emotional behavior will be enhanced in proportion to the magnitude of residual excitation prevailing.

3. Both the period of time in which transfer can manifest itself and the magnitude of transferable residues are a function of (a) the magnitude of the preceding excitatory response and/or (b) the rate of recovery from the excitatory state.

Assuming appreciable individual differences in excitatory responsiveness and recovery proficiency, proposition 3 yields the following corollaries.

(a) The individual's potential for transfer varies proportionally with his excitatory responsiveness.

(b) The individual's potential for transfer is inversely proportional to his proficiency to recover from states of excitatory elevation.

Clearly, the magnitude of excitatory residues depends directly upon the magnitude of the excitatory response these residues derive from. The more responsive the individual is, the larger are the residues provided for transfer. Also, the less efficiently the individual recovers, i.e., controls his own responsiveness, the more likely it is that the conditions for excitation transfer will be met. Other things equal, the highly proficient recoverer retains transferable excitatory residues for a shorter period of time than the less proficient recoverer.

For the purpose of the present investigation it is posited that there are appreciable and consistent differences in (a) individuals' excitatory responses to strenuous exercise, and/or (b) their proficiency to recover from the excitatory responses thus induced (cf. Schneider & Truesdell, 1922; LeBlanc, 1957; Monod, 1967; Campbell, 1969). It is proposed that, with exertion held constant, individuals who display pronounced excitatory elevation and/or fail to recover efficiently are more likely to transfer residual excitation into subsequent behavior than those who are less responsive and/or recover more efficiently. Since low responsiveness and high recovery proficiency are generally considered salient criteria of physical fitness, this proposition may be alternatively expressed by stating that the potential for excitation transfer is negatively related to physical fitness.

In order to explore the validity of the postulated relationship, the present study involved the division of a population into subpopulations representing various levels of responsiveness and/or recovery proficiency (high, intermediate, low). This division was accomplished by assessing each individual's excitatory recovery from strenuous exercise. In a factorial design, levels of recovery proficiency were varied with the absence (delay) vs. presence (no delay) of apparent cues of prior arousal.

Involving the entire design, it is expected, then, that under conditions in which apparent cues linking arousal to its prior induction are absent, aggressive behavior should augment as a function of the incompleteness of recovery, that is, the least fit individuals should display the greatest aggression-intensifying transfer effects. In contrast, it is expected that under conditions in which apparent cues link arousal to prior exertion, aggressive behavior should be at similar, low levels in all conditions of recovery proficiency.

It may, of course, be argued that the grouping of recovery proficiency inadvertently effects a grouping of personality traits with relevant implications for aggression. Conceivably, in comparison to the person in bad shape, the physically fit person is more skillful as an aggressor, has developed a greater habit strength for aggressiveness, is less inhibited to aggress against a tormentor, and so on. The excellent recoverer may thus be expected to display altogether more rather than less aggressiveness. To cope with such an alternative explanation, the present investigation involved an assessment of unprovoked aggressiveness in the various conditions.

Method

Pretest[1]

SUBJECTS

Sixty male undergraduates from a large-enrollment introductory communications course at Indiana University were recruited to participate in two experimental sessions. The students met a course requirement by serving as subjects.

PROCEDURE

All instructions where tape-recorded. The subject was informed that the purpose of the first experimental session was to determine his ability to recall complex communication content under conditions of physical distraction. Specifically, he was told that he would be exposed to visual stimuli while riding a bicycle and that physiological measures would be taken to assess the degree of his physical involvement. Each subject was seated on an exercise bicycle and was hooked up to physiological measuring devices. Electrodes were placed on both arms to obtain the cardiogram, and a brachial artery cuff was placed on the left arm to record blood pressures intermittently. After base level measures were taken, the subject was exposed to slides, projected in front of him. While being exposed to these slides, he pedaled the bicycle ergometer for 1 min and 30 sec with a work-load setting of 1500 kilopond m per min, or 215.3 W. After completing this strenuous task, he continued to be exposed to slides for another 8 min, remaining seated on the bicycle. During this period, physiological measures were obtained immediately after termination of the riding task and in 2-min intervals, that is 2, 4, 6, and 8 min after termination. At these times, heart rate was measured during a 20-sec interval, and blood pressures were recorded immediately thereafter. Finally, in order to disguise the true purpose of the pretest, the subject was given a series of highly specific questions about the content of the slides. After completing this task, he was informed that he would be assigned a particular role in the second experimental session according to his score in the first part.

MATERIALS

The visual stimuli involved were not related to aggression or to anything that potentially could produce nontrivial degrees of arousal. The slides displayed campus scenery, wildlife, complex woven designs, and the like. Each slide was shown for 15 sec.

---

[1]Jennings Bryant conducted the pretest.

APPARATUS

A Schwinn bicycle ergometer was used for the exertion task. Blood pressures were recorded on a Sears sphygmomanometergraph, and heart rate on a Sanborn cardiograph.

DETERMINATION OF LEVELS OF RECOVERY PROFICIENCY

Systolic blood pressure taken 6 min after exertion was used as the blocking criterion (a) because earlier research showed systolic pressure to be the most reliable single index of sympathetic activation induced by exertion (cf. Zillmann et al., 1972), (b) because at this time of measurement maximal between-subjects variability was observed, and (c) because at this time apparent cues of prior arousal should have vanished (cf. Cantor et al., in press). Subjects were rank ordered on this criterion, and the ranked sequence was broken down into pairs of adjacently placed subjects. Three levels of recovery proficiency, high, intermediate, and low, were formed by dividing the sequence of ranked pairs into thirds. One subject in each pair was then randomly assigned to the no-delay condition, and the other was placed in the delay condition.

An analysis of mean scores revealed that recovery to base level was achieved after 4 min in the high proficiency condition and after 8 min in the intermediate proficiency condition. In the low-proficiency condition, recovery was not achieved during the period in which measures were taken: after 8 min, systolic blood pressure was still 10 mm of mercury above base level. Thus, recovery proficiency differed markedly within the population sampled, justifying the blocking of that variable as planned for the main experiment.

Main Experiment[2]

SUBJECTS

Forty-eight of the 60 subjects who participated in the pretest served as subjects in the main experiment. Of the remaining 12 pretested subjects, 10 did not return for the main experiment: one who proved to be physically incapacitated, eight who were not available during the time allotted for completion of the experiment, and one who was

excluded in the interest of equal cell size. In addition, one subject was dismissed because he spontaneously reported having participated in a "similar aggression study," and another refused to participate because he objected to the use of shock.

To prevent any discussion of the experiment or its purpose during class sessions which would bring former and potential subjects together, the entire main experiment was conducted in the period between two successive meetings of the class from which the subjects were recruited. All subjects served in the main experiment between 7 and 14 days after the pretest.

PROCEDURE

All instructions were tape-recorded. The subject was informed that the purpose of this second part of the experiment was to investigate the relationship between the ability to recall complex visual materials and the ability to teach by providing coded information to a learner together with positive and negative feedback about his progress. The subject was told that he had received a rather high score on the retention pretest, and that he was assigned to an experimental condition in which a high-scorer taught a low-scorer. It was explained that he was to play the part of the teacher and that another subject would be the learner. The subject as told that the other subject (actually a confederate of the experimenter) had been scheduled to come earlier and was already well under way on his learning task in the adjoining room. He was told that both subjects would interact over an intercom, but that to maintain strict experimental control they would never meet each other in person. The subject was then informed that, in the experiment, negative feedback would be operationalized in the delivery of electric shock, and he was given an opportunity to withdraw from the experiment if the use of shock was unacceptable to him.

The subject was then given instructions on how to provide the learner with coded information and how to give him negative feedback whenever he made erroneous responses (cf. Zillmann et al., 1972 for further details). The subject was told that he had to deliver shock every time his apparatus signalled that the learner had made an error, but that he could vary the intensity of the shocks from "quite mild" (button #1) through "rather painful" (#10). It was suggested that he choose *the intensity he felt was most appropriate in this particular*

---

[2] KDD conducted the main experiment.

learning situation. The subject was left alone during this teaching task, in which the learner made five prescheduled errors in 12 responses.

After this task, the subject was informed that, since the rapport between teacher and learner critically influences the learning process, it would be necessary to take a measure of how the two were "in tune with one another." Following procedures reported in earlier studies (e.g., Zillmann et al., 1972), the subject was given a list of 12 controversial issues on which he stated his opinion over the intercom. For each attitude expressed by the subject, the learner signalled his agreement by illuminating a light signal or his disagreement by administering shock to the subject. No matter what opinions the subject expressed, he received painful shocks in response to nine out of his 12 expressed opinions. This procedure was employed to induce anger in the subject and to give him the impression that the learner was disagreeable and obnoxious.

The subject was then informed that a measure of his ability to retrieve complex verbal communication content was needed (the pretest involved nonverbal stimuli only). The subject was exposed to slides and, depending on the condition to which he had been randomly assigned, he viewed the slides either while first sitting in a chair for 6 min and then engaging in strenuous exercise for 1.5 min (no decay) or while first engaging in strenuous exercise for 1.5 min and then sitting in a chair for 6 min (partial decay). Subjects in the no-decay condition were not informed about the forthcoming exercise until it was time for them to perform it. The strenuous exercise consisted of bicycle riding under conditions identical to those of the pretest.

After completion of the exercise session, the subject was told that the learner would now be ready for a final exchange similar to the first teaching task. Prior to this, no mention was made of this final teacher-learner encounter. The subject was given a list of coded items and was told to use the procedure he had used before, giving shocks in response to the learner's errors. The subject started the teaching task about 30 sec after having completed the exercise portion of the session. The task involved 28 responses to coded information, 18 of which were prescheduled as erroneous.

Finally, the subject was taken to another room and was asked to fill out a questionnaire concerning the content of the slides he had seen. As in the pretest, this was for the purpose of effective disguise only. Two questions concerning the subject's response to the strenuous exercise were added: he rated (a) the degree to which he had experienced the task as physically demanding, and (b) the degree to which he had liked or disliked the task. The subject was then dismissed. All subjects were given a delayed debriefing by their instructors after the experiment had been completed.

MATERIALS

The slides used were copies of recent magazine advertisements. Each slide was shown for 15 sec.

APPARATUS

Electric shock was generated by a Harvard shock inducer. Eight volts were delivered for about .5 sec to the distal pads of the index and ring fingers of one hand.

Shock was ostensibly delivered via a so-called aggression machine and was recorded on a Gerbrands multichannel event recorder.

DEPENDENT MEASURES

Both intensity and duration of shock ostensibly delivered to the learner were employed as indices of aggressiveness. The mean of the five preprovocation scores served as a measure of unprovoked aggressiveness. It also served as a base level of aggressiveness in the determination of difference scores, the measure of aggressiveness after provocation. For analysis, the 18 difference scores obtained ($\Delta_{ij} = X_{ij} - B_i$, where X_{ij} is the jth retaliation score of the ith subject, and B_i is the arithmetic mean of all preprovocation scores of that subject) were reduced to six blocks of three responses each.

The difficulty of the strenuous task was assessed on a scale ranging from "extremely easy" (-100) to "extremely strenuous" (100). The attitude toward this task was assessed on a scale ranging from "I really hated it" (-100) to "I really loved it" (100). Both scales were marked at intervals of 10.

Results

Recovery Proficiency

The difference scores (deviations from basal measures) of the physiological measures taken in the pretest on the 48 subjects who participated in the main experiment were subjected to analyses of variance (a) to validate the proficiency blocking and (b) to guard against possible sampling bias in the no-delay vs. delay conditions. No sampling bias was detected. Randomization in the decay conditions proved fully satisfactory, since all effects of the resulting grouping were trivial and insignificant.

The main effect of recovery proficiency on systolic blood pressure was highly significant ($F(2,42) = 37.86$; $p < .001$). The means were differentiated as required: 1.262 mm of mercury for high recovery proficiency, 18.80 for intermediate proficiency, and 36.40 for low proficiency, all contrasting significantly ($p < .001$) from one another. The main effect of repeated measures was also highly significant ($F(4,168) = 103.12$; conservatively corrected by the Geisser–Greenhouse method, $p < .001$). All the means in the sequence, 49.75, 32.21, 14.08, 3.12, –5.06, differed significantly ($p < .05$) from each other. There was, however, no appreciable interaction between recovery proficiency and repeated measures ($F < 1$). Given the highly significant differentiation of recovery proficiency and the lack of an interaction, differences in de facto recovery, measured in time, clearly resulted from a well-differentiated initial excitatory response to exertion rather than from differential decay gradients.

On heart rate, the differentiation of proficiency conditions paralleled that of systolic blood pressure, but it failed to be statistically reliable. There was only a negligible interaction between proficiency and decay, and deceleration over time was highly significant and nonlinear (cf. Monod, 1967). The analysis of mean blood pressure (estimated as the systolic pressure minus one third of the systolic-diastolic difference) and that of sympathetic activation (estimated as the product of mean blood pressure and heart rate) both yielded results which were redundant with those reported for systolic blood pressure.

Table 1 shows the mean changes in systolic blood pressure, the primary index of excitation, which were obtained in the pretest and which have been treated as estimates of the excitation prevailing at the outset of the retaliatory encounter in the main experiment. As can be seen, the means are differentiated as required. Comparisons on sympathetic activation closely paralleled those on systolic blood pressure.

The postexperimental ratings concerning the strenuous exercise indicated that subjects tended to perceive the difficulty of the task as a function of their proficiency to recover from it. Subjects in all conditions found it strenuous, but those in the high-proficiency conditions found it less so than those in the intermediate and low conditions. Mean ratings were 16.06, as compared to 32.00 and 32.50, respectively. The differences were not statistically reliable, however. Subjects in all conditions formed the tusk unenjoyable, but their ratings bore no consistent relationship to recovery proficiency. The mean ratings were –8.81,–4.81, and –11.06 from high through low proficiency. Again, the differentiation was statistically unreliable.

For both rated difficulty and disliking of the task, there were no significant effects of the decay manipulation or of the interaction of decay with recovery proficiency.

Aggressive Behavior

As in earlier studies (e.g., Zillmann, 1971; Zillmann et al., 1972), no statistically reliable effects were obtained in the duration of shock. Given the repeatedly observed within-subject consistency of duration over trials, it would appear that this measure assesses mainly the subject's habit of pressing buttons. Shock duration as a measure of aggressiveness will thus be omitted from further discussion.

The analysis of variance performed on the mean shock intensity of the five punitive responses made prior to provocation disclosed entirely negligible effects for all sources of variation (all F's ≈ 1).

As the most pertinent finding, the analysis of variance on the difference scores of shock intensity

TABLE 1. Indices of Excitation Prior to Retaliation and Measure of Unprovoked and Provoked Aggressiveness

	Exertion-induced excitation					
	Undecayed			Partially decayed		
	Recovery proficiency			Recovery proficiency		
Dependent measure	High	Inter-mediate	Low	High	Inter-mediate	Low
Excitation:						
Δ Systolic blood pressure	37.62^{cd}	45.00^d	70.12^e	−16.50^a	3.25^b	23.50^c
Aggression:						
Shock intensity						
before provocation	2.40^A	3.90^A	3.90^A	3.35^A	3.35^A	3.30^A
after provocation	3.09^A	4.52^A	4.33^A	3.36^A	5.05^B	5.28^B
Δ Shock intensity	0.69^{ab}	0.62^{ab}	0.43^a	0.01^a	1.70^b	1.98^b

Note. Comparisons across conditions (horizontal) are denoted by lower-case superscripts, those on repeated measures within conditions (vertical), by upper-case superscripts. Means having no letter in the superscripts in common differ significantly at $p < .05$.

revealed the expected interaction between decay and recovery proficiency ($F(2,42) = 3.36, p < .05$). The associated differentiation of means is displayed in Table 1. Whereas under conditions of undecayed excitation all differences between means were negligible, under conditions of partially decayed excitation measured aggressiveness decreased with recovery proficiency. Shock intensity in the high-proficiency condition was significantly lower than in the intermediate-proficiency condition; in the intermediate-proficiency condition it was lower than in the low-proficiency condition, the latter difference not being statistically reliable, however.

The main effect of the decay variation fell short of significance ($F(1,42) = 3.08, p < .10$). Similarly, the main effect of recovery proficiency was insignificant ($F(2.42) = 2.26. p > .10$). In contrast, the main effect of the six shock blocks was significant ($F(5.210) = 7.95$; conservatively corrected, $p < .01$). The associated differentiation of means (−0.096, 0.647, 1.140, 1.231, 1.306, 1.198) exhibits the repeatedly observed (cf. Baron & Kepner, 1970; Zillmann et al., 1972) successive increment of shock intensity. All interactions involving shock blocks were negligible (all p's > .10).

The analysis of the raw shock-intensity scores paralleled the analysis of the difference scores, but failed to yield a reliable interaction between proficiency and decay conditions. However, when a repeated-measures analysis was performed on the means of the shock intensities employed prior to

and following the provocation treatment, the significant interaction reported for the difference scores was corroborated. As can be seen from Table 1, the increase in shock intensity due to provocation was significant only for low and intermediate recovery proficiency under conditions of delay (both comparisons are associated with $p < .001$). This increase was negligible in all remaining conditions (for all comparisons, $p > .10$).

Discussion

The findings are consistent with the proposition that the facilitatory effect which residual excitation can exert on aggressive behavior presupposes the absence of a decisive attribution of experienced arousal, or portions thereof, to prior stimulation. Under conditions in which apparent extero- and/or interoceptive cues of prior arousal were present, provocation failed to increase aggressiveness significantly, and the magnitude of residual arousal failed to affect aggressiveness. In contrast, significant increments of aggressiveness were observed under conditions in which cues of prior arousal were no longer present but excitatory residues still prevailed. Considering all conditions, provoked aggressiveness was not found to be proportional to the magnitude of arousal active at the time retaliatory opportunities were provided. Together with earlier findings (Zillmann et al., 1972), the present results constitute evidence against the proposal that residual excitation will energize and facilitate, as a simple function of its magnitude, any and every behavior the individual engages in. [...]

REFERENCES

Baron, R. A., & Kepner, R. (1970). Model's behavior and attraction toward the model as determinants of adult aggressive behavior. *Journal of Personality and Social Psychology, 14,* 335–344.

Campbell, D. E. (1969). Trend analysis of heart rate deceleration following graded intensities of exercise of two groups of pubescent boys. *Journal of Sports Medicine and Physical Fitness, 9,* 110–118.

Cantor, J. R., Zillmann, D., & Bryant, J. (in press). Enhancement of experienced sexual arousal in response to erotic stimuli through misattribution of unrelated residual excitation. *Journal of Personality and Social Psychology.*

Le Blanc, J. A. (1957). Use of heart rate as an index of work output. *Journal of Applied Physiology, 10,* 275–280.

Monod, H. (1967). La validité des mesures de fréquence cardiaque en ergonomie. *Ergonomics, 10,* 485–537.

Schachter, S. (1964). The interaction of cognitive and physiological determinants of emotional state. In P. H. Leiderman & D. Shapiro (Eds.), *Psychobiological approaches to social behavior.* Stanford: Stanford University Press.

Schachter, S. (1970). The assumption of identity and peripheralist-centralist controversies in motivation and emotion. In M. B. Arnold (Ed.), *Feelings and emotion.* New York: Academic Press.

Schneider, E. C., Truesdell, D. (1922). A statistical study of the pulse rate and the arterial blood pressures in recumbency, standing, and after a standard exercise. *American Journal of Physiology, 61,* 429–434.

Zillman, D. (1971). Excitation transfer in communication-mediated aggressive behavior. *Journal of Experimental Social Psychology, 7,* 419–434.

Zillmann, D. (1972). The role of excitation in aggressive behavior. In *Proceedings of the Seventeenth International Congress of Applied Psychology, 1971.* Brussels: Editest.

Zilmann, D., & Bryant, J. (in press). The effect of residual excitation on the emotional response to provocation and delayed aggressive behavior. *Journal of Personality and Social Psychology.*

Zilmann, D., Katcher, A. H., & Milavsky, B. (1972). Excitation transfer from physical exercise to subsequent aggressive behavior. *Journal of Experimental Social Psychology, 8,* 117–259.

Appendix: How to Read a Journal Article in Social Psychology

Christian H. Jordan and Mark P. Zanna • University of Waterloo

How to Read a Journal Article in Social Psychology

When approaching a journal article for the first time, and often on subsequent occasions, most people try to digest it as they would any piece of prose. They start at the beginning and read word for word, until eventually they arrive at the end, perhaps a little bewildered, but with a vague sense of relief. This is not an altogether terrible strategy; journal articles do have a logical structure that lends itself to this sort of reading. There are, however, more efficient approaches–approaches that enable you, a student of social psychology, to cut through peripheral details, avoid sophisticated statistics with which you may not be familiar, and focus on the central ideas in an article. Arming yourself with a little foreknowledge of what is contained in journal articles, as well some practical advice on how to read them, should help you read journal articles more effectively. If this sounds tempting, read on.

Journal articles offer a window into the inner workings of social psychology. They document how social psychologists formulate hypotheses, design empirical studies, analyze the observations they collect, and interpret their results. Journal articles also serve an invaluable archival function: They contain the full store of common and cumulative knowledge of social psychology. Having documentation of past research allows researchers to build on past findings and advance our understanding of social behavior, without pursuing avenues of investigation that have already been explored. Perhaps most importantly, a research study is never complete until its results have been shared with others, colleagues and students alike. Journal articles are a primary means of communicating research findings. As such, they can be genuinely exciting and interesting to read.

That last claim may have caught you off guard. For beginning readers, journal articles may seem anything but interesting and exciting. They may, on the contrary, appear daunting and esoteric, laden with jargon and obscured by menacing statistics. Recognizing this fact, we hope to arm you, through this paper, with the basic information you will need to read journal articles with a greater sense of comfort and perspective.

Social psychologists study many fascinating topics, ranging from prejudice and discrimination, to culture, persuasion, liking and love, conformity and obedience, aggression, and the self. In our daily lives, these are issues we often struggle to understand. Social psychologists present systematic observations of, as well as a wealth of ideas about, such issues in journal articles. It would be a shame if the fascination and intrigue these topics have were lost in their translation into journal publications. We don't think they are, and by the end of this paper, hopefully you won't either.

Journal articles come in a variety of forms, including research reports, review articles, and theoretical articles. Put briefly, a *research report* is a formal presentation of an original research study, or series of studies. A *review article* is an evaluative survey of previously published work, usually organized by a guiding theory or point of view. The author of a review article summarizes previous investigations of a circumscribed problem, comments on what progress has been made toward its resolution, and suggests areas of the problem that require further study. A *theoretical article* also evaluates past research, but focuses on the development of theories used to explain empirical findings. Here, the author may present a new theory to explain a set of findings, or may compare and contrast a set of competing theories, suggesting why one theory might be the superior one.

This paper focuses primarily on how to read research reports, for several reasons. First, the bulk of published literature in social psychology consists of research reports. Second, the summaries presented in review articles, and the ideas set forth in theoretical articles, are built on findings presented in research reports. To get a deep understanding of how research is done in social psychology, fluency in reading original research reports is essential. Moreover, theoretical articles frequently report new studies that pit one theory against another, or test a novel prediction derived from a new theory. In order to appraise the validity of such theoretical contentions, a grounded understanding of basic findings is invaluable. Finally, most research reports are written in a standard format that is likely unfamiliar to new readers. The format of review and theoretical articles is less standardized, and more like that of textbooks and other scholarly writings, with which most readers are familiar. This is not to suggest that such articles are easier to read and comprehend than research reports; they can be quite challenging indeed. It is simply the case that, because more rules apply to the writing of research reports, more guidelines can be offered on how to read them.

The Anatomy of Research Reports

Most research reports in social psychology, and in psychology in general, are written in a standard format prescribed by the American Psychological Association (1994). This is a great boon to both readers and writers. It allows writers to present their ideas and findings in a clear, systematic manner. Consequently, as a reader, once you understand this format, you will not be on completely foreign ground when you approach a new research report—regardless of its specific content. You will know where in the paper particular information is found, making it easier to locate. No matter what your reasons for reading a research report, a firm understanding of the format in which they are written will ease your task. We discuss the format of research reports next, with some practical suggestions on how to read them. Later, we discuss how this format reflects the process of scientific investigation, illustrating how research reports have a coherent narrative structure.

TITLE AND ABSTRACT

Though you can't judge a book by its cover, you can learn a lot about a research report simply by reading its title. The title presents a concise statement of the theoretical issues investigated, and/or the variables that were studied. For example, the following title was taken almost at random from a prestigious journal in social psychology: "Sad and guilty? Affective influences on the explanation of conflict in close relationships" (Forgas, 1994, p.

56). Just by reading the title, it can be inferred that the study investigated how emotional states change the way people explain conflict in close relationships. It also suggests that when feeling sad, people accept more personal blame for such conflicts (i.e., feel more guilty).

The abstract is also an invaluable source of information. It is a brief synopsis of the study, and packs a lot of information into 150 words or less. The abstract contains information about the problem that was investigated, how it was investigated, the major findings of the study, and hints at the theoretical and practical implications of the findings. Thus, the abstract is a useful summary of the research that provides the gist of the investigation. Reading this outline first can be very helpful, because it tells you where the report is going, and gives you a useful framework for organizing information contained in the article.

The title and abstract of a research report are like a movie preview. A movie preview highlights the important aspects of a movie's plot, and provides just enough information for one to decide whether to watch the whole movie. Just so with titles and abstracts; they highlight the key features of a research report to allow you to decide if you want to read the whole paper. And just as with movie previews, they do not give the whole story. Reading just the title and abstract is never enough to fully understand a research report.

INTRODUCTION

A research report has four main sections: introduction, method, results, and discussion. Though it is not explicitly labeled, the introduction begins the main body of a research report. Here, the researchers set the stage for the study. They present the problem under investigation, and state why it was important to study. By providing a brief review of past research and theory relevant to the central issue of investigation, the researchers place the study in an historical context and suggest how the study advances knowledge of the problem. Beginning with broad theoretical and practical considerations, the researchers delineate the rationale that led them to the specific set of hypotheses tested in the study. They also describe how they decided on their research strategy (e.g., why they chose an experiment or a correlational study).

The introduction generally begins with a broad consideration of the problem investigated. Here, the researchers want to illustrate that the problem they studied is a real problem about which people should care. If the researchers are studying prejudice, they may cite statistics that suggest discrimination is prevalent, or describe specific cases of discrimination. Such information helps illustrate why the research is both practically and theoretically meaningful, and why you should bother reading about it. Such discussions are often quite interesting and useful. They can help you decide for yourself if the research has merit. But they may not be essential for understanding the study at hand. Read the introduction carefully, but choose judiciously what to focus on and remember. To understand a study, what you really need to understand is what the researchers' hypotheses were, and how they were derived from theory, informal observation, or intuition. Other background information may be intriguing, but may not be critical to understand what the researchers did and why they did it.

While reading the introduction, try answering these questions: What problem was studied, and why? How does this study relate to, and go beyond, past investigations of the problem? How did the researchers derive their hypotheses? What questions do the researchers hope to answer with this study?

METHOD

In the method section, the researchers translate their hypotheses into a set of specific, testable questions. Here, the researchers introduce the main characters of the study—the subjects or participants—describing their characteristics (gender, age, etc.) and how many of them were involved. Then, they describe the materials (or apparatus), such as any questionnaires or special equipment, used in the study. Finally, they describe chronologically the procedures of the study; that is, how the study was conducted. Often, an overview of the research design will begin the method section. This overview provides a broad outline of the design, alerting you to what you should attend.

The method is presented in great detail so that other researchers can recreate the study to confirm (or question) its results. This degree of detail is normally not necessary to understand a study, so don't get bogged down trying to memorize the particulars of the procedures. Focus on how the independent variables were manipulated (or measured) and how the dependent variables were measured.

Measuring variables adequately is not always an easy matter. Many of the variables psychologists are interested in cannot be directly observed, so they must be inferred from participants' behavior. Happiness, for example, cannot be directly observed. Thus, researchers interested in how being happy influences people's judgments must infer happiness (or its absence) from their behavior—perhaps by asking people how happy they are, and judging their degree of happiness from their responses; perhaps by studying people's facial expressions for signs of happiness, such as smiling. Think about the measures researchers use while reading the method section. Do they adequately reflect or capture the concepts they are meant to measure? If a measure seems odd, consider carefully how the researchers justify its use.

Oftentimes in social psychology, getting there is half the fun. In other words, how a result is obtained can be just as interesting as the result itself. Social psychologists often strive to have participants behave in a natural, spontaneous manner, while controlling enough of their environment to pinpoint the causes of their behavior. Sometimes, the major contribution of a research report is its presentation of a novel method of investigation. When this is the case, the method will be discussed in some detail in the introduction.

Participants in social psychology studies are intelligent and inquisitive people who are responsive to what happens around them. Because of this, they are not always initially told the true purpose of a study. If they were told, they might not act naturally. Thus, researchers frequently need to be creative, presenting a credible rationale for complying with procedures, without revealing the study's purpose. This rationale is known as a *cover story,* and is often an elaborate scenario. While reading the method section, try putting yourself in the shoes of a participant in the study, and ask yourself if the instructions given to participants seem sensible, realistic, and engaging. Imagining what it was like to be in the study will also help you remember the study's procedure, and aid you in interpreting the study's results.

While reading the method section, try answering these questions: How were the hypotheses translated into testable questions? How were the variables of interest manipulated and/or measured? Did the measures used adequately reflect the variables of interest? For example, is self-reported income an adequate measure of social class? Why or why not?

RESULTS

The results section describes how the observations collected were analyzed to determine whether the original hypotheses were supported. Here, the data (observations of behavior) are described, and statistical tests are presented. Because of this, the results section is often intimidating to readers who have little or no training in statistics. Wading through complex and unfamiliar statistical analyses is understandably confusing and frustrating. As a result, many students are tempted to skip over reading this section. We advise you not to do so. Empirical findings are the foundation of any science and results sections are where such findings are presented.

Take heart. Even the most prestigious researchers were once in your shoes and sympathize with you. Though space in psychology journals is limited, researchers try to strike a balance between the need to be clear and the need to be brief in describing their results. In an influential paper on how to write good research reports, Bem (1987) offered this advice to researchers:

> No matter how technical or abstruse your article is in its particulars, intelligent nonpsychologists with no expertise in statistics or experimental design should be able to comprehend the broad outlines of what you did and why. They should understand in general terms what was learned. (p. 74)

Generally speaking, social psychologists try to practice this advice.

Most statistical analyses presented in research reports test specific hypotheses. Often, each analysis presented is preceded by a reminder of the hypothesis it is meant to test. After an analysis is presented, researchers usually provide a narrative description of the result in plain English. When the hypothesis tested by a statistical analysis is not explicitly stated, you can usually determine the hypothesis that was tested by reading this narrative description of the result, and referring back to the introduction to locate an hypothesis that corresponds to that result. After even the most complex statistical analysis, there will be a written description of what the result means conceptually. Turn your attention to these descriptions. Focus on the conceptual meaning of research findings, not on the mechanics of how they were obtained (unless you're comfortable with statistics).

Aside from statistical tests and narrative descriptions of results, results sections also frequently contain tables and graphs. These are efficient summaries of data. Even if you are not familiar with statistics, look closely at tables and graphs, and pay attention to the means or correlations presented in them. Researchers always include written descriptions of the pertinent aspects of tables and graphs. While reading these descriptions, check the tables and graphs to make sure what the researchers say accurately reflects their data. If they say there was a difference between two groups on a particular dependent measure, look at the means in the table that correspond to those two groups, and see if the means do differ as described. Occasionally, results seem to become stronger in their narrative description than an examination of the data would warrant.

Statistics *can* be misused. When they are, results are difficult to interpret. Having said this, a lack of statistical knowledge should not make you overly cautious while reading results sections. Though not a perfect antidote, journal articles undergo extensive review by professional researchers before publication. Thus, most misapplications of statistics are caught and corrected before an article is published. So, if you are unfamiliar with statistics, you can be reasonably confident that findings are accurately reported.

While reading the results section, try answering these questions: Did the researchers provide evidence that any independent variable manipulations were effective? For example, if testing for behavioral differences between happy and sad participants, did the researchers demonstrate that one group was in fact happier than the other? What were the major findings of the study? Were the researchers' original hypotheses supported by their observations? If not, look in the discussion section for how the researchers explain the findings that were obtained.

DISCUSSION

The discussion section frequently opens with a summary of what the study found, and an evaluation of whether the findings supported the original hypotheses. Here, the researchers evaluate the theoretical and practical implications of their results. This can be particularly interesting when the results did not work out exactly as the researchers anticipated. When such is the case, consider the researchers' explanations carefully, and see if they seem plausible to you. Often, researchers will also report any aspects of their study that limit their interpretation of its results, and suggest further research that could overcome these limitations to provide a better understanding of the problem under investigation.

Some readers find it useful to read the first few paragraphs of the discussion section before reading any other part of a research report. Like the abstract, these few paragraphs usually contain all of the main ideas of a research report: What the hypotheses were, the major findings and whether they supported the original hypotheses, and how the findings relate to past research and theory. Having this information before reading a research report can guide your reading, allowing you to focus on the specific details you need to complete your understanding of a study. The description of the results, for example, will alert you to the major variables that were studied. If they are unfamiliar to you, you can pay special attention to how they are defined in the introduction, and how they are operationalized in the method section.

After you have finished reading an article, it can also be helpful to reread the first few paragraphs of the discussion and the abstract. As noted, these two passages present highly distilled summaries of the major ideas in a research report. Just as they can help guide your reading of a report, they can also help you consolidate your understanding of a report once you have finished reading it. They provide a check on whether you have understood the main points of a report, and offer a succinct digest of the research in the authors' own words.

While reading the discussion section, try answering these questions: What conclusions can be drawn from the study? What new information does the study provide about the problem under investigation? Does the study help resolve the problem? What are the practical and theoretical implications of the study's findings? Did the results contradict past research findings? If so, how do the researchers explain this discrepancy?

Some Notes on Reports of Multiple Studies

Up to this point, we have implicitly assumed that a research report describes just one study. It is also quite common, however, for a research report to describe a series of studies of the same problem in a single article. When such is the case, each study reported will have the same basic structure (introduction, method, results, and discussion sections) that we have outlined, with the notable exception that sometimes the results and discussion section for each study are combined. Combined "results and discussion" sections contain the same information that separate results and discussion sections normally contain. Sometimes, the authors present all their results first, and only then discuss the implications of these results, just as they would in separate results and discussion sections. Other times, however, the authors alternate between describing results and discussing their implications, as each result is presented. In either case, you should be on the lookout for the same information, as outlined above in our consideration of separate results and discussion sections.

Reports including multiple studies also differ from single study reports in that they include more general introduction and discussion sections. The general introduction, which begins the main body of a research report, is similar in essence to the introduction of a single study report. In both cases, the researchers describe the problem investigated and its practical and theoretical significance. They also demonstrate how they derived their hypotheses, and explain how their research relates to past investigations of the problem. In contrast, the separate introductions to each individual study in reports of multiple studies are usually quite brief, and focus more specifically on the logic and rationale of each particular study presented. Such introductions generally describe the methods used in the particular study, outlining how they answer questions that have not been adequately addressed by past research, including studies reported earlier in the same article.

General discussion sections parallel discussions of single studies, except on a somewhat grander scale. They present all of the information contained in discussions of single studies, but consider the implications of all the studies presented together. A general discussion section brings the main ideas of a research program into bold relief. It typically begins with a concise summary of a research program's main findings, their relation to the original hypotheses, and their practical and theoretical implications. Thus, the summaries that begin general discussion sections are counterparts of the summaries that begin discussion sections of single study reports. Each presents a digest of the research presented in an article that can serve as both an organizing framework (when read first), and as a check on how well you have understood the main points of an article (when read last).

Research Reporting as Story Telling

A research report tells the story of how a researcher or group of researchers investigated a specific problem. Thus, a research report has a linear, narrative structure with a beginning, middle, and end. In his paper on writing research reports, Bem noted that a research report:

> . . .is shaped like an hourglass. It begins with broad general statements, progressively narrows down to the specifics of [the] study, and then broadens out again to more general considerations. (1987, p. 175)

This format roughly mirrors the process of scientific investigation, wherein researchers do the following: (1) start with a broad idea from which they formulate a narrower set of hypotheses, informed by past empirical findings (introduction); (2) design a specific set of concrete operations to test these hypotheses (method); (3) analyze the observations collected in this way, and decide if they support the original hypotheses (results); and (4) explore the broader theoretical and practical implications of the findings, and consider how they contribute to an understanding of the problem under investigation (discussion). Though these stages are somewhat arbitrary distinctions—research actually proceeds in a number of different ways—they help elucidate the inner logic of research reports.

While reading a research report, keep this linear structure in mind. Though it is difficult to remember a series of seemingly disjointed facts, when these facts are joined together in a logical, narrative structure, they become easier to comprehend and recall. Thus, always remember that a research report tells a story. It will help you to organize the information you read, and remember it later.

Describing research reports as stories is not just a convenient metaphor. Research reports are stories. Stories can be said to consist of two components: A telling of what happened, and an explanation of why it happened. It is tempting to view science as an endeavor that simply catalogues facts, but nothing is further from the truth. The goal of science, social psychology included, is to *explain* facts, to explain *why* what happened happened. Social psychology is built on the dynamic interplay of discovery and justification, the dialogue between systematic observation of relations and their theoretical explanation. Though research reports do present novel facts based on systematic observation, these facts are presented in the service of ideas. Facts in isolation are trivia. Facts tied together by an explanatory theory are science. Therein lies the story. To really understand what researchers have to say, you need consider how their explanations relate to their findings.

The Rest of the Story

> There is really no such thing as research. There is only search, more search, keep on searching. (Bowering, 1988, p. 95)

Once you have read through a research report, and understand the researchers' findings and their explanations of them, the story does not end there. There is more than one interpretation for any set of findings. Different researchers often explain the same set of facts in different ways.

Let's take a moment to dispel a nasty rumor. The rumor is this: Researchers present their studies in a dispassionate manner, intending only to inform readers of their findings and their interpretation of those findings. In truth, researchers aim not only to inform readers, but also to *persuade* them (Sternberg, 1995). Researchers want to convince you their ideas are right. There is never only one explanation for a set of findings. Certainly, some explanations are better than others; some fit the available data better, are more parsimonious, or require fewer questionable assumptions. The point here is that researchers are very passionate about their ideas, and want you to believe them. It's up to you to decide if you want to buy their ideas or not.

Let's compare social psychologists to salesclerks. Both social psychologists and salesclerks want to sell you something; either their ideas, or their wares. You need to decide if you want to buy what they're selling or not—and there are potentially negative consequences for either decision. If you let a sales clerk dazzle you with a sales pitch, without thinking about it carefully, you might end up buying a substandard product that you don't really need. After having done this a few times, people tend to become cynical, steeling themselves against any and all sales pitches. This too is dangerous. If you are overly critical of sales pitches, you could end up foregoing genuinely useful products. Thus, by analogy, when you are too critical in your reading of research reports, you might dismiss, out of hand, some genuinely useful ideas—ideas that can help shed light on why people behave the way they do.

This discussion raises the important question of how critical one should be while reading a research report. In part, this will depend on why one is reading the report. If you are reading it simply to learn what the researchers have to say about a particular issue, for example, then there is usually no need to be overly critical. If you want to use the research as a basis for planning a new study, then you should be more critical. As you develop an understanding of psychological theory and research methods, you will also develop an ability to criticize research on many different levels. And *any* piece of research can be criticized at some level. As Jacob Cohen put it, "A successful piece of research doesn't conclusively settle an issue, it just makes some theoretical proposition to some degree more likely" (1990, p. 1311). Thus, as a consumer of research reports, you have to strike a delicate balance between being overly critical and overly accepting.

While reading a research report, at least initially, try to suspend your disbelief. Try to understand the researchers' story; that is, try to understand the facts—the findings and how they were obtained—and the suggested explanation of those facts—the researchers' interpretation of the findings and what they mean. Take the research to task only after you feel you understand what the authors are trying to say.

Research reports serve not only an important archival function, documenting research and its findings, but also an invaluable stimulus function. They can excite other researchers to join the investigation of a particular issue, or to apply new methods or theory to a different, perhaps novel, issue. It is this stimulus function that Elliot Aronson, an eminent social psychologist, referred to when he admitted that, in publishing a study, he hopes his colleagues will "look at it, be stimulated by it, be provoked by it, annoyed by it, and then go ahead and do it better.... That's the exciting thing about science; it progresses by people taking off on one another's work" (1995, p. 5). Science is indeed a cumulative enterprise, and each new study builds on what has (or, sometimes, has not) gone before it. In this way, research articles keep social psychology vibrant.

A study can inspire new research in a number of different ways, such as: (1) it can lead one to conduct a better test of the hypotheses, trying to rule out alternative explanations of the findings; (2) it can lead one to explore the limits of the findings, to see how widely applicable they are, perhaps exploring situations to which they do not apply; (3) it can lead one to test the implications of the findings, furthering scientific investigation of the phenomenon; (4) it can inspire one to apply the findings, or a novel methodology, to a different area of investigation; and (5) it can provoke one to test the findings in the context of a specific real world problem, to see if they can shed light on it. All of these are excellent extensions of the original research, and there are, undoubtedly, other ways that research findings can spur new investigations.

The problem with being too critical, too soon, while reading research reports is that the only further research one may be willing to attempt is research of the first type: Redoing a study better. Sometimes this is desirable, particularly in the early stages of investigating a particular issue, when the findings are novel and perhaps unexpected. But redoing a reasonably compelling study, without extending it in any way, does little to advance our understanding of human behavior. Although the new study might be "better," it will not be "perfect," so *it* would have to be run again, and again, likely never reaching a stage where it is beyond criticism. At some point, researchers have to decide that the evidence is compelling enough to warrant investigation of the last four types. It is these types of studies that most advance our knowledge of social behavior. As you read more research reports, you will become more comfortable deciding when a study is "good enough" to move beyond it. This is a somewhat subjective judgment, and should be made carefully.

When social psychologists write up a research report for publication, it is because they believe they have something new and exciting to communicate about social behavior. Most research reports that are submitted for publication are rejected. Thus, the reports that are eventually published are deemed pertinent not only by the researchers who wrote them, but also by the reviewers and editors of the journals in which they are published. These people, at least, believe the research reports they write and publish have something important and interesting to say. Sometimes, you'll disagree; not all journal articles are created equal, after all. But we recommend that you, at least initially, give these well-meaning social psychologists the benefit of the doubt. Look for what they're excited about. Try to understand the authors' story, and see where it leads you.

Author Notes

Preparation of this paper was facilitated by a Natural Sciences and Engineering Research Council of Canada doctoral fellowship to Christian H. Jordan. Thanks to Roy Baumeister, Arie Kruglanski, Ziva Kunda, John Levine, Geoff MacDonald, Richard Moreland, Ian Newby-Clark, Steve Spencer, and Adam Zanna for their insightful comments on, and appraisals of, various drafts of this paper. Thanks also to Arie Kruglanski and four anonymous editors of volumes in the series, *Key Readings in Social Psychology* for their helpful critiques of an initial outline of this paper. Correspondence concerning this article should be addressed to Christian H. Jordan, Department of Psychology, University of Waterloo, Waterloo, Ontario, Canada N2L 3G1. Electronic mail can be sent to chjordan@watarts.uwaterloo.ca

REFERENCES

American Psychological Association (1994). *Publication manual* (4th ed.). Washington, D.C.

Aronson, E. (1995). Research in social psychology as a leap of faith. In E. Aronson (Ed.), *Readings about the social animal* (7th ed., pp. 3–9). New York: W. H. Freeman and Company.

Bem, D. J. (1987). Writing the empirical journal article. In M. P. Zanna & J. M. Darley (Eds.), *The compleat academic: A practical guide for the beginning social scientist* (pp. 171–201). New York: Random House.

Bowering, G. (1988). *Errata.* Red Deer, Alta.: Red Deer College Press.

Cohen, J. (1990). Things I have learned (so far). *American Psychologist, 45,* 1304–1312.

Forgas, J. P. (1994). Sad and guilty? Affective influences on the explanation of conflict in close relationships. *Journal of Personality and Social Psychology, 66,* 56–68.

Sternberg, R. J. (1995). *The psychologist's companion: A guide to scientific writing for students and researchers* (3rd ed.). Cambridge: Cambridge University Press.

Author Index

Subject Index